CRITICAL INQUIRIES

CRITICAL INQUIRIES

A Reader in Studies of Canada

edited by Lynn Caldwell, Carrianne Leung and Darryl Leroux

Fernwood Publishing • Halifax and Winnipeg

Editing: Brenda Conroy
Cover design: ALL CAPS Design
Printed and bound in Canada by Hignell Book Printing

Published in Canada by Fernwood Publishing
32 Oceanvista Lane, Black Point, Nova Scotia, B0J 1B0
and 748 Broadway Avenue, Winnipeg, Manitoba, R3G 0X3
www.fernwoodpublishing.ca

Fernwood Publishing Company Limited gratefully acknowledges the financial support of the Government
of Canada through the Canada Book Fund and the Canada Council for the Arts, the Nova Scotia Department
of Communities, Culture and Heritage, the Manitoba Department of Culture, Heritage and Tourism under
the Manitoba Book Publishers Marketing Assistance Program and the Province of Manitoba, through the Book
Publishing Tax Credit, for our publishing program.

Library and Archives Canada Cataloguing in Publication

Critical inquiries : a reader in studies of Canada / Lynn Caldwell,
Carrianne Leung and Darryl Leroux, editors ; foreword by Rinaldo
Walcott ; afterword by Sherene Razack.

Includes bibliographical references and index.
ISBN 978-1-55266-551-0

1. Canada--Cultural policy. 2. Canada--Colonization. 3. Canada--
Race relations. 4. Critical theory--Canada. I. Caldwell, Lynn, 1968-
II. Leung, Carrianne K. Y III. Leroux, Darryl, 1978-

FC95.C75 2013   971   C2012-908248-1

Contents

Acknowledgements

As editors in a collaborative project, our gratitude goes first to those who contributed chapters to this collection. The idea for the book comes from a deep recognition that critical inquiries into Canada must engage many voices, and we are grateful to those among them who have shared their work in this book: Andrea, Eve, Stephanie, Michele, Robinder, Damien, Oren and Mary-Jo. All contributors have many projects on the go, and we are very thankful that they gave their time and commitment to this one.

We add a special word of gratitude to Sherene and to Rinaldo, who generously lent their support and scholarship in commentaries on this work and through placing their own work in these pages. Both continue to inspire in their unflinching commitment to social and political justice. Thanks also go out to Emily Gilbert and the anonymous reviewer, both of whom read multiple variations of this book, which is no doubt stronger due to their constructive feedback.

And we acknowledge that this work is taken up by many other scholars, with whom we aim to be in conversation. We hope we have captured this desire in what follows.

Each of the editors has many colleagues, family and friends who have lent encouragement, advice and support throughout the process. Among them, Carrianne thanks her family and friends, especially Andrew Archdekin and Fenn Archdekin-Leung for their unwavering support. She would also like to thank Darryl, Lynn and the contributors, who made this project both a joy and a passion to work on. Lynn is grateful to her family, to colleagues and students in Saskatoon, and she gives extra special thanks to Moe Roberts, HyeRan Kim-Cragg and Melanie Knight for their encouragement in this work and in all things. She also shares big gratitude for Carrianne and Darryl and this opportunity to work closely with two such fine thinkers, teachers and friends. Darryl would like to acknowledge his Mom, Dad, brother Shawn, Eloginy Tharmendran, Lindsey McKay and Ekua Quansah for their continued support, as well as Sirma Bilge, Xiaobei Chen and Gada Mahrouse, who read and commented on previous versions of his chapter. Lynn and Carrianne were a joy to work with and continue to be collaborators extraordinaire.

In addition, a big thank-you to the team at Fernwood: Errol, Beverley, Deb and Brenda, whose professionalism and competence greatly facilitated the publication of this book.

And finally, at the time that this manuscript went to print, Chief Theresa Spence is on a hunger strike and the Idle No More movement is igniting a broad public discourse on questions of sovereignty, nationhood, justice and more generally, restoring treaty relationships. We are humbled by these efforts and stand in solidarity with the communities and activists — Indigenous, settler, racialized — who are engaged in this struggle. We can only hope that this collection contributes to this work in some small way.

Contributors

Michele Byers is an associate professor in the Department of Sociology and Criminology at Saint Mary's University.

Lynn Caldwell completed a PhD in sociology and equity studies in education at the Ontario Institute for Studies in Education (OISE/UT). She currently lives in Saskatoon, where she works as a sessional lecturer and instructor affiliated with the University of Saskatchewan (Education), St. Thomas More College (Sociology) and St. Andrew's College (Social Ethics).

Andrea Fatona is an assistant professor in the Criticism and Curatorial Practice Program at the Ontario College of Art and Design University (OCADU) and formerly Curator of Contemporary Art at the Ottawa Art Gallery.

Eve Haque is an associate professor in the Department of Languages, Literatures and Linguistics at York University.

Oren Howlett is a PhD candidate in the School of Canadian Studies at Carleton University. His research is driven by a critical approach to negotiations of race, gender, sexuality and class in Canadian societies with a specific focus on GLBTQ communities in Toronto.

Damien Lee is a PhD candidate in Indigenous governance and politics at the University of Manitoba. He wrote a chapter for the edited collection *This Is an Honour Song: Twenty Years after the Blockades,* a book that analyzes the meaning of the Oka crisis.

Darryl Leroux completed a PhD in Sociology at Carleton University. He is an assistant professor in the Department of Sociology and Criminology at Saint Mary's University, where he teaches classes on Canadian history and society and social theory, with a focus on the politics of multiculturalism.

Carrianne Leung completed a PhD in sociology and equity studies in education at the Ontario Institute for Studies in Education (OISE/UT). Her dissertation takes up the question of how notions of "multiculturalism" are employed as resources for the production of Canadian national heritage. She is a sessional instructor at the Ontario College of Art and Design University (OCADU).

Mary-Jo Nadeau received her doctorate from York University (Toronto) and has taught as a full-time contract faculty in sociology at Trent University, Wilfrid Laurier University and University of Toronto — Mississauga.

Sherene Razack is a professor in the Department of Humanities, Social Sciences & Social Justice Education, at the Ontario Institute for Studies in Education of the University of Toronto. Her most recent books are *Casting Out: The Eviction of Muslims from Western Law and Politics* and a co-edited anthology (with Malinda Smith and Sunera Thobani), *States of Race* (2011).

Stephanie Tara Schwartz received her PhD in the University of Ottawa's Department of Classics and Religious Studies. She has taught part-time at the University of Ottawa and McGill University. She is working on a project examining the political history of Shephardic Jewish communities in Montréal.

Robinder Kaur Sehdev holds a PhD in cultural studies from York and Ryerson Universities. Her current research asks how the concept of sovereignty is conceptualized and taken up by anti-racist feminists seeking solidarity with Indigenous peoples in Canada and Australia. Her work can be found in *Cultural Studies Review, Critical Race and Whiteness Studies Journal* and *Topia: The Canadian Journal of Cultural Studies* as well as several anthologies on race and Indigenous studies.

Rinaldo Walcott is an associate professor and chair of the Department of Humanities, Social Sciences & Social Justice Education. His research and teaching is in the area of Black Diaspora cultural studies with an emphasis on queer sexualities, masculinity and cultural politics. A secondary research area is multicultural and transnational debates with an emphasis on nation, citizenship and coloniality.

Foreword

TOWARDS A CRITICAL AND NEW CANADIAN STUDIES

Lessons on Coloniality

Rinaldo Walcott

What it means to be human is continually defined against Black people and blackness. The profound consequences of having humanness defined against Black personhood means that the project of colonialism and the ongoing workings of coloniality produce for Black peoples a perverse relationship to the category of the human, in which our existence as human beings remains constantly in question. This global anti-Black condition, most profoundly produced in the post-Columbus era, manifests itself in numerous ways that limit how Black peoples lay claim to humanness and therefore how Black peoples alter what it means to be human.

Taking seriously Sylvia Wynter's (2003) claim that the human is always hybrid — that is, *bios* and *logos* — we might begin to glean how Black peoples' insistence on their humanness continually changes the category of human. In the realm of the post-Columbus colonial project and its resultant "coloniality of being," Black peoples are its most phantasmatic creation. While forms of captivity existed prior to the transatlantic slave trade, the unique ways in which transatlantic slavery became a central plank of the European colonial project and one of the most important ideological frames of coloniality require careful consideration. As Frank B. Wilderson (2010: 18) points out:

> But *African*, or more precisely *Blackness*, refers to an individual who is by definition always already void of relationality. Thus modernity marks the emergence of a new ontology because it is an era in which an entire race appears, people who, a priori, that is prior to the contingency of the "transgressive act" (such as losing a war or being convicted of a crime), stand as socially dead in relation to the rest of the world. This, I will argue, is as true for those who were herded onto the slave ships as it is for those who had no knowledge whatsoever of the coffles.

Wilderson narrates Black coming-into-being and thus Black being. The relations that post-Columbus colonial expansion frame for experiencing humanness and the lack there-of continue to frame modern conversations in which the possibilities for making significant and lasting cross-racial and indeed cross-human solidarities evade our desire to bring to a close this continuing dreadful duration of human organization and life.

I sat down to write this commentary in the midst of the debates, protests and inves-

1

tigations into the murder of Trayvon Martin. A neighbourhood watch captain, George Zimmerman in Sanford, Florida, stalked and shot Martin while the latter was walking in a gated community. The murdered Martin, a Black seventeen-year-old, was carrying candy and pop and reportedly speaking with his girlfriend on the phone. His murderer at the time of this writing has used self-defence, and most likely what is euphemistically called the "stand your ground" law in Florida, as his excuse for taking Martin's life. It seems clear from the available evidence that Zimmerman understood two things about Martin: a) he was a Black teenager and b) he could not have legitimately been in the place where he was shot. Such assumptions condition how Black people occupy the zones of North America and other parts of the North Atlantic considered not to be their natural homes. One of the central conceits that remove Black people from humanness is that Black people are constantly understood to be out of place. The out-of-placeness that Black people, especially poor Black people, continually experience is one which has life-and-death consequences, as Martin's death demonstrates, and which is highlighted by the U.S. carceral state (see Gilmore 2007) and by practices like the enormously disproportionate stop-and-frisk and "carding" measures used against young Black men across the North Atlantic zones (New York City, Toronto, London).

I begin with Martin's death in a book about Canada to point to the ways in which similar issues frame the ongoing coloniality of the Canadian nation-state. In Canada, generally speaking, Black people remain out of place. This out-of-placeness must be understood as a larger part of the colonial project of Canada and of Canada's production by and participation in global coloniality. Differently to Martin's death, Black Canadian youth die at the hands of police, since Canadian gun laws result in fewer civilian-on-civilian murders than in the United States. Such deaths are an element of the coloniality of the Canadian nation-state, and they mark the non-humanness of Black people and demand that Black people struggle to alter what being human means. These deaths extend transatlantic slavery into the present, centring its deadly anti-human and anti-Black foundations. These deaths are the logical outcomes of the underpinnings of technologies of sociality (a perverse sociality) that seek to produce whiteness as a norm against which any "logic of relationality" (Wilderson 2010) might be possible.

Indeed, that modern nation-states like Canada take their very existence from the post-Columbus colonial project means that Black people are central to the ways in which this nation's violent origins must hold at bay the historical and contemporary violences that constitute them as "White nations." However, I contend that the technologies of post-Columbus colonial practices renew themselves in inventive ways, thus producing a global coloniality of which there is no outside for anyone. For example, in the contemporary Canadian context, there is almost universal silence on the record number of Aboriginal Conservatives who are members of Parliament (Leona Aglukkaq, Rob Clarke, Peter Penashue, Rod Bruinooge, Shelly Glover); very little critical attention is paid to these individuals and to this political trend. Given the ways in which Aboriginal abjection is shaped by the ongoing colonial project of the Canadian nation-state, the language for considering Aboriginal coloniality of being remains fairly inchoate and/or not possible. And yet, a push for Aboriginal capitalism, alongside the attempt to produce wasted populations of "non-resourced" Aboriginal communities, is an important example of the adaptability of late modern capitalism. But, most importantly, these practices and incorporations call for relational political logics, which might begin to undo the coloniality of our being(s).

One of the central and complicated dynamics of geo-political spaces like Canada is how to think through the complex dynamics of historical and contemporary colonialism as these practices overlap, producing new neoliberal modes of individualism, citizenship and belonging. In the United States, the Cherokee Nation's attempts to evict the descendants of the freedmen from the tribe are but one complicated strand of the ways in which coloniality functions to produce Black people as out of place. The Black and "mixed raced" descendants of freed Cherokee slaves had long held citizenship in the nation, until 2007, when a vote was taken to deny them their citizenship. This "battle" over who is a Cherokee highlights the ways in which the asymmetries of contemporary neoliberal politics and culture work in our time (Nieves 2007; Stremlau 2011). We can see how modern capitalist discourses and distribution of resources, access and ownership, or proprietary relations to resources, often coincide with neoliberal orderings of the world, in which multiple forms of dispossession produce relationships to capital in ways that allow for non-White groups to act within the historical legacies of racial ordering and its many outcomes in our contemporary cultural moment. The Cherokee example is a case in point. Indeed, one of the shortcomings of making sense of Canada as a colonial entity is to assume that its colonial practices end at the geographical border. Scholars such as Peter James Hudson (2010) who study the history of Canada's now-vaunted banking system can teach us much about the ways in which the colonial project of Canada has a long reach. Hudson's work on the Canadian banking industry and exploitation of the Caribbean region reminds us that colonialism is not only the occupation and exploitation of land and resources and the curtailment of peoples' rights and movements. Colonialism is also the ways in which the invention of modern nation-states demarcates economic and cultural activities, which move beyond the traditional markers of colonial practice.

In the case of Caribbean banking, a number of major Canadian banks (Royal Bank of Canada, Canadian Imperial Bank of Commerce, Bank of Nova Scotia) have long occupied the financial landscape of that "archipelago of poverty." These financial institutions did not seek to service or invest in the region, but rather to extract from it, like Alcan and other Canadian mining giants of the past, "resources" to be returned to Canada. This overseas colonialism, coupled with an "at home" colonial project, produces complicated conceptual dilemmas for thinking about the culture of coloniality in Canada. And, importantly, that Canada's colonial project goes beyond its geo-political borders means that how different bodies are placed within or arrive at the borders of the nation-state is a complex story of arrival and becoming.

A critical engagement with coloniality demands that we see the imprint and the overlap among the reserve, the housing project and "the priority neighbourhood" (as the archipelagoes of poverty are called in Toronto). In each case the language marks a specific space and place of out-of-placeness for those marked as abject and waste within the boundaries of the nation-state of Canada. Such abjection is only possible in terms of the ongoing dynamic practices of coloniality. Those spaces and the ideas of them, as well as the bodies that constitute them, leak into and out of each other.

A critical Canadian studies engages those conditions and ideas, revealing their euphemisms and most importantly their material practices and realities as the logics and practices of coloniality. Thus relational logics require us to take seriously that the colonial project of Canada is skilled at producing what can too easily appear to be non-relational dynamics. "Priority neighbourhoods" have nothing to do with *banlieues*, and none of them have anything to do with European colonial practices in the past and the present. Such pedagogies of coloniality require us to reside in notions of the human that have as their foundation global anti-Black ontologies, for it is upon the body of the Black being that coloniality configured and practised its most significant anti-human projects. Consequently, the Black body is not the most abject body in a war of abjection and oppression, but the Black body is the template of how to produce abjection of/for the other.

The challenge of the essays in this book is to not merely add new voices to a stale and largely White Canadian studies, but rather to account forcefully for the ways in which coloniality frames the nation-state of Canada and Canadian studies. The contributors open up the conceptual terrain that calls for a deep engagement with the ways in which the colonial project and indeed Canada's production by it and of it, as well as the nation-state's perpetuation of coloniality, is central to contemporary questions of global human existence. Furthermore, the chapters in this book necessarily open up conceptual terrain that might produce logics of relationality as coloniality's reach shapes different desiring subjects within and against the nation-state. Such social and political configurations require us to contend with the ways in which the seductions of capitalism in late modernity do not merely replicate colonialism's "Red, White and Black" past. After all, a Black man sits in the White House, and in the Canadian nation-state Aboriginal people sit in Stephen Harper's government of austerity.

Significantly, at a 2012 gathering between First Nations leaders and the Canadian government in Ottawa, the seductions of capitalism framed the conversation of justice. A cynical read would be that an invitation to participate more fully in capitalism was offered as a form of justice by the colonial state. Indeed, former prime minister Paul Martin has set up a foundation to make sure that First Nations/Aboriginal people can be more intimately tied to contemporary capitalism. The foundation, with support from the banking industry (notably, Scotiabank), teaches Aboriginal students how to produce business plans as a part of one of its education programs. These programs are driven by Aboriginal demographics and a desire to secure the future of capitalism by incorporating a previously ignored population into some of its small rewards. However, the kinds of justice Aboriginal communities might require if their forms of life are to be fully acknowledged might mean significant opposition to capitalism. It is indeed my argument that what we might call "Black freedom" is in distinct opposition to something called capitalism. Given that the Black body was an instrument of capital, as well as a significant producer of it — both commodity and labour — the question of freedom and capital is a particularly knotty one for Black personhood. At the same time, given the intimate crossing of black-ness and capitalism, Black freedom as an "authentic" possibility inaugurates a challenge of the imagination to produce new modes of living that might be in accord with some of the most radical global Indigenous calls for a different kind of world.

Given the above, this new critical Canadian studies cannot be merely critical, in that its primary focus is to make visible that which has not been clearly seen before. Instead, the emphasis on critical here points to the networks of Canada's ongoing coloniality and the need for scholars to examine the stakes of the colonial project. The scholars in this book produce analyses that point to the ways in which colonial projects are not only intrusive but also incorporative. At this late stage of capitalist modernity the Canadian nation-state's flexible conceptions of sovereignty, of nation and of self-determination ensure capitalist futurity when and if the stakes of capitalist relations can be secured through incorporation. In the case of places like Attawapiskat, no such flexibility is evident in the face of no resources.[1] Critical Canadian studies enables us to read the historical and the contemporary temporally, rather than in a linear and progressive fashion, and thereby opens up contradictory and illogic neoliberal attempts to make capitalism appear as a rational form of resource distribution and organization of human life.

Given that the Black body and indeed Black personhood is a creation of these contradictory and irrational logics of capitalism, it is often in the face of Black personhood that late capitalism's illogics come into focus. The disposability of Black bodies in the Canadian scene requires appreciative logics of relation as Black people remain deeply estranged from the geo-politics of nationhood, no matter how broadly or inclusively defined nations might be. Even in contemporary "Black" nation-states, forged from the resistance to colonization and enslavement and now governed by the emancipated elites, what Fanon (1963) called the "national bourgeoisie" are sites of this continuing estrangement in "problem-spaces" (Scott 1999) of postcolonial nation-states of former European colonies. These conditions then, mean that Black people share with other colonized peoples struggles over selfhood at the same time that Black peoples' humanity remains in doubt and out of place.

The devastating impact of European coloniality for Black personhood should be understood as the template for the enactment of other atrocities of which the bare life conditions of mid-century concentration camps represent a particularly poignant moment. We must also read the plantation and the reserve together and as constituting each other if a reckoning of history can allow us to imagine different kinds of intimate futures. Comparatively then, we conceive of anti-Black racism as a signally important element of the ongoing flows of coloniality in which the Black subject is never able to fully occupy the site of incorporation into the nation-state given that both nation-state and blackness come into being simultaneously and indeed disjunctively, with Black personhood constituted as one of the elements that could not be constitutive of nationhood. A fundamental and ongoing out-of-placeness for Black bodies still exists, if only ambivalently attenuated by partial incorporations in late capitalism as it seeks bodies in its constant crises. But the more fulsome social reality is that Black bodies become so much human (non-human) waste and suffer excision more so than incorporation.

Critical Canadian studies thus unmoors the silences that condition our contemporary moment by risking identity in favour of a politics of thought. By "politics of thought" I mean to signal the ways in which coloniality's most profound operations work at the level of what it means to know, and how knowing places some bodies out of place. Knowing and what it means to know produce the death-worlds for the Trayvon Martins and Black people generally. These death-worlds are both historical and urgently present, and through them we can conceive of forms of relationality in which new modes of humanness might be possible. The demand here then is to think new possibilities for human life beyond capitalism. In a post-communist and neoliberal world, thinking, articulating and moving towards different modes of human life is our challenge. As a critical Canadian studies unmasks, unearths, repositions, rereads, reworks and remakes, it also works to produce new modes of relational logics and conditions in which the intimacies that European colonial expansion produced for us might be refashioned.

Refashioning in this sense is a radical project of political urgency and agency in which an acknowledgement of the intervention of history produces new modes of living our present intimacies. These new modes call for moving beyond and maybe even against the "romance stories" of a progressive liberation, especially for those who have been formerly colonized, into the bounty of rights and freedoms. To refuse such a romance story is not to deny history, but rather to account for the ways in which history might offer us a better calculation of how to alter the human yet again in our time (Walcott 2011a). Such an alternative will require the production of "new indigenisms" of our globe, and those new indigenisms will require of us conversations, debates, politics and maybe even policies that begin with the "catastrophic culture" that has brought us together.[2] But such a catastrophe also produced and continues to produce profound human possibilities, practices and potentialities. If neoliberalism does anything, it attempts to interrupt human creativity and imagination. A critical Canadian studies works the ruins of catastrophe to produce more hopeful tales of our present human intimacies and to allow the opportunity to reimagine the self.

NOTES

1. Attawapiskat is an interesting case for many reasons. As a territory lacking in natural resources and a site not needed for the transportation of those resources, its appeals to the national government are treated with disdain. This disdain is for me the evidence that those territories that possess the resources to continue to aid in the production of capital can find a place in the late capitalist modern nation regardless of racial history, and those without resources cannot. The point is that capitalism continually modifies and "includes" on its own terms and gives way to "old" designations if those designations can now fuel its engines. Attawapiskat cannot fuel its engines thus it must be managed.
2. Kamau Brathwaite (2006) articulates what he calls "the literature of catastrophe" as the byproduct of European colonial expansion. Brathwaite points out that this catastrophe of colonialism produces death, racism, environmental degradation and so on but it also produces jazz, Caribbean, African American and Indigenous literatures and other cultural forms and practices that have reshaped the globe and human life. I adapt his term to articulate a culture of catastrophe, which draws on his insights.

Introduction

BUILDING A SPACE FOR CRITICAL CANADIAN STUDIES

Lynn Caldwell, Darryl Leroux and Carrianne Leung

As students, scholars, activists and artists thirsty for spaces to rethink and challenge inequitable social relations in Canada, we often find ourselves in situations where dominant forms of Canadian nationalism subjugate and appropriate the very idea of an oppositional politics. We know that terms such as "critical" and "resistance" are often used for purposes that in many ways resituate Canadian forms of domination, however unintentional that might be. Thus, a key task in any conceptual re-imagining intent on disrupting Canada's long and continuing history of colonial subjugation is to define the particular parameters of critique. Such a task is before us here.

In the first instance, we employ the term "critical" in its most basic sense: contestation in studies of the nation and/or debates about Canada that underwrite its constitution in ongoing colonial violence. Whether in representations of Canada's role as a global beacon of peace and tolerance, in discussions of Canada's role as a Western nation intent on contributing to the so-called "War on Terror" or in debates about Canada's role in apologizing for past wrongs, we situate our work outside normative debates about the relative goodness or innocence of Canadians. That is, we problematize many of the ideas and concepts relied on and reproduced by politics in the form of a Conservative–Liberal–New Democratic–Green–Bloc regime on Parliament Hill and by many of the institutionalized academic and scholarly centres of Canadian studies.

Our use of the term "critical," while oppositional in spirit, also points to the need for a sustained focus on Canada as an object of inquiry. This is a second sense in our employment of the term. However one approaches such work theoretically, we argue that interrogating the making of Canada, or the commonsense, everyday understandings of what Canada is and perhaps more importantly, what discourses of Canada produce and what Canadians do, is a crucial intellectual project that lends complexity to the project of studying the nation. We identify the work in this collection, and the broader academic work in which it is situated, as critical in the sense of urgent and needed. It is critical to engage complex questions about Canada and Canadianness in ways that do not take much for granted. In the past ten to fifteen years much work has been done in this vein, including groundbreaking work, such as Himani Bannerji's *The Dark Side of the Nation*, Eva Mackey's *The House of Difference*, Richard Day's *Multiculturalism and the History of Canadian Diversity*, Rinaldo Walcott's *Black Like Who?* and Sherene Razack's *Race, Space and the Law*.

This work is also, as Rinaldo Walcott so succinctly points out in the foreword of this collection, a challenge posed to the many colonial conditions in Canada that place racialized and Indigenous bodies outside the terrain and category of human. Citing examples of the commodification and disposability of Black bodies and Indigenous bodies *vis-à-vis* the nation, Walcott calls for a theorization of how different forms of colonialism constitute each other. Walcott asks us to consider how to read the reserve and the plantation — two strategies of colonial containment and violence — simultaneously, in order to bring about new terms of self and of our intimacies. Following in this trajectory, the essays in this collection intervene in our neoliberal moment by attempting to alter the logics of the national and the global, and by so doing, rework the relationality of bodies and territories.

The work that follows such a path is often placed outside the boundaries of studies of Canada proper, despite its analytical focus on the Canadian nation. This work is usually assigned to the periphery, allocated to courses on race and representation, gender studies or equity studies. Yet we argue that the analytics of such work facilitates a rich, multidisciplinary, historicized engagement with the production of Canada and Canadians that challenges current national projects, including the re-valorization of the Canadian military, the incredible growth in the prison-industrial complex, the criminalization of refugee claimants and immigrants and the marked increase in temporary worker schemes during the 2005–2012 period.

The strength of this book is that it presents disparate empirical sites such as cultural productions, state policies, institutional practices, commemorative events and museum exhibits, to name but a few. What ties these all together, besides identifying them as critical work in the sense of the two broad strokes we introduce above, is their focus on analyses of the racialized, gendered, classed and sexualized dimensions of what constitutes Canada. This sustained intersectional, interdisciplinary approach sees the inherent contradictions in the Canadian nation-building project and attempts to highlight the techniques of power that produce national hierarchies of difference. To reach these goals, we divide the book into three themes, each offering rich empirical analyses and theoretical engagements with crucial aspects in the production of Canada and Canadians.

Our theoretical framework is eclectic; it approaches the study of Canada as a critical project that must and does proceed from a variety of analytical and disciplinary traditions, and we left the question of theoretical frameworks open to individual authors, building on the flexible, yet crucial study of Canada as a White settler colonial project. The key to such analyses is not theoretical purity, but analytical rigour. Despite our reluctance to limit contributors to a strict theoretical interpretation, our vision for the collection depends on several emerging themes in social theory, as we reflect in our thematic organization.

MULTICULTURALISM, DIFFERENCE AND THE POLITICS OF DIVERSITY

The focus of the first section emerges from the longstanding intellectual and creative work that contests the status of multiculturalism as a strategy and vision for conceiving of difference and relationality in Canada. As scholars of nationalism have long maintained, nation-states rely on myths of origin. For White settler nations like Canada, the concept of multiculturalism has emerged as a tool in imagining a coherent national identity by bringing racialized subjects into a narrative that reiterates settler myths of origin, an origin which in fact relied on the very violent eviction of racialized bodies. Perhaps more insidiously, White settlers are equally called into the heroic story of Canadian multiculturalism, since it provides them with ample evidence that racism as a systematic ideological system that favours those people constituted as "white" is a thing of the Canadian past. Through the implementation of state policy and programs, the concept of "multiculturalism" has become foundational to articulations and practices of Canada as a nation.

As editors, we are committed to situating this collection as a contribution to and as encouragement for continued efforts to debate multiculturalism in the interest of addressing ongoing and emerging inequalities in Canada and in the spaces in which Canada is implicated globally. We do not present this text as "assessments" of multiculturalism as a defined practice within Canada. As we explained previously, we start from a critical premise that is meant to interrogate the already-existing inequalities in Canada. As such, we identify multiculturalism as a route through which the very conditions for and limits of Canadianness are constituted and continually revised. Among the places where this is evident are in efforts to reclaim Canadian multiculturalism as a liberatory framework or as an inherently anti-racist endeavour. For example, in the fall of 2011, the Association for Canadian Studies and the Canadian Ethnic Studies Association jointly hosted a conference titled "Revisiting 40 Years of Multicultural Policy in Canada." This was one of the many sites and conversations in which normative assessments of multiculturalism were confronted with an unsettling critique of Canada's past, present and/or future. As one intervention in the debates and accounts at the conference demonstrated, those of us who would draw attention to multiculturalism in Canada must remember that Canada's official founding logic was colonial, since it was founded on the dispossession and displacement of Indigenous peoples and epistemologies, the enslavement of people of African descent and the concomitant ascent of European modernity on a planetary level. Emerging in and as a colonial formation, multiculturalism has always and inevitably been a site for struggles with ruling relations. Contemporary debates about multiculturalism, then, must engage integrally with present-day colonial realities.

This positioning has implications for various debates and strategies, including the notion of "interculturalism" in Québec — presented as an alternative to multiculturalism. It also matters in terms of locating debates about multiculturalism (including who speaks of it, in it, for it, against it) and the terms for locating such interventions. Importantly, we largely agree with Walcott's (2011b) recent work, in that we are not against the *idea* of multiculturalism, but instead, we read current multicultural logics in Canada as deeply embedded in forms of inequality.

Notably, we argue that the Canadian narrative of multiculturalism interpellates national subjects into a story of innocence, one where ongoing systems of differentiation in Canada are conveniently forgotten and erased. The essays included in this section contribute to critical analysis by questioning how official multiculturalism operates through the placement of subjects in formations of belonging/non-belonging, through attempts to subsume Indigenous origins and contemporary Indigenous nationhoods and identities into settler narratives of diversity and through organizing desirable/undesirable difference, practices of containment and surveillance and management of racialized bodies. In order to situate our concern with state practices of multiculturalism and their discursive circulation in Canadian society, the first three chapters of this section examine high-profile national commissions of inquiry in Canada: the Massey Commission (1950s), the Laurendeau-Dunton Commission (1960s) and the Bouchard-Taylor Commission (2007–2008).

In "The Bilingual Limits of Canadian Multiculturalism: The Politics of Language and Race," Eve Haque considers current debates about the possibilities of multiculturalism as a framework for addressing racism and exclusion in Canada. She demonstrates how multiculturalism itself has become a term with great elasticity, which allows it to be taken up across the political spectrum, despite its demise and irrelevance being heralded time and time again. Yet, multiculturalism has proven to be an incredibly resilient signifier, and nowhere is this truer than in Canada, often invoked as the birthplace of the institutional practice.

Haque lays out the limits of multiculturalism in Canada in order to engage with the im/possibilities of a revalorized multiculturalism through an examination of the Royal Commission on Bilingualism and Biculturalism documents related to official multiculturalism's bilingual origins. She argues that attention to the specific genealogy of multiculturalism in Canada shows us that multiculturalism, official or otherwise, can never be considered outside of its "bilingual framework." Although there has been a slow decoupling of multiculturalism and bilingualism over the last thirty-five years or so, again and again the limit upon which the visions of a revalorized, bottom-up notion of multiculturalism founders is that of bilingualism; that is, of a White settler nation with two founding peoples, whose collective claims are at the forefront. Through her rereading of multiculturalism through bilingualism, Haque argues that the federal government's bid to accommodate the claims of Francophone communities within a White settler national framework entrenches a hierarchy of collective belonging so deeply that all attempts to reappropriate and rework multiculturalism will continue to be limited until the impossibility of multiculturalism within a bilingual framework is acknowledged. According to Haque, between multiculturalism and bilingualism lies the aporetic gap, from where, perhaps, the possibilities of challenging the racist exclusions of White settler nationalism might emerge.

In "Arts Funding, the State and Canadian Nation-Making: Producing Governable Subjects," Andrea Fatona demonstrates how a number of concerns regarding nation, culture, class and race underline Canadian policies geared towards the distribution of state funds to the arts. These concerns can be characterized as simultaneously philosophical and pragmatic in nature. As an example, she argues that early state patronage of the arts through the establishment of the Canada Council for the Arts highlights a politics of arts funding that was concerned with elite discourses on aesthetic, cultural and social values and deliberate practices of imagining, shaping and narrating the fledgling Canadian nation as White, middle-class, modern and European. Through her analysis, Fatona demonstrates how this racialized and classed imaginary produced a system of exclusionary arts funding practices that persist into the current moment through definitions of what counts as culture, who counts as cultural producers and artists and even how the Canada Council, for instance, judges "excellence."

Fatona begins her investigation by focusing on the relationship between cultural policy and governance on a theoretical level. She then unpacks the relationships among race, government cultural policy and sovereignty in the Massey Report, which recommended the formation of the Canada Council for the Arts in 1957. Fatona, drawing on interventions in multiculturalism discourse in Canada, discusses how official multiculturalism functions to regulate racialized bodies by offering limited forms of legitimacy within the terms of institutions like the Canada Council, while delegitimizing claims by artists of colour for systemic change. This forecloses entrance to "other" scholars, who stress the lived nature of race as a category of exclusion and assimilation within colonial conventions of government and view race as constitutive of Western political design. Given the focus on a colour-blind, race-neutral approach to race politics in Canada, Fatona's analysis provides us with some important conceptual tools through which to consider alternative modalities.

Darryl Leroux's chapter, "The Many Paradoxes of Race in Québec: Civilization, *Laïcité* and Gender Equality," sketches the genealogy of race in Québec from its inception under the discursive terms of the French imperial model of *mission civilisatrice* to the incipient "two founding nations" discourse of the twentieth century to very recent events, including the Bouchard-Taylor Commission of 2007–2008. Using the concept of "double colonization," Leroux demonstrates how discursive regimes in Québec situate French Canadian Québécois outside the realm of present-day colonial relations. From there, he explains how racial discourses in Québec are organized according to what Wendy Brown calls the "depoliticization" of tolerance, a process that she identifies in Western liberal democracies since the 1980s. Under the terms of this discourse, race and culture are seen as static characteristics of non-Western subjects, pitting the liberal West against an illiberal, racialized other.

In order to situate racial discourses in Québec within this broader civilizational frame, Leroux takes us through a series of documents related to the Bouchard-Taylor Commission of 2007–2008 and demonstrates how dominant Québécois subjects situate themselves within such a grid of intelligibility — one that locates Québec within Western colonial logics. His analysis pushes beyond the normative Canada-Québec national debate towards an understanding of the similarities between racial discourses in Québec and the rest of Canada — similarities borne of historical processes of differentiation based in European White supremacies.

Picking up on the question of the production of racialized difference, Michele Byers and Stephanie Tara Schwartz consider an under-theorized dimension of multicultural discourses in Canada: where do Jews fit into the story of Canadian multiculturalism? In "Creating Space for Difference: Theorizing Multicultural Jewish Identity in Canada," Byers and Schwartz argue that, on the one hand, Jews often align themselves economically, socially and politically with Canadian conservatism, creating an impression of an alliance with racial hegemony. This can be seen in the current Conservative government's embrace of the Jewish question, notably its unabashed support for Israel and the marginalization of anti-Zionist (whether Jewish, Muslim, Christian or secular) organizing in Canada. The Canadian Parliamentary Coalition to Combat Anti-Semitism, founded in 2010, lays bare the relationship between mainstream Jewishness in Canada and conservative political causes that seek to situate all critiques of Israel as anti-semitic. On the other hand, anti-semitism, tolerance of Jewish difference by national communities (for example, Orthodox Jews in Québec) and racialization within the Canadian Jewish community itself continue to be areas of research that are underdeveloped.

Byers and Schwartz maintain that the shifting boundaries of Canadian Jewishness manifest a compelling identity politics within the framework of multiculturalism that deserves sustained attention. They locate their analysis in critical cultural studies scholarship, identifying a need for distinct attention to Canadian contexts and questions in order to examine how diversities of Jewishness are constrained in projects of multiculturalism that privilege whiteness. They argue for distrupting the constraints that work to homogenize Jewishness and demonstrate how lived realities of difference contest such homogeneity. In demonstrating the efforts required to recognize Jews as multicultural, Byers and Schwartz reveal limitations in constructions of Canadian multiculturalism that exclude attention to cultural productions and lived experiences of multiplicity and diversity in Jewishness. Thus, they open up discursive space for attention to difference in ways that unsettle monolithic categories in order to render more visible that Jewishness in Canada is lived and expressed as a subject position inhabited in diverse and shifting ways.

SPACE, PLACE AND TERRITORY

The chapters in this section take up the turn to "space," a concept in social theory that has been influential in a number of disciplines. This is especially true in studies of national communities, given, for example, the geographical dimensions of national borders, the global struggles for Indigenous sovereignties and territory and the complex dynamics of international migration. Captured in a re-imagined attention on border control post-9/11, the national is often conceived through specific techniques of governance relying on competing visions of space.

Many scholars attribute the turn to geography in studies of Canada to Kay J. Anderson's 1991 monograph *Vancouver's Chinatown*, which examines the relationships among space, place, nation and race. Research in the Canadian context has taken up this challenge, studying national, urban and rural spaces, as well as bodies and institutions as spaces of interest. Some studies (Kobayashi and Peake 2000 ; Razack 2002; McKittrick 2006; Teelucksingh 2006; Nelson 2008) direct us to what is to be gained by a sustained focus on the empirical base of geography in the production of national subjects. This collection contributes to one of the lasting results of the spatial turn — the concerted effort to "unmap" systems of social differentiation.

The first chapter in this section, "Chinese Canada in Moose Jaw: A Story Told in Two Parts," situates the tensions between history and memory and between fact and fiction at the forefront of the debate over public space. Carrianne Leung provides an account of the Tunnels of Moose Jaw, a privately owned enterprise in the business of selling the past through its interactive, multimedia tours of the town's underground labyrinth. Consisting of two tours, the Chicago Connection and the Passage to Fortune, the Tunnels presents historical narratives about Moose Jaw: the former depicts the town's bootlegging history involving Al Capone, and the latter alleges that the violent treatment of Chinese Canadians in the late 1800s and early 1900s drove them to seek safety in the town's underground tunnels. Although there is little evidence to substantiate either of these stories, the chapter discusses how the discourse of the Chinese model minority found in the Passage of Fortune is a powerful technique in constituting, regulating and ordering racialized bodies and their subjectivities in the nation. While the radically re-spatialized Tunnels is presented as a universal story of national redemption, Leung demonstrates how racialized bodies are now "out of place" in the underground, troubling notions of space that rely on the very eviction of Chinese Canadians from the nation.

From there, Leung takes us to a second site of interest, Crossings, also located in Moose Jaw, but offering a very different story of Chinese Canadians inhabiting the city. As opposed to the redemptive narrative of Passage to Fortune, Crossings presents the long and at times thriving history of Chinese settlement above ground, locating Moose Jaw as an important space of Chinese Canadian history. By bringing the two sites together, Leung explicates the contradictions, tensions and ambivalences of narrating racialized bodies in national space.

Lynn Caldwell's chapter, "Unsettling the Middle Ground: Could the World Use a More Questionable Saskatchewan?," examines whiteness in the making of a Prairie Province as Canadian space, arguing that the articulation of Saskatchewan's place in the nation relies on sticky colonial fictions to maintain conditions and structures of racism. Drawing from a study of Saskatchewan Centennial commemorations, Caldwell demonstrates how attachments to colonialism operate through representations of Saskatchewan as a conciliatory and mediating space. Countering Saskatchewan's static discourse, the author pushes towards thinking of space as questionable and dynamic and as the grounds for social change and collective life, particularly in the context of twenty-first century "reconciliation" projects and of shifting discourses of Saskatchewan as place.

Robinder Sedhev's chapter, "Home at the Bridge: Indigenous Belonging and the Settler Border," looks at the Rainbow Bridge in Niagara Falls as a site of contestation. The primary focus is on First Nations' struggles for passage across the bridge as their sovereign right of mobility in their territories. Sedhev's attention to the act of crossing as well as the Tuscarora Nation's annual Bridge Crossing Ceremony brings into relief the border as the site of policing and disciplining of settler spaces.

This crossing/non-crossing highlights the tensions, contradictions and assumptions within settler and nationalist logics. In using this representation, Sedhev interrogates different positions on settler/indigeneity, belonging, diaspora and home/lessness and articulates an "epistemology of rootedness" that seeks to resituate Indigenous sovereignties. By bringing the political stakes of the bridge's crossing to the forefront, Sedhev argues for Indigenous sovereignty and non-essentialist forms of identity politics.

SYMBOLS AND SAMENESS

This last section of the collection brings together a variety of analyses of Canadian national symbols. Included among these are analyses of the "Indian" moccasin, the Famous Five monument on Parliament Hill and same-sex marriage in Canada, all of which speak to Canadian national preoccupations. What brings these analyses together is their focus on examining the dynamics of making sameness — and by implication, difference — in contemporary Canada. In other words, how do national symbols, whether heritage sites or consumer products, arrange subjects along a continuum of sameness and difference?

National identifications, such as notions of Canadian national space and a national past, operate both materially and symbolically to produce and mobilize citizen-subjects and to configure a collective public imagined and governed as the "Canadian people." Symbols of collective identification and legislative practices of managing citizen identity (e.g., the *Indian Act*, language policies, national anthems and state cultural institutions) function paradoxically to both subsume *and* exclude diasporic, Aboriginal and mobile subjects into and from national sameness. State-managed national symbolizing, working in concert with everyday forms of identity-making, presume sameness in the exclusions produced through their own practices of managing national identification; not only are national subjects called into a shared "Canadian" identity, but such practices also attempt to homogenize and manage subjects presumed to fall outside the bounds of Canadianness.

Recently, Canada has seen an explosion of large-scale events celebrating the European settler project. In particular, the Alberta-Saskatchewan Centennial in 2005, the Québec 400 in 2008 and the Plains of Abraham 250th anniversary controversy that erupted in 2009 all demonstrated the role collective memory plays in popularizing national narratives of conquest and colonization. Efforts at organizing events for Canada's 150th anniversary by a variety of actors (e.g., PEI 2014–2017 and the Institute of Public Administration's sesquicentennial conference and report in 2010) demonstrate the continued salience of public remembrance.

This section on symbols and sameness is situated in fields of scholarly work that attend to memory's role in nation-building and the production of national subjects.

Elizabeth Furniss' *The Burden of History: Colonialism and the Frontier Myth in a Rural Canadian Community* (1999), for example, locates such narratives in three domains of public history celebrating "pioneer" and "frontier" life in Williams Lake, British Columbia — school curriculum, popular historical literature and public museums. Mackey's work (2002) on the Canada 125 commemorations reveals how symbols were deliberately and strategically designed to de-politicize tensions around belonging and citizenship and explicit state interests in the avoidance of "controversy." Critical studies of memory that inform the works in this text act to disrupt the heroic and homogenizing narratives of the past and illustrate the very instability of historical narratives.

Damien Lee's chapter, "In the Shoes of the Other: Indigenous Authenticities and Colonial Logics of Difference," picks up on many themes of the collection, most notably the colonial imaginings at the heart of Canadian narratives of settler belonging. Using an indigenist theoretical framework, he makes the point that "Canadian" identity relies on the continued dispossession and displacement of Indigenous epistemologies. As an example, he examines the circulation of the "Indian" moccasin in Canadian narratives of nationhood and circuits of exchange. Juxtaposing his own experiences of moccasin-making with the settler obsession with becoming Indigenous, Lee demonstrates how Canadian identity is premised on the impossible desire to become Indian. What he calls "mock-asins," then, are symbols of a deep desire to be other, a desire that appears in sites as disparate as department stores, cultural events and stories about settler belonging.

In "Homonormativity and the Loss of Queer: Re-contextualizing Canada's Sexual Politics," Oren Howlett offers a homonormative re-reading of sexuality politics in Canada that accounts for the loss of queer and liberationist politics in Canada. In order to do so, Howlett takes us through a history of regimes of sexuality in Canada, with a focus on the current phase, what he calls "homonormative" politics. He looks specifically at the adoption of same-sex marriage in 2005 in order to re-conceptualize the ways in which Canadian nation-building operates according to a homo-normative discursive framework that works to depoliticize queer political struggles.

In "Monumental Performances: The Famous Five, Gendered Whiteness and the Making of Canada's Colonial Present," Mary-Jo Nadeau takes us on a tour of a relatively new iconic national monument in Ottawa — the Women are Persons! Famous Five Monument, installed in the northeast quadrant of Parliament Hill in 2000. Since its unveiling at a major ceremony, the monument has been incorporated into the national story and celebrated as a definitive Canadian feminist achievement. Nadeau traces the practices and conditions that have allowed for this public history project to achieve an apparently seamless and uncontested representation of the Canadian feminist body politic. Through engaging in a disruptive reading of its sedimented narrative, Nadeau examines the monument and its ongoing production as a performative act of nationalized gendered whiteness. She calls particular attention to the social organization of forgetting and remembering typical of multiculturalist public memorializing in Canada, including the persistent dismembering of histories of racial and colonial hegemony in Canadian feminist representations of gendered embodiment. In this sense, Nadeau's work traces the production of sameness around the category of Canadian women, directing us to the practices of silencing racialized experiences.

The collection closes with an afterword by Sherene Razack, who reminds us of the "race to innocence," a concept Razack and Mary Louise Fellows developed in a 1998 essay as a call to feminists to refrain from competing for the most marginal status in any given social context (Fellows and Razack 1998). In our work as critical scholars, we must be ever mindful of the interlocking nature of systems of oppression. Our positions on the margins are not disconnected or even distant. As we are marginalized, we are also complicit in the suborbination of others, and thus, we are never fully "innocent." The "race to innocence" is not a productive endeavour; it in fact reproduces the conditions of coloniality, as Razack argues through examples from her most recent work on ongoing colonial forms of violence in Canada. Echoing Walcott, Razack sounds a clarion call for critical analyses that account for all bodies at all moments, as our collective liberation relies on precisely such analytical and political efforts.

This collection is intended as a contribution to studies of Canada across diverse disciplinary and geographical contexts; this includes undergraduate courses in the social sciences, humanities and education as well as those specifically designated as Canadian studies. The editors and contributors also hope that it may serve as a resource to critical studies of Canada taken up in diverse global spaces. Its rich empirical analyses also bridge academic and non-academic interests. Whether in the study of museum exhibits, commissions of inquiry, monuments, clothing and a selection of other cultural productions, our collection opens up space to think the nation otherwise. We are aware that similar conversations are taking place at other sites (particularly the TransCanada and R.A.C.E. series of conferences) and in a number of other recent works (particularly Chazan et al. 2011; Fleishman et al. 2011; Mathur et al. 2011). We are delighted to contribute to these important conversations through this collection.

Part One
MULTICULTURALISM, DIFFERENCE AND THE POLITICS OF DIVERSITY

Chapter 1

THE BILINGUAL LIMITS OF CANADIAN MULTICULTURALISM

The Politics of Language and Race

Eve Haque

On October 8, 1971, Prime Minister Pierre Elliott Trudeau stood up in the House of Commons and declared Canada to be "multicultural within a bilingual framework," ushering in Canada's first policy on multiculturalism. Since that moment, multiculturalism has become a term with great elasticity, which has allowed it to be taken up across the political spectrum even as its demise has been heralded time and time again. As the resilience and polyvalence of multiculturalism as a signifier of various national ideals has become apparent, its connection to bilingualism has been overtly severed to the point that on the one hand multiculturalism has come to indicate a preoccupation with racialized others in the nation, and on the other, bilingualism has become the given White settler foundation of the nation. The normalization of this national framework can be traced in a genealogy of its emergence through the Royal Commission on Bilingualism and Biculturalism (RCBB) (1963–1970). In fact, Trudeau's declaration that Canada was to be multicultural within a bilingual framework is part of his response to the tabled *Book IV: The Cultural Contribution of Other Ethnic Groups* of the RCBB's final report.

In this chapter, I trace a genealogy of the emergence of multiculturalism within a bilingual framework and its eventual sedimentation as a racialized hierarchy of national belonging. Specifically, I show that the culturalization of difference — particularly racialized difference — through the RCBB in the post–World War II era has meant that bilingualism continues to limit any attempt to revision or revalorize multiculturalism's inclusive and emancipatory potential by foregrounding the collective claims of the two "founding" nations — the English and the French — over all others. It is through a genealogy of the RCBB that the culturalization and reinscription of this racially hierarchized national narrative can be traced, as it is the RCBB that gave rise to the *Official Languages Act* (1969) and Trudeau's multiculturalism policy (1971).

A GENEALOGY OF ROYAL COMMISSIONS

Foucault states that genealogy "operates on a field of entangled and confused parchments, on documents that have been scratched over and recopied many times" (1977: 139). This documentary basis of the genealogical approach means that a broad and heterogeneous array of documents can be drawn upon, including, in the case of this chapter, transcripts of royal commission hearings, related research reports, memos, associated conference proceedings, commission briefs, parliamentary debates, newspaper articles and two of the five volumes of the RCBB's final report. The genealogical method eschews the search for origins or beginnings and is instead oriented towards discontinuities even in present social formations. Genealogy is a "history of the present" which evaluates the present by reflecting upon the ways the discursive and institutional practices of the past impinge on the constitution of the present (Tamboukou 1999: 205). Foucault outlines the three main elements of the genealogical method as eventalization, descent and emergence. For Foucault, eventalization seeks to record the singularity of events in the most unpromising places and define even those instances when "they are absent, the moment in which they remain unrealized" (139). This forces the event under scrutiny to be analyzed within the matrix of discursive and non-discursive practices that have given rise to its existence and forces a rethinking of "power relations that at a certain historical moment decisively influenced the way things were socially and historically established" (Tamboukou 1999: 207). Descent disrupts the notion of any uninterrupted continuity by maintaining the passing of events in their proper dispersion. That is, through the identification of accidents, minute deviations or reversals, errors and faulty calculations, the birth of those things "that continue to exist and have value" shows that "truth or being does not lie at the root of what we know and what we are, but the exteriority of accidents" (Foucault 1977: 144). Finally, emergence is the moment of arising that Foucault locates in the interstices of the "endless repeated play of dominations" between distant adversaries that "established marks of power and engrave memories on things and even within bodies" (144). In this way, genealogy is situated within the articulation of the body and history, and its task is to expose a "body totally imprinted by history and the process of history's total destruction of the body" 146). Thus, eventalization, descent and emergence can operate to disrupt the continuity and historical development of the national narrative, revealing discontinuities and forcing a multiplication of causes to be considered in this historical imprinting of different bodies in the nation.

There have been several hundred royal commissions in Canada since Confederation, and as Jenson (1994: 40) states, royal commissions are institutions that go beyond mere policy-making and serve as a platform through which Canadians debate the representation of themselves in order to "set out the terms of who we are, where we have been and what we might become." Corrigan and Sayer (1985) add that commissions also serve to increase the density of state regulation through the centralization of knowledge, that is, the legitimization of some forms of knowledge in order to justify features and forms of particular state policies. Ashforth (1990: 6) describes commissions of inquiry as schemes of legitimization whereby some principles underlying policy are systematized and explained in the language of "objective" knowledge of facts. He outlines three phases of the inquiry. The first of these is the investigative phase, where the official representatives chosen by the state — the commissioners — engage with representatives of selected social interests within the parameters of the inquiry. These engagements are not merely modes of investigation but are in fact performances which serve ultimately to authorize a form of social discourse. In the persuasive phase, the publication of the final reports of the commission as the authoritative statement also symbolizes an invitation for dialogue between a purportedly neutral state and civil society (7). In the archival phase, the reports become part of the nation's interpretative framework and history — in the case of the RCBB, the founding of Canada as a bilingual nation with a policy of multiculturalism. Central to the commission's work is the investigation of the "problem," which can be tackled rationally and singularly as an object of inquiry. Ultimately, in the case of the RCBB, it was the terms of reference[1] that served to delineate the singularity of the problem to be investigated.

HISTORICAL CONTEXT FOR THE RCBB

The federal government established the RCBB at a particular historical juncture when challenges to Anglo-Celtic dominance by others within the nation posed a threat to national social cohesion. These challenges were being posed not only by Francophones, but also by Indigenous peoples and what at the time were lumped together by the royal commission as "other ethnic groups." Although the federal government eventually created the RCBB to tackle the task of crafting a new articulation of national community, concurrent changes to immigration policy, proposed changes to the *Indian Act* and the transformations ushered by the Quiet Revolution in Québec also framed the formation of the RCBB.

The 1960s were a time of great changes in Canadian society, and one area of critical change was in relation to immigration policy. A paradigmatic shift in immigration regulations was presented by the immigration minister, Ellen Fairclough, to the House of Commons in early 1962. These new regulations foregrounded education, training and skills as the main criteria for admission regardless of the country of origin of the applicant over the previous admission criteria, which openly discriminated on the basis of racial and geographical exclusions. This was the first set of proposed immigration regulations in the history of Canada which were not explicitly racist in wording and intent, that is, discouraging of non-White and non-European immigration (Hawkins 1988: 91). These changes in immigration policy were developed in conjunction with the decline in numbers of immigrants from Europe, a strong demand for labour and a growing belief — at least in government — of the benefits of immigration. This is not to say all discriminatory elements of immigration were eliminated, since restrictive sponsorship criteria and uneven distribution of Canadian immigration offices around the world still maintained a level of less overt racialized discrimination in immigration policy. However, these changes resulted in an overall shift in source countries for immigration, and by the 1970s, it was clear that the new immigrants arriving in Canada were an increasingly racialized group. If multiculturalism emerged as policy out of the RCBB, it was as a result of pressures mainly from those whose ancestry was European in origin and for whom language was the most salient marker of identity and difference. However, as multiculturalism became policy and immigrants became an increasingly racialized category, multiculturalism increasingly came to be associated with racialized communities as the European "other ethnic groups" slowly assimilated into the White settler category (Burnet 1978; Lupul 1983).

In the 1960s, another paradigmatic change that the federal government attempted to institutionalize was the forced assimilation of the Indigenous peoples of Canada through the abolition of the *Indian Act*. In 1969, the minister of Indian affairs and northern development, Jean Chrétien, proposed the *Statement of the Government of Canada on Indian Policy* (Government of Canada 1969a), better known as the White Paper. The White Paper was based on the idea that any disadvantages that Indigenous peoples suffered in Canadian society were based on their different legal status from non-Indigenous Canadian citizens; thus, assimilation as regular Canadian citizens could be justified — within a rapid five-year transitional period — even if this meant the continued and in some cases, accelerated abrogation of treaties and land claims. The White Paper was based on an individual notion of equality and pointedly ignored input from Indigenous leaders, which had been sought during consultations in the previous summer of 1968 and also ignored a previous report, *The Hawthorn Report* (1967), commissioned by the Department of Citizenship and Immigration, which had rejected assimilation and also recommended a "citizens plus" status for Indigenous groups. Indigenous communities also reacted to the White Paper, and in 1970 drafted a brief called *Citizens Plus* (see Indians Chiefs of Alberta 2011 for a reprinted version), also known as the Red Paper, and presented it to the federal cabinet. The Red Paper called for the maintenance of the special status of Indigenous groups and reaffirmed the importance of treaties, rejecting the White Paper outright. Shortly thereafter, the White Paper was withdrawn. The federal government's plans for assimilating Indigenous groups during this period meant that there was no mention of them in the terms of reference for the RCBB; a plan which fit well with the assertion in the terms of reference that Canada had only two founding nations, the English and the French, a strategy to reinscribe the White settler logic of the nation. However, Indigenous groups did mount a challenge to this foundational bicultural logic, even if the outcome of a policy on multiculturalism was not necessarily what they had envisioned.

In the wake of the Quiet Revolution,[2] the 1960s ushered in an era in which French Canadian demands for equality — particularly those in Québec — could no longer be ignored by the federal government. Although at Confederation language rights for both English and French were enshrined in section 133 of the *British North America Act*, increasing immigration and industrialization meant the Anglicization of the economy as the English language moved more rapidly than the French out of farming into manufacturing. This meant that immigrant assimilation was oriented more towards English-speaking communities, which exacerbated the marginalization of French in the economy and the federal civil service. Thus, by the 1950s, most of the major economic institutions and industries in Québec were controlled by Anglophones, making English the language of work at higher levels of management. This in turn relegated Francophones to smaller and more peripheral levels of economic activity, all of which translated into significant economic disparities between the two groups, particularly in Montréal (Levine 1990). These economic disparities, alongside the growing urban Francophone middle class in the aftermath of the Quiet Revolution, all worked to mobilize Québec's nationalist movement, with language rights at its centre.

In the post–World War II period, immigrants began to arrive in increasing numbers to Montréal so that by 1970, they accounted for 23 percent of Montréal's population (Levine 1990: 55). As well, the majority of these immigrants chose to send their children to schools with English as the medium of instruction in order to ensure some sort of future economic mobility for their children, but also because of the poor schooling offered to their children at French-language schools — a problem compounded by the fact that the French Catholic school board would not admit non-Catholic children. With the publication of sensationalist demographic projections about the declining Francophone birthrate and increase in immigration rates (Levine 1990), the schooling choices of immigrant children ignited nationalist sentiments and became the site for nationalist action including agitation for unilingual French schooling. These increasing pressures led to riots in Montréal's Saint Leonard neighbourhood — a neighbourhood with a growing Italian immigrant population — on September 10, 1969, in which a hundred people were injured and fifty were arrested and the *Riot Act* was imposed to set curfews and restore order (Levine 1990: 78; Mills 2010: 142–43). In the aftermath of the riots, the provincial government issued Bill 63, which guaranteed parents a choice in language schooling. Ensuing activism on the part of Francophones would see this bill replaced with future legislation that would guarantee much stronger protections for the French language and the eventual loss of any choice in language of public schooling for immigrant parents. In this era, nationalist sentiment was growing throughout many segments of Francophone society; however, it was the extreme fringes of this movement which garnered the most publicity and ultimately influenced political will. This was emblematized in the example of the Front de libération du Québec (FLQ) which was responsible for over 160 violent incidents between 1960 and 1970, including bombings, kidnapping and deaths, all culminating in the October Crisis of 1970[3] (Levine 1990: 90).

The 1960s were a period of great social upheaval in Canadian society, which included the questioning of existing national narratives; hence the adoption of the Canadian flag (1965), the extensive centennial celebrations (1967) and the Royal Commission on the Status of Women (1968). Although the RCBB was a way for the federal government to respond to the perceived challenges to national unity triggered by French Canadian demands, the increasingly visible Indigenous activism and the sea changes in immigration policy and immigrant demographics made the 1960s a time when established modes of organizing national belonging were being called into question and the reworking and rearticulation of a new basis of Canadian national identity had to be considered. It was in the midst of these pressures for social and political changes in Canadian society that calls for a royal commission on bilingualism and biculturalism were made, foremost in a seminal editorial by André Laurendeau in *Le Devoir*, on January 1962. This editorial triggered other calls for an inquiry, and when the federal Liberals were elected with a minority government in 1963, Prime Minister Lester B. Pearson immediately established the RCBB, foregrounding his primary concern with the French Canadian challenges to national unity: "The greater Canada that is in our power to make will be built not on uniformity but on continuing diversity, and particularly on the basic partnership of English speaking and French speaking people" (Government of Canada 1963a: 6). The commission's terms of reference were finalized as an order-in-council on July 19, 1963:

> To inquire into and report upon the existing state of bilingualism and biculturalism in Canada and to recommend what steps should be taken to develop the Canadian confederation on the basis of an equal partnership between the two founding races, taking into account the contribution made by the other ethnic

groups to the cultural enrichment of Canada and the measures that should be taken to safeguard that contribution.[4] (Government of Canada 1965a: 151–52)

In response to a letter from Prime Minister Pearson to the provincial premiers that asked whether they would "favour" an inquiry, the majority of the provinces expressed support for the RCBB terms of reference, and shortly thereafter ten commissioners were appointed, including co-chairs André Laurendeau and Davidson Dunton.

THE PRELIMINARY PHASE

The RCBB entered the investigative phase of the inquiry with preliminary hearings held November 7 and 8, 1963, in Ottawa. The key task of these preliminary hearings — which would be extended as regional hearings across the country the following year — and the ensuing preliminary report was to confirm the "problem" as set out in the terms of reference: that is, that the greatest crisis facing Canada was relations between the English and French. However, the framing of the French-English crisis as the singular "problem" for the RCBB to tackle was contested vigorously by members of other ethnic groups throughout the hearings.

Members of other ethnic groups contested the RCBB's singular framing through a variety of strategies; however, two main ones were contesting the hierarchy implied amongst groups in the terms of reference and questioning the historical claims upon which the category founding races was restricted to only the English and French. At the hearing, a representative from the Canadian Polish Congress began by questioning the hierarchy suggested in the very name of the commission, "Although it is stated that the Commission is to study other ethnic groups and cultures, the very name of the Commission suggests that Canadian culture is or should be bicultural" (Government of Canada 1963b: 183–84). He went on to caution that "we cannot limit a culture in a mechanical way to one or two or three or four elements … multiculture is a necessity" (Government of Canada 1963b: 183–84). This suggestion of the necessity for "multiculture" foreshadowed the ensuing hearing discussions, which would also advocate multiculturalism as a way to break out of the bicultural binary being foregrounded by the commission.

This query over the name of the commission gave rise to a concern with the terms of reference and the hierarchy among groups it implied. Thus, a representative from the Ukrainian Canadian Congress argued that the terms of reference implied a division of Canadian citizens into "first and second class citizens" and that the hierarchization of one group of Canadians over another on the basis of a "so-called prior historic right" would ultimately mean a "return to colonial status" (Government of Canada 1963b: 83). These concerns gave way to contentions around particular terms such as "new Canadians," which was used with great frequency throughout the hearings to refer to all groups other than the English, French and Indigenous communities. For example, the president of the National Council of Women of Canada (NCWC) argued that the term "new Canadian" had shifted from describing those who had come after 1947, to meaning "all those who are in Canada after 1759 who are not of French or Anglo-Saxon origin," which would mean that, "if a person came from England in 1960, he is Canadian, but if a Pole or a Ukrainian or a Jew traces his origin in Canada to his great grandfather in

1799, he is a 'new Canadian'" (Government of Canada 1963b: 488). This example was given to show the contradictions embedded within the hierarchy between "Canadian" and "new Canadian," which was paralleled in the terms of reference by the labels "other ethnic groups" and "founding races." As the president of the NCWC continued, the use of these terms suggested "a kind of a priori conclusion — that, whatever the findings of the Commissioners should be, this is a conclusion that they must, by the very terms of reference, arrive at" (Government of Canada 1963b: 452).

Although many spoke out at the hearings about the hierarchization of communities in the terms of reference, another strategy also extensively used at the hearings was not to necessarily challenge the distinctions between groups but to widen their inclusion. Specifically, the idea of a "prior historic right" was an ongoing point of contention and one that various groups representing the Ukrainian community in particular used to make their claims for also fitting into the founding race category. For example, a representative from the Ukrainian Professional and Businessmen's Club spoke about how "Canadian Ukrainian citizens felt that they too are a founding race since to a large extent it was the Ukrainians that did the work of building the railways, and … opened up the backwoods … and transformed [Canada] into the Canadian breadbasket of the world" (Government of Canada 1963b: 220). It was on the basis of these prior historical claims that a territorial argument for language rights was made by the same presenter:

> When you consider the fact that now we have third generation Canadians and now my children are fourth generation and speak Ukrainian, having learned it in Canada, these people find themselves in a milieu which enables them to speak that language and be understood … in Winnipeg or in many Manitoba and Saskatchewan towns, one can shop during a complete day and do business during that day using only this language which has been learned in Canada … this is a Canadian language. (Government of Canada 1963b: 231)

Not only did members of other ethnic groups come to the preliminary hearings, but a member of the National Indian Council of Canada also made a bid for Indigenous peoples to be considered as a founding race and therefore to have their language rights also acknowledged: "We respectfully submit that Canada is a tri-lingual country. Our imprint is indelibly on this land … Indians possess a culture quite distinct from biculturalism" (Government of Canada 1963b: 144). Although Indigenous groups were explicitly excluded from the terms of reference, they did come to hearings and participated in the public portion of the commission in order to make clear that they also had a stake in the deliberations of the RCBB.

The preliminary hearings were a forum for groups other than the English and French to contest the hegemony of the idea of two founding races. However, it was clear that for the commissioners, the primary task was to generate agreement on the singularity of the "problem" facing the RCBB as defined through the terms of reference. Published on February 1, 1965, the preliminary report was a surprise best-seller, indicating the depth of national interest in the initial findings of the commission. The publication of the report inaugurated the persuasive phase of the commission as the "truth" (Ashforth 1990:

9) of the hearings. The report opened with the statement that the commissioners "have been driven to the conclusion that Canada, without being fully conscious of the fact, is passing through the greatest crisis in its history" (Government of Canada 1965a: 13). At the end of the report, in a postscript from the commissioners, the exact nature of the crisis is reiterated: "The present crisis is reminiscent of the situation described by Lord Durham in 1838: 'I found two nations warring in the bosom of a single state'" (144). Thus, the extensive deputations from the other ethnic groups challenging the fundamentally binaristic framing of the terms of reference were minimized in favour of reasserting the central crisis as one between the English and French, that is, a primary concern with the "totality of the two societies in Canada" (144). Challenges from groups other than the English and French were set aside using a number of discursive strategies, but primarily the report relied on presenting the opinions of other ethnic groups as fragmented and atomized, as exemplified in this passage from the report: "An attempt was made at some regional meetings to discover what unifying values are held in common by Canadians of German, Italian, Chinese, Ukrainian and other ethnic extraction, but a full discussion didn't seem to follow, and this variant on the multicultural theme tended to blend with the mosaic idea" (51). Although here in the preliminary phase of the RCBB, the term multicultural emerged as a way to define other ethnic groups, its primacy over other terms such as "mosaic" and "new Canadians" had not yet been established; this would only happen during the course of the public hearings.

THE PUBLIC HEARINGS

Even as the publication of the preliminary report ushered in the persuasive phase of the RCBB, the investigative phase continued concurrently as the much more extensive cross-country public hearings began in March 1965. The key difference between the preliminary and public hearings was that groups/people had to submit briefs — which had specific guidelines for discussion points — to the commission. The ensuing discussions at the hearings were then specific to the issues raised in the briefs. The constraints imposed by having to first submit a brief before being able to participate in the public hearings did limit the involvement of many racialized communities, although there were a few submissions from the Japanese community. Ultimately, it was the longer established Ukrainian community who made the largest number of submissions at the public hearings.

If the call for multiculturalism was only one of many ways in which other ethnic groups tried to petition for inclusion at the preliminary hearings, at the public hearings multiculturalism became a prominent term around which the inclusion, and limits thereof, of Aboriginal and other ethnic groups began to coalesce. For example, the Social Study Club of Edmonton established their historical claims as "homesteaders" who had come in the early days of Alberta and managed to work and mingle with each other "without bothering about bilingualism, or giving too much thought to the fact that we were helping to form a basic Canadian culture" (1964: 4). As the brief clarified, they were against the idea of compensating "economic injustices with an artificial form of bi-culturalism which will try, through an artificial bi-lingualism, to overcome an economic problem with a cultural remedy … rather than recognizing the actual fact that multi-culturalism has already been adopted spontaneously by the people themselves" (4). This brief exemplified the emerging consensus among many other ethnic groups that multiculturalism was already an everyday fact of Canadian life and that official recognition of only two languages in Canada would in fact be counter to this grounded spirit of multiculturalism.

Citing data from the 1961 census, the Mutual Co-operation League of Toronto argued that there was "neither one race nor language in this country forming a clear majority"; therefore, "the advancement of bilingualism was insufficient in scope, and that of biculturalism was limited in vision" (1964: 1). The Canadian Mennonite Association also agreed that biculturalism/bilingualism was limited, arguing that it was a useful idea only insofar as "it moves society from a monocultural status to multilingualism and multiculturalism," and hoped that for the RCBB, "the larger frame of reference will be multilingualism and multiculturalism" (1965: 3). This was echoed by the International Institute of Metropolitan Toronto, a community-wide voluntary settlement organization, which argued that the increasingly diverse range of immigrants settling in Toronto meant that "the City is moving from a largely monocultural society to a multicultural world now"; thus, "a new idea of citizenship is developing which transcends culture and language," giving Canada an "opportunity to demonstrate to the world the idea of a multicultural country" (1964: 1). In these and other briefs, both the contemporary shifts in immigration demographics as well as the historical diversity of immigration to Canada were mobilized as arguments against a limited bicultural and bilingual conceptualization of the nation, instead, biculturalism/bilingualism were seen at best as stepping stones to the official recognition of a de facto multicultural nation. In this way, multiculturalism was naturalized as an already existing Canadian reality, both in the past and into an increasingly cosmopolitan future.

The RCBB garnered extensive press coverage during the hearings, not only in the mainstream press but also in the ethnic press. The ethnic press, 80 percent of which was published in languages other than English and French, played an important role in keeping various communities updated on developments throughout the inquiry, and royal commission researchers also collected related press clippings the various ethnic media in order to remain informed throughout the inquiry. Given the extensive coverage and analysis generated in the ethnic media, the Canada Ethnic Press Federation also submitted a substantive brief on behalf of the other ethnic groups. An overarching theme in the brief was that of "unity in diversity" as a basic Canadian principle (1964: 15). Similar to many other ethnic groups, for the Canada Ethnic Press Federation (1964: 15), the substantive element of "unity in diversity" or multiculturalism was multilingualism:

> The language of origin is the most powerful instrument in the hands of an ethnic group for retaining its cultural heritage ... the selection of English or French (or both) does not mean that the ethnic groups will or should discard their languages — the best media available to them for the preservation of their cultures and integration into Canadian cultural streams.

During the course of the public hearings, the linking of language preservation to cultural retention became a central argument for many other ethnic groups for moving beyond biculturalism and bilingualism to multiculturalism materialized as multilingual rights. However, not all briefs from other ethnic groups embraced multiculturalism and multilingualism.

Members of both the Polish and German communities made strong demands in community newspapers for multiculturalism even as they did not make any substantive demands for community language support. For example, a German community newspaper article stated: "Canada is not expected to become a Tower of Babel ... but to lay down the rule that Canada should have two cultures is illogical and outright wrong" ("Once Again: Two Languages" 1964); furthermore, the article went on to argue that Canada was built on the roots of many cultures, all of which should be officially recognized. In a brief from the National Japanese Canadian Citizens Association, members of the Japanese community made no demands for any community language preservation support or multiculturalism, arguing that this would promote a "hyphenated Canadian" identity; rather, they argued for "'Canadianism' — one and indivisible," based on their "bitter experiences during the war years," which they attributed in part to "hyphenated Canadianism" (1965: 3). The Toronto-based Italian Aid Society, which was essentially a settlement organization for newly arriving Italian immigrants, echoed the Japanese brief in that they fully endorsed the terms of reference of the commission, arguing that "there should be no special treatment afforded any other ethnic groups towards the perpetuation of the cultures, languages, customs, etc. of these groups" (Bagnato 1963: 1). The only request for language learning support was for multilingual staff at the various levels of government in order to "expedite the handling of the problems of those who have not, as yet, mastered the English language" (2). However, the more established Italian community in Montréal, represented in a brief from the Canadian-Italian Business and Professional Men's Association, did argue for support for community language preservation since there was a concern that without the maintenance of Italian, "it is definite that in 30 to 50 years we will not have a medium of communication between us" (Government of Canada 1965b: 4273). Finally, the Ukrainian community, which submitted over half of all the briefs from the other ethnic groups, came out strongly in favour of both multiculturalism and a territorial multilingualism as proposed during the preliminary hearings, exemplified in a community paper: "Since Canadian is not merely bi-lingual and bi-cultural but multilingual and multicultural, our principle is an absolute equality of all Canadians" ("Canada is Ours" 1965: n.p.).

Although not mentioned in the terms of reference, pressure from Indigenous communities and coverage of Indigenous issues in the mainstream media meant that Indigenous groups were able to participate in the public hearings. The briefs from Indigenous groups focused on their extensive socioeconomic marginalization from mainstream Canadian society and emphasized their unique identity as a way to challenge their original erasure from the RCBB. As well, the briefs challenged the limited notion of founding races in the terms of reference and emphasized their status as the "first citizens," which made them "more Canadian than any other groups that have arrived since European settlement" (Indian-Eskimo Association of Canada 1965: 2). The threat of assimilation to cultural survival was concretized extensively as the urgent need for Indigenous language preservation and revitalization over English and French bilingualism: "As to two languages, it has long been accepted that Red Men are entitled to their own original ancient language which precedes that of the languages of the Western world by thousands of years" (Caughnawaga Defence Committee 1965: 3). Ultimately, even Indigenous groups gave little support to the commission's notion of biculturalism, arguing instead that "'equality' of groups … should also include Indians and bring into it 'multi' instead of 'bi'" (Caughnawaga Defence Committee 1965: 4). The public hearings were the central element of the investigative phase in the RCBB, and many other ethnic groups and well as Indigenous groups used this as an opportunity to make clear the exact nature of their opposition to the commission's terms of reference. As well, they used these hearings as a venue to articulate their vision for inclusion and belonging in this moment when the national narrative was being rearticulated, with multiculturalism — substantiated through support for community languages — emerging as a contested idea for other ethnic and Indigenous groups to challenge the commission's limited framework of biculturalism.

BOOK I TO THE OFFICIAL LANGUAGES ACT

The end of the public hearings indicated the close of the investigative phase of the RCBB, and the first volume of the final report, *Book I: The Official Languages*, was tabled in the House of Commons on December 5, 1967, ushering in a new persuasive phase of the commission and entering the archival phase by providing the foundation for the *Official Languages Act*. This report began with a general introduction, which examined the key terms from the commission's terms of reference. One of the most contentious terms discussed in this introduction was "race." The authors of the report admitted that this term had been a source of great "misunderstanding" throughout the hearings and that in fact, "the word 'race' is used in an older meaning as referring to a national group, and carries no biological significance" (Government of Canada 1967: xxii). Given the necessity of divorcing any biological connotations from the word race, the authors were quick to de-emphasize race in favour of language and culture: "We feel that language and culture and truly central concepts in the terms of reference … we shall give them more emphasis than the notions 'race,' 'people,' or even 'ethnic groups'" (xxii). The authors foregrounded language and culture over race and ethnicity as a response to the critiques made during the hearings that there was an implied hierarchy of founding races over other ethnic groups.

However, even as the report disavowed this hierarchy by citing the openness of language ("membership in a linguistic group is a matter of personal choice"), they brought it back in by demarcating "two classes of citizens, one consisting of Anglophones of British origin and Francophones of French origin, and the other of Anglophones and Francophones of other origins" (xxiv). Thus, the original distinctions between founding races and other ethnic groups were transposed onto linguistic divisions. These distinctions were concretized as the report stated that for the two founding races "the life of the two cultures implies in principle the life of the two languages" (xxxviii), which was the rationale for proposing an official languages act that would declare English and French to be the official languages of Canada. However, with respect to the other ethnic groups, the report argued that "much of the culture of one's forbears could be preserved even when one no longer spoke their language" (xxiii). This was the critical difference then between founding races and other ethnic groups; the former needed language to retain their culture and the latter could manage their culture without language. This disparity in the right to language would set the mode for differential inclusion between these two groups and reinstall the hierarchy of difference of the original terms of reference, but this time on the terrain of language and culture.

Despite the original omission from the terms of reference, Indigenous groups had made great efforts to participate in the hearings, and, in turn, the commission spent resources researching issues related to Indigenous communities. Reports were commissioned, memos were written, experts were consulted and meetings were arranged.

At the end of these efforts, the conclusions drawn by the commission were clear: "The Canadian Indian problem is so complex that an inquiry into the existing situation of this large and important group should be handled by a special Royal Commission" (Varjassy 1964: 5). The pathologization of Indigenous issues by the RCBB served to set them outside of the ambit of the inquiry and also exempted the commission from having to consider the cultural and linguistic claims of the Indigenous founding peoples: "The social and economic problems of the Indians are so great, deep and bitter, that the cultural and language problems must wait until they realize them" (Varjassy 1964: 3). All this culminated in the clear statement in *Book I* of the report, which handily discounted the one undeniable challenge to a bicultural notion of founding races: "We should point out here that the Commission will not examine the question of the Indians and Eskimos … since it is obvious that these two groups do not form part of the 'founding races' as the phrase is used in the terms of reference" (Government of Canada 1967: xxvi).

With challenges from other ethnic and Indigenous groups set aside in this report, the proposal to declare English and French the official languages of Canada could go ahead, and in the final chapter of the report, "The Necessary Legislation," the proposed principles for an official language policy were spelled out in detail. As Bill C-120 regarding the Official Languages of Canada was presented in the House on October 17, 1968, Trudeau echoed the terms of reference and gave a glimpse at his future formulation of official multiculturalism: "We believe in two official languages and in a pluralist society, not merely as a political necessity but as an enrichment" (Government of Canada 1968: 1509).

BOOK IV TO MULTICULTURALISM WITHIN A BILINGUAL FRAMEWORK

Book IV: The Cultural Contribution of Other Ethnic Groups was published in October 1969. Even before the publication of this volume of the final report, the commissioners were grappling with the impact of the other ethnic groups, particularly their desire for multiculturalism over biculturalism. One internal working paper concluded: "In summary we can say that the mainspring (*l'idée force*) of the terms of reference is the question of bilingualism and biculturalism (i.e., English and French) adding immediately that this mainspring is working in a situation where there is a fact of multiculturalism" (Study Group D 1963: 1). This multicultural fact was not one to necessarily be celebrated, but rather one to watch out for as another internal commission memorandum warned that "the most striking characteristic of Other Ethnic Group immigration is its increased strength at the expense of the British element," and, therefore, "the imposing growth of the number of the Other Ethnic Groups has disturbed the balance of the core societies' strength" (Wyczynski 1966: 4). Given these concerns, it is not surprising that when the report was finally published, it repudiated multiculturalism altogether and began the introduction from the position that, "while the terms of reference deal with the question of those of ethnic origin other than British or French, they do so in relation to the basic problem of bilingualism and biculturalism from which they are inseparable" (Government of Canada 1969b: 3).

In *Book I*, the commission made the shift from race and ethnicity to language and culture for identifying and delineating groups within the nation. Here in *Book IV*, the shift away from race and ethnicity was emphasized right from the introduction as contact between groups and the contribution of other ethnic groups was couched in terms of language and culture: "We will look at the contribution to Canadian life, and especially to the enrichment that results from the meeting of a number of languages and cultures" (Government of Canada 1969b: 3). As well, if in *Book I* this shift meant that founding races had now putatively become Anglophones and Francophones, here in the *Book IV*, the shift was completed as "we would rather regard the 'other ethnic groups' as cultural groups" (11). The crucial difference was that, in the case of other ethnic groups, culture was foregrounded and language was not. The hierarchy between founding races and other ethnic groups that was transposed onto language and culture was clearly reiterated throughout the report: "It is thus clear that we must not overlook Canada's culture diversity, keeping in mind that there are two dominant cultures, the French and the English" (13). Although *Book I* set the foundations for the *Official Languages Act*, in *Book IV* commensurate support for the languages of cultural groups was clearly lacking and language preservation for these groups was essentially to be privatized:

> The presence of other cultural groups in Canada is something for which all Canadians should be thankful. The members must always enjoy the right — a basic one — to safeguard their languages and cultures. The exercise of this right requires an extra effort on their part, for which their fellow Canadians owe them a debt of gratitude. (14)

The extra effort would clearly stem from the limited enforceable legislation and lack of constitutional protections for languages other than English and French, as well as the limited funding that would be allocated for this purpose. On these matters, the report was clear: "The learning of third languages [languages other than the two official languages] should not be carried on at the expense of public support for learning the second official language" (138). Ultimately, the authors of *Book IV* remained unequivocal in their support for biculturalism; however, cultural groups across Canada did not let the matter rest, and several conferences on the report were organized. Among these was the Canadian Cultural Rights Concern conference held in Toronto in December 1968, which ended with six resolutions specific to the demands of cultural groups, stating "the Conference unequivocally rejects the concept of biculturalism and seeks official recognition of the multicultural character of Canada" (Canadian Cultural Rights Committee 1968: iii).

These resolutions were sent out to the provincial ministers as well as the Prime Minister's Office and garnered mainstream media coverage, generating headlines such as "Ethnics Attack Biculturalism" in the *Toronto Telegram*.

Book IV was published in 1969, but it wasn't until October of 1971 that Prime Minister Trudeau made his now famous speech announcing the implementation of a policy of multiculturalism within a bilingual framework, "For although there are two official languages, there is no official culture, nor does any ethnic group take precedence over any other … a policy of multiculturalism within a bilingual framework commends itself to the government as the most suitable means of assuring the cultural freedom of Canadians" (Government of Canada 1971: 8545). Even as Trudeau repealed the report's support for biculturalism, he reprised the hierarchy by maintaining that there were two official languages even if there was no official culture. Trudeau concluded his speech by emphasizing "the view of the government that a policy of multiculturalism within a bilingual framework is basically the conscious support of individual freedom of choice" (8546). Therefore, as Trudeau cast his new formulation for national belonging as individual rights, he also maintained the collective rights to language of the English and French over other cultural groups. This entrenched a critical difference between the rights of cultural groups and those accorded to the English and French, even as it was stated that there was no official culture and that henceforth Canada was to be multicultural. Ultimately, although Trudeau had ushered in a policy of multiculturalism, this was a very different idea from the substantive and grounded notion of multiculturalism that had been advanced by other ethnic groups at the hearings.

Materially nothing much had changed in this formulation of multiculturalism as Trudeau based most of the actual details of his multiculturalism policy on the recommendations of *Book IV*; originally recommendations for a bicultural Canada. As well, the clear funding imbalance also concretized this hierarchy, as was pointed out by members of other ethnic groups: "This year, the Federal government has allocated fifty million dollars for French language and culture development outside the province of Québec. For all other minorities combined in all of Canada, the budget is forty thousand" (Multiculturalism for Canada Conference 1970: 30). This disparity was also noted by politicians such as leader of the opposition Robert Stanfield, who in response to Trudeau's announcement of a policy of multiculturalism within a bilingual framework stated: "I do not think that members of other cultural groups with other cultural traditions are at all happy with the relatively pitiful amounts that have been allocated to this other aspect of the diversity about which the Prime Minister spoke this morning, multiculturalism" (Government of Canada 1971: 8547). In short, Trudeau's announcement of a policy of multiculturalism within a bilingual framework as a response to the recommendation of biculturalism in *Book IV* grew out his need to balance the interests of national unity from competing claims put forward by Francophones, Québec and other ethnic groups, among others. However, adopting the recommendations of *Book IV* almost wholesale ensured collective rights to language only for the English and French and essentially relegated community language rights to the private sphere, through a paucity of legislation and underfunding. Thus, the multiculturalism policy did little to disrupt the original White settler formulation of bilingualism and biculturalism put forward in the original terms of reference for the RCBB.

CONCLUSION

The RCBB was established at a particular historical moment when demands from various communities within the nation meant that the federal government had to rearticulate its formulation for nation building. A genealogy of the RCBB shows that in the present, multiculturalism as a narrative of Canadian national identity cannot be considered outside the constraints of bilingualism. The need to always consider the dual poles of this formulation in tandem is critical if we are to understand the limits of multiculturalism in Canada. Even with the shift from race and ethnicity onto the terrain of language and culture, the original racialized hierarchy of difference and belonging remains; however, they are now articulated through a differential set of linguistic rights. These differential rights are now entrenched in the *Canadian Charter of Rights and Freedoms*, where, as Meyerhoff (1994: 918) argued, the collective rights of linguistic dualism in sections 16–23 in comparison to those for multicultural rights in section 27 result in a significant disparity between ethnic minorities and official language minorities with respect to the rights and status each enjoy.[5] Specifically, Meyerhoff showed that section 27 has never been interpreted as a collective right and therefore is no way a substantive provision of rights (Meyerhoff 1994: 935), unlike sections 16–23, which guarantee substantive collective official language rights. Thus, the hegemony of linguistic dualism has not only limited the current conception of multiculturalism but also concretized a racially ordered disparity of rights. The cultural equality and substantive pluralism that other ethnic groups originally sought in their vision of multiculturalism is now entrenched as a single limited interpretative section in the Charter. Ultimately, any future attempt to re-envision, rehabilitate or revalorize multiculturalism's inclusive and emancipatory potential must first address the limitation that official bilingualism presents. This is essential if the goal to move beyond a White settler national narrative in Canada is to be realized.

NOTES

1. There terms of reference were "to inquire into and report upon the existing state of bilingualism and biculturalism in Canada and to recommend what steps should be taken to develop the Canadian confederation on the basis of an equal partnership between the two founding races, taking into account the contribution made by the other ethnic groups to the cultural enrichment of Canada and the measures that should be taken to safeguard that contribution" (Government of Canada 1965a: 151–52).
2. After the death of Duplessis in 1959 and the subsequent death of his successor, Paul Sauvé, Jean Lesage led his Liberal Party to victory over the Union Nationale in 1960, propelling Québec into an era now commonly known as the "Quiet Revolution" — a time of accelerated social, political and economic reforms spanning the early to late 1960s.
3. During the October Crisis of 1970, British Trade Commissioner James Cross was kidnapped and Québec Labour Minister Pierre Laporte was murdered. This crisis led to Prime Minister Trudeau's implementation of the *War Measures Act*, the arrest of almost 500 people and the deployment of federal troops in Montréal.
4. For the full text of the terms of reference, see Government of Canada 1965a: 151–52.
5. Section 27 of the *Charter of Rights and Freedoms* states: "This Charter shall be interpreted in a manner consistent with the preservation and enhancement of the multicultural heritage of Canadians" (Government of Canada 1982a).

Chapter 2

ARTS FUNDING, THE STATE AND CANADIAN NATION-MAKING

Producing Governable Subjects

Andrea Fatona

A number of concerns regarding nation, sovereignty, culture and race underline Canadian state policies for arts funding. These concerns can be characterized as simultaneously philosophical and pragmatic in nature. In this chapter I engage with macro theories of state, governmentality and culture in order to argue that early state patronage of the arts, through the establishment of the Canada Council for the Arts, highlights a politics of arts funding concerned with elite discourses on aesthetic, cultural and social values. Early state funding of the arts produced practices of imagining, shaping and narrating the fledgling Canadian nation as White, modern and European. This imaginary produced a system of exclusionary arts funding practices that persists to this day. The questions that arise as I examine the institution of federal arts funding are the following: What constitutes culture? What are the forms in which culture and art are manifested? Who produces culture and art? And how do institutions such as the Canada Council for the Arts produce, shape and disseminate meanings about what art and culture are? These questions arise from my ongoing research into the implementation of racial equity arts policies at the Canada Council for the Arts, an arms-length federal arts funding agency. This research is motivated by my own work as an emerging video maker and curator, which began in the late 1980s.

I begin my investigation with a primarily theoretical discussion on culture and governance. I then conduct a genealogy of the formation of the Massey Commission (1949) and its final report, which led to the formation of the Canada Council for the Arts (1957), highlighting the discourses that underpin the ideas expressed by the commissioners. I focus my attention on the emergence of issues of race and representation dating back to the Massey Report and the development of racial equity policies in the 1990s. Employing Foucault's concept of governmentality, I argue that the Massey commissioners deployed the concept and practices of culture in an anthropological manner predicated on European mores and sensibilities to create a similitude of a Canadian way of life. I argue that this anthropological deployment of culture galvanized support for their nation-building project, while downplaying questions of aesthetics. This strategy was used to engender alliance-building across various elite constituents and their meaning-making practices in the name of an independent, bicultural Canadian nation, one newly buttressed by official multiculturalism.

GOVERNING CULTURE/CULTURE OF GOVERNING

Contemporary cultural theorists have moved past earlier conceptions of culture as merely signifying practices and implicate state policy in the production of culture. Within these discussions of culture (Bourdieu 1984; Miller and Rose 1992; Bennett 1992, 2003; Yúdice 2003), culture is viewed as normalized through various pedagogical mechanisms, or it is seen as a product of contestations over meaning and social and economic relations (Williams 1981; Hall 2000; Yúdice 2003).[1] Further, within these accounts there is an acknowledgement that culture is connected to state policy and is invoked in two registers: the anthropological and the aesthetic (Bourdieu 1984; Bennett 1992; Miller and Yúdice 2002). In the *anthropological* register, the term "culture" is used to refer to what is distinctive about the "way of life" of a people, community, nation or social group. In the *aesthetic* register, the creative products of individuals are assessed on the basis of formal criteria regarding beauty, derived from the fields of art history and cultural criticism. According to Bennett (1992: 26), culture is best thought of as

> a historically specific set of institutionally embedded relations of government in which the forms of thought and conduct of extended populations are targeted for transformation — in part via the extension through the social body of the forms, techniques, and regimes of aesthetic and intellectual culture.

Bennett's definition of culture provides an entry point for understanding the formation of the Canada Council and its relationship to the state. Bennett moves away from earlier articulations of culture as "way of life" or signifying practices and positions culture as a concern of the state and as a target of governance and regulation. Culture, in this view, is a historically contingent set of non-coercive practices deployed by the state to produce a cultivated population.

In the aesthetic register, the notion of taste or preference for particular types of cultural practices and products is foundational to discussions as to what constitutes culture and how cultural expressions and subjects are classified. The work of Pierre Bourdieu makes strong claims that aesthetic, high cultural tastes and values are socially constituted. In *Distinction*, a book based on empirical material gathered in France in the 1960s, Bourdieu (1984) argues that taste is an acquired "cultural competence" that is used to legitimize social differences. Bourdieu asserts that taste is imbricated with social class and status. On such terms, an elite assessment of culture favours high-culture, and this assessment is used to differentiate between social classes.[2] Cultural policy scholars such as George Yúdice (2003) examine "culture" in the context of neoliberal globalization and the ways in which culture has become an important economic "resource" or commodity. Yúdice further argues that in the current era of globalization, culture is legitimized based on its utility as an object of exchange in the global marketplace. In this marketplace, migration and contact with difference have disturbed the foundation upon which a unified culture was previously used to express "a national expedient" (Yúdice 2003: 11), making way for claims over cultural citizenship and cultural recognition by culturally defined groups.

In addition to Bourdieu's and Yúdice's understanding of "culture," Foucault's argument about the role of the state in managing populations is central to my discussions on cultural policy in general and the formation of the Canada Council for the Arts in particular. I use the term "managing population" to refer to the production of detailed knowledge and expertise developed by institutions of the state that allow for the categorization, organization and care of a given population within a given territorial boundary. Foucault's argument also serves as grounding for my later examination of the Canada Council's establishment of the Racial Equity Office (1991). Foucauldian analyses of the liberal state (Foucault 1991; Gordon 1991; Miller and Rose 1992; Dean 2002) are concerned with the materiality of practices of the state or how the state comes into being through precise institutional practices such as surveillance, regulation and discipline.

For Foucault, part of the work of the liberal state is to perfect what he calls the art of governance — to know and account for its subjects and while doing so, produce subjects who are self-regulating and governable. In his later work, Foucault employs the concept of governmentality, or "governmental rationality" — discourses that make up the logic of governmental authority — as descriptors of the following: processes and practices by which states manage populations within territorial spaces, the governance of the conduct of subjects and the governance of the self by the self. Foucault was concerned with the ways in which populations are problematized, objectified and managed through the activities of social institutions. This form of power is exercised over members of a population to constitute their subjectivity in accordance with state policies. In other words, the role of government is to produce governable subjects. But Foucault was critical of contemporary Marxists who identified all power with the state; hence he also developed the concept of governmentality to signal that much governing takes place beyond the purview of the state.

Foucault's concept of governmentality serves as an analytic framework for understanding different elements of state formation, the ways in which subjects govern themselves and exercise agency, the technologies employed to enable both domination and contestation and the ways in which subjects are constituted. This conceptual lens focuses attention on the ideological[3] function of the liberal state as well as the multiple ways in which the state is implicated in activities within civil society. It specifically allows us to shed light on the dynamic relationships that exist among the Canadian state, the Canada Council for the Arts and its administration of culture in civil society, and the mechanisms through which cultured subjects are produced.

Foucault (1988) refers to this "working on" one's self and the maintenance of certain ways of being and social practices as the "cultivation of the self." Through government intervention and institutional practices, behaviours are shaped in order to produce morally uplifted individuals and a civilized population. These practices are normalized within the sphere of everyday activities via various forms of education practices and cultural institutions. It is through education and the establishment of taste-shaping institutions such as arts funding agencies, museums, libraries and art galleries that the subject learns the art of cultural consumption and production within the parameters of the cultural sphere. A specific instance of how governmentality gets played out in the public realm can be seen in the establishment and execution of commissions of inquiry.

As discussed in the previous chapter, the work of Adam Ashforth (1990) is useful in guiding an understanding of the symbolic and material work that commissions of inquiry engage in as part of a process of state legitimation, especially through the construction of purportedly "objective" knowledge. As Ashforth explains, commissions of inquiry are exercises in standardizing and explaining the rules and outcomes of state policy formation; they actively produce publics that participate, intervene and shape public opinion (Ashforth 1990: 6). I use Ashforth's (1990: 12) typology of the three symbolic and ritualistic phases of commissions of inquiry: the investigative phase, in which representatives chosen by the state — the commissioners — engage with representatives of selected interests within processes of engagement bound by institutional, jurisdictional epistemological and juridical parameters; the persuasive phase, which is marked by the publication of the report/s of the inquiry, which "symbolize a sort of dialogue between the State on the one hand and Society on the other" (7); and the final, or "archival" phase, when the report becomes an instrument of policy formation and serves as a way to interpret events and enter into dialogue with national history.

Ashforth characterizes commissions of inquiry as theatres of power where performances are scripted and the parameters in which the performance unfolds is bounded by codes that govern the performance. Each phase of an inquiry contributes to the process of truth-making, out of which specific plans can be devised to ameliorate a problematic social condition. The production of rational public space for dialogue and debate serves to transform "contentious matters of political struggle into discourses of reasoned argument" (Ashforth 1990: 12). These ideas on the symbolic and material work of commissions, read in relation to Foucault's work on the art of government, are helpful for analyzing the Canadian Massey Commission.

THE CANADIAN GOVERNMENT AND ITS RESPONSIBILITY FOR CULTURE

The Royal Commission on National Development in the Arts, Letters and Sciences, chaired by Vincent Massey (former Canadian envoy to the United States and high commissioner to the United Kingdom), was struck in 1949 by Liberal Prime Minister Louis St. Laurent to examine "broadcasting, federal cultural institutions, government relations with voluntary cultural associations, and federal university scholarships" (Litt 1992: 3). The Massey Commission made its recommendations to Parliament two years later, and in 1957, through the *Canada Council Act*, the Canada Council for the Enjoyment of Arts, Humanities and Social Sciences (herein Canada Council) came into existence. The commission and the subsequent creation of the government agency charged with responsibility for the arts and social sciences can be viewed as technologies designed to draw clear parameters around the types of creative and intellectual knowledges that the Canadian state would privilege as representing the Canadian nation at a time when it was differentiating itself from other nations on the world stage.

The Massey Commission was struck at a time when intellectuals and artists were actively organizing and lobbying for the creation of a funding agency to support the arts and universities. The establishment of the Arts Council of Britain in 1945 played an influential role in informing the sentiments of intellectuals and artists, who were primarily of British "stock," regarding the need to establish a Canadian institutional body that would shape and oversee national cultural production and dissemination (see Whittaker 1965). According to some scholars (Whittaker 1965; Cummings and Katz 1987; Litt 1992;

Beale 1993), the commission interpreted its mandate as part of a broader campaign to galvanize Canadian nationalism in order to distinguish postwar Canada as distinct from its southern neighbour and from Britain. The postwar period was a significant one in which art, culture, research and education were deemed important tools for preventing the re-emergence of fascism and socialism.

The Massey Commission

The Massey Commission was composed of members of Canada's cultural establishment who were affiliated with national voluntary associations such as the League of Nations Society, the Société d'éducation des adultes du Québec, the Canadian Institute for International Affairs, the Société des écrivains canadiens, the Association of Canadian Clubs and the Canadian League.[4] Not only were the commissioners drawn from Canada's cultural elite, but almost all of the commissioners were "friends-of-government insiders" (Litt 1992: 35). Litt (1992: 21) describes the commissioners as "generally well educated, White, middle class, and male, and their interactions led to friendships which reinforced their shared interests." Although one female academic was appointed to the group, the Massey Commission was otherwise a homogeneous assemblage with regard to gender, race, ethnicity, ideology, education and class. It should be noted that not one single artist was appointed to the commission. The commission excluded the rank of the "average" Canadian citizen and drew from a pool of Canadian intellectuals who advocated for state support of the arts and letters as a way to foster the development of a distinctly Canadian culture, one that symbolized Canada's transformation from the status of a colony to that of an independent, bicultural, yet unified nation.

During the investigative phase of their work, the commissioners held hearings in "sixteen cities across Canada, making sure that every province had been visited. Travelling some 10,000 miles, it held 224 meetings, 114 of which were public sessions; 462 briefs were presented to it and about 1,200 witnesses appeared before it" (Royal Commission on National Development in the Arts, Letters and Sciences (1949–1951) 1951: 8). Associations such as the Canadian Arts Council,[5] which later became known as the Canadian Conference of the Arts, and the Canada Foundation played a pivotal role in providing support for the commission's work. Their ideology and goals were in keeping with those of the members of the Massey Commission regarding the central role of the arts and culture in shaping the Canadian nation and the need for public funding to support this nation-building endeavour.

The cultural lobby articulated a logic that was based on what Litt (1992) refers to as a liberal humanistic philosophical perspective on culture and the social and psychological development of democratic society. In their quest to better society and the individual in society, the cultural lobby favoured state interventions that enabled and furthered the project of the production of universal knowledge and practices. Their perspective was in keeping with that of the Massey commissioners. The cultural lobby and the Massey commissioners were committed to Enlightenment notions of progress and freedom that emphasize the universality of aesthetic judgments and the transcendental potential of Western aesthetic sensibilities. The commissioners saw elite culture as being central to the mission of democracy and were interested in the arts and culture as apparatuses that could improve the spiritual, moral and intellectual capacities of the "ordinary" citizen. The growing influence of broadcast media and of American productions was also an important factor that fuelled the concerns of the cultural lobby. Litt appropriately conjectures that the cultural elites' concern to halt the proliferation of mass culture was an attempt to further the project of the betterment of the masses. More importantly, Litt claims, it was an indication of class struggles being played out in the cultural sphere.

The development of the collective and individual self of the nation is implicitly bound up in the notion of "working on" the spiritual foundation of Canadians. In such practices, we see at work the "cultivation of self" identified by Foucault, in that these practices aim to normalize the conduct of national subjects. As such, the state is involved in securing the nation while institutions in civil society take on the role of moulding social practices concerned with the care of the self and self-sovereignty. Prime Minister Louis St. Laurent expressed sentiments similar to those of the commissioners with respect to the subject's care of self and the role of the state in relation to the welfare, education and upliftment of its citizenry: "There is another side of human life that is as important as the dollars resulting from trade. Upon that side of the normal activities of civilized, Christian human beings, sufficient attention has not been focused nationwide" (Litt 1992: 31). Thus, the commission's effects as an element of governmentality work to employ culture and the arts to produce, maintain and transform the Canadian citizenry into respectable subjects with strong Christian moral principles.

The Massey Commission was concerned with the production and consumption of taste as much as the development of a nationalist sentiment. The commissioners strategically downplayed the use of the terms "art" and "culture" on their tour across the country so as not to draw attention to their elitist interpretations of the terms. Instead, they opted to market the commission as a nationalist project that was concerned with the average person. This is apparent in the rhetoric employed by the commission over its two-year period of public consultation. Litt (1992: 65–66) states that "the commission remained wary of associating itself with culture" and "the commissioners would continue to pitch this combination of lowbrow pretence and patriotic purpose as they moved across the country." The move towards appealing to the "average" person, or to the lowbrow, was ironic and somewhat patronizing as the commission was composed of a sampling of the elite who themselves were concerned with highbrow cultural practices. The term culture was excluded from public discourse and replaced by ideas about the public good and the development of a nationalist sentiment. This shift served to protect the commissioners from being challenged about their highbrow affiliations and the elitist connotations the terms "art" and "culture" carry; thus, their role in the management and production of a particular form of public good could operate relatively unimpeded.

The commissioners viewed the increase in the leisure time of Canadians as allowing the spectre of mass culture to creep into the national psyche and expressed the following opinion about the role of the arts and letters in halting this phenomenon:

> Canadian achievement in every field depends mainly on the quality of the Canadian mind and spirit. This quality is determined by what Canadians think, and think about; by the books they read, the pictures they see and the

programmes they hear. These things, whether we call them arts and letters or use other words to describe them, we believe to lie at the roots of our life as a nation. (Royal Commission on National Development in the Arts, Letters and Sciences (1949–1951) 1951: 271)

This cultural elite also sought to differentiate Canadian culture from the culture of the rest of the world, and specifically from the United States. There was fear that American mass culture would bastardize the Canadian cultural persona. The immediacy of the fear of the proliferation of American mass culture was fuelled by the fact that Canada lacked a history of arts patronage from the economic elite to stoke the engine of creativity and the market for art and high culture. To ameliorate the position of artists and Canadian cultural producers *vis-à-vis* the influence of their southern neighbour, various cultural power brokers called upon the state to intervene and provide the necessary infrastructure and financial support to generate distinctly Canadian cultural products while building an independent Canadian nation.

The commissioners were not only concerned with the American cultural presence in Canada; they were equally concerned with Canada's cultural presence abroad. They called upon the state to participate in the engineering of a coherent articulation of Canadianness that could be exported. To meet that need, the commissioners recommended that the Canada Council act as a "clearinghouse" of products that could be distinctly catalogued and labelled "Canadian." The Massey Report stresses the need for a centralized, state-supported agency that would oversee and manage any Canadian cultural presence on the international scene.

The commissioners prescribed the creation of and a role for the Canada Council. The Canada Council was called upon to possess expert knowledge of Canadian culture and to participate in the dissemination of the nation's cultural products on the national and international stages. Their concern was to hold the state responsible for developing public policy that would (a) aid in differentiating the culture of Canada from that of other nation states, (b) create the conditions in which Canadian high culture would be produced and consumed and (c) enable the "spiritual foundations" of the Canadian citizenry to flourish. This concern with the management (creation and enabling) of culture drew on both the anthropological and aesthetic registers of culture for resonance and legitimacy, even though the aesthetic was prioritized. The commissioners sought to throw off the yoke of colonial domination while engaging in a love affair with the cultures of their colonial pasts. The goal then was to create a Canadian culture or way of life that was distinctly different from those of other nations, yet the "art" forms of Western Europe were espoused as the benchmarks of valuable cultural expression. These forms represented a nation's arrival at the pinnacle of cultural evolution and moral development.

Culture, Race and the Massey Report

The Massey Commission presented its written report and recommendations to the prime minister in 1951, during the height of the Korean War. As an element of this persuasive phase, the commissioners employed the rhetoric of the "defence of Canadian culture," which meant a Canadian culture that represented English and French Canadians, as one of the justifications for the formation of a federal arts funding body. The commissioners not only championed the defence and enrichment of Canadian culture through the activities of the state, they anchored the notion of progress and civilization on the concepts of "national" culture and sovereignty. By employing dominant symbols of national culture, the commissioners presented themselves as advocating for the "common good," in keeping with the schemes of legitimation underwriting their work. Enlightenment notions of progress informed the types of representational national culture espoused by the commissioners in the Massey Report, which touts the two "founding races" of Canada as the producers of culture and hence the defenders of civility and civilization. The term "race" was further used to denote who legitimate national subjects were, and it appears in the report under subheadings such as "the conduct of the inquiry," "the mandate," "general and specific contributions to Canadian life," "radio broadcasting" and "Indian art" to denote individuals and groups of French and English origins, as well as their First Nations other. All non-English or non-French European ethnicities and racialized peoples are placed within the category of "ethnic." In other words, Canadians of British and French descent were at once raced and erased of ethnic affiliations. In contrast, non-European cultural producers are deliberately removed from the palette that symbolizes the nation. Culture in the Canadian context would reflect the achievements of Canada's French and English populations. As Eve Haque points out in the previous chapter, the notion of the two founding races was highly disputed by Indigenous peoples and a range of other non-British and non-French ethnic groups in the Royal Commission on Bilingualism and Biculturalism hearings of the 1960s, which is not surprising given the ways in which the Massey Commission upheld dominant notions of race and culture through the 1950s. The Massey Report makes explicit the hierarchies and worth ascribed to the cultural expressions and products of various racial/ethnic groups in Canada by privileging art forms based in European traditions. The commissioners' discussions on the authenticity of "Indian Art" and the cultural contributions of groups from other European ethnicities illustrate the racist thinking of the commissioners:

> Indians should not be encouraged to prolong the existence of arts which at best must be artificial and at worst are degenerate. It is argued that Indian arts emerged naturally from that combination of religious practices and economic and social customs which constituted the culture of the tribe and the region. The impact of the white man with his more advanced civilization and his infinitely superior techniques resulted in the gradual destruction of the Indian way of life. The Indian arts thus survive only as ghosts or shadows of a dead society. They can never, it is said, regain real form or substance. Indians with creative talent should therefore develop it as other Canadians do, and should receive every encouragement for this purpose; but Indian art as such cannot be revived. (240)

The obliteration of Indigenous art from the legitimate categories of Canadian art permitted the Massey commissioners to imagine and produce referents that gestured back to European conventions and logics unhampered by the ghosts of First Nations others. Accordingly, such racial logics allowed for the establishment of European culture and art as dominant in the order of cultural things. In the minds of the commissioners, Indigenous cultural production was unimaginable as a possibility because settlement practices had eradicated the conditions necessary for the production of this Indigenous form of art. The tropes of the advanced and the pre-modern allowed the commissioners to presume a form of innocence based in and on violence and a racist ideology of cultural development.

Elsewhere in the final report, the commissioners discuss the briefings received by groups who were "proud to be able to trace their origins back to various countries in continental Europe" (72). The report goes on to state that the commissioners "were impressed by what they were doing to enrich our national heritage by preserving their distinctive and vigorous cultural activities. We were particularly struck by the contribution of these groups to Canadian music and to Canadian ballet" (270). Up until 1947, Canadian immigration policy favoured immigrants from select European countries while discouraging and placing barriers to other potential immigrants including Blacks (see Gogia and Slade 2011). By the 1960s, non-Europeans were recruited in greater numbers to Canada to meet labour market requirements. The racial composition of Canada began to undergo transformations that would eventually shape later conversations on citizenship and participation. The Massey Report and its recommendations on "Indian Art" served as one mechanism that excised contemporary First Nations peoples from the images that represented the nation and simultaneously allayed the fears of the dominant White elite regarding the contamination of their imaginations of the Canadian collective self by racialized immigrants.

The commissioners managed to engineer the creation of the Canada Council for the Arts in a Canadian cultural and political ecology that was circumscribed by a practice of biculturalism that gave precedence to the cultural traditions of English and French Canadians. The Massey Commission hearings were themselves part of the practice and performance of governance. The hearings enacted deliberative participatory democracy by providing spaces in which a range of publics could engage in the field of the performance of politics.

THE BIRTH AND FUNDING OF THE CANADA COUNCIL FOR THE ARTS

Heralding the advent of the archival phase, Prime Minister St. Laurent made public the government's intention to form the Canada Council for the Arts in his Throne Speech on January 8, 1957 (Ostry 1978: 69); a bill to that effect was debated in Parliament some three months later. The debate about the bill highlighted anxieties and competing notions regarding the role of culture among politicians. Ostry (1978: 71) writes: "These anxieties were based on the Puritan view that the arts were merely to be enjoyed and that enjoyment was somehow wicked — or at least something to be put off to the end of the day of hard work."

Issues of geographical or regional representation peppered discussions amongst politicians in Ottawa regarding the Canada Council and its ability to represent the nation. This is evident during the debate on the *Canada Council Act* in St. Laurent's response to questions in the House of Commons about the composition of the Canada Council board and the criteria employed to choose the members of the board:

> It will not be possible to have representatives of each branch of the arts or of each branch of the humanities and the social sciences, neither should every racial group be represented because one is of that racial group, nor should any person be excluded from the Council because of his racial origin. (quoted in Whittaker 1965 : 156)

There exists a close relationship between the Canada Council and government, although the Council is set up as an arms-length agency of the federal government. This relationship is played out in Parliament regularly as the Council receives an annual appropriation from the government. This puts the Council in a precarious position as it is subject to the ideologies and strategies of the political process. In the beginning, the Council's activities were funded by an endowment fund derived from the death duties of two Nova Scotian industrialists, but by "1965 the federal government increasingly provided subventions; by 1969, it had become an automatic vote" (Davies 1995: 7). The Council receives an annual appropriation from Parliament that is supplemented by its endowment income, donations and bequests. The Canada Council competes with a number of government cultural agencies — the National Gallery, the CBC, National Library and Archives, the National Film Board, the Canadian Museum of Civilization, the National Arts Centre — for financial assistance. An investment committee was appointed to "aid and advise the Council, in making, managing and disposing of investments under this Act" and the Auditor General of Canada audits its finances (*Canada Council Act* 1957: 18(2)). From the Council's inception, insufficient financial resources have plagued its directors.

A significant change in the Canada Council's reporting relationship to Parliament also occurred in the 1960s. The direct reporting relationship enjoyed by the Canada Council transformed into one that saw reporting to Parliament via the minister of communications. Over the Council's fifty-year history it has also reported to Parliament through the secretary of state and the minister of Canadian heritage (Robertson 2006: 114–19). Despite these changes in the chain of accountability to Parliament, the Council is assigned full responsibility, through the *Canada Council Act*, for its policies, programs and the expenditure of its funds.

Funding to Artists and Arts Organizations
Since the early years of the Canada Council's existence, two overlapping questions have arisen on a recurrent basis: *what* constitutes art and *who* produces it. The Council's own role in defining the boundaries for inclusion and exclusion in these categories has functioned to secure state practices of governmentality, such as those set out in the Massey Commission deliberations. Over the years, the Council has paid attention to and expanded its notions of what constitutes art and who produces culture in Canada to accommodate those who have contested the Council's definitions and practices. The *Canada Council Act* of 1957 defined what counted as art, setting up parameters around the disciplines and genres that would be supported through state subsidies. At the beginning, the Council provided support to established Western European disciplines in the arts: theatre, music, ballet, painting, sculpture and literature, as laid out in the *Act*.[6] Individual artists were funded through programs of Senior Fellowships and Junior Scholarships. Grants were

awarded to organizations on a yearly basis, and according to the Council's first annual report, funding decisions were made by both Council officers and committees of experts drawn from organizations such as the Canadian Foundation, the Canadian Social Science Research Council and the Humanities Research Council of Canada. Council staff would vet applications to determine eligibility, and expert opinions were sought when deemed necessary.

Special emphasis was placed on funding "the two or three leading organizations in the country having world standards to enable them to reach more people and to stimulate improvement in standards of performance and appreciation" (Canada Council for the Arts 1958: 25). The rationale for the focus on a few leading organizations, located in urban centres, was based on the Council's image of itself as facilitating the development of excellence in an environment of limited financial resources. Key cultural organizations such as the CBC Orchestra, the Montréal Symphony Orchestra, the Opera Festival Association of Toronto, the Toronto Symphony, the National Ballet Guild of Canada, the Royal Winnipeg Ballet, the Stratford Shakespearean Festival, the Banff School of Fine Arts, the Canadian Film Institute and the Canadian Art Journal were prioritized for funding with the hope that the injection of financial resources would enhance the quality of the work produced and disseminated by these organizations.[7] Whittaker (1965 : 232–33) argues that the principle underlying this decision to fund the *best* was based on the Council's recognition of itself as a national body whose primary role was to uphold national standards.

The notion of quality or excellence was connected to the professionalization of both artists and organizations served by the Canada Council. The ability of an artist or arts organization to achieve excellence and international notoriety was equated with the ability to engage in artistic endeavours on a full-time basis (see Ostry 1978). This emphasis on the full-time artist or arts organization served to weed out the categories of artists often referred to as "Sunday painters" or "amateur artists," as well as local community-based arts organizations. Large urban organizations received the bulk of the arts funding and continue to receive the biggest slice of the Canada Council pie. With the concentration of funding accruing to a few large organizations, Council staff and directors saw it as necessary to strategize and disseminate cultural products to Canadian audiences outside of the metropolitan areas. The Council's concern with the dissemination of quality artistic works and the acculturation of the Canadian populace is expressed in the following statement about the accessibility of quality theatre productions:

> The Council has for some time been bothered by the lack of good professional theatre in a number of Canadian cities which might have been expected to support a company. Apart from one or two tentative forays there has recently been no well-established professional theatre outside Montréal, Toronto, Stratford, and Winnipeg. Other cities have had to rely largely upon the uncertain glory of touring companies. This would be bad enough in itself, since it is generally considered among civilized people that the theatre (particularly as a commentary upon contemporary society) is as essential to well-being, like wheat and steel. At the moment, however, nobody is making much theatrical hay out in the grasslands.

There are, of course, a great many amateur theatres doing excellent work, but this — as any professional actor will explain without any prompting — is not at all the same thing. (Canada Council for the Arts 1961: 9)

The Canada Council's support of national and international touring activities and festivals became one of the ways of promoting the arts and encouraging the enjoyment of the arts in Canada.[8] Cultural products were exported to the Canadian populace in the hinterland who otherwise would be exposed to parochial amateur art.

From the outset, the Canada Council's staff liaised with artists and cultural producers in order to legitimate the work of the Council to artists and to the government as well as to better serve the needs of art communities. During the first six years of its operation, the small staff of five at the Canada Council organized a series of national consultations and networking meetings of Canadian artists and curators. Consultations with artists and representatives of art organizations aided in the development of the Council's early operational guidelines and principles for conducting the business of providing support to artists and art organizations in the early days. This practice of consultation continues today in the Council's use of advisory committees and juries.

Culture and Representation

By the mid-1970s there was a proliferation of ethno-cultural community-based organizations across Canada that had garnered funding from federal multicultural programs to facilitate capacity building and celebrations of their cultures of origins (Pal 1993). However, the primary desire of artists of colour was to create cultural products that referenced the contemporary hyphenated nature of Canadian identity and not merely to produce nostalgic narratives about a place of origin. This is a classic example of what Mackey (2002) refers to as the limiting effect of multiculturalism and its policies *vis-à-vis* resource distribution to ethno-cultural groups: "State recognition of diversity also limits diversity. Trudeau's announcement of the policy defined and limited the specific forms of support for multiculturalisms that the government would provide" (65). To extend her argument, multicultural funding also limited and defined the kinds of performances of ethno-cultural specificity that were allowable in the nation and fundable by the Canada Council.

During the decade of the 1970s, the Canada Council began to address questions of representation as they pertained to the working of juries and advisory panels, access to programs by a broader cross-section of artists, regional issues and marketing. At the same time, demands for access to state funding for the arts through the Canada Council's programs were made from beyond the institution by artists living in regions outside of central Canada and Québec, "alternative" galleries, production and distribution centres, women, artists working in new genres and artists and producers who located their works "in between" or outside of European traditions. New programs that focused on touring, ameliorating regional disparities and new innovations in art-making were developed by the Council. The category of "other art forms" shows up during this period in the Council's accounts of itself and funding activities, and as a result, regional juries were implemented, the first artist-run organizations were supported and the Canada Council expanded into the marketing of Canadian art through the Art Bank program. During this period, the video program was established as part of the Visual Arts section and the Council funded multidisciplinary work and performance art. Despite the recognition of disparities in funding to its clientele, the Canada Council's tradition of providing large operating funds to big, urban-based organizations that were considered bastions of European artistic traditions persisted into the 1970s and continues today.

In the wake of the calls for access to Canada Council funding from new and smaller experimental art venues across the country, the Visual Arts section of the Canada Council opened up its assistance program to new organizations and art collectives in the 1970s. These new organizations, or artist-run centres, critiqued the traditional museum and art gallery systems for "their particular administrative allegiances and self-interpretations of inherited mandates and resource allocation" (Robertson 2006: 7). The forms of organizational cultures that existed within the traditional museum and art gallery sphere resulted in exclusionary practices that continued to shut out new forms and genres of contemporary art.

In 1973 a significant shift in what was seen to constitute art and where it was produced took place at the Canada Council when it set up a regional office in the Atlantic region as part of a pilot project to ensure that all regions of Canada had equal access to Canada Council funds. This was also the year that the Canadian Horizons program was reinvented, renamed Explorations, and allocated a budget of $1 million.[9] The Explorations program was designed "to include grants for new forms of expression, communication, and public participation in the arts, humanities and social sciences" (Canada Council for the Arts 1972: 63). The program served new categories of art, such as community-based productions that did not fit into the Council's disciplinary silos. It was also meant to open up definitions of the category of the artist and reach out to artists from other conventions and cultures, hence fostering diversity in the types of works supported by the Council.

The Explorations program was set up in response to changing conceptions and realities as to whom and what the Canada Council represented. The program was created to serve the "new": new genres, new forms and new immigrants. The Council's Explorations brochure outlines the mandate of the program:

> Through the Exploration Program, the Canada Council acknowledges that to ensure continued growth and development in the arts it is essential to assist new artists and to encourage fresh ideas. Thus, Explorations both encourages artists in the early stages of their practice and new forms of artistic expression by offering project grants toward the creation and presentation of new works drawn from any cultural context. Equally, it encourages initiatives that challenge creative possibilities within or across any arts discipline. As a regionally-structured program, it assists in the development of artists within their respective communities. (Canada Council for the Arts 1995: 2)

The concern with fostering regional representation and culture is an acknowledgement of Canada as a pluralist entity constituted by multiple cultural centres that produce a range of cultural expressions. Yet, how *new* were these supposed new forms, practices and insights into Canadian cultural heritage? The term "new" operates to denote a boundary without the politics the boundary assumes, particularly the politics of distribution, since this interest in the "new" did not affect how the "old" continued to be funded. The Canada Council now supported cultural production — disciplines, genres and contents — that represented those outside of the status quo. The Explorations program ran until 1998, when the budget for the program was cut in a process of bureaucratic rationalization.

It is not surprising that the Explorations program took up issues of race, as its precursor, the Canadian Horizons, also supported work that dealt with cultural diversity and heritage. Although the Explorations program was set up to ameliorate some of the disparities with regard to Canada Council funding to its clients, the Council did not address the question of opening up the frameworks upon which the Canada Council's disciplinary sections hinged their sense of collective self. The disciplines remained committed to European conceptions of art and disciplinary boundaries.

By 1977, serious questions were being asked by racialized artists and cultural producers outside of the Council, as well as by officers and section heads inside the Council itself, about the reach of the Council's programs. These questions addressed the workings of juries and advisory panels, the notion of excellence and marketing.[10] Artistic excellence, one of the bedrocks of Canada Council criteria for funding, was deemed by the Council as congruent with its ideas and practices of cultural democratization and decentralization. However, this was not the sentiment of the Canada Council's experts who made up the Advisory Arts Panel. They advocated for an expanded notion of excellence, one that took into consideration regional concerns, the conditions under which artists produce work and the cultural milieu in which, and for whom, it is produced.

The remarks regarding the notion of excellence and its operationalization in the context of the Council's work were inflections of a growing dissatisfaction amongst artists and arts organizations regarding the continued elitist nature of Canada Council activities and resulting exclusions. In their report entitled *The Future of the Canada Council*, the Advisory Arts Panel stated that they preferred "the term *standards of quality* as indicating that excellence is more to be found with an open and sensitive mind than to be applied from a single preconceived idea" (Canada Council for the Arts 1978: 19, emphasis in original).

The Advisory Arts Panel's response highlighted the areas of diversity and equality and the role of the Canadian government in supporting the development of diversity in Canadian culture. The authors offered up several reasons for government support to assist in the production of cultural products that would otherwise be undervalued in the marketplace:

> The pressures and influences from its neighbour, the AMERICAN GIANT make it more vulnerable than others. Moreover, it faces specific problems, such as the dispersal of a small group of individuals (21 million) over the second largest NATIONAL SURFACE AREA in the world and the diversity of ethnic and linguistic groups. (Canada Council for the Arts 1978: x, emphasis in original)

The messiness of Canadian culture is acknowledged and geography is pinpointed as working against the possibilities of the nation; hence the state is called upon to intervene in the problem that this diverse and dispersed population posed. With concerns for regional issues and diversity on the table, it was not "business as usual" at the Canada Council; an impending crisis was on the horizon.

DIVERSITY YEARS, 1980S AND 1990S

Artists of colour and First Nations artists formed coalitions and organized to demand that cultural institutions including the Canada Council address inequities within the cultural sphere. Questions were being posed about what it meant to be "Canadian," who and what defined artistic merit and who were being privileged as creators of Canadian culture (Nourbese Philip 1992; Fung and Gagnon 2002; Gagnon and McFarlane 2003). In short, artists and cultural producers of colour contested the received notions of Canada's commitment to cultural diversity in the arts that emerged following the Biculturalism and Bilingualism Commission. Racialized artists questioned cultural institutions for the exclusion of their works and the positioning/categorizing of the symbolic products produced by those artists as "folk" art. These categorizations contained their art within the paradigm of tradition or a way of life based on notions of origins based outside of the confines of the Canadian nation. The residual effects of Canada Council funding to artists and arts organizations working within European art traditions were being felt by the burgeoning numbers of First Nations artists and immigrant artists of colour producing contemporary art.

The Canada Council's language regarding Canada's diverse population changed in tone in the Council's report entitled *The Canada Council in the 1980s: The Applebaum-Hébert Report and Beyond* (Canada Council for the Arts 1982). Diversity here referred to the distinctness of Canada's cultural and geographical regions but also to ethnicities other than English and French. The authors stress the need for the "accommodation" of French and English cultural expression while "taking into account" the other satellite cultures that existed around them. Nonetheless, their main concern was with the representation of Francophone cultures outside of Québec:

> It is however, our firm belief that a single, uniform culture is neither possible nor desirable in Canada and that, accordingly, federal arts funding must recognize and respect the diversity of the Canadian population. Where French- and English-speaking Canadians have distinctive forms of expressions, institutions, or needs, these must be accommodated in policies and programs. Other forms of cultural diversity must be recognized, understood, and taken into account. (Canada Council for the Arts 1982: 5)

The passage above draws attention to the hierarchical foundation of biculturalism, in which Francophone and Anglophone cultures assume dominance over "other" cultures, which are "taken into account" almost as an afterthought. The Council's distant relationship to multiculturalism would change in the late 1980s to one that saw the Council directly negotiating with "multiculturalism and its discontents," even though in many ways, diversity came to be seen as a problem to be governed through its policies and practices. Given the social context Haque outlines well in the previous chapter, many racialized artists gained legitimacy in their claims for inclusion in this multiculturalism era. As a result, the Council tried to regulate these "new" players on the national arts scene by developing programs such as Explorations.

At the same time, at the grassroots level, racialized artists raised objections and protested against practices of appropriation and exclusion taking place within cultural institutions. For example, in Ontario, members of various Black communities and their allies spoke out against exhibits held at the Royal Ontario Museum and the Art Gallery of Ontario, and the Women's Press was also called upon to respond to charges of exclusion by women of colour writers. In British Columbia, artists confronted the Vancouver Art Gallery for its exclusionary practices, and in Alberta, "The Spirit Sings" exhibition at the Glenbow Museum was called into question by First Nations chiefs and artists.[11] Conversations taking place in marginalized communities entered into the Council through various channels, including alternative community publications. An ex-director stated: "I wasn't unaware of the issues around diversity because I read *FUSE* magazine[12] that dealt with these issues from the perspective of communities who did not feel that the Canada Council was serving them well."[13] Equity became one of the Council's priorities in the late 1980s and a commitment was made to serve First Nations artists and artists from racialized communities because of "discussions within the Council of a need for its policies, programs and practices to comply with two federal laws" — the *Employment Equity Act* (1986) and the *Multiculturalism Act* (1985) (Robertson 2006: 53).

In April 1989, Council director Joyce Zemans focused attention on issues of racial equity and diversity, even though the Council was plagued by years of underfunding from the federal government. Reflecting the priorities set by the prevalent multiculturalism discourse of the 1980s, an internal multiculturalism committee was formed to focus on such issues and engage in long-term strategic development. The committee recommended a number of strategies to facilitate the inclusion of racialized and First Nations artists into the milieu and culture of the Council. The recommendations covered the following areas: human resource policy development in keeping with the *Employment Equity Act*, staff sensitization, eligibility and assessment criteria, representation of artists of colour and First Nations artists on juries and training of artists of colour and First Nations artists (Creighton-Kelly 1991). A racial equity consultant was hired in 1990 to start the process of institutional change by assisting "the Council in developing policies and strategies relating to cultural diversity and aboriginal art" (Robertson 2006: 53).

The Racial Equity Committee, made up of racialized artists and a First Nations artist, was struck in 1990 to assist the consultant in the task of policy development. The separate First Peoples Advisory Committee was created at the same time as the issues being dealt with by these two constituents of artists, although similar in many ways, diverged because of historical differences in the groups' relationship to the Canadian nation-state. The first racial equity officer was appointed in December 1991; the following year an Aboriginal coordinator was hired. The Council began the development of outreach activities to artists of colour and First Nations artists in the late 1980s, and in 1991–1992 the Council established an internship program for First Nations and "visible minority" artists. The program served artists of Aboriginal, African and Asian backgrounds, as well as artists from other racialized groups. Interns were hired "to work with the Council and the artistic community in the development of communication, recruitment, and outreach strategies and to participate in the regular work of Council" (Canada Council for the Arts 1991: 16).

Throughout the 1990s new programs geared toward First Nations artists in theatre, music, visual arts, media arts, writing and publishing and dance were created. Programs catering to culturally diverse artists and arts organizations, such as the Quest program for new and emerging culturally diverse artists and the Visual Arts section's assistance to culturally diverse curators, were developed. The programs were designed to address racial equity at the Council and took place both within a climate of major cutbacks of federal funding to federal institutions and the threat of an amalgamation with the Social Science and Humanities Research Council by virtue of the introduction of Bill C93 in 1992.

Bill C93 was introduced to Parliament "to amalgamate or eliminate forty-six agencies and/or commissions" in an attempt to rationalize further government bureaucracies (Robertson 2006: 118). The bill was defeated, but the Council proceeded with its cost cutting agenda because the Treasury Board requested that the Council reduce its administrative costs by $2 million over three years (Canada Council for the Arts 1993: 10). Programs and staff were eliminated as employee and community dissent grew. Several Council staff resigned or opted for early retirement packages, signalling their opposition to a top-down, government-directed style of governance at the Council. The Council reported that, "as a result of voluntary measures, a total of twenty-six positions out of a total of 260 regular and temporary employees were cut" (Canada Council for the Arts 1993: 12). The style of governance was in direct contrast to the culture of the Council to date. Many of the staff members were themselves artists who believed in the principles of arms-length funding and democratic governance practices.

The Council articulated its vision for long-term streamlining in its strategic plan published in 1995, entitled *The Canada Council: Design for the Future*. In this document, the Council reiterated its commitment to cultural diversity. The plan identified five priority areas — investment in the arts; leadership, advocacy and appreciation of the arts; partnerships and other forms of support; equity, access and new practices; and improving program delivery — and action plans for meeting these goals. Within the objectives set out under the priority of "equity, access, and new practices" the Council undertook to address issues pertaining to regionalism, First Nations peoples, culturally diverse communities, interdisciplinary art and new technologies. This was also a time when reform and restructuring came to the forefront in the government and public sectors more generally. Budget cuts and the introduction of more market-like, neoliberal practices to government and the public sector were the order of the day.

Representation and jury composition were addressed under two of the priority areas — equity, access and new practices and improving program delivery and administrative reform. There is a dissonance in the ways in which the Council articulated the action plan for transformation in each area. With regard to equity and cultural diversity the plan states: "The Council will *try* to ensure that the perspective of artists from culturally diverse backgrounds is better reflected in the Canada Council by such means as jury and advisory committee representation, Council staff representation, program guidelines and criteria" (Canada Council for the Arts 1995: 17, emphasis added). Later on in the document, the Council commits to improving the practice of peer assessment by taking into account issues of diversity and representation.

At the same time as peer assessment was being upheld as a key principle, the workings of the system were under threat of erosion because of the implementation of cost saving practices. Cuts were made to the budgets for juries and advisory committees, and the frequency of juried assessments decreased. The administrative system was centralized, the Art Bank was closed and a separate Arts Awards Section was handed over to disciplinary sections (Robertson 2006: 119). The culture of the organization evolved to one that embraced the practices and principles of the corporate world. The Council's first Corporate Plan was unveiled in 1997–98, and by the close of the decade, the Council was rewarded with new funds from the government, which enabled the development of new programs, such as the world music program, geared towards culturally diverse artists and First Nations artists.

CONCLUSION

I have provided an overview of the history of the Canada Council for the Arts, starting with its antecedents, the Massey Commission and the Massey Report. I have argued that the Council was a nation-building project spearheaded by elite intellectuals and cultural producers to differentiate the Canadian nation from other nations and to disseminate culture and civility over a large geographical and regionally diverse territory. More importantly, this nation-making project produced a particular type of nation — European, liberal, modern and "democratic." The architects of the Council imagined, designed and created the Council to support the production and reproduction of English and French cultures. Over the years, this imaginary of the nation and the role of the Council in fostering and supporting nation-making opened up to include women, people of colour and gays as part of the imaginary. Although the Council transformed from a conservative supporter of high culture to an institution responding to new practices, genres and demographics, the residual effects of highbrow interpretations of culture continue to shape the Council's decisions. It continues to provide its largest support to arts and organizations based on European aesthetic traditions, while at the same time making formal commitments to equity. Since its inception, the Council has taken a responsive role in dealing with issues of representation, including race, an issue that surfaced early in its history and resurfaced again in the late 1980s. In this case, the "art of government," as Foucault called it, produced acceptable and governable forms of art and culture among racialized cultural producers, further rationalizing the work of the Canada Council. The practices of government, including multiculturalism and its policies, found their way into the Council, highlighting the ways in which the state and the social and political are intertwined and difficult to disentangle.

NOTES

1. Miller and Yúdice (2002: 7–8) discuss Raymond Williams' application of the Gramscian concept of hegemony to culture, in their discussion of historical changes in taste and power: "When the dominant culture uses education, philosophy, religion, advertising and art to make its dominance appear normal and natural to the heterogeneous groups that constitute society.

The accomplishment of this 'consensus' instantiates what then appears to be an 'ethical state,' which deserves universal loyalty and transcends class identifications."

2. In *Distinction*, Bourdieu (1984) discusses the notion of "good taste" and its acquisition. Good taste is dependent upon a separation from the requirements of manual labour. It is through class power that such social inequities are reproduced.

3. Foucault distances himself from this term; he is more interested in the politics of truth than the politics of untruth linked to ideology. See, for instance, Foucault's (1980: 109–33) own discussion of the concept of "ideology" or Hunt and Purvis's (1993) work reconciling the concepts of ideology and discourse in social theory.

4. Other members of the commission were Norman A. M. Mackenzie, president of the University of British Columbia; Georges-Hénri Lévesque, dean of the Faculty of Social Sciences at Université Laval; Arthur Surveyer, civil engineer from Montréal; and Hilda Neatby, acting head of the Department of History, University of Saskatchewan (see Litt 1992 for a more detailed description of the backgrounds and affiliations of the commissioners).

5. In 1946, the Canadian Arts Council took on the role of administering culture out of concerns for the well-being of artists and in an effort to create a unified sense of national culture. It represented the following sixteen organizations: the Royal Canadian Academy of Arts, the Royal Architectural Institute of Canada, the Sculptors' Society of Canada, the Canadian Society of Painters in Water Colour, the Society of Canadian Painters, Etchers and Engravers, the Canadian Group of Painters, the Canadian Society of Graphic Art, the Federation of Canadian Artists, the Canadian Authors' Association, la Société des écrivains canadiens, the Music Committee, the Canadian Society of Landscape Architects and Town Planners, the Dominion Drama Festival, the Canadian Handicrafts Guild, the Canadian Guild of Potters and the Arts and Letters Club (Centre for Contemporary Canadian Art 2011).

6. These disciplines are outlined in the *Canada Council Act* of 1957 as "expressions" of what constitutes the arts.

7. A full list of grant recipients for 1957–1958 can be found in Annex J of the Canada Council's first annual report (Canada Council for the Arts 1957).

8. Extensive details of the touring and festival programs are outlined in annual reports of the Canada Council for the Arts over the years 1957–62.

9. The Canadian Horizons program was "inaugurated by the Council in 1971 to create a heightened awareness of Canada's cultural diversity and heritage in the humanities and social sciences" (Canada Council for the Arts 1973: 82).

10. In a discussion paper put by the Canada Council's Advisory Art Panel in November of 1977 entitled "Twenty Plus Five," the Council outlines three areas for development — policies, programs and structures.

11. The exhibit was one of the showcases for the Calgary Winter Olympics in 1988. The Lubicon Cree Nation of northern Alberta, along with several other Indigenous nations and communities in British Columbia, Newfoundland, Saskatchewan, Alberta and Ontario, boycotted "The Spirit Sings" on the grounds of the Museum's cultural appropriation of Indigenous "artefacts," provincial and federal inaction on land claims and treaty recognitions and to protest the oil industry's involvement in the exhibit (Shell Canada Ltd., which was drilling on Crown land in Lubicon territory, was the principal sponsor). As Heather Devine (2010: 218) sums up: "The subsequent boycott of the exhibition and the withdrawal of many of the museums that had agreed to participate as donors sent shock waves throughout the Canadian heritage community. The controversy over "The Spirit Sings" had not only revealed Canada's history of shameful Aboriginal policies to the world, but had also exposed the profound gulf that existed between the largely non-Native administrators, curators, designers, and educators, and the Indigenous

peoples whose heritage they presumed to interpret to the rest of the world."

12. Formerly known as *Centrefold, FUSE* was founded over thirty years ago at the same time as the national artist-run centre movement. *FUSE* is one of Canada's art and culture periodicals with a history of engagement with political and cultural issues and has evolved to include perspectives from diverse and racialized communities.

13. Interview with an ex-director of the Canada Council for the Arts in July 2006.

Chapter 3

THE MANY PARADOXES OF RACE IN QUÉBEC

Civilization, *Laïcité* and Gender Equality

Darryl Leroux

In order to study the dynamics of race-making in Québec, this chapter looks at how Québec and the Québécois re-claim the project of European modernity, Western civilization and the history of Euro-American White supremacy through several recent events and documents. In particular, I examine the formation of the Consultation Commission on Accommodation Practices Related to Cultural Differences (Bouchard-Taylor Commission) and, particularly, a sample of one hundred briefs that individuals and organizations presented to the Commission. A majority of the briefs I review express what I call a "discourse of opposition" to racialized diversity through two interrelated tropes: values of *laïcité* and gender equality. Through this analysis, I tease out elements of the particular and changing constitution and expression of racialized discourses in Québec.

This chapter begins with a historical overview of White settler colonialism in Québec through an encounter with the concept of "double colonization." It proceeds to a discussion of what some scholars have identified as the culturalization of race in twenty-first-century Western liberal democracies. Finally, I analyze a sample of the Bouchard-Taylor briefs and point to the specificities of racialized discourses in Québec.

DOUBLE COLONIZATION AND THE CULTURALIZATION OF RACE

Understandings of race have shifted considerably in the history of New France, French Canada and Québec. In many ways, these shifts in racial knowledge have shadowed the overlapping histories of Euro-American imperialism and colonialism, nationally and globally. Since French colonial policy in New France was originally constructed along the imperial model of the *mission civilisatrice*, ideas about race and civilization belied a deep desire to assimilate Indigenous peoples in the Americas. The now largely accepted version of this early colonial history, including notably in Québec, celebrates early French settlers for their humanistic appeals to justice and fairness in their relations with Indigenous peoples and peoples of African descent. Bereft of violent impulses, French colonizers are reclaimed as near heroic. The year-long celebration of the 400th anniversary of the founding of Québec City by Samuel de Champlain in 2008 provided an opportune time for just such hagiographic work, readily on display in a number of historical works displaying Champlain's genius (see, for an example of such work, Fischer 2008). The celebratory tone of Champlain historiography is not surprising, for as historian Saliha Belmessous (2005: ¶1) writes, "the French are either credited with a generous vision and treatment of Amerindians or they are kept in limbo [in studies of colonialism]." Thanks in part to the long historiographic tradition that positions French colonial policy as enlightened *vis-à-vis* British and Spanish policies in the Americas, many French Canadians and Québécois by and large still uphold a strong belief in an innate, cultural and social *rapprochement* with Indigenous peoples.[1] Of course, much scholarship places this exalting discourse into question, including scholarly work that questions the particular social and economic factors that led to French colonial policies (Trigger 1985; White 1991); that reconsiders French colonial history with a critical eye on practices of gendered violence (Anderson, K. 1991; Cooper 2006); and that reads French colonial history through a historical lens intent on unpacking its racialized character (Aubert 2004; Belmessous 2005; Rushforth 2006). With this body of scholarly research in mind, Christopher Hodson and Brett Rushforth (2010: 107) stated: "It has become clear that [the] assertion that the French exhibited a unique 'openness to peoples of other race and cultures' is no longer tenable."

Added to the complexity of race-making and violence under French colonial regimes are the results of the British conquest of New France in the mid-eighteenth century. Besides the already overarching European obsession with civilizational discourses that placed Indigenous peoples and peoples of African descent within de-humanizing Euro-centric epistemological frames, a point Frantz Fanon (1967) made amply clear in *Black Skin, White Masks*, French settlers were suddenly faced with their own colonized experience. From an early colonial focus on Indigenous and African difference, French discourses on race shifted to respond to the new colonial situation in what then became known as Lower Canada.

In recognition of these colonial machinations, analytically I locate my work within studies of Canada and Québec as *settler* societies, in which the racial order of society is put in motion through European colonial projects. Ronald Weitzer (1990: 24) defines settler societies as "founded by migrant groups who assume a super-ordinate position *vis-à-vis* native inhabitants and build self-sustaining states that are *de jure* or de facto independent from the mother country and organized around settlers' political domination over the indigenous population." Added to the political dimensions of domination in settler societies, Sherene Razack (2002: 1, 2) argues that White settler societies "continue to be structured by a racial hierarchy" that enables the denial of the European conquest and colonization of North America "through the fantasy that North America was peacefully settled and not colonized." Yet, as Daiva Stasiulis and Nira Yuval-Davis (1995: 7) claim, there is no inherent coherence in such settler projects, as is apparent in the continued Canada-Québec political divide, one that highlights the many divisions within Canadian and Québécois settler projects. The tensions in the Canadian nation-building project are numerous, including in the mid-twentieth century rise of Québécois nationalism.

Unlike the history of many settler societies (e.g., United States, Australia, New Zealand), the history of Québec is doubly complex, since not only did French settlers colonize what is now Québec (and extensive areas of what later became Canada and the U.S.), but they were also later colonized by British and American settlers, who treated New France quite like many overseas British colonies. To analyze race-making, and follow my claim that the process of colonization was central in the making of French Canadian society, it is necessary to consider this multi-layered colonial situation.

Critical race and legal scholar Laura Gómez (2007) offers useful tools for describing and analyzing similar processes. Writing in the Mexican-American context, Gómez introduces the notion of "double colonization" to characterize the multiple systems of racialized inequality — what Razack calls a racial hierarchy — that marked the context of the making of what she calls the "Mexican American race." Her understanding of the concept explains that "double colonization resulted in a situation in which everyone, including elites of all races, jockeyed for position and defined themselves and others in an undeniably multi-racial terrain" (48). Within this social and political terrain, "Mexican-American" has become a trope in a flexible racial ideology that continues to shift meaning in different spatial and temporal contexts.

For instance, the concept is often used by a variety of actors to mark a social division between Indigenous peoples and Mexican Americans claiming a "Spanish" heritage in the state of New Mexico. Regardless of the precise dynamics of the double-colonization process, Gómez (2007: 10) reminds us that "both the Spanish and British colonial enterprises were grounded in racism, though their precise ideologies of white supremacy differed." As a scholar of colonialism, explicating the precise nature of White supremacy[2] and colonial relations is crucial to the contributions my research makes to multi-dimensional understandings of inequality and difference in Québec society.

The concept of double-colonization adapted to the British-French Canadian-Québécois context can help delineate three regimes: the French colonial-settler project of the seventeenth and eighteenth centuries, the British colonial-settler project of the eighteenth and nineteenth centuries and contemporary Canada-Québec political regimes. The concept draws attention to the different systems of racial order imposed by each regime. A racial discourse of White supremacy is central to all three; however, the particular variants of this discourse, including the category of "white," differ under each regime. Colonized by the British, yet itself a colonial society founded through French imperial ideologies, Québec inherited a position in North America not unlike that of Mexican-Americans in New Mexico. The unique racialization processes in Québec necessarily make for a particular organization of racial hierarchies, whose significance for the national Québécois subject is produced through public events like those I discuss later in this chapter.

It is my contention that due to Québec's history of "double colonization," current exclusionary practices on the part of the majority French Canadian Québécois population are often forgiven or forgotten in mainstream Québec society, whether in academia, the media or everyday practices. There are many reasons for such efforts to displace any talk of race and racisms in Québec, including among them a response to the persistent critique in English Canada of Québec's inferior social status (i.e., Québec as more intolerant, reactionary and unstable); an effort to construct a national discourse in Québec that positions itself as an enlightened, progressive counterpart to neighbouring Anglo-dominated societies (i.e., Canada and the U.S.); and an investment in French republican ideologies that strive to maintain universal notions of citizenship (see Peabody and Stovall 2003; Thomas 2007; Miller 2008; Marshall 2009 for critiques). To be sure, I do not contend that Québec society is either more or less exclusionary than Canada (or the United States for that matter). Advancing such a polemical idea would do little to better understand the social dynamics of race and exclusion in Québec. Instead, as I stated above, I aim to study the specificities of race in Québécois contexts and to call attention to the ways that race-making operates in Québec.

From the relatively overt use of the language of race (i.e., two founding "races") in the post-conquest period until the mid-twentieth century to today's dominant language of "cultural difference" in Québec and in Western liberal democracies more generally, race talk has shifted considerably in French Canada and Québec. Yet, as recent work on the persistence of liberal "colour-blindness" across different spatial and temporal contexts demonstrates (see, for example, Williams 1998; Wiegman 1999; Bonilla-Silva 2006), under such discursive regimes, race continues to hold salience as a complex of meanings with tangible social effects. Such is the case in Québec, where racial dynamics usually take a back seat to now-dominant national, cultural and linguistic claims. As David Austin (2010: 19) argues: "Québec's own version of a founding national narrative is a tale of innocence and victimhood that conveniently omits the colonization of Indigenous peoples, the practice of slavery and racial exclusion." A body of work questioning such discourses on race in Québec has emerged (Marhraoui 2005; Salée 2007, 2010; Leroux 2010b; Mahrouse 2010a), and in so doing, challenges the two founding nations/races discourse (see Haque and Fatona in this collection for genealogies of this concept) that is a shared founding principle in both Canada and Québec.

THEORIES OF RACE: FLEXIBLE AND SHIFTING MEANINGS

The ontological status of race has come under sustained criticism over the course of the past half-century (e.g., Banton 1967; Hall 1989; Miles 1989; Goldberg 1993; Gilroy 2000). What I take from these reflections on the status of race is that as a discredited biological concept, race is without any analytical value of its own. In other words, race does not explain social phenomena independent of its construction. In light of this, Robert Miles (1989) takes the position that we should abandon the use of race as an analytical tool altogether, in favour of concepts such as racism and racialization, otherwise we risk reifying "race" through utilizing it as an explanatory category.[3]

Many other critical race scholars find the dismissal of the concept of race unsatisfactory because the vexing question is then what to do about the fact that race, though not a biological phenomenon, nonetheless has social significance (Omi and Winant 1986; Razack 2002; Das Gupta et al. 2007). Taking the position that race does not exist *at all* or that speaking about race further exacerbates forms of racism, makes political claims against racist exclusions nearly impossible. After all, if there is no such thing as race as a social category, how could claims against racism be justified on any political grounds? Many scholars (Alcoff 1998; Dei et al. 2005) see theoretical moves to eliminate race in the face of massive racial inequalities globally as a sign of the re-constitution of global White supremacy. Alcoff (1998: 31) explains this concern well:

> So today race has no semantic respectability, biological basis or philosophical legitimacy. However, at the same time, and in a striking parallel to the earlier Liberal attitude towards the relevance and irrelevance of race, in the very midst

of our contemporary skepticism toward race stands the compelling social reality that race, or racialised identities, have as much political, sociological and economic salience as they ever had.

As some scholars point out, the refusal to recognize the salience of racial categories within our current social configurations is accompanied by the depoliticization and culturalization of race, two interrelated *political* processes that exacerbate inequalities based on forms of racial differentiation. For instance, Wendy Brown (2006: 15) argues that the process of depoliticization has very real material effects: "Depoliticization involves construing inequality, subordination, marginalization, and social conflict, which all require political analysis and political solutions, as personal and individual, on the one hand, or as natural, religious, or cultural on the other."

The discourses surrounding the idea of "reasonable accommodation" in Québec, which I analyze below, clearly articulate the conflation between culture and politics that Brown recognizes, in which culture is reduced to a natural human trait, to simply what some people *do*. In this sense, culture at times stands in for biology as the marker *par excellence* of racial difference. And as Sourayan Mookerjea (2009: 180), also writing about the debate over reasonable accommodation in Québec, explains, "signifiers of 'culture' serve as a racializing code," where fantasies of a clash of civilizations between the West and the rest are continually revived (see Hall 1996).

Ghassan Hage, in his work on the liberal concepts of multiculturalism and tolerance, echoes Brown and Mookerjea, indicating how tolerance discourses depoliticize what are essentially effects of power. Hage (2000: 87) shows how "multicultural tolerance ... is a strategy aimed at reproducing and disguising relationships of power in society, or being reproduced through that disguise. It is a form of symbolic violence in which a mode of domination is presented as a form of egalitarianism." Tolerance, as it is articulated in my empirical material, is a legitimating practice of power, one that positions the "French Canadian Québécois," as the authors of the Bouchard-Taylor final report call them, as normative governing subjects.

As a component of this shift in racial knowledge and discourse, I speak of the whiteness of nation-building processes in Québec in order to highlight the specificity of exalting a particular connection to European (French) civilization, as various social actors in Québec do quite clearly during the Bouchard-Taylor proceedings. This is not an attempt to flatten differences within the category of "white," but it is an important element of a theoretical approach aimed at explaining what Sneja Gunew (2007: 142) calls "interpellations of whiteness." Despite historical forms of exclusion from the family of White supremacy, my contention is that "French Canadian Québécois" subjects aspire to whiteness and the power flowing from it.

I carry forward two conceptual threads from this section throughout my chapter: a focus on the cultural practices and discursive strategies employed by those aspiring to whiteness in Québec and, in particular, the depoliticization and culturalization of race essential to these aspirations. As such, I pay close attention to the racial re-imaginings and reconfigurations currently taking place in Québec society. The next section turns to my empirical analysis of the briefs presented to the Bouchard-Taylor Commission.

THE BOUCHARD-TAYLOR COMMISSION

As a key political event in Québec, during 2007–2008, the Bouchard-Taylor Commission has received extensive academic and non-academic analysis (Geadah 2007; Côté 2008; Potvin 2008, 2010; Heinrich and Dufour 2008; Sharify-Funk 2010; Adelman 2011, among many others). Thus, I offer just a brief overview before turning to my analysis of a sample of the written briefs presented to the commission.

The Government of Québec formed the Bouchard-Taylor Commission in February 2007 (Government of Québec 2007a, 2007b) in order to address several instances of conflict over the concept of "reasonable accommodation." A debate about the appropriate level of accommodation that Québec society should afford to those positioned as making specific cultural or religious claims in the public sphere began to gain steam in the weeks leading to the Québec general election in 2007. Several events in the preceding few years conspired to make this an important campaign issue. Among the stories that circulated during this period were the acceptance in March 2006 of an offer by the Yetev Lev Orthodox Jewish congregation in Montréal to pay for the frosting of windows in the gymnasium of the YMCA du Parc, to block from public view the sight of women who were exercising (a decision the YMCA reversed on March 19, 2007, following protests by its members) and the order by the Commission des droits de la personne et des droits de la jeunesse [the Québec Human Rights Tribunal] on September 22, 2006, after an initial complaint by the Mouvement laïque québécois [the Québec Movement for Secularism], that the City of Laval halt its practice of reciting a non-denominational prayer at public meetings of the municipal council.[4]

Yet, many scholars and journalists identify the ruling in February 2002 that a Sikh student, Gurbaj Singh Multani, could not wear his *kirpan* (a ceremonial knife) to school and the subsequent overturning of the decision by the Supreme Court of Canada in March 2006 as the lightning rod behind the recent focus on "reasonable accommodation" in Québec society. The Supreme Court ruling was extremely unpopular among a large majority of French Canadian Québécois. First, it was seen as delegitimizing Québec's juridical and legislative independence from the Canadian state, a longstanding contention among a very broad constituency in Québec. In addition, it was seen as opening up the possibility of allowing for the accommodation of any number of religious and cultural practices that may threaten French Canadian Québécois culture.

Mario Dumont, the leader of the major conservative political party in Québec, Action démocratique du Québec (ADQ), sensed this unease and throughout the election campaign in 2007 added fire to the debate about the appropriate level of accommodation in Québec. Dumont repeatedly voiced the ADQ's opposition to what he called the "unreasonable" accommodation of religious and cultural minorities, relying on an anti-immigrant discourse to mobilize his conservative political base. On January 16, 2007, Dumont went a step further when he released an open letter to the people of Québec in which he argued in defence of Québécois values and identity. In the letter, published in several major, Québec-based, French-language newspapers, he urged people in Québec to "get rid of the old minority reflex" in which Québécois "continue to submit when we should keep our chin up high." He goes on to propose that people in Québec "should act in a way that reinforces our national identity and, especially, protects the values that are so dear to us" (Dumont 2007, my translation). In his estimation, Québec was under threat, as was evidenced by "multiple episodes that demonstrated how public-sector leaders choose to push aside our shared values in order to satisfy demands advanced by certain communities." Above all, Québec must return to its "European roots, by virtue of who founded Québec … our shared values were actualized and are now a part of Western thinking." In this last sentence Dumont most clearly expressed the *racial* character of the Québécois, a people who are undeniably connected to the Western family of nations through their European roots.

The ADQ subsequently won forty-one seats and increased its share of the popular vote by nearly thirteen percentage points, finishing a very narrow second place to the Québec Liberal Party. Importantly, it was into this firestorm of public debate that Québec Premier Jean Charest formed the Bouchard-Taylor Commission, with the following broad mandate, as enumerated in the commission's final report: to survey harmonization practices in Québec; to compare Québec society's issues with cultural pluralism to those of other societies; to conduct extensive consultations on these questions; and, finally, to make recommendations to the Government (Government of Québec 2008: 7).

To accomplish these tasks, the commission received a budget of $5 million, which it distributed among a vast array of research activities. Besides organizing thirteen research projects at different Québec universities and thirty-one focus groups with individuals, the commissioners and their staff also held fifty-nine meetings with experts and representatives of civil-society organizations. The largest part of the commission's work occurred during public hearings, which took place in the final months of 2007. The commission held thirty-one days of public hearings throughout the province and collected over 900 briefs at the hearings. Its members later met with many of the authors during 328 individual hearings. The bulk of my analysis at the end of this section looks specifically at a sample of one hundred of these written briefs.

In order to situate my analysis, it seems important to further contextualize the debate over "reasonable accommodation" in Québec. In their analysis of the concept, Yasmeen Abu-Laban and Bahu Abu-Laban (2007) describe its historical origins in Canada. They claim that as far back as 1978, the Ontario Human Rights Commission invoked the term to settle a workplace dispute, while in subsequent years the term was used in relation to employment practices relating to individuals with disabilities. The term has taken many different forms over the last decades — for example, in the mid-1980s, regulating relations between landlords and tenants and smokers and non-smokers under the Alberta Human Rights Commission. Yet Abu-Laban and Abu-Laban (2007 30) argue for the importance of the *Multani v. Commission scolaire* decision to the context of Québec:

> The great catalyst for the contemporary popularization of the term "reasonable accommodation," and in particular its association with religious groups, appears to stem from the March 2006 Supreme Court of Canada ruling on whether a Québec schoolboy, who is an orthodox Sikh, could wear his *kirpan* to school.

Marie McAndrew also cites the Multani decision as a turning point in the debate over "reasonable accommodation" in Québec. In her estimation, the debate leading up to the Bouchard-Taylor Commission was a "bad dream" evoking signs of a time when the racialized other was seen as an inherent threat to a homogeneous Québec national identity:

> But the dichotomization of "Us/Them" is not the only worrying aspect of the current debate on ethnic relations. It is actually accompanied by a tendency to inferiorize, whether through the devalorization of the others' behaviors or cultural traits or through the generalization of negative representations of minority groups. (2007: 50, my translation)

McAndrew identifies a key element of the debate in Québec: much of the popular debate revolved around the *cultural* traits unique to racialized others. Culture, in this sense, comes to stand in for "race." It is clear that the older, broader understanding of "reasonable accommodation" in Québec shifted semantically to what Sirma Bilge (2010: 209) distinguishes as a new commonsense understanding that focuses almost exclusively on religious and/or cultural practices. In this sense, coding racially what certain people *do* has become a key component of racial discourses in Québec.

With this debate about "reasonable accommodation" in Québec framing its origins, the commission set out to evaluate the appropriate levels and modes of accommodation in Québec. The commission's final report, released amidst intense media saturation, manifests the accepted liberal approach common in Québec society, grounded as it is in the notions of Western civilization I discuss above — one that ultimately seeks balanced opinions in the face of an inequitable social context (Government of Québec 2008, 241–43).

In their attempts at balance, Bouchard and Taylor do acknowledge the fears raised by many scholars (e.g., MacAndrew above) and organizations representing the interests of racialized minorities, as well as the widespread belief that accommodation has perhaps gone too far. As I argue elsewhere (Leroux 2010b), despite their best efforts to strike a moderate tone (e.g., they acknowledge that Islamophobia is a problem in Québec), in many ways the commissioners contribute to normative discourses in Québec society that problematize and naturalize racialized differences. But beyond the work of the commissioners, including the much-discussed and widely disseminated final report, what did people living in Québec have to say about these issues? The next section provides some answers to this question, through an analysis of what I call the "discourse of opposition" individuals and organizations expressed in the briefs presented to the commission.

THE DISCOURSE OF OPPOSITION IN QUÉBEC

I examine elements of the social and political opposition to the concept of "reasonable accommodation" in Québec through a close empirical analysis. The 901 written briefs submitted to the Bouchard-Taylor Commission provide scholars with rich documentary material through which to explore the many dimensions of opposition to reasonable accommodation and/or racialized diversity in Québec (see Freake et al. 2011 for a tangential analysis). For the purposes of this chapter, I reviewed a sample of one hundred of these briefs in order to examine the broader discourse of opposition contained within the corpus. For the most part, the briefs are responses that include reflections by individuals, groups and organizations thinking through the varied meanings of reasonable accommodation, immigrant integration, human rights legislation and their relationship with Québécois identity.

Despite the broad range of views expressed among those who opposed or had serious misgivings about reasonable accommodation and/or racialized diversity, a consistent narrative justifying this resistance emerged. The most common elements among the briefs opposing reasonable accommodation were a sustained focus on defining and underlining a set of unique Québec values to potential newcomers, of which the two most important were far and away *laïcité* and gender equality, both elements Bouchard and Taylor argue are fundamental to Québec's post-Quiet Revolution cultural heritage. The following sections provide an analysis of these two elements of the discourse of opposition, expressed as they were in many different forms, through a selection of passages from the briefs presented to the commission.

Québec Values: Laïcité

As stated above, one of the central concerns for those articulating a discourse of opposition to reasonable accommodation was Québec's assumed secular nature. The focus on *laïcité*[5] dealt with a variety of questions revolving around religion, including the neutrality of the state, the separation of religion and state, and especially, public displays of religiosity, among others. The overwhelming majority of respondents who tackled the question of *laïcité* in their briefs did so in order to express their support for it being a fundamental and non-negotiable Québec value. This was expressed in many different ways.

In the case of an untitled brief written by twenty-one members of a self-identified seniors' (over fifty years of age) group, the focus was entirely on Québec's unique brand of secularism. The authors explain: "What motivates us, is being confronted in the public sphere with protests, requests and demands that for certain people challenge values that we see as fundamental in Québec society" (Arseneau et al. 2007: 1, my translation). In this sense, the authors repeat a well-rehearsed concern in the briefs with the question of accommodation practices that pit a benevolent host society to the rather "unreasonable" demands of religious newcomers. Reiterating the importance of the fundamental values to Québec society, the authors explain that it is essential "to announce clearly the colours [of Québec society] to those we welcome," more or less repeating the infamous Hérouxville town council's missive to potential newcomers.[6] In order to accomplish this task, the authors develop a proposal for a Québec charter of secularism, which they explain is inspired by a similar proposal by the French-based Mouvement Europe et Laïcité for a European charter that "defends secularism where it is threatened in France ... and in Europe" (Mouvement Europe et Laïcité 2010). The Mouvement national des Québécoises et Québécois (MNQQ), a Québec-wide independence organization, echoed this call for a Québec charter of secularism, in this case one that would resemble France's 1905 law on the separation of church and state. In their opinion, this charter would

> state certain limits on religious freedoms, including an interdiction against political meetings in places of worship, any incitation to civil disobedience by ministers of religion, religious signs on public monuments other than places of worship,

weapons in school and other sensitive public places, and clothing that entirely covers the face. (2007: 13, my translation)

Several other individuals and organizations, including the second-largest union in Québec, the Confédération des syndicats nationaux, which spoke out very strongly against the discrimination immigrants and refugees experienced during the heated debate on "reasonable accommodation," and the Centrale des syndicats du Québec (CSQ), a union representing thousands of workers in the public education sector, set out the broad parameters for such a charter, making it among the most common recommendations in my sample.

Besides a very general call for a charter of secularism, several respondents fleshed out what precisely such a charter would encompass. For instance, Québec-based anthropologist, writer and former president of the Mouvement laïque québécois, Daniel Baril (2007), argued explicitly that such a charter would ensure that religious freedoms do not take precedence over "other fundamental rights." A number of other individuals and organizations in Québec made similar calls for a special law that would favour certain rights over others. The rights to be protected varied by respondent, though as we will see below, most who shared such a concern made it clear that in their opinions the main right threatened in the public sphere was that of gender equality. The CSQ explained in their brief: "This law must also recognize that the exercise of a liberty or right enshrined in the Charters should not deny or restrict the right to equality between women and men" (2007: 19, my translation). Thus, in many ways, the charter of secularism would mark out the terrain between various opposing rights (i.e., religious freedom versus gender equality), which according to a number of respondents, existing legislation (e.g., Canadian and Québec *Charters of Rights and Freedoms*) leave undefined.

In most cases where a Québec charter of secularism was promoted, the briefs articulated a particular vision of a threatened Québec struggling against the spectre of religious fundamentalism(s), or what the CSQ called the "return of religion" to Québec[7] (16, my translation). These documents highlight certain values that have been key to the debate about difference in Western liberal democracies more generally and in Québec more specifically: secular humanism, tolerance and the place of individual rights. These briefs and the many others opposing reasonable accommodation on the grounds of protecting Québec's secular values position Québec firmly on the path of Western civilization and progress. For instance, many individual respondents made straightforward arguments to this effect, including the following by an individual respondent expressing pride at Québec's adoption of Enlightenment ideals, which now mean that "Québec, Canada and the United States are the safest societies in History" (Claveau 2007: 2, my translation). Another man, describing himself as representing the Franco-Québécois "silent majority," followed through on this Enlightenment logic: "We have Western customs of liberty, tolerance and of generosity. Often immigrants who arrive in Canada are not used to this way of life" (Gauthier 2007: 2, my translation). Importantly, what I am calling a discourse of opposition makes no mention of the social barriers to integration in Québec society; instead we are faced with strangers who naturally do not understand our ways. As Hage (2000: 87) explains, this invariably leads to a desire to govern racialized others:

Those addressed, or to use a technically more correct word, those interpellated, by the discourse of tolerance see in the very address a confirmation of their power to be intolerant. In fact, they would not be interpellated by this discourse if they did not recognize that they are already in a position of power which allows them to be intolerant.

Not surprisingly, given the current constellation of geo-political and social forces in North America that pit the West versus Islam (see Mamdani 2004), respondents who identified particular religious and/or cultural practices as especially problematic in Québec most often used examples of a presumed "Muslim" difference. For instance, an individual captured this concern in the following passage:

> Over the past few years, it has been difficult not to notice that certain fundamentalist elements of Montréal's Muslim community look down on the host society's values and customs with contempt. They claim rights far beyond what is necessary under the precepts of religious pluralism and attack the rights and liberties of others. (Réhel 2007: 9, my translation)

While most briefs steer clear of problematizing any specific religion, practices that are most often associated with Islam in the social imaginary (e.g., wearing the hijab, separation between men and women) are among the most common to elicit direct comment, followed by practices associated with orthodox Judaism.

A specific element of the briefs that takes on a uniquely Québec flavour is the evocation of Québec's history struggling against the shackles of an oppressive Catholic Church in order to become a secular society. In the opinion of many of the authors of briefs to the commission, requests for accommodation on religious grounds and displays of religious symbols and affiliations in the public sphere bring society back to an unacceptable past before the social gains of the Quiet Revolution in the 1960s and 1970s. However, a large number of people who stated that position also argued, paradoxically, that there is no problem with keeping symbols of Québec's religious past on public display, for they are an intrinsic part of Québec's history. The Société Saint-Jean-Baptiste de Montréal, a Montréal-based nationalist organization, explains this seeming contradiction:

> We opt for moderation: installing a crucifix in a school or a municipal hall in 2007, for example, does not have the same significance as leaving one that has been there for generations. The first act is to be avoided; in the second case, the site that is directly concerned must judge local sensibilities. And also History. (2007: 7, my translation)

In another instance of this argument for the *historical* and *cultural* value of Catholicism in Québec, the MNQQ, despite their concerns for the neutrality of the state *vis-à-vis* religion, argued: "All interpretation of the proposed charter must promote Québec's spiritual heritage as much as possible" (2007: 14, my translation). In this sense, many of the respondents defined the acceptable limits of Catholic and in some cases Protestant religion in the public sphere, though there was little discussion in these same briefs of how the public sphere might legitimately integrate non-Christian religious symbols or practices. Echoing many of the respondents in my sample, when portions of the Bouchard-Taylor report calling for the removal of the crucifix in the National Assembly were leaked to the media, the Québec Legislature unanimously passed a motion supporting the crucifix. Defending the vote, Premier Jean Charest was quoted as saying: "We cannot erase our history. The crucifix is about 350 years of history in Québec that none of us are ever going to erase, and of a very strong presence, in particular of the Catholic Church" (CTV News 2008). Yet, despite his support for Québec's religious history, in his address to the National Assembly earlier in the day Charest stated unequivocally that Québec had been secular since the Quiet Revolution, the first time any sitting premier of Québec made such a statement (Milot 2009: 69). Why then, is there a need to reiterate the importance of Québec's religious "heritage" while at the same time arguing that Québec is for all intents and purposes secular?

In her analysis of the very recent construction of secularism as a fundamental Québécois value, Micheline Milot (2009) points out that through most of the history of French Canada, secularism was cast to the wayside as a symbol of republican anti-clericalism. Her study demonstrates that until 1990, the use of the term "secularism" was almost non-existent in government-appointed commissions or councils, and that it was not until 2007 that the Government of Québec first used the term "*laïcité*," and this in a document aimed at potential immigrants to Québec (31–54). While she acknowledges that secularism has attained sudden popularity in Québec, she encourages us to consider what its emergence as a "fundamental value" might tell us: "When an idea emerges in everyday language, we can assume that it reveals new expectations, concerns or social perceptions towards the phenomena it is intended to signify" (30, my translation). Indeed, the written briefs demonstrate how secularism has become a key component of Québec's normative identity, one intimately linked to the threats posed by racialized outsiders.

In conjunction with many of the arguments in the briefs and in Québec, well-known Québec intellectual Jean-François Lisée made a similar call for the continued importance of the Catholic religion in Québec's secular society. While Lisée calls for the further secularization of the public school system in Québec, for instance, he also unabashedly calls for the importance of Catholicism in the public sphere as a sign of Québec history: "Québec exists because its majority has lived a unique history, speaks French and is the bearer of a religious tradition. To evacuate or devalue this is to lose ones' self-esteem, and in the long run, to detest the other" (2007: 3, my translation). The only way to stop this flirtation with postmodernism, as he calls it, is for the "French-Québécois majority to establish in a much clearer way its predominance over history, language and religion" (5, my translation). Another individual author expresses a similar nationalist sentiment: "The Québécois must rediscover the essence of their roots. They have collectively painted the most beautiful of landscapes throughout their eventful and unfinished history. They mustn't accept that others, from elsewhere, undo what they built with much effort" (Turcotte 2007: 10, my translation). Through this first element of the discourse of opposition in the briefs, it becomes clear that religion is an important marker of identity in Québec, though the respondents almost unanimously mark religious practices as coming from outside Québec. As Milot (2009: 56) demonstrates further, the adoption of secularism as a key social value by the majority in Québec at a time of social crisis can be read as a discursive strategy to limit the expression of minority religious and cultural practices.[8]

Québec Values: Gender Equality

Besides the notable attention on Québec's secular values in the written briefs, the most common element tying the briefs together is the defence of gender equality as a fundamental Québécois value. As such, it stands out as the most important part of the opposition to "reasonable accommodation" in my sample.

In many ways, the question of gender equality was at the forefront of the reasonable accommodation debate. Québec is not unique in this regard, as feminist scholars across a wide spectrum have written about the Western preoccupation with the figure of the endangered Muslim woman struggling against patriarchal norms (Yegenoglu 1998; Jiwani 2006; Razack 2008; Haque 2010). In the aftermath of the Bouchard-Taylor Commission, several Québec-based feminists argue that a narrow understanding of gender equality generally operates to uphold Western civilizing norms in Québec (among them, Mahrouse 2008; Chew 2009). With this context in mind, Tanisha Ramachandran (2009: 37) argues that in Canada and Québec, the "Muslim woman's body becomes the site of contestation where struggles over nation and citizenship are waged."

The discourse opposing so-called Western values of gender equality with purported non-Western patriarchal practices was on very clear display ten days into the commission's hearings when the Conseil du statut de la femme du Québec (CSFQ), a government advocacy and research agency focused on gender equality, proposed that the Québec *Charter of Rights and Freedoms* be amended to ensure that the equality of men and women supersedes the freedom of religion, much like in the hierarchy of rights I discussed in the previous section. Despite legal advice suggesting that any new legislation would be redundant since both Canadian and Québec law already prevented violating women's rights (Mahrouse 2010a: 92–93) and the CSFQ's own acknowledgement in their brief to the Bouchard-Taylor Commission that requests for religious accommodation are very rare in Québec, the government later tabled legislation modifying the Québec Charter, in many ways pre-determining the commission's hearings.

Nevertheless, a look at some of the briefs articulating opposition to accommodation through the gender equality versus religious freedom binary is instructive. For example, the brief entitled "L'égalité des sexes, une valeur fondamentale au Québec" [Sex Equality: A Fundamental Value in Québec] makes this argument quite clear. In the words of the author: "Québec must take all legal means necessary to ensure the lasting nature of women's equality, to affirm it loudly and with pride, and demonstrate to the entire world that it is possible to accomplish this" (Dion 2007: 5, my translation). The author goes on to state unequivocally that since "very few religions consider women equal to men" and that Islamic fundamentalism is a major problem globally, then we must hold firm to Québec's Western values. In the author's words: "Québec is a member of the Western countries, and accordingly, articulates the same values as they do" (7, my translation). In this way, the author picks up on the theme of Québec as a model student of Western civilization, with a global mission to spread its superior values and norms. As I noted above, this theme is common in the briefs I examined, particularly among individual authors.

In their own brief to the commission, entitled "Droit à l'égalité entre les femmes et les hommes et liberté religieuse" [The Right to Equality Between Men and Women and Religious Freedom], the CSFQ explains that their first foray into the question of religious freedom was in 1995, when they wrote a report on Muslim veils in schools. Since that time, they have organized much of their activity around the debate about values common to Québec society, in ways consistent with their lobbying in regards to the Québec *Charter of Rights and Freedoms* above. Notably, nowhere in their brief is there any mention of ongoing forms of violence against women or other modes of gender inequality in Québec other than those originating in the minority Muslim community. Accordingly, the CSFQ provides two hypothetical cases involving ostensibly "Muslim" practices. In both cases, it is evident that the CSFQ sees the threat to gender equality as coming from values foreign to Québec's superior value set and not from patriarchal practices and values fundamental to Québec society, despite a long tradition of radical feminism in Québec.[9]

In fact, another women's organization, the South Shore University Women's Club (SSUWC), repeats this concern with values foreign to Québec, but in a way that more explicitly enumerates acceptable women's conduct. Much like the CSFQ, the Hérouxville Code of Conduct and the City of Gatineau's "Statement on Values" (see note 6), "immigrant" values and norms become responsible for women's subjugation:

> We must ensure that the immigrant girl be provided with the opportunity to engage in critical thinking with respect to parental pressure if that interferes with her opportunity to pursue further education or make enlightened career choices. And, beyond that, we must be able to support her when faced with the consequences of choices that run counter to traditions that restrict her choices. (South Shore University Women's Club 2007: 10)

Again, we see here how this discourse blames naturalized immigrant "traditions" for gender inequality in Québec society, not practices inherent to Québec, which, in contrast, is held up as an egalitarian space for women. The majority of respondents who discussed gender equality did so according to the same framework used by organizations such as the CSFQ and the SSUWC.

The CSQ, an important Québec-based social and political institution, also made their call for limits related to cultural and especially, religious practices quite plain: "In the *majority* of cases, requests for reasonable accommodation have had as an effect the exclusion of women from the public sphere or the denial of their fundamental rights" (2007: 7, my translation and emphasis). Here the CSQ repeats a commonsense formulation that in many ways has become "fact" in Québec: the idea that human rights commissions and courts are overrun with requests for accommodation that infringe on norms of gender equality, what they previously called the "return of religion" in the public sphere. Yet, as Yolande Geadah (2007) demonstrates, no more than 85 of the 5,482 official requests for accommodation to the Commission des droits de la personne et des droits de la jeunesse [Québec Human Rights Tribunal] in the five-year period preceding the Bouchard-Taylor Commission (2000–2005) were of a religious nature, and only fifty-five of these made requests for accommodation. Of these, Geadah (2007: 23–25) confirms that the majority was made by Protestants, including mainstream Christians and Jehovah's Witnesses. Since we know that many of these nearly fifty-five requests were about religious symbols and practices in the public sphere (e.g., establishing prayer rooms, the wearing of religious symbols, etc.) and were made primarily by *Christians*, then what purpose does it serve to suggest that the *majority* of the requests for accommodation involved conflicts between minority religious demands and gender equality, as the CSQ does quite explicitly? Sirma Bilge (2010: 198, my translation), writing specifically about the discourse on gender equality in Québec, argues that "the gender equality and sexual freedoms discourse is an integral part of the homogenizing and totalizing processes that go hand in hand with the constitution and reaffirmation of national identity [in Québec]." Indeed, for many respondents, gender equality becomes the legitimating practices and/or value that points to Québec's national genius and places it within a civilizational order based on European White supremacist discourses. In other words, gender equality becomes Québec's contribution to Western civilization. In such a discourse, we need only focus on the cultural practices of racialized others, even when similar practices occur regularly in Québec society (e.g., violence against women). In this way, none of the respondents speak explicitly about race; the silences and omissions point to the overwhelming depoliticization underwriting race-making in Québec society.

Despite the overwhelming focus on Islam and gender equality in the briefs I examined, a small minority of respondents drew heavily on a variety of social indicators that paint a rather different picture of the place of Muslim women in Québec society. For instance, in a telling contrast to the CSFQ brief, three Québec-based organizations, the Canadian Council of Muslim Women (CCMW), Présence musulmane Montréal (PMM) and the Centre culturel islamique de Québec (CCIQ) also wrote briefs to the commission that resituated the discussion about Muslim women in Québec.[10] In their reflections on the two public consultations held by the Bouchard-Taylor Commission in immigrant, west-end Montréal, the CCMW stated that the two most pressing concerns for the Muslim women participants in the consultations were better access to employment and the alleviation of racism and discrimination in Québec society. The PMM comes to similar conclusions in their brief, outlining how Québec Muslims have an unemployment rate over three times the provincial average (25 percent to 8 percent for those twenty-five to forty-four years old), despite significantly higher university graduation rates. Perhaps most saliently, the PMM argues that when it comes to the debate about gender equality, "the problem is that we often only recognize one model of modernity and the emancipation of women, a particular Western model" (Présence mMusulmane Montréal 2007: 9, my translation). They explain that this specifically Western "phantasm" continues in Québec today through placing an interdiction on the Muslim headscarf,[11] rather than focusing on policies to ensure, for instance, employment equity. The PMM echoes many scholars in Québec who argue that mainstream definitions of feminism and gender equality do not support Muslim women wearing a veil in their many struggles against sexist attacks and racist exclusions. "The implicit message," Dolores Chew (2009: 87) argues, "is that support is forthcoming just as long as one conforms to the accepted mainstream definition of feminism." And yet, mainstream definitions of feminism remain difficult to pin down, precisely because they rely on commonsense notions of what it means to be Québécoise, notions that are at once unspecified (universal) and ultimately contingent (particular) on civilizing norms. The effect is to further marginalize Muslim women in Québec, especially those wearing a veil, while at the same time calling for their equality.

The CCIQ, a Québec City-based Muslim community centre, spoke out quite forcefully against the discrimination faced by Muslim women along the terms I develop above. In fact, they chose to respond directly to the CSFQ's efforts to lobby the Québec government on behalf of women in Québec:

> The Conseil du statut de la femme never consulted us women wearing the hijab on our lot; instead they shamelessly present their own courageous positions on current issues involving the wearing of the hijab. What do they know about our problems with unemployment? Of the discriminations and insults of all kinds that we must face as women and upon which they never take a stand? Is this a Conseil du statut de la femme for old stock, White, sexually liberated women who have renounced the church and Christ? Are we — Muslim women — worthy of your interest? (2007: 12, my translation)

In this sense, a number of briefs in my sample resist the common discourse of opposition that pits Québec values to those emanating from elsewhere (spatially, religiously, cultur-ally), laying bare the problematic *racial* assumptions that are at its foundation. As I state above, nowhere in these briefs is there an explicit discussion of racial difference; instead, in following the culturalized approach to race, respondents enumerate a number of values and practices that position Québec and the Québécois within frameworks of Western civilization and White supremacy.

CONCLUSION

This analysis demonstrates an approach to the study of race-making in societies such as Québec. The double-colonization process in French Canadian society has produced particular ways to imagine and construct race in Québec. Many respondents in the briefs I examined employ the dominant approach to race-making common in Western societies, one that presents itself as unquestionably committed to equality and justice. Yet, through both the particular and universal ways in which this discourse is employed, race and racial difference continue to take on further salience. For instance, the discourse of opposition in the Bouchard-Taylor briefs articulates a civilizational logic that places Québec within the Western family of nations (civilized) and the threats to Québec's purported values as outside the civilizational norm (uncivilized). From this seemingly natural civilizational divide flows the power to make decisions about the appropriate levels of accommoda-tion. This discourse points to a continuity with colonial discourses in Québec society that underwrote the dispossession and exploitation of Indigenous peoples, a process ongoing today. Ultimately, as Mahrouse (2010a: 90) argues, the debate over reasonable accommo-dation in Québec paves the way for legislation and other forms of regulation that increase surveillance on racialized populations and in fact decrease economic opportunities for Muslim women (e.g., Bill 94). Any research that challenges the many silences on race in

Québec society and in other French Canadian societies would go far in dispelling the commonplace notion that race and racism are of no consequence in Québec.

NOTES

1. See for examples of this, my analysis of the commemorative events celebrating Québec's 400th anniversary in 2008 (Leroux 2010a) and Daniel Salée's critique of two major historical works released in 2009 underlining the friendship between early French settlers and Indigenous peoples (Salée 2010). Claude Couture (2010 and 2011) expresses this position rather well in two texts lauding David Hackett Fischer's (2008) *Champlain's Dream: The Visionary Adventurer Who Made a New World in Canada*.

2. By "White supremacy" I refer to political, economic and cultural systems that favour those constructed as "white" in our society. According to Gillborn (2006: 320), "white supremacy is not only, nor indeed primarily, associated with relatively small and extreme political movements that openly mobilize on the basis of race hatred (important and dangerous though such groups are): rather, supremacy is seen to relate to the operation of forces that saturate the everyday, mundane actions and policies that shape the world in the interests of white people."

3. Micheline Labelle (2010), writing in the Québec context, takes a similar position. Her study *Racisme et anti-racisme au Québec* provides a good overview of debates over racism in Québec society and points to the dominance of the colour-blind approach.

4. See the Bouchard-Taylor final report for a lengthy discussion of such cases (Government of Québec 2008: 48–60).

5. While there is a slight, yet important differentiation between the concepts of *laïcité* in French and secularism in English, I have decided to retain the English-language term as a stylistic decision.

6. In the heat of the bitterly fought election campaign in winter 2007, the Hérouxville (pop. 1,300) town council passed a Code of Conduct aimed at potential immigrants that specifically prohibited stoning or burning women alive, female circumcision and a number of other practices. This provoked an international media storm, on both the Code and Québec's treatment of immigrant minorities. See the following analyses of the Hérouxville "affair" (Ahadi 2009; Gilbert 2009; Mookerjea 2009; Nieguth and Lacassagne 2009). Notably, in November 2009, the Canadian Government released a new citizenship study guide, *Discover Canada: The Rights and Responsibilities of Citizenship*, which used some of the same language as the Hérouxville Code, including a reference to "barbaric cultural practices." In addition, the City of Gatineau, Québec's fifth largest municipality (pop. 220,000), released a twenty-page document intended for immigrants, entitled *Énoncé de valeurs* [Statement of Values] on November 28, 2011, that lists sixteen core Québécois values, including gender equality, punctuality, personal hygiene and respect for private property.

7. Victor Armony, a leading scholar of immigration in Québec, ruefully pointed out in his brief that over 400 municipal councils in Québec continue to open their sessions with a Christian prayer.

8. On February 9, 2011, Pauline Marois, the leader of the Parti Québécois and Member of the National Assembly for Charlevoix, re-introduced Bill 391 (An Act to assert the fundamental values of the Québec nation), which would amend the Québec *Charter of Rights and Freedoms* to include equality of women and men, the primacy of French and the separation of state and religion as fundamental values of the Québec nation.

9. Chantal Maillé's (2010) work situates such feminist responses in Québec theoretically, while Sean Mills' (2010) work on the history of radical activism in 1960s Montréal has a useful chapter devoted to radical feminism.

10. Micheline Labelle, François Rocher and Rachad Antonius have written about Arab-Muslim political organizations and the dynamics of race-making and difference in Québec (see Antonius 2008; Labelle, Rocher and Antonius 2009).

11. On March 24, 2010, the Government of Québec introduced Bill 94 (An Act to establish guidelines governing accommodation requests within the administration and certain institutions), which prohibits people covering their faces from accessing almost all public services and employment. Concordia University's Simone de Beauvoir Institute prepared a response to the bill in the Québec National Assembly (delivered by Prof. Vivian Namaste on May 20, 2010), which in many ways reflects the positions taken by organizations representing Arab and/or Muslim women in the briefs. A video of the Institute's response can be accessed online (Assemblée Nationale 2010). The bill was adopted in principle in the National Assembly on February 15, 2011.

Chapter 4

CREATING SPACE FOR DIFFERENCE

Theorizing Multicultural Jewish Identity in Canada

Michele Byers and Stephanie Tara Schwartz

What does it mean to be Jewish within the context of state-sanctioned Canadian multiculturalism? What happens to Jewishness as the meaning of multiculturalism changes and is challenged? How do we begin to conceptualize a critical theoretical model through which we might engage these questions? In the summer of 2010, we presented our work as part of a panel on Jewishness and Canadian multiculturalism at the Association for Canadian Jewish Studies in Montréal. During the panel, we and two of our colleagues raised questions about the invisibility of Jewish difference, as well as the lack of interrogation within Jewish studies of the constitution of Canadian Jewish identity within problematic colonial tropes like multiculturalism. We found the audience extremely generous and willing to engage with us on these issues. But one of the questions stood out: why were all of our presentations so strongly rooted in American literatures, even as the object of our inquiry was Canadian Jewishness?

In writing this chapter, we begin with this question because it is often asked of Canadian scholars. The simplest answer is that there *is* no (or very little) scholarship in the area of critical Jewish studies and/or Jewish cultural studies in Canada. The one event either of us has participated in where this type of work was presented in some quantity was the 2007 conference of the Canadian Society for Jewish Studies in Ottawa, perhaps because it brought out a host of scholars who work at or near the boundaries of Jewish studies, but whose work is relevant because it engages the question of Jewish identity within representations of various kinds — fiction, art, film, television, material culture and theatre. This type of work has been well articulated within the American context for the past fifteen to twenty years. Indeed, the vastness and complexity of the literature on American Jewishness are impossible to chronicle in a paper such as this one. But in reading those studies, there is always the following question for us: what about Canada?

In Michele's home office there are three full shelves devoted to books on Jewishness, emanating primarily from the U.S., many of them written from a cultural studies orientation.[1] This rich work has complicated conceptions of Jewish identity in the North American diaspora. Barbara Kirshenblatt-Gimblett (2005: 449–50) links the emergence of this type of perspective to the "corporeal turn" in Jewish studies, which marked "a more inclusive and pluralist view of Jewish cultures" and cultural artifacts. In the U.S. there was a great deal of gatekeeping around the development of these critical discourses and concern over whether they were properly Jewish or good for Jews. Many traditional Jewish studies scholars continue to be uncomfortable with the idea that Jewish identity is made up of multiple, unstable, shifting and constructed identity categories and cultural practices. In the new paradigm we are asked to consider the categories "Jews" and "Jewish" as exactly this: unstable, shifting and constructed (Stratton 2000); we are asked to consider Jewishness as a text whose meaning is produced as it intersects with a multitude of socially, culturally and historically situated audiences.[2]

The corporeal or cultural turn in American Jewish cultural studies also encouraged scholarly engagement with the place of Jews within multiculturalism (e.g., Biale et al. 1998; Boyarin and Boyarin 1996 Gilman 2006), which included taking a probing look at how multiculturalism produces/privileges particular forms of Jewishness. In this chapter, we are interested in linking state-sanctioned multiculturalism and the production of ways of being and understanding Jewishness as a practice of embodiment, in order to understand the role whiteness plays in that discursive space. That is, we argue that Jewishness becomes visible within Canadian multiculturalism as a certain kind of whiteness. From the American literature we can draw an understanding of whiteness as a constellation of privileges that allows us to ask how multiculturalism as policy has facilitated the possibility for some Jews to draw upon those privileges. Our work here also examines examples of cultural production and lived experience whose representations of complicated and dynamic Jewish identities and histories help us consider what happens to Jews who do not fit so neatly into the model supported by multiculturalism. Further, through these examples we interrogate how multiculturalism mitigates the precariousness of privilege. That is, multicultural tolerance for marginal forms of whiteness has mitigated the vulnerability of Jewish otherness for several decades, but at the cost of the invisibility of Jewish difference and internal xenophobia within many Jewish communities.

In the analyses that follow, we create discursive space within which to speak about the implications of understanding Jews as one (that is, as a single, monolithic) part of multiculturalism and a part that enables us to move towards finding ways of speaking, thinking and representing Jews as multicultural. We begin with a discussion of some of the ways in which Jewish cultural studies has developed in the U.S. context and contrast this with the existence and absence of similar work in Canada. We follow this with a discussion of the ways Jewish difference emerges into both discourse and lived experience in the Canadian context. In the final sections of this chapter we return to our desire to formulate ways of creating a more comprehensive and fully felt paradigm shift in Canadian Jewish studies (and Jewish studies in Canada) and critical Canadian studies.

WRITING CANADIAN JEWISH CULTURE

To do Jewish cultural studies means more than just taking cultural studies terms and using them to study aspects of Jewish culture, which would leave Jewish studies as a discipline more or less unchallenged. The tradition of Jewish cultural studies is quite different, politically and theoretically, than Jewish studies. As the editors of *Queer Theory and the Jewish Question* articulate very well:

> Both Jewish cultural studies and queer theory find an alternative impetus, grounded less in the positivism of identities than in the shifting terrain of discourse....

That said, it is not as if Jewish cultural studies and queer theory are strangers to the political claims that energized Jewish studies and lesbian and gay studies in their earlier incarnations. We want to recognize the ongoing pull of identity and identity politics, even as we mark the necessary trouble and incitement of identities that refuse to come clean or become simple. (Boyarin et al. 2003: 6)

To illustrate some of the conundrums of Jewish cultural studies, we examine a few areas in which there exists a strong tradition of scholarship in the U.S. In each case, the work exists to showcase Jewishness in its particularities, but also positions itself within a broader interrogation of American culture, of which Jewishness is understood to be an important part.

Jewishness and Whiteness

Studies of "whiteness" have been quite extensive in the U.S. context, with books on how Jews (Jacobson 1998; Brodkin 2000; Goldstein 2006), Irish (Ignatiev 1996; Negra 2006) and Italians (Guglielmo and Salerno 2003) came to be seen as "white." Again, there is surprisingly little work in the area of whiteness in the Canadian context, with particularly few studies of the specific histories through which ethnicized immigrant communities have been organized and assimilated in relation to dominant White norms. The Canadian literature on whiteness has tended to focus on histories of colonialism that continue to be felt in the contemporary experiences of racialized and ethnicized Canadians and First Nations peoples (Clarke 1997; Harper 2002; Levine-Rasky 2002; Razack 2002; Carr and Lund 2007). The interrogation of struggles for whiteness and processes through which differently ethnicized groups or claim White privilege, as well as histories of racialized and otherwise marginalized Canadian Jews, are still needed.

American Jewish cultural studies has explored questions of Jewish multiplicity, both the relationship between "Jews" (as a monolithic category) and multiculturalism as social policy, and "Jewishness" as a subject position that can be inhabited by people of all racialized, ethnicized, sexually oriented, linguistic and class positions (often several at the same time). Much of this work is focused on problematizing the assumption that Jews are what you think they are and look like what you think they do.

There have been many historical shifts in the production of and understanding of "race" as a subject position. In particular, understandings of whiteness — who is/is not considered White, but also whether White is a "race" — are contested. Carstairs (2001), in her discussion of a conference on "whiteness" held at the University of Toronto, addresses two particularly salient issues: first, the link between racialization/racism and national histories, for example, the self-congratulatory sense of Canada's difference from the U.S. and a subsequent turn away from rigorous interrogations of White histories and supremacies in Canada. Without falling back on the unhelpful old dichotomy of mosaic and melting pot, it is important to acknowledge that in the U.S. issues of identity and plurality exist within a national history that is centred on a bifurcation of "whiteness" and African-Americanness. This situation is not paralleled in Canada, and that difference has been used as a way of positioning Canadian "tolerance" as a corrective to American racism. Second, there is a concern that some histories of whiteness collapse distinctions between the histories of White ethnic groups and those of racialized populations.[3] What needs to be further complicated, in our minds, is the assumption that Jews are White, keeping the problems and risks of doing this work always in mind.

Rather than claim that Jews are *not* White, what needs to be made visible is that whiteness need not be a condition of Jewishness. Jews may belong to any and all racialized groups. We recognize that the term White is conceptually limiting and problematic. As stated earlier, we think about it less as a singular, bounded identity than as a constellation of privileges that accrue via proximity to a series of norms around race and racialization that are highly situational. While "Jew" may have functioned as a non-White racial category in many historical periods, it largely does not do so in North America today. At the same time, Jewishness remains an ambiguous space to inhabit within structures of White privilege, and there has been little room to theorize — literally to make visible — Jews who do not have access to White privilege. Analyzing some of the ways Jews are racialized is a starting point to develop these ideas further, and this is one of the tasks we have set for ourselves in this chapter.

Entry into Discourse
Before turning to a discussion of racialization in the context of Canadian Jewish culture, it is important to consider how Jewish nationalism has complicated the issue of race for world Jewry. The establishment of Israel in 1948 triggered a process by which Jews of various geographical, national and cultural contexts were uprooted and reterritorialized within an idealistically envisioned Jewish nation-state. A conundrum emerged that not all Jewish immigrants to Israel shared the same physical appearance, language, culture and values of the European Zionists who founded the country and many were, as a result, racialized and treated differently on a national scale. Jewish racial/ethnic concepts and practices solidified in state policies and ideology, whereas in the diaspora, they remained more difficult to pin down as Jews negotiated their self-definition *vis-à-vis* diverse majority cultures.

The treatment of Mizrahi Jews by Ashkenazi Jews during the founding years of the State of Israel is one example of this. Israel was founded by a Eurocentric and Orientalist vision of nationalism that idealized emancipated Jewish pioneers and defenders throwing off the shackles of their lives in the diaspora and the burden of rabbinic Judaism (Almog 2000; Ram 2008). In the 1950s, Zionist ideologues were faced with mass immigration of Eastern European holocaust survivors and Jews from Arab and Muslim countries, many of whom remained observant of the *halakha* (Jewish religious law). Jews from the Muslim countries of North Africa and the Middle East, *Mizrahim* (a Hebrew term meaning "easterners"), were subject to racial discrimination that included being deloused with DDT, having children kidnapped and given to Ashkenazi families for adoption, being forcibly separated from their families and being settled in *ma'abarot* (refugee absorption camps) and development towns far from the centres of Tel Aviv and Jerusalem (Segev 1986; Massad 1996; Shohat 1999). Ethiopian Jews who were airlifted to Israel in the late 1980s and early 1990s also experienced significant racism in the Jewish state, to the point of having their authenticity as Jews undermined by Ashkenazi religious leaders.[4]

One scholarly approach that critiques the racist treatment of Mizrahim by Ashkenazi

Zionism is Mizrahi studies. This interdisciplinary body of works aims to challenge the stigma of Arabness imposed by Zionist ideology and enacted through state policies upon Arab Israelis (both Jewish and non-Jewish) and Palestinians (Shohat 1999, 2006). This relational method of inquiry interrupts the teleology of Jewish history, which presumes a European and now Israeli centre and challenges instances of Jewish material and discursive oppressive power. Mizrahi studies stretches beyond the dichotomy of Israel-diaspora and places questions of Jewish racialized difference at the centre of its critical analysis. Applied to the Canadian context, a turn to Mizrahi studies prompts us to ask: what power differences exist among differently racialized Canadian Jews (the Mizrahim being just one example)? What can this teach us about processes of racialization, racism and configurations of power between Canadian Jews and other Canadians in the context of multiculturalism as a state policy?

Because of the political situation in Israel, Arabness, viewed by many as a characteristic of the enemy, has come to function like "blackness" as a cultural trope. A consciousness of blackness, as Fanon (1967) articulates, derives from a relationship between the body and the world. The "fact" of blackness is not merely an appearance but part of a historical and cultural system that organizes Black bodies as objects to be feared for (what is imagined to be) their primitive biology or culture and their "otherness," which might *infect* White society. In Canada, as in Israel, Sephardi and Mizrahi/Arab Jews[5] experience racialization, the attribution of the trope of blackness, primitiveness and otherness upon their bodies. In Québec, this is further compounded by the problems of language. Jacques Bensimon's 1977 film *20 ans après* documents struggles on behalf of the Francophone Sephardic Jews in Montréal to fight for their cultural and linguistic rights *vis-à-vis* the Anglophone Jewish community and Québécois society (Bensimon 1977). In this rare cultural artifact of Jewish internal difference, the Sephardim speak out against both the Anglophone Jewish community and Québécois society, which assert hegemonic pressure for the group to assimilate to their visions of either Jewish or Francophone culture.

Bensimon's documentary reveals that Canadian Jews occupy multiple subjectivities in different times and locations; the work challenges us to question the reductive vision of Jewishness that multiculturalism privileges. Indeed, Train (2006) calls the establishment of the Sephardic Kehila Centre in Thornhill, Ontario — founded to counter the refusal by Ashkenazi Jewish institutions to include Sephardic culture — a claim for racialized space. The building, constructed in 1997 in the colourful Moorish styles of Spain and North Africa, interrupts both the Canadian and the Jewish landscapes of its neighbourhood, asserting a different kind of Jewish space.

Despite this evidence of Jewish difference, multicultural discourse in Canada generally sees Jews as a single ethnic/cultural unit within multiculturalism, rather than as multicultural themselves. The reality is substantially more complex. Menkis (2011: 287) writes that the Canadian Jewish Congress (a leading voice for the combined Jewish community in Canada) only cautiously participated in the preliminary hearings of the 1963 Royal Commission on Bilingualism and Biculturalism, recommending that the Canadian Confederation recognize two founding "languages" and/or "cultures" rather than "races." The organization, based in Montréal (home of the largest Canadian Jewish demographic at the time) was worried about introducing a multiculturalism that would offend the dominant French population of their province. (Indeed, Québec would reject the concept of multiculturalism and prefer a model of interculturalism; see Leroux 2010b for discussion.) Further, the group saw more advantages to defining their community as a religious rather than an ethnic group.[6] Menkis's observations reveal the anxieties felt by Canadian Jews who were victims of discriminatory treatment by both French and English Canada in the years prior to the "Announcement of the Implementation of a Policy of Multiculturalism within the Bilingual Framework" in 1971, a process explained in Haque's chapter in this collection.

Michael Brown (2007: 3–4) offers another perspective on Jewish ethnic claims in Canada before, and during, the multicultural era: "In the words of Henry Srebrnik, Canada was a place where 'ethnicity [was] legitimated as the primary basis for political interaction.' And so, like French and Anglo-Canadians, Jews in Canada organized themselves as an ethnic group, a nationality." This, according to Brown, resulted in the strong tendency of Canadian Jews to identify as a single ethnicity closely affiliated to both Judaism and Zionism. Official multiculturalism offered institutions promoting this mode of Jewish identity the financial support to enhance a single Jewish ethnic heritage through festival, public education, arts and culture. Brown (2007: 3–4) further writes:

> Multiculturalism in Canada has meant, then, that Jews no longer fell into a constitutional lacuna. Instead, they were full-fledged members of the Canadian polity. In strengthening their own institutions and their own culture, Jews were no longer acting as outsiders but, rather, as model Canadians. To be a good Jew was now to be a better Canadian.

With the growing critiques in critical Canadian studies on what constitutes a model Canadian (e.g., Thobani 2007) and questions emerging from Jewish cultural studies and Mizrahi studies on Jewish internal difference, it is time to examine the positions Jews have been offered and adopted within Canadian multiculturalism.[7] Jews are depicted as a distinct group, caught between the nation's two founding communities, who capitalized on the shift from bi- to multiculturalism (Abella 1996). Jews whose embodiment or cultural/political heritage challenge the type of Jewish ethnicity (Ashkenazi, Zionist) promoted by the dominant communal institutions, accrue a designation of cultural blackness — a tainted and threatening element distinguished from the normative community, as Walcott explains in his foreword to this collection. But ethnicity is a problematic category for Jewish identity, especially in Canadian spaces that increasingly circumvent traditional modes of top-down representation (discussed later). The focus on Jewish unity or Jews as a single ethnicity ignores the realities of racialized and other forms of Jewish difference in Canada. A cultural studies approach helps to expose the complexities lying beneath this veneer of unity. To shift the discourse, we must ask serious questions about who has been "invited" to represent the Jewish community "racially," linguistically, politically and in popular culture. Who has been given space to speak the nation? Who else may be speaking? Who is listening? To attempt an answer we move now to a discussion of some voices on the margins of mainstream Canadian Jewish culture.

LIVING AND PRODUCING CANADIAN JEWISH DIFFERENCE

We started by asking: How do Jews fit into discourses of multiculturalism? How do we theorize Jewish difference rather than Jews as difference? How/can cultural studies add complexity to the way we think about Canadian Jewry? The U.S. and Israel provide us with entry points into discourse but fall short because Canadian historical and material realities are not exactly the same. Theorizing Canadian Jewish difference involves a recognition of the multiple and sometimes counter-subjectivities that Jews can claim, the complicated routes Jews have taken from one place to another and the recombinant cultures that have been created in their wake in the particularities that create the Canadian context. This means understanding how history and politics, including multicultural policy, have shaped Jewish identities in Canada. It means interrogating how different ways of being/ embodying/performing Jewishness have been privileged in the Canadian imaginary, as well as within the material realities of lived experience and popular representation. Jewish culture in Canada (especially forms produced on the margins) labours to make itself known within a language that exceeds the confines into which Jews and Jewishness as identity and cultural categories have been, to some degree, fixed within policy, community and the public imagination. The interdisciplinary media art of b.h. Yael, the music of Geoff Berner and the festival Le Mood provide three sites for analyzing the ways that groups and individuals are creating spaces, events and material artifacts through which they can claim and create Jewishness that is post-Jewish, that is, that expands the recognizable limits of Jewishness in Canada today.

b.h. Yael: Hybrid Identities and Bridging the Margins

The experimental and multimedia art of Toronto-based filmmaker and video installation artist b. h. Yael is one such productive space that exists on the margins of Canadian Jewish culture. Yael is a professor of integrated media at the Ontario College of Art and Design University in Toronto. In 2009, Yael was one of eight Jewish Israeli and Canadian women who occupied the Israeli Consulate in Toronto in protest of the Israeli attacks on Gaza, calling upon the Canadian government to impose sanctions on the Israeli government to end its abuses of human rights (Rabble 2009). Yael's oeuvre and public profile bridge activism, art and intellectual criticism and offer a potent site for the representation and theorization of Jewish difference.

Yael's *Fresh Blood* (1996) is a hybrid documentary that explores the filmmaker's racialized Jewish identity. The narrative follows Yael as she journeys from Canada, her current home, to Israel, the place of her birth. Over the course of this trip, Yael engages with Jewishness at the intersection of a mess of other, sometimes conflicting, identities along the lines of race, sexuality, nationality, gender and political positioning. Most importantly, *Fresh Blood* paints a portrait of a Canadian Jew who does not settle neatly into the commonly perceived Jewish ethnic profile proffered by American television or Canadian scholarship.

Yael's work undermines the trope of Jewish whiteness in two significant ways. First, she exposes Jewish diversity by deliberately exploring the Arabness of her identity, drawing from Mizrahi studies and examining her mother's Iraqi culture. An Arab Jewish identity emphasizes Jewish difference on two counts: one is political, insisting on an affiliation with

Palestinians and linking their shared experiences of oppression by the Jewish state; the second is a disruption of the idea of Jewishness as a monolithic race/ethnicity. Though born to a Jewish mother in Israel, Yael was brought up as a Christian when her mother immigrated to Canada and converted. Beyond the division between Arab and Jew, Yael critiques the identity categories that label her gender, sexuality, nation and class.

Second, in her commitment to building bridges across the margins of Canadian difference Yael's work undermines the trope of Jewish "whiteness." In 2011 Yael was featured in a conversation with Cree/Métis interdisciplinary artist, singer/songwriter and curator Cheryl L'Hirondelle and Plains Cree singer/songwriter, storyteller and actor Joseph Naytowhow in *Cultivating Canada*, a book published by the Aboriginal Healing Foundation Research Series. The three artists discuss differences and connections between the experiences of First Nations Cree and Métis in Canada and Arab Jews and Palestinians in Israel. Creating solidarity through dialogue with members of Canada's First Nations, Yael breaks the trend observed by Thobani (2007) that immigrants generally opt to emulate the exalted national subject when moving to a new host nation. Yael's commitment to connecting with other marginalized groups in Canada thus further challenges the monolithic association of Jews, whiteness and power.[8]

The meaning of whiteness and the place Jews occupy within or in relation to it varies across time and space. Mizrahi studies and the critical analysis of how racialization occurs between Jews push us to challenge discourses that frame Jews as a homogenous unit within Canadian multiculturalism. Yael's work creates discursive space for minority and marginalized voices within Canadian Jewish communities. It is an example of how Canadian Jews are living and producing multicultural identities that resist the designation of whiteness that has been afforded to and occupied by some Canadian Jews.

Geoff Berner: Questioning Jewish Privilege

Vancouver-based musician Geoff Berner is a cultural producer in the thriving klezmer[9] music scene in Canada. This scene, while not-exclusively Jewish, has become a place for some young Jews to negotiate identities that are alternative to the Canadian Jewish mainstream (including atheist, socialist and diaspora-centric). Tour-mate Daniel Kahn (American born, Berlin-based front man of the band Daniel Kahn and the Painted Bird) describes himself, Josh Dolgin (a.k.a. DJ Socalled[10]) and Berner as representatives of the "Klezmer Bund," elaborated in the bio section of Berner's website as: "the flowering of a reborn radical Jewish culture." Another quote from Berner's bio page reads: "We're all trying to put out a vision of Jewish culture that's the opposite of the conservative, knee-jerk pro-Israel, judgmental bullshit that's emerged in recent decades" (Berner 2012). This radical shift is a self-consciously political aspect of Berner and his colleagues' works.

The lyrics of Berner's 2005 song "Lucky Goddamn Jew" are evidence of his willingness to challenge the Canadian Jewish status quo. In an interview with *HEEB* magazine (2010) he explains his lyrics:

> I mean, I didn't just mean Israel when I said that "I live in a country where I am free to persecute people with less luck than me." I don't make any ethical or political distinction between the Israelis in their Occupation, and the general

behavior of the Canadian and U.S. governments toward their indigenous people. It's sort of a depressing thought, but one of the major things that the song is supposed to convey is the sad fact that suffering does not ennoble most people. When we were taught in Hebrew school the whole "Never Again" thing, was it "Never Again" genocide, or "Never Again" to us? (*HEEB* 2010)

Berner complicates the category "Jew" by using his Jewish difference to challenge the normative (often Zionist) political vision of Canadian Jews. Yet he also acknowledges that he is "lucky" and has been offered a place of privilege and power in Canadian society. In one breath Berner is both persecuted and persecutor, marginal and majority. His participation in the klezmer scene speaks to the desire for some young Jews to reclaim Ashkenazi Jewishness as a particular form of minority culture rather than as the Jewish norm (Smulyan 2010). The subtext of this engagement with Jewish privilege is the re-assertion of a Jewish "blackness"/visibility: the costumes, the music, the colour, the politics of Jewish difference from the mainstream (the invisible White Canadian subject). This is another moment of recognition of and resistance to the mechanisms of power and subjectivity that form and curtail expressions of Jewish difference and subjectivity in the Canadian context.

Le Mood: Creating Spaces for Alternatives
Held on June 6, 2011, Le Mood: A Festival of Unexpected Jewish Learning, Arts & Culture in Montréal marks a major shift in the mainstream Jewish community's acknowledgment of Jewish difference in Canada. The event, spearheaded by Mike Savatovsky, Director, Young Adult Outreach & Engagement at the Federation Combined Jewish Appeal,[11] and run mostly by volunteers, brought together several hundred people in day-long panel sessions on topics that included "Beyond Bagels and Bannock: Tribal Eco-Action," "Loaded: Jews and Money" and "Campus Strife, Community Struggles: Experiences of the Globalised Israel-Palestinian Conflict." Le Mood is striking for its postmodern style of organization, which, in its first year, called upon young artists, scholars and activists in the Jewish community to curate and speak on panels that addressed issues directly relevant to their experiences as Jews.

Le Mood offered a novel forum for some members of the Jewish community to engage reciprocally with critical Jewish scholarship. In the "Campus Strife" session, organized by Dr. Eric Abitbol, a lecturer in the Department of Political Science at Concordia University, participants used narrative to chronicle their experiences of the Israel and Palestine conflict on university campuses. Though most participants were of a Jewish left-wing or liberal political orientation, the discussion reflected a desire for better ways of understanding the complexities of Jewishness and for developing better tools to dialogue with both right-wing Jews and Palestinians. Another interesting session, on Jewish masculinities, asked partici-pants to reflect on stereotypes versus lived experiences of performing specifically Jewish gender roles. The session, though provocatively titled "Nice Jewish Boys? A Conversation on Jewish Masculinities amongst Ashkenazim and Sephardim," drew heavily on stereo-types of American Ashkenazim. A handful of audience members pointed this out and challenged the group (and session organizers) to think about how Israeli, and specifically

Mizrahi masculinities, complicate the discourse on Jewish men. This kind of dialogue is particularly relevant considering that the marginalization of Francophone Sephardi culture continues to exist in Montréal. The success of Le Mood is that it created a safe space in which to start some of these controversial conversations.

In some ways, Le Mood reproduced certain power dynamics in the Canadian Jewish community. Middle-class, university-educated, non-Hasidic, Ashkenazi Jews appeared to be the dominant demographic represented at this event. Yet, there was a deliberate attempt to include multiple voices: Francophone, queer, Sephardi, Hasidic, Russian and others within the space. There was also a deliberate attempt to contemplate the kinds of positions (rich? White? secular? religious? activist? oppressor?) that Canadian Jews occupy. Le Mood, like Berner's klezmer-punk approach to cultural production and Yael's interdisciplinary art, demonstrates the changes in the ways in which Jewish identity is being conceived in Canada today.

b.h. Yael's work, Geoff Berner's music and Le Mood are important sites of Canadian Jewish cultural production and lived experiences that complicate the singular space that Canadian Jews have both been offered and claimed with the nation's multicultural framework. Canadian Jewish diversity need not undermine the privileges of protection from anti-semitism and financial support of heritage preservation that Canadian Jews have received in the thriving years of multiculturalism. Rather, contemplating Jewish cultural diversity and the discussion of Jewish privilege in the Canadian state — aspects that have rarely been theorized in discussions of Canadian Jewishness within multiculturalism — should plug back into the struggle to create political frameworks where all people can live with dignity and without oppression.

CONCLUSION: THEORIZING CANADIAN JEWISH DIFFERENCE

One of the most recent discursive shifts in discussions of Jewishness is described in the U.S. as "post-Jewish." This type of language is certainly contentious, as is well chronicled in a recent issue of *The Journal of Critical Inquiry*. Indeed, we are well warned to remember that racism, sexism, anti-semitism, classism and homophobia (and other forms of oppression and marginalization) continue to exist and, at times, "post" functions as a way of delegitimizing such claims. As Kent Ono (2010: 228) writes:

> That a Black man became the president of the United States implies that past racial barriers to occupying that office are now gone. Racism is passé. Today, anything — even tremendous political and international power — is possible. The example of a postracial interpretation of Obama's presidency illustrates one of the major functions of postracial discourse: to minimize the reality of racism.

As Ono frames it, the discourse of postracism delegitimizes the ongoing reality of racially based forms of privilege and oppression, revokes gains made through social justice, anti-racist and coalitionist initiatives and furthers a neoliberal system that has no use for the state and imagines all people to be equally able to care and be responsible for themselves.

Post-Jewish discourse is, we would argue, somewhat different. David Hollinger (2009: 23) suggests that the idea of post-Jewishness "tries to balance an appreciation for the indispensable function of natal communities with a capacity for making new communities and for developing multiple identities." While Jewishness as an identity is not something that can be owned, contained or controlled within reductive, pre-existing (or even antici-pated) ideas about Jews/Jewishness, to be post-Jewish is still to be Jewish. This demands that we think about the complexity and increasing commodification of multigenerational diasporic experiences that may well include multiple national histories and points of identification. But it also reminds us that Jewishness has been exclusionary. The dangers of postracial discourses articulated so clearly by Kent Ono and others are embedded in many of the discourses through which traditional modes of understanding "Jew" and "Jewish" have been knowable. That is, "Jewish" as an identity category has often been predicated on the exclusion of Jews not raced, classed, sexually oriented, located, edu-cated and so on in particular ways. Post-Jewishness thus aims to push conceptualizations and representations of Jewishness *beyond* the limits that are traditionally ascribed to them. This includes acknowledging that traditional conceptions of Jewishness have privileged certain identities and have maintained and fostered oppression, invisibility and racism within Jewish communities.

Literary scholar Linda Hutcheon (1997) argues that Canada has been characterized as a postmodern nation since at least the late 1980s. She describes postmodernism as "undercut[ting] the notion that authorial authority rests on a single meaning, fixed in the past, by materially reminding us of the process of re-interpretation that we call the act of reading"; this is what we see in the grassroots eruptions of artistic, political and communitarian post-Jewishness described above. Hutcheon (1997: 69) notes that in fiction the postmodern erupts as a rethinking of narrative convention, "especially the so-called 'transparency' of stories and storytelling, whether in novels or history-writing." Today, Jews on the margins are struggling to find languages to represent their Jewish identities to the world; to find and give public expression to ways of being that break with convention and challenge the transparency through which Jews and Jewishness have been understood, both by those outside but also by those inside its communities. A young cantor/rabbi wrote a moving letter to the Halifax-based *Chronicle Herald* newspaper in honour of Pride Week. In it he talked about learning that his brother was gay and his struggle regarding making this fact public given his role in a religious community where there remains a lot of homophobia:

> Consider, if you will, the amount of sheer hatred, injustice, intolerance and shame resulting from this classical understanding of the unique Hebrew text. That a text can be sacred need not preclude a process of interpretation. In fact, the Jewish tradition encourages multiple layers of interpretation of all elements of its foundational text.... In light of what we know is true, that homosexuality is a perfectly normal and natural variation of human sexual orientation, the two phrases in the Bible [that appear to prohibit same-sex relations] cry out to us: "Re-read me! Re-interpret me! Understand me anew!" (Isenberg 2011)

This is precisely what we suggest that Jewish cultural studies allows: re-reading, re-presen-tation, re-vision, re-conceptualization, re-interpretation and re-narration.

But where is multiculturalism in all this? It is important to note that Jewish cultural studies emerged primarily in the U.S. and that multiculturalism is understood quite differently there than in Canada, where the dominant national myth is of a culturally diverse mosaic overtop the two founding White nations rather than on a White/Black binary.

In the context of Canadian multiculturalism, theorizing Jewishness involves a look at agency within multicultural environments. Further to this, the idea of the Jewish diaspora needs to be retheorized as a site of multiplicity, where culture is formed with attention to multiple and competing spaces as people move along different diasporic routes. As Aviv and Schneer (2005) posit, are we at *The End of the Jewish Diaspora?* Their work interrupts the discourse through which Jews are imagined as outsiders yearning for a home, elsewhere; a discourse which imagines, in a way, a monolithic Jewish identity with a single home as a single site of desire. But to some degree their book resituates the U.S. as the site through which American Jews come home. With different experiences of dislocation and relations to Israel, what we need is to create space for the theorizing of these questions in other national spaces, such as Canada, the U.K., Iran, Morocco, France, Australia and even Israel.

With *this* work, we are pushing for the inauguration of a cultural studies approach to Jewishness that begins in Canada. A cultural studies approach entails a political shift in conceptualizing "Jewish" that involves a combination of, but is not limited to, the following:

- a focus on active and engaged identities that acknowledge "Jewish" as one significant component among many possible and multiple axes of identity and an insistence that there is no thing that one must or cannot be to claim Jewishness as part of one's identity;
- a shift from seeing Jews as part of multiculturalism to Jews as multicultural;
- a recognition that Jews, Judaism and Jewishness change across time and space;
- an approach to group identity that moves beyond insularity based on fear of anti-semitism, assimilation or binaries of religious-secular, Zionist-anti-Zionist, Israel-diaspora, etc.;
- recognition of structures of power, privilege and racism/oppression within Jewish communities;
- creation of space for multiple definitions of Jewishness, including those that emanate from the bottom up or from the margins to the centre; and
- recognition of the importance of cultural production and lived experiences, in multiple languages, which present complicated and dynamic Jewish identities and histories.

Canadian Jewish culture defined according to this paradigm opens up whole new realms — and asks us to revisit many old ones — for further scholarship. Indeed examples of this paradigm shift are burgeoning on the margins of the Canadian Jewish mainstream. It manifests in the creation of progressive Jewish organizations, in the fostering of new communities, including online communities, and in the work of cultural producers and their products. It is now time for the intellectual community to follow their lead.

NOTES

1. We situate this orientation in relation to cultural studies more broadly, which we understand to mean work that engages via critical theoretical (and political) interventions with cultural texts and culture as text. Cultural studies is not easily defined, but we might begin with Nelson, Treichler and Grossberg's (1992: 4) description of it as an "interdisciplinary, transdiciplinary, and sometimes counter-disciplinary field…. It is typically interpretive and evaluative … it rejects the exclusive equation of culture with high culture and argues that all forms of cultural production need to be studied in relation to other cultural practices and to social and historical structures." Thus, works that use cultural studies terms without an understanding of their politico-theoretical linkages are not works of cultural studies; they may engage with the theoretical tensions of cultural studies and its languages without necessarily claiming to situate themselves explicitly within the discipline (as opposed to the work of some U.S. authors who identify explicitly as engaging in Jewish cultural studies).

2. It may be that internal difference has not always been problematic within Jewish thought. However, within the context of multiculturalism and the specific racist demands of Canadian identity, Jewish difference has become increasingly difficult to theorize within mainstream public cultures.

3. We refer here to the way that some groups now considered white could not always access white privilege, but also, as difference becomes a more valuable commodity, the way that those with white privilege may also try to claim a racialized (even if historical) identity.

4. The complex racialized experiences of Ethiopian immigrants to Israel received cinematic representation in the film *Live and Become* (2005).

5. The Jewish community is generally thought of as divided into two religious subdivisions: Ashkenazim (Jews of Eastern European descent) and Sephardim (Jews of Iberian origins). This binary division obscures internal differentiation of both groups and the suppression of Arab identities under the European tint that "Sephardi" implies (see Benbassa and Rodrigue 2000; Shohat 2006). In the Canadian context, Sephardi is the term most often used for the Jews from the Middle East and North Africa.

6. Particularly because the number of Jews who declared themselves by religion far outnumbered the number of Jews who declared themselves by ethnic group on the 1961 Canadian census (Menkis 2011: 290).

7. This indeed was the question that David Koffman and Stephanie posed to the Working Group on Jews and Multiculturalism in Canada that inspired the presentation that Michele and Stephanie along with Sheryl Nestel and David presented at the 2010 Association for Canadian Jewish Studies Conference mentioned in the introduction of this paper.

8. Yael's work consistently forms bridges with other marginalized communities. *Triskaidekaphobia*, for example, was commissioned by Inside/Out (Toronto LGBT Film and Video Festival) focusing on conversations with her son about phobias, theories of sexuality and mothers. See also *Palestine Trilogy* (Yael 2006).

9. Klezmer is a genre of music traditionally played by the Yiddish-speaking Ashkenazi Jews of Central and Eastern Europe and now a popular, innovated form played by Jewish and non-Jewish musicians across the globe.

10. DJ Socalled is a Canadian rapper, musician and producer known for his fusion of hip-hop and klezmer music. He produced Berner's 2011 album *Victory Party*. See Margolis 2011 for an analysis of DJ Socalled's work and of klezmer as a cultural phenomenon.

11. Other funders included: Federation CJA, Gen J, A Bit off the Top and the Jewish Community Foundation of Montréal.

Part Two
SPACE, PLACE AND TERRITORY

Chapter 5

CHINESE CANADA IN MOOSE JAW

A Story Told in Two Parts

Carrianne Leung

"An exciting new way to discover the past!" —from the Tunnels of Moose Jaw guestbook

For the past 150 years, representations of Chineseness from filmic characters like Charlie Chan to the spatial landscapes of "Chinatown" have been indicative of the prevalence of Chinese presences in Western imagined landscapes. But how do these representations insert the Chinese body into the Canadian nation? What roles do racialized bodies play in the narration of the nation, and indeed to the notions of authenticity and coherence? Representational strategies of "inclusion" in the nation highlight the politics of belonging and the complex dynamics of commodity culture, identity politics and diasporic longings.

In this chapter, I argue that notions of inclusion and recognition of difference are integral to the discourse of official multiculturalism in Canada. Representations of racialized people in the nation's past help produce the discourse of multiculturalism as part of Canadian heritage today. Through visiting two exhibits about Chinese Canada in a small city in Saskatchewan, I discuss the representational strategies of inclusion, maintaining that the emplacement of racialized bodies is deliberate, setting the terms of how multiculturalism gets produced as Canadian heritage.

Often, representations of racialized bodies in sites of national memory are called upon to write the celebratory discourse of official multiculturalism and to narrate a nascent multiculturalism alongside nation building. In some instances racialized bodies are used as rhetorical devices to reify notions of progress and diversity. The first exhibit I examine, a permanent installation entitled Passage to Fortune, is part of the Tunnels of Moose Jaw tourist attraction. Passage to Fortune makes the unfounded claim that Chinese labourers, driven west by anti-Asian groups in British Columbia in the nineteenth century, escaped further violence in Moose Jaw by living virtually underground in tunnels. The second exhibit, entitled Crossings: A Portrait of the Chinese Community of Moose Jaw, was part of the 2005 Saskatchewan Centennial celebrations and was housed in the Moose Jaw Museum and Art Gallery. Crossings displayed the material life of the Chinese Canadian community in Moose Jaw from the early 1900s to the present. The narratives, while claiming to tell the story of the same community, contradict one another. Throughout this essay, I explicate how these two narratives reify or undo constructions and performances of Chinese Canadians as "model minorities."[1] Through this analysis, I interrogate how the racialized body of Chinese Canadians figures in the nation's past and what this means in the placement of bodies in the nation-scape of the present. As such, I explicate the possible meanings of both narratives and what it means for them to occupy the same space. I begin with a sketch of the city of Moose Jaw, where both of the exhibits took place.

MOOSE JAW: MOST CANADIAN OF CITIES

Peter Gzowski, the late writer and CBC personality, described Moose Jaw as the "most Canadian of cities" (Larsen and Libby 2001: i). This statement, coming from someone frequently hailed as a Canadian icon himself, warrants elaboration. Like other small cities and towns in western Canada, Moose Jaw is filled with representations of what Elizabeth Furniss (1999: 53) characterizes as "histories commemorating the arrival of early explorers, settlers, missionaries, and industries," images that "constitute the master narratives of Canadian nationalism."

Moose Jaw is a city actualized by the Canadian Pacific Railway (CPR), whose early surveyors depicted the land around the city as "rough bush country" (Shaw 1970: 19). Their narratives are replete with images akin to those found in popular Victorian adventure stories set in Canada. Charles Aeneus Shaw, a CPR surveyor sent to Saskatchewan to collect detailed information about the land in order to encourage British settlement in 1871, wrote as he was nearing Moose Jaw that the expedition group feared a "certain death from starvation and hostile Indians" (Shaw 1970: 97). The extreme temperatures, harsh terrain, lack of food and water and threat of attacks from Aboriginal people were all conflated to an imagery associated with the conquest of European men over the land. In fact, Richard Phillips (1997) maintains that it is through these stories of fur traders and adventurers that British hegemonic masculine identities were forged.

The first mayor of Moose Jaw in 1881 proclaimed, "There was nothing here at the time" (Larsen and Libby 2001: 7), thus legitimizing claims over the territory long inhabited by the Cree, the Blackfoot, the Assiniboine and the Sioux. With the European encroachment came the railroad, White hunters and agricultural cultivation, which all brought the buffalo to near extinction in the Prairies. Organized murders like the Cypress Hills massacre of 1878 (Hildebrandt and Hubner 1994) and the formation of the Royal Canadian Mounted Police ensured the subjugation and eviction of First Nations people from what became highly coveted land of the Dominion. Furniss (1999: 69) states that there "are characteristic silences of frontier histories." The selective silences or historical amnesia around the violent taking and construction of Canada is necessary to sustain its White settler mythology.

Walking around Moose Jaw, there are few signs that First Nations peoples inhabited this part of Canada prior to European encroachment. In a local history book on Moose Jaw published in 2001, there is scant mention of First Nations peoples. They are disappeared from the text with this paragraph:

> It was the beginning of a very difficult time for the prairie First Nations. Within a decade of the arrival of the CPR, the sea of grass that had sustained the buffalo — and, through them, the First Nations — had been replaced by seas of wheat, the foundations of the settler economy. (Larsen and Libby 2001: 5)

Meanwhile, the Chinese presence in Moose Jaw can be traced back to the mid-1880s. Upon the completion of the CPR in British Columbia in 1885, there was an active "driving out" campaign against the estimated 15,000 Chinese labourers who had been recruited to build the railroad. Escaping violent uprisings and lack of opportunity, the labourers migrated eastward. Moose Jaw was at one time the largest Chinese settlement east of British Columbia. In 1911, the Canadian census showed a population numbering 160, with over twenty Chinese-owned businesses (Con et al. 1982: 91). For such a small community, the Chinese in Moose Jaw were quite established, having formed their own associations, youth centres and churches in the early part of the century. Although Moose Jaw's White opposition to the Chinese was not as consistent and organized as the violent uprisings in B.C., life was far from idyllic. In 1908, a group of White labourers, armed with pick axes, mounted an attack on CPR Chinese labourers at the train station. According to the Tunnels of Moose Jaw, it was around this time that the Chinese began to take refuge in the tunnels. In a history book about Moose Jaw, third-generation Moose Jaw resident Eric Chow muses that it was possible that Chinese workers lived in the tunnels and explains that "there were two things happening. One is that [the Chinese] were scared they'd get beaten up … and the other thing was that the early Chinese settlement was really poor, limiting the choice of accommodations" (Larsen and Libby 2001: 31). The infamous *White Women's Labour Law* of 1912, which made it illegal for White women to work for Chinese businesses in Saskatchewan, Manitoba and Ontario as a way to protect their virtue, was initiated in Moose Jaw.[2] It was also a Chinese restaurant owner in Moose Jaw who challenged this law all the way to the Supreme Court of Canada, which upheld it in 1914 (Backhouse 1999: 148).

In the 1920s, Moose Jaw became known as the "red light district" of Regina, a city nearly seventy kilometres away. The convergence of many rail lines, including the Soo line from Minneapolis, a major metropolitan centre in the U.S. Midwest, Moose Jaw became the "happy hunting ground for Regina gamblers, philandering husbands, stagpartyers, unattached tom-catters, drinking preachers, service club sports and unclassified scofflaws" (Gray 1971: 78). There were several brothels, bars, gambling rooms and opium dens concentrated on the famed River Street. The space of River Street contrasted greatly with the rest of the "respectable" town. Many of the restaurants on River Street were Chinese-owned; in fact the Tunnels of Moose Jaw creators reference Chinese involvement in opium and gambling dens during this period. As Kay J. Anderson's (1991) work demonstrates, representations of Chinese bodies and spaces in Canada are often conflated with spaces of prostitution, alcohol, gambling and drugs.

I contend that the making of race in Canada has been spatially organized as the regulation of space through policed, contained and excluded racialized bodies in the nation.[3] The mystique of Moose Jaw's frontier past, coupled with the continued fetishism of Chineseness as degeneracy, is now being commodified to benefit the contemporary economic development of Moose Jaw. The Tunnels of Moose Jaw tours are leading the way in the economic revitalization of Moose Jaw as a tourist destination by playing on this degenerate past and remaking it as a "heritage attraction."

A PASSAGE TO FORTUNE

The Tunnels of Moose Jaw proclaims boldly on its pamphlet "An exciting new way to discover the past!" The Tunnels tourist attraction is privately owned and operated by Historical Xperiences Inc., a company based in Vancouver. Since its opening in 2000, an estimated 100,000 people from over forty-five countries have toured through the Tunnels. The Tunnels and a mineral spa that opened the same year are the biggest draws for visitors to Moose Jaw. As a result, other businesses are experiencing economic growth for the first time in decades. The Tunnels themselves received provincial and national tourism awards and ample media attention over the last decade (HXP 2006).

The actual tunnels, built in the early 1900s to house the steam boilers that heated the city, have taken out a new lease on life via the Tunnels of Moose Jaw tours. Positing itself as an historical exhibition, the tunnels offer two tours. One focuses on Chinese Canadian history in Moose Jaw and is titled Passage to Fortune; the other tells the story of infamous gangster Al Capone's visit to the city in the 1920s and is called the Chicago Connection.

The Passage to Fortune tour suggests that the Chinese literally went underground in order to escape violent opposition from the White community, and lived and worked in these spaces for decades. I visited the Tunnels in 2001, upon reading a newspaper clipping about its history, and then again in 2005. Struck by the tragedy of this event, I was compelled to go to Saskatchewan to find out more. Once there and after an interview with the Tunnels of Moose Jaw's main researcher, I quickly realized that there was no historical evidence to support this story of the tunnels. The authenticity of the Tunnels of Moose Jaw narratives was also challenged in Will Ferguson's (2005) travelogue *Beauty Tips from Moose Jaw*. As well, the debate around the lack of evidence surrounding the Chinese and the tunnels has played out in the local newspaper, the *Moose Jaw Times Herald* (2004a, 2004b). Yet, despite these debates, the story of the Chinese "inhabitants" captures the imagination of the visitors who tour the site.[4] The subterranean location is evocative of rats and other unwanted vermin, implying that the bodies within had "no place" and did not belong above-ground, in the legitimate landscape of respectable nation-building. It is not a large leap of logic to see why the creators of the Tunnels of Moose Jaw would choose to memorialize Chinese Canadian history in the tunnels, a "placeless" place. It is also not difficult to understand why this historical fabrication is so believable, given the violent and institutionalized opposition to the Chinese in Canada in the late 1800s and early 1900s. While the liberties taken by the Tunnels of Moose Jaw to create these fictional accounts and pass them off as "history" warrants further attention, I focus on the discursive journey upon which the Passage to Fortune tour takes its visitors and the kinds of identities that are constructed within it.

The tour begins in a reconstructed laundry storefront where the name "Burrows" is tiled into the floor. A guide narrates the tour by taking us through the storefront and through passageways and stairs that descend into what are known as the tunnels. The guide gives their first name, but in different moments in the tour assumes character portrayals. If the guide is a man, he becomes a character named Dawson, who is the engineer of the boiler rooms as well as the foreman of the Chinese workers underground. If the guide is a woman, she becomes Mrs. Burrows, who owns the laundry.

The tour consists of several *in situ* exhibits with a series of full-size dioramas. Once in the tunnels, visitors enter a large room divided into two parts. It is cold and damp, with dimmer lights. The first part of the room is a diorama of the supposed living quarters of the Chinese underground. Chopsticks and bowls cover a long dining table with a stove with woks and pans adjacent to it. Further down are bunk beds, and the guide tells visitors that up to three men would share one narrow sleeping surface. Across from the beds are two toilet stalls — each one containing a wooden pail. Rounding the corner, visitors come to the laundry. Large tin washing bins, dirty laundry on clotheslines, ironing boards and ancient washing contraptions fill the room. The guide states that this room would house from eighty to a hundred workers at a time, each man working up to sixteen-hour shifts in the laundry. Interspersed with these details, the guide goes into the character of the foreman or laundry owner and calls the visitors "coolies," accusing them of being lazy and needing to be kept in line. From these rooms, visitors are led to an opium den, where the guide tells us Chinese workers would form addictions as a response to the harsh life they led. A burlap factory follows, where the guide states that this was one of the better job opportunities for the Chinese workers, who faced restrictions on the kinds of professions they could practise in Canada. Visitors are then taken to a Chinese café, as the guide describes ownership of such an establishment as the ultimate achievement for the Chinese. The last room in the tunnels is a reconstructed immigration office. There are suitcases, a desk with office chairs, what looks like some kind of ledger on the table and an old adding apparatus. File cabinets line the walls. In this room, the guide summarizes the immigration policies that affected Chinese mobility and settlement into Canada including the Head Tax and the *Chinese Exclusion Act*. The guide's parting words are that freedom is an important thing, one that we should all value. As visitors exit the tunnels on their way back to the lobby of the laundry, they pass a hall lined with photos. The guide encourages us to view the photo gallery on our way out. The photos are all visual documents of Chinese people in Canada. There are personal and family photos, images of Chinese associations and Chinese CPR workers, and photos of Chinese Canadian soldiers in World War II.

Journey from Degeneracy to Respectability

Sherene Razack maintains that "white, bourgeois subjects" visit spaces of degeneracy in order to constitute themselves as respectable. This transgression necessitates the dominant body's enactment of violence against the body of the other, where the former emerges from these spaces "unscathed and strengthened" (Razack 1999: 352). Ethnic enclaves, like Chinatowns, as depicted in Kay J. Anderson's (1991) work, are also often constructed as degenerate spaces. Anderson demonstrates in *Vancouver's Chinatown* that Chinatown is a product of the White imagination, one in which White identity can be made against what it defines itself against. As an example, in Canada, Chinatowns were effectively produced as spaces of degeneracy through such policies as public health regulations and municipal zoning bylaws. Anderson states that spaces that were defined as "Chinese," such as Chinatown, were criminalized and stigmatized as sites of vice and filth. In this sense, I argue that the Passage to Fortune tour, although fictitious, is produced as a degenerate space through which White bodies reassert White subjectivity.

While the tunnels are spaces of degeneracy, the name of the tour, Passage to Fortune, implies a journey towards respectability. This is made clear during the tour as we travel from room to room, from the laundry to the burlap factory to the Chinese-owned restaurant. Each room on the tour is symbolic of a progression towards legitimacy culminating in the immigration office where a limited form of national identity is secured. The last passage, the corridor full of photos, is meant as a tribute to the participation of Chinese in the national story. Our tour guide's narrative traces this journey from hardship to persever- ance to emerging as bona fide national subjects. This narrative is a familiar trope in the official multicultural discourse. The Chinese as the "model minority" is often employed to demonstrate to national subjects that the discourse of multiculturalism as Canadian heritage works (Osajima 2005).

This "passage to fortune" and resulting respectability is made possible through the continual abjection, containment and border marking of Indigenous and other racialized bodies in the political landscape of Canada. This exhibit presents Chinese Canadians as having a "toehold on respectability" in the racial hierarchy.[5] This is not to diminish the injustices that have occurred and continue to occur against the Chinese as a racial- ized group. Rather, the making of the model minority discourse acts as a disciplining mechanism to other racialized bodies. It is a precarious position to occupy, since not only do structural inequities remain, but at moments of crisis, model minorities can become alien enemies.

Throughout the city, there are no official markers to show that First Nations people ever existed before colonialism. A history outlining the violent occupation and eviction of First Nations people could not be presented under the same terms as Passage to Fortune. The state requires Aboriginal spaces to be continually produced as degenerate spaces and used as an ideological tool to control and manage contestations over Indigenous land claims and self-government (Mawani 2009). For this reason, Aboriginal spaces and bodies are not recuperated into the national political landscape. This would cause the White settler identity to confront its own contradictions, an act that would cause its col- lapse and is thus evaded. The historical perspective presented in Passage to Fortune is produced in the same stroke that further erases Aboriginal peoples, histories and spaces. It must be noted also that the creators of Passage to Fortune chose renderings of Chinese Canadian history in order to sustain the model minority myth. For example, the tour does not explain that while head taxpayers from 1885 to 1923 were allowed entry, they were not considered citizens or naturalized Canadians. It was only after World War II, with the entry of Chinese Canadian soldiers, that citizenship rights and the lifting of the ban on immigration was "earned."[6] While the Chinese body is allowed conditionally to transcend and ascend from the "underground" in the Passage to Fortune, the Aboriginal body and other racialized bodies are forced into further erasure.

The Liberal Discourse of Passage to Fortune
A liberal discourse that relies on the production of subjects as autonomous individuals with equal agency and universal rights, existing within a temporal framework of progress, is an overarching theme in Passage to Fortune. These hallmarks of liberalism naturalize the violence of racism by individualizing responsibility and ignoring socio-structural factors.

By inserting itself into such a framework, the Passage to Fortune exempts visitors from any implication and/or responsibility for past violations that continue to shape current realities.

In attempting to offer an explanation for the anti-Chinese climate of the late nineteenth and early twentieth centuries, the tour guide frames it as an issue of labour, eliding it as an issue of race, stating that many White people were worried that Chinese workers would steal their jobs. Without elaborating, the tour guide states that "now of course" we know that this reasoning was wrong, suggesting that White people at that time were simply misinformed and mistaken. By failing to mention the deliberate policies and practices that made clear the state's intent on building a White Canada, this narrative naturalizes the systemic, historical violence against the Chinese (which included nation-wide anti-Chinese organizations and campaigns that were responsible for murders, injuries and destruction to Chinatowns and successful lobbying for racist policies), framing it as actions inflicted by a few ignorant individuals (Chan 1983; Anderson, K.J. 1991; Li 1998).

This elision is evident at another moment on the tour. The guide states that the reason so many of the Chinese population were engaged in laundry, restaurant and domestic work is that they were denied access to most professions. He does not mention that the majority of White settlers to Moose Jaw in the late 1800s came as homesteaders who worked the land for farming and ranching. The settlement of the west had everything to do with land. The *Dominion Land Act* of 1872 distributed 160 acres of free land to any person who could prove that they were the head of a household, was a British subject and could pay the ten-dollar fee for the Letters Patent (Saskatchewan Settlement Experience 2005). The *Land Act* was an imperial, spatial act that mapped spaces and subjects, a process rendered invisible in the tour's narrative. Kathleen Kirby (1996: 46) states that "cartography selectively emphasizes boundaries over sites" and that this mapping emphasizes ownership. Kirby argues that European colonialism demonstrated its mastery by spatially demarcating rational, ordered spaces and a White national identity separate from the chaotic and inferior bodies and spaces of the racialized other that were placed external to it. This boundary between inside/outside necessitates a vigilant maintenance, one that is always producing racialized bodies and their spatial practices as inferior. It is in this context that the continual eviction of First Nations, the Chinese and other racialized bodies must be theorized as a consequence of the *Land Act* and how the impact of landlessness continues to shape racialized subjects as inferior and degenerate. It is therefore ironic that the Tunnels of Moose Jaw are housed in the old Dominion Land Claims Office, where thousands of White settlers passed through a century ago to acquire their private allotments. This further underscores the limitations placed on Chinese Canadians through the denial of British subjecthood and, consequently, entitlement to this land claim, as well as the violent evictions of Indigenous peoples in and around the time of Confederation and following the passing of the *Indian Act*.

To underscore the exclusion to British subjectivity, the guide (in his role as Dawson) loudly ponders whether we, the "coolies" are "illegals." He elaborates later that some of the Chinese went underground in order to escape paying their head tax. From 1885 to 1923, Chinese people were not allowed to enter Canada without paying a head tax. The enforcement of this law was strict, and there is no evidence that people were able to avoid the fee and trespass the border. In the context of this period, an institutional discourse around legal or illegal status in Canada did not exist as it does currently. The tour plays on contemporary backlashes against immigrants and people of colour as perpetually trying to "sneak in the back door" (Sharma and Wright 2008). The tour is operating from the same worldview of immigration that Razack (1999: 170) explains as "a clearly demarcated field of activity," one in which there exists "a sharp distinction between moral and immoral actors." The distinction made between legal and illegal re-inscribes the distinction between respectable and degenerate actors while occluding the question of the very legitimacy of White settler colonialism in Canada.

The White Body in the Tunnels

The absence of Chinese voices in the tour implies that acts of resistance and activism never occurred throughout the history of the Chinese in Moose Jaw. This silence normalizes Chinese communities as passive recipients of racist treatment. Contrasted with the Chicago Connection tour, which valorizes the popular cultural portrayal of mafia violence in the 1920s United States, the lack of active agency presented in Passage to Fortune reifies a portrayal of the effeminate, submissive Chinese male subject. This tour not only reinstates a raced, White subjectivity but also reconstitutes a hegemonic masculine identity.

The tour guide's use of the pronoun "we," as in "we were once very bad towards the Chinese," makes it clear that the tour presents a hegemonic White narrative and not a Chinese Canadian or an anti-racist one. Given this, the White body is implied as the hero of the story for recuperating the Chinese body from abjection since the Chinese are naturalized as degenerate actors, unable to rescue themselves. This dominant White body is theorized within liberal democratic discourse as having the ability to transcend itself, into a metaphysical realm where it is endowed with moral reasoning. This moral reasoning then is threaded throughout the narrative of Passage to Fortune, which results in a moral pronouncement by the White body on this particular history. In turn, the racialized body functions as a discursive device that produces White national subjects.

The distanciation from the past is normalized, therefore erasing the trace of historical and social relations that continue to shape current social and spatial practices. The White body, restored as the normative body, allows whiteness to recede into universal invisibility. Alcoff (1998: 10) states that the appeal of a universal racelessness "may entitle whites to believe they/we don't need to acknowledge the salience of White identity and thus to avoid the moral discomfort that identity cannot help but present." Finally, by treating tourists as Chinese "coolies," there is an assumption that tourists would somehow get a feeling of what it must have been like for Chinese men in the tunnels. This particular role-play in the tour points to a notion that empathy is sufficient redemption. For me, being addressed in this way as a racialized body, as a Chinese body, was a re-inscription of violence not experienced solely as a historical event but as a very present and visceral one. This alerted me to the fact that this tour was not meant for my body or other racialized bodies. The tunnels were never intended as a site for Chinese Canadians to claim resistance or memory or to even disturb the White settler ontology of the nation.

Ghosts?

I did not initially visit the Passage to Fortune knowing that the story was fictional. Even after emerging from the tour, I was left with mixed feelings in response to the tour's narrative as well as to events that I assumed had happened. It was only after visiting the Tunnels that I discovered through more research that the stories had no historical basis and that "Chinese tunnels" are widely mythologized in the U.S., but have never been proven.[7] In fact, "edutainment" tours like the Passage to Fortune also exist in U.S. cities, and yet the narrative acquires authority and legitimacy through its exhibitionary practices. A perusal of the guestbook reveals the following comments from visitors:

- Fun and exciting! Felt Chinese!
- Great way to learn Canadian history!
- Most informative. Shameful part of Canadian history.
- Great history lesson for the grandchildren.
- Not so bad. I've seen worse places to live.
- Sad but true.
- We like history!

And yet, even knowing the falsity of the claim and after tracing the limits of the Tunnels, I still felt haunted. I was disturbed by the "absent presence" of bodies assigned to the imagined tunnels. My desire to "know" the lives of Chinese Canadians in Moose Jaw only intensified, given shape by what was not said, not knowable and not named. On another research visit to Moose Jaw in September 2005, I was given a second opportunity to glimpse the lives of Chinese Canadians in the Prairies.

FROM PASSING TO CROSSINGS ...

Passage to Fortune maps Chinese Canada onto the nation's past, yet it represents this presence as illegitimate and "out of place." During the 2005 Saskatchewan Centennial, another representation of Chinese Canada in Moose Jaw was launched. During the Centennial celebrations, the whole province celebrated with performances, homecomings, exhibits and fireworks (see Lynn Caldwell's chapter in this collection). Moose Jaw is once again thriving, boosted by the growing success of the Tunnels of Moose Jaw, the Temple Mineral Springs Spa and the opening of Casino Moose Jaw in September 2002. As one of the Centennial markers, the Moose Jaw Museum and Art Gallery installed an exhibit entitled "Crossings: A Portrait of the Chinese Community in Moose Jaw."

The Moose Jaw Museum and Art Gallery is housed in the lower level of the Moose Jaw Public Library. The space is outfitted with the accoutrements befitting a modern gallery. The ceilings are high, the rooms well-lit and spacious, with the hum and hush often characteristic of gallery/museum spaces. On one side of the entrance, there is a gallery exhibiting two art installations. On the other side, there is the entry to a historical display of Moose Jaw. Since both are housed in the same building and administered under the same curator, there is little distinction between the two spaces, with one being solely an art museum and the other functioning as a historical museum. The exhibit Crossings employs a mix of display modes. Housed in a rectangular room, glass-enclosed exhibits line three walls, and three more glass-encased tabletop counters sit in the middle. In these cases, there are photos and objects that narrate a non-linear history of the Chinese presence in Moose Jaw. The exhibit is organized thematically and each cabinet has its own subject. Accompanying the exhibit is a report that expands on the exhibit through interviews with Moose Jaw's long-time residents of Chinese descent. While most of the objects displayed are "artifacts," on the fourth wall, the newly purchased work of Toronto artist Brenda Joy Lem is displayed.

Crossings is, in many ways, a counter-narrative to Passage to Fortune. Chronicling the history of Chinese Canadian families in Moose Jaw spanning three generations, the Crossings exhibit provides material evidence that Chinese Canadian lives were firmly established "above ground." Crossings responds to Passage to Fortune as not only a counter-narrative of recuperation from the "underground," but also as an interrogation of truth claims and collective memory.

The entrance to the exhibit is signalled by English- and French-language banners bidding welcome. A text hangs on the wall that reads:

> The Chinese made a unique contribution to life on the Prairies. The research for this project began with the goal, on the occasion of Saskatchewan's Centennial celebrations, to recognize the significant role that the Chinese community played in the history of Moose Jaw and the district. Implicit within this goal has been the desire to record the history of this community, which has been composed of so many remarkable lives: the many generations that have settled here, left and returned, drawn back by the sense of community that makes "this a really special place for the Chinese."

The Crossings exhibit was initiated by the Museum and Art Gallery Curator, Heather Smith. Crossings was in fact a direct response to Passage to Fortune. In an email exchange I n November 2006, Smith explains:

> I had found it impossible to reconcile the Chinese community I knew in Moose Jaw with the presentation of a version of the Chinese immigrant experience that I saw being told in the "Passage to Fortune" Tunnels tour. I was also very uneasy with the Tunnels manipulative presentation of history — using phrases like "It could have been like this in Moose Jaw."

Smith took advantage of the Celebrating Community Centennial Grant Program initiative, which included among its objectives, "To increase awareness and understanding of the cultural heritage of the province through encouraging diverse peoples to come together and explore their diversity as they build bridges to the future."

Smith was able to secure a sizable grant from this provincial funding source as well as other grants from the Multicultural Initiatives Fund and Heritage Moose Jaw. In a personal communication, Smith observes that, "After many years working in museums and art galleries and competing for grant money I have come to grips with the idea that when my curatorial work is in sync with the goals of funders, then we have much more money to work with." The funding enabled Smith to hire a researcher and writer to publish an accompanying catalogue/report as well as launch the exhibit (Lee 2005). Smith also acknowledges that Crossings follows on a community-based model she has employed in the past, including most notably a project with a local First Nations community entitled *Dana Claxton: Sitting Bull and the Moose Jaw Sioux*. In the exhibit, Dana Claxton, a contemporary Indigenous artist, highlighted the complicated history of place, describing Sioux resistance to the White settlement of the American west, resulting in the eventual crossing into Canada of Lakota Sioux leader Sitting Bull to Wood Mountain, near Moose Jaw in 1877. Smith relays that "this is a model of doing museum work here … doing exhibits that are relevant to the community … attract good public funding, and facilitate the collection of real and sometimes new history (rather than the history we already think we know)." Therefore, the curatorial process of Crossings distinguishes itself from Passage to Fortune primarily through collaboration with "communities" and therefore, attempts to present a more "real" representation of Chinese Canadian experiences in Moose Jaw. Its multiple objectives to be "relevant to the community" and to work "in synch with the goal of funders" (through state grants) present a tension in the ways that nationhood is presented through the display of minority history. In the following sections, I examine the politics of belonging in Crossings to further think through how this "counter-narrative" at once unravels and remakes the nation in three key moments of the exhibit: institutions, racial/sexual anxieties and family, and finally, representation of the mundane.

Chinese Cafés as Institution

In Crossings, there is a display cabinet illustrating the labour history of the community. Unlike many narratives of Chinese Canadian history, the exhibit does not start with the building of the railroad or even with the Chinese hand laundries that used to dot River Street in the centre of town. Rather, it begins with the emergence of Chinese-owned fruit and grocery stores and Chinese cafés that once flourished in Moose Jaw and across the Prairies in the 1920s, when Chinese hand laundries were replaced with washing machines (Lee 2005: 24). The Crossings catalogue notes that in the two decades that spanned the 1950s and 1970s, Chinese families ran nearly all of the forty corner stores or groceries throughout Moose Jaw, as well as a high percentage of the restaurants (Lee 2005: 17). There is also a photo of the Exchange Café, the largest café in Moose Jaw, which once stood across the street from the CPR station (now the site of Capone Hideaway Motel). The accompanying label tells of it employing over a hundred workers at its zenith. This display offers a glimpse into how integral these establishments were to the Chinese communities in the Prairies. The cafés and small groceries are represented as sites of multiple functions. They served as the place of entry for many Chinese migrants to gain employment, find their kin relations, develop networks, exchange news from "back home" and collectively organize socially and politically.

They were also important to White residents of Moose Jaw as the cafés provided important gathering spaces in the small city. Thus, they were the primary contact zones between Whites and Chinese for many decades. Beyond being "above ground" operations, they are represented as providing important public spaces to the Chinese community as well as the whole city. Establishing that the cafés were important economic and social networks for Chinese Canadians in this part of the Prairies, the exhibit catalogue goes on to cite Anthony Chan's documentary *Chinese Cafés in Rural Saskatchewan*. Chan writes that the process of filming the documentary broke some of his preconceived notions of extensive racism in small towns, "When people of colour have life sustaining and community building institutions like cafes to offer to the community, need overcomes racial prejudice. Utility overcomes people's fears of the unknown, the foreign, the exotic, and alien" (quoted in Lee 2005: 19). Therefore, although racist practices existed, "overt prejudice seems to have taken a back seat to necessity and practicality," and Chinese-run businesses and services became "institutions that were central to community life" (Lee 2005: 19).

However, Chinese businesses and all spaces deemed "Chinese" were also lightning rods for racist backlash at that time, as evidenced in the *White Women's Labour Law*, which had a particularly strong impact in Moose Jaw. This law banned White women from working in Chinese establishments, purporting as it did to protect "white women's decency from the threat of men of Chinese descent" (Lee 2005: 33). The law was a backlash against Chinese immigration, with as its rationale the protection of White Canada against the debasement caused by the Chinese presence. Many stories of struggle are interwoven throughout the exhibit, complicating any singular celebratory story. The exhibit focuses on Chinese spaces like cafés, groceries, associations, church and homes as sites of celebration and resilience. However, it is important to note that the mapping of Moose Jaw, while not as polemic as Passage's representation, was deeply racialized. For instance, while Chinese-operated cafés were important public zones in the daily life of Moose Jaw, Chinese community members were not always welcomed at "mainstream" public spaces in the city.[8]

Racial/Sexual Anxieties and the "Family"
Early Chinese Canadian communities are often called "bachelor societies" to describe the disproportionate population of men to women. The Crossings report by Soo Wen Lee (2005: 5) notes that in 1912, only two Chinese women were recorded as residents in Moose Jaw and that the lack of women "exacerbated prejudice by intensifying the suspicions of Chinese abnormality." Crossings does not explicitly state the homophobic/erotic tensions that the Chinese "bachelor societies" posed to White Canada or Chinese Canadians themselves. Instead of naming these "suspicions" and "abnormalities," Crossings glides over these omissions and focuses instead on two examples of interracial heterosexual relations.

One of the glass-enclosed display cases chronicles "Rex v. Quong Wing," the test case against the *White Women's Labour Law*. The law would have a big impact on Chinese businesses, barring Chinese employers from an important gendered labour source. Quong's suit was supported through fundraising conducted by the entire Chinese community in Moose Jaw and beyond. The exhibit report notes that Quong's court challenge was the catalyst for debates regarding definitions of "Chinese" and "Canadian," thus opening up an interrogation of racial markers. Quong argued that he held a certificate of naturalization and that, therefore, his status must factor into the interpretation of the law. Quong lost the case and the law was not repealed in Saskatchewan until 1969, but it is evident that the suit against the state brought to the fore the racial and sexual anxieties that the Chinese presence brought to Canada. It also illustrates that many Chinese at that time already had strong stakes in the nation by bringing the case to the Supreme Court. While the hostility towards interracial relations between Chinese men and White women seems clear in White Canada, Crossings also revealed a more complex portrayal of the Chinese community's anxieties regarding miscegenation.

One of the tabletop glass displays in the middle of the room is devoted to the Chows, a multi-generational family in Moose Jaw. Charlie Chow, one of the most prominent Chinese Canadians in Saskatchewan, arrived in Moose Jaw in 1901. He owned grocery stores and cafés in Moose Jaw and even acted as the principal liaison between the English-speaking and Chinese communities, particularly as a court interpreter. The Crossings publication notes that in 1910, Chow married a Romanian immigrant, Mary Feica, an event which the Crossings report states "must have caused some waves" because it made frontpage news: "Chow to Wed — Court Interpreter to Marry Western Girl" (Lee 2005: 30). This was only two years before Saskatchewan passed the *White Women's Labour Law*, so the general resistance to miscegenation can be assumed to have existed during the time of this marriage. But rather than addressing the furor that may have existed, the exhibit's emphasis is on the large family that followed this union. The Chow family is an anomaly in a history that is characterized by the formation of bachelor societies. In the cabinet, there is a family portrait of Charlie, Mary and several of their children. The Chow family is presented as noteworthy within the Chinese community as an example of a traditional, heterosexual nuclear family. They were an exception to the bachelor society during the period between the late 1880s and 1947. Their daughter Helen remembers making the annual visits at Chinese New Year to all the Chinese establishments in town and receiving many customary "red envelope" gifts, which are traditionally given to children. She recalls: "At that time in the thirties we were the only Chinese family. They were all very indulgent with us" (Lee 2005: 31). It is evident that while Crossings disrupts an essentializing discourse about Chinese Canadian historical narratives, it does reify traditional forms of family, heterosexual relations and structures within Chinese Canadian communities as normative, even overriding the racial anxiety of mixed-race marriages and children.

In discussing parallel representations of Chicano cultural forms, Karen Mary Davalos (2001: 59) warns:

> So-called minority museums and cultural centres were informed by the public museum and its image of the nation and citizen. The goals and services of these institutions did not reflect the public museum but responded to it. They have not become antimuseums, however, as they also incorporate the mandate of nationalism (albeit combinations of American, Chicano, or Mexican nationalisms) by representing the ideologies that make nationalism a success, specifically, patriarchy, homophobia, and essentialist visions of "race."

This caution is relevant here, considering how Crossings differentiates what Jennifer Ting (1995) calls "deviant heterosexuality" (signified by the bachelor society and non-conjugal sex) from "normative heterosexuality" (signified by the emergence of families and conjugal sex) in the representation of Chinese histories in the Americas. She states:

"Family" is always (but not exclusively) about gender and sexuality, the Asian American studies discourse on family is also a discourse on sexuality.... A particular kind of heterosexuality constructed within the historiographic tradition of the bachelor society is working, at the level of representation, to develop, secure, and reproduce certain cultural logics (such) as those underpinning the racial and class meanings of Asians and Asian Americans or ideas of U.S. national identity. (Ting 1995: 271–78)

Passage focuses solely on the bachelor sojourner, cast as the inassimilable other while Crossings represents the transitional moment from bachelor society to family as the beginning of assimilation and of national belonging.

The theme of continuity is significant in Crossings. Both the exhibit and publication outline the memories of first, second and third generations of Chinese Canadians in Moose Jaw. The network of familial, clan and community ties can be seen throughout the themes from the list of paper sons on the back of the Exchange Café menu to the exhibit of photos of Chinese vegetable gardens that fed three generations and are entitled "Putting Down Roots." It is the affirmation of heteronormative marriage and traditional nuclear family formations that are called upon to illustrate this continuity. The obvious intimacy and relationships that formed between men are invisible beyond the descriptions of benevolent associations that adhere to established norms based on familial and clan ties. "Bachelor societies" continue to be treated as "deviant heterosexuality" with the advent of families (largely post-Exclusion period) as the beginning of assimilation to the nation.

The Mundane

The installation entitled *Fan Ngukkei* by Brenda Joy Lem, consisting of long silk-screened banners, hangs from the ceiling on bamboo sticks on the back wall of the exhibit. The banners are each inscribed with oral history and photographs of members of Lem's family. For example, one of the banners is an homage to Lem's Aunt Marg. She is shown in a photograph as a beautiful, stylish young woman sitting on the hood of a car. It is hard to determine when the photo was taken, but it is sepia toned and from the style of dress and car, it appears to be from the 1950s. Below, there is this inscription: "Aunt Marg could have been a beauty queen." Even further down the banner is an account of Marg's small wages from her labour in a laundry. Another banner shows Lem's Uncle Jim, a pilot in the U.S. Navy during World War II who succeeded in finding his lost sisters while stationed in China. These images and oral histories are intimate narratives from Lem to her family. Cultural producer Min Sook Lee (2006: ¶5) reviewed Lem's *Fan Ngukkei* while on exhibit at Mercer Union Gallery in Toronto prior to its exhibition in Moose Jaw:

The intimacy of Brenda Joy Lem's work can be unsettling. Her work denies the viewer that anonymity of the voyeur with which art is so often appraised. Why? Because her stated audiences first and foremost are Asian women, second it is her Asian community. When speaking to a sister you cannot help but direct honesty, clarity and specificity into your communication. To create artwork primarily for Asian women is to proffer a resounding affirmation of re-spect and re-cognition for their lives. Necessarily this is challenging work because it is work that disrupts the accustomed/accultured/gendered cycle of artist and audience.

Lem's Aunt Dora was the first Chinese baby born in Moose Jaw, and a collection of some of her aunt's things are displayed beneath the glass of one of the central counters. There are letters with stamps intact, correspondences between family members across distance and time. There is a paper fan, some photos — personal mementos of familial ties and keepsakes. Lem's artwork blends seamlessly with the objects displayed, connected through the tone of personal narrative and objects, thereby blurring together the exhibit's ethnographic and artistic intention. Mostly, the objects in the Crossings exhibit describe everyday life. There is poignancy in the objects, as ordinary as they seem. This poignancy reflects Lee's review of Lem's exhibit in the "re-cognition" of lives through the clarity and honesty of their everyday. Unlike the Passage to Fortune, Crossings does not offer a tour or linear narrative. Visitors can organize their tour of the space in the order they want and therefore assemble and re-assemble their engagement and readings of the exhibit. The age and wear of the letters and personal mementos evoke and fill the gallery space with ghosts. But unlike the ghosts in the Tunnels, these ghosts have names, stories and relationships.

The exhibit acknowledges a much diminished Chinese Canadian community in Moose Jaw, attributed to the flight of younger generations to urban centres across Canada. Yet, Crossings shifts the geographical origin of the Chinese diaspora as China/Hong Kong to a focus on Moose Jaw. While the exhibit does show documents describing associations in Moose Jaw that were supporting Dr. Sun Yat Sen and the Nationalist movement in China, there is no overtly strong link to China as reference point of identity-making. This is challenging to notions of diasporic formation with an origin as a point of reference. Instead, Crossings attempts to highlight a moment, a resting place, a contested space for Chinese Canadians as well as the telling of the nation that has not been told. It is an exhibit firmly placed in Moose Jaw. I consciously use the term "placed" over "rooted" to convey the sensibility of Crossings as a people in movement. The "community" asserts its history in multiple ways, each stating that Chinese Canadians were/are "here," negotiating through the different and changing terms and conditions that being "here" required/requires. It also avoids essentializing a Chinese Canadian identity by polyphonically telling the yearnings, challenges and celebrations without fixed resolutions of identity or even a strong assertion of future continuation as the numbers of self-identified Chinese Canadians leave Moose Jaw.

Therefore, Crossings defines a community through the complex, dynamic and fluid conditions that shape this "here-ness" and this "being-here-ness" rather than Passage to Fortune's orientalist representation of a bounded, homogenous culture and people forever immobilized and separated in the underground. The "out-of-placeness" of Chinese bodies dwelling outside urban Chinatowns also marks a defiant presence of marginalized bodies in the spaces of Canada's margins. Crossings represents a community changing, moving, still negotiating through the spaces of Moose Jaw and the world while trying to understand what continuity and generational memory means, all the while making and remaking the nation and creating new pathways to diaspora through its remembering.

Crossings' insistence on representing a living culture leaves the work necessarily incomplete. Therefore Crossings could be called "hybrid" in the sense that Hall (1997a: 226) refers to hybridity: "a process of cultural translation, which is agonistic because it is never completed, but rests with its undecidability."

TWO NARRATIVES COLLIDE

While Crossings is a counter-narrative in the sense that it dispels the sensationalist fiction of Passage to Fortune, I am not implying that Crossings is itself not a staging or that it does not take the trajectory of the model minority discourse. In many ways, an insistence on Chinese Canadian settlement and survival can/will always run the risk of being read as a celebration of official multiculturalism through the making of the model minority subject.

Crossings, housed in a room that travels through a permanent exhibit of "local history" in Moose Jaw (including a wide array of Aboriginal objects belonging to one of the first White settlers) is still an inserted history, an added appendage to the White settler story. It is also another layer in the representations of Chinese Canadians in the nation, however resistant of stereotypical narratives of the "immigrant does good" rhetoric. Yet Crossings is told through voices of long-time Chinese Canadian residents of Moose Jaw and at the very least, bodies deemed Chinese Canadian have some agency in their own subject-making, even if this practice is to make another kind of coherence or essentialism of Chinese Canadian identity. Although celebratory in the survival of Chinese Canadianness in Moose Jaw, Crossings also reveals the ambivalences and tensions of occupying such space, as noted earlier. As Tony Kushner (1999: 86) acknowledges, the construct of minority peoples in multicultural nation-spaces are usually "either at one extreme as victims in order to represent the impact of slavery and/or imperialist-inspired racist discourse or, at the other as global citizens representing the romantic projections of romanticism." I believe Crossings is a more complicated representation, which plays with, but does not completely fall into either one of the tropes. It demands a more complex reading precisely due to its shared geography with the Passage to Fortune narrative. Crossings should not be read solely as a corrective to the Tunnels' story, although it is obviously based on more material evidence as presented through objects and texts. The question is not of authenticity, but of the discursive potency of each narrative and the oscillation between the two sites. It is this movement that is disruptive. Passage to Fortune resonates with the canonical immigrant story and the making/disciplinary narrative of Chinese Canadians as model minority. Meanwhile, Crossings is a practice of the everyday through the remembering of a community's life. What does it mean to "pass" and "cross" in simultaneity in the context of a multicultural White settler nation?

In this ambivalence of the nation-space lies the possibility for a disruption of the official narrative. Crossings' performance of everyday life interrupts Passage's journey from degeneracy to respectability. It intervenes with its rough patches, gaps and uneasy silences even as Passage attempts to obscure the everyday life of "people" with the grand epic of the nation's multiculturalism.

Setting these temporalities and meanings against one another reveals the ambivalence in the memory of race in the national narrative and necessarily redefines the process of heritage-making, challenging us to rethink the nation without the moment of transcendence. This is precisely what an engagement between Passage and Crossings does — it prevents the kind of passing or crossing that produces a liberal discourse of transcendence to occur.

The forgetting — or rather "being obliged to forget" that constitutes the narrative of the nation — becomes "remembering the nation, peopling it anew, imagining the possibility of other contending and liberating forms of cultural identification" (Bhabha 1994: 161). The "remembering," situated as "minority histories," reveals the incommensurability of the grand narrative of the nation. It defies a totalizing gaze, driven by the will of the nation. Instead, these minor narratives rip apart the illusion that makes a panoramic view of the nation possible. Homi Bhabha (1994: 155) states that the minority does not simply pose a counter-narrative to the master discourse, but by "insinuating itself not in the terms of reference of the dominant discourse, the supplementary antagonizes the implicit power to generalize, to produce sociological solidity." The ambiguity produced in the encounter of these two sites clears new space for re-imagining a representation of Chinese Canada that not only attempts to chronicle the history of a racially bounded community but to perform a contrapuntal reading of an entangled past/present/future of Canada's nation-building project. Therefore, I am proposing a practice that goes beyond a revisioning project or a rewriting of "minority history." What is at stake is much more. I am suggesting a practice that could unsettle the very notions of history, nation, race and what constitutes a Canadian story and subjectivity.

CONCLUSION

Is it possible to represent another kind of presence/absence of memory of Chinese Canada that does not require the use of a dichotomy of sexuality as deviant or normative (either a heterosexual or queer spectrum) as a route to recuperate the racialized body? The constant interpellation of concepts such as "bachelor society" and family within the telling of Chinese Canada must be continually interrogated. Work like Richard Fung's (1996) video *Dirty Laundry* is one such example that explodes the categories of masculinity and sexuality in Chinese Canadian narratives by queering the story of Chinese Canada past and present.

Another question to consider: is it possible to narrate/place the racialized body against the nation and reshuffle the terms and borders of belonging, community and nation? We engage in difficult telling and risky reading practices. The presencing of race runs the risk of reinscribing the representations of the model minority as a condition of belonging within the national discourses. Racialized people grapple with the multiple notions of "belonging" in storytelling. There is yearning in this act. But what does this yearning mean? What does this yearning want? More than anything, the lingering sensibility I was left with in leaving Moose Jaw can be summed up by Elaine Kim's (1995: 15) thoughts on Asian American identity: "Perhaps after all there is no 'home,' except for a place of contestation that negates as well as affirms." The ambivalence of home is also fitting when considering the name of Lem's artwork is *Fan Nggukei*, which means "returning home" in Cantonese. Perhaps both the questions and the answers lie in the impossibility of an untroubled return to the imagined spaces of "home." Or perhaps there is a reminder that we are already "here" — wherever we happen to be — and the act of the telling, however "incoherent," is what makes "here" possible. How does the process of "here" make and unmake the nation? Kim's claim that "home" is a site of contention and multiple meanings defies the use of Chinese Canada in the making of a heritage of multiculturalism discourse. When the nation is revealed as neither a refuge nor a place to belong, it fragments under the weight of its own impossibility. Kim (1995: 15) maintains that,

> inevitably, the Asian American identity offered by cultural nationalism could not but produce conflicts that portended its own undoing: what was excluded and rendered invisible — the unruly, the transgressive, and the disruptive — begins to seep out from under the grids and appear from between the cracks. Eventually the seams burst and are exposed.

I want to reintroduce a third narrative. The silence of the tunnels is still a formidable presence, a palpable ghost. It bespeaks the ultimate unknowability of lives lived in the past, the irreducibility of the nuances, the complexities of a history of joys and violences, the displacement of bodies in a displaced land. It is this spectral encounter that struck me precisely for its defiance of being captured in the well-trodden narratives of Chinese Canada and therefore makes me attentive to silences. For instance, Lisa Chalykoff (1999: 157), in *Encountering Anomalies*, traces the silent narratives of the migrants who never desired to make Canada "home" or the early Chinese women whose lives cannot be told within the net of patriarchal family structures. Chalykoff suggests a Foucauldian analysis to investigate what is produced through the "reclaiming" of some experiences over others. It becomes clearer what stakes are at work in particular representations and how the "salvaging" of other narratives risks the toehold of belonging.

The question of entanglement remains in the complicated terrain of what Edward Said called "overlapping territories" in *Culture and Imperialism*:

> So vast and yet so detailed is imperialism as an experience with crucial cultural dimensions, that we must speak of overlapping territories, intertwined histories common to men and women, Whites and non-whites, dwellers in the metropolis and on the peripheries, past as well as present and future; these territories and histories can only be seen from the perspective of the whole of secular human history. (1993: 61)

Said, reading the European canon as the cultural production of imperialism, reveals the polyphonic resonances of histories excised. In doing so, he provides us with a methodology of breaking apart the official imaginary of the nation to peer into the history of the present where ghosts haunt, "harbour(ing) the violence, the *witchcraft* and denial that made it, and *the exile of our longing*, the utopian" (Gordon 1997: 207, emphasis in original). Ghosts prevail and sit alongside each telling, each representation with its patient and incoherent silence. It is the ghostly absence/presence in the tunnels that made me want to know more about the stories of the Chinese in Moose Jaw. But after Passage, I realize that all journeys are necessarily incomplete. As Avery Gordon (1997: 22) writes, ghost stories are "stories that not only repair representational mistakes, but also strive to understand the conditions under which a memory was produced in the first place, toward a counter-memory, for the future." The signposts are there, in the exhibits in museums and heritage sites, as they are in the entangled practices of everyday life in the nation.

The representation of Chinese Canada in the nation's past through the lens of justice and remembrance is messy work considering the over-determined narrative of the model minority figure. We can try to reconfigure the nation through the rubrics of entanglement that assume bodies, territories and histories are inextricable and mutually constitutive.

NOTES

1. The model minority myth constructs Asian Canadians/Americans (particularly Chinese) as examples of integration into "mainstream" Canada or America. The myth implies that Asian Canadians/Americans exemplify the immigrant success story based on the perceived economic and class gains of Asians as a group.

2. The *White Women's Labour Law* marks the "first overt racial recognition of 'whiteness' in Canadian law" (Backhouse 1999: 136). First enacted in 1912 in Manitoba, Saskatchewan and Ontario, the law banned the employment of white women by Chinese businesses that relied on their labour. Backhouse (1999: 141) discusses the law as a gendered and raced construct in which the protection of white women, "as symbolic emblem of the 'white race', became a crucial cornerstone in the attempt to establish and defend white racial superiority and white racism."

3. Sherene Razack's (2002) edited book *Race, Space, Citizenship*, Katherine McKittrick's (2006) *Demonic Grounds* and Kay J. Anderson's (1991) *Vancouver Chinatown* are examples of work that theorize race/space and identity in Canada.

4. Historical Xperiences Inc, the owner of the Tunnels, responded in the *Moose Jaw Times Herald* that, "immediately upon entering the tour, our guests are told that our characters are fictional and the story is representative of the Canadian story of Chinese immigration to this country." I do not recall being told that the characters were fictional, and more importantly, I certainly do not remember being told the story was fictional. Comments left in the guestbook indicate that most visitors felt the story was factual.

5. I am using the statement by Mary Louise Fellows and Sherene Razack (1998: 350) that if "our liberation leaves intact the subordination of other women, then we have not achieved liberation but only a toehold on respectability."

6. Jeri Osbourne's NFB film *Unwanted Soldier* is a thorough examination of the link between Chinese Canadians' entry in World War II and the securing of citizenship rights.

7. Dr. Priscilla Wegers, an anthropologist at the University of Idaho, has conducted extensive studies across the United States in cities that had or have large communities of Chinese Americans to investigate claims of "Chinese tunnels." She has never found substantive evidence of Chinese people living in tunnels yet maintains that the myth continues to be perpetuated. For an unpublished paper, contact pwegars@moscow.com. Other ventures that capitalize on this long-standing rumour include the Pendleton Underground in Pendleton, Oregon.

8. There are examples cited in Crossings: for instance, the report that describe public dances and social events where Chinese Canadians were not desired. For example, a Chinese Canadian woman recalls that while growing up in the 20s and 30s, her and her siblings were asked to leave public dances and Temple Gardens, the community hall. She states: "And you know of course, we were not allowed in Temple Gardens. My brother went there and was asked to leave, and then we all knew: it was an absolute no-no" (Lee 2005: 10).

Chapter 6

UNSETTLING THE MIDDLE GROUND

Could the World Use a More Questionable Saskatchewan?

Lynn Caldwell

> We're very unusual, this province. This landlocked place of 652 thousand square
> kilometers. —Former Saskatchewan Lieutenant Governor Lynda Haverstock

A description of Saskatchewan as *land-locked* implies relation to many seas, to their histories and to their contemporary activities that contour much on the planet. The implied relation is one of distance, a suggestion that Saskatchewan is buffered from and not touched by these presumably distant seas and their movements. Mapped lines indeed exist as demarcations of the Canadian province of Saskatchewan, and they do lock that space in a particular way; the provincial borders do not edge upon or open into a vast expanse of ocean or sea as do some other mapped borders. The border lines are there, but to name that place *as* Saskatchewan and as land-locked in such a way that demarcates it as separate from waters' edges is a thin and readily contested story. It does not require much of a stretch to shift one's gaze from those recently mapped lines declaring the space as a Canadian province and to see it otherwise. Just as that mapped gaze is neither pre-eminent nor primary, so too the containment on which such a gaze might rest is quite easily and always unsettled. Those borderlines do actually traverse waterways; many rivers flow across the marked space of Saskatchewan and move beyond those provincial edges. That flow of water in a significant way counters the declaration of a land-locked space. The containment countered in this chapter, however, is more particularly that of how the lines of Saskatchewan as a space, an identity, and as Canadian, conceal movements that are peopled, are embodied. That is, peoples' lives, relations and identities, their histories and futures in that space are not fixed by such provincial boundaries or by gazes that delineate cohesive lines of history and geography. These are flows that run counter to any notions of Saskatchewan as locked space.

This chapter confirms the ease of contesting a land-locked story of Saskatchewan and addresses the coexistence of such ease with the tenacity of Saskatchewan as a bound space. The analysis presented here is offered as part of the critical work of imagining and living a Canada that unsettles containments — of citizens, citizenship, bodies, identities, and of histories and possibilities. Such work is a call to imagine and recognize a Canada that is marked by unsettling, by openness to fluidity and by remembrance of possibility, all of which cross and transcend nations and borders. The analysis in this chapter specifically calls us to imagine a Canada that draws (on) a more fluid Saskatchewan than a view of it as "land-locked" recognizes or declares. As will also be argued in this paper, such analysis bears circulation in studies of Canada because the practices that work to conceal that fluidity rely on and perpetuate exclusionary and dangerously problematic forms of Canadianness.

The research from which this analysis is derived is a study of materials from a commemorative event designed to celebrate one hundred years of the provincial space of Saskatchewan — the 2005 Saskatchewan Centennial. Based on that research, presented here is an analytic approach to understanding the persistence of a settler-colonial Canada in spite of long articulated and lived counter-narratives and practices. It is the work of this chapter to describe a production of Saskatchewan as a "sticky fiction" in Canada and to reveal how understanding that production contributes to the resituating of ourselves in geographic and social possibilities as we engage anti-oppressive work and futures. In the commemorative event are moves that shape Saskatchewan as a known, specific and enduring space in Canada, and these moves reiterate untenable and destructive settler-colonialism. Beyond a critique of settler-colonial spatiality, I argue that understanding the *particularity* of the moves revealed through this celebration of Saskatchewan as Saskatchewan provides a useful and needed analytical tool for the work of decolonization in Canada.

SITUATING THIS PROJECT IN STUDIES OF CANADA

Claims about the normalization of colonial violence through constructions and reiterations of particular forms of Canadianness are well-documented — and much has been detailed about these workings in the making of Canada and of Canadian space and citizenship (e.g., Furniss 1999; Razack 2002; Mackey 2002; Lawrence 2004; Thobani 2007 and others cited elsewhere in this collection). The intent of my research on Saskatchewan is situated with the commitments and contexts of such work, and intersects also with studies that investigate everyday, normalized racism in many contemporary contexts (e.g., Hage 2000; Essed 2002; Goldberg 2002); these include studies that recognize how racist categorizations organize cultures and state practices. This categorizing operates through different forms of belonging in and claims of entitlement to national spaces (see Hage 2000 in particular). Not all studies that investigate the embeddings of racism in state and culture deploy this notion of the "everyday" as articulated by Philomena Essed (2002: 178), but it is useful to recall her succinct explanation that, "because everyday racism is infused into familiar practices, it involves socialized attitudes and behaviour." In that vein, the questioning of Saskatchewan presented here seeks to make explicit that as a site in a Canadian landscape and nation, the processes through which Saskatchewan becomes familiar involve racialized processes of settler colonial state formation. Making the familiar questionable is critical in ongoing efforts to understand the lingering effects of racism and to generate new anti-racist possibilities and solidarities.

The form of questioning presented here specifically adds to the ongoing work of addressing how attempts toward social justice — such as in anti-racist education (Schick 2002; St. Denis and Schick 2003; St. Denis 2007) and in social justice activism (Heron

2007; Mahrouse 2010b) — can have the effect of perpetuating rather than disrupting colonial power relations and specifically have the effect of centring White subjects as if normative. As these and other studies demonstrate, attempts toward social justice through education and activism rely on and produce experiences and ideas about the *spaces* in which such education and activism are enacted. As Mahrouse (2010b: 183) explicitly reminds us through her work studying the efforts, by those privileged in a racist society, to "do good" through social justice interventions, "race must be understood as an insidious conceptual and political structure, and not as an event." Attempting to do good and to rectify historical inequalities and forms of divisiveness in contemporary society organized around race requires more disruption and reconceptualization of familiar notions of space and self than some Canadians may have been socialized to accept. The particular questioning of Saskatchewan I present here is explicitly in the interests of recognizing and giving more strength to a Canada that does not secure White normativity as its past or its future — and, most directly, strength to a Canada that is not centred on the interests of colonial privilege or settler perspective.

Further, understanding the social and spatial construction of purportedly reconciliatory terrain as a particularly generative characteristic of the Saskatchewan space-making described below is critical in light of recent and ongoing projects of reconciliation and of compensation for colonial violences[1]. Research, activism and community responses in relation to twenty-first-century reconciliation projects on national, global and local scales raise many questions about what such projects accomplish and about how they conceive what is possible and just (e.g., Grattan 2000; Ahmed 2004; Mathur, Dewar and DeGagne 2011; Simpson 2011). How the spaces for such acts and intentions for reconciliation are conceived as terrains of encounter is of course an ongoing concern. In the context of this collection of critical work on Canada, the present chapter points to Saskatchewan as constructed Canadian space as a contribution to the calls to think carefully about spaces imagined as mediating between unjust pasts and reconciled futures.

How is space conceived and known? What difference does Saskatchewan make in conceptions of twenty-first-century Canadian space, and particularly in conceiving of such space as generative of a more cohesive and just society? This is not to assume nor desire that there would be only one way of articulating such a conception, but as other chapters in this collection attest, there is much effort made through government and popular initiatives to shape and celebrate a Canada that does well with diversity and can justify and maintain claims to being a site of tolerance, multiculturalism and peace. How the space of Canada is imagined or asserted through such efforts requires much scrutiny.

I specifically problematize the ways that Saskatchewan is reiterated as a Canadian space that purportedly bears awareness of a colonial dispossessing past while verging on a productive reconciliatory future. Saskatchewan at its hundredth year as a Canadian province was celebrated as just such a conciliatory space within Canada, spatially and temporally. I contend that the process and effects of this particular reiteration of Saskatchewan reveal troubling possibilities in shared space declared as reconciliatory. Understanding how Saskatchewan works as such a space in Canada exposes the ways that certain constructions of "mediating" space within the bounds of colonialism function to maintain rather than disrupt its violence.

Before detailing what I refer to as the static of Saskatchewan and discuss how the construction of that space and its possibilities reveal some sticky issues in relation to problematic constructions of twenty-first-century century "reconciliation" in various forms, I turn to the work of Sara Ahmed.

WHAT STICKS? SARA AHMED AND THE CULTURAL POLITICS OF EMOTION

Investigating and questioning calls for positive collective feelings of social cohesion in an invader-settler space[2] is a central contribution of the analysis presented here and very much tied to the impetus for the broader project in which it is situated. I align concerns regarding colonial commemorations and productions of positive feeling with a question that Sara Ahmed (2004: 12) names in her work on "the cultural politics of emotion," in which she asks: "Why are relations of power so intractable and enduring, even in the face of collective forms of resistance?" In her analysis, Ahmed conceptualizes this intractability and endurance as "what sticks" and by this she explains forms of investment in social norms and structures — such as, for example, the nation as object of love — as a process involving both movement and attachments. Regarding emotion and its effects, Ahmed explores how such objects of emotion, which may be nations, images or bodies, "become sticky, or saturated with affect, as sites of personal and social tension" (11).

On emotion, Ahmed says: "What moves us, what makes us feel, is also that which holds us in place, or gives us a dwelling place" (11). Her approach to emotion as a factor in perpetuating oppressive social norms and power relations focuses on the social and bodily effects of contacts with circulating objects. Objects, suggests Ahmed, can include texts, memories and imagined phenomena, as well as the immediate physical presence of another person or material thing. She states an interest in how such objects "impress" on us through various forms of contact:

> How the object impresses (upon) us may depend on histories that remain alive insofar as they have already left their impressions. The object may stand in for other objects, or may be proximate to other objects. Feelings may stick to some objects, and slide over others. (8)

Significant to her analytic approach is that she emphasizes how emotions do not reside in either the subject (perhaps you or I) or the object (perhaps Canada or Saskatchewan, an image or words on a newspaper page, or someone who walks through the door of a classroom or passes us on the street). Rather, emotions are produced as effects of circulation. Ahmed argues that the association between objects (the nation, the image, the person) and emotions (fear, shame, pride, love) is "contingent (it involves contact), but that these associations are 'sticky'" (18 n. 13).

Of Saskatchewan's place in perpetuating colonial attachments, my research explores and poses conclusions about what "moves" and "holds in place" identifications with Saskatchewan — identifications that obscure not only its place in the workings of race and nation but also the always present efforts to disrupt and resist them. These inquiries have been shaped by interest in releasing invader-settler Saskatchewan fictions from their hold on possibility. This investigation — through a study of the Saskatchewan materialized, narrated and commemorated in the 2005 Centennial celebrations — revealed some insights into what I refer to as this "static possibility" of Saskatchewan. That notion of "static" possibility is an attempt to draw together Ahmed's work on the social stickiness of emotions with my attention to Saskatchewan as a particular, known and conciliatory, Canadian space. Ahmed's work helps to understand how certain constructions "stick" around through material and symbolic processes of nation-making.

CELEBRATING AND COMMEMORATING: THE CENTENNIAL

This work investigates Saskatchewan as a powerful fiction, and as a particular fiction. In my use of that language, I draw from Avery Gordon's (1997) description of sociological research in which she describes the fictive, its power and forms of its investigation. Further, in my analysis I seek to do as Michael Taussig (1993: 255) suggests and live "reality as really made up" and to insist on attention to what Sara Ahmed (2004: 180) names as recognizing "the world as something that does not have to be, and as something that came to be, over time, and with work." Specifically, I investigate Saskatchewan's *sticky* fictions of past, place and people that were writ large in the 2005 Centennial celebrations and how Saskatchewan fictions of past, place and people operate in national imagining and as domains of possibility within Saskatchewan. I do so with the awareness that Saskatchewan space is always already contested and is also always already experienced otherwise.

The designation of the Saskatchewan Centennial year occasioned festivities organized by the provincial government, local municipalities, museums, community organizations and individuals. Many communities organized homecomings, the lieutenant governor hosted a nationally televised gala of performing arts and several other arts-based initiatives, Queen Elizabeth and Prince Phillip visited the province from Britain, and newspapers published special editions featuring images and stories about and from a Saskatchewan past. There were contests, concerts and parades throughout the year, particularly during the summer months, commemorative calendars, t-shirts, coffee table books, theatre productions and commemorative songs. The provincial Western Development Museum, which has branches in four Saskatchewan cities, launched a commemorative exhibition called Winning the Prairie Gamble. To accompany this exhibition, the museum set up a website to collect "family stories" of "survival and success," which they invited as personal illustrations of a provincial tale of a gamble won.

The Saskatchewan commemorated as a province created in 1905 is of course the name for a place and history marked by the violence, legislation, labour and constructions of colonial settlement in the Canadian West — within broader Canadian and global activities of imperialism and colonialism. It is also the name for a place comprised of multiple names and histories. The place called Saskatchewan is peopled by and remembered as, lived in and related to through diverse global migrations and through Indigenous life, including Indigenous mobilities and cultural variances — all of which disrupt and defy any colonial or cohesive claims to territory and history, for whatever purposes such cohesive claims may be articulated. The museum exhibits and stories, and the festivities encouraged by the government's publicity through the provincial 2005 Centennial office[3] therefore, faced this tale of European colonial invasions that capitalized on the fertilities of soil, on the labours of homesteaders and on an official policy of aggression toward Aboriginal peoples, including the *Indian Act*[4] and the establishment of the reserve system. Commemorative and cohesive tales of a knowable Saskatchewan organized through the official Centennial diverted from the contemporary varied and uneven conditions of life embodied by people, lands and communities in Saskatchewan. To call such telling to account, as I do here, is not a call for attention to a regrettable colonialism presumably now past, nor is it premised on a notion that colonialism is a readily known monolith that could be named as such within the contours of the commemorated province. Rather, such a call to account is a call to recognize the varied mobilities and histories that shaped and shape the place *as* a place.

That the task of commemorative telling ought to recognize diverse mobilities and varying forms of identification with and aside from Saskatchewan and its Centennial among those inhabiting the space, was not apparent in ready evocations of a hundred years of shared success and survival. It may be no surprise that a Centennial event of this sort emphasized cohesion over complication, and survival and success over loss and aggression, and such commemorations in the context of colonization and resistance to it are certainly neither unusual nor unquestioned in contemporary activist culture and scholarship. However, while the analysis I offer here does call to account Centennial practices that reinscribe colonial identifications as an outcome of state commemoration, the focus of my contribution has more to do with how *Saskatchewan is available and accessed* in very particular ways in the sticking of colonial racism to nation in Canada and how certain attachments to Saskatchewan as a knowable place, population and past contribute uniquely and persistently to ongoing racist national formations. The 2005 Centennial presented a vital opportunity to decipher such attachments and their particularities.

My Centennial research involves studying *discursive* processes; analysis of the textual, observed, photographed and conversational data from Centennial activities recognizes a constructed character to the subjects, places, stories and meanings ascribed to them in these materials. My approach recognizes that bodies of knowledge — or, domains of possibility — both "constrain and enable" (McHoul and Grace 1993: 37) the construction of possible subjects, spaces, stories and their meanings. A question guiding my discursive analysis is: what *occurs* in Centennial moments? This is informed by Derek Hook's (2001: 532) approach to such analyses, and particularly his call to "approach discourse less as a language, or as a textuality, than as an active 'occurring' — something that implements power and action and that also is power and action."

This analysis also recognizes the commemorative processes as *performative*. Centennial moments were occurrences of power and action, within broader fields of activity and meaning. As performative occurrences, the productions in texts, museums, stages, images and speeches do perform a kind of theatre in the sense of being "staged," as well as bearing the sense of performative as "citing norms and conventions that already exist" (Ahmed 2004: 93). I deliberately use the word "moment" in my analysis of the Centennial to convey these connected operations of discourse and performance. Framing the Centennial material as moments in this way also derives from Diana Taylor's (2003: 13) identification of "scenario," which she describes as "a paradigmatic setup that relies on supposedly live participants, structured around a schematic plot, with an intended (though adaptable) end." Scenarios "exist as culturally specific imaginaries — sets of possibilities, ways of conceiving of conflict, crisis, or resolution — activated with more or less theatricality" (13) and rely on more than language for their repetitions; a prominent example Taylor notes for scenarios is that of repeated stagings of colonial encounters. There are repeated stagings of paradigmatic setups in the commemorations and celebrations of Saskatchewan's genesis as a province; I encountered these through observation at various events, readings of text, viewing of visual material and in conversation about Centennial productions through interviews with organizers.

The Centennial commemorations invoked Saskatchewan as a knowable and known place, and such claims to knowability are forms of containment in their presumption that Saskatchewan *is* a shared geographic story and experience. I approach this analysis of Saskatchewan with a view of space as questionable. This is a stance situated in critical work and lived experience that contests hegemonies, including the hegemonies of the everyday and familiar, and that specifically contests the givenness of space. In this view my research is aligned with critical work such as that cited above, which recognizes space as a social product (see the introduction to Razack 2002 for a detailed account), and that which recognizes the alterability and multiplicity of geographic tellings (see McKittrick 2006).

These inquiries into paradigmatic Centennial moments are a route to understanding Saskatchewan's knowable and accessible form as mobilized for the purposes of celebratory commemoration. Identifying Saskatchewan as a *static* domain of possibility derives from observing how Saskatchewan as a space of Canadianness functions not as a mobile or flexible notion, but as a kind of stasis — as the static, or stuck, domain in which the future *and* past are contained.

CENTENNIAL MOMENTS THAT PLACED SASKATCHEWAN

The intent of commemorations to be instructive and particularly to teach about the nation and national belonging is well documented in the contexts of Canadian national commemorations; for example, Eva Mackey (2002: 71) identifies the "pedagogies of patriotism" carried out through authoritative narrations of Canada. In the context of the national commemoration of Canada's 125th anniversary as a nation, Mackey reports a "linear narrative of Canada's past, present and future" and describes how the construction of national identity received official government sanction. Mackey's account of the processes through which the Canada 125 celebrations and related developments in national multicultural policies contributed to the securing of normative subject-citizen formations such as "*Canadian*-Canadians" very much informs my query into Saskatchewan commemorations. Mackey's attention to this formation proceeding through "the subtle and mobile powers of liberal inclusionary forms of national imagining and national culture" (5) contributes much to my analysis of positive collective feelings mobilized through inclusionary imaginings of Saskatchewan. This is evident for example, in the often repeated refrain during the Centennial: "We are many and we are one, and we love this place, Saskatchewan."[5] The "we" and the oneness of such a refraining sentiment is an inclusionary imagining of a singular voice of love, a not unexpected effect of commemorative practice. Not unexpected, but questionable.

Like Mackey's study, this investigation of 2005 established as an occasion to commemorate Saskatchewan also investigates sanctioned practices of commemorative activity and questions managed productions that form and reiterate a depoliticized and normative Canadian national belonging. The insights I draw from this investigation, however, are also quite particular to how *Saskatchewan* "belongs in" Canada. Through this analysis of Centennial moments, I argue for dislodging some powerful fictions that perpetuate a static shape to how Saskatchewan "belongs" in Canada and who "belongs" in Saskatchewan.

Four themes, or "interpretive repertoires" (see Wetherell and Potter 1992: 88–93) emerged in this analysis from which I make these claims about how Saskatchewan particularly functions as this "static." The themes are of Saskatchewan constructed as "middle landscape," "terrain of disharmony and displacement," "mapped on a nation" and "a place with a future." These themes emerged repeatedly and are revealing of how racialized space within Saskatchewan and of Saskatchewan in Canada was effectively and affectively reiterated through the Centennial. They are revealing of how the "we" of Saskatchewan and the possibilities for belonging and shaping the space are embedded in naturalized portrayals of Saskatchewan as a constructed social, political and colonial reality. The shape of these celebrated versions of Saskatchewan space conceals their implications in and reliance on not only early twentieth-century forms of Canadian colonialism, but also their ongoing productions and practices as twenty-first-century conceptions of a reconciled Canadianness. I turn to each of these themes in turn.

Middle Landscape

The notion of "middle landscape" comes from Leo Marx's study titled *The Machine in the Garden*, from 1964. Middle landscape describes a space conceived as one formed within but tempering what are imagined as the extremities of European civilization and industrialism and one that is invigorated by but tames what is imaged as "wilderness," providing a "moral position perfectly represented by the image of a rural order, neither wild nor urban, as the setting of man's best hope" (Marx 1964: 101). This reconciliatory image actively situates agrarianism as an embodiment of this "middle state" of "the desirable, or at any rate the best attainable, human condition" (88), in ways that Leo Marx illustrates have been productive of political, artistic and economic manipulations of desire to retreat or to be sheltered from the countered extremities of city or wilderness. The middle landscape exists in between two "wilds" and is presented as a moral space where progress, in the terms of European modernities and technologies, thrives but is restrained.

The Centennial offered many textual *personifications* of the province that portray Saskatchewan as such a natural mediating "character." The province was frequently characterized as a place with an inferiority complex and an ever-expansive heart: many Centennial moments featured references to the province's "ego." In an article in the *Moose Jaw Times Herald* (2005a), for example, the writer celebrates Centennial commemorations and simultaneously critiques the emphasis in Centennial advertising on the fact that some people choose to stay in the province instead of moving out. The writer of the newspaper account muses on this ego fragility, asking, "why else would a province celebrate the fact that people chose not to leave it if did not have a major league inferiority complex?" The geography in this chastisement is visible in relation to repeated occurrences of celebrated mediocrity and critiques of such. This writer makes a distinction between pride and the form of the celebrations to which he responds; the effect being that Saskatchewan is humble (and in this rendering, *too* humble). In other moments, the choice of Saskatchewan over the many advantages/temptations/differences of elsewhere takes the form of pride: pride in Saskatchewan as a chosen home-place:

> Over time, the oil bonanza attracted the go-west go-getters to Alberta, the kids determined to put their muscles to work, the hot graduates seeking fast promotions in lucrative careers, the socialites in search of a party town, the risk takers with dollar signs in their eyes. Saskatchewan, by contrast, kept the homebodies. (*Moose Jaw Times Herald* 2005a)

This prideful or chastised attribute of mediocrity in comparison to "elsewhere" is geographic in the ways that these attributions collude with various Centennial moments that invoke Saskatchewan as place and with linked practices that inscribe Saskatchewan within and as Canada's imagined rural heritage.

The Centennial marks a particular rurality of Saskatchewan in repeated contrasts between the social and political economies of Alberta and Saskatchewan. This includes contrasts between the character of Centennial celebrations in Alberta and in Saskatchewan, held in the same year. There are many elements to the refrain that Saskatchewan is not Alberta. The differences feature in comparisons between the events of the two Centennial celebrations and also in some discussion about what might have happened if the two provinces had become one instead of two in 1905. The contrasts between social and political economies and between the character of Centennial celebrations, *and* the musing about the arbitrariness of the border, function *together* to place Saskatchewan as the middle landscape; relatedly, these contrasts place Alberta as signifier of a different and perhaps more advanced modernity.

In Centennial moments that place Saskatchewan as middle landscape, celebrations of prairie heart and sometimes impatient, sometimes laudatory, tellings of Saskatchewan as self-deprecating or backward-looking mobilize notions of the rural/agrarian/agricultural as contrary or oppositional to forms of community imagined (and sometimes also personified) as elsewhere. The telling of Saskatchewan's rural character as counter to a specified (such as the neighbouring province of Alberta) or unspecified elsewhere reveals ways that Centennial moments serve to fix Saskatchewan as a mediating space in relation to these elsewheres.

Together, these are recurrent moves that place Saskatchewan somewhere in between what is imagined as pre-history/wilderness/primitive land and forms of human social and economic life characterized as more decidedly modern/urban/industrial. Leo Marx emphasizes, in his account of the functioning of a middle landscape in American imaginings, that this form of idealized terrain colludes with notions of "civilization" as a state laudably removed/improved from "wilderness." That is, this moderate landscape is not conceived of as somehow absolutely removed from colonial modernity, but rather as having adopted its technologies in such a way that the landscape remains marked as a space of nature. Saskatchewan, in this sense, has adopted the technologies of and exists in the teleology of Canada's formation as a nation but yet exists as a space shaped by a kind of restraint or resistance to modernity's excesses.

The Saskatchewan settler geographic story bracketed in the one hundred years of 1905–2005 includes the technology, politics and commerce that turned soil and forest and waterways into farms, towns, railway lines, schools, mines and money. It remains rural through keeping community and cooperation somehow central and attached to agricultural origins, but it is not out of touch with/untouched by North American modernity. As one form of this placement of Saskatchewan, the province's premier at the time repeatedly celebrated the province as such in Centennial speeches, as an example, his claim that, "for goodness sakes, we invented the automated teller" (Calvert 2005). The Saskatchewan settler geographic story is in these terms a version of that middle and mediating state. The geographic story neutralized in a story of moderate modernity is how the turn to farm, town, railway, school, mine and money was and is a *colonial* turn in all the violence of that endeavour. These "modernities," celebrated as somewhat unexpected marks of progress in a place conceived of as resistant to modernity's excess, are technologies attached to the colonial project of Canadian nation-making.

The common refrain that "we are First Nations and Métis and the descendants of immigrant pioneers" (Calvert 2005) does reference a geography of colonialism in Saskatchewan, but in this speaking deflects attention from the specifics of history in and among those subject positions. This is a refrain, and a deflection, that occurs in many Centennial moments and is an effect of attempts to conceal and naturalize the fact of colonialism and to deflect historical and political questions about relationships among Aboriginal, Métis and "immigrant pioneers." The very different conditions of presence for Aboriginal, Métis and the multiple diverse immigrant and diasporic histories in Saskatchewan are glossed over in the repeated sequence of shared space in the present, as voiced by that refrain and in other repeated scenarios of the Centennial. The presumed invisibility or negligibility of historical conditions that shape and stratify current encounters is very much at the heart of the racialization of space and its production of subject distinctions. The refrain invokes identification with shared space; this mediating terrain of the cooperatives-producing, automated-teller-inventing Saskatchewan is presumed as shared contemporary home for the distinctly named groups of inhabitants. Such "sameness" is, in invader-settler Canadian space, a racialized condition of encounter that disavows violent histories and varied conditions of contemporary difference, and it is by implication a disavowal of race as present in the encounter (for a detailed discussion of such disavowal see Gill 2000: 160). The middle landscape identifications of Saskatchewan repeat this disavowal when this middle state is claimed, through self-deprecating personifications of a modest landscape or contrasts to imagined less moderate elsewheres, in ways that presume equivalent and homogenous identifications for all in and of Saskatchewan.

Yet, as the next section illustrates, the neutralizing of a geographic story in Centennial intonations of an Aboriginal/settler/immigrant population was not consistently in the form of open disavowals or insistent deflections from acknowledging colonial violence. Repeatedly, there *were* moments that named displacements of Aboriginal cultures and community, and inequities in patterns and policies of immigration. Conflicted positionalities did feature in the commemorations, and the commemorated Saskatchewan was in various ways placed as a conflicted space. The presence of such conflict also marks the conciliatory shape of the space, with conflict as a precondition for the need, desire or hope for reconciliation.

Terrain of Disharmony and Displacement

There were Centennial tellings and exhibits of a colonial geography, along with naming of conflict and struggle within and about the boundaries of Saskatchewan. Three of the four Western Development Museum's Winning the Prairie Gamble Centennial exhibits included an "Introduction" room that displayed a painted wall mural on one side: blue sky, a river waterway, buffalo, green and golden landscape and Aboriginal community in the foreground.[6] An adjacent wall, directly opposite the room's entrance, displays four mannequin figures: two standing together on the left, near the painted mural and two together on the right. Behind these four mannequins is a wall with an aerial depiction of green land and water and the words, "Winning the Prairie Gamble: The Saskatchewan Story"; the wall space between the two sets of figures, representing the land area of Saskatchewan, becomes a projection screen for video. At the foot of each mannequin figure is a placard with a title that places each figure in relation to this "prairie gamble" narrative, and echoes the designations in that refrain often repeated about Saskatchewan inhabitants. The titles are "We are the First Peoples," "We are the Métis," "We are Newcomers" and "We are a New Province."

In the sung and spoken narrative in the video projected into this scenario, Aboriginal losses and colonial violence are directly named. Aboriginal culture and community are represented. Stories of settler arrivals describe uncertainty and grief. Thus, the story is not seamlessly celebratory nor overtly an erasure of Aboriginal presence or of colonial invasion; rather, these realities are made evident. The exhibit introduction rooms place First Nations, Métis and settler figures, voices, stories and artefacts alongside each other to tell a story of Saskatchewan's genesis as a province. Proximity and juxtaposition in these displays repeat the story of encounters and of inhabited land; however, they do so without directly addressing the specific conditions of encounter or indicating the presence of communities and histories that do not conform to this story of origin. While this introduction room depicts the landscape of Saskatchewan as inhabited and as having a long history, this scenario attempts to appropriate all histories and inhabitance into a tale of Saskatchewan's genesis. Specifically, the display heralds this "new province" as the culmination of these *different* sets of struggles and losses as if it is provincehood in Canada that secures the ground for such losses to turn into a shared reality and identification with the place. While the fourth mannequin in the display bearing the sign "We are a New Province" is a single figure just as those before him — the Newcomers, Métis and First Peoples — the "we" of the new province stands in for all who come before. The exhibit poses and personifies this new Saskatchewan "we" as the singular condition of possibility for the future of all those represented in the story preceding this genesis.

Other moments contribute to grounding reconciliatory possibility as an accomplishment of Saskatchewan's formation. Official commemorations also included a travelling Centennial theatre performance titled *All My Relations — Wahkotowin,*[7] which juxtaposed settler and Aboriginal voices to tell a settler/immigrant story of seeking religious freedom and new hope together with an Aboriginal story of lost land, residential schools and policing of sacred ritual. In one scene, an Aboriginal man and a Euro-Canadian man at either side of the stage speak of memories of the land from their different perspectives — one speaks of "Pasqua ... a sacred place to me" and the other of "McCallum's home quarter ... still feels like home." In another, an Aboriginal family and a settler family pick saskatoon berries on stage, then the music changes and the two families (all six actors) look in different directions from where they stand and speak in turns:

> I came to find a land with no borders.
> I was sent to live on a reserve.
> I came for religious freedom.
> I had to hide my sweatlodge under the table.
> I came to live in a wild land.
> I know this land as gentle.
> I came to plant a seed.
> The buffalo are gone.
> A new province is born.
> A people are forgotten.[8]

These voices name in short sentences that violence and loss has happened in this shared land they portray together; they are sentences that rely on much "longer histories of articulation" (Ahmed 2004: 2).[9]

Saskatchewan, the same place personified as a mediating middle landscape, is thus in some moments and scenes also this terrain of disharmony and displacement. Pleas for harmony, calls to step outside a comfort zone and calls to celebrate the Centennial as a bringing together of cultures and differences gesture to losses and conflict as constitutive of the commemorated place. In such a story, disharmony is constitutive, and it coexists with the naturally reconciliatory landscape such that the assumed middle landscape not only mediates between contrasting "elsewheres," but also conflict in Saskatchewan itself. As detailed next, this is a landscape of reconciliation that is placed in a Canadian national narrative.

On the Maps of a Nation

The Centennial commemoration marks a hundred years of Saskatchewan's existence, making provincehood the story, the place and the "where" of Saskatchewan. The commemorated origin of Saskatchewan as a province of course places it within Canada. In part, the specific naming of originary moments of provincehood reinscribe the geopolitical borders of the province on a printed national map — those straight line boundaries that demarcate Saskatchewan from Alberta to the west, Manitoba to the east, the North West Territories to the north and the United States (specifically Montana and North Dakota) to the south. However, Centennial moments that place Saskatchewan in Canada did not always explicitly rely on or call to mind those specific borderlines. Saskatchewan is mapped in the nation, as Canadian and as particular in Canada, in ways that call upon imaginative processes other than cartography.[10]

For example, the director's message printed in the official program for a nationally televised Centennial Gala describes how the set was designed to represent the Canadian "heartland." This representation is made through "its open, living, windswept skies. Its multicultural mosaic. Its colourful yet quietly understated history of people, places and events that have shaped who we are today" (Boileau 2005: 4). The stage was literally set for a performance of Saskatchewan as Canada, and to Canada. The Gala was designed to reveal, and as described below, to surprise the Canadian viewing audience with things such an audience might not know about Saskatchewan.

One moment in the Gala that played overtly on a "surprise" motif was when the host, comedian Brent Butt,[11] introduced Regina-born singer Dione Taylor:

> Our next singer began her career touring the jazz circuit in Regina.... And, after that day and a half [laughter from Gala audience] she moved to Toronto. Back in Tisdale, we didn't really have a jazz quarter, per se [laughter]. Although the street I lived on did eventually become known as Bourbon Street for some reason [laughter]. Please I want you now to join me in welcoming ... she's one of Canada's most exciting and fastest rising jazz performers ... please welcome the lovely and talented Dione Taylor![12]

Thus, in the very same moment that the Gala stage included Taylor among performers *from* and performances *of* Saskatchewan, Butt's jokes marked jazz music and culture as somehow surprising and somehow actually "out of place" in Saskatchewan. In order to present Saskatchewan "to Canada" and a Canadian audience, Butt first reiterated *an improbability of Saskatchewan having a jazz quarter or a jazz circuit* as the stage on which to surprise the audience.

Katherine McKittrick provides a detailed account of Black women's geographies rendered surprising in the dominant geographical narratives of Canada, "a nation that has and is still defining its history as Euro-white or nonblack" (2006: 92). That Gala moment in which the host Brent Butt introduced Dione Taylor with reference to jazz culture as a surprise in Saskatchewan, implicitly places Black culture (jazz) and Black persons (Taylor) as somehow not in synch with the geography of Saskatchewan. Reading this moment along with reiterations of the continuous and now shared landscape reveals the making of a racial story as "second nature" (Taussig 1993: xiii) in Saskatchewan: that is, a naturalized racial story of White settlement and nation-building. Moments that presume and restate Saskatchewan as the heart of nation-building rely on and produce many racialized "surprises" of the sort that McKittrick (2006: 92) describes:

> In terms of geography, the element of surprise is contained in the material, political, and social landscape that presumes — and fundamentally requires — that subaltern populations have no relationship to the production of space. The surprise takes place when ... these populations are recognized as viable geographic subjects who live and negotiate the world around them in complex ways.

The documenting of surprise in Centennial descriptions of Saskatchewan collaborates with the dominant racial, colonial narrative of nation and nation-building and of

Saskatchewan's place therein. That surprise is visible *as* surprise when Saskatchewan's Canadian geography and geographic story is accepted to be that of the humble prairie heartland peopled by modest unassuming, White, rural people attached to histories and geographies of European settlement. As I explain below, the binding of such geography works not only through a fashioning of Saskatchewan's past but also through securing the boundaries of a future.

Place with a Future
In the travelling play *All My Relations — Wahkotowin,* "Crazy Rosie" is both a character in the narrative and is also a large mask forming the backdrop to the stage. "She" is the place and the land of stories in this performance. As the play opens and the large mask of Crazy Rosie is positioned at the centre background, a recorded voice speaks:

> She's been known by many names. Some say she is made of uranium and hydro- gen. Some say circles and seasons. Others have sworn she is not made of atoms, she is made of stories. She changes forms like we all do. A face made by ice and water. We are, all of us, tied to her by our body's need for food and our spirit's longing to be at home.[13]

Rosie as character and backdrop personifies a place and land that from ice and wa- ter and atoms, and as varied stories, *becomes* Saskatchewan. The "Rosie" of a long and pre-human geography provides background to and embodies the past of this narration of Saskatchewan's history. The introduction room displays in the Western Development Museum exhibits similarly situate the land as a background and also as the site for transi- tions of people and cultures from Aboriginal communities to "newcomers" who together share the new province of Saskatchewan. Textual invocations including newspaper com- mentary and political speeches also draw upon land as the ground of a continuous and anticipated Saskatchewan, which made its full arrival in 1905. As well as, and in collu- sion with, such extensions to the past, Centennial commentary reveals and produces another kind of continuity to place and landscape; this appears particularly in the form of Saskatchewan's *next century.*

A particular brief articulation — "Saskatchewan's second century" — shifts the continuity from a land on or through which changing cultures and political formations occur to a land that continues into the future as this specific knowable cultural and political formation of Saskatchewan. Among what disappears into that continuity is possibility: the possibility for a radically different geopolitical "century" or centuries and also for the possibilities that emerge from recognizing lives and identities that do not conform to the contours of the dominant Saskatchewan colonial story. Continuity in the fictions of Saskatchewan as landscape functions to unite its predicted future as this province and in this nation with political, cultural and geographic forms that precede the political forma- tion of Saskatchewan. Repeated references to Saskatchewan as the future structure a teleological claim in which Saskatchewan as land/landscape exceeds the bounds of the hundred years of Saskatchewan as province. I regard this as a production of a particu- lar continuity that sustains these moments of "surprise" and that forecloses possibilities for future configurations, thus countering the geographical questionability inherent in emancipatory projects.

Commemorative speeches that extend Saskatchewan into a future century were accompanied by placements of that future figuratively into the *present* landscape. The premier repeatedly placed the future in his celebrations and accounts of Saskatchewan in Centennial speeches. He repeated phrases such as there is a lot of "future" or "tomorrow" in Saskatchewan (for example, Calvert 2004), and he, along with other speechmakers, used the image of a prairie horizon to place the future in the province. Then Prime Minister Paul Martin, in a Centennial address, described this as a form of pride for Saskatchewan's "forebears":

> "Your forebears would be proud," Martin told a group of more than 200 people who gathered to watch events in Regina. "They would be proud that, for the people of Saskatchewan, the future stretches out as far as the plains themselves, rich, enduring, wondrous." (*Moose Jaw Times Herald* 2005b)

Federal MP Ralph Goodale drew on the horizon as well (along with the repeated trope of "next year," which calls up the rural/agricultural context), with "We keep our eyes on that vast Saskatchewan horizon. We dream of 'next year.' And we know we can build our tomorrows to be just as bold and exciting as we dare to imagine" (Goodale 2005).

"The World Could Use a Little More Saskatchewan"

The forms of fixed knowledge that appear as the self-deprecating mediating middle landscape, the reconciliatory terrain of disharmony and displacement, the surprisingly productive and diverse rural heartland of the nation and the fixed future of continued political/cultural identity as Saskatchewan — all rely on a hundred-year story of Saskatchewan in a static domain of knowledge.

A refrain that the world could use *more* of this "Saskatchewan" appeared repeatedly in speeches at Centennial events and in multiple pages on the official Centennial website, including the message posted on the home page at the close of the Centennial year — a message repeated in the final edition of the official Centennial souvenir newspaper:

> Saskatchewan — you showed your heart throughout 2005 as we commemorated and celebrated our home. You sang our song and wrote your own poems and stories. You raised the flag and wore the gear. You picked a place in Saskatchewan you'd never been to before and you went there (maybe even twice). You discovered your roots and planted a centennial tree. You planned events and special projects that built lasting — and living — legacies. You proved that nobody throws a party like Saskatchewan! You celebrated with family and friends and created memories to last another 100 years. You shared your centennial spirit and provincial pride with the many visitors that enjoyed our birthday celebrations! *You showed the world it could use a little more Saskatchewan.* And you're not stopping anytime soon! Keep your provincial pride close to your heart; keep telling the world just how much we love this place — Saskatchewan! For making us all Saskatchewan proud — thank

you — from the bottom of our 100 years of heart! (Saskatchewan Centennial newspaper insert, emphasis added)

This refrain was repeatedly linked to Saskatchewan as a place with a particular inheritance as the heart of the nation and to a collective subjectivity formed by the terrain of a middle landscape, as discussed above. My reading of this repetitious claim, in the context of these Centennial moments, is that it functions as an invitation into a nostalgic and sticky feeling in which Saskatchewan is a return "home." Saskatchewan, bound in this hundred years story, is the possibility of a homeplace in modernity — or, in a world of "elsewheres." This is a nostalgia bound up in the colonialism that maps the relations of this as a home to such elsewheres. The "world's need" for more Saskatchewan contains and reproduces transnational imperialisms in which home as a settler space serves as an attempt to redeem the violences of imperial acquisition.

Saskatchewan as a return home features in many Centennial moments, an occurrence that is deeply twined[14] with the repetition of Saskatchewan as heart of the nation. For example, in CBC commentary about Queen Elizabeth's visit to Saskatchewan's provincial legislature, the reporters remark on how the queen has described experiencing Saskatchewan as a "home away from home"; they can see "how relaxed she is here," which seems to them to uphold her observations of that homeliness.[15] The Canadian prime minister, on the same occasion of the official welcome to Queen Elizabeth II and Prince Phillip, named the Saskatchewan Centennial as an opportunity to welcome the queen to "Canada's heartland," and, in a now familiar recounting of the tough practicality of settlers and how "First Nations shared this bountiful land," the prime minister muses that "those who dare to dream look up at the stars in the prairie sky and they know that this is their home."[16] The repeated celebrations of Saskatchewan as home and heart of a nation in speeches and text commemorating the Centennial and this repeated claim that Saskatchewan bears particular value for "the world," fixed Saskatchewan as a reliably productive site.

That repeated short sentence, "the world could use a little more Saskatchewan," was an articulation bolstered by moments such as one on a Centennial stage when four dancers came forward, holding bread and wheat, at the end of a "multicultural extravaganza" danced to the Centennial theme song. The dancers held up the sheaves of wheat and loaves of bread during the final chorus of "We are many and we are one, and we love this place, Saskatchewan." When the premier and others echoed that celebration of cohesion and love in the related refrain about the world's need for more Saskatchewan, what gets held up is bound in a colonial story that has materialized in geography, economy, culture and politics.

Holding up a particular configuration of cohesion and shared love for place, in a symbolic gesture of raised bread and wheat or in the repeated refrain that holds up Saskatchewan as a place-bound exemplar of human solidarity and social formation, is not determinate of the forms of recognition or identification for participants in or observers of such moments. However, the holding up of bread, and throughout the Centennial the holding up of volunteerism, community and a reconciliatory terrain that is home to a continuing story of Saskatchewan as home to the heart of a nation — positions colonial/

teleological Saskatchewan as the shape of possibility for the place, people and past of this terrain. Bread and wheat are symbolic and also (though not the only) material effects of Saskatchewan as a site in the Canadian nation, and, their production is deeply entwined with incursions on land and with the global structures of colonialism that support them even though there have been many shifts in the agricultural economies of Saskatchewan and Canada since the time of the province's formation in the context of Canadian colonial expansion. What can be found in tracing the mobilities of bread include the divisions and violence of race and racism in the wheat economy and in immigration experiences, in legalized racism toward Aboriginal peoples, in policing, in schooling, in the theft of land and in other practices that constitute the place as Saskatchewan. There are also past and present diasporic mobilities in that bread, and in Saskatchewan, which are not easily traced through bounded stories of shared love. The evocative power of bread as a wholesome organic affirmation explains something of what perpetuates celebrative accounts of benign togetherness. This is also taken up in Ahmed's (2010) more recent work on productions of happiness and "happy subjects" of multiculturalism in which Ahmed observes that "happiness is thus promised in return for loyalty to the nation, where loyalty is defined in terms of playing its [the nation's] game" (122).

CONCLUSION: OR PERHAPS A MORE QUESTIONABLE SASKATCHEWAN

Centennial moments draw attention to fictions that do press upon inhabitants of Saskatchewan terrain (invoking here Ahmed's attention to the "press" that happens through encounters with objects, the "press" that forms impressions). However, recounting these moments and interpreting the shape of some dominant fictions that secure particular guises of Saskatchewan as knowable and as objects of affection is also intended as revealing invention itself. A middle landscape in the heart of an invader-settler nation may be "what sticks" through circulations of Saskatchewan as object of collective love and object of desire to return to a homeplace. However, this powerful, sticky, fictive Saskatchewan as naturally productive of reconciliation and homeplace for the "world's needs" reveals its own concealments when it is regarded with a view toward broader horizons of possibility that extend beyond perceived boundaries of time, space and Saskatchewan.

Broader horizons of possibility and new fictions in and of Saskatchewan do not mean a turn toward a future not yet in place. The place named/mapped as Saskatchewan is always already also peopled by and remembered as, lived in and related to through global migrations and through Indigenous life, including Indigenous mobilities, which disrupt and defy any colonial claims to territory and history. However, coaxing colonial hegemonies loose from their workings of power is of course an effort that exceeds pointing to their illegitimacies and narrowness or to the fact of their invention. What I seek to accomplish here is to contribute an analysis that reveals particular forms of concealment and normativity attached to and activated by Saskatchewan's presumably land-locked borders. As such, this is an analysis that asks for unsettling the forms of ease and attachment that reside in associating Saskatchewan's place in Canada with formations of possibility for twenty-first-century reconciliations.

We might ask how Canada, its national subject-citizens and boundaries of national belonging, would be differently configured with a Saskatchewan opened to continual question and not reliably/repeatedly situated as a bounded and mediating space in a colonial teleology. Could Canada, and the world, use a little more unpredictable and contested Saskatchewan … *as* the current ground of our lives? What possibilities reside in prioritizing the flows and instabilities as constitutive of the place?

Such questioning has particular resonance as Saskatchewan takes up space in the shifting national discourses and economies of the twenty-first century. What is learned through an analysis of how Saskatchewan operates as a static possibility in Canada opens up routes of interrogation for Saskatchewan's so-called "second century" — and discourses/occurrences of a future-oriented spatial demarcation. Saskatchewan is increasingly reiterated as having become an "it" province (from "have-not" to "have" in popular Canadian vernacular) and a place of economic "boom" in the midst of a global recession. Any such claims to transformation and to shifts in the characterization of Saskatchewan of course rely on relations to prior characterizations of the place and do press questions of what is it that changes and what makes Saskatchewan *Saskatchewan*. For example, Simon Enoch (2011) takes up a discussion of "New Saskatchewan" discourse in which he argues that claiming new prosperity in contrast to an "old" Saskatchewan is not particularly novel. Enoch traces continuities of emerging neoliberal policies that seek to obscure such continuity and to "establish a binary between a stagnant past and a prosperous future" (206). In this intervention into the discourse of new prosperity, Enoch draws attention to long debates over Saskatchewan's "economic potential." What happens to such debates about change and potential when the knowability of Saskatchewan is drawn into question? This shifts the debate and characterizations from questions of new prosperity, survival and success, old stagnancy or untapped potential — toward asking how to make visible that it is difference that constitutes the space as a space.

Further, this analysis speaks to the ongoing work of addressing the challenges of and calls to reconciliation in what function as Canadian spaces. Reconciliation (in TRCs and in engagements and discourse productive of reconciliation as national "work" and "opportunity") involves imagining and materializing terrains of encounter for the work of reconciliation and for the future space of lived relations meant to emerge from such processes. In a discussion of the politics of reconciliation, Rinaldo Walcott (2011a: 345) names a critical question: "How are we to make other conceptions of being human and of traversing the globe appear?" Walcott asks this alongside the critique that "reconciliation does not ask us to rethink where we are" (346). That is, the politics of reconciliation conceived in notions of humanity and space enforced through colonial European mapping of the world ask about reconciliation in keeping with the terms of that map itself. As well as reconciliation projects such as truth and reconciliation commissions, there are spaces such as anti-oppressive classrooms and organizations (where the specific focus is on recognizing and contending with social differences and social identities that are secured by White settler Canadian processes) — where what is attempted is the creation of space that is equitable, inclusive and specifically not dominated by or productive of whiteness as normative. There too it is worth persistently living the open question of "where are we?"

This sticky fiction of Saskatchewan as middle landscape, when recognized as sticky and as fictive, demonstrates how the work of decolonized space means being alert to the static and to what is static in our efforts to live counter to settler-colonial boundaries of possibility.

NOTES

1. At the time of this writing a prominent example is the Truth and Reconciliation Commission of Canada established as an outcome of the Indian Residential Schools Settlement Agreement.

2. Terms such as invasion and conquer recognize the context as one founded in and functioning through violence. My use of the term invader-settler space is particularly informed by Diana Brydon's (2004) account of reading postcoloniality in Canada. Brydon makes clear that settlement was and is an invasion. See in particular her discussion (2004: 177, n.2) of this terminology in postcolonial critique.

3. The 2005 Centennial was chaired by an elected member of the Legislative Assembly, Glenn Hagel, who was given the title of legislative secretary to the premier and responsibility for coordinating celebrations with staff members at the 2005 Centennial office, which brought together several departments and ministries of the provincial government. The organizational structure and activities for the official celebrations were established as an outcome of a four-year study and public consultation process conducted by the nineteen-member Citizens' Advisory Council to the Anniversaries Secretariat (Citizens' Advisory Council 2001).

4. The *Indian Act* of 1876 merged federal laws relating to and treaties with Aboriginal peoples into one statute constructed with the intent to define and regulate all aspects of "status Indian" life, and it still functions with this intent and effects today. For this description of the *Indian Act*, I rely on Bonita Lawrence's (2004) work. See also the discussion in the chapter by Lee in this collection.

5. This is a phrase from the official song of the Saskatchewan Centennial.

6. The three are Moose Jaw, North Battleford, and Yorkton. The Saskatoon exhibit did not include an Introduction room.

7. This play, *All My Relations — Wahkotowin*, was performed by the Dancing Sky Theatre Company at various outdoor sites throughout the province in the summer of 2005.

8. These lines are transcribed from my notes as an audience member at two of the performances of this play.

9. Ahmed's discussion of short articulations is a reminder of the histories embedded in and conveyed through such abbreviations.

10. Which is to identify cartography as also an imaginative process.

11. Brent Butt is the creator of and part of the cast of the CBC sitcom *Corner Gas*, now in syndication.

12. The words are transcribed from the video recording of the Lieutenant Governor's Centennial Gala.

13. Transcribed from performances of the play.

14. This word is a deliberate play on the notions of "intertwined" and "twinned."

15. CBC televised news special May 18, 2005.

16. Ibid.

Chapter 7

HOME AT THE BRIDGE

Indigenous Belonging and the Settler Border

Robinder Kaur Sehdev

The bridges at Niagara Falls are deeply symbolic. In addition to metaphorically controlling the landscape by spanning the powerful river, they are border zones defining and linking settler nations, and so the bridges are politically powerful.[1] By crossing these bridges, the crosser is literally located in the settler national project of drawing and policing settler borders. Through two images, one of a failed bridge and another of an interrupted crossing, both at Niagara, I present an argument about Canadian nationalism and its fitful relationship with universalism and particularism in relation to Indigenous belonging.

The limits of visibility and knowability are determined at national borders. Jody Berland (2001) describes borders as unsuccessful binary oppositions where one is marked as either inside or outside, and they are unsuccessful because (metaphorically, literally, culturally and ideologically) living at and crossing the border continuously fractures this binary. For most Canadians, living at the border is literal, and the overwhelming imperial power of the United States threatens to engulf as it undeniably shapes our nation and national identity. Thus, according to Berland, all Canadians live the border. Critical race scholars such as Himani Bannerji (2000), Sherene Razack (2002) and Sunera Thobani (2007) importantly note that while all Canadians might live the border, the relationship between people, Canadianness and the borders is importantly structured by power and violence. I argue that the border not only separates Canada from the United States, but that in parcelling out land among settler states, it also acts as a colonial enforcer; the border is a marker of the settler states' power and presumed entitlement to occupy and portion out Indigenous lands, thus alienating Indigenous peoples, forms of governance and politics from Indigenous space.

Challenges to Canadian nationalism that the persistent universalism-particularism debates present offer no new space for Indigenous belonging; such debates accept the terms of settler nationalism and close off the potential to investigate modes of settler-First Peoples belonging beyond the strictures of Eurocentric governance. Universalism is best embodied in sentiments of undifferentiated nationalism, for example, "we are all Canadian," while particularism in sentiments of special status as per the signifier "Native-Canadian." Particularism is invariably accompanied by the discourses of special status, preferential treatment and reverse racism — all discourses that attempt to make the structural nature of racial power invisible. Indigenous belonging is markedly different from other kinds of belonging within the nation, unique in its relationship with land and with settler colonial authority.

My call for an epistemology of roots comes from the struggle of Indigenous nations to cross the settler border at Niagara and the Tuscarora Nation's subsequent Bridge Crossing Ceremony. At issue in the struggle to cross the border is the centrality of roots and land to Indigenous sovereignty and life. While the relationship between community and roots is necessarily affected by the violence of colonization, and settler colonization in turn, the need for roots has not been eroded or erased. The bridges at Niagara are spaces of Indigenous action which aims to radically alter the nations the bridges connect; thus decolonial action here at the site of the bridge challenges settler home and belonging. The challenge that decolonial action presents productively unsettles the normalcy of the settler's rightfulness to home and nation on this land.

PRECARIOUS BRIDGES AND RISKY CROSSINGS

Today the Rainbow, Peace and Queenston/Lewiston Bridges span the Niagara River and the Canada-U.S. border. The Rainbow Bridge is closest to the cataract and was built on the site of the collapsed Honeymoon Bridge, the bridge whose collapse serves as an organizing metaphor for this chapter. Niagara has seen several bridges in its settler history, and throughout that history these bridges have been surrounded by the discourses of "civilization," "progress" and "mastery over nature." This is not to suggest that Indigenous peoples did not have bridges at Niagara Falls, but that the implementation of settler technologies was seen as a natural expression of the colonial imperative. On the subject of the early adoption of settler technologies at Niagara, Joyce Chaplin (2001) argues that settler approaches to Indigenous peoples' use of technology gradually shifted over time. Often woefully equipped, ill or malnourished, "explorers" and early colonists relied heavily on Indigenous peoples' knowledge of the environment and how to live with it. This relationship began with the mutual exchange of knowledge (particularly instrumental to the newcomers were ecological and geographical knowledges) and transformed to a state of the settlers imposing and withholding technologies. At this point, Chaplin argues, it was assumed that Indigenous peoples had no more knowledge to offer Europeans. "Innovation" in the form of technology was conflated with human progress, and newcomer technologies were tightly policed to guard against Indigenous adaptations in order to preserve the discourse of colonial manifest destiny. The notion that Western technology is an indicator of human progress, that is, the supremacy of European ideas of progress, stubbornly persists.[2]

When the Honeymoon Bridge (also called the Fallsview Bridge) fell down in 1938, the prospect of a romantic stroll over the Niagara River collapsed along it. Oscar Wilde wrote in 1882 of Niagara Falls: "Every American bride is taken there, and the sight of the stupendous waterfall must be one of the earliest, if not the keenest, disappointments in American married life" (quoted in Dubinsky 1999: n.p.). He would likely have found the collapse of the Honeymoon Bridge strangely fitting. The day the bridge fell, CBC journalist John Kannawin (1938) reported that an ice jam in the river had caused the bridge's supports to twist in place and suddenly give way. The bridge went down, shooting snow and ice in the air, yet in spite of the dramatic spectacle, there were no injuries or loss of life. The collapse had been anticipated hours in advance and crowds were kept at a distance at either side of the river, where they could safely witness the show. In keeping with the popular discourse of scientific mastery over nature, Kannawin (1938) ends his report of the wrecked bridge with musings on Canada-U.S. cooperation, the symbolic value of the Honeymoon Bridge and the promise of modern science:

> Niagara Falls, one of the wonders of the world, and here we have disaster penetrating that which in itself is a super-colossal example of nature's great work. Niagara Falls in the summertime, a glorious resort. Niagara Falls in the wintertime, an awe-inspiring sight of just what King Winter can do to nature's fortress. Man has spanned the Niagara Falls and now one of those spans has gone down. But then, civilization goes on. Nature itself will go on. Another bridge will be built. And people will travel across from the United States where we're all brothers on this great continent, and all proud of our associations with one another. The Fallsview Bridge during this great number of years has represented something a great deal more than just a point of entry from one country to another. It's been a sort of scientific hand-clasp from one nation to another, and it can't be allowed to remain down there at the bottom of the gorge. Another bridge must rise to take its place.

According to historian Sherman Zavitz (1999), the ice jam formed two days before the bridge collapsed, and it crushed the docking area for the Maid of the Mist tour boats, pushing two of the boats from their wintertime berths and knocking the caretaker's home from its foundation. Maintenance crews were sent out at 4.00 a.m. on January 26, 1938, to clear the ice from the bridge's supports, but there was little they could do as ice continued to flow over the waterfalls and compact at the bridge's base. Word quickly spread through the community that the bridge would surely fall. Zavitz (1999: 57) and Seibel (1991: 156) report that a "death watch" began at 9:15 a.m. and crowds began to collect at both sides of the shore to witness the spectacular destruction. When the bridge did fall, the media described it as a death and a disaster. Kannawin's description of what the Honeymoon meant and why a new bridge must replace it, hyperbolic though it is, reflects the general faith in technology and its presumed ability to bind nations and secure futures that was characteristic of the time. More than this, the call to rebuild reflects an unwavering faith in the settler's right to the land, as well as the natural connection between bridge building and civilization. Rather than being seen as a technological failure, the fallen Honeymoon became emblematic of the imperative to innovate, to connect two nations and to express the manifest destiny of "civilization" over nature. In Kannawin's own words, this event was about more than the collapse of a bridge, it was about an unshaken technological imperative in which we, as citizens of civilized nations, must place our faith. The structural failure of a single bridge then becomes the rallying point of renewed effort and faith in this "scientific hand-clasp" between settler nations.

The Honeymoon's replacement, the Rainbow Bridge, was completed in 1941. It is the closest bridge to the waterfalls and serves as an access point to various tourist attractions on both sides of the border. It is considered part of the complete tourist experience and the only pedestrian walkway on the bridge is positioned on the falls' side. In other words, the Rainbow Bridge is the Honeymoon's copy. The collapse of the Honeymoon should serve as a reminder of the precarious nature of seemingly permanent structures in a geography where impermanence is inevitable. In spite of this persistent precariousness and the attention that the collapsed Honeymoon attracted, the construction of the replacement bridge was inevitable, and its actual construction is less significant to my discussion of "home at the bridge" than the creative powers upon which it depended. Indeed, the imaginative construction of the Rainbow began the moment the Honeymoon broke and fell to the bottom of the frozen gorge. The prefigured image of the Rainbow Bridge symbolized settler belonging and directed understanding of the collapsed bridge as an opportunity to simply build again. This is a creativity that settles settlement and so normalizes colonialism.

Not all bridges are created equal. While to some, Niagara's bridges might serve as a platform for a spectacular view, to others they serve as pathways through colonial law. The same shores at which the spectators amassed to witness the collapse of the bridge and the paradoxical reinforcement of settler nationalism were a space of struggle for citizens of the Haudenosaunee Confederacy, where the act of crossing Niagara's bridges was absolutely critical to their assertions of sovereignty and home on their land. Since the bridges are slung over the international Canada-U.S. border, they are places where settler law is brought to bear, and subsequently, they became the nexus point of Indigenous decolonial action.

Through the imposition of immigration quotas, the *Johnson Act* of 1924 barred Indigenous peoples from freely entering the U.S. from Canada.[3] This was a violation of the Jay Treaty of 1794 and the Treaty of Ghent of 1814 (see Brunyeel 2004). The Jay Treaty was negotiated after the American Revolution, in part to secure peace and trade relations between the young American Republic and the British Empire. The treaty also formalized the borderlines between the British colony of Canada and the American Republic. The Haudenosaunee Confederacy had not fought on the side of the Americans in their revolution, and their territories spanned the newly formed colonial border. As such, the Jay Treaty ensured that Haudenosaunee territories remained intact and that the Haudenosaunee could freely cross the colonial border.[4] The Treaty of Ghent, formed after the War of 1812, affirms the commitments made in Jay, and it too was formed to secure peace and trade between the American Republic and the British Empire.

A week after the *Johnson Act*, barring Indigenous movement across the border, was passed in the U.S. Congress, Indigenous peoples in the U.S. were patriated under the *Indian Citizenship Act* of June 2, 1924. Making Indigenous peoples citizens under the settler state restricted their physical mobility and threatened their sovereignty, which served as a way of solidifying U.S. national borders. On the Canadian side of the settler border, Indigenous sovereignty was threatened through various amendments to the *Indian Act*, where Indian status[5] could be revoked: Indigenous peoples could be forcibly enfranchised if they were deemed to have met various criteria of "civilization" (for example, serving in the military or earning a university degree). During the 1920s, the Canadian settler state also sought to neutralize Indigenous nationalism, which threatened colonial-imposed forms of governance, by suppressing traditional forms of governance. Six Nations at Grand River (of the Haudenosaunee Confederacy), asserting its sovereignty as a nation, sought the Crown's recognition of its treaty responsibilities to them, arguing that this would ensure that Haudenosaunee lands remained in Haudenosaunee hands and out of the reach of quickly encroaching settler communities. They saw the Crown's annexation of reserve lands as a violation of its treaty obligations to not interfere with Indigenous land tenure. Levi General, a Cayuga chief with the title of Deskaheh (to this day, Levi General is commonly referred to by this chiefly title, Deskaheh), was charged with the responsibility of arguing for Six Nations' rights. To this end, Deskaheh submitted a petition asserting the sovereignty of Six Nations to the Supreme Court. According to Yale Belanger, "after consulting the Department of Justice, the Privy Council determined, in its order-in-council of 27 November 1920, the Six Nations' sovereignty claims to be unfounded" (2007: 36). Six Nations responded by then appealing to the Crown's representative, the governor gneral, to protect their rights from settlers and the settler government. When it became apparent that the governor general would not hear him, Deskaheh wrote to England. Colonial Secretary Winston Churchill directed him back to the Canadian government, saying that this was a dominion matter and must be addressed there.

In 1923, Deskaheh and his followers, using Six Nations passports, travelled to Geneva (Switzerland was the only European nation to recognize the validity of those passports) to appeal to the League of Nations.[6] Winston Churchill, who had previously been eager to lay responsibility at the distant feet of the Canadian dominion government, blocked Deskaheh's appeal by claiming that this was an internal (that is, British imperial) matter. He condemned Persia, Panama, Ireland and Estonia's support of Deskaheh as "impertinent interference in the internal affairs of the British empire" (quoted in Wright 1993: 324). In one final attempt to appeal to reason, Deskaheh wrote directly to King George V, reminding him of his treaty commitment to the Haudenosaunee and of their service to him during England's many wars. On October 7, 1924, while Deskaheh was still in Europe, RCMP officers raided Six Nations' Council House, dissolved the Six Nations governance system[7] by dominion decree, confiscated a number of documents that were relevant to their sovereignty claim and seized wampum from the homes of wampum keepers. After this coup, Deskaheh risked arrest were he to return to Canada and so he elected to stay with his friend, Chief Clinton Rickard, on Tuscarora Territory at Niagara Falls on the American side of the settler border. Fatally ill, Deskaheh asked Chief Rickard to send for medicine men from Six Nations at Grand River. They were turned away at the border due to the border guards' fastidious application of the *Johnson Act*. Not long before Deskaheh died, he urged Rickard to "fight for the line" (Rickard 1973: 68), meaning the Haudenosaunee's right to cross the settler border as a sovereign people.

Rickard, along with other influential neighbouring chiefs and supporters formed the Indian Defense League in 1926, with the aim of securing the border crossing rights of all Indigenous peoples on both sides of the colonial border. Both Deskaheh and Chief Rickard held firm to their commitment to affirm Indigenous sovereignty in spite of the demands that the border crossing process placed on Indigenous people: proof of American or Canadian citizenship. To Niagara's border guards, Haudenosaunee citizenship and passports were simply not enough to merit the right to cross the bridge. Rickard (1973:

72) reports advocating for Job Henry, an Indigenous man, and his right to cross into the United States:

> I took up the case of Job Henry immediately. I wrote letters to Senator Wadsworth and to the Immigration Bureau in Washington. Senator Wadsworth gave us much assistance in supporting our right to cross the border at will. I myself went to the main office of the district director of immigration in Buffalo to protest this unjust exclusion and to plead the case of our Indian people who wished to cross the border. I had told the immigration officials that Job Henry was a native American whose ancestors had been here for centuries and who had been unjustly stopped at the border and separated from his wife and children. I did not consider that there was any such thing as "Canadian Indian" or "United States Indian." All Indians are one people. We were here long before there was any border to make an artificial division of our people.

In 1927, Rickard appeared before the Committee on Immigration and Naturalization in Washington to defend the rights of all First Peoples to cross the settler border, even while the right had been recognized specifically for the Haudenosaunee: "The congressmen … asked me what the Jay Treaty said, and I told him that it referred to Indians in general but not specifically to any tribe or tribes. I added that I was working to restore the Jay Treaty as read" (Rickard 1973: 81). Rickard reports that he appealed to Niagara tourists for support. Wearing Algonquin traditional dress and carrying wampum from Lake of Two Mountains (in this way representing many different Indigenous nations), Rickard would walk through Niagara's tourist area to speak with tourists about the right of all Indigenous peoples to cross Niagara's bridges. He became a visible spokesperson for Indigenous sovereignty in an area where occupants typically did not meaningfully encounter Indigenous people beyond the souvenirs and images they consumed. Tourist reaction was, Rickard reports, overwhelmingly supportive. On April 2, 1928, the right to cross into the United States was won, and Indigenous peoples, regardless of nation, were recognized as having the right to cross the settler border without restriction (O'Brien 1984). To mark the occasion, every third weekend of July since 1928, the Tuscarora Nation marches with the Indian Defense League across the Niagara, sometimes on the Queenston-Lewiston Bridge, at other times upstream on the Rainbow Bridge, in the Border Crossing Ceremony, which exercises their right to cross the settler border and thereby defend their sovereignty.

The significance of this bridge crossing extends well beyond the particulars of Niagara Falls and serves as a lesson in decolonial action. As a reporter for *Indian Country Today* declared, the event "could very well be the oldest continuous Native protest movement in northern America" (Adams 2004). The very real threat that colonial law would subsume Indigenous law and its citizenship through coercive belonging meant that crossing and not crossing were equally fraught. Bridge crossing as a political strategy confronts the settler's assumption of their right to draw and defend borders, and reminds the settler that the imposition of citizenship that lies at the heart of this conflict has not been resolved.[8] The event is a critical assertion of Indigenous sovereignty in settler states that would strategically deploy settler nationalism to suppress its Indigenous counterpart. Bridge crossing as decolonial strategy remains a political necessity.

BELONGING AND HOME IN THE SETTLER NATION

Niagara Falls is both home and not-home. The tourist industry's marketing presented the space as one to be done or experienced rather than lived, and it bears mentioning that while Niagara Falls is one point in an international tourist network, it is simultaneously a tourist, settler and First Nations space. In short, it is a space where belonging is experienced in a dramatic diversity of ways, and as such, the bridge is not a universal metaphor. This means that crossing a bridge might, to some, amount to a challenge to colonial legal strictures, and to others it might simply serve as a platform for a spectacular view, as a means to safely and quickly access tourist attractions or as a way of crossing international borderlines. In other words, not all bridges are created equal and not all homes are the same.

"The land is what holds us together; without our land we are nothing" (Rickard 1973: 138).[9] Chief Rickard's explanation of the bonds between his community and their territory would be decidedly out of place in much of today's political thought. Community belonging, or to put it more specifically, the belonging of particular ethnic, cultural or racial group to a specific place — that is, the validity of homeland — has been roundly condemned amongst postmodernist critics. After all, the examples of the Nazi *Volksgemeinschaft* (meaning "people's community," or "national community"), Afrikaner *Volkstaat* (meaning "people's state") and United States' homeland all issue powerful warnings about the potential to alienate and persecute in the invocation of homeland. In all cases, homeland is predicated on belief in "the people's" exclusive right of inhabitance. However, the association of homeland with right does not end at the right to a specific space. "Homeland" necessarily encompasses the right, perhaps the imperative, to determine who constitutes the community that inhabits specific spaces.

In his attempts to understand the nature of community through the extreme example of Nazi Germany, Jean Luc Nancy begins from the position that communities are based upon loss, which is not an actual, material or experiential loss, but the notion that the people have lost something they never had in the first place. This sense of loss invokes the relationship between community and its other. Nazi Germany's sense of loss of ancient Greece had the Deuschland looking back to another time and place in order to map its vision of its future community. This was not the other as defined by postcolonial thought (the abject or subaltern), but an equal, perhaps even superior other who can never co-exist with us, but must remain accessible to us only through our sense of loss and feelings of having just missed them. Spatial and temporal distance matters little here: "the 'I' and the 'other' do not live in the same time, are never together (synchronously), can therefore not be contemporary, but separated (even when united) by a 'not yet' which goes hand in hand with an 'already no longer'" (Nancy quoted in Bernasconi 1993: 8). Thus, the myth of origins is interrupted from the outset, indeed cannot operate as a myth were it anything but fundamentally interrupted. The yearning for the unrealizable communion with the other is what structures the definition and direction of community. In this nostalgia for a community that never was and will never be lies the threat of totalitarianism, which can be brought to the surface through attempts to redeem community from its apparently wayward path. Nazi policies of segregation, persecution and genocide were justified as ensuring the purity of the Aryan race and the *Volksgemeinschaft* from racial and moral pollution. This looking back to move forward, this "inoperative community" based on the "interrupted myth" of an original, pure, innocent, intact and simpler time must be the focus of our suspicion, Nancy argues (1991: 10). How the vicissitudes of Western community formation and identification have come to stand in for community globally has in turn become the focus of considerable suspicion.

Charles Taylor's now-canonical work on difference in Canada, "The Politics of Recognition," has inspired many responses that further query the nature of Canadian national identity and the structures of power and privilege that determine it. Taylor (1994: 42) argues that freedoms flow from the recognition of differences. Therefore, in order to defend the "principle of human equality," which he prizes, *we* must recognize *them*. This means extending *our* understanding of national community to encompass *them*. Just who constitutes this "we" and "them," and how this "we" has seemed to amass such power in relation to "them" are questions that remain unanswered in Taylor's theory of liberal inclusion in the nation. These are questions Ian Angus asks of Taylor's politics of recognition. When Taylor speaks of the recognition of cultural difference in pluralist societies he bypasses any meaningful discussion of the nature of the culture-which-recognizes (the "we" who appear to have the uncontested power to recognize) (Angus 1997). Angus notes that "we" is a difficult term to employ in the case of Canadian cultural recognition because all cultures aside from those of First Nations come from elsewhere. The analysis of difference must actively question this invocation of those-who-recognize and those-who-are-recognized, and such invocations obliquely reference vastly uneven relations to power. In his questioning of the national "we" that Taylor invokes, Angus argues that inclusion in the nation without having constitutive access to that nation is another form of colonization. In other words, the idea that domination is the result of a lack of recognition, as Taylor contends, is simply insufficient. The conversation must be turned from the recognition of difference to a confrontation with the ways that power and domination organize the nation.

Himani Bannerji (2000: 96) further criticizes Taylor's imperative of inclusive recognition, arguing that he over-emphasizes the importance of recognition and thereby further obscures the profound structural problems that ensure racial dominance involved in the definition and disciplining of Canadianness. Bannerji revisits the discourse of official multiculturalism as a method of outward inclusion, which preserves the authority of White settlers to define the terms and limits of Canadian citizenship and belonging. Bannerji's focus on racism in Canada enables the identification of how whiteness is encoded in national identity. Imbalances in power are made apparent in the production and articulation of colonial knowledge (of what is considered worth knowing, saying, defending, experiencing). Sherene Razack argues: "We need to direct our efforts to the conditions of communication and knowledge production that prevail, calculating not only who can speak and how they are likely to be heard but also how we know what we know and the interests we protect through our knowing" (1998: 10). In other words, the terms of communication and knowledge were and remain coercive. It is the responsibility of the scholar not to avoid these problems, but to confront them. The imperative to "return the gaze" (Bannerji 1993) or "look white people in the eye" (Razack 1998) attempts to redirect the question of self-representation in a political context where spectacular difference is desired, expected and holds considerable market value. In other words, when the racialized other is expected to perform and embody their otherness (which often entails the performance of "disadvantage"), the ability to counter the dominating gaze with a critical gaze of one's own turns dominant expectations on its ear. "When are those of you who inflict racism, who appropriate pain, who speak with no knowledge or respect when you ought to know to listen and accept, going to take hard looks at yourself instead of me. How can you continue to look to me to carry what is your responsibility?" asks Patricia Monture-Angus (1995: 21). Such questions both direct the gaze to whiteness while attempting to disengage from the entitlement and power implicit in colonial looking and knowing. Settler national myths are space-bound because they explain and perpetuate settler claims to Indigenous place. In this sense, marking boundaries is a deeply ideological and carefully mystified act that needs to be exposed (Razack 2002: 5). Likewise the making of Niagara as a settler space through its bridges and the policing of access to those bridges needs also to be revealed as part of the process of settler colonization.

According to Taylor, "we" must recognize "others." This does not mean that the culture-to-be-recognized must mimic the dominant, but that it is the responsibility of the dominant culture to recognize its other. In order for citizenship to have substantive value in a society that balances the universal with the particular, differences between citizens must be respected. This recognition of difference, or the politics of recognition as Taylor calls it, is remarkably different from the political imperative for social harmony by way of the refusal to recognize or weigh difference differently.

> Where the politics of universal dignity fought for forms of nondiscrimination that were quite "blind" to the ways in which citizens differ, the politics of difference often redefines nondiscrimination as requiring that we make these distinctions the basis of differential treatment. So members of aboriginal bands [sic] will get certain rights and powers not enjoyed by other Canadians, if the demands for native self-government are finally agreed on, and certain minorities will get the right to exclude others in order to preserve their cultural integrity. (Taylor 1994: 39–40)

This is a seemingly apt endorsement of the principle of equity in modern liberal societies: equality can only be achieved through the recognition of difference and the implementation of differential treatment when the need is apparent. It means that the relationship between the particular citizen and the nation (as well as its society) differs according to the citizen's difference. It also means that *we* must ensure the just distribution of material, cultural and political resources. In spite of his endorsement of plurality in the service of the singular nation and universalist principles of human rights, Taylor fails to recognize that the very same hands that open to embrace difference can close around the necks of others. Ostensibly inclusive gestures amount to another exclusion, this version more insidious than explicit exclusion because it appears transformatively inclusive.

Glen Coulthard (2008) argues that Fanon is important for understanding contemporary Canadian colonial politics because Fanon recognizes the interplay between the subjective and objective in colonialism. In other words, yes, misrecognition is vastly damaging to those misrecognized. More than this, however, Fanon argues that misrecognition of the other must be met with more than a liberalist expansion of recognition, which would focus attention on increased recognition rather than the social and political structures which secure the practice of colonial (mis)recognition. It must rather be met with radical struggle for the reorganization of power. Treaty must be understood to be a living feature of Indigenous sovereignty, if the lot of the settler is ever to move toward an ethical position in relation to Indigenous nations.

Treaty according to settler law and political philosophy asphyxiates true recognition and fatally reduces Indigenous sovereignty. Patricia Monture-Angus (1999: 28) makes the case for full recognition by pointing to the failings of our current state of affairs: "Whites can accept that Aboriginal people have politics (albeit not fully) but do not recognize that we equally have theologies, epistemologies, knowledge systems, pedagogy and history. These are all collapsed into mere 'perspective,' thus making actual the white fallacy of Aboriginal inferiority." In the classification of Indigenous political and intellectual life as "perspective" (as in "the Indigenous perspective") the image of the White settler as the bringer of knowledge is thus enforced.

Ian Angus's work on radical homelessness is useful in thinking through the potential for philosophies that speak to the universal without homogenizing the specific. Angus offers a means of building English Canadian philosophy beyond the impulse to seek out, invent or impose origins or completion through his concept of radical homelessness. Located between empires (the United States and Britain), Canada is at the hinterland and so drawing a border means positing an answer to Northrop Frye's (1971: 220, emphasis in original) riddle: "Canadians are bedeviled not by the question of *Who am I?* but by the riddle *Where is here?*" "Here" is the space of the drawn border, a space that is more about politics and power than actual place. Radical homelessness necessitates this border and through this border productive difference is revealed. The other is not abject or (spatially and temporally) removed, but internal to us:

> It is the drawing of a line, a border that separates here from there, that lets there appear an Other, a mismatch, a difference. In relation to this difference we are not fused with origin, but drawn towards the Other. Origin is plural if it is traced back elsewhere; origin is wilderness here. [English Canadian philosophy] must begin in this radical incompletion itself, this struggling on. (Angus 1997: 126)

Radical homelessness is the "struggling on" in spite of the "radical incompletion" of national identity and philosophy. It is, in other words, purposeful work. Angus argues that in order to build a philosophy that is reflexive and diverse, we must abandon the notion of origins, so that we may struggle on, taking up homelessness as a foundation for our thinking and action. This philosophical imperative of struggling on is the only reasonable way to live and be in the settler nation in a way that does not write over Indigenous philosophical, national or lived belongings. Abandoning the notion of epistemic origins releases us from the temptations of claiming truth or knowledge that is exclusively, narrowly determined.

Angus describes radical homelessness as integral to Canadian (and by way of generalization, settler) philosophy and nation-building. But in the settler state homelessness must first be understood as dispossession and injustice, rather than as a general metapolitical and epistemic necessity. There are different ontologies of home, and radical homelessness must be a response to a particular politico-historical situation: that of the settler. English Canadian philosophies must embark on the stated task of radical homelessness, which is not the abandonment of rootedness or home generally, but of the philosophical rootedness and home of Western knowledge. On Nancy's work on community and its other, Bernasconi (1993: 15) says, "[focus] has fallen ... on the margins of Western philosophy, but not, for the most part, on the philosophies that we have consigned to the margins or have denied the name of philosophy altogether, for no better reason than that the identity of philosophy has been decided in advance." The universalization of Western experience in Nancy's work, Bernasconi argues, occurs at the expense of the colonized world.[10] This is no incidental criticism, rather it points to the growing skepticism about Western philosophy's place within colonial domination. Indigenous philosophies, to say nothing of Indigenous ontologies, have been pulled from their place as central to the understanding of home, land and community through colonization. This is why, at first glance, Angus's argument might arouse considerable suspicion: Indigenous philosophies already are in a state of homelessness, made so by the aggressive universalization of Western experience and the conflation of Western knowledge with legitimacy itself.

Take Patricia Monture-Angus's experience of academic homelessness; she writes that because Indigenous epistemologies are considered to be peripheral to so-called legitimate academic pursuits, within the university she experienced a profound and alienating homelessness (2002; 1995: 53–73; see also Eisenkraft 2010). Understood as another mechanism of colonial displacement, this homelessness cannot be redeemed.[11] Radical homelessness, this time meant to dislodge Western philosophy from pride of place as the unqualified philosophy, offers the promise of radical displacement in the service of those philosophies that Bernasconi identified as confined to the margins of knowability. Angus's work on the place of Western philosophy, specifically on the need to take on radical homelessness as an organizing principle, is critical to unsettling the colonizing potential of normative philosophy. Radical homelessness acknowledges how Western philosophies rely on the epistemological homelessness of the marginalized and disenfranchised. Rather than creating a philosophical tradition based on the fundamental and silenced upheaval of Indigenous philosophies, radical homelessness takes on this displacement, and in so doing, creates room for Indigenous epistemological re-homing through bridge-crossing, the operation of treaty.

ROOTS AND THE SPECTRES OF PURITY

Contemporary thinking about community, home and roots is far from a seemingly decontextualized state of knowledge production, the workings of which Angus indicates and never endorses. Reversing Nancy's arguments that spectral loss is community-forming, scholars such as Homi Bhabha and Paul Gilroy rearticulate loss as yearning or nostalgia for home and purity, the result of which is cultural stagnation, intolerance and ultimately, oppression. They write of home and movement as intermingling; more than a necessity of global politics, home and movement are traits of cultural and political advancement. Skepticism about community origins and homeland informs Bhabha's writings on the nature of culture in postcolonial and postmodern times (the "new" internationalism, as he wryly calls it). These are times marked by displacements and relocations that accompany the often-violent reorganization of state borders resulting from wars and the spasms of empires in decline. The "new" internationalism is anything but; Bhabha indicates that the Middle Passage (the transportation of African slaves to the Americas) operates as a meta-phor for postmodern-postcolonial diasporas, and as Du Bois (1896), Cox (1959) and Gilroy (1993) have demonstrated, the Middle Passage was critical to the formation of European modernity and nationalisms in the Americas and the global economic supremacy of the West.[12] Movement compels community to rethink its relationship to spatial belonging and cultural practice, both historically and in the future.

According to Bhabha, "new" internationalism (our present context of rhizomatic movement) was enabled by the massive and traumatic dis- and relocations of the slave trade. Cultures on the move come to occupy spaces and times "in-between" physical space and linear time, indicated by the shorthand "new:" "The borderline work of cul-ture demands an encounter with 'newness' that is not part of the continuum of past and present…. The 'past-present' becomes part of the necessity, not the nostalgia, of living" (1994: 7). In other words, global movements have radically reorganized what it is to live in and create culture because cultures have had no choice but to adapt. This means that we can no longer locate our notion of rootedness or home in the past or the future; "new-ness" as a necessity of living, Bhabha suggests, cannot afford the nostalgic attachments of rootedness. Rather, we live in the past as we live in the present, and as we live between home and the reality of global belonging. This in-betweenness is born of necessity, not desire, and our understanding of time and place becomes indistinct as we no longer live at home, but are "at home in the world." In the face of this, calls to return home appear facile and out of place. We cannot go back home, says Bhabha, because our movement has formed us and challenged what it means to belong. Now that we are at home in our movement, belonging in movement, there is no longer any home to which we can return. Bhabha (1994) uses the metaphor of the bridge to describe the hybrid's perpetual embar-kation into new territories, where the limits of time and space are differently lived. The bridge figures as the emblem of movement, rootlessness (a more neutral designation than uprootedness) and cultural liminality, which brings forth creativity and forward motion not otherwise realizable: "the boundary becomes the place from which something begins its presencing in a movement not dissimilar to the ambulant, ambivalent articulation of the beyond" (1994: 5). Home without movement (or, situated and material home) is now unfathomable except as nostalgia and regression.

Rending peoples from their homes has formed the basis of contemporary nations, and now those made homeless shake up contemporary nationalisms by moving to impe-rial centres. The "new" subject raises a mocking eyebrow to the racist taunt, "go back to where you came from," knowing, to borrow from Paul Gilroy (1991), that "we are here because you were there." As nationalisms are radically reconsidered, nations demand that their "new" citizens demonstrate their belongingness in ways that the "old" citizens never had to. These demands have become far more strident, reactionary and divisive and are expressed through a civic panic concerning how prepared immigrants are to be full citizens.

Thatcher's demand that "new" British citizens demonstrate their Britishness at the expense of all other allegiances (made evident in her query to Britons: "Are you one of us?") is met with Hall's (1997b: 26) observation: "Hardly anybody is one of us any longer." The idea of the true blue-blooded British subject and the accompanying idea of the purity of British belonging, Hall says and Bhabha would agree, is and has always been a powerful and formative myth: powerful because it justifies violence and formative because it structures belonging. But it is a myth nonetheless. It is this confluence of racism and nationalism that incites Bhabha's position that the intersections of home and nation are not places where difference will be countenanced. For Bhabha, diasporic cultures emerge as the protagonists of this international drama, and the central problem of this drama arises when diasporic cultures relocate to specific nations where their difference and in-betweenness are not only considered strange, but treacherous.[13]

Are all expressions of home and rootedness in this "new" internationalism the thin edge of the fascist wedge? Bhabha and Gilroy think so. Both see these expressions of rooted belonging as symptomatic of the desire for cultural and racial purity. To Gilroy (2000), movement is not only inevitable, it is laudable, while rootedness is stagnation and nostalgia. Positioning the question of roots and home as the source of the problem of racist violence, Gilroy (2000: 111) condemns what he sees as a "sedentary poetics of … blood [and] soil" in favour of "movement" which "asks [us] to consider what might be gained if the powerful claims of soil, roots, and territory could be set aside." Who, according to Gilroy, is guilty of fencing in cultural and social potential by forcing community into the enclosure of rooted belonging? Even Nelson Mandela is guilty; after being elected the first president of post-apartheid South Africa he spoke of the nation moving into the post-apartheid future renewed by their "intimate attachment" to the soil and united in their collective homeland (quoted in Gilroy 2000: 111). Gilroy argues that Mandela's expression of national belonging is essentialist, that it fuses the notions of community (a cultural phenomenon) and land (a natural phenomenon as he understands it) while confusing constructions for what lies beyond the reach of human influence. Gilroy condemns Mandela's words for what he sees to be national essentialism, fascism's kissing cousin. Mandela's vision of national belonging, of rootedness in the context of a nation whose Indigenous peoples were rendered homeless in profound and violent ways, is truly a vision of struggle and of overcoming a historical practice of enforced national alienation. Yet, says Gilroy, roots essentialize.

If we are to accept that movement is fundamental to diasporic subjectivities because it radically reformulates our relationships with space and time, as both Bhabha and Gilroy wish us to, surely we must also accept that the notions of soil, roots and territory are also formative. If formative, they are also potentially transformative. Practically and ethically, how then can these formative and essential (not, by default, essentializing) factors be set aside? Conflating the very specific conditions of fascism and apartheid with rootedness means that any and all articulations of roots become both the originator and the symptom of totalitarianism. Such assumptions prevent Gilroy from recognizing the difference in colonial invocations of soil, roots and territory for the purposes of colonial expansion and subjugation and the validity of soil, roots and territory for anti-colonial movements.

What is the value of Bhabha's "in-between" and Gilroy's exuberant diaspora? If one is "in-between," embarking on "new" territories that trouble normative understandings of our relationship with space and time, how does "in-betweeness" retain its "in-betweenness," the zone that is allegedly safe from threats of fascist decay? (Or if not "safe," at least the liminal zone where creative politics are reformulated). When does "in-between" become a destination, and so vulnerable to the intertwined evils of roots, nostalgia and purity? If we now belong in movement, rather than on the land, it would seem that Bhabha and Gilroy locate the evils of racism and fascism in the land itself, rather than in specific historical, economic and political conditions and articulations of belonging. In the effort to theorize the creative potential afforded by diaspora, another hierarchy has been reinforced, one that associates movement with the natural evolution of culture and people.

Hybridity, in-betweenness and diaspora — all of these are synonyms for inherently painful processes of dislocation and relocation, yet Gilroy and Bhabha present these as states of being or destinations at which to arrive. The modern sojourner who can pick up and make home anew is an ideal-type, embodied for Bhabha in the form of Salman Rushdie, who is iconic because he is in between nationalisms, ethnicities, languages and literary traditions. Yet Rushdie as the icon of diaspora is disingenuous. He is, after all, a celebrated author, educated in Western and Eastern literary traditions and in spite of the fatwa that was on his life, Rushdie has enjoyed the security of the British police and moved between nations in airplanes. The modern diasporic subject, were Bhabha faithful to his original invocation of the Middle Passage, is unnamable, not because this subject has no name, but because this name has been cast aside.[14]

She does not cross nations in planes or by Bhabha's celebrated bridge (for him, the emblem of creative motion). In the Middle Passage she is made chattel, and her humanity, sovereignty and community are left behind on the vanishing shores. This reality of enforced movement in modernity demands justice, rather than the jettisoning of home and roots. But once roots and home are cast aside because they are thought to be the source of stagnation, what place is there for justice? Bhabha's attempt to find redemption for the diasporic subject in her new location, in an idea of a metaphysical home, results in his also jettisoning the immediacy of the need and demand for justice in spite of historical distance. Movement does not break the links between roots and home, and the fact of diaspora does not make the need for justice vanish.

The idealization of the diasporic subject at the expense of grounded or rooted treatment of home and justice suggests that contemporary struggles for justice on the basis of displacement are out of time and place. But roots do matter and they can provide the grounds for radical action. It is precisely because land and belonging on it matter that Indigenous communities in the colonized world were and are displaced, and it is the way that roots matter that matters here. Not a question of the cultural ability to adapt to rhizomatic movement, this is a question of ontological difference and supremacy on colonized lands. This problem of the displacement of Indigenous ontologies and its effects on our conceptions and misconceptions about what it might mean to belong to particular places is central to the question of justice in settler societies. We, First Nations and settler (newcomer and new-newcomer), must accept the gravity of the continued offence of colonialism; we must believe in the possibility of restorative justice and in our agency to affect this.

The question of home and roots becomes increasing complex in the case of Indigenous nations which have been displaced not once, but multiple times. Aileen Moreton-Robinson (2003) explains how colonial dispossessions mean that Indigenous people come to find refuge on other Indigenous nations' lands, as settler states interfere with and undermine Indigenous sovereignties and force Indigenous people to move again and again. The difference between Indigenous and settler-immigrant migrancies, she argues, is "an incommensurate doubleness superimposed by marginality and centring. Marginality is the result of colonization and the proximity to whiteness, while centring is achieved through the continuity of ontology and cultural protocols between and amongst Indigenous peoples" (2003: 53). The crucial significance of Indigenous ontology and protocols surrounds the settler state but seldom passes its borders in meaningful ways. This means that Indigenous ways of knowing and doing are made strange in the settler state, and this, coupled with forced migrancies of Indigenous peoples, produces an at-home homelessness, or a state of dispossession in another Indigenous nation's traditional territories.

The Tuscarora Nation's traditional territories are in what we now call the Carolinas of the U.S., but in the 1710s and 1720s aggressive White settlers forced them north (Dubinsky 1999). Dispossessed, they appealed to the Five Nations Confederacy for refuge at Niagara, a region they were permitted to share with the Seneca Nation of the Five Nations Confederacy, who eventually adopted the Tuscarora, making the Six Nations Confederacy of today. The fact of their dispossession does not erase the intimate connection between the nation and its territories in the recently renamed Carolinas; moreover the way that Niagara matters to the Tuscarora is central to the nation's relationship with the Confederacy. The significance is also cosmological: Niagara plays an important role in the creation stories of the Tuscarora Nation and several other First Nations. Indigenous refugees in the territories of other Indigenous nations develop multiple understandings of the ways that they are rooted to the territories they currently inhabit as well as their traditional territories, the spaces that are central to their ways of knowing and being "a people." This is no easy belonging since the violence that necessitated diaspora is dismissed and blanketed in the settler discourse of "human progress" and continues to threaten Indigenous belonging in diaspora. Moreton-Robinson explains how the result is that Indigenous peoples come to belong in the settler state when White people permit them to belong. To be clear, Moreton-Robinson is speaking of forced migrations of Indigenous peoples, in Indigenous territories that have been seized by settler states. For the Indigenous person, the settler state is no postcolonial reality: its continual unhoming of Indigenous protocols and ontologies is a perpetual colonialism.

Home, roots and belonging are cast in a new light with these multiple displacements of Indigenous peoples. Conventional historical narratives of the Americas begin with theories that Indigenous peoples are descendants of prehistoric intercontinental migrants. Such a position causes great offence to a people who are of the land, whether "people of the land" references humans formed from the soil,[15] or the community-forming power of the land, it matters little when the assumption that Indigenous peoples are stateless wanderers dominates historical records and modern conviction. Tom Flanagan (2000: 25), whose scholarly contribution to Indigenous and Canadian histories and political thought is hotly debated, nevertheless gives voice to this still-operative position when he says:

> Why not consider the coming of Europeans as [the latest in a series of] migration[s], a new set of tribes pushing others in front of them? Should we hesitate to do so because the European colonists had lighter-coloured skin, hair, and eyes than the older inhabitants? At bottom, the assertion of an inherent right of aboriginal self-government is a kind of racism. It contends that the only legitimate inhabitants of the Americas have been the Indians and Inuit. According to this view, they had the right to drive each other from different territories as much as they liked, even to the point of destroying whole peoples and taking over their land, but Europeans had no similar right to push their way in.

The temptation to scoff at the claim of reverse racism against the backdrop of colonial invasion should not detract from the importance of what Flanagan is arguing: colonialism is just another migration and there is no significant difference between European and Indigenous movements (and atrocities) save phenotype and time. For Flanagan, the settler, to modify the words of Mahmood Mamdani (1996), has become native. The doctrine of the statute of limitations on indigeneity is clearly visible throughout Flanagan's work and was fully operative in the bridge-border disputes of the 1920s. In other words, Flanagan believes that given enough time, Indigenous people's indigeneity, along with their connections to their often resource-rich lands, will invariably fade away. In this line of thinking, time is the determining factor and any consideration of Indigenous people's pre-existing rights is a symptom of reverse racism.[16]

The United States and Canada, like other former colonies turned settler states, are characterized by what Pal Ahluwalia calls "settler independence" (2001). Unlike former colonies that experienced a period of decolonization, where the place of colonizers and settlers within the decolonizing nation was (variously) precarious, settler states have had no such decolonizing moment. Ahluwalia says that place of birth becomes the occasion of settler native-ness as settler law determines belonging within its nascent borders on the basis of conquest. Here, the confusion between race and belonging to the land is demonstrated in full colour. The United States revolted against Britain's imperial chokehold, only to continue to dispossess and oppress Indigenous nations inside its still-forming borders. That the Boston Tea Party (a protest against the British that is widely acknowledged as the first major act of the American Revolution) was instigated by men "playing Indian" (dressed in feathers, dancing and "war whooping") is no coincidence; Philip Deloria (1998) argues that in these early days of American nationalism, settlers sought and found credibility for their revolutionary aspirations by dressing up and acting out as "Indians." Of course, the "Indians" they played were stereotypes in the most crassly literal sense, but this turn to Indianness, stereotypic as it surely was, demonstrated a deep need to gain legitimacy by constructing and performing this other. These acts of settler revolt drew the proverbial line, this time at Boston Harbor, beyond which British imperial law would not be allowed to pass. Settler law transforms into colonial law when it assumes the subjugating role of colonial law. After 9/11, newspapers were ablaze with the slogan, "We are all Americans now." Far from a rallying cry, this daunting message threatened Indigenous nations centuries ago.

HOMECOMING AT THE BRIDGE

In this chapter I offer images of two bridges, one whose purpose is to link shores and carry the settler national imperative over the gorge, the second bridge (more a process than a thing) enunciates Indigenous sovereignty by denying the settler national imperative. The processual nature of the decolonial bridge is critical; rather than simply and immediately reproducing the bridge in unstable times, the process of embarking out over the Niagara River to assert sovereignty demonstrates a conscious and critical commitment to challenging the normativity of settler borders, envisioning and connecting community, and claiming belonging in spaces considered un-homeable.

Bridges are nothing without roots to anchor them. Roots, home and belonging, in other words, matter, but as I argue, they matter differently, and it is the terms of that difference that matters in settler national politics. The terms of settler belonging on the land must include the recognition of the limits of settler entitlement to home on the land and the acknowledgement that settler nationalism is fatally incomplete without meaningfully recognizing and engaging treaty and Indigenous sovereignty. This demands far more than the attempt to force Indigenous sovereignty into the particularist-universalist debates that often lie at the centre of Canadian nationalism's confrontation with difference. Rather than tearing down settler bridges or awaiting their inevitable and dramatic collapse, the settler home needs to be grounded in the lived experiences and ontologies of Indigenous home, and this demands a demonstrable commitment to Indigenous sovereignty and treaty. Indigenous home is the normative, determining factor to settler belonging.

NOTES

1. My sincere thanks to the editors, Carrianne Leung, Darryl Leroux and Lynn Caldwell for their careful edits and thoughtful questions. Jody Berland, John O'Neill and Ato Sekyi-Otu read and critiqued much earlier versions of this chapter, and I warmly thank them for their generous work, guidance and support.
2. Early tourist manuals exalted Niagara's bridges. One manual describes the reaction of Red Jacket, an important Seneca chief and orator, to American settlers' successful completion of a bridge joining the mainland on the U.S. side to Goat Island: "His mind seemed to be busy both with the past and the present, reflecting upon the vast territory his race once possessed, and intensely conscious of the fact that it was theirs no longer. Apparently mortified, and vexed that its paleface owners should so successfully develop and improve it he rose from his seat, and, uttering the well-known Indian guttural 'Ugh, ugh!' he exclaimed: 'D—n Yankee! d—n Yankee'! Then, gathering his blanket-cloak around him, with his usual dignity and downcast eyes, he slowly walked away, and never returned to the spot" (Holley 1883: 77). This report differs slightly from John Niles Hubbard's historical report (1886: 328–29): "After its [the bridge's] completion, Red Jacket, in company with General Porter, was passing over it one day, when the chief, whose curiosity was excited, examined minutely every part of its

construction, evidently regarding it, as a great wonder. At length discovering the secret, he exclaimed, 'Ugh! still water!' and immediately added, 'd—n Yankee.'" Both examples demonstrate the settler's keen interest in Native reception of their technologies, and by extension, their presumed superiority. Holley's account highlights the significance of the "achievement" of the bridge as a marker of colonial superiority and as a point of tourist interest. Hubbard's, on the other hand, purports to chronicle the noble savagery of Red Jacket as he confronted the so-called inevitable destruction of his nation. This illustrates the conjoined discourses of noble savagery and technological progress.

3. The *Johnson Act* was created to exclude non-white people, specifically South and East Asians from U.S. citizenship. The *American Citizenship Act* of 1924 imposed American citizenship on Indigenous peoples born within U.S. borders. South and East Asians were excluded from U.S. citizenship because they were considered to be unable to assimilate and therefore deemed to be threats to the whiteness of the nation, while the imposition of U.S. citizenship on Indigenous peoples was seen as an important step in the neutralization of Indigenous nationhood and in securing white, American settlement. For a detailed analysis of the *American Citizenship Act*, see Bruyneel (2004). Hauptman and Campisi (1988) offer an exhaustive historical account of the American Chicago Conference, which helped to galvanize pan-American Indian response to the U.S.'s anti-American Indian political and cultural climate.

4. As I explain below, in the 1920s Haudenosaunee activists argued that all Indigenous nations had the right to cross the settler border without restriction. However, U.S. border guards, in their policing of Niagara's bridges, disagreed and refused to permit Indigenous peoples from other nations to cross the bridges into the U.S.

5. "Indian status" is a federal invention, used to define people who are included in the *Indian Act*. See the next chapter in this collection for a more in-depth discussion of the politics of the *Indian Act*.

6. See Wright (1993) and Dickason and McNab (2009) for excellent descriptions of the following attacks on Indigenous governance and diplomacy.

7. The Haudenosaunee system of governance is comprised of chiefs and clan mothers and is rooted in Haudenosaunee political philosophy, namely the Great Law of Peace. In the 1920s, this form of governance replaced *Indian Act*-imposed band councils, and as such, represented a threat to the imposition of settler governance on Indigenous peoples.

8. As recently as 2010 the matter of Indigenous sovereignty and settler nationalisms emerged when the players of the Iroquois National Lacrosse Team, all of whom were travelling with Haudenosaunee passports, were denied visas to the U.K. where the Lacrosse World Championships were held. Ironically, lacrosse is Haudenosaunee, and it is also Canada's official national sport.

9. I have taken this quote out of context: Rickard is specifically responding to the Tuscarora Nation's battle to protect their reservation lands from the New York State Power Authority, which wanted to annex significant portions of those territories to build a hydroelectric power station, replacing the Schoellkopf Power Station, which collapsed into the gorge in 1956.

10. Ali Rattansi (1994) makes a similar argument in his writing on postmodernity, arguing that Western philosophies of postmodernity universalize Western experience and in doing so, neglect the manifestations of power in the lives of others upon which Western postmodernity utterly depends.

11. Monture-Angus's (2002) arguments that colonial homelessness continues within the walls of the academy requires further investigation into justice-oriented pedagogy, recruitment and retention rates of Indigenous students (including graduate students) and faculty. On the organized dismemberment of Indigenous knowledge by school systems, Lee Maracle (1996: 87)

writes: "The desire of our people to gain a foothold in this society is arrogantly interpreted as a desire to be like Europeans. We have never feared or rejected new things, new knowledge. But quite frankly, we do not respect the ways of European CanAmerica. We seek knowledge that we may turn it to our own use. Do not be surprised when I tell you that your knowledge is not the only knowledge we seek."

12. Stuart Hall (Grossberg and Hall 1996: 132) argues against the notion of "postmodernity" as a global phenomenon. According to him, postmodernism is, "in my view, being deployed in an essentialist and uncritical way. And it is irrevocably Euro- or Western-centric in its whole episteme."

13. This is precisely the kind of problem that is central to Paul Gilroy's analysis of racism in Thatcherite Britain (1991). Kobena Mercer (1994) examines the influence of Thatcherism on Black cultural politics in Britain. More locally, Sunera Thobani's (2000) work on policies of exclusion of women of colour from immigration into Canada demystifies the image of the welcoming nation, while Sherene Razack (2004) casts doubt on the validity of the myth of Canadian peacekeeping. These works map the contours of difference and conflict that make and mark Western postmodernity.

14. Not all expressions of diaspora from the Middle Passage are as celebratory as Bhabha's becomes. Glissant considers the Middle Passage as exile into plantation slavery and exile as brutal constraint. This radically recasts relationality in ways that force a vocal reckoning with justice and universalism: "For three centuries of constraint had borne down so hard that, when this speech took root, it sprouted in the very midst of the field of modernity; that is, it grew for everyone. This is the only sort of universality there is: when, from a specific enclosure, the deepest voice cries out" (2000: 74).

15. Many First Nations' oral traditions trace the people's origins to the soil itself. See Monet and Skanu'u (1992) for a critical and creative analysis of the treatment of these oral traditions of the origins of the Gitksan and Wet'suwet'en Nations in the courts.

16. "Reverse racism" relies on the assumption that all social actors are equal. Racism never occurs on an equal social plane; rather, it is dependent on structural inequalities that manifest in systemic violence against racialized people.

Part Three
SYMBOLS OF SAMENESS

Chapter 8

IN THE SHOES OF THE OTHER

Indigenous Authenticities and Colonial Logics of Difference

Damien Lee

> We love to *use them as instruments* to behold ourselves, maintaining thereby a narcissistic relation of me to me, still me and always me. —Trinh T. Minh-ha 1989

The process of defining difference in Canada has long served the state's domination of Indigenous peoples. I have come to understand that, like many things that can be controlled by the dominant group in a colonial context, whoever defines difference holds the power to define the nature of political relationships. In Canada, the defining of difference between settlers[1] and Indigenous peoples has manifested itself in the creation of the image of the Indian — an image imagined in Western consciousness to serve the state's ongoing goal of gaining and maintaining access to resources in Indigenous territories (Lawrence 2003: 6). The state continues to regulate difference by upholding the image of the Indian in legislation, such as the *Indian Act*. In a context where some of our people have been colonized into accepting that the image of the Indian is the only authentic way to be Cree, Anishinabe, etc., reclaiming difference must move beyond the Western tools available to us. How do we move away from the image of the Indian and other logics of difference regulated by the settler state without re-centring Eurocentric thinking?

Colonialism works so well in part because it establishes back doors in our minds that we do not even know are there, often reproducing colonial logics even when we mean to critique them (Lawrence 2003: 18, 24). For example, some Indigenous individuals, in particular Indigenous men, have reasserted colonial logics of difference to protect what little separation exists between Indigenous peoples and settler society, even if this has meant performing the role of the Indian or oppressing Indigenous women (13–25). Yet indigenist[2] scholars have been addressing the paradoxes of reproducing colonialism in a number of ways: some, including myself, argue that our decolonization must be based in the intellectual and political traditions unique to our individual nations. However, this has led to discussions about authenticity where we face a plethora of conundrums, including how to explain indigeneity without putting it on trial for settlers (22–23) and ultimately how to define our differences from settler society without legitimizing in any way the image of the Indian that is regulated *by* the state, *for* settlers.

The concept of the moccasin or, in Anishinabemowin,[3] makazin,[4] has become important to my personal decolonization process. In this, my nokomis,[5] Geraldine MacLaurin-ba, who I called "grams," was pivotal. While my grams had her own identity that inevitably took on elements of Western culture, she was still Anishinabekwe — an Anishinabe woman. After years of trying to makazinan, and with no one able to teach her, she had a dream in the late 1950s through which this knowledge came to her. While the colonized context she grew up in demanded that she at times minimize her Anishinabe identity, her dream delivered some Anishinabe knowledge at a time when it was safer for her to be an Anishinabe woman. From then on, she made and sold her makazinan, and she taught others in my community her design. I remember her giving me several pairs of makazinan as gifts throughout my childhood. In 2010, exactly one year before she passed away, she gave me a different gift: she taught me how to make the makazin from her dream. For two weeks we sat in her kitchen on our reserve — Fort William First Nation — and drove around the city of Thunder Bay, Ontario, talking about her unique makazin design. It became my responsibility to respect that knowledge and dream through coming-to-know the essence of what that knowledge means in the context of my own life.

I use the example of my training in how to make makazinan here to discuss how settlers support the state's regulated Indian image in ways that maintain dominance over Indigenous peoples in Canada. I argue that settlers reify the state's regulation of indigeneity by producing and wearing material objects that express the colonized image of indigeneity — the Indian — thereby obfuscating Indigenous peoples through commodifying the Indian image, or materially manifesting the logics of difference regulated by the state. While material products that embody Indian imagery alone are not the cause of the continued dominance, my analysis of such products demonstrates how the state regulates Indian imagery and how settlers manifest that imagery at the cost of Indigenous peoples' political and cultural presence in their own territories.

DEFINING DIFFERENCES

The image of the Indian has defined differences between Indigenous peoples and settlers in Canada for generations. Scholars such as Linda Tuhiwai Smith (1999), James Blaut (1993) and James Sákéj Youngblood Henderson (2000a) have shown that this image is an invention of European ethnocentrism; when European explorers and settlers interacted with non-European peoples, such as Indigenous peoples in Canada, these interactions were recorded and relayed back to Europe through the only lens they had to work with: European eyes. This way of defining difference between Europeans and others, in this case Indigenous peoples, served Western interests, which in the case of present-day Canada meant accessing resources in Indigenous peoples' territories. Difference was defined in a binary framework and assigned either positive or negative values: where Europeans were inventive, others could only imitate; where Europeans were rational, others used instinct and emotion and were irrational; where Europeans had science, others had sorcery; where Europeans had the maturity of civilization, others were children in need of teaching (Blaut 1993: 17).

Each of these differences not only gives primacy to Europeans, but the binaries of difference are framed in such a way as to assign inferior values to anything other than

Europeanness (Henderson 2000a: 65–70). There is almost no way for racialized others, or in this case, Indigenous peoples, to escape the negativity assigned to their ways of being in this framework of difference. For example, whereas Indigenous peoples have their own forms of science, these were labelled "sorcery" by Eurocentric thinkers because such forms do not fit seamlessly into Eurocentric definitions of science (Blaut 1993: 17). Indigenous sciences are re-classified as utterly *non-scientific* and assigned negative connotations, because they fall outside of Eurocentrism's basic tenets of positivism and objectivism. Indigenous ways of knowing the world are just as valid as Western ways, but due to the ways in which the binaries are constructed and totalized, no room is left for discussing Indigenous sciences without recasting them as inferior to Eurocentric ways of knowing, thereby implicitly leaving colonialism intact. For example, Indigenous peoples' botanical knowledge has historically been mined by colonizers, and in the process, colonizers fostered the idea that such knowledge was inferior to their own, leading to the destruction of Indigenous knowledge systems (Geniusz 2009: 3). While this example is about botanical knowledge, it demonstrates a superior/inferior binary that colonizers have applied broadly to Indigenous peoples and their knowledges (Smith 1999): even forms of knowledge that were deemed less "savage" (and therefore more "civilized") according to colonizers would still ultimately be a form of "primitive" knowledge, thus inferior to European science. European science always reproduces itself as superior to Indigenous knowledges in these ways.

Eurocentric thought positions the West above all non-European peoples, creating a perpetual binary of civilization and savagery. Due to this way of thinking, Europeans deemed themselves not only "civilized" but at the apex of civilization, where other peoples in the world could only be defined in relation to how they measured up to the European. European thought developed the idea of civilization as the antithesis of living in a state of nature, for to be in a state of nature, argued early European scholars such as Hobbes, was to be in a state of constant chaos and war, with no laws or systems of government to organize human communities in ways that protected a person's property and autonomy (Henderson 2000b: 17). Indigenous peoples were cast in the role of the savage, the uncivilized, to allow Europeans to contrast themselves as civilized. The idea of a civilized Western state therefore requires that Indigenous peoples remain in an uncivilized state, close to nature, and without European cultural, political or technological contamination (to be "contaminated" would disrupt the civilized-savage binary, and thus upset the colonizer's "civilized" self-image).

These binary ways of defining difference continue to be problematic for many Indigenous peoples. For example, in the Anishinabe context, a position from which I write, having our relationship to lands caricatured in a way that renders us as "stuck" in a state of nature is dehumanizing. Our worldview positions everything we do in a reciprocal ecological relationship; respecting this relationship is always implied in the essence of Anishinabe actions. This means that to be Anishinabe, which for me is to be human, my relationship with the ecology is broader than fulfilling the role of a "noble savage" simply to allow colonizers to define themselves. Being Anishinabe for me is in part living according to the teachings that arose from generations of people living with the land in relationships that constantly demanded innovation, invention and honourable governance. These innovations and ways of being shaped a specific Anishinabe identity, in a specific place along the northwestern shore of Lake Superior. Yet, Canadian colonialism dehumanizes my family and my wider community by assigning the label "uncivilized" to us because our relationship to the land differs from Western notions of relating to land. But I engage in decolonizing myself by re-centring Anishinabe teachings in my everyday actions in order to live a more human existence within Anishinabe aki.[6] To do otherwise is to suppress my humanity in the name of becoming "civilized," which is the same as serving the Canadian settler state by perpetuating my own colonization.

Whereas differences do exist between Indigenous peoples and the settler society, part of the colonial context today is that the differences defined by the state always renew settlers' colonial privileges. For example, the state's creation and continued assertion of the category "Indian" as a race-based form of determining difference situates Indigenous peoples within the state's regulatory objectives, one being the legislating away of Indigenous peoples' claims to their territories and forms of governance so that settlers can benefit from the wealth generated from Indigenous territories. In discussing a piece by Janice Acoose, Bonita Lawrence (2003: 5, emphasis in original) writes:

> Being classified by the Canadian government as a status Indian under the Indian Act represented a violation of the rights of [Acoose's] Cree/Métis and Saulteaux cultures to define her as *Nehiowe* or *Nahkawe*, which removed her, in common-sense ways, from any sense of being part of the destiny of her own nation(s) and instead placed her as a powerless and racialized individual at the bottom of the hierarchy of Eurocanadian society. For Indigenous peoples, to be defined as a race is synonymous with having our Nations dismembered.

Lawrence and Acoose point to how the very system of difference used by the Canadian settler state is constructed in such a way as to reproduce Eurocentric epistemological and axiological underpinnings whenever the state's logics of difference are employed. For example, reclaiming Anishinabe ways of determining "citizenship" by using race-based logics of difference, as found in the *Indian Act*, would only serve to re-centre the state's logics of defining difference within Indigenous peoples' cultural and political resurgences, as is the case with several Anishinabe communities in Ontario that are reclaiming control of their membership by merely employing *Indian Act* logics such as blood quantum and paternal heredity.[7]

The image of the Indian is based on Eurocentric interpretations of indigeneity that sometimes overlap in paradoxical ways. On the one hand, Indians are conceptualized as childlike, drunks, criminals and a whole series of other descriptors that position them as living in perpetual chaos, quite unlike "civilized" settler society. On the other hand, Indians are positioned as having close connections to the natural landscapes in what is currently known as Canada, and while this supposedly means they lack civilization, it also means that on some level the state recognizes that Indigenous peoples have a legitimate claim to their national territories even if this claim is only recognized by the state when Indigenous peoples are forced to conform to roles[8] prescribed to them by the state as Indians. This is complicated by the history of political relationships the British Crown and subsequent Canadian governments have had with Indigenous peoples, such as the treaty order, demonstrating that earlier settlers recognized Indigenous peoples' governance and leadership systems and, therefore, that Indigenous peoples are more "civilized" than Canada's official civilizing narratives have traditionally allowed (for such narratives play on the superior-inferior binary in order to justify and obfuscate the state's historical expropriation of lands, political interference and residential school genocide). Conceptualizing Indigenous peoples in such polarized ways — that is, as either the indigene of society or the deeply spiritual, natural other — while also recognizing that such concepts do not explain the existence of Indigenous peoples' highly developed political and legal systems, has necessitated the image of the Indian. The Indian image is regulated to ensure settlers can assign what they need to it in order to serve their own interests.

Settlers in Canada, similar to the philosophers of the seventeenth- and eighteenth-centuries who needed an uncivilized antithesis to define their own civility, need the image of the Indian to define their Canadianness. For example, in the early colonization period, settlers rigidly defined differences between themselves and Indigenous peoples in order to maintain solidarity within settlements (Lawrence 2003: 8).[9] With the mixing of settler and Indigenous individuals through marriage and sexual relations, however, came new problems of difference for settlers to solve, as now it was not so simple to differentiate between settlers and Indigenous people. It is for this reason that governments of Upper and Lower Canada in 1850 invented the legal definition of who is an Indian along gendered lines:[10]

> Social control was predicated on legally identifying who was "white," who was "Indian," and which children were legitimate progeny; citizens rather than subjugated "Natives" (Stoler 1991: 53). Clearly, if the mixed-race offspring of white men who married Native women were to inherit property, they had to be legally classified as white. Creating the legal category of "status Indian" enabled the settler society to create the fiction of a Native person who was by law no longer Native, whose offspring could be considered white. Because of the racist patriarchal framework governing white identities, European women who married Native men were considered to have stepped outside the social boundaries of whiteness. They became, officially, status Indians. (Lawrence 2003: 8)

In other words, regulating Indigenous identities through the image of the Indian created and commodified race-based differences according to Eurocentric thought. The image of the Indian vested the power to determine difference in the state, enabling the state to go so far as to change a person's "race" from Indian to White, or from White to Indian to suit the patriarchal, colonial interests of particularly elite male settlers.

Canada enacted legislation to embody and entrench this racism in the state itself. While such racist sentiments towards Indigenous peoples were a fundamental part of the earliest colonial periods, the first *Indian Act*, of 1876, consolidated these ideas into official legislation. The *Act* has changed several times since then, but its role remains the same, namely, to enable Canada to dominate Indigenous peoples based on its own intentions instead of interacting with them to fulfill its responsibilities embodied either in existing treaties or in accordance with the fact that Indigenous peoples have inherent sovereignty that necessitates nation-to-nation relationships.

Today, the *Indian Act* continues to define who is an "Indian" based on race or what has been called notional blood quantum.[11] Section 2(1) of the *Indian Act, 1985*, defines an Indian as "a person who pursuant to this *Act* is registered as an Indian or is entitled to be registered as an Indian" (Government of Canada 1985). Section 6 of the *Act* determines a person's eligibility for registration, which is determined by notional blood quantum: if a person has enough Indian blood, which is determined by descent in ways that favour the paternal line, they might be registered under section 6(1) of the *Act*, meaning they will be able to pass on Indian status to their children (especially if they are a man) (Palmater 2011: 34). Those with 50 percent Indian blood or less might be registered as a status Indian under section 6(2) of the *Act*, which means they are not allowed to pass on status. Of course, status Indians do not exclusively marry other status Indians, so the number of status Indians being born with 6(1) status, or those who can pass their Indian status onto their children, is decreasing. Those people from Indigenous nations who do not have enough Indian blood according to the *Indian Act, 1985,* might be considered non-status Indians, to whom Canada owes no responsibilities in terms of treaty rights, Aboriginal rights or cultural programs and services (Palmater 2011: 47). Looking at this broadly, it is clear that there will be no status Indians left within a few generations (see Palmater 2011: 46). Thus, regulating who is entitled to Indian status is suspect, as the state is clearly in the business of fostering the legislative extinction of Indigenous peoples (29).

This is important because for many people today, being a status Indian has become conflated with being an Indigenous person due to generations of interference by the state. As Palmater (2011: 23) argues, "traditional ways of determining identity and belonging have been twisted to meet legislated rules in order to satisfy unrelated factors, such as Canada's funding restrictions or a band's own financial predicament." Whereas the state regulates Indian identity through the race-based logics of the *Indian Act*, which Indigenous peoples do not control, Indian status has become tied to being an Indigenous person as far as the state is concerned. In order to access the rights and resources according to existing treaties and/or Aboriginal rights, which include "land, natural resources, and seats at self-government negotiating tables, the real question is not whether one is a citizen of the Mi'kmaq, Cree, or Mohawk, but whether one is an Indian and a band member" (Palmater 2011: 39). The ultimate goal of the state regulating difference through the Indian image is thus to assimilate Indigenous peoples into the dominant society as Aboriginal Canadians who in only a few generations will not be able to claim their rights supposedly protected in the *Indian Act*. The *Act* itself is legally erasing the very people it purports to protect.[12]

The state has made significant headway towards this legislated extinction. As Lawrence (2003: 6) points out: "By 1985 there were twice as many non-status Indians and Métis as status Indians in Canada." As another example, the state has not yet recognized me as a status Indian based on my customary adoption — something that occurred according to how my grams and my father interpreted Anishinabe "adoption" laws when I was a one-year-old baby. This, despite the fact that Anishinabe have specific ways of adopting people in accordance with their own forms of self-determination; when adopted into the Anishinabe nation, people become Anishinabe regardless of their race (Auger 2001: 177–202; Atkinson 2010: 51).

Born in the 1930s, my grams lived through a time when Canada was making strident attempts at committing genocide against Indigenous peoples through its partnership with various Christian churches in the residential schools era. Though her parents kept her from residential school, the time period demanded that Anishinabek be careful about their identity. Before my grams was born, her father adopted non-Indigenous children through Anishinabe custom when he married a woman from Europe — these children became Anishinabe according to Anishinabe laws. Yet, due to how the state and settler society viewed Indigenous peoples throughout her childhood and adult years, my grams had to take on some Western ways of thinking and doing in order to survive in other parts of life. She and her family, and subsequently my immediate family, had to take on the image of the Indian to do simple things like live on our reserve and to access the rights we are entitled to through the Robinson Superior Treaty of 1850. Whereas customary adoption was recognized as a way for individuals to be entitled to registration as a status Indian in the original *Indian Act, 1876*, by 1980, when I was born, the state's position on customary adoption was that it did not entitle adoptees to registration as a status Indian, despite sections of the *Act* that should have protected customary adoption as an Aboriginal right (Gilbert 1996: 76–77).[13] That said, while I was made a part of the Anishinabek nation when my family chose to care for me and to protect me as one of their own, the chances of me being given access to my community's land to build a home someday are limited, as are my chances of accessing the other treaty rights my ancestors reserved for me, such as participating in Anishinabe self-governance or the ability to pass these rights on to my children, because my community still uses the *Indian Act* to determine who "officially" belongs. In the eyes of the Government of Canada I am not permitted to participate in the affairs of my community in an "official" way,[14] despite the fact that the settlers my ancestors treatied with now exploit the resources we were meant to share.

Whereas the state encroaches on Indigenous peoples' identities by inventing and wielding the image of the Indian for its own purposes, settlers also encroach(ed) on that identity and our territories to the point that the perceived differences between Indians and settlers needed to be secured. Political leaders thought Indigenous peoples needed to be protected from the corrupting elements of settler society, an idea imbued with the notion that indigeneity is predicated on purity of blood lines and cultural norms. Securing this difference was enshrined in subsection 91(24) of the *Constitution Act, 1867* — the part of Canada's Constitution in which the federal government assumes control of Indians in a paternal and arbitrary manner, giving rise to the creation of the *Indian Act* in 1876.[15] The final report of the Royal Commission on Aboriginal Peoples (RCAP) (1996) demonstrates that Canada's Indian policies are a mix of protection, civilization and assimilation ideologies. Before Confederation, the British Crown felt that Indigenous peoples needed its protection from settlers who were encroaching on Indigenous communities and territories. The British Crown considered Indigenous nations as valuable commercial and military allies, subsequently developing policies to protect Indigenous peoples from the influx of settlers, respecting, for example, the lands that Indigenous peoples who treatied with the Crown reserved for their exclusive use (RCAP 1996: 9.3).

However, the British eventually sought to "civilize" Indigenous peoples, particularly after they were no longer needed by the British Crown as military allies. To "civilize" Indigenous peoples, British policies were developed to "help" Indigenous peoples learn how to become farmers and tradespeople, and were implemented with the help of missionaries (9.4). Other colonialists, viewing Indigenous peoples as impossible to civilize, argued for the abandonment of civilizing policies, instead promoting the concept of "protecting" Indigenous peoples by removing them from settler society altogether (9.3).[16] Later, others developed official policies for assimilation as a means to allow Indigenous peoples to enjoy "full citizenship" in the settler society, which combined the notions of "protection" and "assimilation" into the idea of the Indian: Indigenous peoples could be included in settler society as Indians regulated by the *Indian Act*, while doing so in a way that maintained state-defined difference between settlers and Indigenous peoples. This notion of protection was threaded into the fabric of the *Indian Act* so that the *Act* could be used to protect Indigenous peoples *until* they were ready to become part of settler society, that is, *until* they were deemed civilized.

Within this brutally assimilationist context, the Indian image became a way to maintain Indigenous difference, even though the image is paradoxically based directly in assimilationist policy. Indigenous peoples sometimes are forced to employ the Indian image in order to protect their Indigenous identities and their lands. This is another layer of colonialism because Indigenous peoples are then forced to define *themselves* as the Indians the state and settlers want to see. Lawrence (2003: 21) notes:

> Not the least of the problem is that we still live under conditions of colonization, where it is vital for Native people to practice some sort of boundary to maintain Indian land in Indian hands — but where traditional forms of regulating who was or who was not a member of a Native society have been deliberately and viciously suppressed. In the interests of survival, communities often find it safer to maintain "the devil they know," embracing colonial frameworks about Native identity because they represent tried and true ways of maintaining boundaries against white society.

This is further complicated by how Canadian colonialism works: to access treaty rights such as certain resources as well as to be protected from settler society through Canadian laws, one has to be recognized as an Indian according to Canada's race-based logics of determining difference. Difference is thus regulated by making Indigenous peoples play the role of the Indian to access treaty rights, *on the state's terms*.

In critiquing the state's regulation of Indigenous difference through the enforcement of the Indian image, it is imperative that we do so in a way that does not rely on the "binary essentialisms" designed by the state and Western thought, as this would lead "us back to the very stereotypes we are resisting" (LaRocque 2010: 139). However, if we are not using the state's versions of essentialism and authenticity, how do we define Indigenous authenticity in ways that honour Indigenous traditions while also reclaiming difference in ways that promote Indigenous peoples' self-determination?

DIFFERING AUTHENTICITIES

What makes the Indian real is how settlers manifest the idea of the Indian in material forms. For instance, settlers often produce consumer goods and products expressing the colonized Indian image for other settlers. While there are Indigenous peoples who engage in making products for sale to settlers and Indigenous peoples alike, here I am speaking about the mass-produced products that give expression to the generic Indian image that displaces Indigenous peoples, their political struggles with the Canadian state and their very authenticity, such as mass-produced "moccasins."

One of the most useful written pieces I have found about Indigenous authenticity is Manulani Meyer's (2004) doctoral dissertation. Her discussion about the authenticity of Indigenous Hawaiian epistemology is useful in discussing Indigenous authenticity in the Canadian context. In both locations authenticity (and ways to determine authenticity) is questioned by settler society when it is claimed by Indigenous peoples. Further, there is a strong similarity between Hawaii and Canada in that generations of Native Hawaiians have now been forced to interact with settlers and hegemonic state governments, with much of that interaction over the past century characterized by the state and settlers asserting their control and culture onto Native Hawaiians against their will and against their sovereignty (Trask 1999: 87–97).

Meyer argues that there is an authentic Indigenous Hawaiian culture despite generations of colonial impacts, and that living an Indigenous life today is meaningless if one is not encouraged to change and grow. Our cultures are not crystalized in some pre-contact time — this line of argument inevitably leads nowhere because we cannot (and many of us would not) go back in time; Indigenous peoples have contemporary authenticity, found in renewing ourselves in contemporary contexts. She accepts the idea that cultural exchanges have happened, but that these exchanges do not undermine Indigenous Hawaiian authenticity. Meyer argues that accepting such exchanges as part of our authenticity does not mean we are automatically assimilated. Drawing on Cornel West's thoughts regarding cultural representation, Meyer (2004: 83) demonstrates that the go-it-alone approach — an "extreme rejectionist perspective that shuns the mainstream" — is "Impossible to sustain if one is to grow, as some dialogue with community is necessary." She advocates a more organic way of approaching the arena of culture, where one "stays attuned to the best of what the mainstream has to offer, while clearly being aligned with [keeping] alive potent traditions of critique and resistance" (83).

For Meyer, culture is defined as the best practices of a people over time in a specific place (188). This means that in a colonized context, culture has adapted but remains authentic, even though settlers sometimes claim that Indigenous peoples are "inventing culture" when cultural changes disrupt the myth that Indigenous cultures are frozen at the time of contact. Transcending such denigrating and racist arguments, Meyer contends that cultural authenticity is defined through the lens of one's culture, where practices and ways of being and knowing are defined as authentic according to the norms and teachings of that culture, which are constantly shifting; put simply, culture defines culture. I take this to mean that cultural authenticity is defined in a colonized context by Indigenous peoples themselves, relying on culturally based traditions of discernment. For me, culture includes the traditions and ways of living a people embodies as a result of their ongoing, constantly changing relationship with the ecology. Moving towards a decolonized future in ways that do not reproduce colonial thinking does not mean simply accepting everything as it is and calling it "authentic," but rather it is a process of re-placing our peoples and traditions at the centre of our thoughts and actions while recognizing that we and our ancestors exercised agency despite colonialism in choosing to take on certain aspects of Western culture that made/make sense within our cultural worldviews. The task then becomes teasing out those aspects of the colonial mentality[17] that we do not want in our lives.

Emma LaRocque (2010: 137–38) outlines some of the ways that discussions about authenticity can be co-opted to re-centre the state's visions of how difference should be defined through the image of the Indian. For her, authenticity demands that we be different from settler society, but she questions by whose definitions we are authentic and different. If our difference is defined only by settlers or the state, our own ways of defining ourselves are silenced. Authenticity is not about living in a way found only in the prehistoric past; it recognizes that cultural exchanges *have* taken place over 500 years of interactions between Indigenous peoples and settler society. She questions whether difference even matters to our authenticity, asking "What if we were not different but still original to this land? What is the colonizer's agenda for keeping us different?" (138). LaRocque shows us that difference can become a commodity for settlers and the state to assert Canada's domination over Indigenous peoples; this is done, in part, by imagining and reifying the Indian.

My grams taught me one way that Anishinabe culture acts as a lens through which to discern what is Anishinabe culture. When she taught me to make makazinan, the pairs I made looked exactly like the ones she gave me when I was a child for Christmas presents and birthdays. In learning how to make them, however, I had to embody the dream she had in the 1950s. Otherwise, if my makazinan did not embody the essence of that dream perfectly, they were not "right," they were not authentic expressions of *her* dream. Each time I had to re-stitch the makazin after making a mistake, I had to pay closer attention to her description of the dream. Each detail was already given, I had only to learn it.

What makes makazinan authentic is the fact that they embody our relationships with our territories and other Anishinabek. Makazinan are something more than simply a material object. As Betasamosake notes:

> For me, making makazinan is much more than actually just making the makazinan. Anishinaabeg people need new makazinan at certain times of year — to dance the manomin in the fall, or when they are dancing out of a fasting ceremony, for instance. New babies are given their first pair of makazinan with a small hole in them, so that they will always wear out their makazinan and have a good, long life. Makazinan making then, is an important way of acknowledging and celebrating life stages, ceremonies, and seasonal activities. In order to begin, I must have strong relationships to the land or to people who have strong relationships to the land — otherwise, I cannot get the appropriate materials.
>
> Making makazinan really begins with a hunter putting semaa down and asking for a deer or moose to give up his or her life. There is a lot of intricate environmental and spiritual knowledge involved in tracking and hunting moose

or deer. There is a lot of complex knowledge in processing the hide into a usable material. So in order to have the appropriate materials to make makazinan, I need to either possess this knowledge or have a strong relationship to someone who does. I also must have a strong relationship with (usually) an Anishinaabekwe artist and knowledge holder.

Making makazinan in an Anishinaabeg way cannot be learned online or from a book. One needs to have a respectful, reciprocal, long-term relationship with someone who is a master makazinan maker. That way, one will be able to learn and understand the philosophical, metaphorical and conceptual knowledge embedded in designs and in the stitching together of leather. For instance, when done in the correct way, the stitching together of two pieces of leather binds those two pieces together to create a new object, in essence the stitching is an act of transformation, and can be thought of as a metaphor for family. Beading has similar meaning. The word for bead, "manidoominens," means "little spirit," and the complex patterns and designs of the beadwork often encode all of these relationships in a storied form. To me, making makazinan stitches the maker to the land, to our language, to our ancient stories and traditions. To me, makazinan hold our traditions, our knowledge, our connections to our territories and to our connections to Elders. They mark our ceremonies and seasons, and they hold our stories — and all of this knowledge is under the sovereignty of Anishinaabekwewag.[18]

Clearly, makazinan connect Anishinabek to places, knowledge systems and ways of relating that cannot be reproduced by purchasing a mass-produced "moccasin" that intentionally employs Eurocentric projections of Indianness.

Embodied in mass-produced "moccasins" are the logics of difference that manifest the Indian image. While these products may look like makazinan, they are at best representations of what settlers think of makazinan, as they lack peoples' reciprocal relationships to territories. Again, makazinan embody a deep and broad collective relationship to the land that cannot be picked up and reproduced simply to make money without compromising and/or recolonizing Indigenous peoples in the process. These "moccasins," like the invented Indian image, mock Indigenous peoples by controlling a symbol of indigeneity that is actually a production of what settler logics of difference consider a makazin to be. For this reason, I call these "moccasins" *mockasins* — a reproduction of the Indian image that aids settlers in mocking Indigenous presences in our territories by displacing us, forcing Western forms of governance systems in our communities and then pillaging our lands.

This mocking can be likened to a mirror image. While LaRocque (2010: 168) discusses Indigenous peoples as mirroring back to settler society the problems it has forced on Indigenous nations, I use the concept of the mirror in a different way. A mirror does two things: it reflects an image projected onto it, while also obfuscating what lies behind it. It is "considered an instrument of self-knowledge … [and] bears a magical character that has always transcended its functional nature. In this encounter of I with I, the power of identification is often such that reality and appearance merge while the tool itself becomes invisible" (Minh-ha 1989: 22). In this light, the mockasin is both a mirror in the sense that settlers no longer question its origins or political impacts on Indigenous peoples and their on-going political struggles and resistances, while also being the mirror image of what settlers project indigeneity to be. In the case of the former, the mockasin as a mirror becomes invisible to settlers as, in Henderson's (2000a: 60) words, these misrepresentations "gain acceptance without supporting evidence [because] they are properly Eurocentric." The interplay between the invisible mirror and the reflected image silences Indigenous peoples, as it is the infinite reflection of the Indian that settlers see, drowning out the authenticity of Indigenous peoples: appropriating Indigenous images and rendering them into Indian form thus enables settler society to engage "in a conversation with itself, using First Nations people to measure itself, to define who it is or is not" (Crosby 1991: 271). The relationship settlers have with the Indian image renders Indigenous peoples voiceless in settler society, exemplified by how Canada and Canadians maintain that they know what is best for Indigenous peoples through the development of failed Indian policy after failed Indian policy.

Indeed, as Sarah Hunt (2011: n.p.) notes in an online article, replacing Indigenous images with Indian images obfuscates the identities of authentic Indigenous peoples, their authentic struggles and their authentic relationships to land. The images act as a mirror that obfuscates Indigenous peoples and their historical struggles against the Canadian state. Hunt tells settlers: "For close to 100 years, in an effort to get rid of 'the Indian problem' in Canada, the *Indian Act* made it illegal for us to practice our traditions" because settlers' ancestors "wanted to obliterate us in order to clear up the land for colonial expansion." She reminds settlers of how they are contributing to colonialism in Canada today:

> Separating native people from our culture, and the politics and history from the images, serves to erase us. It makes it easier for native people like me ... to remain marginalized and silent while our imagery becomes a consumer object as part of mainstream culture. This is an old tactic, part of broader political efforts to forget the history of colonialism upon which this country is founded.

While some might say that wearing mockasins is not such a big deal, the fact remains that such an act mocks the Indigenous peoples who have struggled to keep the authentic images alive as manifestations of cultures that settlers' ancestors tried to destroy. As Hunt argues, mockasins might be considered "trendy" by settler society at the moment and wearing them might even help to assuage settler guilt about their continued occupation of Indigenous territories.

It might be a surprise to some settlers when they find out wearing mockasins is making it harder for Indigenous peoples to reclaim their identities from the regulated Indian image now being reified on the bodies of settlers. This reification occurs when wearing Indian images, which moves "ideas from brains to bodies, from the realm of abstraction to the physical world of concrete experience," which, when witnessed by other settlers, renews and entrenches the image of the Indian "as a marker of essential [North] Americanness" (Deloria 1998: 184).

Through making makazinan with my grams I was able to use the knowledge she gave me to discern authenticity in a new way. I was able to discern among different types of makazinan as well as between makazinan and mockasins. For example, other makazinan from our area have different designs, but they are still Anishinabe makazinan because they are grounded in cultural practices that connect them to that specific part of Anishinabe aki. My grams' design is unique: the way the "tongue" of her makazin is sewn is different than other designs in our territory. The tongue of most other makazinan I have seen in the north shore of Lake Superior area is often cut so that there is an excess of leather that is then sewn under the edges of the front and side walls of the slipper, requiring the tongue leather to be bunched up at short intervals. Bunching up the excess of the tongue leather and sewing it into the walls like this makes a distinct "pucker" design, sort of like if you tucked a shirt slightly too big for you into your belt-line — more bunchy than pleated pants, but still bunched enough to make the leather look slightly like puckered lips. Most designs I have seen achieve the *pucker* (an art unto its own) by sewing the excess leather into place while the unfinished makazin is still turned inside-out. When turned right side-out, if done properly, the pucker is a neat bunching that emerges from the side and front walls, which can be further decorated with beadwork or other materials.

However, my grams' makazinan are different in that the pucker is achieved not by sewing it into place while the makazin is inside out. Rather, the pucker is achieved by sewing it into place when the makazin is right side-out. This process still results in a pucker, but also a crown along the seam, as the excess tongue leather and the side walls bunch and shoot upwards as they are not sewn under themselves; the rest of the makazin is mostly the same as other makazinan I have seen from around the north shore of Lake Superior. Neither one form of makazin is more Anishinabe than the other — both are Anishinabe. In the case of my grams', hers are Anishinabe not only because she was Anishinabe, but also because that knowledge came to her from the spiritual world of the lands around our reserve and was renewed within her familial and community relationships.

When settlers consume products that mock indigeneity, they commoditize our relationships with our lands while also obfuscating our identities as place-based peoples. Disconnecting us from our territories to exploit resources is central to the state's larger project of regulating Indian images and identities; settlers help to reify the state's regulated Indian image by materially asserting this image in the physical spaces where Indigenous resistance struggles have always taken place, such as the streets of any town or city in Canada.

INVISIBILIZING INDIGENOUS PEOPLES

Lost in the consumption of Indian logics of difference are Indigenous peoples. The mockasin resembles the authentic image, but is never fully accurate because it is a copy produced through a Eurocentric lens, which can never fully understand indigeneity.[19] While the products might look similar, the processes are not the same. In the case of Indians and mockasins replacing Indigenous peoples and makazinan in settler consciousness, the fact that Indigenous peoples exist beyond the image of the Indian becomes forgotten or at least invisibilized. However, settlers still need the images that originate within Indigenous peoples' relationships to their territories: for colonial domination to be complete in Canada, settlers must also become Indians (Deloria 1998), literally trying to move into the mirror. In other words, settlers seek to be in the shoes of the other.

Making Indian images allows settlers to purchase those images and wear them on their bodies in an attempt to "Indigenize" themselves to the Canadian landscape. Goldie (1989: 13) defines Indigenization as the settler's "need to become 'native,' to belong here … in Canada…. A peculiar word [suggesting] the impossible necessity of becoming indigenous." Philip Deloria (1998: 120) discusses this process not as imitation, but of literally becoming the Indian, or the mirror, in a mimetic process:

> Mimesis seems to insist that Self and Other are, in fact, the same. Mimesis was not simply the copying of something Other. Rather, [settlers attempting to Indigenize themselves] imitated and appropriated the Other viscerally through the medium of their bodies…. The channeling of mimetic contact with an Other through one's body forced it into concrete social, political and cultural realities, where it helped define individual and group identities.

The makazinan knowledge my grams passed on to me enables me to critique settler commodification of our differences. The process of learning how to make makazinan not only enabled me to discern between Anishinabek makazinan, but also between authentic makazinan and mockasins. In renewing her dream in my hands, I had to renew the essence of the knowledge my grams saw, even if what she dreamt included useful elements of Western culture, including plastic beads, processed leather and a synthetic liner. Applying this to difference, settlers engaging in consuming Indianness attempt to blur the lines between themselves as settlers and the image of the Indian as a projection of Canadianness. They are attempting to become the projection of Indianness, which is not Indigenous at all.

Deloria discusses settlers' paradoxical need for accessible Indian identities. Settlers involved with state-building needed to assert differences between colonial societies and Europe and looked to the Indian image as "a revolutionary identity, drawing on the deeply rooted power of familiar ideologies surrounding Native Americans" (Deloria 1998: 20). He goes on to show that this need ultimately necessitates the absence of Indigenous peoples, for "in order to complete their rite of passage" from Europe to North America, Americans had to displace Indigenous peoples in one way or another (1998: 36). The image of the Indian, though constructed and regulated by settlers and the state, thus came to represent both Indigenous peoples and settlers within settler consciousness (36). The paradox is that settlers need their representations of Indigenous peoples (i.e., the Indian) in an accessible form in order to establish a distinct Canadian identity, while at the same time there is no way for Canadian identity to come to fruition so long as Indigenous peoples exist, their presence implicitly challenging the image of the Indian as a misrepresentation (37).

In this light, the goal of the settler interested in Indigenization is not to *imitate* the reflection of the Indian in order to gain Canadianness, but it is instead to *become* the mirror itself to "emit" an Indian and therefore Canadian identity by removing all differences between themselves and Indianness. The function of the mockasin is thus to give settlers an opportunity to become the image they have created. Mockasins are consumed as part of settlers' Indigenization processes.

Reclaiming Indigenous identities requires that we recognize that settlers have invented images of Indigenous peoples in the form of the Indian, which are then used for their own goals. While they consume those images, they impact us because the state controls who can access treaty rights and other aspects of our nation-to-nation relationship; the erosion of difference based on the reification of the Indian helps to legitimate the state's assertion that Indigenous peoples are actually just Aboriginal Canadians — Indians — who do not have a nation-to-nation relationship with the state.

CONCLUSION

To echo Emma LaRocque (2010: 138) again, when difference is defined for us by the Canadian state and settlers, such definitions must be held suspect for who and what they serve. Like LaRocque, I ask whose interests are being served when the Indian image is so tenaciously clung to by the Canadian settler state. Clearly, the state's interests in silencing and undermining Indigenous peoples are at play in creating and reifying the Indian image.

The process of making makazinan has shown me one way to determine authenticity within the Anishinabe context, allowing me also to discern appropriation of Anishinabe cultural images for what they are: tools used by settler society to further entrench Canadian colonialism. Reclaiming differences that work *for* us rather than *against* us requires reasserting our authenticity, which for me was accomplished in part by learning how to make makazinan; it showed me how to discern authenticity through living it. I was picking up a piece of our culture that was almost lost in my family. The experience renewed my relationship with my broader family and community, as now others are coming to me to learn the design, thereby in part renewing their own identity as Anishinabek.

What I have tried to show here is that the Indian image is not only regulated by the state, but that the state requires settlers to take up that image by wearing it. This creates a number of problems for reclaiming differences in a way that supports Indigenous peoples' anti-colonialism, as not only do we need to assert our differences in a positive way, we also have to reclaim the very way that difference is defined. Authenticity is often the next step in demonstrating our differences; but authenticity has become a site of decolonization as well, since claims of authenticity are often called into question for inventing culture, as if Indigenous cultures are not allowed to change if they are to remain authentically Indigenous. It then becomes even more imperative for Indigenous peoples to not employ colonizing tools to reclaim our difference. Indeed, we have our own ways to define difference that are often right in front of us.

NOTES

1. In this chapter, settler is defined as any person who is living within an Indigenous people's territory and is not living according to the laws and political systems of those people. Being a settler is not based on race; it is based on the way one lives one's life, meaning one is living-out a settler existence when one is privileging Eurocentric ways of being at the expense of place-based Indigenous ways of being (Geniusz 2009: 196). I also use the word "settler" in

the place of "Canadian" to underscore the notion that Canada as a state is not permanent and is relatively new.

2. Indigenist research privileges specific Indigenous peoples' intellectual traditions in research and activist projects, and locates the liberation of Indigenous peoples and their territories from colonial occupation as its highest political goal. See Simpson (2009: 143–47) and Smith (1999: 146–47) as examples.

3. The Anishinabe language.

4. I have specifically not italicized Anishinabe words in this chapter to assert the validity of Anishinabemowin in its own right. Italicization renders Anishinabe words as something exotic within English texts, hinting towards the colonial history of seeing the other and their languages and customs as quaint, obscure and, ultimately, not as valid as Western ways of being and languages.

5. Grandmother.

6. Anishinabe territory.

7. I discuss blood quantum and its relatedness to the *Indian Act* later in this chapter. However, it is worth noting here that though the *Indian Act* does not mention blood quantum specifically, it nonetheless establishes a *de facto*, or notional, blood quantum rubric by using out-marriage (when a status Indian marries a non-status Indian) to limit which child is considered a status Indian when born (Palmater 2011: 29). And while many Anishinabe communities in Ontario are reclaiming control of their citizenship, Clatworthy (2010: 9) has shown that, as of 2005, thirty of the forty (75 percent) Anishinabe communities represented by the Union of Ontario Indians were "using the rules governing Indian registration or Section 10 [of the *Indian Act*] which were identified to be equivalent to those for determining Indian registration"; four of forty (10 percent) were using a 50 percent blood quantum membership rule to determine community membership; one of forty (2 percent) was using a 25 percent blood quantum membership rule. The remaining five of forty (13 percent) were using an unlimited one-parent rule, where a person is considered a community member if at least one of their parents is a member, regardless of whether that parent is entitled to being registered as a status Indian under the *Indian Act* (Clatworthy 2010: 7, 9).

8. By roles I mean those images and positions in society that the Canadian state and settlers have invented or imagined for Indigenous peoples. For example, whereas the *Indian Act* forces Indigenous communities to adopt a municipal-style chief and council structure for governance, such a structure is not a traditional form of governance for Indigenous peoples in Canada. Yet, most Indigenous communities cannot access transfer payments or other resources associated with our nation-to-nation relationship with Canada without first having a chief and council in place. The chief and council system is designed to be filled with Indians, and in doing so invents Indians. In this way, Indigenous peoples find themselves having to play the role of Indians in order to access resources that were guaranteed to them when either colonial or imperial Crowns recognized them as Indigenous nations.

9. Lawrence cites Stoler (1991: 53) in her argument here.

10. Prior to 1850 there was no need for a precise definition of Indian, as Crown representatives used Indian, Native, Aboriginal, Band and Tribe to refer to Indigenous peoples (Acton 2011). However, 1850 marked the first attempt by legislators of Upper and Lower Canada to define in statute Indigenous peoples as Indians in two parallel acts: *An Act for the Protection of Indians in Upper Canada from Imposition, and the Property Occupied or Enjoyed by Them from Trespass and Injury* and *An Act for the Better Protection of the Lands and Property of Indians in Lower Canada* (Library of Parliament 2003 [1996]: endnote 2). The Lower Canada statute defined an Indian as "All persons of Indian blood, reputed to belong to the particular Band or Tribe of Indians ...

and their descendants; All persons intermarried with any such Indians and residing amongst them, and the descendants of all such persons; All persons residing among such Indians, whose parents on either side were or are Indians of such Body or Tribe, or entitled to be considered as such; And all persons adopted in infancy by any such Indians, and residing in the Village or upon the lands of such Tribe or Body of Indians, and their descendants" (Province of Lower Canada 1850: 1248). The definition of who is an Indian continued to be unilaterally redefined by Canadian legislators in increasingly complex ways, and in 1876 *An Act to Amend and Consolidate the Laws Respecting Indians* (short title: *Indian Act*) was passed to combine all previous statutes pertaining to Indigenous peoples into one Act. It is worth noting that the practice of redefining who is an Indian within the *Indian Act* continues today (e.g., the Bill C-31 *Indian Act* amendment in 1985, and the Bill C-3 amendment to the *Indian Act* in 2011) (see Palmater 2011).

11. Mi'kmaq scholar and lawyer Pamela Palmater (2011: 29) notes that while the *Indian Act, 1985* does not explicitly use blood quantum in the process of registering status Indians, "through its reliance on specific degrees of birth descent, Canada has, in effect, incorporated a type of blood quantum by birth descent for status Indians born after April 17, 1985, when Bill C-31 amended the *Indian Act*. In other words, one generation of marrying out [i.e., a status Indian marrying a non-status Indian] equals 50 per cent notional Indian blood quantum, two generations equals 25 per cent, and so on." One reason the *Indian Act* relies on blood quantum to determine Indian status is to allow Canada to judge a person's biological relatedness to a presumed biological purity of Indigenous peoples at a point frozen at the time of contact (Palmater 2011: 32).

12. This enables the state to claim Indigenous peoples as Aboriginal Canadians (or Indians) within its body politic as a group of people that do not have a nation-to-nation relationship with the state.

13. Gilbert (1996: 77) notes that subsection 48(16) of the *Indian Act* between the years of 1956 and 1988 defined an Indian child as one who could have been adopted through Indian custom. However, in describing Canada's application of its laws in reference to Indian status and custom adoptions, Gilbert (1996: 77) notes that "the right to have a child adopted by custom recognized as being entitled to have his or her name registered [as a status Indian] under the *Indian Act* prior to the 1985 amendments by virtue of the exercise of that custom has not been determined by the courts.... The Government of Canada created the Indian register and maintains it under the *Indian Act* and since that government also controls most of the programs and services which flow to the registered Indian population, the argument that custom adoption means inclusion into the community stops at the border of that community." The *Indian Act, 1985*, now recognizes customary adoptions as entitling people to registration as a status Indian, though in a way highly regulated by the state (Gilbert 1996: 67).

14. This is not a blanket statement that can be applied to all people who are a part of an Indigenous nation without also being a status Indian, and thus needs to be clarified here. My community, Fort William First Nation, has not yet opted out of the *Indian Act*'s control of band membership; section 10 of the *Indian Act, 1985*, allows for federally recognized First Nations to opt out of the *Act*'s band membership provisions (Library of Parliament 2003 [1996]), in which case a First Nation establishes its own membership rules. A membership code may or may not rely on notional blood quantum to determine band membership, and membership codes in and of themselves do not make non-status individuals status Indians in the eyes of the federal government. As Fort William First Nation has not yet reclaimed control of membership from the *Indian Act*, band membership is determined by the *Act* itself, meaning one must be a status Indian to "officially" enjoy land, political participation and treaty rights within my reserve.

15. S.91(24) of the *Constitution Act, 1867*, which remains in the *Constitution Act, 1982*, is the Parliament of Canada's paternalistic claim to have responsibility for "Indians and lands reserved for the Indians" (Government of Canada 1982b). Palmater (2011: 39) notes that this responsibility was taken without input from Indigenous peoples, enabling Canada through its legislation to regulate the identity of individual Indigenous people.

16. For example, Sir Francis Bond Head concluded after visiting communities where "civilizing" efforts were taking place that Indigenous people could not be civilized. His proposed solution was to relocate Indigenous people to the periphery of settler society at the time, particularly to Manitoulin Island, "where they could be protected in a traditional lifestyle until their inevitable disappearance as separate peoples" (RCAP 1996: 9.3). This proposal, as with the proposals to "civilize" Indigenous people, was based on the notion that Indigenous people inherently could not respond to the new settler society — they would eventually die off. Bond Head's "protection" scheme was imagined as a way for Indigenous peoples to enjoy their cultures and ways of life in the limited time they had left.

17. Alfred (2009: 94) defines the colonial mentality in this way: "Most Native lives continue to be lived in a world of ideas imposed on them by others. The same set of factors that creates internalized oppression, blinding people to the true source of their pain and hostility, also allows them to accept, and even to defend, the continuation of an unjust power relationship. The 'colonial mentality' is the intellectual dimension in the group of emotional and psychological pathologies associated with internalized oppression.... The colonial mentality can be thought of as a mental state that blocks recognition of the existence or viability of traditional perspectives. It prevents people from seeing beyond the conditions created by the white society to serve its own interests."

18. Betasamosake (Leanne Simpson), personal communication via email, September 30, 2011.

19. Henderson (2008: 21–22) writes that Eurocentric thought inherently cannot understand indigeneity, exemplified by the rise of *sui generis* concepts of law in Canadian jurisprudence — a recognition in Canadian law that Indigenous peoples developed their polities, cultures and legal systems completely outside those of European origin, meaning English and French legal traditions cannot adequately describe Indigenous peoples' sovereignty, laws or rights. This difference in worldview, argues Deloria (1994: 62–77), is based on spatial vs. temporal conceptualizations of humans' relationships to land: Indigenous peoples centre their reciprocal relationships with places in their worldviews, economies, languages and political systems; European thought places humans in a temporal relationship with land, promoting the idea that land must be dominated in order for humans to achieve progress.

Chapter 9

HOMONORMATIVITY AND THE LOSS OF QUEER

Re-contextualizing Canada's Sexual Politics

Oren Howlett

Scholarship on Canada's sexual politics has increased significantly over the last fifteen years. Emerging interest in explaining the relationship between the Canadian nation-state and queer sexualities is due, in large part, to the devolution of equality rights to gays and lesbians that has occurred over the last thirty years. Consequently, the attention of scholars has focused squarely on examining this complex relationship through an equality-seeking political frame, which places the Canadian nation-state as a neutral, uninterested entity in the achievement of equality for gays and lesbians. In much of this work, gay and lesbian movements are the actors who compel Canadian governments and courts to change laws and recognize the equality of gays and lesbians by way of human rights protections, social policies, relationship recognition and marriage. In the end, by employing such an equality-seeking frame, the Canadian nation-state is able to maintain its reputation of tolerance and benevolence of these previously marginalized communities.

This chapter, however, employs a critical lens to re-read the sequence of events described above. Drawing on scholarship examining Canada's sexual politics (Kinsman 1996; Rayside 1998; Smith 1998, 1999, 2004; Adam 1999), I reposition the Canadian nation-state and its relationship to sexual minorities. Unlike the equality-seeking approach mentioned above, I argue that a much more active and protective state sought to control, manage and regulate the threat of sexual minorities. As such, a critical re-reading of sexual politics in Canada offers an opportunity to think differently about the Canadian nation-state's actions towards alternative sexualities. Moreover, when placed within a broader context of queer struggles, the management of the "sexual threat" has succeeded in the Canadian state's homonormalization of gays and lesbians, which has consequently led to the de-politicization of queer communities. Homonormativity — the sexual politics of neoliberalism — is a useful lens through which to understand the current context of queer rights.

I begin with an overview of three periods of sexual regulation that structure the sexuality of those individuals who live within what are now largely understood as Canadian borders over the course of the past four hundred years or so. While efforts to exercise control over the sexuality of Indigenous populations coincided especially with European missionary contact in the late 1600s, I suggest that the first period of sexual regulation becomes fully identifiable with the beginnings of state governance. Governments and the laws they created supported the imagined nation and sought to perpetuate the nation's growth through the encouragement of heterosexuality. During the second period of sexual regulation, which lasted from the 1920s to 1960s, sexuality and gender roles were regulated increasingly by the Canadian state. For instance, during the early twentieth century, the prevailing climate of moral regulation contributed to the pathologization of the homosexual. Later, the post-World War II Canadian welfare state and anti-homosexual campaigns in the 1950s and 1960s reinforced the nation's compulsory heterosexuality and discouraged alternative sexualities. In addition, this period gave rise to the public perpetuation of gender norms to ease concerns of gender anxiety that resulted from the social change occurring in this period. Finally, the current period of sexual regulation began in the early 1970s and is characterized by the deconstruction of regulation and the institution of normalization. Actors within the English Canadian nation-state are in the midst of legislatively dismantling the Canadian sexual regime. I argue, however, that the final result of this project has been the rise of homonormative politics, which have depoliticized queer communities and diminished the radical potential of alternative sexualities in Canada.

These periods of sexual regulation are closely related to what I call "sexual regimes" throughout this chapter. I use the terms sexual regulation and sexual regimes interchangeably to reinforce the fact that each period is supported by structures through which the exclusion of homosexuality and the regulation of sexualities and gender were maintained. These sexual regimes, a term inspired by the race regime framework developed by Jill Vickers (2000a), create and sustain a climate in which heterosexuality is sanctioned, rewarded and accepted as the hegemonic national sexuality by those included within the nation-state. As a result, I believe that such sexual regimes continue to derive and exert their force from and within both the nation-state and society at large.

Canada's three sexual regimes, outlined below, sketch the existence and operationalization of sexual regulation from first contact to the present day. My historical survey of sexual regimes does not attempt to address the agents/methods of change between periods of sexual regulation. Instead, my purpose is to explore the manifestation of Canada's three sexual regimes over time. I am interested in the trends and themes that shape the ways in which homosexuality was viewed in each period with the goal of tracing those themes into the present day. Themes and trends witnessed in one sexual regime may not appear in the subsequent regimes and may also shift within the same regime, like the deconstruction currently occurring. Most importantly, I seek to lend a critical eye to the events and forces that construct each sexual regime affecting gays and lesbians.

Finally, I offer a caveat. Despite my focus on homosexualities, I do not address the full spectrum of sexualities or gender in detail, but recognize the variation in exclusion created by gender and alternative sexualities that differentiate the experiences of lesbians, gay men and those of other sexual attractions within each period of sexual regulation. In the end, my goal is to present a critical view of a national queer history — Canada's queer history — that has largely focused on gays and lesbians and presents the current climate of queer acceptance in the context of a past based on regulation, control and managed integration. As such, the hard fought equality gained by gays and lesbians through (homo) normative, rights-based politics has been successful, but at a cost that has left many, who adopt alternative and queer sexualities that do not conform to the (homo)norm, still unable to love openly and fully in relationships of their choosing. Let us turn our attention to the three periods of sexual regulation.

THE FIRST PERIOD OF SEXUAL REGULATION: THE COLONIAL IMPLEMENTATION

In Canada, efforts to regulate the sexuality of Indigenous populations in North America emerged long before the founding of the Canadian nation-state. In his exploration of this early regulation, Martin Cannon (1998: 2–3) writes:

> Even prior to Confederation and the first statute entitled the Indian Act in 1876, the colonial enterprise in Canada had virtually enforced a system of Eurocentric policies, beliefs, and value systems upon First Nations. The earliest missionaries, for example, were determined to "civilize" the Indian populations by attempting to indoctrinate a Christian ethos and patriarchal family structure. It was within the context of such a conversions mission that same-sex erotic and sexual diversity was negatively evaluated and often condemned. This mission was a project fuelled by heterosexism.

The foundation of such regulation is apparent in the racist and heterosexist beliefs of religious missionaries sent to "civilize" Indigenous peoples. Sexual regulation took the form of condoned heterosexuality and, acting in tandem with the ideologies of racial superiority, began to cement the oppression and destruction of Aboriginal customs and sexual relations.

Sexual freedom among women, social and biological diversity in third and fourth genders and various erotic relations, including European-defined sodomy, are some examples of the open sexuality expressed within North American Indigenous groups (Lang 1997: 100–101). Following contact, these practices were immediately characterized as inferior, and missionaries, among other colonial officials, pursued measures to encourage Eurocentric heterosexual models. Cannon (1998: 3) cites the journals of French administrative official Jean Bernard Bossu, who resided intermittently in New France from 1751 to 1771, to provide insight into Christian perceptions of North American Aboriginal sexuality:

> The people of this nation are generally of a brutal and coarse nature. You can talk to them as much as you want about the mysteries of our religion; they always reply that is beyond their comprehension. They are morally quite perverted, and most of them are addicted to sodomy. These corrupt men, who have long hair and wear short skirts like women, are held in great contempt.

Bossu's words illustrate a deep disdain for the sexual diversity present in Aboriginal cultures. The initial perceptions of European settlers set the tone for Aboriginal-missionary relations. Indeed, such prejudices against diverse Aboriginal sexualities laid the foundations upon which the first sexual regime was built and heterosexuality entrenched in "civilized" North America. For example, during the fur trade, European efforts to exercise control over Aboriginal sexualities were difficult to enforce, given the absence of institutionalized state structures and the vested interests both the British and French had in solidifying trade and military relationships with Aboriginal nations. Yet, during this same period, French royal initiatives such as *les filles du roi*[1] suggested that colonial authorities wanted to ensure that proper family units and heterosexual couples were populating the colonies (Gagner 2001).

During this colonial period, tensions within the first period of sexual regulation are evident. Administrative control over family relationships was tenuous as, arguably, control over the settler populations focused primarily on the growth of settler colonies, rather than intimate sexual practices. It was not until state control was established and entrenched in the post-Confederation period that the sexual regime took a more regulatory turn. For instance, working and military men were presented with increased opportunities for same-sex relations during this period. It was not uncommon for men in logging towns, remote work stations or in military settings to engage in many forms of sexual contact, including buggery and sodomy, which were considered criminal acts during this period (Kinsman 1996: 110). As a result, relations between men in these settings became highly regulated to avoid these crimes. In Upper and Lower Canada, the consequences for those caught could result in death. This maximum penalty, however, rarely was applied. Instead, the criminal was often imprisoned or banished from the communities in which they lived (Kinsman 1996: 99).

The above point raises a number of interesting observations surrounding this first period of sexual regulation. First, sexual regulation, when employed, focused mainly on men's sexual activities. Relationships between "independent women" were not subject to the same level of criminalization as those between men.[2] Second, regulation was a community effort since certain sexual activities between opposite sexes were sanctioned both by colonial governments and settlers. Finally, the punishments for sodomy and buggery reveal the extent to which such behaviour was pathologized amongst the settlers. That men who engaged in such activities were often removed or banished from colonies illustrates the perceived threat of these deviant sexual practices to the survival of the colonies.

Sexual regulation strengthened in post-Confederation Canada. As a result, "the social relations in which English legal history and practice had developed were thereby integrated into the foundations of the Canadian state" (Kinsman 1996: 110). In addition to legal reinforcement, ideas about both appropriate sexual behaviour and what it meant to behave as a good citizen of the nation were spread through the education system, a key tool of civic nationalism that not only reinforced state power and compulsory heterosexuality but also inculcated populations, both Aboriginal and non-Aboriginal, with norms and values about the nation and nationalism.[3]

Sexual stereotypes are unmistakably witnessed in the writings of Jean Bernard Bossu. Descriptions of Aboriginals as "morally perverse" and "addicted to sodomy" contributed to the sexual stereotypes imposed on these groups in order to maintain the supremacy of European ideas about heterosexuality. These sexual stereotypes of North American Indigenous peoples, combined with their perceived racial inferiority, resulted in assessments of their sexual practices as inferior and deviant. In turn, sexual stereotypes justified missionaries' and colonial officials' perceptions that the alternative sexual practices among Aboriginals should be eliminated and controlled.

The perceived necessity to control and eradicate the diverse sexualities among Aboriginal peoples and the desire to impose similar restraints on colonial settlers demonstrate the perceived threat of alternative sexualities to the founding of the Canadian nation-state. As a result, all Aboriginals became the targets of conversion, "civilization" and regulation due to the intersection of racial and sexual hierarchies, while European settler men faced sexual regimes of regulation as described above. In post-Confederation Canada, state regulation increasingly replaced community and self-regulation. Laws were adopted and, in the case of the *Indian Act, 1876* (Cannon 1998: 9–13), created to maintain the domination of heterosexuality within the colonies and the emerging Canadian nation.

As the Canadian nation developed in the post-Confederation period, the state's preoccupation with the marriage and procreation of its citizens increased, producing a climate in which the endorsement and enforcement of heterosexuality was regarded as integral to the survival and future of Canadian society. Yet, the second sexual regime would take on a much more coercive and state-enforced approach as the Canadian nation-state entered the twentieth century.

THE SECOND PERIOD OF SEXUAL REGULATION: ENFORCING NATIONAL SECURITY

As Canada matured, negative attitudes towards vice and "immoral" sexual practices continued to have a significant impact on the way sexuality could be expressed within English Canadian society. To maintain order within the nation, the regulation of poverty, crime and vice was commonplace by moral reformers through the early decades of the twentieth century (Valverde 1991: 130–31). Homosexuality was among the many social experiences deemed as vices in need of regulation. During the early twentieth century, homosexuality received much attention from psychologists. Homosexuals were the subjects of many unflattering studies that reduced their sexual attractions to sexual perversions. In Richard von Krafft Ebing's *Psychopathia Sexualis*, homosexuals were defined as individuals with a "physiologically based psychiatric pathology attributable to congenital weakness of the nervous system" (Warner 2002: 22–23). Thus, the medical and social stigma attached to homosexuality required gays and lesbians to remain inconspicuous and unnamed.

Increasingly marginalized from mainstream society, gays and lesbians developed submerged networks in cities where they could gather, express their sexuality and find companionship after World War II (Warner 2002: 49–51). Yet, because cities continued to be highly community regulated through social and kinship networks, gay and lesbian sexual and social systems existed underground and relied heavily upon secrecy and custom. Strengthened networks in urban areas soon spread into rural English Canada throughout the post–World War II period. This set of connections fostered and produced safe spaces for same-sex experiences. Public, private and semi-private spaces, like clubs, parks, public washrooms and homes, provided areas through which lesbians and gays could meet others who shared their attractions and explore their same-sex desires. Public lesbian and gay communities emerged from these networks and built a sense of kinship, commonality and belonging for gays and lesbians. Public communities, however, made gays and lesbians prone to increased surveillance.

The entrenchment of this second period of sexual regulation accelerated after World War II. This important period of nation-building saw the introduction of Canadian citizenship legislation and the adoption of national symbols such as the Canadian flag, designed to create a Canadian identity separate from that of the nation's British origins (Martin Sr. 1993). Additionally, the development of a national federal welfare system strengthened the institutionalization of heterosexuality throughout English Canada. Financial support, such as family allowances, benefited those citizens who produced Canadian children (Martin Sr. 1993: 67). While supporting the nation-building project of the day, these monetary incentives for citizens within heterosexual relationships reinforced traditional gender roles and social interactions between the sexes and entrenched heterosexuality further within Canadian legislation. As Smith (quoted in Kinsman 1996: 135) observes:

> The state enacted legislation "constitutive of a family in which dependence of women and children ... became legally enforceable and ... progressively incorporated into the administrative policies of welfare agencies, education, health care, etc.... The man as breadwinner and the woman as dependent become the legally enforceable and administratively constituted relation."

Clearly, heterosexuality was deemed integral to the growth of the Canadian nation-state. Furthermore, the Canadian nation-building project of financial support to the family through the development of the welfare state and programs, such as family allowances, made heterosexuality the only sanctioned vehicle for inclusion within the national community.

The 1950s marked a new period of sexual regulation focused on the homosexual. Ushered in by the McCarthy era's "Red Scare," the numerous groups identified as enemies of the Canadian nation-state included feminists, Québec sovereigntists, youth, Black and Native political activists, immigrants and unionists to name a few (Kinsman, Buse and Steedman 2000: 3). Gays and lesbians, also identified as enemies of the state, became the subject of intense scrutiny by officers of the Royal Canadian Mounted Police (RCMP) and local police departments. Security officials believed homosexuals to be untrustworthy because of their allegedly deviant sexuality. As a result, gays and lesbians were labelled threats to the nation. This classification prompted the allocation of increased resources to oversee the removal of homosexuals from the Canadian civil service and armed forces. To justify this expenditure, state officials invented "character weaknesses" to ensure gays and lesbians fulfilled the "enemy" role.

"Character weaknesses," linked solely to gay and lesbian individuals, became the main rationalization security officials used to decry homosexuality within the public service (Kinsman 1995: 144). These "weaknesses" supposedly increased gay and lesbian vulnerability to blackmail, coercion and other illicit behaviours, such as "drunkenness, adultery, and 'promiscuity'" (145). As a result, the term assumed a gradually more homosexual connotation and became a code word for homosexuality within Canadian security practices.[4]

The association of character weaknesses with homosexuals justified increased surveillance of homosexuality within the civil service.[5] Security Panel documents confirm this preoccupation. An internal memo by D.F. Wall, secretary of the Security Panel, the interdepartmental committee responsible for coordinating national security, states, "It is the Prime Minister's wish that the matter be examined to determine whether it might be possible to treat cases of character weaknesses differently than those involving ideological beliefs, without of course weakening present security safeguards" (Kinsman 1995: 145). This quotation reveals the distinction made between political disloyalty and that of character weaknesses (or homosexuality) within the security discourse, which, in turn, legitimated the expansion of homosexual surveillance and regulation by the state and RCMP.

In conjunction with these state-sanctioned anti-homosexual campaigns, the second period of sexual regulation also drew on the public reinforcement of gender roles through media and national displays, a factor unique to this period of regulation. One example within the public service was the establishment of the "Miss Civil Service" beauty pageant and the "Ottawa Man." According to Patrizia Gentile (1996: 33–34), during the Cold War period, gender/sexual anxiety created the need to establish stable models of femininity and masculinity:

> Yet, even at the apex of the seemingly "natural" reintegration of traditional family values and reinforcement of heterosexuality, the "witch hunts of the early '50s directed against homosexuals spoke to a pervasive fear of Otherness" [Irvine 1990]. The influx of women in the labour force and the challenges to the traditional roles articulated by the feminist movement in the mid to late sixties, further contributed to gender anxiety and the need to re-order society along conservative lines. (34)

The increased regulation of sexuality within this climate of gender anxiety shows a clear relationship among anti-homosexual campaigns, the extent of gender role stability and the broader goal of social regulation within Canadian society. One productive way to ensure the dissemination and success of these models was through the civil service — the public face of the nation-state, which Canadian citizens should emulate.

As Gentile documents, civil service efforts at social regulation culminated in the creation of the Miss Civil Service contest and the Ottawa Man ideal. By stabilizing gender roles within the government, these models were an alternate method of ensuring security within the nation-state's civil service. The Miss Civil Service contest, which began in 1950 and lasted through 1973, created an idealized image of the female government worker and represented "'proper' codes of femininity, beauty, and sexuality in the federal community" (Gentile 2000: 133). In addition to being a model of femininity to her fellow civil servant workers, Miss Civil Servant was a model of femininity to the Canadian public. Conversely, the Ottawa Man, in keeping with the image of the most powerful male civil servants, was "heterosexual and virile, but not flamboyant" (138). As such, Ottawa Men were highly educated, well mannered, articulate and discerning. The contrasts between the ideal government guy and gal were consistent with traditional gender roles.

These beauty contests and the image of Ottawa Man, in conjunction with the anti-homosexual campaigns, stand as powerful evidence of the social and sexual regulation that attempted to define proper gender scripts in the Cold War period. While directed at the civil service, public appearances by Miss Civil Service and news articles on Ottawa Man suggest that these gender ideals functioned as part of official, state-directed nationalism and also permeated popular, societal discourses around English Canadian nationalism. Furthermore, these models were designed to ease fears of social change by reinforcing traditional values, sex roles and the pre-eminence of the family within the civil service and Canadian society. While regulating societal norms, the government guy and gal marginalized gays and lesbians because of the latter's inability to meet the former's heterosexual prerequisite, which further reinforced the compulsory heterosexuality of the nation.

The emerging historical record in this area reveals that Canada's sexual regulation during this time was multifaceted and complex. Moral regulation and urban growth facilitated the spread of submerged gay and lesbian networks, which later developed into English Canada's queer communities. While the secrecy and custom of gay and lesbian associations characterized the lifestyles of homosexuals throughout this period, the Canadian government simultaneously promoted heterosexuality and traditional gender roles with the establishment of civil service gender models and monetary incentives, such as family allowances, to further the nation-building project. Nation-building was not, however, only concerned with heterosexuality, but also with the discovery of the homosexual threat to the nation. As the Canadian anti-homosexual campaign reveals, government officials directed great efforts and financial resources into the surveillance, detection and regulation of gay and lesbian civil servants and emerging gay and lesbian communities. The modernization of Canadian society and state permitted increased preoccupation with the maintenance of compulsory heterosexuality and rhetoric that insisted on the need for the protection of the nation from homosexual influence and activity.

Taking a step back, we can discern some differences between the first and second periods of sexual regulation in Canada. Early in this second period, the investigation of "homosexual pathology" supported the regulation of vice and excess by moral reformers. These practices contributed first to the creation of underground networks that eventually developed into public gay and lesbian communities following World War II. The redefinition of the homosexual security risk, during this same postwar period, was based on sexual stereotypes of homosexuals as "promiscuous" and "untrustworthy." These "character weaknesses" rationalized the exclusion of homosexuality and the reinforcement of heterosexuality. The alleged character weaknesses of gays and lesbians separated homosexuals from ideological security threats (communists and socialists) and resulted in the increased observation and surveillance of gay and lesbian communities. Although these arguments were placed under the rubric of Cold War threats, the breakdown and specific targeting of gays and lesbians speaks to a larger, multifaceted project seen as integral to the survival of the nation-state.

The public appearances of Miss Civil Service and the construct of Ottawa Man reinforced the heterosexuality of Canadian society. They provided models of the ideal gender/sexual roles and traditional values to be emulated by Canadians and provided Canadian citizens at large with a model of who belonged and who did not, most specifically gays and lesbians. Efforts at social and gender regulation during the second sexual regime, therefore, supported the nation-building process that coincided with the Cold War period, the entrenchment of the Canadian welfare state and the solidification of traditional gender roles within Canadian society. Within this context, the anti-homosexual campaigns and the Government Girl/Ottawa Man take on a much more important role, highlighting a backlash against any diversion from the nation-state's attempt to strengthen its heterosexual foundations through support for the traditional family unit. As a consequence, gays and lesbians, framed as enemies of the nation, proved to be a potent threat requiring a multifaceted program of intense surveillance and regulation.

THE THIRD PERIOD OF SEXUAL REGULATION: MANAGED INTEGRATION AND THE POLITICS OF HOMONORMATIVITY

The two periods of sexual regulation outlined above illustrate their breadth and diversity over Canada's history. While homosexuals and heterosexuals alike were subject to sexual regulation, the difference was in how sexual regimes constructed homosexuals as immoral, deviant and criminal. This pattern of homosexual exclusion is often assumed to have ceased with the oft quoted statement by former prime minister Pierre Elliott Trudeau: "The state has no place in the bedrooms of the nation" (quoted in Rankin 2000: 176). Nevertheless, Rankin astutely observes:

> Despite the federal government's apparent liberalisation of policies around homosexuality, then, as now, the construction and maintenance of pan-Canadian nationalism demanded that the state remain keenly interested in the bedrooms of its citizens. In fact, the project of defining national identities in Canada has always involved significant attention to the regulation of the sexual preferences and practices of Canadians. (177)

While "officially" removing themselves from the bedrooms of the nation in the late 1960s, the Canadian government, in effect, became more involved in the public regulation of sexuality in the 1960s, 1970s and 1980s.

The third Canadian period of sexual regulation coincides with the rapid social change that occurred during the 1960s and 1970s. The introduction of many of modern English Canadian nationalism's pillars, such as multiculturalism, bilingualism, the 1982 Canadian Constitution and the *Canadian Charter of Rights and Freedoms*, signified the beginning of a new Canadian era replete with a discourse promoting citizen equality and perhaps most notably, gender equality. Officials presented the 1982 Canadian Constitution as marking the maturation of the Canadian nation-state and its nationalism. Canada, at least in the eyes of its English Canadian citizens, was now an independent, modern nation that adhered to values of democracy, equality and freedom for all. For gays and lesbians, the most important development was the *Charter of Rights and Freedoms* and the equality rights it potentially guaranteed.

The *Charter of Rights and Freedoms* offered gays and lesbians a new route for pursuing inclusion and belonging within the Canadian community. For many, including feminist activists, whose successful struggles for sex equality guarantees had opened the door for the entrenchment of minority rights and values of equality and non-discrimination, the *Charter* was a momentous occasion for those who long felt the exclusion of previous political regimes. Yet, the *Charter* did nothing immediately to acknowledge the discrimination and exclusion of "out" gay and lesbian Canadians, who wished for explicit recognition of their sexual orientation. Section 15(1) states:

> Every individual is equal before and under the law and has the right to the equal protection and equal benefit of the law without discrimination and, in particular, without discrimination based on race, national or ethnic origin, colour, religion, sex, age or mental or physical disability. (Government of Canada 1999: 568)

The omission of sexual orientation in section 15 was not unintentional. During the process to amend the *British North America Act* in 1980, a Special Joint Committee of the Senate and House of Commons was asked repeatedly to include sexual orientation among the enumerated groups within the *Charter*. In spite of a Liberal Party resolution to champion equality rights on the basis of sexual orientation, this committee voted down the appeal twelve to two (Lahey 1999: 33). One member, so enraged by the attempted inclusion, stated that "Parliament could not 'include every barnacle and eavestrough in the Constitution of Canada'" (quoted in Lahey 1999: 33). In consolation, it was commonly agreed that the open-ended wording of section 15 (the Charter's equality clause), secured by NDP Member of Parliament Svend Robinson (Rayside 1998: 109), permitted future flexibility in rendering court decisions that would be favourable for gays and lesbians. As such, even as "non-enumerated" groups, gays and lesbians would be able to gain access to equality rights.

The omission of sexual orientation from the enumerated groups in Section 15 calls into question the potential deconstruction efforts of actors within the third sexual regime. The judiciary's non-inclusive interpretation of section 15 until 1995 is evidence of this point (Lahey 1999; Macdougall 1999; Warner 2002). As a result, gay and lesbian exclusion was prolonged because of the judiciary's strict reading of the apparently "openly" worded *Charter* clause. In addition, the achievement of sexual orientation being "read" into section 15 did not accelerate the transfer of gay and lesbian rights through court and/or legislative avenues (Lahey and Alderson 2004: 74–75). Instead, the status quo of heterosexuality, entrenched by earlier sexual regulation, remained firmly in place.

The steps towards equality for gays and lesbians have been slow, piecemeal and incomplete at best. This trend emulates Walby's (1997: 109) rounds of restructuring:

> Rather than this notion of one critical period of "nation-formation," it is more appropriate to talk of "rounds of restructuring" of the nation-state.... It is useful in carrying the notion of change built upon foundations which remain, and that layer upon layer of change can take place, each of which leaves its sediment which significantly affects future practices.

Read through this idea of rounds of restructuring, the current sexual regime allows for the gradual inclusion of those gays and lesbians who 1) remain single individuals who practice their sexuality within the privacy of their homes or publicly during festivals or celebrations and/or 2) assimilate to the heterosexual majority's relationship models, which match the patriarchal and gendered foundations upon which the heterosexual regime relies. Proof of this fact is most obvious in the area of relationship recognition (i.e., partner insurance, pension and spousal benefits), which allows for the inclusion of gay and lesbian relationships that mimic those heterosexual relationship models commonly accepted within and by the dominant sexual regime. At the same time, the benefits of inclusion and belonging continue to elude gays and lesbians who do not match heterosexual relationship models. These non-conformist individuals embrace a publicly announced, displayed and enjoyed "alternative" gay and lesbian lifestyle of promiscuity, public sex and deviant sexual acts outside of hetero-like relationships. Thus, given the entrenchment of the homonormative discourse, which excludes such displays of alternative relationships, the heterosexual foundations of the nation remain intact despite the extension of relationship recognition to gays and lesbians.

For most Canadians, the exclusion of homosexuality is thought to have changed as the third sexual regime developed. For instance, with the passage of the *Civil Marriage Act*, gays and lesbians reached a significant milestone, imagined by many as the last step to gaining full equality and belonging within the Canadian community. Within the context of relationship recognition, the deconstruction of sexual regulation in this third period is demonstrated by the partial acknowledgement of gay and lesbian relationships. The same-sex marriage debates flow from the judicial decisions in Ontario, British Columbia and Québec, which extended marriage to gays and lesbians. Because the courts amended the traditional definition of marriage with gender-neutral language, federal politicians then faced the task of reconciling government legislation with the court-ordered definition of marriage. Out of this need for reconciliation, actors for and against same-sex marriage asserted their positions in an effort to influence public opinion and gain legislative change or protect the status quo in keeping with their vision of the Canadian nation.

The pillars of Canadian society were invoked throughout the debates on same-sex marriage. The opponents of same-sex marriage regularly drew upon the sanctity of the institution of marriage and family to support their position. These individuals tapped into the "deviance of homosexuality" and the heterosexual origins of marriage and of the so-called traditional family to convince Canadians that same-sex marriage would be detrimental to English Canadian society. Here, the arguments stirred fear over the unknown changes that same-sex marriage might imply for Canada. To reinforce their positions, opponents of same-sex marriage also delegitimized institutions and legislation, such as the courts and the *Charter of Rights and Freedoms*, to forward their argument. These tactics sought to undermine the legitimacy of the Canadian courts with arguments of judicial activism and sought re-negotiation of the meaning of rights and Canadian values that form the basis of the *Charter of Rights and Freedoms*. This double-pronged strategy shored up a very powerful position that effectively reinforced the status quo.

In contrast, supporters of same-sex marriage conveyed their positions through the use of rights talk, the *Charter of Rights and Freedoms* and Canadian values of equality and non-discrimination. These tactics deployed progressive language forwarded through

Canadian values and ideas designed to deconstruct previously perpetuated exclusions within the third sexual regime. Gay and lesbian activists effectively utilized rights talk to justify same-sex marriage to politicians and Canadians. However, the concept of rights was employed in different ways: activists conjured images of human rights discourses and struggles for equality and politicians used rights within a national context, separate from international or human rights. In both cases, these arguments lent support to the image of inevitability that politicians created to encourage English Canadian society's acceptance of change and difference. Nevertheless, rights-based arguments also created room for gay and lesbian equality to be compromised by same-sex marriage supporters in government. In an effort to get marriage "at any cost," politicians relied on a climate of resignation about same-sex marriage within Canadian society, which allowed for the protection of religious freedoms within Canada to take precedence over the right of gays and lesbians to marry through the institution of their choice (civic or religious).

The efforts of actors to deconstruct sexual regulation in this third period through ideologies of non-discrimination, equality and democracy continue. While the current period does provide protection from discrimination and access to a degree of equality to certain groups or individuals, it does so on its own terms. For gays and lesbians, inclusion comes at the cost of adopting a "behind closed doors" homosexuality, an acceptable "public" homosexuality or conforming to heterosexual relationship models and gender roles. Deconstruction efforts, therefore, are incapable of fully dismantling the (heterosexual) foundations that open up room for the acceptance of sexual diversity that previously existed in North America among Indigenous communities. As a result, the current period of sexual regulation promotes a limited and managed integration of hetero-conforming gays and lesbians, with the potential for full belonging of all queers still unrealized.

The measured integration of gays and lesbians, I argue, is tied to the shift in politics that has recently occurred throughout North America and Western liberal democracies. Not only have nation-states become more welcoming to gays and lesbians, but they have also de-mobilized their communities and politics. Lisa Duggan (2002: 179) links this trend of inclusion to the neoliberal politics that now dominate Western liberal democracies. While largely unspoken, the cultural politics of neoliberalism gave rise to a cultural imperialism that has adopted a successful sexual politics that, in many cases, achieved the gains listed above. Duggan terms this neoliberal sexual politics "homonormativity": "a sexual politics that does not contest dominant heteronormative assumptions and institutions but upholds and sustains them while promising the possibility of a demobilized gay constituency and a privatized, depoliticized gay culture anchored in domesticity and consumption." Homonormativity creates a politics that speaks with two voices: one that addresses an imagined gay public and another that speaks to a national mainstream shaped by neoliberalism. It offers hope to queers seeking inclusion, but allows entry through a non-radical and integrationist discourse that promises no challenge to heterosexist institutions.

Unlike the second period of sexual regulation, Canada in the current period is less concerned with overt regulation and exclusion of gays and lesbians. In contrast, it seeks to protect the Canadian nation-state through the controlled management and integration of once-excluded gays and lesbians. The adaptation of sexual regulation occurs because the nation-state can no longer openly regulate the sexuality of gays and lesbians. New values entrenched within the *Charter of Rights and Freedoms* allow citizens of the nation the freedom to do whatever they please behind the closed doors of their bedrooms. However, the public expression of sexuality in the nation becomes a threat to be managed through legislation, rights and selected exclusion.

Thus, the trends of inclusion gained by gays and lesbians, such as same-sex marriage, the right to join the military and the acceptance of gay and lesbian families all fit within the definition of homonormativity and its accompanying politics. The entry of gay and lesbian individuals to these national symbols does not contest the fundamental heterosexual underpinnings of these dominant institutions. Rather, it integrates gays and lesbians into them with no challenge to their heteronormative assumptions. Further, homonormativity, in my view, simultaneously gives rise to an insidious trend that narrows the forms of activism and sexual expression available to all queer individuals by tightening the hetero/homo binary to a point where the terms almost subsume one another through a process of normalization.

While in the past, hetero- and homo-sexualities would be used as reference points against which each defined the other, the normalization witnessed in homonormative politics results in a process whereby homosexuality becomes neutralized through its integration and normalization. It loses its radical potential because it becomes part of the norm with no challenge to the heterosexist assumptions that underpins how the nation-state conceives of sexuality. As such, the security afforded gays and lesbians is limited to those queers who conform to heterosexist models of behaviour and sexual expression in public, such as adopting monogamous relationships or professional personas that deny explicit expressions of sexual orientation. Although homonormativity does not challenge heteronormativity or the heterosexual foundations of the nation, it does shift the ways one must think about core experiences aligned with the experience and expression of sexual orientation.

As a result, the deconstruction of the third period of sexual regulation remains incomplete. Limited integration of "acceptable" gays and lesbians still displays a reliance on stereotypes of homosexual deviance and immorality. The slow transfer of rights and piecemeal legal integration of gays and lesbians reflect the hesitation among many policymakers to reject previous notions of the gay and lesbian threat to the nation. Therefore, the continued marginalization of homosexuals and their relationships demonstrates that attempts to shift the basis upon which the nation-state recognizes and accepts alternative sexualities is far from complete. Yet, Canadian gay and lesbian political movements have lost focus with the achievement of marriage and equity in the recognition of their relationships. With these goals accomplished, gay and lesbian politics, in short, have been co-opted by neoliberalism's homonormative politics, which have de-politicized a movement and moved the community into complacency. This, for any movement, is a dangerous place to be, and I explore possibilities for change in my closing thoughts.

LENDING A CRITICAL EYE TO THE FUTURE OF CANADIAN QUEER HISTORY

Throughout this chapter, I argue that three periods of sexual regulation can be discerned in Canada's history since European contact. The first predated Confederation and continued to the 1920s. Based on the oppression of Aboriginal sexual diversity and the regulation of colonial sexuality, this first period was driven by a desire to support and build the new Canadian nation according to strict heterosexist, patriarchal norms and values. Gradually, the second period emerged and relied much more heavily on governmental regulation of homosexuality and promotion of heterosexuality. The creation of the welfare state supplied heterosexual couples with monetary incentives to increase the Canadian population and entrenched further the ideal of the heterosexual family with well-defined gender roles. As well, the "red scare" provided a convenient guise for the Canadian government and security officers to target and exclude gays and lesbians from the national community. The current period of sexual regulation is based on the managed integration of gays and lesbians into the national community. Inclusion is, however, only guaranteed for those in relationship models that mimic those of their heterosexual counterparts.

In spite of the inclusion granted through rights entrenched in Canada's Constitution, gays and lesbians still find themselves struggling for the piecemeal transfer of rights that, in the end, do not fundamentally alter the heterosexual nature of the Canadian nation-state. Rather, I contend that the politics of homonormativity are being employed to include those gays and lesbians that assimilate to models of heterosexual, monogamous companionship. Simultaneously, heterosexuality remains privileged, as the societal norm of sexual orientation to which all those who wish to be fully integrated as Canadian citizens should aspire. The three periods of sexual regulation examined show how, despite an undeniable improvement in the rights of gay and lesbian Canadians, the nation-state continues to work to exclude and/or contain the inclusion of gay and lesbian within the state.

With a critical eye to the future, it is hard to tell what lies ahead for gay and lesbian movements in Canada. The rise of homonormative politics works to silence a political movement that still has a great deal to do. Work on the rights of the transgendered, while advanced, remains a point around which even more radical mobilization could be beneficial. The introduction of Bill C-389, an *Act to Amend the Canadian Human Rights Act and the Criminal Code* (gender identity and gender expression), in 2011, is a key example that work continues to be done.[6] However, the absence of mass mobilization around gay and lesbian rights, to me, signifies the depoliticization of a community that has become complacent and comfortable with the equality currently offered by the Canadian nation-state. Moreover, the solidarity politics that would see queers engaged with political movements with those oppressed within Canadian borders and beyond continue to be challenged both within the community and around it. One only need to think about the controversy surrounding the participation of Queers Against Israeli Apartheid at Toronto's Pride Celebrations over the last two years to grasp the effects of homonormative politics on the depoliticization of queer (McCann 2010).

These trends signal what I call the success of homonormativity in Canada. Gays and lesbians are now sufficiently integrated into the national community. We have become placated with the recognition of our relationships such that we contribute to the marginalization of the struggles that remain to be fought through social movement politics. We have forgotten about the radical change that liberationist activists before us hoped to bring to Canadians. These activists believed in change that would shift ideas of sexuality, allowing individuals the opportunity to express their sexual desires without the fear of reprisal and violence of exclusion as full citizens with unalienable rights. Instead, the Canadian version of homonormative politics keeps us in line and fearful that rights may one day be taken away. Yet, while I may lament a de-politicized gay and lesbian community, hope springs eternal for the radical groups that continue to push the boundaries and remind our communities of past struggles and struggles that continue in Canada and around the world. It is a sign that although the stage on which gay and lesbian politics takes place has shifted, the potential for its rediscovery is always present.

NOTES

1. Between 1663 and 1673, over 700 young women, called *filles du roi*, were sent to North America by Louis XIV. Concerned with the growth of New France, Louis XIV subsidized the migration of these women to strengthen the development of the colony. Each woman, while not an actual daughter of the king, had all their travel expenses paid. In many cases, they were also provided a dowry and a chest with needles, thread and other supplies to help them begin their households. Once in New France, these women were expected to marry and procreate.
2. Becki Ross (1998) observes that independent women were perceived much differently than men who engaged in sodomy or buggery. Instead of being characterized as "criminal" or "deviant," "independent women" who eschewed their patriotic obligation to motherhood and wifedom were widely perceived as disorderly, amoral and a threat to the foundations of civil society and the "laws of nature."
3. The education system played a strong role in the maintenance of gender roles and heterosexuality. As Kinsman (1996: 107) notes of the mid-1800s to early twentieth century, "The school system played an ever more important role as it extended to more and more young people in making 'citizens' and a Canadian public." As a key tool of nationalism, residential schools, run by Anglican, Roman Catholic and United Church clergy, acted as a means to "civilize" aboriginal children and teach them "proper" European, Christian morals (see Milloy 1999).
4. For a full discussion of the evolution of the term "character weakness" and its relationship to gays and lesbians as created by members of the Security Panel, see Gary Kinsman (1995, 2000). It is important to note, however, that these events had a more significant impact on gays rather than lesbians, given that gender discriminatory practices at the time dictated that fewer women than men held senior posts within the Canadian civil service, and therefore, women were not seen to constitute as serious a security threat.
5. For a thorough review of this period in Canadian queer history, see Kinsman and Gentile 2010.
6. Bill C-389 reached third reading in the House of Commons and passed with votes in favour from members of all political parties. The bill, however, died on the Senate floor due to the vote of non-confidence that brought down the government in March 2011.

Chapter 10

MONUMENTAL PERFORMANCES

The Famous Five, Gendered Whiteness
and the Making of Canada's Colonial Present

Mary-Jo Nadeau

On October 18, 2000, an "over-life-sized" (Dodd 2009: 11) monument titled *Women Are Persons!* was officially inaugurated on Canada's Parliament Hill. This seven-piece statue celebrates Canada's most famous feminists "frozen in serious debate over tea" (*Globe and Mail* 2000), as an embronzed Nellie McClung holds up the news of their 1929 Persons Case victory, which officially recognized women as "legal persons." Five women, an empty chair and a table bearing teacups comprise the basic elements of this silent but palpable "commemoration scene" (Eagan 2003: 34). In addition to a dramatization of the Famous Five's most significant collective moment, the inauguration ceremony also featured speeches, song, dance, a recital and a ribbon-cutting ceremony by several of the nation's highest officials. A thousand-some crowd attended, including a few hundred school children, several of the women's descendants, the sculptor,[1] national and local media and a handful of notable Canadians, from Margaret Trudeau to Shirley Douglas. As the newest installment on a site dominated by individual statues of Canada's "great white men," the monument has been praised as "wonderful and unconventional" (McKenna 2005: 24), and a "bold and cheerful" (Eagan 2003: 47) addition to the Hill. Interactive and participatory by design, the monument is also hailed as unique in commemorating both the group and the individuals who became known as the Famous Five: Henrietta Muir Edwards, Emily Murphy, Louise McKinney, Irene Parlby and Nellie McClung. Facing the Senate, it now stands as a permanent symbolic gesture to the doors that the five are credited with opening for women.

And yet, as one commentator noted at the time, the "drive to commemorate them stirred up a turbid historical context" (Ghosh 1999: 11), igniting a controversy in which Canada's ongoing legacy of racism emerged as a focal concern. The nationally broadcast ceremony that marked the monument's public debut, for example, included protestors carrying placards declaring that "The Famous Five were Infamous Racists" (*Globe and Mail* 2000). Small in numbers, the presence of these protestors was nevertheless a reminder of the simmering public debate that had surrounded the Hill monument and related public memory projects promoted by the Famous Five Foundation, an organization created in 1996 to commemorate the accomplishments of the five women. News coverage surrounding the inauguration ceremony was largely celebratory, emphasizing the feminist aspect of the women's legacy as a "triumph" of these "women's rights giants" (*Ottawa Citizen* 2000a), "trailblazers" (*Toronto Star* 2000a) and "strong women" (*Ottawa Citizen* 2000b). Substantial media ink had also been spilled since the foundation's creation, calling attention to the women's legacy of racism and involvement in eugenics. It would be a full five years before the controversy subsided and the "monumental women" (Shanahan 2008: 26) settled into permanence amongst the pantheon of national honourees on Parliament Hill.

This chapter revisits this public encounter with Canada's past, examining it as one moment in the long and living history of racial-colonial contestation around "white people's primary claim to the land and to the nation" (Razack 2002: 5). In this particular episode, the *Women Are Persons!* controversy invoked the fraught nexus of race, gender, feminism and national space in public history projects. Most explicitly, the central tension revolved around the commemorability of feminist icons associated with Canada's history of racism, hinging primarily around two limiting narratives. Would the five women be remembered as "feminist racists" (Woodard 1998) or as "imperfect heroines" (Eagan 2003: 47)? The Famous Five Foundation advocated a version of the latter, constructing a narrative that was compatible with the hegemonic sensibility of tolerance cultivated through Canada's forty-year-old reinvention of itself as a "non-racist" multicultural nation. Over a decade later, it remains instructive to examine how racism was neutralized in this context and Canada effectively recuperated as a space of White benevolence.

This effective mobilization of multiculturalism as a managerial discourse for cleansing the colonial present was made possible by amplifying the women's feminist legacy and diminishing their racist legacy. Reinserting gendered whiteness as a category of analysis, then, is crucial for examining the broader problematic of how "public space is profoundly implicated in the process of 'othering'" (Burk 2010: 93). How does multiculturalist re-membering, for example, subtly reposition the body and history of White women as the unacknowledged privileged subject for feminist public history in Canada? What does the palatability and popularity of the foundation's appeal to an idealized non-racist present reveal about the salience of gender in securing White hegemony through public commemoration?

While this controversy also generated important critical analyses of race and feminism (Crow 1999; Ghosh 1999; Devereux 2005; Roome 2005), these questions have gone largely unasked and unanswered in scholarship on public history. They remain relevant, however, especially in the current context where the Famous Five as national heroines have become normalized as a "product," packaged and distributed with regularity as an entrenched form of "branded nationalism" (Lorenzkowski and High 2006: 9). In order to unpack these practices of gendered whiteness, this chapter focuses on the processes of reconciliation and recuperation in the Famous Five Foundation's response to the controversy and explores how these responses became authoritative in public debate and in some areas of scholarship.

The chapter begins by casting the story of the Famous Five across three historical moments, providing a preliminary mapping of the contexts and contested terrains through which they have become an "enduring symbol" (Dodd 2009: 8) of feminism and hegemonic nation-building in Canada. This is followed by a review and analysis of the public controversy surrounding the foundation's commemorative project. Here I trace the production and enactment of White multiculturalism as an "institutional script" (Puwar

2004: 88), or a knowable and recognizable set of hegemonic national logics that have been administered and popularized in Canada's modern history of colonial race-thinking (Nadeau 2009a). I illuminate how these scripts were adapted by the foundation and came to resonate and dominate the public debate to legitimate the Famous Five as "imperfect" but commemorable national heroines. My analysis explores how the Famous Five monument functioned as a site for both strategic mobilization and the popular enactment of this script of hegemonic national belonging. The chapter ends with a return to the *Women Are Persons!* monument for analysis of how gendered whiteness functions performatively to sustain a colonial present through an assertion of spatial dominance.

THE FAMOUS FIVE: A BRIEF HISTORY IN THREE PARTS

To understand both its origins and longevity as an "enduring symbol," it is useful to situate the Famous Five across three key moments of intersecting feminist activism and colonial race-making in Canada: first, the life and times of the five women who won the Persons Case (pre-1930s); second, their posthumous recovery as "founding mothers" of Canadian feminism and the anti-racist feminist critique that emerged alongside this reclaiming (1960s–1990s); and, third, their most recent recasting and institutionalization as national heroines by the Famous Five Foundation (since 1996). Through a brief sketch of these distinct but continuous moments, this section traces the history of the Famous Five as connected to hegemonic White feminist currents in Canadian women's movements, particularly foregrounding their contradictory location "as agents of nationalism and feminism" (Vickers 2000b: 144). The fraught dual legacy of feminism and White nationalism has shaped activism in Canadian women's movements, past and present. A sizeable and growing historiography of the first moment now exists, with general consensus that the original five were major figures in the production of the colonial nation-building project through "racialized maternal feminism" (Devereux 2005: 11). There is also a growing literature analyzing the post-1960s moment as a period of sustained struggle against establishing White feminist dominance in women's movements and challenging this through anti-racist feminism (Carty 1993; Carty and Brand 1993; Rebick and Roach 1996; Lee and Cardinal 1998; Stasiulis 1999; Vickers 2000b; Rebick 2005; Srivastava 2007; Nadeau 2009b). A small literature has also emerged around the *Women Are Persons!* monument (Crow 1999; Eagan 2003; McKenna 2005; Roome 2005; Dodd 2009; Strong-Boag 2009). This third moment, however, remains in need of further theorization particularly with respect to situating the Famous Five Foundation as a site of elite feminist activism in the service of advancing neoliberal multiculturalism. The following summary account of the Famous Five as an "enduring symbol" through these three periods provides some necessary context for this chapter, particularly for understanding the emergence and specificity of the most recent moment (post-1996).

The Original Five: A Dual Legacy of Feminism and White Nationalism
Collectively speaking, the women who became known as the Famous Five were highly influential figures during the early 1900s across two overlapping realms of public activism — women's rights and social reform. Their "greatest achievements" (Glasbeek 2009) around women's rights activism include the suffrage victory (winning the vote for women,

narrowly defined[2]), having women recognized as legal "persons" and, by extension, gaining representation for women in the Senate and public office. While Emily Murphy and Nellie McClung were the most prominent of the five, all were attached to these movements as a core commitment. Indeed, all except McKinney first met through the struggle for women's political rights as part of McClung's post-suffrage Provincial Law Committee (Sharpe and McMahon 2007). To a large extent their rights-based activism overlapped with their shared experience as founding and active members of organizations associated with the "first wave" women's movement, including the National Council of Women of Canada (NCWC) and the Womens' Christian Temperance Union. As well-known social reformers across various causes (prisons, drugs, prostitution, immigration, labour, temperance, child welfare and peace), their lives also overlapped as they "linked politics and social betterment" (Sharpe and McMahon 2007: 41). It is through this combined involvement as women's rights activists and social reformers that all five (to varying degrees) shaped, and were shaped by, the period's mutually reinforcing "framework of eugenic feminism and maternalist ideology" (Devereux 2005: 57) and by "colonial nationalism" (Vickers 2000b: 134). Contemporary scholarship recognizes and assesses their feminist projects as contradictory and heavily influenced by "a nation-building project that sought to establish Canada as a 'white settler nation'" (Kinahan 2008: 6). As such, it is now widely acknowledged that their gender politics (i.e., expanding rights for women) cannot be treated separately from the discourses and practices of racism and imperialism (i.e., exclusionary racialized citizenship) that were foundational to this earlier period of Canadian feminism and social reform (Bacchi 1983; McLaren 1990; Valverde 1991, 1992; Perry 2001; Henderson 2003; Carter et al. 2005; Kinahan 2008; Glasbeek 2009). Indeed, as others argue, it is crucial to grasp "the complicated role that women and gender played in Canada's colonial and nation-building projects" (Carter et al. 2005: 4).

While acknowledging that a "politics of racialized maternal feminism" (Devereux 2005: 11) dominated the period, scholars have also emphasized that a "monolithic racism" (Fiamengo 2006: 146) cannot be easily inferred. The historical record indicates unevenness across their biographies and contradictions within each, and recent feminist scholarship argues for the need to grasp a "diversity of motives and ambitions" (Cavanaugh 2000: 101). Amongst the five women, for example, Murphy and McClung were the most outspoken advocates of eugenics, while Edwards is described as having "more progressive views on race than Murphy or many other maternal feminists" (Sharpe and McMahon 2007: 43). The description of "maternal imperialist" also applies to each in specific ways, often reflecting key distinctions across their social locations. Edwards, for example, lived for several years in a direct if complicated colonizer positionality with Indigenous communities in the North-West Territories (Roome 2005), while Parlby's elite "allegiances to Empire" (Cavanaugh 2000: 104) and White settler sensibility shaped her suffrage activism.

While biographical analyses are critical for mapping a broader terrain of the encounter between feminism and White settler nation-building, an over-emphasis on individuals can also obscure that which the women shared amongst themselves and with other women and men across class and geography. Unevenness and contradiction notwithstanding, there is little evidence that any of the five women "addressed White privilege adequately" (Roome 2005: 72). Rather, the dominant feminist politics of the period was grounded in reinforcing, not challenging, the collective position of White settler dominance in the colonial-racial order. As Kinahan (2008: 5) argues, the feminist politics of this period was "literally and figuratively concerned with enfranchising White women." These are the grounds on which the women "publicly endorsed their province's aggressive eugenics policy" (Ghosh 1999: 10), and it is on these terms that we can best understand the meaning and significance of their feminist activism as integrally linked to the politics of gendered whiteness.

The Persons Case victory of 1929 essentially marked the end of the women's collective activism and the beginning of the practice of memorializing the Famous Five. In 1938, not long after the deaths of three of the five women, a bronze plaque to the Persons Case was placed in the lobby of the Senate Building. The public speeches by Nellie McClung and Prime Minister W.L. McKenzie King at the event are noteworthy. Together they highlighted two key aspects of the women's legacy, with McClung foregrounding the "epic story" of the "rise of women" and McKenzie King situating the women in the national story by stating: "It is well that our national existence should be fortified by the participation in its affairs by those who are so exceptionally qualified to contribute to human well-being and to the preservation of the foundations of home and community life" (CBC 1938). Left unspoken by both were the racial and colonial grounds of the women's activism. As discussed below, this erasure would continue to dominate the commemoration of the Famous Five into the next significant wave of memorialization.

The Famous Five and Post-1960s Canadian Feminism
Between 1939 and 1966 each of the five women received a modicum of individual commemoration, particularly in being designated as significant "Persons" in the Parks Canada Women's History program (Dodd 2009). As a group, however, the Famous Five would not return to widespread feminist and public exposure until the post-1960s Canadian women's movement cast renewed attention to the women's rights side of their legacy. This focus, and its entrenchment in key feminist institutions, helped ensure that the women and their collective activism would be preserved in public memory. This renewed attention to their legacy also aided in legitimating the emerging elite White liberal strand of feminism, which sought to secure its place as the public face and national voice of the post-1960s Canadian women's movement through the Royal Commission on the Status of Women (Williams 1990; Freeman 2001; Nadeau 2009b). By 1979, the five were institutionalized at the state level through the creation of an annual Governor General's Persons Case Awards, thus marking the fiftieth anniversary of the legal case that "declared women to be full persons under the law" (Sharpe and McMahon 2007: x).

The formative political culture of the National Action Committee on the Status of Women (NAC) was a significant site for this canonization process. With its creation in 1972, the NAC was initially modelled around a White liberal parliamentary feminist space, casting deep associations with selected aspects of the activism of the five women and their contemporaries. The idea of a general affiliation with the Famous Five, as the authentic "first" feminists, was naturalized through frequent articulations in familial and generational terms, as the "foremothers" and "pioneers" of Canadian feminism. Emily Murphy and Nellie McClung figured prominently in naturalizing this idealized sense of generational affiliation. Much of this iconization is captured on the pages of the NAC's first newsletter, *Status of Women News*. This practice, which endured throughout most of the 1970s, helped institutionalize a political culture of White liberal feminist parliamentary activism in the NAC.

In 1979, for example, the NAC decided to publicize the anniversary of the Persons Case in the media and to lobby for a commemorative plaque to be installed near the Supreme Court. As part of these celebrations, and as a fundraising effort, it issued both a "Persons Case Medallion" and a "commemorative seal, for use on the back of correspondence and on communications of all types" (NAC 1979: 11). Essays were commissioned and photos of the "Five Persons" (NAC 1978: 2) were published, including Emily Murphy and Nellie McClung (who were already familiar to *Status* readers in prominent representations over the first five years). While not all feminists participated in this iconization, the Famous Five as a prototype of White feminist commemoration and generational affiliation circulated widely in the women's movement as a staple in the lexicon of second-wave organizations, activism, popular culture, scholarship and women's studies curricula.

As this White feminist script shaped the general tenor and direction of the dominant strands of the movement throughout the 1970s and into the 1980s, it also generated an influential early critique of the race politics of first-wave feminism. In her widely read critical study of English Canadian suffragists at that time, for example, Carol Lee Bacchi (1983: 104) examined how the various strands of the suffragist and reform movements were unified around "a concern for the future of the Anglo-Saxon race." This terrain of anti-racist feminist critique consolidated throughout the 1980s under the leadership of feminists of colour, ultimately expanding and reshaping women's movements in Canada (Bannerji 1993; Rebick and Roach 1996; Lee and Cardinal 1998; Dua and Robertson 1999; Srivastava 2005; Bunjun 2010). This process took many forms, including the creation of women of colour caucuses as a mechanism for organizing change within mainstream White-dominated feminist organizations and institutional sites (including women's studies); anti-racist feminist conferences; feminist publishing venues created by and for women of colour, as well as political challenges to the exclusionary White feminist press; anti-racist affirmative action and equity policies inside mainstream feminist and other social movement organizations; the creation of anti-racist spaces and political cultures in coalitions; struggles over racism in women's services organizations; and much more. Much of the critical race research and writing that has unpacked White feminism in turn-of-the-century women's movements (including on the Famous Five) builds on these earlier victories won by feminists of colour and allies (Valverde 1992; Devereux 2005; Roome 2005; Fiamengo 2006; Kinahan 2008).

The NAC itself became a central site of this expanding struggle over racism in the women's movement, resulting in the organization changing its constitution to include an anti-racist mandate in 1991 (Gottlieb 1993; Robertson 1999; Nadeau 2009b). As is discussed below, the NAC definitively departed from its earlier attachments to the Famous Five by deciding against supporting the Famous Five Foundation in its 1997 motion requesting state approval to place the monument on Parliament Hill (Ghosh 1999; Devereux 2005; Roome 2005).

The Famous Five Foundation

The third and most recent reinvention of the Famous Five can be traced back to the creation of the Famous Five Foundation, which, since 1996, has directed elite activism to commemorate the original five as "feminist nation-builders" (Dodd 2009: 11). Initiated and led by Calgary-based businesswoman Frances Wright, this "conservative feminist group" (Dodd 2009: 19) expanded rapidly into a high-profile organization funded privately by a substantial roster of corporate donors and individual supporters. Within its first five years Wright had secured over $1 million from private donations by "five prominent individual Canadian women willing to donate $200,000 each to fund the Famous 5 monument" (NCWC 2000). This funding was crucial for putting the foundation's extensive public memory project in motion, particularly enabling it to design and build twin *Women Are Persons!* monuments (one on Ottawa's Parliament Hill and the other in Calgary's downtown Olympic Plaza).

In addition to this privileged access to large sums of money, the foundation's success is likely attributable to the appeal of the message of national loss that launched its signature commemorative campaign. As Wright claimed at the time, the monument was needed because "there was nothing for them as a group, nothing vis-á-vis the Persons Case" (quoted in Lahey 1997: 10). This claim of national amnesia around the women became the foundation's rallying call and legitimated its primary aims for redress — "first to honour the Famous Five, and then to establish a pattern of celebrating" around their legacy (Lahey 1997: 10). As its primary vehicle for winning public legitimation, the foundation's claim of an overwhelming absence of the Famous Five in public discourse was maintained until the unveiling of the monument on Parliament Hill. Just three days before the Ottawa inauguration ceremonies, for example, Wright asserted to journalist Peter Mansbridge in a national television interview that "unfortunately they have disappeared" (CBC 2000).

While this framing lament of presumed national erasure around the feminist icons would diminish after this inaugural event, it had been enormously productive. The now fifteen-year-old signature brand of the foundation has become a recognizable feature of the public history landscape. Self-promoted as the "most popular monument on Parliament Hill" (Famous Five Foundation 2011), the *Women Are Persons!* monument was neither the first nor the last project in the foundation's mission to address this claimed historical gap in the national story. School curricula (1997), commemorative stamps (1999), a replica monument near Calgary City Hall (1999) and a "Nation Builders" image on the fifty-dollar bill (2004) now carry the Famous Five brand. Fifteen annual Speakers' Series have been held in their name in the nation's capital, the foundation's founder was celebrated with a Governor General's Award in Commemoration of the Persons Case in 2004, and the five famous women were posthumously designated as honorary senators in 2009. Having firmly established itself and its "products" on the national terrain, the Famous Five Foundation has since attended to growing its brand through a veritable memory-making industry. Its acquisition of substantial corporate sponsors, including partnerships with Enbridge and Esso Oil, secures further longevity to its bronze-clad inaugural project.

In recent years the foundation has shifted its framing discourse from a focus on national forgetting to an emphasis on the Famous Five as "a stirring example of the power of women who work together as leaders and nation builders" (Famous Five Foundation 2011). On the one hand this subtle change is indicative of the foundation's success in achieving the first stage of their campaign (i.e., "first to honour the Famous Five"), and implementing its rollout into the second phase (i.e., "establish a pattern of celebrating"). The infrastructure for celebrating was thus well-established in its first ten years and maintained with ongoing corporate donations, programming, annual awards ceremonies and an institutional base.

Receptivity to the foundation's ideas (including its ability to draw in substantial funding) needs to be understood in the context of shifts underway in the mid-1990s both nationally and globally. This was a fertile context in which the foundation could emerge, find ground and articulate a politics of feminism that was compatible with the turn to White neoliberal multiculturalism. First, as a "private initiative" (Dodd 2009: 11) the foundation held special appeal for corporate donors in a political economic climate that had turned definitively in favour of market expansion, markedly so in Canadian institutions (including universities, hospitals and schools). The foundation's capacity to attract substantial funds from private donors and the private sector also made it attractive to a Canadian state seeking to expand the idea and practice of "public-private partnerships" (PPPs). In this case, the controversial 1997 motion to Parliament tabled by Liberal MP Jean Augustine to gain approval for the monument on the Hill (discussed further below) required that the "statue ... be donated by the Calgary based Famous Five Foundation who will establish an endowment fund for landscaping and maintenance" (House of Commons 1997). While framed around philanthropic language of "donations," this stipulation nonetheless amounted to a private organization providing funding to develop public monumental space. In a neoliberalizing context, these kinds of subtle agreements are significant for validating the contested ideal of public-private partnerships being sought by the state.

Second, the liberal Canadian state was also facing a severe crisis of legitimacy around its neoliberal restructuring agenda at the time, including deeply unpopular funding cuts and regulatory changes that would advance privatization while dismantling the public sector. Cuts to state funding for social movement organizations were well underway as early as 1989, when the federal budget decreased grants by $10 million, a decision which affected "primarily women's, native and visible minority" groups (McKeen 2004: 135). By 1997 the cuts had reached such a crisis that the NAC launched a campaign with over twenty national women's organizations to politicize the issue and raise funds to sustain the organizations that were feeling the effects of an accumulated 75 percent decrease in funding (Decter 1998). In this context, state support for the foundation carried the appearance of a commitment to women's advocacy activism while it stealthily dismantled the longstanding "infrastructure of dissent," the complex "variety of shared political, cultural, educational and social spaces" built and sustained by grassroots movements for almost three decades (Sears 2008: 7). This gradual dissolution of the NAC in the latter half of the 1990s reflects the generalized attack on grassroots women's movement and activist organizations, but it also reflects a particularized backlash against the growing transformative feminist anti-racist/anti-colonial and queer/transgender movements of the period. Indeed, while the mid-1990s marked simultaneously a high point in the Canadian women's movement particularly with the expansion of anti-racist feminist infrastructure, this was also a moment of fragmentation and destructive backlash as the neoliberal rollout was fully underway on all fronts (from restructuring work, to dismantling the welfare state protections, to tightening immigration controls and racialized criminalization).

Finally, the period of the foundation's formation and expansion can also be characterized as a moment of heightened contestation over race, space and the foundational belief in dominant White Canada "as a space structured around a White culture" (Hage 2000: 18). On the one hand, the mid-1990s saw unprecedented and highly effective anti-racist organizing at the national level. The national women's movement had shifted decisively such that the NAC had become a recognized anti-racist organization. As characterized by its president, Joan Grant-Cummings, in the period: "You have women of colour and you have Aboriginal women, and you have allies in White women who are taking the anti-racism struggle to the next step. There's been a building, a widening of who's pushing the anti-racism agenda in NAC" (quoted in Decter 1998: 19). Similarly, sustained challenges to the labour movement by workers of colour pushed the Canadian Labour Congress to redefine its priorities and redistribute its organizational resources to anti-racist change. These two major organizations teamed up in 1996 for the NAC-CLC Women's March Against Poverty, the largest cross-country feminist-labour popular mobilization in their histories, and an action that involved an unprecedented level of participation from women and workers of colour (Robertson 1999). On the other hand, a simmering "crisis of whiteness" (Thobani 2007: 148) was evident in the periodic racial panics that erupted, signalling that the nation was perceived, through the lens of dominant White hegemony, to be at risk of being dominated by racial others. Anti-immigrant backlash, attacks on multiculturalism and racist media discourse around fears that White Canadians will become a minority in Canada's urban centres were common in the period.[3] This racist reaction to a perceived loss of historical White entitlement also helps explain public receptivity to the foundation's founding lament that the Famous Five had been "forgotten." Hegemonic nationalist projects — like the Famous Five Foundation — are implicated in these moments as they become sites for (re)naturalizing the pairing of whiteness and privileged national belonging. In this case, the foundation asserted a narrative of multicultural inclusivity as an inherent national trait. This framing allowed it to distance itself from the explicitly racist and exclusionary foundations of Canada as a colonizing White settler state, while also providing it with a language for distancing itself from anti-racist critique and claims of racism by women of colour and First Nations women. It could thus project non-racism as a national trait of the colonial present, leaving whiteness intact at the centre while assuming the position of benevolent managers of the nation. The state also derived acclaim for its role in supporting a project dedicated to women. Indeed, its inauguration ceremony for the monument on Parliament Hill was assessed positively by some feminists as a "distinctly Canadian" accomplishment and a model for representing women's history in "a new, more diverse and open social order" (Eagan 2003: 48). Through this embrace of Canada's national mythology then, the foundation's remobilization of the Famous Five and its support from the state furthered the re-whitening of Canadian feminism on the terrain of neoliberal multiculturalism. To demonstrate how this was accomplished in the foundation's formative years, from 1996–2000, the next section returns to the original debates over the monument and its broader commemorative project.

"FEMINIST RACISTS" OR "IMPERFECT HEROINES"?
ENACTING MULTICULTURALIST SCRIPTS

As Canadian cultural studies theorists Druick and Kotsopolous (2008: 8–9) argue, projects "explicitly focused on nation-building paradoxically call the nation into question, if only momentarily, by historicizing it; they are essentially self-conscious." In this case, the national question was ignited into controversy as the Famous Five Foundation sought to access the national stage as its venue of choice for its public history project. The Hill, the Senate, the House of Commons, the Governor General's Awards, Canada Post stamps and the national currency were all engaged as key sites of memorialization.

Public debate around the foundation's plans erupted during four key moments in the implementation of its memory project, marking a turbulent start to its first five years. These moments were the parliamentary resolution required to approve the *Women Are Persons!* monument on Parliament Hill (1997), the proposed installment and eventual inauguration of the monument in Calgary (1999), the commemoration ceremonies for the Parliament Hill monument in Ottawa (2000) and finally, the decision around minting the image of the monument on the fifty-dollar bill (REAL Women 2001). While each took on a specific character, this brief review focuses on summarizing the main lines of debate as instructive for demonstrating how public memorializing of national subjects in Canada is shaped through contestations over race and space. It also provides an example of how a persistent racial logic of multiculturalist benevolence was successfully mobilized as an institutional script for recuperating the national past to accommodate the reproduction of the colonial present.

The foundation's endeavour in 1997 to have the state dedicate a vaunted piece of national real estate to monumental space for the Famous Five became a hallmark moment in its early history, signalling the debates that would follow. At issue were the exclusionary criteria circumscribing admittance to the highest site of official national memory: monuments on the Hill had been reserved solely for three narrow categories of honorees: "deceased Prime Ministers, Fathers of Confederation, and monarchs" (Dodd 2009: 11). To gain access to this space for its *Women Are Persons!* Monument, the foundation made an appeal for gender equality on nationalist terms by invoking a rhetorical reinvention of the Famous Five as "Mothers of Confederation" (CBC 2000; Devereux 2005). The main opposition in the parliamentary debate came from an Independent MP, likely reflecting the views of other "traditionalist" parliamentarians who hoped to preserve the existing narrow selection criteria for Parliament Hill monuments (Ebner 1997; Ghosh 1999; Dodd 2009). After months of lobbying and three attempts at a vote, the final all-party resolution achieved the required "unanimous consent" in the House of Commons (Parliament of Canada 1997). With the resolution passing in December 1997, approval was rendered for the foundation's request around the Famous Five, "allowing a statue commemorating them to be placed on Parliament Hill" (House of Commons 1997).

In large part an outcome of the foundation's successful request to the Liberal Women's Caucus for support (Steele 2002), the project was vigorously promoted amongst parliamentarians by Liberal MP Jean Augustine (who presented the motion to the House of Commons) and by Canadian Heritage Minister Sheila Copps, who praised the women as "monumental groundbreakers for all women and for all Canadians" (Status of Women

Canada 1997: 1). While Augustine was accused of "unethical tactics" by the conservative women's organization REAL Women (2001: 10), all parties, including the conservative Reform Party, were ultimately outspoken in their support (Ebner 1997). This resolution became the "crowning achievement" (Ghosh 1999: 11) that activated the ensuing "pattern of celebrating" around the Famous Five.

As others accurately note, subsequent public debate about the *Women Are Persons!* monument "rose from the right, middle and the left" (Eagan 2003: 47). Furthermore, and crucially, most hinged on the stakes of foundational racial-national logics. While the parliamentary right eventually supported the monument, anti-feminists and conservative anti-abortion groups generally did not, with most focusing on identifying the women as "feminist racists" (Woodard 1998). The feminist left mapped out a more complex territory of anti-racist repudiation of the commemorative project. The foundation itself took up the so-called "middle" ground, arguing that it was valid — indeed imperative — to commemorate these women even if they were "imperfect heroines" (Eagan 2003: 47). Ultimately, as noted earlier, the public debate was won and settled in favour of this "middle" position, particularly as the mainstream media adopted this as its dominant frame. The remainder of this section reviews the play of these debates to highlight the use of multiculturalism as a persuasive institutional script that ultimately advanced the foundation's project of re-membering the Famous Five through unmarked gendered whiteness.

Two anti-abortion and anti-feminist groups, REAL Women and Campaign Life,[4] captured the media spotlight by appropriating the language of anti-racism to promote and reignite the longstanding lobby for a legal ban on abortion. Arguing that "racists should not be honoured," for example, allowed REAL Women to foreground the message that gave their anti-abortion position most traction. Their rally on Parliament Hill expressed the protest position that it was "very critical of politicians and others who are overlooking the well documented advocacy of racism and eugenics by some of these women being honoured today" (LifeSite 2000). This group shared with Campaign Life an interest in highlighting the historical fact that put the politics of reproduction in the spotlight — the "Famous Five supported eugenics" (LifeSite 2000). To achieve the same end, Campaign Life took a different angle by harnessing the language of equity. Agreeing that the Famous Five had rightly challenged the Supreme Court for discriminating against women as a "class of people" allowed them to smuggle in the argument that "The Discrimination Continues" in the courts today against another "class" of people — "unborn children" (LifeSite 2000). Successful in attracting media attention, particularly surrounding the installment of the first monument in Calgary (1999), the anti-abortion lobby's charge of "infamous racists" (REAL Women 2001: 10) provided both a spark and an anchor that invigorated the debates on racism and feminism.

The feminist left also engaged the discourse of anti-racist arguments to repudiate the foundation's Famous Five commemorative project. It did so, however, through a movement-based articulation grounded in a history of social justice organizing. Reflecting the strength drawn from a decade of difficult and transformative struggle over racism in the women's movement, the National Action Committee on the Status of Women denounced the proposed project. Calling it "offensive," President Joan Grant- Cummings explained that the NAC would not celebrate the Famous Five because their actions were "done in a very partial way, in a racist way, in a classist and ablest way" (quoted in Ghosh 1999: 11). From this anti-racist feminist position, the NAC thus challenged the foundation's White feminist framing by arguing that the advancement of women's rights was not, in and of itself, sufficient cause for commemoration and celebration. This intersectional feminist analysis was elaborated as follows: "Women aren't cut up into little pieces. I can't say, 'Oh I'll be a woman this day, and of colour the next.' If we say feminism is about equality of women in every aspect of women's lives, then all those human rights pillars must be in place. We have to look at all those things — race, poverty, abilities, gender — simultaneously" (11–12).

The NAC's was the most complex and challenging line of opposition to the monuments. Its position foregrounded how gender is mobilized to further entrench hegemonic whiteness as a privileged site of national representation in Canadian public history. Despite the potential for this position to both displace the right and to rearticulate a more powerful anti-racist feminist left basis of unity, it nonetheless remained in the minority. It was ignored by the mainstream media and rendered almost entirely invisible in public debate.

Ultimately, it was the foundation's representation of the Famous Five as "imperfect heroines" that prevailed as dominant. While often treated as a universal claim shared by all Canadians, this position was actually mobilized in direct support of the project and was greatly facilitated by the White multiculturalist script of racial innocence generated and articulated by the foundation itself. Through this framing, three standard responses to charges of racism were typically repeated. First and foremost, the foundation represented the Famous Five as "products of their time." This use of the past had a dual effect; it positioned racism as predominantly an artifact of Canada's past while simultaneously treating past racism as accepted in its time and therefore not accountable in the present. As Frances Wright stated on national television: "Had they known then what we know now I'm sure they would have said different things" (CBC 2000). The foundation was able to assert confidently their public memory project as non-racist by situating these as "values" that belonged to the past and by advocating that "these views are not appropriate for today" (Wright, quoted in Ghosh 1999: 12). The second type of scripted response involved sanitizing the Famous Five by erasing explicit references to racism from public accounts. This included referring to the women's racist ideas and actions as "mistakes" and "errors" (Wright, quoted in Woodard 1998: 38) or suggesting language for diminishing public attention to race. In her television interview with journalist Peter Mansbridge, for example, Wright "corrected" his statement that "some of their views were considered racist" by suggesting that "prejudiced perhaps is a better word" (CBC 2000). This was justified through reference to a narrow and individualist definition of racism, namely that "they did not hate, they did not say you must exclude people. But they had their preferences" (CBC 2000). A third stock response by the foundation involved attributing and amplifying universal and timeless worthiness and benevolence to the five women. Adapting the multiculturalist script through gendered invocations was pivotal because it allowed their achievements for women to be treated as separate from, and to outweigh, their racism. As articulated by a supporter of the foundation at the time: "In the end though, they fought for us all" (Jivraj, quoted in Ghosh 1999: 12) or, in reference to one of the five, Wright argued that ultimately "the doors she opened, she opened for everybody" (CBC 2000).

The following media quote from a surviving ancestor of Emily Murphy neatly encapsulates all aspects of the foundation's script: "Emily was a person of her times. She believed what everyone believed. She did the best she could for her times. She was not a racist. She was a very strong woman. A little feisty. To get anything done, you had to be aggressive" (Gillespie 2000). Emphasizing that she was a woman "of her times" allows for racial innocence to prevail on the grounds that Murphy's beliefs were acceptable in the past because that's "what everyone believed." While "racism" is explicitly stated and permitted here, it is also denied as an attribute of Murphy and held up as incompatible with her attribution as "a very strong woman." Racism thus disappears into the shadow of her gendered achievements — as a "feisty" woman she simply got things "done."

This script was clearly effective in securing rhetorical support for the foundation's campaign, ultimately rendering the Famous Five palatable for national celebration. Echoed widely in the mainstream media, it popularized the foundation's campaign as a reasonable and well-intentioned "balanced" position. Reporters, for example, tended to remove the word "racism," replacing it with phrases like "politically incorrect statements." Where racism was explicitly mentioned, it was typically offset with an excess of text that highlighted the Famous Five's positive achievements. Framing headlines were prominent in this regard and included "Honouring/honoured," "feminist pioneers," "women's rights giants," "return in triumph to Hill" and "bronzes of trailblazers."

While powerful and clearly useful as an effective marketing campaign for media coverage and for winning space for their public history projects, the foundation's "middle-ground" script does not sufficiently explain why this particular narrative of hegemonic gendered whiteness found resonance in the public sphere. To answer this question it is crucial to recognize the script's shared foundations with the racial-national script of multiculturalism. While direct references to multiculturalism were rare in this debate, their occasional appearance is instructive, as in this comment made by a foundation supporter at the unveiling of the Calgary statue:

> Canada has come a long way in the last 70 years.… People have realized that multiculturalism and pluralism is a strength. But at the time of the Persons Case, they thought differently. The women of the Famous five were very white-oriented. In the end, though, they fought for us all. Seventy years later, it doesn't make a difference. (Dr. Munira Jivraj, quoted in Ghosh 1999: 10)

This stated multiculturalist logic incorporates the standard assumptions of Canada's official multiculturalism rhetoric — in particular, the claim of a non-racist "pluralism" in the present replacing a regrettable racism of the past. The overlapping logics between the foundation's script and that of official multiculturalism are evident in this passage. As in the foundation's script, Canada's history of systemic racism is sanitized — in this case, "white-oriented" stands in for an acknowledgement of systemic racism and White racial privilege. Both scripts also assert a "narrative of progressive inclusivity" (Nadeau 2009a: 9) in which the nation's shift to diversity or "pluralism" is assumed to signify a transformative shift to non-racism in the present. As Jivraj states: "Canada has come a long way" through "multiculturalism," to the point that "it doesn't make a difference" that racist acts occurred in the past. In this logic and language of idealized multiculturalism, contemporary racism and the colonial present disappear under the umbrella of "pluralism." At the same time, Canada's racist past becomes irrelevant, and universal unmarked White benevolence is secured as a timeless national trait. The most relevant point in this discursive frame is that "in the end ... they fought for us all." Ultimately, it was the articulation of this liberal feminist argument of the women's universal achievements, with minimal and coded acknowledgment of their "regrettable" racism that prevailed. As *Globe and Mail* columnist Jan Wong stated at a Famous Five Foundation charity event: "The Famous Five stood up for women like themselves ... White, upper-class Protestants. But they created conditions that have benefited me as a woman" (quoted in Woodard 1998: 38).

The main public debate around the foundation's memory project was essentially over by the time the Parliament Hill monument was inaugurated, celebrated and had received full state endorsement, including Prime Minister Chrétien's approval of their "noble actions" (*Toronto Star* 2000a). While some controversy resurfaced a year later with REAL Women's (2001: 10) campaign to pressure the government "to drop the image of the Famous Five from our currency," the pattern of celebrating had largely been established. As with its success in the previous projects, the foundation's brand image on the fifty dollar bill was approved in 2001 and celebrated in a state-sponsored ceremony on the seventy-fifth anniversary of the Persons Case (October 2004). Five years later, on the eightieth anniversary of the case, the Senate passed a motion to make the Famous Five honorary senators. And in October 2011, the federal Conservative government declared the Persons Case to be a National Historic Event (Parks Canada 2011). Today, the only remaining hint of this early round of controversy on the foundation's website is an obscure FAQ link that directs readers on how to address "negative things about some members of the Famous Five." The script's answer is that these "heroes" are "complex beings" who "operated from the basis of compassion, rather than hate."

Gendered Whiteness, Spatial Dominance and the Colonial Present
In her book *Space Invaders*, feminist critical race scholar Nirmal Puwar (2004: 4) interrogates the hegemonic effects that emerge through the racial, national and gender normative practice of the "coupling of particular bodies with specific spaces." As she argues: "There is a connection between bodies and space, which is built, repeated and contested over time ... it is certain types of bodies that are tacitly designated as being the 'natural' occupants of specific positions" (8). It is precisely this privileged space of the "somatic norm" (8), or the naturalized and idealized embodied self attached to a space or position, that the Famous Five occupy in Canada's national and feminist public memory. And yet, their commemorative placement on Parliament Hill has not been addressed in the feminist literature as an act of gendered whiteness implicated in sanitizing and normalizing Canada's racialized colonial present. Rather, unexamined praise for certain features of the monument itself prevails, even in scholarship that is critical of the five women and the history they represent. It has become axiomatic, for example, to celebrate the monument's "over life-size" character as "appropriately larger than life" (Strong-Boag 2009:

57) and to applaud the human-like qualities of the statues as befitting the "humanity of heroes" (Crow 1999: 24), even "imperfect" ones (Eagan 2003: 47). Two of the monument's non-human features have also been objects of substantial praise. The tea cups are now heavily associated with celebration of their collective achievements for women, and the empty chair is treated as an innocent and inherently positive space of interaction where "young women and girls can sit … and dream about their futures" (Metcalfe, quoted in Ghosh 1999: 13).

I return to the bodily space of the monument to trouble the easy characterizations of its features and their meanings. Recasting them as emblematic of the colonial present provides grounds for a more critical reading, one which situates the story of the monument amongst "the stories the West most often tells itself about itself [that] are indeed stories of self-production, a practice that … does induce blindness" (Gregory 2004: 4). Examining the monument and its afterlife on these terms shifts the analytical centre of the debate on public memorialization to contemporary race-thinking. Specifically, it requires us to consider how White nationalism is accomplished as a practical matter in contested racial-colonial space. By extension, this focus directs attention to an analysis of persistent erasures in contemporary feminist scholarship on the monument, particularly the lack of attention to hegemonic gendered whiteness as a social location that has been central to reproducing the colonial present.

How has the *Women Are Persons!* monument intensified the naturalized validation of these embodied subjects as having "an undisputed right to currently pass as the universal figure of leadership" (Puwar 2004: 5) for Canadian women and feminism? How has it obscured this somatic norm while itself resting upon the privilege of unmarked whiteness? After a brief description of the monumental site, three points of analysis are developed to address these questions: first, the written text and teacups as "erasing race" from the site and sanitizing the colonial present; second, the embodied statues as asserting spatial dominance; and third, the empty chair as a site for performing gendered whiteness.

The monument's design as a "collective sculpture" is fitting for the Famous Five as it "combines the role of individual historical figures with recognition of the importance of the group" (Eagan 2003: 46). This is clearly established in both the written text and the individual statues. The primary written description is contained within three bronze plaques situated on the perimeter of the monument, placed together atop a row of cement blocks about three feet high. Two of the plaques (in French and English) tell the story of the Persons Case, highlighting it as broadening the definition of the Canadian Constitution as a "living tree" and as opening the doors of the Senate to women. The five women are described as "determined nation builders" who "paved the way for women to participate in other aspects of public life." Short biographical statements for each of the women highlight their individual achievements. Two secondary sites of written text are also embedded in the monument: the newspaper tablet held by Nellie McClung reads "Journal, October 15, 1929, Women are Persons … Les femmes sont des personnes …," highlighting their collective story, and each woman's handwritten signature carved into the stone platform near their feet accentuates the individuals. While the five bodies are individualized through their separate placement in an expansive circular fashion, they are also collectively joined through a focal centre (the tablet), which ensures that all face each other across the empty inner space. Two of the women are sitting at a teacup-laden table and three are standing, with one draping her arm over an empty chair. The spacious site is large enough for several individuals to simultaneously walk between the statues and to stand beside them, or for groups to gather in the centre amongst them.

WRITTEN TEXTS AND TEACUPS: ERASING RACISM THROUGH GENDER AND UNMARKED WHITENESS

The written text contributes significantly to establishing the tone and context for interaction on the site, namely by "erasing race" from the monumental space and effectively "retaining the basic structure of power and privilege of White dominance" (Jiwani 2006: xvii) in public discourse. Indeed, a fundamental erasure is embedded in the written texts, where the history of racism and Canada's colonial story is rendered completely absent. This is typical of hegemonic "nation builders" discourse and, as others note, this focus was required "in order to meet existing criteria at the federal level" (Dodd 2009: 19). This erasure is also compatible with the sanitized version of the Famous Five pursued and promoted by the foundation. Expunging the legacy of racism from the commemorative site thus permits a uni-dimensional gendered focus to prevail, one that is easily celebratory because it is unhinged from the historical frame of colonization and racism. In this context of erasure even the teacups appear innocent, completely shorn of their colonial symbolism. Foregrounded instead is their more celebratory meaning, as in the "Pink Teas," or women's private strategy meetings held by early suffragists (Famous Five Foundation 2011). While this permits a celebration of women's activism, it also romanticizes Canada's colonial past and forecloses consideration of the exclusionary history of whiteness and space in women's movements past and present.

Instead of a more nuanced and critical recognition then, the women are commemorated for what they have achieved for others in the nation (particularly White women). Far from acknowledging Canadian racism, for example, the site's text writes Nellie McClung into history as one who worked to "improve the rights of women, immigrants, farmers and factory workers." While this kind of erasure and inversion is standard script for the commemorative projects of White nationalist states, scholarship and critical commentary are presumably not bound in this same way. And yet, critical analysis of the written text is strikingly absent in the feminist public history literature that examines the monuments (Eagan 2003; McKenna 2005; Dodd 2009; Strong-Boag 2009). The original erasure on the site has thus been compounded by the fact that the written text, which establishes a tone of erasing racism and cleansing colonialism, has neither been named nor analyzed in scholarly research on public history.

The Bodies: Humanized, "Real" and Spatially Dominant

The erasure of the women's legacy of racism from the site established the conditions for popular and celebratory identifications and interactions with the monument through a singular gender reading of the Famous Five (i.e., uni-dimensional affirmations of their achievements for gender equality). Reflecting and appealing to a distinctly White feminist sensibility, the "bronzes on the Hill" (*Toronto Star* 2000b) thus function in and for dominant White culture, providing a site for recuperation of racial hegemony rather than a space for critical remembering of racism and the colonial present. The following analysis, however, considers their gender and race meanings simultaneously, thus re-evaluating the meaning of the statues' "larger than life" size not as inherently celebratory, but rather, as performing spatial dominance through gendered whiteness. By restoring race to the analysis of the commemorative scene, I read the over-life-size bodies (and the public fascination surrounding them) as an act of White nationalism in which White women "construct themselves as spatially dominant" (Hage 2000: 48). From this perspective the super-humanization of these particular bodies, and their placement on privileged national terrain, reflects a move to re-whiten Canadian feminism in public memory.

The "performances of space" (Gregory 2004: 19) enacted through the five embodied statues can be viewed through this critical race lens as a "resistant response" (Srivastava 2005: 29) to anti-racist feminism's rupturing of the White feminist claim to be the natural spokeswoman for Canadian women. The NAC's definitive shift away from a White-dominated leadership model in that period, most notably, disrupted the pattern of the idealized somatic norm in which White feminists had spatially dominated the organization and its leadership positions for over two decades. As activists from the period have widely attested (Gottlieb 1993; Rebick and Roach 1996; Robertson 1999), this interruption of a "racialized episteme" provoked both a physical and symbolic "disorientation" for White feminism in Canada (Puwar 2004: 42). It effectively broke the pattern of performativity that had created the entrenched singular association between White bodies and spaces of feminist leadership.

Through the representation of the women as super-human-sized figures of benevolent leadership, the embodied statues can thus be viewed as performatively asserting the return and re-naturalization of the White body as the somatic norm of Canadian women. The mask of benevolence, or White tolerance, is projected here through the humanizing features of the statues. The statues' open and "real" eyes elicit a sense of trust, their extended hands and arms suggest openness and their individual handwritten signatures on the platform invoke familiarity through personalized naming. The attributes most associated with leadership are also accentuated through the bodies — the super-enlarged hands are guiding and assertive (particularly in the three standing figures), the gesturing bodies suggest agency and capability, the open eyes suggest wisdom and knowledge and the extended height evokes confidence. The statues might also be easily read as masculinized, a feature that further deepens the association with ideals of "natural" leadership, particularly when coupled with implicit whiteness. By simultaneously amplifying their gendered traits and decontextualizing whiteness from the nation's racial-colonial history, these disproportionately humanized and over-sized heroine figures are iconized through the monument as benevolent "mothers of the nation." Reading the statues as performing race through spatial dominance however, permits analysis of this representation as a contemporary attempt to assert and re-authenticate their presence as the prototypical White Canadian feminist leadership.

The Empty Chair: Gendered Whiteness as Monumental Performance
As with the other features of the monument, the empty chair is typically appraised positively. Some call attention to its unique feature, as an "empty chair that invites the viewer

to interact with the sculpture" (*Ottawa Citizen* 2000b). Others, however, capture more precisely its deeper ideological associations, as in the following quote: "an empty chair, representing generations of Canadian women to come, and Catherine will sit in it as their embodiment" (*Ottawa Citizen* 2000c). As the first description suggests, the chair is, of course, open to multiple and contested interpretations and interactions. The second description suggests a greater urgency to unpack its discursive foundations, however, particularly in terms of the associations it implies for an assumed and idealized mode of participation and belonging in this space. It indicates, in particular, that a more limiting set of discursive associations is already operating to impose a particular interpretive frame. Most notably, the chair is assumed to be "representing generations," it is nationalized as "Canadian" and the idea of a shared "embodiment" is invoked. Far from being an innocent interactive space and open text then, the "empty chair" is already framed within a narrow institutional script of hegemonic national belonging. Surrounded by unacknowledged gendered whiteness in the form of the Famous Five and in a context marked by significant historical erasures, the chair's imagined and projected "embodiment" of "generations of Canadian women" requires further inquiry. As a basic starting point, it needs to be acknowledged that the context of spatial dominance reflects and refracts the imagined shared generational history of White national feminism. Located on Parliament Hill and aligned with the Senate doors, the chair and its inhabitants are scripted into a generational story that narrates directly back to the ideals and practices of White maternalist feminism pursued by the original famous five women. While this spatial arrangement does not prohibit participants from imagining broader feminist lineages, it certainly reinforces an othering of histories and belongings that contradict these hegemonic parameters or do not easily fit the intended script. In this context, the over-sized embrace of the chair's inhabitants by an omnipresent "mother of the nation" is best read as a suturing practice that intends a hegemonic reading of both national and feminist history. While further research is required to examine the meanings drawn from the experience of meaning-making at the monument, it is clear that critical inquiry requires stepping outside of the scripted focus on the celebrated "interactive" chair.

To close this section and conclude this chapter, I raise here a different route of inquiry into these interrogations. By all accounts, the empty chair has been treated as an interactive and playful feature designed solely for visitors to the monument. On these terms it is assumed to be a space of engagement, an opening for dialogue and interaction that is aimed primarily at the site user. Alternately, however, we might also view the empty chair as a site whose main subject is not just the user, but also the producer. This would require a shift to thinking about the chair as driven by concerns about the "self-production" (Gregory 2004: 4) of the foundation and its investments in reproducing a White hegemonic colonial present. From this view its primary aim is to solidify hegemony around the ideal of feminism associated with gendered whiteness and forms of neoliberal multiculturalist participation being advanced by the Famous Five Foundation.

At issue then, and the focus of this chapter's interrogation, is the contested but ultimately successful mobilization of White national feminist interests around the making of the *Women Are Persons!* monument. The Famous Five Foundation's vision for a monument was not initially shared in the women's movement. Of particular relevance, the project was rejected outright by the organized anti-racist feminist movement in the form of the newly transformed NAC. To explain how state support and public acceptance was eventually secured in favour of the monument requires a multilayered analysis. First, in tracing the uneven history of the Famous Five as an "enduring symbol," it is clear that its popularity declined substantially during the consolidation of anti-racist feminist movements through the 1980s and much of the 1990s. What emerges then is a story of the re-whitening of Canadian feminism as anti-racist feminism and the broader "infrastructure of dissent" struggled against backlash and fragmentation. As the context of neoliberalism intensified in the 1990s, so too did a crisis of whiteness converge with anti-feminist and anti-immigrant backlash. It is in this turbulent context that the Famous Five Foundation was able to successfully revive the symbol. Second, I argue that the struggle over the commemorability of the monument was won, in significant part, through mobilizing the script of institutionalized multiculturalism at a time of ascending popularity around White racial-national identifications. My discussion of the monument as a site of spatial dominance and racial erasure provides some preliminary analysis of how national space was mobilized by hegemonic feminism to reproduce and popularize the colonial present. This included, most notably, the foundation's successful over-amplification of gender-based claims while substantially erasing historical markers of racial dominance associated with the Famous Five. Third, the analysis of the foundation and its efforts to recuperate the Famous Five provide some insight into the operations of the "new self-assertive and self-confident white feminism" (Thobani, quoted in Khan 2007: 51) that emerged nationally and globally in the late 1990s. Its successful proliferation of this public memory enterprise rested heavily on disavowing gendered whiteness as a category of analysis. Clearly, the foundation's White nation-builders' discourse needs to be explored and troubled on many levels, not least because its colonial foundations can be easily mobilized in support of the imperial projects of "the West" that increasingly rely on liberal feminist discourse.

NOTES

1. Information about the sculptor, Barbara Paterson, and images of the monuments can be found at heroines.ca/celebrate/statuepersons.html
2. The 1918 decision to extend voting rights to "women" federally was, in fact, partial and grounded in the systemic racial exclusions and hierarchies produced by the colonial white settler state in that period. As Crow (1999: 26) succinctly summarizes it, "the franchise was not extended to people of Japanese ancestry until 1948, to Québec women until 1940, to the Inuit until 1950, or to First Nations people living on reserves until 1960."
3. Significantly, this crisis of whiteness reverberated throughout the women's movement, where organizations had taken the lead in effectively challenging entrenched forms of white hegemony. Sunera Thobani stated of NAC in this period: "We shook up the whole country when we put forward that agenda [of anti-racist feminism]" (quoted in Khan 2007: 54). In the lead-up to her election in 1993 as NAC's first woman of colour president, Thobani was publicly attacked by a member of Parliament who falsely called her an illegal immigrant. She and the NAC challenged this racist discourse, particularly exposing how it situated women of colour as "outsiders" and unfit for positions of national feminist leadership. While this was a crucial struggle against the backlash, the defence of white Canadian feminist entitlement nonetheless continued to have traction inside and outside the women's movement.

4. Campaign Life (now called Campaign Life Coalition) was created in 1978 as a lobbying organization formed by anti-abortion groups from across Canada. In 1997 it launched LifeSiteNews, an internet news service whose primary audience is social conservatives and anti-abortion movements in the United States and Canada. One of Campaign Life's founding members, Gwen Landolt, is currently also the vice-president and public face of REAL (Realistic, Equal, Active, for Life) Women of Canada. Created in 1983 as an explicitly anti-feminist women's organization, REAL Women formed to counter the growth and success of the feminist National Action Committee on the Status of Women. REAL Women is the most widely recognized women's anti-abortion lobby in Canada. As with Campaign Life Coalition, its anti-liberal and socially conservative position is used to lobby against equity and the expansion of rights-based laws, including those pertaining to pornography, affirmative action, universal childcare, prostitution and same-sex marriage.

Afterword

UNMAPPING CANADA

Starting with Bodies and Repressed Truths

Sherene Razack

> At the end of all our theorizing, there is someone's body, so I start there. —Mari
> Matsuda 2010

The scholars in this collection confidently launch their contributions to what they describe as a critical Canadian studies approach. They set about contesting the liberal roots of multiculturalism, unmapping Canada as a White settler society and subjecting nationalism to full critical scrutiny. The word critical, they avow, is meant to underline that studies of the nation must begin with the understanding that Canada is a White settler society, one that is constituted in ongoing colonial violence.

This book invites readers to think about the salience of race and colonialism in the Canadian context. Racial exclusion is built into the Canadian story of multiculturalism, Haque argues, showing that multiculturalism emerged as a compromise between two colonizing nations that were negotiating their respective powers, powers that cohere around the management of Indigenous and racialized others. Although each colonizing group imagines itself as White, whiteness is differently constituted. Leroux traces how Québec crafts its own version of a White settler society based on its history as colonizer (of Indigenous peoples) and colonized (by the English). Cleaving to the idea of being colonized, Québecers readily acquiesce in the subordination of racial others in a bid to protect what they view as their own endangered patrimony.

What the national mythology declares to be true, that Canada is a society founded by Europeans, must be *made* true on the ground. White mythologies are underwritten by material practices such as arts funding. As Fatona shows, arts funding prioritizes European elite arts. Indeed, a thousand commemorative acts teach citizens that we live in a society peacefully settled by Europeans and without a long history of the dispossession of Indigenous peoples and the exploitation of racialized groups. A museum made of the tunnels of Moose Jaw, where Chinese workers are supposed to have lived after working on the railroad, tells a story of a benevolent White Canada transcending its racist past (Leung's chapter). The Saskatchewan Centennial commemorates the initiatives of pioneers and disavows Indigenous nations (Caldwell's chapter). In these pedagogical enterprises, no stone is left unturned. Monuments commemorating White feminists (Nadeau's chapter), the iconic status of Indian moccasins (Lee's chapter) and the Rainbow Bridge at Niagara Falls connecting Canada to the U.S (Sehdev's chapter) all must be enlisted in the symbolic and material production of a White Canada and a benevolent nation. Anyone hoping to enter the national story must tell a story of White enterprise and innocence. Some Jews, Byers and Schwartz argue, turn to Zionism to negotiate their own passage into the nation as people of European origin. Sexual minorities, Howlett suggests, mimic a White heteronormativity to gain the right to marriage. If we are inducted into the national mythology at every turn, it is surely because the colonial project is unstable. First Nations who assert their sovereignty through the right to move between the two countries that the Rainbow Bridge separates, for instance, remind us all *whose* ground we really stand on and what it takes to make it ours.

What are the challenges facing critical scholars in a White settler society? Unlike the recent turn (and of course return) in the academy to a scholarship that refuses to start from a commitment to social justice, the contributors to this book are absolutely clear that scholarship must be at the outset anti-racist and anti-colonial. I am inspired by the unabashed politics of the scholars in this anthology. I would like to use the space of this afterword to consider some directions for critical scholars in mapping the contours of a White settler society. I believe that critical scholars must start with bodies, as Mari Matsuda maintains. For Matsuda, starting with bodies is about pursuing an "understanding of those places where race meets power, where people are hurt, where people survive, where people thrive" (Matsuda 2010: 350). I would like to begin with the Indigenous body and end with a consideration of where other bodies are on the landscape.

STARTING WITH INDIGENOUS BODIES

If, as Mari Matsuda states, there is a body at the end of our theorizing, a violated, marginalized and sometimes murdered person, then at the beginning of our theorizing is the body of the colonizer, rapist or murderer. For me, a pre-eminent challenge is to make *colonizers* visible and to explain why they do what they do *in order that they are held to account*, both at the individual and collective levels. The theoretical scaffold on which accountability is built may draw on a variety of disciplines, but its point of departure, if the context is Canada, is that this is a White settler society where the theft of Indigenous land is an ongoing project that requires a vigorous White supremacy at its core. In scholarship and in law (where accountability is pursued), the challenge for me is to understand the violence of the colonial project and the colonial subjects it both requires and produces.

Some scholars have turned to psychoanalysis for answers to the problem of violence against the Indigenous in settler colonial societies, for example, Brunner's work on Zionism as a form of settler occupation that is deeply narcissistic and therefore fearful of and violent towards Palestinians (Brunner 2010). Nationalisms that are described as narcissistic, as Brunner describes Israeli nationalism (and arguably all nationalisms are to some degree narcissistic), are organized around protecting the material basis of *normative* citizens. It is therefore necessary to theorize the role that race plays in the making of the nation's psyche, constituting some citizens as within the national community and others as threats to it. Psychoanalysis offers insight into the persistence of violence against racial others in White settler societies. As Renée Bergland (2000) explains, drawing on Etienne Balibar, the settler subject internalizes the colonial relation, believing that it is through enterprise, moral superiority and courage that the land belongs to White settlers, while at the same time these same settlers remain haunted by those they have dispossessed. The American subject is obsessed with Indians, Bergland writes, often imagining that Indians are ghosts and not living subjects, because it is only through Indians that the settler subject feels both entitlement and anxiety. Both "Aliens [Black slaves and later other groups exploited for labour] and Indians are repressed because they represent the fearsome possibility of non-citizenship" (18). The connection among individual settler identity, violence against Indigenous people and the settler collective is established and is traceable through land. This connection becomes visible when we begin to account for the persistent violence against Indigenous people and the widespread indifference to it. The nexus of violence, terror and subjectivity, as Saidye Hartman (1997) writes with respect to slavery and as I attempt to trace with respect to Indigenous peoples, can be examined in moments of shocking and terrible violence as well as in moments of routinized violence. The challenge is to see how terror is enacted in the everyday.

In my research on Indigenous deaths in custody, I am quite literally starting with bodies: dead Indigenous men and some women whose bodies are found in the snow with handcuff marks on the wrists, in custody in hospital with boot prints on the chest and in dark city alleys. For example, focusing on inquests and public inquiries, I track what is said in law about a sixty-seven-year-old Shuswap man who dies in hospital in police custody with a large, visible, purple boot print on his chest, a mark no one notices (Razack 2011a, 2011b). Both the boot print and the indifference to it require explanation. In another death in custody case, I analyze what is said in the commission of inquiry into the actions of the police, who dropped off a barely conscious alcoholic older Indigenous man in a dark alley on a cold Vancouver night (Razack forthcoming). These deaths, and others, give rise to patterns involving an everyday failure to care, a systemic indifference and callousness, and sometimes, outright murder. Inquests and public inquiries reveal these patterns and offer the same recommendations time after time. We ought to care more, they conclude, offering a plethora of recommendations that have little impact. Such legal accounts of Indigenous death *do something.* I advance the argument that the inquest and the inquiry are sites which produce the settler subject, whose entitlement to the land is secured through a performance of Indigenous people as a dying race whom no one can kill or harm since they are dying anyway. It is only when I bring together the violence itself and the persistent indifference to it in law that I see that White settler society has a strong vested interest in violence against Indigenous peoples. The violence provides settlers with a sense of themselves as modern and capable, and as legitimate owners of the land. Race and land come together in these moments of violence and in law's treatment of it.

Writing about a public inquiry into the death of Neil Stonechild, a seventeen-year-old Indigenous youth whose frozen body was found on the outskirts of Saskatoon, Joyce Green (2006) examines Stonechild's death and the related terrible fact of three frozen Indigenous bodies turning up in the same area, around the same time that Stonechild was found. She offers the argument that racism killed Neil Stonechild. Recalling that two police officers had a bloody and battered Stonechild in their cruiser hours before he died and reviewing the evidence at the inquiry that Stonechild had handcuff marks on his wrists and scrapes on his face consistent with handcuffs being slammed into it, Green considers what could have led police to engage in the practice of dumping Indigenous men to freeze to death. Drawing on Albert Memmi's theorizing of the oppressor's hatred for the colonized, a hatred Memmi maintained was born in the oppressor's theft of land, Green suggests that it is this hate, nurtured in a structural privilege and systemic racism, that explains why the two officers, Larry Hartwig and Brad Senger, may have driven Neil Stonechild to his death. Power and hatred came together that night, she suggests, to produce the outcome of two cops brutalizing a young boy and leaving him to die in subzero temperatures in a field outside of town. The same power and malice come together to prompt other police officers to protect Hartwig and Senger, and for the system to delay a thorough investigation of his death until ten years later, when similar deaths finally prompted an RCMP investigation and ultimately a public inquiry. Although Hartwig and Senger were ultimately fired for lying about the fact that they had Stonechild in their custody a few hours before he died, they were not charged with manslaughter or murder.

The first challenge that arises when Indigenous bodies with handcuff marks on the wrists turn up in the snow is to prove the connection between the two officers and Stonechild's death. The second challenge is to show that Hartwig and Senger are not simply rogue police officers but White men who share in a widespread dehumanization of Indigenous peoples. Critical scholars have little to contribute on the first point since this is a matter best left to detectives, pathologists and forensic experts, among others. Our domain is the second challenge. We track dehumanization, and we are tasked, so to speak (to use police and military language) with showing how little anyone White cared or considered Indigenous life to be valuable. If a widespread dehumanization is in evidence, then we can begin to see how bodies may have ended up in snowy fields and why so few cared about how they met their fate. Green begins the argument that racism kills by bridging the gap between the individual and the systemic. Citing my own work on the murder of Pamela George, an Indigenous woman killed by two White men in Regina, she proposes that we consider that Neil Stonechild was evicted from the city because the city is established historically and in the present as belonging to White settlers (see Razack 2000). In their individual acts, two White police officers were simply doing the work required of them in a White settler society, the work of cleansing the city of Indigenous bodies.

As I argue in my study of Indigenous deaths in custody and in my exploration of the death of Pamela George, colonizers lay claim to the land through the practice of violating with impunity those whom they have dispossessed. Racial entitlement, fuelled by a devaluing of the lives of the colonized, must be continually performed if colonizers are to know themselves as owners *and if they are to actually become owners*. Violence towards the colonized confirms who is in charge, as nothing else can, but it also dispenses with bodies who can contest the settler claim to land. Thus, a making of self through violence against the Indigenous other characterizes White settler society. Such a self is in evidence when two ordinary White college students kill an Indigenous woman in a drunken spree, when police drop Indigenous people on the outskirts of prairie cities on cold winter nights and when any of us who considers frozen Indigenous bodies in the snow and wrists with handcuff marks, fail to ask ourselves how they came to be there. If there remains, however, something under-theorized in this argument, a gap that persists between the individual and the systemic, something that would explain the murderous impulses one sees in the high rates of Indigenous deaths in custody and the hundreds of missing and murdered Indigenous women but also in societal indifference to these bodies, it is because the racial subject defies easy tracking as a subject who is full of rage. Rage has many manifestations and the psyche is hard to track empirically.

What To Do with Larry Hartwig's Smile?

What to do, for example, when those who commit racial violence are the loudest voices proclaiming their love and respect for Indigenous peoples? Consider Larry Hartwig as a prototype in this regard. Filmmaker Tasha Hubbard talked about her encounter with Larry Hartwig while making a film about freezing deaths early in 2000. In Hubbard's film, *Two Worlds Colliding*, there are two vignettes of Hartwig. In the first, in an on-camera interview well before Hartwig's appearance at the inquiry into the death of Neil Stonechild, Hartwig, one of the new (White) cultural liaison officers, describes his healthy respect for Indigenous communities and his conviction that it is he who must learn from them. "We must never abuse our authority," he tells Hubbard emphatically. "We have the author-ity to destroy lives and we must always be careful that that authority is *never ever* abused" (Hubbard 2004). One's hair stands on end when next we see Hartwig testifying at the inquiry into the freezing death of Neil Stonechild. We learn that Hartwig was one of the officers who had Neil Stonechild in custody that night.

When I asked Hubbard about this horrifying moment in her film, she elaborated on how she came to shoot the two vignettes:

> When I met him for the first time, I was attending a diversity conference where 20+ Saskatoon police officers were in attendance. I knew some of them, and was asking them for short interviews. One refused, saying he did not want to go on camera, but suggested I ask Hartwig for an interview. I was told that he likes to talk, and indeed, he readily agreed to be interviewed. The first words out of his mouth were "we as a police force have developed a culture of secrecy." I actually committed a director's gaffe by turning to my camera operator and asking him if the camera was on. Most police were reluctant to talk about abuse of power, and it would often take me many questions before they would begin to talk about the issues on the table. But not Hartwig. At the end of the interview, as he walked back into the conference, my crew and I commented on the anomalous nature of his interview. It wasn't until six months later that it became public that he was one of the officers being investigated for Neil Stonechild's death. I now wonder if that reluctant officer pushed me in Hartwig's direction because it was known within the force that he was a suspect.

> When it was Hartwig's turn to testify at the Commission of Inquiry, we filmed his entire testimony. Something told me to make sure we filmed him as he exited the stand. His growing smile as he gets further away from the stand disturbs me greatly. Smugly celebrating his avoidance of responsibility? I in turn avoided watching Hartwig's footage for weeks. When I finally brought myself to watch, I read the transcripts alongside. A few times, I knew there was nothing

> useable in specific sections of testimony, so would fast forward and it was then
> I made the following observation: at regular intervals, Hartwig turned his head
> from right to left. Both his interview and his testimony at the inquiry began to
> remind me of a performance. It is as though officers like Hartwig and Munsen
> (the senior officer responsible for Darrell Night's abandonment) "perform" their
> role as trustworthy police officers while masking their true intentions and actions
> towards Indigenous peoples, choosing to replicate the power dynamic with tragic
> results. (Hubbard and Razack 2011: 321)

Hubbard's insights about what police officers perform in legal settings suggest that Hartwig exhibits aspects of a psychopathology. It is Hartwig's "growing smile" that we need to explore here. Does the smile indicate that Hartwig is gleeful that he got away with murder? Is he smiling because he believes that the system will protect him? Colonialism produces someone like Hartwig. We can see the connection between Hartwig and the White collective during the inquiry when it became clear that for so many police officers and administrators, Stonechild's death was not something to be concerned about. Hartwig (and Senger) were clearly part of a wider police collective for whom Indigenous life held little value. Hartwig's performance was matched by several police officers who testified at the inquiry.

From his commissioner's seat, Mr. Justice David Wright had to watch a seemingly endless parade of police witnesses, from investigators to the chain of command, whose conduct the commissioner could only conclude was inexcusable. From the investigator who closed the Stonechild file in a matter of hours, to the deputy police chief who misled the press about how much effort had been expended to find Stonechild's killers, few police officers behaved ethically with respect to Neil Stonechild. Some lied; others could not remember, and all but two (tellingly, an Indigenous officer and a White officer who had an adopted Indigenous son who knew Neil Stonechild) could not find it in their hearts to pursue the story of what happened to Neil Stonechild.

In the Stonechild Inquiry, confronted with what appeared inescapably as a *collective* impulse to dehumanize, Mr. Justice Wright refused to begin with colonialism, which would bring the White collective into view. Instead, the judge finds that Indigenous people and the police are equally to blame for what came to pass on the frozen prairie that night, and in the subsequent widespread failure to care. Here, as Green points out, Wright is walking a path that depends on accepting that colonizer and colonized are somehow equivalent. Presumably, Indigenous people are to blame because some are alcoholics who are difficult to handle; the police are to blame because they do not have effective ways (and presumably non-lethal ones) of handling the problem that indigeneity poses, namely public drunkenness and widespread addiction. Things would all work better if everyone understood each other culturally, the judge concluded. Armed with cultural knowledge, perhaps non-Indigenous cops would not indulge so quickly in devaluing Indigenous life. Unable to entirely ignore the pathology of what unfolded before him, the commissioner recommends race relations and anger management training and strategies to promote better cross-cultural relations. As Green (2006: 520) observes: "Wright misunderstood the toxic gulf [between Indigenous people and police] because he saw it as personal and relational, and as being equally the responsibility of the dominant and Indigenous communities. He did not conceptualise it as a logical consequence of the processes of colonialism." The only way to avoid taking the wrong turn that Mr. Justice Wright takes, Green concludes, is to understand where a racist political culture comes from. As she ruefully acknowledges, however, how can we expect this understanding from those who benefit most from the arrangements?

If we can track a persistent dehumanization, the "toxic gulf" of which Green speaks, we must connect it to the materialities of the colonial project and not only to the psyche. The rage/anxiety that prompts the dehumanization comes from some place and that place is the material structure in which White colonizers are at the top of the racial hierarchy and Indigenous peoples are at the bottom. As settlers, who must we be and who do we become when our individual and collective selves depend on a storyline about innocent besieged settlers and Indigenous peoples who are unable to bear the stresses of modern life? If we don't begin with the fact of colonialism, we will end up where Mr. Justice Wright did, turning a murder and collective complicity in it into a misunderstanding between two cultures.

Leslie Thielen-Wilson (2012) offers just such an anti-colonial analysis in her remarkable exploration of the Canadian government's and the law's responses to Indigenous demands for redress for the genocidal violence of Indian residential schools (IRS). Thielen-Wilson argues that we must first understand the institutions of the schools and the justice system as integral to the colonial quest to control land and resources. As Indigenous scholars emphasize repeatedly, the violence of IRS was aimed at nothing less than eradicating a culture and a people. Once we appreciate that residential schools were central to the acquisition of land and resources, we can begin to see how Canada's response to Indigenous claims for IRS redress is also part of a continuing acquisition. The government's and the law's responses to Indigenous demands re-assert colonial sovereignty *today* not only by disavowing colonization altogether but by casting Indigenous peoples as too damaged to become modern subjects, and thus not fit to be present owners of the land. Arguing that the *ongoing* colonial project is secured when courts refuse to recognise the violence of Indian residential schools, Thielen-Wilson demonstrates what she terms the triadic relationship of land, terror and White identity that structures settler colonialism. Building on Fanon, who made clear that colonialism is not only a project of accumulation, but crucially a quest for identity, Thielen-Wilson demonstrates that "white racial identity and hegemony are constructed and solidified *through* relations of accumulation" (8). Put more directly, "just as settler control of land is always about white identity, so too, white identity is always about land (even when land is not explicitly visible or tangible)" (8).

The inextricable link between White identity and land is, I propose, a critical part of the methodological foundation of critical scholarship. The dehumanization of Indigenous people, Fanon showed, *symbolically and materially* produces the settler as entitled to the land. If we start here, we can follow, as Thielen-Wilson does, how Whites as a collective are secured whenever violence is directed against Indigenous people, and whenever that violence is denied. We cannot explore the Larry Hartwigs of the world, and indeed Mr. Justice Wright or ourselves, unless we consider both the psyche and its material base. When we ask what would prompt two White police officers to batter an Indigenous man and leave him to die, and what would enable so many to disregard such a death or to view it as inevitable in view of Indigenous dysfunction, these questions must be explored within the context of a history and ongoing theft of land, and within a context of ongoing structures and institutions that perpetuate the supremacy of one group over another. These questions cannot be pursued if we continue to believe that our encounters with each other are merely encounters between individuals, and that we are born again each day, fresh and innocent, outside of history. They cannot be pursued if we refuse to acknowledge *where* we are and who we become. What would interrupt the cycle of violence that begins with the theft of the land and continues with the persistent dehumanization of Indigenous peoples? Our answer to this question cannot be limited to the recommendation that settlers should better understand Indigenous people culturally. We will need to stop stealing and to give back some of what was stolen. The fact of the matter is that the bodies continue to pile up.

OTHER RACIALIZED BODIES

If we must start with Indigenous bodies, understanding that the settler state is profoundly structured by the theft of Indigenous lands and the ever constant necessity of ensuring that Indigenous people must always be disappearing, as Andrea Smith has succinctly put it, the White settler state is also structured by other imperatives: the commodification of the Black body as property (slavery) and the exploitation of the labour of marginalized groups. Unless we believe that White supremacy structures all racialized bodies in the same way, the critical scholar must consider the meaning of differently racialized bodies, unpacking the violence that is directed at each and considering how these are related to each other in the project of making a White settler society. As Bergland reminds us, all disenfranchised groups must be spectral, denied personhood yet returning in uncanny moments to remind the settlers that they are not the enterprising and innocent subject of their fantasies (Bergland 2000: 18). The challenge for critical scholars is to understand the relationship between these spectral subjects in the White settler unconscious.

Canadian critical scholars, myself included, have been particularly challenged to theorize the violence directed at Black bodies. Because Canada did not have plantation slavery (it had other forms), we easily elide slavery in our analyses, believing that transatlantic slavery did not leave its mark on Black bodies in Canada as it did in the United States. In effect, many of us fail to see the continuous eviction from humanity that is the lot of Black people regardless of whether they are the descendents of slaves or recent immigrants from countries in Africa and/or the Caribbean.

Jared Sexton has carefully explained what it means to theorize blackness, or more specifically, anti-blackness, the obsessive need of North American White settler society to commodify and obliterate Black bodies. We must begin, as Sexton advises, (drawing on Hartman 1997) with the absoluteness of power that converged on the Black slave's body. The Black slave was property and the slave's life had value only in relation to this fact. The commodification of human existence that was so unprecedented until the transatlantic slave trade means that the Black slave lost not his land or even his community but in fact his very existence as human. It is this "crushing objecthood," of which Fanon writes, that continues to define Black bodies today, and it is this singular condition that we lose when we engage in facile comparisons of forms of violence. For example, to compare the torture at Abu Ghraib to the lynchings of Blacks after slavery, as I did in my own work (Razack 2008), is to elide the specific history and meaning of the Black body, and the specific violence of anti-blackness (Sexton 2010: 43). We must attend to the singularity of racial slavery and its legacy of dehumanization of the Black body (44). In comparison to other racialized groups, "antiblackness seems invariant and limitless" (44). Sexton is careful to note, however, that it is not comparison that matters, as much as a relational analysis: "Black existence does not represent the total reality of the racial formation — it is not the beginning and the end of the story — but it does relate to the totality; it indicates the (repressed) truth of the political and economic system" (48). The truth of Black labour must be denied if the structure of White settler society is to stand, an argument made by Achille Mbembe with respect to apartheid South Africa. Mbembe writes of the racial city and its economy. Under apartheid, where Black people did all the work, the use value of Black labour had to be obfuscated and repressed, and the Black body rendered both indispensible and expendable (Mbembe 2003: 381).

An urgent question confronting critical theorists is what happens if we fail to attend to Black existence in our theorizing. What happens to my own theorizing of Indigenous deaths in custody? For Sexton, Blacks are "the prototypical targets of the panoply of police practices and the juridical infrastructure built up around them" (48). If, then, I do not take into account what happens to Blacks, I will miss something about how policing and the justice system are both organized. However, Sexton's observations about Blacks as prototypical targets does not hold true for Canada. The contemporary parameters of policing emerged most clearly with respect to the policing of Indigenous bodies in the late ninetenth century (Edmonds 2010). Vagrancy laws, for instance, emerged in the context of settlers claiming the city as White space at a time when it was urgent for White settlers to evict Indigenous people from cities and confine them to reserves. But Sexton is correct in one respect. When we consider why jails and prisons are filling up with Indigenous peoples, we would do well to look to the policing of Blacks in the U.S. to understand some of the *contemporary* practices that have gained currency in Canada. The school-to-prison pipeline, for instance, while differently organized for Indigenous peoples (one need only think of the history of residential schools), now draws on schooling practices that developed in the United States, where the schooling, or more accurately non-schooling, of Blacks occurs in a context where the Black body is criminalized from the start. The apparatus of schooling and even teaching practices revolved around the need to control Black bodies always understood as threat. I might also ask in turn what Sexton misses when he "forgets" colonialism. Andrea Smith (2010) comments that when Sexton relegates all non-Black racialized groups to a single category, lumping Indigenous people into the category of racial minority immigrants, this simply reifies the settler colonial project. Land claims disappear, as does genocide, into the fiction that Indigenous people have simply progressed into (been assimilated into) the White settler population. To believe in this fiction not only flies in the face of the facts but, more importantly, misses the ongoing and active efforts on the part of the settler state to destroy Indigenous communities.

If the commodification of human existence that structures responses to Black bodies is the repressed truth of White settler society, another (and prior) repressed truth structures White settler society: the land is stolen. Each repressed truth gives rise to particular violence, but these strains of violence and the truths they repress operate to install White settlers both as owners of the land and as dominant over all others. When we come to consider how the status of Asians as foreigners within the nation, or racialized migrants (a tautology since White Anglo Saxons are very rarely confined to the category of migrant) as outsiders whose labour we rely on but who are not entitled to the benefits of citizenship, we can see how the foundations of North American White settler society (stolen land and the commodification of Black bodies as property) is protected by the logic that only Whites are citizens and that citizenship is organized to "make live" White communities and let die others, to use Foucault's terms (Foucault 2003: 256).

Attempting to capture the various strains that make up White settler society as a racial formation, Andrea Smith (2010 : ¶2) articulates the following three "primary logics of white supremacy" at play in a White settler society: "(1) slaveability/anti-black racism, which anchors capitalism; (2) genocide, which anchors colonialism; and (3) orientalism, which anchors war." Smith takes issue with such scholars as Jared Sexton and Angela Harris who stress (1) and ignore or minimize (2). But she also takes to task Indigenous American scholars who fight for recognition within a capitalist settler state that remains structured by the logic that White bodies count more than any other. Smith's categories do not shed light on the nature of violence directed at each group — why for example a widespread killing rage at Indigenous people, gratuitous violence against Blacks and a willingness to abandon Muslim men to torture and solitary confinement? Even more significant, in these apparently discrete practices, we cannot see how the three logics sustain each other, as for example when young Black men with few options are recruited into the U.S. military and participate in military rule over racial others. Smith's categories still require that we work out how at any one site these three aspects of White settler society operate to shore up the settler as owner of the land.

It has been difficult for critical scholars to hold all the repressed truths of settler society in mind. We slip easily into analyses that end up privileging one set of claims over the other and claiming innocence in the oppression of others. Are racialized groups implicated in settler colonialism, as are Whites? Are people of colour settlers? If "contempt for blacks is part of the ritual through which immigrant groups become 'American'" then are all non-Blacks implicated in the subordination of Blacks? (Harris quoted in Smith 2010 : ¶14). How are Blacks implicated in the colonial project? These are the kinds of questions that have torn apart both scholarly and political coalitions (for a Canadian example of such a conflict, see Lawrence and Dua 2005; Sharma and Wright 2008). As critical scholars, we lose our way politically when we are unable to explore the multiple logics of White settler society as they operate in and through each other.

CONCLUSION: THE RACE TO INNOCENCE

In an article in 1998, Mary Louise Fellows and I explored why solidarity among feminists so often fell apart around the problem of competing marginalities (Fellows and Razack 1998). We proposed that these "moments of conflict and political immobility seem to center around the deeply felt belief that each of us, as women, is not implicated in the subordination of other women" (335). When each woman claimed her own marginality as the worst one, she raced to innocence. While we knew that the race to innocence made it impossible to consider relationships among hierarchical systems and how systems of oppression relied on each other (White supremacy could not function without patriarchy, for instance), we were repeatedly torn apart because we could not *feel* ourselves as simultaneously marginal and complicit in the subordination of another. We concluded that "the systems of domination that position white, middle-class, heterosexual, nondisabled men at the center continue to operate among all other groups, limiting in various ways what women *know* and *feel* about one another" (336).

The race to innocence does not happen simply because we do not know about each other's realities, although this is crucial. We view our places on the margins as unconnected to each other, an analytical approach that derives from viewing systems of domination as discrete. The analytical problem is compounded by the fact that the race to innocence is productive for us. First, if we do not secure our own place on the margins, we will be erased. For example, if Indigenous peoples do not insist that colonialism is ongoing, the chances are high that this will fall off the scholarly and political table. Second, when we act from our position of marginality, this is the first step towards our own liberation. We must name our oppression in order to challenge it. A third reason why the race to innocence happens, however, is that we hear the narratives of others through dominant frames, and given how productive the race to innocence is for us, we find it hard to develop the critical consciousness that would enable us to cut through dominant representations. It is, for example, hard to see that colonialism is ongoing if we do not know about the elevated rates of deaths in custody or the ever rising incarceration rates for Blacks and Indigenous people, and if we are ill equipped to understand what such patterns reveal.

It goes without saying that the reasons behind the race to innocence are beyond the cognitive. No matter how many times I remind myself to consider how all the systems are operating to position me as both dominant and marginal, I continually race to innocence. Even when writing this conclusion, I found myself anxious to make a case for the things I have been studying (Indigenous deaths in custody and the torture of Muslim men) and made uneasy by the things I had so easily suppressed (the singularity of anti-blackness). When Mary Louise Fellows and I wrote "The Race to Innocence," we urged feminists to recognise how systems of domination interlock (rather than intersect), producing us in varying relations of dominance and marginality. Appreciating that as scholars we had settled on yet another cognitive solution to a problem that was so clearly about feelings, we could only recommend, with a nod to Raymond Williams, that we ask how repressions are socially produced (Williams cited in Fellows and Razack 1998: 341: note 5). It is here that I find myself well over a decade later, venturing with trepidation into the unconscious of White settler society while reckoning with what is repressed in my own scholarship.

References

Abella, I. 1996. "Foreword: Multiculturalism, Jews and Forging a Canadian Identity." In H. Adelman and J.H. Simpson (eds.), *Multiculturalism, Jews, and Identities in Canada*. Jerusalem: Magnes Press.

Abrams, N. 2010. "Hidden: Jewish Film in the United Kingdom, Past and Present." *Journal of European Popular Culture* 1(1): 53–68.

___ (ed.). 2008. *Jews & Sex*. Nottingham, UK: Five Leaves Publications.

Abu-Laban, Y., and B. Abu-Laban. 2007. "Reasonable Accommodation in a Global Village." *Policy Options* Fall: 28–33.

Acton, A. 2011. "Indian Registration and Membership: Bill C-3." Presentation to Union of Ontario Indians E'Dbendaagzijig Conference. December 13, 2011 at Munsee Delaware First Nation.

Adam, B. 1999. "Moral Regulation and Disintegration of the Canadian State." In B. Adam, J.W. Duyvendak and A. Krouwel. (eds.), *The Global Emergence of Gay and Lesbian Politics: National Imprints of a Worldwide Movement*. Philadelphia, PA: Temple University Press.

Adams, J. 2004. "Activist Roots Still Thrive in Canada Border Crossing." *Indian Country Today* July 23.

Adelman, H. 2011. "Contrasting Commissions on Interculturalism: The Hijab and the Workings of Interculturalism in Quebec and France." *Journal of Intercultural Studies* 32(3): 245–59.

Ahadi, D. 2009. "L'Affaire Hérouxville in Context: Conflicting Narratives on Islam, Muslim Women, and Identity." *Journal of Arab and Muslim Media Research* 2(3): 241–60.

Ahluwalia, P. 2001. "When Does a Settler Become a Native? Citizenship and Identity in a Settler Society." *Pretexts: Literary and Cultural Studies* 10(1): 63–73.

Ahmed, S. 2010. *The Promise of Happiness*. Durham, NC: Duke University Press.

___. 2004. *The Cultural Politics of Emotion*. New York: Routledge.

Alcoff, L.M. 1998. "Philosophy and Racial Identity." In M. Bulmer and J. Solomos (eds.), *Ethnic and Racial Studies Today*. London: Routledge.

Alfred, T. 2009. *Peace, Power and Righteousness: An Indigenous Manifesto*. Toronto: Oxford University Press.

Almog, O. 2000. *The Sabra: The Creation of the New Jew* (trans. H. Watzman). Berkeley, CA: University of California Press.

Anderson, K. 1991. *Chain Her by One Foot: The Subjugation of Native Women in Seventeenth-Century New France*. New York: Routledge.

Anderson, K.J. 1991. *Vancouver's Chinatown: Racial Discourse in Canada, 1975–1980*. Montreal: McGill-Queen's University Press.

Angus, I. 1997. *A Border Within: National Identity, Cultural Plurality, and Wilderness*. Montreal: McGill-Queen's University Press.

Anidjar, G. 2008. *Semites: Race, Religion, Literature*. Palo Alto, CA: Stanford University Press.

Antonius, R. 2008. "L'islam au Québec: Les complexités d'un processus de racisation." *Cahiers de recherche sociologique* 46: 11–28.

Arseneau, R., et al. 2007. "Mémoire présenté à la Commission de consultaion sur les pratiques d'accommodement reliées aux differences culturelles." At <accommodements.qc.ca/documentation/ memoires/Montreal/trepanier-reginald-memoire-presente-a-la-ccpardc.pdf>.

Ashforth, A. 1990. "Reckoning Schemes of Legitimation: On Commissions of Inquiry as Power/ Knowledge Forms." *Journal of Historical Sociology* 3(1): 1–22.

Assemblée Nationale du Québec. 2010. "Audition — Institut Simone-De-Beauvoir." At <assnat.qc.ca/ fr/video-audio/AudioVideo-22373.html> May 20.

Atkinson, G. 2010. "Adoption Practices: A First Nation Perspective." In J. Carrière (ed.), *Aski Awasis/ Children of the Earth: First Peoples Speaking on Adoption*. Halifax, NS: Fernwood Publishing.

Aubert, G. 2004. "'The Blood of France:' Race and Purity of Blood in the French Atlantic World." *The William & Mary Quarterly* 61(3): 51 pars.

Auger, D. 2001. "Northern Ojibway and Their Family Law." Unpublished PhD thesis. Toronto: Osgoode Hall Law School, York University.

Austin, D. 2010. "Narratives of Power: Historical Mythologies in Contemporary Québec and Canada." *Race & Class* 52(1): 19–32.

Aviv, C., and D. Schneer. 2005. *New Jews: The End of Jewish Diaspora*. New York: New York University Press.

Bacchi, C.L. 1983. *Liberation Deferred? The Ideas of the English-Canadian Suffragists, 1877–1918*. Toronto: University of Toronto Press.

Backhouse, C. 1999. *Colour-Coded: A Legal History of Racism in Canada, 1900–1950*. Toronto: University of Toronto Press.

Bagnato, V.E. 1963. Library and Archives Canada, Italian Immigrant Aid Society. November 19.

Bannerji, H. 2000. *The Dark Side of the Nation: Essays on Multiculturalism, Nationalism and Gender*. Toronto: Canadian Scholar's Press.

___ (ed.). 1993. *Returning the Gaze: Essays on Racism, Feminism and Politics*. Toronto: Sister Vision Press.

Banton, M. 1967. *Race Relations*. London: Tavistock.

Baril, D. 2007. "L'approche judiciaire européenne de la gestion des accommodements religieux." At <accommodements.qc.ca/documentation/memoires/Montreal/baril-daniel-l-approche-judiciaire-europeenne-de-la-gestion-des-accommodements-religieux-montreal.pdf>.

Beale, A. 1993. "Harold Innis and Canadian Cultural Policy in the 1940s." *Continuum: The Australian Journal of Media & Culture* 7(1): 75–90.

Belanger, Yale D. 2007. "The Six Nations of Grand River Territory's Attempts at Renewing International Political Relationships, 1921–1924." *Canadian Foreign Policy* 13(3).

Belmessous, S. 2005. "Assimilation and Racialism in Seventeenth and Eighteenth-Century French Colonial Policy." *The American Historical Review* 110(2): 56 pars.

Benbassa, E., and A. Rodrigue. 2000. *Sephardi Jewry: A History of the Judeo-Spanish Community, 14th–20th Centuries*. Berkeley, CA: University of California Press.

Bennett, T. 2003. "Culture and Governmentality." In J. Z. Bratich, J. Packer and C. McCarthy (eds.), *Foucault, Cultural Studies and Governmentality*. Albany, NY: State University of New York Press.

___. 1995. *The Birth of the Museum: History, Theory, Politics*. New York: Routledge.

___. 1992. "Putting Policy into Cultural Studies." In L. Grossberg, C. Nelson and P. Treichler (eds.), *Cultural Studies*. New York: Routledge.

Bensimon, J. 1977. *20 ans après*. National Film Board of Canada.

Bergland, R.L. 2000. *The National Uncanny: Indian Ghosts and American Subjects*. Hanover, NH: University Press of New England.

Berland, J. 2001. "Writing on the Border." *The New Centennial Review* 1(2): 139–70.

Bernasconi, R. 1993. "On Deconstructing Nostalgia for Community within the West: The Debate between Nancy and Blanchot." *Research in Phenomenology* 23: 3–21.

Berner, G. 2012. "Bio." At <http://geoffberner.com/?page_id=2>.

Bhabha, H. 1994. *The Location of Culture*. New York: Routledge.

___. 1990. "Introduction: Narrating the Nation." In H. Bhabha (ed.), *Nation and Narration*. New York: Routledge.

Bial, H. 2005. *Acting Jewish: Negotiating Ethnicity on the American Stage and Screen*. Ann Arbor, MI: University of Michigan Press.

Biale, D., M. Galchinsky and S. Heschel. 1998. *Insider/Outsider*. Berkeley, CA: University of California Press.

Bilge, S. 2010. "'... alors que nous, Québécois, nos femmes sont égales à nous et nous les aimons ainsi' : la patrouille des frontières au nom de l'égalité de genre dans une 'nation' en quête de souveraineté." *Sociologie et sociétés* 42(1): 197–226.

Blaut J.M. 1993. *The Colonizer's Model of the World: Geographical Diffusionism and Eurocentric History*. New York: Guilford Press.

Bloom, J.D. 2003. *Gravity Fails: The Comic Jewish Shaping of Modern America*. Westport, CT: Preager.

Boileau, P. 2005. "A Message from the Director." *Lieutenant Governor's Celebration of the Arts*. Official program.

Bonilla-Silva, E. 2006. *Racism Without Racists: Color-Blind Racism and the Persistence of Racial Inequality in the United States*. Lanham, MD: Rowman & Littlefield.

Boris, S. 2007. *The New Authentics: Artists of the Post-Jewish Generation*. Chicago: Spertus Press.

Bourdieu, P. 1984. *Distinction: A Social Critique of the Judgement of Taste* (trans. R. Nice). Cambridge, MA: Harvard University Press.

Boyarin, J., and D. Boyarin. 2002. *Power of Diaspora*. Minneapolis, MN: University of Minnesota Press.

___. 1996. *Jews and Other Differences*. Minneapolis, MN: University of Minnesota Press.

Boyarin, D., D. Itzkovitz and A. Pellegrini. 2003. *Queer Theory and the Jewish Question*. New York: Columbia University Press.

Brathwaite, K. 2006. *Middle Passages: A Lecture*. Toronto: Sanberry Press.

Brodkin, K. 2000. *How Jews Became White Folks*. New York: Routledge.

Brook, V. 2009. "Convergent Ethnicity and the Neo-Platoon Show." *Television & New Media* 10(4): 331–53.

———. 2003. *Something Ain't Kosher Here*. Piscataway, NJ: Rutgers University Press.

Brown, M. 2007. "Canadian Jews and Multiculturalism: Myths and Realities." *Jewish Political Studies Review* 19(3–4): n.p.

Brown, W. 2006. *Regulating Aversion: Tolerance in the Age of Identity and Empire*. Princeton, NJ: Princeton University Press.

Brunner, J. 2010. "Contentious Origins: Psychoanalytic Comments on the Debate over Israel's Creation." In J. Bunzl and B. Beit-Hallahmi (eds.), *Psychoanalysis, Identity, and Ideology: Critical Essays on the Israel/Palestine Case*. Boston, MA: Kluwer Academic Publishers.

Bruyneel, K. 2004. "Challenging American Boundaries: Indigenous People and the 'Gift' of U.S. Citizenship." *Studies in American Political Development* 18.

Brydon, D. 2004. "Reading Postcoloniality. Reading Canada" In C. Sugars (ed.), *Unhomely States: Theorizing English-Canadian Postcolonialism*. Peterborough, ON: Broadview Press.

Buhle, P. 2003. *From Lower East Side to Hollywood*. New York: Verso Press.

Bunjun, B. 2010. "Feminist Organizations and Intersectionality: Contesting Hegemonic Feminism." *Atlantis* 34(2): 115–26.

Burk, A.L. 2010. *Speaking for A Long Time: Public Space and Social Memory in Vancouver*. Vancouver: University of British Columbia Press.

Burnet, J. 1978. "The Policy of Multiculturalism within a Bilingual Framework: A Stock-Taking." *Canadian Ethnic Studies* 10(2): 107–13.

Byers, M. 2011. "Post-Jewish? Theorizing the Emergence of Jewishness in Canadian Television." *Contemporary Jewry* 31(3): 247–71.

———. 2009. "The Pariah Princess: Agency, Representation, and Neoliberal Jewish Girlhood." *Girlhood Studies: An Interdisciplinary Journal* 2(2): 33–54.

Calvert, L. 2005. Premier's Speech: Centennial Saskatchewan Summit, Saskatoon, Saskatchewan, January 24.

———. 2004. Premier's Speech: Centennial Launch, Yorkton, Saskatchewan, September 23.

Canada Council Act. 1957. "An Act for the Establishment of a Canada Council for the Encouragement of the Arts, Humanities and Social Sciences." Ottawa: Queen's Printer

Canada Council for the Arts. 1995. *The Explorations Program Brochure*. Ottawa: Queen's Printer.

———. 1995. *A Design for the Future*. Ottawa: Queen's Printer.

———. 1993. *37th Annual Report, The Canada Council for the Arts, 1993–1994*. Ottawa: Queen's Printer.

———. 1991. *35th Annual Report, The Canada Council for the Arts, 1991–1992*. Ottawa: Queen's Printer.

———. 1982. *The Canada Council in the 1980s: Applebaum-Hébert Report*. Ottawa: Queen's Printer.

———. 1978. *The Future of the Canada Council: A Report to the Canada Council from the Advisory Arts Panel*. Ottawa: Canada Council for the Arts.

———. 1973. *17th Annual Report, The Canada Council for the Arts, 1973–1974*. Ottawa: Queen's Printer.

———. 1972. *16th Annual Report, The Canada Council for the Arts, 1972–1973*. Ottawa: Queen's Printer.

———. 1961. *5th Annual Report, The Canada Council for the Arts, 1961–1962*. Ottawa: Queen's Printer.

———. 1958. *2nd Annual Report, The Canada Council for the Arts, 1958–1959*. Ottawa: Queen's Printer.

———. 1957. *1st Annual Report, The Canada Council for the Arts, 1957–1958*. Ottawa: Queen's Printer.

Canada Ethnic Press Federation. 1964. "Brief Presented to the Royal Commission on Bilingualism and Biculturalism."

"Canada Is Ours." 1965. June. *Zhinochyi Svit*. Department of Citizenship and Immigration, Canadian Citizenship Branch, Foreign Language Press Review Service. Library and Archives Canada.

Canadian Cultural Rights Committee. 1968. December 13–15. "Canadian Cultural Rights Concern: A Conference to Study Canada's Multicultural Patterns in the Sixties." Toronto.

Canadian Mennonite Association. 1965. "Brief to the Royal Commission on Bilingualism and Biculturalism." Winnipeg.

Cannon, M. 1998. "The Regulation of First Nations Sexuality." *The Canadian Journal of Native Studies* 17(1): 1–18.

Carr, P., and D. Lund. 2007. *The Great White North?* Rotterdam, Netherlands: Sense Pubs.

Carstairs, C. 2001. "Defining Whiteness: Race, Class, and Gender Perspectives in North American History." *International Labour and Working-Class History* 60: 203–21.

Carter, S., L. Erickson, P. Roome and C. Smith (eds.). 2005. *Unsettled Pasts: Reconceiving the West Through Women's History.* Calgary: University of Calgary Press.

Carty, L. 1993. "Combining Our Efforts: Making Feminism Relevant to the Changing Sociality." In L. Carty (ed.), *And Still We Rise: Feminist Political Mobilizing in Contemporary Canada.* Toronto: Women's Press.

Carty, L., and D. Brand. 1993. "Visible Minority Women: A Creation of the Canadian State." In H. Bannerji (ed.), *Returning the Gaze: Essays on Racism, Feminism and Politics.* Toronto: Sister Vision Press.

Caughnawaga Defence Committee. 1965. "Brief to the Royal Commission on Bilingualism and Biculturalism." Caughnawaga.

Cavanaugh, C.A. 2000. "Irene Marryat Parlby: An 'Imperial Daughter' in the Canadian West, 1896–1934." In C.A. Cavanaugh and R.R. Varne (eds.), *Telling Tales: Essays in Western Women's History.* Vancouver: University of British Columbia Press.

CBC (Canadian Broadcasting Corporation). 2000. "Mansbridge One on One: Frances Wright." At <archives.cbc.ca/politics/federal_politics/clips/14998/> October 15.

___. 1938. "Women Become Persons." At <archives.cbc.ca/politics/rights_freedoms/clips/1801/> June 11.

Centrale des syndicats du Québec. 2007. "Définir les balises du vivre ensemble au Québec." At <accommodements.qc.ca/documentation/memoires/A-N-Montreal/centre-des-syndicats-du-quebec.pdf>.

Centre for Contemporary Canadian Art. 2011. "Canadian Arts Council." At <ccca.ca/c/ writing/d/ duval/duv001t.html>.

Centre culturel Islamique de Québec. 2007. "Mémoire." At <accommodements.qc.ca/ documentation/memoires/Quebec/centre-cultuel-islamique-de-quebec-memoire-elabore-en-reponse-a-la-consultation-accommodements-et-differences-vers-un-terrain-d-entente-la-parole-aux-citoyens.pdf>.

Chalykoff, L. 1999. "Encountering Anomalies: A Cultural Study of Chinese Migrants to Early Canada." In V. Strong-Boag, S. Grace, A. Eisenberg and J. Anderson (eds.), *Painting the Maple: Essays on Race, Gender, and the Construction of Canada.* Vancouver: University of British Columbia Press.

Chan, A. 1983. *Gold Mountain: The Chinese in the New World.* Vancouver: New Star Books.

Chaplin, J.E. 2001. *Subject Matter: Technology, the Body, and Science on the Anglo-American Frontier, 1500–1676.* Cambridge, MA: Harvard University Press.

Chazan, M., L. Helps, A. Stanley and S. Thakkar (eds.). 2011. *Home and Native Land: Unsettling Multiculturalism in Canada.* Toronto: Between the Lines.

Chevlowe, S. 2005. *The Jewish Identity Project.* New Haven, CT: Yale University Press.

Chew, D. 2009. "Feminism and Multiculturalism: An/Other Perspective." *Canadian Woman Studies* 27(2/3): 84–92.

Citizens' Advisory Council. 2001. *Celebrating Saskatchewan: Celebrating a Century of Progress 1905–2005.* Regina, SK: Saskatchewan Government Publications.

Claveau, C. 2007. "Mémoire présenté par Clément Claveau." At <http://accommodements-quebec. ca/documentation/memoires/Rimouski/claveau-clement-memoire-presente-a-la-commission-de-consultation-sur-les-accommodements-reliees-aux-differences-culturelles-au-quebec.pdf>.

Clarke, G.E. 1997. "White Like Canada." *Transition* 73(1): 98–109.

Clatworthy, S. 2010. *Estimating the Population Impacts of the E-Dbendaagzijig Aaknigewin.* Winnipeg: Four Directions Project Consultants.

Cohen, Y. 2011. "The Migrations of Moroccan Jews to Montreal: Memory, (Oral) History and Historical Narrative." *Journal of Modern Jewish Studies* 10(2): 245–62.

Con, H., R.J. Con, G. Johnson, E. Wickberg, W.E. Willmott (eds.). 1982. *From China to Canada: A History of the Chinese Communities in Canada.* Toronto: McClelland and Stewart.

Cooper, A. 2006. *The Hanging of Angélique: The Untold Story of Canadian Slavery and the Burning of Old Montreal.* Toronto: Penguin.

Corrigan, P., and D. Sayer. 1985. *The Great Arch: English State Formation as Cultural Revolution.* New York:

Blackwell.

Côté, P. 2008. "Québec and Reasonable Accommodation: Uses and Misuses of Public Consultation." In L.G. Beaman and P. Beyer (eds.), *Religion and Diversity in Canada*. Leiden, Netherlands: Brill.

Coulthard, G. 2008. "Beyond Recognition: Indigenous Self-Determination as Prefigurative Practice." In L. Simpson (ed.), *Lighting the Eighth Fire: The Liberation, Resurgence, and Protection of Indigenous Nations*. Winnipeg: Arbeiter Ring.

Couture, C. 2011. "Introduction." *Canadian Issues/Thèmes canadiens* 3–5(Summer).

___. 2010. "Racism, Nationalism and Literature: The Case of French Canada." In W. Zach and U. Pallua (eds.), *Racism, Slavery and Literature*. Frankfurt: Peter Lang.

Cox, O. 1959. *The Foundations of Capitalism*. New York: Philosophical Library.

Creighton-Kelly, C. 1991. *Report on Racial Equality in the Arts at the Canada Council*. Ottawa: Canada Council for the Arts.

Crosby, M. 1991. "Construction of the Imaginary Indian." In S. Douglas (ed.), *Vancouver Anthology: The Institutional Politics of Art*. Vancouver: Talonbooks.

Crow, B. 1999. "The Humanity of Heroes: The Famous Five." *Alberta Views* 24–28 (Fall).

CTV News Online. 2008. "Minority Accommodation No Threat to Quebec: Report." At <ctv.ca/CTVNews/TopStories/20080522/quebec_commission_080522/> May 22.

Cummings Jr., M., and R.S. Katz (eds.). 1987. *The Patron State: Government and the Arts in Europe, North America, and Japan*. Oxford, UK: Oxford University Press.

Das Gupta, T., C.E. James, R.C.A. Maaka, G.-E. Galabuzi and C. Andersen, C. (eds.). 2007. *Race and Racialization: Essential Readings*. Toronto: Canadian Scholars' Press.

Davalos, K.M. 2001. *Exhibiting Mestizaje: Mexican (American) Museums in the Diaspora*. Albuquerque, NM: University of New Mexico Press.

Davies, I. 1995. "Theory and Creativity in English Canada: Magazines, the State and Cultural Movement." *Journal of Canadian Studies* 30(1): 5–19.

Day, R.J.F. 2000. *Multiculturalism and the History of Canadian Diversity*. Toronto: University of Toronto Press.

Dean, M. 2002. "Liberal Government and Authoritarianism." *Economy and Society* 31(1): 37–61.

Decter, A. 1998. "Working from the Ground Up: An Interview with Joan Grant-Cummings." *Herizons* 12(1): 17–19.

Dei, G., L.L. Karumanchery and N. Karumanchery-Luik. 2005. *Playing the Race Card: Exposing White Power and Privilege*. New York: Peter Lang.

Deloria, P. 1998. *Playing Indian*. New Haven, CT: Yale University Press.

Deloria Jr., V. 1994. *God Is Red: A Native View of Religion*. Golden, CO: Fulcrum Publishing.

Devereux, C. 2005. *Growing a Race: Nellie L. McClung and the Fiction of Eugenic Feminism*. Montreal: McGill-Queen's University Press.

Devine, H. 2010. "After the Spirit Sang: Aboriginal Canadians and Museum Policy in the New Millenium." In B. Beaty, D. Briton, G. Filax and R. Sullivan (eds.), *How Canadians Communicate III: Contexts of Canadian Popular Culture*. Edmonton: Athabasca University Press.

Dickason, O.P., and D. McNab. 2009. *Canada's First Nations: A History of Founding Peoples from Earliest Times*. Toronto: Oxford University Press.

Dion, A. 2007. "L'égalité des sexes, une valeur fondamentale au Québec." At <accommodements.qc.ca/documentation/memoires/Montreal/dion-arlette-l-egalite-des-sexes-une-valeur-fondamentale-au-quebec-montreal.pdf>.

Dodd, D. 2009. "Canadian Historic Sites and Plaques: Heroines, Trailblazers, The Famous Five." *CRM: The Journal of Heritage Stewardship* 6(2): 29–66.

Druick, Z., and A. Kotsopoulos. 2008. "Introduction." In Z. Druick and A. Kotsopolous (eds.), *Programming Reality: Perspectives on English-Canadian Television*. Waterloo, ON: Wilfrid Laurier University Press.

Dua, E., and A. Robertson (eds.). 1999. *Scratching the Surface: Canadian Anti-Racist Feminist Thought*. Toronto: Women's Press.

Dubinsky, K. 1999. *The Second Greatest Disappointment: Honeymooning and Tourism at Niagara Falls*. Toronto: Between the Lines Press.

Du Bois, W.E.B. 1896. *The Suppression of the Africa Slave-Trade to the United States of America 1638–1870*. New York: Longmans, Green, and Co.

Duggan, L. 2002. "Materializing Democracy: Toward a Revitalized Cultural Politics." In D.D. Nelson and R. Castronovo (eds.), *Materializing Democracy: Toward a Revitalized Cultural Politics.* Durham, NC: Duke University Press.

Dumont, M. 2007. "Une constitution québécoise pour encadrer les 'accommodements raisonnables' — Pour en finir avec le vieux réflexe de minoritaire." At <bulletin.adq.qc.ca/ bulletins/2007-01-17_25. html> January 16.

Eagan, E. 2003. "Immortalizing Women: Finding Meaning in Public Sculpture." In P. Welts Kaufman and K.T. Corbett (eds.), *Her Past Around Us: Interpreting Sites for Women's History.* Malabar, FL: Krieger Publishing Company.

Ebner, D. 1997. "Famous Five Make History Again." *Ottawa Citizen,* December 19: A1–A2.

Edmonds, P. 2010. *Urbanizing Frontiers: Indigenous Peoples and Settlers in 19th-Century Pacific Rim Cities.* Vancouver: University of British Columbia Press.

Eisenkraft, H. 2010. "Racism in the Academy." At <universityaffairs.ca/racism-in-the-academy.aspx> October 12.

Enoch, S. 2011. "The 'New Saskatchewan:' Neoliberal Renewal or Redux?" *Socialist Studies* 7(1/2): 191–215.

Epstein, L.J. 2001. *The Haunted Smile: The Story of Jewish Comedians in America.* New York: Public Affairs.

Erdman, H. 1995. *Staging the Jew.* Piscataway, NJ: Rutgers University Press.

Erens, P. 1988. *The Jew in American Cinema.* Indianapolis, IN: Indiana University Press.

Essed, P. 2002. "Everyday Racism: A New Approach to the Study of Racism." In P. Essed and D.T. Goldberg (eds.), *Race Critical Theories.* Malden, MA: Blackwell Publishers.

Famous Five Foundation. 2011. "Sponsors and Donors: About Us." At <famous5.ca/sponsors.html> and <famous5.ca/about.html>.

Fanon, F. 1967. *Black Skin, White Masks* (trans. C.L. Markmann). New York: Grove Press.

___. 1963. *The Wretched of the Earth* (trans. C. Farrington). New York: Grove Press.

Fellows, M.L., and S. Razack. 1998. "The Race to Innocence: Confronting Hierarchical Relations Among Women." *The Journal of Gender, Race and Justice* 1(2): 335–52.

Ferguson, W. 2005. *Beauty Tips from Moose Jaw: Travels in Search of Canada.* Toronto: Vintage Canada.

Fiamengo, J. 2006. "Rediscovering Our Foremothers Again: Racial Ideas of Canada's Early Feminists, 1885–1945." In M. Gleason and A. Perry (eds.), *Rethinking Canada: The Promise of Women's History* (fifth edition). Toronto: Oxford University Press.

Fischer, D.H. 2008. *Champlain's Dream: The Visionary Adventurer Who Made a New World in Canada.* Toronto: Vintage Canada.

Flanagan, T. 2000. *First Nations? Second Thoughts.* Montreal: McGill-Queen's University Press.

Fleischmann, A.N.M., N. Van Styvendale and C. McCarroll (eds.). 2011. *Narratives of Citizenship: Indigenous and Diasporic Peoples Unsettle the Nation-State.* Edmonton: University of Alberta Press.

Foucault, M. 2003. *Society Must Be Defended. Lectures at the College de France 1975–1976* (M. Bertani and A. Fontana, eds.; trans. D. Macey). New York: Picador.

___. 1991. "Governmentality." In G. Burchell, C. Gordon and P. Miller (eds.), *The Foucault Effect: Studies in Governmentality.* Chicago: University of Chicago Press.

___. 1988. *The History of Sexuality: The Care of the Self (Volume III)* (trans. R. Hurley). New York: Vintage.

___. 1980. *Power/Knowledge: Selected Interviews and Other Writings, 1972–1977* (trans. C. Gordon, L. Marshall, J. Mepham and K. Soper). New York: Pantheon.

___. 1977. "Nietzsche, Genealogy, History." In D.F. Bouchard (ed.), *Language, Counter-Memory, Practice.* Ithaca, NY: Cornell University Press.

Freake, R., G. Gentil and J. Sheyholislami. 2011. "A Bilingual Corpus-Assisted Discourse Study of the Construction of Nationhood and Belonging in Quebec." *Discourse & Society* 22(1): 21–47.

Freeman, B.M. 2001. *The Satellite Sex: The Media and Women's Issues in English Canada, 1966–1971.* Waterloo, ON: Wilfrid Laurier University Press.

Friedman, L. 1991. *The Jewish Image in American Film.* New York: Citadel Press.

Frye, N. 1971. *The Bush Garden: Essays on the Canadian Imagination.* Toronto: Anansi Press.

Fung, R. 1996. *Dirty Laundry* [videotape]. Fungus Productions.

Fung, R., and M.K. Gagnon (eds.). 2002. *13 Conversations About Art and Cultural Race Politics.* Montreal: Artextes Editions.

Furniss, E. 1999. *The Burden of History: Colonialism and the Frontier Myth in a Rural Canadian Community*. Vancouver: University of British Columbia Press.

Gagner, P. 2001. *The King's Daughters and Founding Mothers: the Filles du Roi, 1663–1673*. Pawtucket, RI: Quintin Publications.

Gagnon, M.K., and S. McFarlane. 2003. "The Capacity of Cultural Difference." Ottawa: Department of Canadian Heritage. At <pch.gc.ca/special/dcforum/info-bg/05_e.cfm>.

Gauthier, M.D. 2007. "Où est le chef?" At <accommodements.qc.ca/documentation/mem oires/St-Jerome/gauthier-michel-memoire-pour-la-commission-bouchard-taylor-ou-est-le-chef.pdf>.

Geadah, Y. 2007. *Accommodements raisonnables. Droit à la différence et non différence des droits*. Montréal: VLB Éditeur.

Geniusz, W. 2009. *Our Knowledge Is Not Primitive: Decolonizing Botanical Anishinaabe Teachings*. Syracuse, NY: Syracuse University Press.

Gentile, P. 2000. "'Government Girls' and 'Ottawa Men:' Cold War Management of Gender Relations in the Civil Service." In G. Kinsman, D.K. Buse and M. Steedman (eds.), *Whose National Security? Canadian State and the Creation of Enemies*. Toronto: Between the Lines.

____. 1996. "Searching for 'Miss Civil Service' and 'Mr. Civil Service:' Gender Anxiety, Beauty Contests and Fruit Machines in the Canadian Civil Service, 1950–1973." Unpublished MA thesis. Ottawa: School of Canadian Studies, Carleton University.

Ghosh, S. 1999. "Monumental Questions: The Human Rights Legacy of the Famous Five." *Catholic New Times* 23(15) (October 17).

Gilbert, L. 2009. "Immigration as Local Politics: Re-Bordering Immigration and Multiculturalism Through Deterrence and Incapacitation." *International Journal of Urban and Regional Research* 33(1): 26–42.

____. 1996. *Entitlement to Indian Status and Membership Codes in Canada*. Scarborough, ON: Carswell.

Gill, S. 2000. "The Unspeakability of Racism: Mapping Law's Complicity in Manitoba's Racialized Spaces." In S. Razack (ed.), *Race, Space and the Law: Unmapping a White Settler Society*. Toronto: Between the Lines.

Gilman, S. 2006. *Multiculturalism and the Jews*. New York: Routledge.

Gillborn, D. 2006. "Rethinking White Supremacy: Who Counts in 'WhiteWorld'" *Ethnicities* 6(3): 318–40.

Gillespie, G. 2000. "Famous Five's Fight Goes On, Women Told." *Ottawa Citizen*, October 19: A11.

Gillis, J.R. (ed.). 1994. *Commemorations: The Politics of National Identity*. Princeton, NJ: Princeton University Press.

Gilmore, R.W. 2007. *Golden Gulag: Prisons, Surplus, Crisis, and Opposition in Globalizing California*. Berkeley, CA: University of California Press.

Gilroy, P. 2000. *Against Race: Imagining Political Culture Beyond the Color Line*. Cambridge, MA: Harvard University Press.

____. 1993. *The Black Atlantic: Modernity and Double-Consciousness*. Cambridge, MA: Harvard University Press.

____. 1991. *"There Ain't No Black in the Union Jack:" The Cultural Politics of Race and Nation*. Chicago: University of Chicago Press.

Glasbeek, A. 2009. *Feminized Justice: The Toronto Women's Court, 1913–34*. Vancouver: University of British Columbia Press.

Glissant, É. 2000. *Poetics of Relation* (trans. B. Wing). Ann Arbor, MI: The University of Michigan Press.

Globe and Mail. 2000. "Five Suffragists Honoured for Role in Legal Victory." October 19: A3.

Gogia, N., and B. Slade. 2011. *About Canada: Immigration*. Halifax, NS: Fernwood Publishing.

Goldberg, D.T. 2002. *The Racial State*. London: Blackwell.

____. 1993. *Racist Culture: Philosophy and the Politics of Meaning*. Malden, MA: Blackwell.

Goldie, T. 1989. *Fear and Temptation: The Image of the Indigene in Canadian, Australian and New Zealand Literatures*. Montreal: McGill-Queen's University Press.

Goldstein, E.L. 2006. *The Price of Whiteness*. Princeton, NJ: Princeton University Press.

Gómez, L. 2007. *Manifest Destinies: The Making of the Mexican American Race*. New York: New York University Press.

Goodale, R. 2005. Speech: Canada Day Provincial Ceremony, Regina, Saskatchewan, July 1.

Gottlieb, A. 1993. "What About Us? Organizing Inclusively in the National Action Committee on the Status of Women." In L. Carty (ed.), *And Still We Rise: Feminist Political Mobilizing in Contemporary Canada*. Toronto: Women's Press.

Gordon, A. 1997. *Ghostly Matters: Haunting and the Sociological Imagination*. Minneapolis, MN: University of Minnesota Press.

Gordon, C. 1991. "Governmental Rationality: An Introduction." In G. Burchell, C. Gordon and P. Miller (eds.), *The Foucault Effect: Studies in Governmentality*. Chicago: University of Chicago Press.

Government of Canada. 1999. "Appendix One: The Constitution Act, 1982." In A.G. Gagnon and J. Bickerton (eds.), *Canadian Politics*. Peterborough, ON: Broadview Press.

___. 1985. "Indian Act R.S.C., 1985, c. I-5." At <laws-lois.justice.gc.ca/eng/acts/I-5/FullText.html>.

___. 1982a. "Charter of Rights and Freedoms." At <laws-lois.justice.gc.ca/eng/charter/>.

___. 1982b. "Constitution Acts, 1867 to 1982." At <laws.justice.gc.ca/eng/Const//FullText.html>.

___. 1971. October 8. House of Commons Debates. Vol. 8, 3rd Session, 28th Parliament. Ottawa: Queen's Printer.

___. 1969a. *Statement of the Government of Canada on Indian Policy*. Presented to the First Session of the 28th Parliament by the Honourable Jean Chretien, Minister of Indian Affairs and Northern Development. Department of Indian Affairs and Northern Development. Ottawa: Queen's Printer.

___. 1969b. *Book IV: The Cultural Contribution of the Other Ethnic Groups*. Ottawa: Queen's Printer.

___. 1968. October 17. House of Commons Debates. Vol. II, 1st Session, 28th Parliament. Ottawa: Queen's Printer.

___. 1967. *Book I: The Official Languages*. Ottawa: Queen's Printer.

___. 1965a. *A Preliminary Report of the Royal Commission on Bilingualism and Biculturalism*. Ottawa: Queen's Printer.

___. 1965b. "Transcripts of Public Hearings." Ottawa. Microfilm.

___. 1963a. May 16. House of Commons Debates. Vol. 1, 1st Session, 26th Parliament. Ottawa: Queen's Printer.

___. 1963b. Royal Commission on Bilingualism and Biculturalism. Transcript of "Preliminary Hearing." Ottawa.

Government of Québec. 2007a. "Extrait de décret du gouvernement du Québec, Numéro 95-2007." At <accommodements.qc.ca/commission/decret.pdf>.

___. 2007b. The Consultation Commission on Accommodation Practices Related to Cultural Differences *Participation Guide*. At <accommodements.qc.ca/documentation/ guide-participation-en.pdf>.

___. 2008. The Consultation Commission on Accommodation Practices Related to Cultural Differences *Final Report* (Complete). At <accommode ments.qc.ca/index-en.html>.

Grattan, M. 2000. *Reconciliation: Essays on Australian Reconciliation*. Melbourne, Australia: Bookman Press.

Gray, J.H. 1971. *Red Lights on the Prairies*. Toronto: Macmillan.

Green, J. 2006. "From *Stonechild* to Social Cohesion: Anti-Racist Challenges for Saskatchewan." *Canadian Journal of Political Science* 39(3): 507–27.

Gregory, D. 2004. *The Colonial Present*. Oxford, UK: Blackwell.

Grossberg, L., and S. Hall. 1996. "On Postmodernism and Articulation: An Interview with Stuart Hall." In D. Morley and K-H Chen (eds.), *Stuart Hall: Critical Dialogues in Cultural Studies*. New York: Routledge.

Guglielmo, J., and S. Salerno (eds.). 2003. *Are Italians White? How Race Is Made in America*. New York: Routledge.

Gunew, S. 2007. "Rethinking Whiteness: An Introduction." *Feminist Theory* 8(2): 141–48.

Hage, G. 2000. *White Nation: Fantasies of White Supremacy in a Multicultural Society*. New York: Routledge.

Hall, S. 2000. "Conclusion: The Multi-cultural Question." In B. Hesse (ed.), *Un/settled Multiculturalisms: Diasporas, Entanglements, Transruptions*. London: Zed Books.

___. 1997a. "The Spectacle of the Other." In S. Hall (ed.), *Representations: Cultural Representations and Signifying Practices*. London: Sage.

___. 1997b. "The Local and the Global: Globalization and Ethnicity." In A.D. King (ed.), *Culture, Globalization and the World-System: Contemporary Conditions for the Representation of Identity*. Minneapolis, MN: University of Minnesota Press.

___. 1996. "The West and the Rest: Discourse and Power." In S. Hall, D. Held, D. Hubert and K. Thompson (eds.), *Modernity: An Introduction to Modern Societies*. Oxford, UK: Blackwell.

___. 1989. "Ethnicity: Identity and Difference." *Radical America* 23(4): 9–20.

Hammersley, M. 2003. "Conversation Analysis and Discourse Analysis: Methods or Paradigms?" *Discourse and Society* 14(6): 751–81.

Haque, E. 2010. "Homegrown, Muslim and Other: Tolerance, Secularism and the Limits of Multiculturalism." *Social Identities* 16(1): 79–101.

___. 2005. "Multiculturalism Within a Bilingual Framework: Language and the Racial Ordering of Difference and Belonging in Canada." Unpublished PhD thesis. Toronto: Ontario Institute of Education at the University of Toronto.

Harper, H. 2002. "When the Big Snow Melts." In C. Levine-Rasky (ed.), *Working Through Whiteness: International Perspectives*. Albany, NY: State University of New York Press.

Hartman, S. 1997. *Scenes of Subjection: Terror, Slavery, and Self-making in Nineteenth Century America*. New York: Oxford University Press.

Hawkins, F. 1988. *Canada and Immigration: Public Policy and Public Concern* (second edition). Montreal: McGill-Queen's University Press.

Hawthorn, H.B. (ed.). 1967. *A Survey of the Contemporary Indians of Canada: Economic, Political, Educational Needs and Policies.* Ottawa: Queen's Printer.

Hauptman, L.M., and J. Campisi. 1988. "The Voice of Eastern Indians: The American Indian Chicago Conference of 1961 and the Movement for Federal Recognition." *Proceedings of the American Philosophical Society* 132(4): 316–29.

HEEB. 2010. "'Lucky Jew': An Interview with Geoff Berner."At <heebmagazine.com/ lucky-jew-an-interview-with-geoff-berner/15834>. June 24.

Heinrich, J., and V. Dufour. 2008. *Circus Quebecus: Sous le chapiteau de la Commission Bouchard-Taylor.* Montreal: Boréal.

Henderson, J. 2003. *Settler Feminism and Race Making in Canada*. Toronto: University of Toronto Press.

Henderson, J.S.Y. 2008. "Treaty Governance." In Y. Belanger (ed.), *Aboriginal Self-Government in Canada: Current Trends and Issues* (third edition). Saskatoon, SK: Purich.

___. 2000a. "Postcolonial Ghost Dancing: Diagnosing European Colonialism." In M. Battiste (ed.), *Reclaiming Indigenous Voice and Vision*. Vancouver: University of British Columbia Press.

___. 2000b. "The Context of the State of Nature." In M. Battiste (ed.), *Reclaiming Indigenous Voice and Vision*. Vancouver: University of British Columbia Press.

Heron, B. 2007. *Desire for Development: The Education of White Women as Development Workers*. Waterloo, ON: Wilfrid Laurier University Press.

Hildebrandt, W., and B. Hubner. 1994. *The Cypress Hills: The Land And Its People*. Saskatoon, SK: Purich.

Hoberman, J., and J. Shandler. 2003. *Entertaining America: Jews, Movies, and Broadcasting*. Princeton, NJ: Princeton University Press.

Hodson, C., and B. Rushforth. 2010. "Absolutely Atlantic: Colonialism and the Early Modern French State in Recent Historiography." *History Compass* 8(1): 101–7.

Holley, G.W. 1883. *The Falls of Niagara*. New York: A.C. Armstrong & Son.

Hollinger, D.A. 2009. "Communalist and Dispersionist Approaches to American Jewish History in an Increasingly Post-Jewish Era." *American Jewish History* 95: 1–32.

Hook, D. 2001. "Discourse, Knowledge, Materiality, History: Foucault and Discourse Analysis." *Theory and Psychology* 11(4): 521–47.

House of Commons. 1997. "Jean Augustine spearheads motion to have Famous Five Statue on Parliament Hill." *Communiqué* December 11.

Hubbard, J.N. 1886. *The Account of Sa-Go-Ye-Wat-Ha or Red Jacket and His People, 1750–1830*. Albany, NY: Joel Munsell's Sons.

Hubbard, T. 2004. *Two Worlds Colliding*. National Film Board of Canada.

Hubbard, T., and S. Razack. 2011. "Reframing *Two Worlds Colliding*: A Conversation Between Tasha Hubbard and Sherene Razack." *Review of Education, Pedagogy and Cultural Studies* 33(4): 318–32.

Hudson, P.J. 2010. "Imperial Designs: The Royal Bank of Canada in the Caribbean." *Race and Class* 52(1): 33–48.

Hunt, A., and T. Purvis. 1993. "Discourse, Ideology, Discourse, Ideology, Discourse, Ideology…" *The British Journal of Sociology* 44: 473–99.

Hunt, S. 2011. "An Open Letter To My Local Hipsters." At <mediaindigena.com/sarah-hunt/issues-and-politics/an-open-letter-to-my-local-hipsters> September 20.

Hutcheon, L. 1997. "The Canadian Postmodern" In E. Cameron (ed.), *Canadian Culture: An Introductory Reader*. Toronto: Canadian Scholars' Press.

HXP. 2006. *Historical xperiences*. At <Hxp.ca>.

Hyman, P.E. 2009. "We Are All Post-Jewish Historians Now: What American Jewish History Brings to the Table." *American Jewish History* 95(1): 53–60.

Ignatiev, N. 1996. *How the Irish Became White*. New York: Routledge.

Indian Chiefs of Alberta. 2011. "Citizens Plus." *Aboriginal Policy Studies* 1(2): 188–281.

Indian-Eskimo Association of Canada. 1965. "A Brief to the Royal Commission on Bilingualism and Biculturalism." Toronto.

International Institute Canada. 1964. "Brief to the Royal Commission on Bilingualism and Biculturalism." Ottawa.

Isenberg, A. 2011. "Verses Cry Out for New Understanding." *Chronicle-Herald* (Halifax) July 18.

Jacobson, M.F. 1998. *Whiteness of a Different Color*. Cambridge, MA: Harvard University Press.

Jenson, J. 1994. "Commissioning Ideas: Representation and Royal Commissions." In S. D. Phillips (ed.), *How Ottawa Spends 1994–95*. Ottawa: Carleton University Press.

Jiwani, Y. 2006. *Discourses of Denial: Mediations of Race, Gender and Violence*. Vancouver: University of British Columbia Press.

Kannawin, J. 1938. "Disaster over Niagara Falls." CBC Radio Archives. At <archives.cbc .ca/400i.asp?IDCat=70&IDDos=530&IDCli=2616&IDLan=1&type=hebdoclip> January 27.

Khan, S. 2007. "The Fight for Feminism: An Interview with Sunera Thobani." *Upping the Anti* 5 At <http://uppingtheanti.org/journal/article/05-the-fight-for-feminism/>

Khazzoom, L. (ed.). 2003. *The Flying Camel: Essays on Identity by Women of North African and Middle Eastern Jewish Heritage*. Berkeley, CA: Seal Press.

Kim, E. 1995. "Beyond Railroads and Internment: Comments on the Past, Present, and Future of Asian American Studies." In G. Okihiro, M. Alquizola, D. Fujita Rony and K.S. Wong (eds.), *Privileging Positions: The Sites of Asian American Studies*. Pullman, WA: Washington State University Press.

Kinahan, A-M. 2008. "Transcendent Citizenship: Suffrage, the National Council of Women of Canada, and the Politics of Organized Womanhood." *Journal of Canadian Studies* 42(3): 5–27.

Kinsman, G. 2000. "Constructing Gay Men and Lesbians as Security Risks, 1950–70." In G. Kinsman, D.K. Buse and M. Steedman (eds.), *Whose National Security? Canadian State and the Creation of Enemies*. Toronto: Between the Lines.

___. 1996. *The Regulation of Desire: Homo and Hetero Sexualities*. Montreal: Black Rose Books.

___. 1995. "'Character Weakness' and 'Fruit Machines:' Towards an Analysis of the Anti-homosexual Security Campaigns in the Canadian Civil Service." *Labour* 35: 133–61.

Kinsman, G., D.K. Buse and M. Steedman. 2000. "How the Centre Holds — National Security as an Ideological Practice." In G. Kinsman, D. K. Buse and M. Steedman (eds.), *Whose National Security? Canadian State and the Creation of Enemies*. Toronto: Between the Lines.

Kinsman, G., and P. Gentile. 2010. *The Canadian War on Queers: National Security as Sexual Regulation*. Vancouver: University of British Columbia Press.

Kirby, K. 1996. *Indifferent Boundaries: Spatial Concepts of Human Subjectivities*. New York: Guilford Press.

Kirshenblatt-Gimblett, B. 2005. "The Corporeal Turn." *The Jewish Quarterly Review* 95(3): 447–61.

Kleeblatt, N. 1996. *Too Jewish? Challenging Traditional Identities*. Piscataway, NJ: Rutgers University Press.

Kobayashi, A., and L. Peake. 2000 "Racism Out of Place: Thoughts on Whiteness and an Anti-Racist Geography in the New Millennium." *Annals of the Association of American Geographers* 90(2): 392–403.

Kugelmass, J. (ed.). 2003. *Key Tests in American Jewish Culture*. Piscataway, NJ: Rutgers University Press.

Kushner, T. 1999. "Selling Racism: History, Heritage, Gender and the (Re)production of Prejudice." *Patterns of Prejudice* 33(4): 67–86.

Labelle, M. 2010. *Racisme et antiracisme au Québec: Discours et déclinaisons*. Québec, QC: Presses de l'Université du Québec.

Labelle, M., F. Rocher and R. Antonius. 2009. *Immigration, diversité et sécurité: Les associations arabo-musulmanes face à l'État au Canada et au Québec*. Québec, QC: Presses de l'Université du Québec.

Lahey, A. 1997. "Foundation to Re-Build History: With the Famous Five." *Herizons* 11(4): 10.

Lahey, K.A. 1999. *Are We "Persons" Yet? Law and Sexuality in Canada*. Toronto: University of Toronto Press.

Lahey, K.A., and K.G. Alderson. 2004. *Same-Sex Marriage: The Personal and the Political.* Toronto: Insomniac Press.

Lang, S. 1997. "Various Kinds of Two-Spirit People: Gender Variance and Homosexuality in Native American Communities." In S. Lang, S.-E. Jacobs and W. Thomas (eds.), *Two-spirit People: Native American Gender Identity, Sexuality, and Spirituality.* Urbana, IL: University of Illinois Press.

LaRocque, E. 2010. *When the Other Is Me: Native Resistance Discourse, 1850–1990.* Winnipeg: University of Manitoba Press.

Larsen, J., and M.R. Libby. 2001. *Moose Jaw: People, Places and History.* Regina, SK: Coteau Books.

Laurendeau, A. 1962. "Pour une enquête sur le bilinguisme." *Le Devoir* January 20.

Lawrence, B. 2004. *"Real" Indians and Others: Mixed Blood Urban Native Peoples and Indigenous Nationhood.* Lincoln, NE: University of Nebraska Press.

___. 2003. "Gender, Race, and the Regulation of Native Identity in Canada and the United States: An Overview." *Hypatia* 18(2): 3.

Lawrence, B., and E. Dua. 2005. "Decolonizing Anti-Racism." *Social Justice* 32(4): 120–43.

Lee, J-A., and L. Cardinal. 1998. "Hegemonic Nationalisms and the Politics of Feminism and Multiculturalism in Canada." In V. Strong-Boag, A. Eisenberg, S. Grace and J. Anderson (eds.), *Painting the Maple: Essays on Race, Gender, and the Construction of Canada.* Vancouver: University of British Columbia Press.

Lee, M.S. 2006. "Brenda Joy Lem: A Conversation With the Artist and Her Work." At <mercerunion. org/lee.html> December 8.

Lee, S.W. 2005. *Crossings: A Portrait of the Chinese Community of Moose Jaw.* Moose Jaw, SK: Moose Jaw Museum and Art Gallery.

Leroux, D. 2010a. "The Spectacle of Champlain: Commemorating Québec." *Borderlands* 9(1): 1–27.

___. 2010b. "Québec Nationalism and the Production of Difference: The Bouchard Taylor Commission, the Hérouxville Code of Conduct, and Québec's Immigrant Integration Policy." *Quebec Studies* 49: 107–26.

Levine, M.V. 1990. *The Re-conquest of Montreal: Language Policy and Social Change in a Bilingual City.* Philadelphia, PA: Temple University Press.

Levine-Rasky, C. (ed.). 2002. *Working Through Whiteness: International Perspectives.* Albany, NY: State University of New York Press.

L'Hirondelle, C., J. Naytowhow and B.H. Yael. 2011. "Land Project: A Conversation Between Canada and Israel/Palestine." In A. Mathur, J. Dewar and M. DeGagné (eds.), *Cultivating Canada: Reconciliation Through the Lens of Cultural Diversity.* Ottawa: Aboriginal Healing Foundation Research Series.

Li, P. 1998. *The Chinese in Canada.* Toronto: Oxford University Press.

Library of Parliament. 2003 [1996]. "Indian Status and Band Membership Issues." At <parl.gc.ca/Content/LOP/researchpublications/bp410-e.htm>.

LifeSite News. 2000. "Famous Five Statue Honours Racism and Eugenics Advocates." At <lifesitenews. com/ldn/2000/oct/001018a.html> October 18.

Lisée, J-F. 2007. "Pour un nouvel équilibre entre tous les 'Nous' Québécois." At <accommodements. qc.ca/documentation/memoires/A-N-Montreal/lisee-jean-francois.pdf>.

Litt, P. 1992. *The Muses, the Masses, and the Massey Commission.* Toronto: University of Toronto Press.

Lorenzkowski, B., and S. High. 2006. "Culture, Canada and the Nation." *Social History/Histoire Sociale* 39(77): 1–10.

Lupul, M.R. 1983. "Multiculturalism and Canada's White Ethnics." *Canadian Ethnic Studies* 15(1): 99–107.

MacDougall, B. 1999. *Queer Judgments: Homosexuality, Expression and the Courts in Canada.* Toronto: University of Toronto Press.

Mackey, E. 2002. *The House of Difference: Cultural Politics and National Identity in Canada.* Toronto: University of Toronto Press.

Mahrouse, G. 2010a. "'Reasonable Accommodation' in Québec: The Limits of Participation and Dialogue." *Race & Class* 52(1): 85–96.

___. 2010b. "Questioning Efforts That Seek To 'Do Good:' Insights from Transnational Solidarity Activism and Socially Responsible Tourism." In S. Razack, M. Smith and S. Thobani (eds.), *States of Race: Critical Race Feminism for the 21st Century.* Toronto: Between The Lines Press.

___. 2008. "'Reasonable Accommodation' in Quebec: A Good-Faith Effort or Insidious State Racism?" *R.A.C.E. link* 2: 18–21.

Maillé, C. 2010. "French and Quebec Feminisms: Influences and Reciprocities." In P.R. Gilbert and M. Santoro (eds.), *Transatlantic Passages: Literary and Cultural Relations Between Quebec and Francophone Europe*. Montreal: McGill-Queen's University Press.

Mamdani, M. 2004. *Good Muslim, Bad Muslim: America, the Cold War and the Roots of Terror.* New York: Pantheon.

___. 1996. *Citizen and Subject: Contemporary Africa and the Legacy of Late Colonialism*. Princeton, NJ: Princeton University Press.

Manning, E. 2003. *Ephemeral Territories: Representing Nation, Home, and Identity in Canada*. Minneapolis, MN: University of Minnesota Press.

Maracle, L. 1996. *I Am Woman: A Native Perspective on Sociology and Feminism*. Vancouver: Press Gang.

Margolis, R. 2011. "*HipHopKhasene*: A Marriage Between Hip Hop and Klezmer." *Studies in Religion* 40(3): 365–80.

Marhraoui, A. 2005. "La lutte contre le racisme en l'absence de politique antiraciste: le cas du Québec (1990–2004)." *Nouvelles pratiques sociales* 17(2): 31–53.

Marshall, B. 2009. *The French Atlantic: Travels in Culture and History*. Liverpool, UK: Liverpool University Press.

Martin Sr., P. 1993. "Citizenship and the People's World." In W. Kaplan (ed.), *Belonging: The Meaning and Future of Canadian Citizenship*. Montreal: McGill-Queens's University Press.

Marx, L. 1964. *The Machine in the Garden: Technology and the Pastoral Ideal in America* (second edition). New York: Oxford University Press.

Massad, J. 2000. "The 'Post-Colonial' Colony: Time, Space, and Bodies in Palestine/Israel." In F. Afzal-Kahn and K. Seshadri-Crooks (eds.), *The Pre-Occupation of Postcolonial Studies*. Durham, NC: Duke University Press.

___. 1996. "Zionism's Internal Others: Israel and the Oriental Jews." *Journal of Palestine Studies* 25(4): 53–68.

Mathur, A., J. Dewar and M. De Gagne (eds.). 2011. *Cultivating Canada: Reconciliation Through the Lens of Cultural Diversity*. Ottawa: The Aboriginal Healing Foundation.

Matsuda, M. 2010. "Poem for Armenian Genocide and Rules for Postcolonials." *JAAS* October: 359–69.

Mawani, R. 2009. *Colonial Proximities: Crossracial Encounters and Juridical Truths in British Columbia 1871–1921*. Vancouver: University of British Columbia Press.

Mbembe, A. 2003. "Necropolitics" (trans. L. Meintjes). *Public Culture* 15(1): 11–40.

McAndrew, M. 2007. "Des balises pour une société ouverte et inclusive." *Policy Options* Fall: 45–51.

McCann, M. 2010. "Pride Toronto plans to censor the term 'Queers Against Israeli Aparthied.'" *Xtra*. At <xtra.ca/public/National/Pride_Toronto_plans_to_ censor_the_term_Queers_Against_Israeli_ Apartheid-8653.aspx> May 13.

McGrath, R. 2006. *Salt Fish & Shmattes: A History of the Jews in Newfoundland and Labrador from 1770*. St. John's, NL: Creative Book Publishing.

McHoul, A., and W. Grace. 1993. *A Foucault Primer: Discourse, Power and the Subject*. New York: New York University Press.

McKeen, W. 2004. *Money in Their Own Name. The Feminist Voice in Poverty Debate in Canada, 1970–1993*. Toronto: University of Toronto Press.

McKenna, K.M.J. 2005. "Women's History, Gender Politics and the Interpretation of Canadian Historic Sites: Some Examples from Ontario." *Atlantis* 30(1): 21–30.

McKittrick, K. 2006. *Demonic Grounds: Black Women and the Cartographies of Struggle*. Minneapolis, MN: University of Minnesota Press.

McLaren, A. 1990. *Our Own Master Race: Eugenics in Canada, 1885–1945*. Toronto: McClelland and Stewart.

Menkis, R. 2011. "Jewish Communal Identity at the Crossroads: Early Jewish Responses to Canadian Multiculturalism, 1963–1965." *Studies in Religion* 40(3): 283–92.

Menkis, R., and N. Ravvin (eds.). 2004. *The Canadian Jewish Studies Reader*. Markham, ON: Red Deer Press.

Mennie, J. 2007. "Hey, Here's an Idea: Let's Ask Muslims What They Think." *Montreal Gazette*. At <canada.com/montrealgazette/columnists/story.html?id=e3bb831c-31fd-4988-a486-190b5d472ba1> September 8.

Mercer, K. 1994. *Welcome to the Jungle: New Positions in Black Cultural Politics*. New York: Routledge.

Meyer, M.A. 2004. *Ho'oulu: Our Time of Becoming, Hawaiian Epistemology and Early Writings.* Honolulu, HI: 'Ai Pokaku Press

Meyerhoff, T. 1994. "Multiculturalism and Language Rights in Canada: Problems and Prospects for Equality and Unity." *American University Journal of International Law and Policy* 9: 913–1013.

Mihaileanu, R. 2005. *Va, Vis et Deviens* [Live and Become]. Menemsha Films.

Miles, R. 1989. *Racism.* New York: Routledge.

Miller, C.L. 2008. *The French Atlantic Triangle: Literature and Culture of the Slave Trade.* Durham, NC: Duke University Press.

Miller, P., and N. Rose. 1992. "Political Power Beyond the State: Problematics of Government." *British Journal of Sociology* 43(2): 173–205.

Miller, T., and G. Yúdice. 2002. *Cultural Policy.* Thousand Oaks, CA: Sage Publications.

Milloy, J.S. 1999. *A National Crime: The Canadian Government and the Residential School System, 1879 to 1986.* Winnipeg, MB: University of Manitoba Press.

Mills, S. 2010. *The Empire Within: Postcolonial Thought and Political Activism in Sixties Montreal.* Montreal: McGill-Queen's University Press.

Milot, M. 2009. "L'émergence de la notion de laïcité au Québec — Résistances, Polysémie et instrumentalisation." In P. Eid, P. Bosset, M. Milot and S. Lebel (eds.), *Appartenances religieuses, appartenance citoyenne: Un équilibre en tension.* Québec, QC: Presses de l'Université de Laval.

Minh-ha, T.T. 1989. *Woman, Native, Other: Writing Postcoloniality and Feminism.* Bloomington, IN: Indiana University Press.

Monet, D., and Skanu'u (A. Wilson). 1992. *Colonialism on Trial: Indigenous Land Rights and the Gitksan and Wet'suwet'en Sovereignty Case.* Philadelphia, PA: New Society Publishers.

Monture-Angus, P. 2002. "On Being Homeless: Aboriginal Experiences of Academic Spaces." In E. Hannah (ed.), *Women in the Canadian Academic Tundra: Challenging the Chill.* Montreal: McGill-Queen's University Press.

___. 1999. *Journeying Forward: Dreaming First Nations' Independence.* Halifax, NS: Fernwood Publishing.

___. 1995. *Thunder in My Soul: A Mohawk Woman Speaks.* Halifax, NS: Fernwood Publishing.

Mookerjea, S. 2009. "Hérouxville's Afghanistan, or, Accumulated Violence." *The Review of Education, Pedagogy, and Cultural Studies* 31(2/3): 177–200.

Moose Jaw Times Herald. 2005a. "Saskatchewan Should Lose its Inferiority Complex." September 22: 4.

___. 2005b. "Pancakes, Powwows, and Plaques Mark First Day of Centennial Events." September 3: 1.

___. 2004a. "Tunnels of Moose Jaw Shrouded in Mystery." November 19: 9.

___. 2004b. "Tunnels Official Takes Exception to Author's Comments in His Book." November 25: 4.

Moreton-Robinson, A. 2003. "I Still Call Australia Home: Indigenous Belonging and Place in a White Postcolonizing Society." In S. Ahmed, C. Castañeda, A. Fortier and M. Sheller (eds.), *Uprootings/Regroundings: Questions of Home and Migration.* Oxford: Berg Publishers.

Mouvement Europe et Laïcité. 2012. At <europe-et-laicite.org/>.

Mouvement national des Québécoises et Québécois. 2007. "L'intégration à la Québécoise: pour une meilleure définition et un renforcement démocratique." At <accom modements.qc.ca/documentation/memoires/A-N-Montreal/mouvement-national-des-quebecoises-et-quebecois.pdf>.

Multiculturalism for Canada Conference. 1970. *Report of the Conference.* University of Alberta. August 28–9.

Mutual Co-Operation League of Canada. 1964. "Brief to the Royal Commission on Bilingualism and Biculturalism." Toronto.

NAC (National Action Committee on the Status of Women). 1979. "Women — 50 Years as Persons." *Status of Women News* 5, 3 (March).

___. 1978. "Five Persons." *Status of Women News* 5, 1 (September).

Nadeau, M-J. 2009a. "Troubling Herstory: Unsettling White Multiculturalism in Canadian Feminism." *Canadian Woman Studies* 27(2/3): 6–13.

___. 2009b. "Rebuilding the House of Canadian Feminism: NAC and the Racial Politics of Participation." In S. Bashevkin (ed.), *Opening Doors Wider: Women's Political Engagement in Canada.* Vancouver: University of British Columbia Press.

Nancy, J.L. 1991. *The Inoperative Community* (trans. P. Connor; L. Garbus; M. Holland and S. Sawhney). Minneapolis, MN: University of Minnesota Press.

National Japanese Canadian Citizens Association. 1965. "Brief to the Royal Commission on Bilingualism and Biculturalism." Toronto.

NCWC (National Council of Women of Canada). 2000. "The Famous Five Foundation: About Council." At <ncwc.ca/aboutUs_five.html> March 29.

Negra, D. (ed.). 2006. *The Irish in Us.* Durham, NC: Duke University Press.

___. 2001. *Off-White Hollywood.* New York: Routledge.

Nelson, C., P.A. Treichler and L. Grossberg. 1992. "Cultural Studies: An Introduction." In L. Grossberg, C. Nelson and P. Treichler (eds.), *Cultural Studies.* New York: Routledge.

Nelson, J.N. 2008. *Razing Africville: A Geography of Racism.* Toronto: University of Toronto Press.

Nieguth, T., and A. Lacassagne. 2009. "Contesting the Nation: Reasonable Accommodation in Rural Québec." *Canadian Political Science Review* 3(1): 1–16.

Nieves, E. 2007. "Putting to a Vote the Question 'Who Is Cherokee'?" *New York Times.* At <nytimes.com/2007/03/03/us/03cherokee.html?_r=2> March 3.

Nourbese Philip, M. 1992. *Frontiers: Essays and Writings on Racism and Culture.* Stratford, ON: Mercury Press.

O'Brien, S. 1984. "The Medicine Line: A Border Dividing Tribal Sovereignty, Economics and Families." *Fordham Law Review* 53(2): 315–50.

O'Donnell, T. 2007. Background Information on Membership and Citizenship. Background document included in Union of Ontario Indians' "Those Who Belong" E-Dbendaagzijig Conference binder. Conference held December 13–14, 2011 at Munsee Delaware First Nation.

Omi, M., and H. Winant. 1986. *Racial Formation in the United States: From the 1960s to the 1980s.* New York: Routledge.

"Once Again: Two Languages — Yes! Only Two Cultures." 1964. September 12. Department of Citizenship and Immigration, Canadian Citizenship Branch, Foreign Language Press Review Service. Library and Archives Canada.

Ono, K.A. 2010. "Postracism: A Theory of the 'Post' — as Political Strategy." *Journal of Communication Inquiry* 34(3): 227–33.

Osajima K. 2005. "Asian Americans as the Model Minority: An Analysis of Popular Press Images in the 1960s and 1980s." In K.A. Ono (ed.), *A Companion to Asian American Studies.* London: Blackwell.

Ostry, B. 1978. *The Cultural Connection: An Essay on Culture and Government Policy in Canada.* Toronto: McClelland and Stewart.

Ottawa Citizen. 2000a. "Tribute to Women's Rights Giants." October 19: A1.

___. 2000b. "Famous Five's fight goes on, women told." October 19: A11.

___. 2000c. "Teen to Take Place Among Famous Five." October 16: B2.

Owram, D. 1992. *Promise of Eden: The Canadian Expansionist Movement and the Idea of the West 1856–1900.* Toronto: University of Toronto Press.

Pal, L. 1993. *Interests of State: The Politics of Language, Multiculturalism and Feminism in Canada.* Montreal: McGill-Queen's University Press.

Palmater, P. 2011. *Beyond Blood: Rethinking Indigenous Identity.* Saskatoon, SK: Purich.

Parks Canada. 2011. "Government of Canada Commemorates the Persons Case: News Releases and Backgrounders." At <pc.gc.ca/apps/cp-nr/release_e.asp?id=1789&andor1 =nr> October 21.

Parliament of Canada. 1997. "Debate in Parliament: Famous Five." *Hansard* December 11: 1720–1735.

Peabody, S., and T. Stovall. 2003. *The Color of Liberty: Histories of Race in France.* Durham, NC: Duke University Press.

Perry, A. 2001. *On the Edge of Empire: Gender, Race, and the Making of British Columbia, 1849–1871.* Toronto: University of Toronto Press.

Phillips, R. 1997. *Mapping Men and Empire: Geographies of Adventure.* New York: Routledge.

Potvin, M. 2010. "Discours sociaux et médiatiques dans le débat sur les accommodements raisonnables." *Nos diverses cités* 7: 83–89.

___. 2008. *Crise des accommodements raisonnables: une fiction médiatique?* Montreal: Athéna.

Présence Musulmane Montréal. 2007. "Plaidoyer pour un *Nous* inclusif." At <accommodements.qc.ca/documentation/memoires/Montreal/presence-musulmane-montreal-plaidoyer-pour-un-nous-inclusif.pdf>.

Province of Lower Canada. 1850. "An Act for the Better Protection of the Lands and Property of Indians in Lower Canada." In *Provincial Statutes of Lower Canada: Being the Third Session of the Third Provincial Parliament of Canada*. At <signatoryindian.tripod.com/routingusedtoenslavethesovereignindigenouspeoples/id16.html>.

Puwar, N. 2004. *Space Invaders: Race, Gender and Bodies Out of Place*. Oxford, UK: Berg.

Rabble. 2009. "Jewish Women Occupy Israeli Consulate in Toronto."At <rabble.ca/rabbletv/program-guide/best-net/jewish-women-occupy-israeli-consulate-toronto-video> January 10.

Ram, U. 2008. "Why Secularism Fails? Secular Nationalism and Religious Revivalism in Israel." *International Journal of Politics, Culture, and Society* 21(1–4): 57–73.

Ramachandran, T. 2009. "Unveiling and the Politics of Liberation in Multi/interculturalism." *Canadian Woman Studies* 27(2/3): 33–38.

Rankin, P. 2000. "Sexualities and National Identities: Reimagining Queer Nationalism." *Journal of Canadian Studies* 35(2): 176–96.

Rattansi, A. 1994. "Western Racisms, Ethnicities and Identities in a 'Postmodern' Frame." In A. Rattansi and S. Westwood (eds.), *Racism, Modernity and Identity on the Western Front*. Cambridge, UK: Polity Press.

Rayside, D.M. 1998. *On the Fringe: Gays and Lesbians in Politics*. Ithaca, NY: Cornell University Press.

Razack, S.H. forthcoming. "Memorializing Colonial Power: The Death of Frank Paul." *Law and Social Inquiry*.

____. 2011a. "Timely Deaths: Medicalizing the Deaths of Indigenous People in Police Custody." *Law, Culture and the Humanities* 1–23.

____. 2011b. "The Space of Difference in Law: Inquests into Indigenous Deaths in Custody." *Somatechnics* 1(1): 87–123.

____. 2008. *Casting Out: The Eviction of Muslims from Western Law and Society*. Toronto: University of Toronto Press.

____. 2004. *Dark Threats and White Knights: The Somali Affair, Peacekeeping and the New Imperialism*. Toronto: University of Toronto Press.

____. 2002. *Race, Space and the Law: Unmapping a White Settler Society*. Toronto: Between the Lines.

____. 2000. "Gendered Racial Violence and Spatialized Justice: The Murder of Pamela George." *Canadian Journal of Law and Society* 15(2): 91–130.

____. 1999. "Making Canada White: Law and the Policing of Bodies in the 1990s." *Canadian Journal of Law and Society* 14(1): 159–84.

____. 1998. *Looking White People in the Eye: Gender, Race, and Culture in Courtrooms and Classrooms*. Toronto: University of Toronto Press.

RCAP (Royal Commission on Aboriginal Peoples). 1996. "Final Report, Volume 1, Section 9: The Indian Act." At <collectionscanada.gc.ca/webarchives/20071124124337/http://www.ainc-inac.gc.ca/ch/rcap/sg/sgm9_e.html>.

REAL Women of Canada. 2001. "Famous Five Image Preserved on Canadian Currency." *REALity Newsletter* XX, 1 (January/February).

Rebick, J. 2005. *Ten Thousand Roses: The Making of a Feminist Revolution*. Toronto: Penguin.

Rebick, J., and K. Roach. 1996. *Politically Speaking*. Vancouver: Douglas & McIntyre.

Réhel, A. 2007. "Réflexions sur les accommodements raisonnables." At <accommodements.qc.ca/documentation/memoires/Quebec/rehel-augustin-reflexion-sur-les-accommodements-raisonnables.pdf>.

Rickard, C. 1973. *Fighting Tuscarora: The Autobiography of Chief Clinton Rickard*. Syracuse, NY: Syracuse University Press.

Robertson, A. 1999. "Continuing on the Ground: Feminists of Colour Discuss Organizing." In E. Dua and A. Robertson (eds.), *Scratching the Surface: Canadian Anti-racist Feminist Thought*. Toronto: Women's Press.

Robertson, C. 2006. *Policy Matters: Administrations of Art and Culture*. Toronto: YYZ Press.

Roome, P. 2005. "'From One Whose Home Is Among the Indians:' Henrietta Muir Edwards and Aboriginal Peoples." In S. Carter, L. Erickson, P. Roome and C. Smith (eds.), *Unsettled Pasts: Reconceiving the West Through Women's History*. Calgary, AB: University of Calgary Press.

Ross, B. 1998. "A Lesbian Politics of Decolonization." In V.J. Strong-Boag, S. Grace, A. Eisenberg and J. Anderson (eds.), *Painting the Maple: Essays on Race, Gender, and the Construction of Canada*. Vancouver: University of British Columbia Press.

Royal Commission on National Development in the Arts, Letters and Sciences (1949–1951). 1951. At <collectionscanada.ca/massey/h5-439-e.html#bibcopyright>.

Rushforth, B. 2006. "Slavery, the Fox Wars, and the Limits of Alliance." *William and Mary Quarterly* 63(1): 53–80.

Said, E. 1993. *Culture and Imperialism*. New York: Knopf.

Salée, D. 2010. "Penser l'aménagement de la diversité ethnoculturelle au Québec: Mythes, limites et possibles de l'interculturalisme." *Politiques et Sociétés* 29(1): 145–80.

___. 2007. "The Quebec State and the Management of Ethnocultural Diversity: Perspectives on an Ambiguous Record." In K. Banting, T. J. Courchene and F. L. Seidle (eds.), *The Art of the State III: Belonging? Diversity, Recognition and Shared Citizenship in Canada*. Montreal: Institute for Research on Public Policy.

Samuel, R. 1994. *Theatres of Memory Volume I: Past and Present in Contemporary Culture*. New York: Verso.

Saskatchewan Settlement Experience. 2005. *Dominion Lands Act*. <sasksettlement.com/display.php?cat=18701880&subcat=Dominion%20Lands%20Act>.

Schick, C. 2002. "Keeping the Ivory Tower White: Discourses of Racial Domination." In S. Razack (ed.), *Race, Space and the Law: Unmapping a White Settler Society*. Toronto: Between the Lines.

Scott, D. 1999. *Refashioning Futures: Criticism after Postcoloniality*. Princeton, NJ: Princeton University Press.

Sears, A. 2008. "Notes towards a Socialism for the Times." *New Socialist Magazine* 63. At <www.newsocialist.org>.

Segev, T. 1986. *1949: The First Israelis*. New York: Free Press.

Seibel, G.A. 1991. *Bridges Over the Niagara Gorge: Rainbow Bridge — 50 years, 1941–1991*. Niagara Falls, ON: Niagara Falls Bridge Commission.

Sexton, J. 2010. "People-of-Color-Blindness. Notes on the Afterlife of Slavery." *Social Text* 28(2): 31–56.

Shanahan, N. 2008. "Monumental Women: A Journey in Search of Our Foremothers." *Herizons* 21, 4 (Spring).

Sharify-Funk, M. 2010. "Muslims and the Politics of 'Reasonable Accommodation:' Analyzing the Bouchard-Taylor Report and its Impact on the Canadian Province of Québec." *Journal of Minority Muslim Affairs* 30(4): 535–53.

Sharma, N., and C. Wright. 2008. "Decolonizing Resistance, Challenging Colonial States." *Social Justice* 35(3): 120–38.

Sharpe, R.J., and P.I. McMahon. 2007. *The Persons Case: The Origins and Legacy of the Fight for Legal Personhood*. Toronto: University of Toronto Press.

Shaw, C.A. 1970. *Tales of a Pioneer Surveyor*. Toronto: Longman.

Shohat, E. 2006. *Taboo Memories: Diasporic Voices*. Durham, NC: Duke University Press.

___. 1999. "The Invention of the Mizrahim." *Journal of Palestine Studies* 29(1): 5–20.

Simon, R. 2005. *The Touch of the Past: Remembrance, Learning and Ethics*. New York: Palgrave MacMillan.

Simpson, L. 2011. *Dancing on Our Turtle's Back: Stories of Nishnaabeg Re-Creation, Resurgence and a New Emergence*. Winnipeg, MB: Arbeiter Ring.

___. 2010. "Indigeneity, Settler Colonialism, White Supremacy." *Global Dialogue* 12(2): 1–13.

___. 2009. "Advancing an Indigenist Agenda: Promoting Indigenous Intellectual Traditions in Research." In J. Oakes, R. Riewe, R. ten Bruggencate and A. Cogswell (eds.), *Sacred Landscapes*. Winnipeg, MB: Aboriginal Issues Press.

Smith, A. 2010. Indigeneity, Settler Colonialism, White Supremacy. *Global Dialogue* 12(2): n.p.

Smith, A. 2005. *Conquest: Sexual Violence and American Indian Genocide*. Cambridge. MA: South End Press.

Smith, L.T. 1999. *Decolonizing Methodologies: Research and Indigenous Peoples*. New York: Zed Books.

Smith, M. 2004. "Segmented Networks: Linguistic Practices in Canadian Gay and Lesbian Rights." *Ethnicities* 4(1): 99–124.

___. 1999. *Lesbian and Gay Rights in Canada: Social Movements and Equality-Seeking, 1971–1995*. Toronto: University of Toronto Press.

___. 1998. "Social Movements and Equality Seeking: The Case of Gay and Lesbian Liberation in Canada." *Canadian Journal of Political Science* 31(2): 285–309.

Smulyan, S. 2010. "Yiddish and 'Deep Ashkenaz.'" At <jewishboston.com/15-boston-workmen-s-circle/blogs/810-yiddish-and-deep-ashkenaz> October 1.

Société Saint-Jean-Baptiste de Montréal. 2007. "Pour un Québec francophone, fier de son passé, laïque et tolérant." At <accommodements.qc.ca/documentation/memoires/A-N-Montreal/societe-saint-jean-baptiste.pdf>.

Social Study Club of Edmonton. 1964. "Brief to the Royal Commission on Bilingualism and Biculturalism." Edmonton.

South Shore University Women's Club. 2007. "The Position of Women in Quebec Society." At <accommodements.qc.ca/documentation/memoires/longueuil/south-shore-university-women-s-club-the-position-of-women-in-quebec-society.pdf>.

Srivastava, S. 2007. "Troubles with 'Anti-Racist Multiculturalism:' The Challenges of Anti-Racist and Feminist Activism." In S.P. Hier and B. Singh Bolaria (eds.), *Race and Racism in 21st Century Canada: Continuity, Complexity and Change*. Peterborough, ON: Broadview Press.

____. 2005. "'You're Calling Me a Racist?' The Moral and Emotional Regulation of Antiracism and Feminism." *Signs* 31(1): 29–62.

St. Denis, V. 2007. "Aboriginal Education and Anti-racist Education: Building Alliances Across Cultural and Racial Identity." *Canadian Journal of Education* 30(4): 1068–1092.

St. Denis, V., and C. Schick. 2003. "What Makes Anti-Racist Pedagogy in Teacher Education Difficult? Three Popular Ideological Assumptions." *The Alberta Journal of Educational Research* XLIX(1): 55–69.

Stasiulis, D. 1999. "Relational Positionalities of Nationalisms, Racisms, and Feminisms." In C. Kaplan, N. Alarcon and M. Moallem (eds.), *Between Woman and Nation: Nationalisms, Transnational Feminisms, and the State*. Durham, NC: Duke University Press.

Stasiulis, D., and N. Yuval-Davis (eds.). 1995. *Unsettling Settler Societies: Articulations of Gender, Race, Ethnicity and Class*. London: Sage.

Status of Women Canada. 1997. "Famous Five Statue on Parliament Hill Wins Unanimous Support." December 11.

Staub, M. 2002. *Torn at the Roots: The Crisis of Jewish Liberalism in Postwar America*. New York: Columbia University Press.

Steele, J. 2002. "The Liberal Women's Caucus." *Canadian Parliamentary Review* 25, 2 (Summer). At <revparl.ca/english/issue.asp?param=83&art=253>.

Stoler, A.L. 2001. "Tense and Tender Ties: The Politics of Comparison in North American History and (Post) Colonial Studies." *The Journal of American History* 88(3): 829–65.

____. 1991. "Carnal Knowledge and Imperial Power: Gender, Race and Morality in Colonial Asia." In M. di Leonardo (ed.), *Gender at the Crossroads: Feminist Anthropology in the Post-Modern Era*. Berkeley, CA: University of California Press.

Stratton, J. 2000. *Coming Out Jewish: Constructing Ambivalent Identities*. New York: Routledge.

Stremlau, J. 2011. "Black Cherokees Exercise Hard-Won Right to Vote." CNN. At <cnn.com/2011/10/19/opinion/stremlau-cherokee-vote/index.html> October 19.

Strong-Boag, V. 2009. "Experts on Our Own Lives: Commemorating Canada at the Beginning of the 21st Century." *The Public Historian* 31(1): 46–68.

Study Group D. 1963. "Working Paper." Library and Archives Canada.

Tamboukou, M. 1999. "Writing Genealogies: An Exploration of Foucault's Strategies for Doing Research." *Discourse: Studies in the Cultural Politics of Education* 20(2): 201–17.

Taussig, M. 2002. "The Beach (A Fantasy)." In W.J.T. Mitchell (ed.), *Landscape and Power* (second edition). Chicago: University of Chicago Press.

____. 1993. *Mimesis and Alterity: A Particular History of the Senses*. New York: Routledge.

Taylor, C. 1994. "The Politics of Recognition." In A. Gutman (ed.), *Multiculturalism: Examining the Politics of Recognition*. Princeton, NJ: Princeton University Press.

Taylor, D. 2003. *The Archive and the Repertoire: Performing Cultural Memory in the Americas*. Durham, NC: Duke University Press.

Teelucksingh, C. (ed.). 2006. *Claiming Space: Racialization in Canadian Cities*. Kitchener-Waterloo, ON: Wilfrid Laurier University Press.

Thielen-Wilson, L. 2012. "White Terror, Canada's Indian Residential Schools and the Colonial Present: From Law Towards A Pedagogy of Recognition." Unpublished PhD thesis. Toronto: Ontario Institute for Studies in Education at the University of Toronto.

Thobani, S. 2007. *Exalted Subjects: Studies in the Making of Race and Nation in Canada.* Toronto: University of Toronto Press.

___. 2000. "Closing Ranks: Racism and Sexism in Canada's Immigration Policy." *Race and Class* 42(1): 35–55.

Thomas, D. 2007. *Black France: Colonialism, Immigration, and Transnationalism.* Bloomington, IN: Indiana University Press.

Ting, J. 1995. "Bachelor Society: Deviant Heterosexuality and Asian American Historiography." In G.Y. Okihiro (ed.), *Privileging Positions: The Sites of Asian American Studies.* Seattle, WA: Washington State University Press.

Toronto Star. 2000a. "Famous Five Honoured for Rights Fight." October 19: A3.

___. 2000b. "Five Who Won Persons Case Return in Triumph to Hill." October 18: A5.

Train, K. 2006. "Carving Out a Space of One's Own: The Sephardic Kehila Centre and the Toronto Jewish Community." In C. Teelucksingh (ed.), *Claiming Space: Racialization in Canadian Cities.* Waterloo, ON: Wilfrid Laurier University Press.

Trask, H.K. 1999. *From a Native Daughter: Colonialism and Sovereignty in Hawaii.* Honolulu, HI: University of Hawaii Press.

Trigger, B.G. 1985. *Natives and Newcomers: Canada's 'Heroic Age' Revisited.* Montreal: McGill-Queen's University Press.

Turcotte. N. 2007. "Le devoir de ne pas disparaître." At <accommodements.qc.ca/documentation/memoires/Rimouski/turcotte-nestor-le-devoir-de-ne-pas-disparaitre.pdf>.

Twine, F.W., and C. Gallagher. 2008. "The Future of Whiteness: The Map of the 'Third Wave.'" *Ethnic and Racial Studies* 31(1): 4–24.

Valverde, M. 1992. "'When the Mother of the Race Is Free:' Race, Reproduction, and Sexuality in First Wave Feminism." In F. Iacovetta and M. Valverde (eds.), *Gender Conflicts: New Essays in Women's History.* Toronto: University of Toronto Press.

___. 1991. *The Age of Light, Soap, and Water: Moral Reform in English Canada, 1885–1925.* Toronto: McClelland & Stewart.

Varjassy, I.M. 1964. "Confidential Distribution: The Ontario Conference of the Indian Eskimo Association." November 20–22. London, ON: Library and Archives Canada.

Vickers, J. 2000a. *The Politics of 'Race:' Canada, Australia and the United States.* Ottawa: Golden Dog Press.

___. 2000b. "Feminisms and Nationalisms in English Canada." *Journal of Canadian Studies* 35(2): 128–48.

Walby, S. 1997. *Gender Transformations.* New York: Routledge.

Walcott, R. 2011a. "Into the Ranks of Man: Vicious Modernism and the Politics of Reconciliation." In A. Mathur, J. Dewar and M. DeGagné (eds.), *Cultivating Canada: Reconciliation Through the Lens of Cultural Diversity.* Ottawa: Aboriginal Healing Foundation Research Series.

___. 2011b. "Disgraceful: Intellectual Dishonesty, White Anxieties, and Multicultural Critique Thirty-Six Years Later." In M. Chazan, L. Helps, A. Stanley and S. Thakkar (eds.), *Home and Native Land: Unsettling Multiculturalism in Canada.* Toronto: Between the Lines Press.

___. 2007. "Homopoetics: Queer Space and the Black Queer Diaspora." In K. McKittrick and C.A. Woods (eds.), *Black Geographies and the Politics of Place.* Toronto: Between the Lines.

___. 2006. "Black Men in Frocks: Sexing Race in a Gay Ghetto (Toronto)." In C. Teelucksingh (ed.), *Claiming Space: Racialization in Canadian Cities.* Waterloo, ON: Wilfred Laurier University Press.

___. 2005. "Outside in Black Studies: Reading from a Queer Place in the Diaspora." In E.P. Johnson and M. Henderson (eds.), *Black Queer Studies: A Critical Anthology.* Durham, NC: Duke University Press.

___. 2003. *Black Like Who? Writing Black Canada.* Toronto: Insomniac Press.

Warner, T. 2002. *Never Going Back: A History of Queer Activism in Canada.* Toronto: University of Toronto Press.

Weitzer, R. 1990. *Transforming Settler States: Communal Conflict and Internal Security in Northern Ireland and Zimbabwe.* Berkeley, CA: University of California Press.

Wells, A. 2009. *Tropical Zion.* Durham, NC: Duke University Press

Wetherell, M., and J. Potter. 1992. *Mapping the Language of Racism: Discourse and the Legitimation of Exploitation.* New York: Columbia University Press.

White, R. 1991. *The Middle Ground: Indians, Empires, and Republics in the Great Lakes Region, 1650–1815.* Cambridge, UK: Cambridge University Press.

Whittaker, W.L. 1965. "The Canada Council for the Encouragement of the Arts, Humanities and Social Sciences — its Origins, Formation, Operation and Influence Upon Theatre in Canada, 1957–1963." Unpublished PhD thesis. Ann Arbor, MI: University of Michigan.

Wiegman, R. 1999. "Whiteness Studies and the Paradox of Particularity." *Boundary 2* 26(3): 115–50.

Wilderson, F.B. 2010. *Red, White and Black: Cinema and the Structure of U.S. Antagonisms*. Durham, NC: Duke University Press.

Williams, P. 1998. *Seeing a Color-Blind Future: The Paradox of Race*. New York: Farrar, Straus and Giroux.

Williams, R. 1981. *Culture*. Glasgow, UK: William Collins Sons.

Williams, T. 1990. "Re-Forming 'Women's Truth:' A Critique of the Report on the Royal Commission on the Status of Women in Canada." *Ottawa Law Review* 22, 3 (Summer).

Wolfe, P. 1999. *Settler Colonialism and the Transformation of Anthropology: The Politics and Poetics of an Ethnographic Event*. New York: Cassell.

Woodard, J. 1998. "But She Was a Feminist Racist: A Columnist Has Some Startling Words About the Famous Five." *Alberta Report* 25, 22 (May).

Wright, R. 1993. *Stolen Continents: The 'New World' through Indian Eyes*. Toronto: Penguin Books.

Wyczynski, P. 1966. May 28. "Les autres groupes ethniques — Rapport Préliminaire." Library and Archives Canada.

Wynter, S. 2003. "Unsettling the Coloniality of Being/Power/Truth/Freedom: Towards the Human, After Man, Its Overrepresentation — An Argument." *CR: The New Centennial Review* 3(3): 257–337.

Yael, b.h. 2006. *Palestine Trilogy: Documents in History, Land & Hope*. VTape.

———. 1996. *Fresh Blood: A Consideration of Belonging*. VTape.

Yegenoglu, M. 1998. *Colonial Fantasies: Towards a Feminist Reading of Orientalism*. Cambridge, UK: Cambridge University Press.

Yúdice, G. 2003. *The Expediency of Culture: Uses of Culture in a Global Era*. Durham, NC: Duke University Press.

Zavitz, S. 1999. *It Happened at Niagara*. Niagara Falls, ON: Lundy's Lane Historical Society.

Index

Health Instruction:
Theory and Application

Health Instruction:

Theory and Application

FOURTH EDITION

JOHN T. FODOR, Ed.D.
>*Professor of Health Science and Director, Instructional Media Center*
>*California State University Northridge*
>*Northridge, California*

GUS T. DALIS, Ed.D.
>*Consultant in Health Education and Teaching Strategies*
>*Los Angeles County Office of Education*
>*Downey, California*

>Foreword by Dr. ANN NOLTE
>*Distinguished Professor Health Education*
>*Illinois State University, Normal, Illinois*

LEA & FEBIGER Philadelphia • London

Lea & Febiger
200 Chester Field Parkway
Malvern, Pennsylvania 19355
U.S.A.
(215) 251-2230
1-800-444-1785

Lea & Febiger (UK) Ltd.
145a Croydon Road
Beckenham, Kent BR3 3RB
U.K.

1st Edition, 1966
Reprinted, 1968
Reprinted, 1970
Reprinted, 1971
2nd Edition, 1974
Reprinted, 1976
Reprinted, 1978
3rd Edition, 1981
Reprinted, 1987
4th Edition, 1989

Library of Congress Cataloging-in-Publication Data

Fodor, John T.
  Health instruction.

  Bibliography: p.
  Includes index.
  1. Health instruction. I. Dalis, Gus T. II. Title
RA440.F59   1989   613'.07'1   88-13741
ISBN 0-8121-1209-1

PRINTED IN THE UNITED STATES OF AMERICA

Print number: 4 3 2

Foreword

Health education in the schools today is one way of investing in the future of our society. Through the promotion of positive health behaviors, the schools are becoming proponents of health rather than reactors to illness.

Actions are occurring that reflect support of school health education by the public. In 1982 the National School Health Education Coalition (NaSHEC) was established. NaSHEC represents over 50 national organizations with an interest in promoting high quality comprehensive school health education. The common bond uniting these organizations is the belief that all children should have access to health instruction during their formative years. NaSHEC is a significant advocate for school health education today.

The federal government has made another commitment to school health education. In addition to the focus on school health education at the U.S. Public Health Service Centers for Disease Control, the Office of Comprehensive School Health Education was reinstituted in 1988. This office will establish linkages that will coordinate activities of the federal government in education for health.

Fodor and Dalis, in the fourth edition of *Health Instruction: Theory and Application*, have skillfully integrated the basic components of curriculum: knowledge of society, knowledge of the human being, and knowledge of health education. Each chapter illustrates the theory of health education, and translates it into very practical suggestions. This edition continues to represent quality in the literature of health education, and reflects the changes that have occurred in health education and education since 1981. Chapter 7, "Evaluating Health Instruction," provides essential information for program facilitators and teachers. It is a critical area in health instruction, and one about which little has been written. "Utilizing Appropriate Teaching Strategies for Health Instruction," Chapter 5, reflects considerable change from the previous edition and contains many practical suggestions.

Since 1981, health education has been integrated into employee wellness programs in business and industry. The techniques of structuring knowledge in health education and developing goals and objectives are as applicable to planning these programs as they are in developing comprehensive health education programs in schools.

The profession of health education is enhanced with this edition of *Health Instruction: Theory and Application.*

Ann E. Nolte, Ph.D.
Distinguished Professor
Health Education
Illinois State University
Normal, IL

Preface

A rationale for planning and implementing health instruction continues to be the focus of this revised edition. This rationale can be applied by teachers planning instruction and by those planning and organizing a comprehensive health curriculum and is applicable to any teaching-learning environment, whether it be the school, community, medical care or work-site setting. Thus, the "teacher" might be a public school teacher, a public health educator, a nurse trainer or a health educator in business and industry. Students might be school-age children in public or private schools, patients in a hospital, senior citizens in a retirement community or company employees.

Beginning with the first edition, the text has been based on the premise that a process for making effective decisions about the development of health instruction is necessary, and that a rationale based on inquiry into curriculum development can serve as the process for making these decisions. Such a rationale should not be considered a recipe or prescription but should serve as a point of departure for productive and creative efforts to upgrade health instruction and give direction to those responsible for its development and implementation.

The following questions are offered as a rationale for making effective decisions about the development and implementation of health instruction and serve as the basis for this text.

- How do points of view concerning health and education influence health instruction (see Chapter 1)?
- How should the content of health instruction be determined (see Chapter 2)?
- How should the knowledge for health instruction be structured (see Chapter 3)?
- How should the goals and objectives of health instruction be formulated (see Chapter 4)?
- What teaching strategies should be utilized to attain the objectives of health instruction (see Chapter 5)?
- How should health instruction be organized (see Chapter 6)?
- What should be considered in evaluating health instruction (see Chapter 7)?
- What should be the competencies of those teaching health (see Chapter 8)?

When reasoned responses to these questions are formulated, the chances of developing a viable program of health instruction are increased. The order in which the responses are given is less important than the totality of all responses. That is, an inquiry about health instruction can begin with any of these questions. Eventually, however, all questions should be confronted.

In Chapter 1, consideration is given to points of view concerning health and education and the influence of these points of view in shaping the instructional program.

Chapter 2 is concerned with sources useful in selecting the content of health instruction. Here, specific consideration is given to individual and societal health needs.

Chapter 3 focuses on health areas / themes / questions and on the development of generalizations and topics as ways of structuring the expanding body of health knowledge.

Chapter 4 deals with formulating goals and objectives. Stress is placed on the development of objectives for a range of cognitive and behavioral outcomes.

Chapter 5 examines the utilization of teaching strategies designed to help learners attain a range of objectives. Emphasis also is given to specific teaching techniques useful in implementing teaching strategies. Illustrative lesson plans for different teaching strategies are provided.

In Chapter 6 the organization of health instruction, from specific lessons to the total health curriculum, is discussed. Principles of learning are applied as a significant basis for organization.

In Chapter 7 a review of basic concepts of evaluation is included. The chapter contains specific illustrations of strengths and limitations of various types of test items, and provides examples of test items related to specific objectives.

Chapter 8 is devoted to an exploration of the competencies of those who should teach health. Consideration is given both to the professional and personal competencies desired for health educators.

Throughout the text an attempt has been made to apply the rationale presented through the use of concrete examples. These examples are not offered as blueprints to be memorized but are intended to serve as guides for the creative efforts of those planning and teaching in health education.

Ultimately the goal of the text is to make health instruction relevant so that it will favorably influence the health behavior of individuals. Ideas presented have evolved from public school, university, community, health care and worksite experience in health education. Ideas presented also have been shaped by administrative, supervisory and consulting experiences within public schools, the university and the larger community setting and from research in curriculum development, teaching strategies and educational psychology.

Gratitude is extended to those individuals whose teachings, research and writings have influenced the points of view expressed in the text. Special acknowledgement is made to Susan Giarratano for her thoughtful review of the third edition and for her helpful suggestions concerning this new edition. Sincere thanks also is extended to the many students who have given us further insight through their use of the text.

Particular appreciation is offered to those who assisted in the original 1966 manuscript. Specifically we offer thanks to Ruth Abernathy, William H. Creswell, Jr., Edward B. Johns, Maria McGann, Richard K. Means, Ann Nolte, Marion B. Pollock, Elena M. Sliepcevich and Wilfred C. Sutton.

We express our affection and gratitude to our wives, Mary J. Fodor and Helen K. Dalis, for their continued support during the preparation of the text.

Any errors or omissions in the text are the responsibility of the authors alone and should in no way reflect upon those mentioned as having contributed to its successful completion.

Northridge, California   JOHN T. FODOR

Downey, California   GUS T. DALIS

CONTENTS

1

Considering Points of View When Planning Health Instruction

Decisions about health instruction are affected by points of view held concerning health, education, and school and community health programs. Instructional decisions in health education about what should be taught, how it should be taught, when it should be taught, and who should teach it are thus influenced by the points of view held by those making these decisions.

Of primary importance are points of view held by the teacher. For it is the teacher's point of view that will prevail in the classroom. One of the purposes of this chapter is to present for the prospective teacher of health education those points of view generally held by health and education professionals regarding the meaning of health, the place of health instruction in education, and the role of school/community health programs. When there is relative agreement on these issues, there is likely to be a more stable and more meaningful health instruction program.

POINTS OF VIEW ABOUT HEALTH

How health is viewed—its meaning, its scope, its importance—by those making curricular decisions partially determines the content of health instruction. If health is viewed primarily as physical fitness, health instruction would be colored by that point of view and emphasis would be on that aspect of health. If health is thought of as healthy organs and tissues, health instruction might focus on anatomic structures and physiology. If health is considered to be dependent on social/emotional factors, the focus of health instruction would probably reflect that point of view. If, however, health is thought of as the interrelatedness of physical, mental, spiritual and social factors, health instruction would reflect this broader point of view and would encompass all aspects of health-influencing behaviors as individuals interact with one another.

Historical Perspective

The meaning of health has changed considerably through the years. In ancient societies, from approximately 3200 B.C. to 1000 A.D. the Egyptians, Hebrews, Greeks, and Romans stressed physical well-being and hygiene. Emphasis on physical health continued through the Renaissance to about 1700 A.D.

During these early years, however, while stress seemed to be placed upon physical well-being, notable exceptions existed. For example, in ancient Athens both physical and spiritual well-being were emphasized. This broader notion of health appeared again during the 1600s and 1700s. During this period John Locke wrote of: "A sound mind in a sound body. . . . " However, during this time emphasis was still placed upon physical well-being and the absence of disease. In the 1840s Horace Mann, as the first secretary of the first board of education in the United States in Massachusetts, further stressed the importance of physical well-being and the importance of "educating for health."

Later, in 1850, Shattuck, in his "Report of the Sanitary Conditions in Massachusetts," emphasized the need for preventive programs and indicated that health was much more than the absence of disease (14).

Health as "optimum well-being," including the interrelatedness of physical, mental, and social well-being, was not appreciably emphasized until after the two great wars.

A Modern Perspective

Health has become so complex a term that it seems to defy definition; precise definitions of health generally place unnecessary boundaries on its meaning and fail to reflect the complexities of the term. Thus, a definition of health will not be given. Rather, a number of descriptives are used to better convey the dynamic and complex quality of health.

Our current concept of health goes far beyond the curing and treating of sickness or preventing disease and infirmity. It includes raising levels of wellness—the goal being to attain, as near as possible, optimum well-being. Dunn aptly captured this point of view in the early 1950's in his discussion of health:

> The goal of health now at mid-century calls for not only the cure or alleviation of disease. It calls for even more than prevention of disease. Rather it looks beyond, to strive for maximum physical, mental, and social efficiency for the individual, for his family, and for the community (7:225).

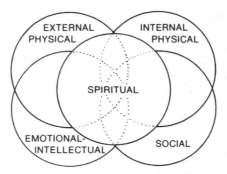

Figure 1. Factors That Interact and Influence Individual Health.

Health also involves the dynamic interactions amoung one's internal physical environment, external physical environment, social environment and emotional/spiritual environment (see Fig. 1).

Those writing about holistic health refer to the integration of mind, body and spirit in a dynamic relationship:

> Holistic health refers quite simply to the integration of mind, body, and spirit in the person, and emphasizes the importance of perceiving the individual—regardless of physical symptoms—in a "whole" sense, as a being who requires balance and harmony in all three dimensions in relationship with himself, the environment and the universe (3).

The concept of wholeness and dynamic interaction also was stressed by the Association for the Advancement of Health Education when it described health in a position statement on health education:

> The term "health" does not relate to a wholly measurable quality or condition. It can best be described in terms of the degree to which the composite or aggregate powers of the human organism are able to function. . . .
> This concept of health embraces the entire being. The individual is not a composite of separate entities, such as body, mind, and spirit, arranged in a presumed ascending order of importance. The individual is a multidimensional unity, with each component existing as an element within a complex of interrelationships. . . . (1).

Willgoose broadened the concept of health even more as he discussed health in a complex society:

> The whole of an individual's capacity for expression is involved in the health spectrum. It is multidimensional—anthropological, biological, psychological, economic, and even political. . . . Thus all human relationships between a community and its environment are somehow health related. There are no set boundaries. Social unrest, inadequate sanitation, and urban dehumanization are as significant in terms of well-being as a bleeding ulcer, a coronary thrombosis, or advanced paranoia (29:1).

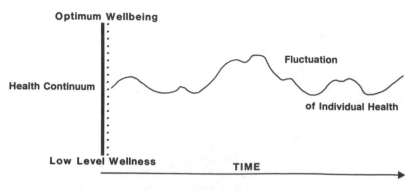

Figure 2.

Health is a dynamic quality of life rather than a static entity. No longer is the individual thought of as being "healthy" or "unhealthy." Rather, health varies during any time span from optimum well-being to low-level wellness. Individuals might function "normally" throughout a day with varying degrees of efficiency, depending upon the many factors which affect their state of well-being. Well-being fluctuates on a health continuum rather than remaining static at any one point (see Fig. 2). Health is not merely a continuum of physical well-being or of mental or spiritual or social well-being but a combination of all four, dynamically interrelated. The individual functions as a whole, or as an integrated unit with each dimension of health having an influence upon the other dimensions. For instance, physical illness has an effect on one's emotional well-being, spiritual state and on one's social relationships. The psychosomatic aspects of health also illustrate the dynamic interrelationship among these dimensions of health. For example, an individual beset with social and emotional conflicts and pressures may develop ailments of a physical nature, such as high blood pressure or peptic ulcers.

Health instruction should reflect a point of view which: (1) takes into account the many forces that affect one's health and (2) integrates the various dimensions believed to influence health. In so doing health instruction becomes realistic and meaningful in helping the learner achieve and maintain a high level of wellness.

THE ROLE OF HEALTH INSTRUCTION IN EDUCATION

Education today encompasses far more than the mastery of academic subject matter. Education is concerned with the whole child, not merely with the student's mental processes or intellectual growth. The child, rather than the subject matter, is considered the focal point. The needs of students become the basic concern, and the purposes of education must then be formulated to meet these needs.

Among the many functions and purposes of education commonly cited by most educators are those related to the health of students. Through the years those in professional education continually have endorsed the importance of health knowledge and values as necessary for making appropriate decisions in our society. This is exemplified and most aptly illustrated by statements concerning educational outcomes formulated by professional educators. Such statements have been included in historical documents, such as the "Cardinal Principles of Education"—1918 (16), "Education for All American Youth"—1952 (9), "The Central Purpose of Education"—1961 (8), "Schools for the Sixties"—1963 (24), and "Schools for the 70's and Beyond"—1971 (25). Perhaps the most significant statement regarding the outcomes of education is reflected in the "Priorities of Schools" as listed in the *Report on the National Education Association's Project on Instruction.* In this report health instruction is included as a designated priority of schools:

> ... the content of health instruction belongs in the school curriculum because such knowledge is necessary, is most efficiently learned in school, and no other public agency provides such instruction (24:31).

Other more recent statements reflect these same points of view. For instance, in the 1979 Surgeon General's report, *Healthy People,* schools were identified as playing a major role in achieving national health goals:

> No group is more able than school teachers to provide information and instruction that can help young people make decisions that promote good health. Comprehensive school health education activities can: enhance a child's skills and personal decision-making; promote understanding of the concepts of health and the causes of disease; and foster knowledge about the ways in which one's health is affected by personal decisions related to smoking, alcohol and drug use, diet, exercise, and sexual activity (12:143).

In its 1981 report, the Education Commission of the States recommended ten specific ways in which state education agencies could develop or strengthen health education in schools:

1. State education agencies should encourage local school boards and administrators to include health education in the curriculum in elementary and secondary schools.
2. State education agencies should promote health education as a responsibility shared by the family, school and community.
3. State education policymakers should support the development and improvement of school health education programs by utilizing the direct and indirect means available to them in their official capacity.

4. State education agencies should provide technical assistance to local districts in planning and implementing school health education programs.
5. State education agencies should promote the development of comprehensive school health education programs.
6. State education agencies should encourage local school boards to undertake a participatory planning process in the development of school health education programs.
7. State and local education agencies should ensure the presence of trained and qualified teachers in school health education programs.
8. State and local education agencies should assist in developing a system of information exchange about health education.
9. State education agencies should encourage the evaluation of school health education programs and assist local districts in developing appropriate evaluation processes.
10. State education agencies should encourage federal agencies to channel categorical funds in a manner that will enhance comprehensive school health education program development (22:1-2).

In the 1983 *Carnegie Report on Secondary Education in America*, the importance of health education for all students was stressed:

> Clearly, no knowledge is more crucial than knowledge about health. Without it, no other life goal can be successfully achieved. Therefore, we recommend that all students study health, learning about the human body, how it changes over the life cycle, what nourishes it and diminishes it, and how a healthy body contributes to emotional well-being (5:112).

In its *Critical Issues Report—Promoting Health Education in Schools* (1985), the American Association of School Administrators identified twelve national health needs and suggested ways in which school health education could alleviate these problems. One of their recommendations was the support of the comprehensive health education curriculum (k-12):

> ... comprehensive health education holds promise for affecting long-term behavior. Students exposed to comprehensive health education, including early warnings about what smoking or drugs do to the human body, are more likely to act in accordance with what they've been taught than those who have had, say, a single-focus antismoking or drug education program....
> The case for a comprehensive curriculum has unfolded gradually during the past decade and researchers began to take note of the gaps and weaknesses of single-topic curricula, such as those on smoking (18:31).

One of the most recent statements supporting the place of health instruction in schools came from William J. Bennet, U. S. Secretary of Education, in his 1986 *Report on Elementary Education in America*:

> Health and nutrition education should also be a part of the elementary curriculum. Children should learn how their bodies function, what kinds of food to eat, how to avoid illness, and what the disastrous effects of

drug use will be. Maintaining children's good health is a shared responsibility of parents, schools, and the community at large. But elementary schools have a special mandate: to provide children with the knowledge, habits, and attitudes that will equip them for a fit and healthy life (4:37).

If health instruction is to become an integral part of the curriculum, it is essential that those engaged in the curriculum process develop a point of view which embraces health knowledge and values as important outcomes of education. The successful health instruction program depends not only upon a mastery of content or subject matter by a capable staff but also upon a sound philosophical base from which to function.

THE SCHOOL HEALTH PROGRAM

When developing and implementing health instruction in schools, it is important to understand the nature of the school health program. Such an understanding helps the teacher place health instruction in a perspective that relates it to other school efforts aimed at protecting and promoting the health of children and youth.

Health Service, Health Environment, Health Instruction

The term *school health program* is used to describe those activities within the school that are directed toward promoting the health of children and youth. The purpose of this program is to provide learning opportunities, experiences, services and an environment that will favorably influence those values, attitudes, practices, and cognitive capabilities which promote individual, family, and community health.

To carry out this purpose the school health program has three distinct, yet interrelated, divisions. These are: *health services, healthful school environment* and *health instruction.*

Health Services. Health services consist of the cooperative activities of teachers, physicians, dentists, nurses, and others for the purposes of appraising, promoting, protecting, and maintaining the health of pupils and school personnel. School health services may be defined as those procedures which are established to: (1) appraise the health status of students and school personnel, (2) counsel students, parents, and others concerning appraisal findings, (3) encourage the correction of remediable defects, (4) assist in the identification and education of handicapped children and youth, (5) help prevent and control disease, and (6) provide emergency service for injury or sudden sickness (9:3).

Healthful School Environment. Every school has a responsibility for providing a healthful environment: physical, social, and emotional. Healthful school living is defined as:

... all efforts to provide at school physical, emotional, and social conditions which are beneficial to the health and safety of pupils. It includes the provision of a safe and healthful physical environment, the organization of a healthful school day, and the establishment of interpersonal relationships favorable to mental health (13:2)

Specific aspects of a healthful school environment include: (1) building construction, (2) safety, (3) lighting and acoustics, (4) heating and ventilation, (5) water supply and waste disposal, (6) school climate, (7) school food services, (8) academic and social pressures, (9) school day and year, (10) reports on pupil progress, (11) pupil grouping and schedules, (12) homework, and (13) teachers and other school personnel. For a complete review of the healthful school environment see Wilson, *Healthful School Environment* (30).

Health Instruction. Health instruction refers to a plan that provides for the sequential arrangement of learnings designed to favorably influence health values, attitudes, practices, and cognitive capabilities that are conducive to the optimum development of the individual, the family, and the community.

A comprehensive health curriculum should cover, at a minimum, the following: community health, consumer health, environmental health, family health, growth and development, nutrition, personal health, prevention and control of diseases and disorders, safety and accident prevention, and substance use and abuse" (18:31).

A national committee suggested that comprehensive school health instruction include:

A. *Instruction intended to motivate health maintenance and promote wellness and not merely the prevention of disease or disability.*
B. *Activities designed to develop decision-making competencies related to health and health behavior.*
C. *A planned, sequential Pre-K to 12 curriculum based upon students' needs and current and emerging health concepts and societal issues.*
D. *Opportunities for all students to develop and demonstrate health-related knowledge, attitudes and practices.*
E. *Integration of the physical, mental, emotional and social dimensions of health as the basis for study....*
F. *Specific program goals and objectives.*
G. *Formative and summative evaluation procedures.*
H. *An effective management system.*
I. *Sufficient resources: budgeted instructional materials, time, management staff and teachers (15:2–4).*

Orientation Toward Service and Education

The school health program can be viewed as having essentially a service function and an educational function. From one perspective the primary responsibility of the school health program might be seen as providing for the "needy" and rendering aid. From another perspective the program might be considered a motivating force aimed at helping individuals to help themselves. The latter does not necessarily negate or minimize possible service functions such as vision, dental, and physical examinations, but it does place the emphasis on education rather than on services.

It is our position that all service functions of the school health program have an educational component. For instance, dental screening examination provides a service for the child and the parent which helps prevent oral disorders. This service is of educational significance when it (1) causes the child and parent to take action which corrects a disorder and thereby makes the child more educable, and (2) includes instruction on practices that help to prevent dental disorders. The eye examination, hearing test, food service program or any other service-oriented school activity should have educational significance if it is to be a part of the school health program. If the educational significance is not evident, the validity of providing a health service activity in the school might be questioned.

THE COMMUNITY HEALTH PROGRAM

The school health program, as part of the total community health effort, should not be developed in isolation from the community. Those working in school health education and health service programs need to have a good understanding of the health efforts within the community and, more importantly, should insure that school health program activities are somehow related to health efforts in the community.

Community health efforts involve private health practitioners; local, county, state, and federal public health agencies; voluntary health agencies, such as the American Heart Association, the Lung Association; professional organizations, such as the American Medical Association, the American Dental Association, the American Public Health Association; local hospitals, and health maintenance organizations; service clubs, such as Rotary, Lions Club, Elks Club; church groups; commercial organizations, such as the automotive industry, insurance agencies, the food industry, pharmaceutical organizations; parents and parent groups. For a comprehensive review of community relationships with school health programs see Pollock, *Planning and Implementing Health Education in Schools (19:327–349)*.

Private Enterprise and Health Education.

One of the most striking developments in recent years has been the involvement of private enterprise in health education activities. This may be due to a lack of public funds or a change in attitude by private enterprise as to the value of health education, or both. Regardless of the reason, health education is being provided in the community at increasing levels by private hospitals, health maintenance organizations and private industry.

Such health education efforts include providing incentives or time off to participate in fitness programs, providing health and fitness facilities at the work site, developing antismoking and drug prevention programs, providing for health screening and medical examinations, providing educational programs and materials relative to health promotion and the prevention of health problems and sponsoring broad, community-based health and fitness activities.

Community Hospitals and Health Maintenance Organizations as Primary Providers of Health Education.

Another important change in recent years has been the involvement of hospitals in health education efforts. In fact, community hospitals and health maintenance organizations seem to be taking primary responsibility for health education activities in the community. They are providing more and better patient and family education regarding specific health problems as well as general health promotion. Inservice education for staff members regarding patient needs and health education skills also is being provided. In addition, hospitals are expanding their efforts to promote general health and to prevent diseases and disorders through "community outreach" activities. Such activities include the use of flyers, pamphlets, bulletins, public meetings, and small-group discussions. Public meetings and discussions are conducted at the hospital site and at different locations within the community (churches, private industry, social clubs, public and private schools and universities).

Cooperative, Comprehensive, Health Education Programs.

One of the most encouraging developments in recent years has been the emergence of cooperative comprehensive health education programs. Such programs bring together public health personnel, hospital staff, volunteer agency personnel, personnel from private industry and schools to plan and implement community health education efforts. The Los Angeles Community Cancer Control Project is an excellent example of such cooperative efforts. In this project over twenty groups and agencies, including official and voluntary health agencies, hospitals, several schools of medicine, a school of public health, public and private schools, universities and private industry, are working together to provide a comprehensive health education program in the greater Los Angeles area to promote general health and to prevent and treat cancer.

Another example of school / community cooperative health education efforts was the establishment of the National School Health Education Coalition in 1983. The coalition was incorporated by several private sector agencies (e.g. the American Lung Association, American Cancer Society, National Center for Health Education, American Red Cross, American School Health Association, etc.) to provide a focal point for facilitating the development and coordination of school health education efforts in the private sector (21:63).

In 1984, the U.S. Department of Health and Human Services brought together over sixty national groups from the public and private sectors to participate in discussions of the health promotion objectives of the nation and formulate recommendations on how to achieve these objectives through schools, business and industry, voluntary organizations, health professions and health care settings (21).

Additional community-wide health promotion programs focusing on other health problems have been established throughout the country. *The Journal of School Health* devoted an entire issue to describing a number of such programs dealing with drug abuse prevention (28).

Cooperation Between School and Community Health Personnel.

The mood of comprehensive health education has fostered greater cooperation between community and school health personnel. Community health educators are working more closely with school personnel in planning and implementing health instruction and in providing school health services. Conversely, school personnel are increasingly participating in planning and implementing a variety of health promotion programs, such as fitness programs, the prevention of sexually transmitted diseases, nutrition programs, and drug abuse programs.

HEALTH EDUCATION AS A SHARED RESPONSIBILITY

The health education of the child should be a responsibility shared among the home, school, and community. In a democratic society the primary responsibility for the health of the individual rests with the home and the family. Because of the enormity and complexity of societal health problems, the question arises as to whether the home can most efficiently "educate" for health. Many believe that the school with its resources is in the most favorable position to provide instruction for healthful and effective living.

Education does not begin or end during the course of a school day, nor does health education occur only during those hours when the child is at home or at school. Because health education is a process that takes place continuously throughout the individual's life and is not confined solely to the home or to the school, it must be considered a shared responsibility.

All available resources and agencies can and should be utilized to preserve that most important possession, health. The attainment of desired health education outcomes and the solution of health problems can best be accomplished through the coordinated efforts of the home, community, and school. This shared responsibility for health is illustrated in the model entitled: *Individual Health as Influenced by Home-School-Community Interaction* (see Fig. 3).

In this model the individual student or citizen is depicted at the apex of the structure as being fully developed physically, intellectually-emotionally, morally, and socially. This optimum development, while difficult or perhaps impossible to attain, becomes the goal of health education. Forces within the community, the school, and the home influence the development of the individual, and are shown by the triangle at the top of the model. The home is shown as forming the base of the triangle. Forces within the home are fundamental and primary influences upon the individual's total development. These forces, however, work in concert with forces emanating from the school and community, as depicted by the arrows connecting the three sides of the triangle.

Forces in the home, school, and community supplement one another and can affect the well-being of the individual child or citizen. The two broad pillars represent forces within the school and within the community which can favorably or adversely influence the individual's health. Some forces within the community are various agencies, hospitals, and service groups. Prominent forces within the school are the three divisions of the health program previously discussed: health instruction, health services, and healthful school environment.

At the bottom of each pillar are the coordinating bodies of the community and of the school that are essential for a coordinated school-community health program. If a coordinated school-community health program is to exist, there must be liaison and cooperation between the school and community. This liaison is illustrated by the arrow connecting the two coordinating bodies.

At the very bottom of the model is the foundation of home-school-community interaction for individual health. This foundation is based upon: points of view concerning health, education, and the school health program; health needs and interests of the individual; and societal health problems and cultural conditions.

Inasmuch as the emphasis of this text is on health instruction and curriculum development, special attention is given to those viewpoints concerned primarily with health instruction. A number of such viewpoints previously identified in the chapter are summarized in the following:

INDIVIDUAL HEALTH AS INFLUENCED BY
HOME-SCHOOL-COMMUNITY INTERACTIONS

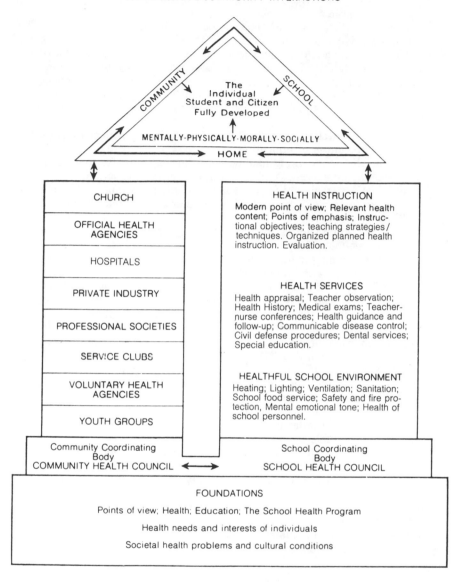

Figure 3.

- The administrator of the school along with those teachers conducting health instruction have a leadership responsibility for the health instruction program.
- The objectives of education include health knowledge and values as a primary educational objective.
- Health content should be included in the school's program of studies because accurate health information is necessary for effective living, and such knowledge is most efficiently developed in a school setting.
- Health instruction should be aimed at closing the gap between that which is known in the health field and that which is practiced by the public.
- The health instruction program should be in keeping with the general aims and objectives of education.
- Points of view concerning health, education, and health instruction influence the effectiveness of the health instruction program.
- Health instruction should focus upon the whole individual and should emphasize the development of physical, mental, spiritual, and social well-being.
- Health instruction should attempt to foster in the individual a greater value for health.
- Health instruction should be directed toward developing individuals who can apply health knowledge to daily living.
- To be effective and meaningful, the health instruction program should be based upon individual and societal health needs, health interests of the learner, and the level of the learner's health knowledge and understandings.
- A comprehensive program of health instruction (k-12) should be provided in each school district.
- Health instruction is one of three divisions of the total school health program and is dynamically interrelated with the other two divisions: health services and healthful school environment.
- There should be continual communication among the school, home, and community in order to enrich the health instruction program and make it more viable.
- There should be a coordinating body in the school and within the community to provide for more effective school-home-community interaction regarding school and community-based health instruction.
- The professional and personal competencies of teachers and their points of view concerning health, education, and health instruction are crucial to effective health instruction.
- There should be continuous evaluation to assess the effectiveness of the health instruction program.

The teacher's point of view concerning health instruction will greatly affect both the selection of health content and the selection and utilization of instructional techniques. The extent to which a health instruction program succeeds or fails is largely dependent upon the points of view held by the individual teaching health. It is suggested that those involved in the teaching of health continually identify, analyze, and evaluate their perception of health, of education, and of the school/community health program.

REFERENCES

1. "A Point of View for School Health Education." *Position Statement.* Reston, Virginia: Association for the Advancement of Health Education, January, 1983.
2. Anderson, C.L. and W.H. Creswell. *School Health Practice.* St. Louis: C.V. Mosby Co., 1985.
3. Ardell, Donald. "Holistic Health Planning." *The Holistic Health Handbook.* Berkeley, California: And-or Press, 1978.
4. Bennett, William J. First Lessons: *A Report on Elementary Education in America.* Washington, D.C.: U.S. Government Printing Office, 1986.
5. Boyer, Ernest. *High School: A Report on Secondary Education in America.* New York: Harper and Row Publishers, 1983.
6. Constitution of the World Health Organization. *Chronicle of the World Health Organization, 1:*29–43. Geneva: World Health Organization, 1947.
7. Dunn, Halbert L. "Points of Attack for Raising the Levels of Wellness." *Journal of the National Medical Association, 49:*225–235, July, 1957.
8. Educational Policies Commission of the National Education Association. *The Central Purpose of Education.* Washington, D.C.: National Education Association, 1961.
9. Educational Policies Commission of the National Education Association and the American Association of School Administrators. *Education for All American Youth.* Washington, D.C.: National Education Association, 1952.
10. Greenberg, J.S. "Health and Wellness: A Conceptual Differentiation." *Journal of School Health. 55:*403–406, October, 1985.
11. "Health Education: Basic to Learning." *Curriculum Report.* Reston, Virginia: National Association of Secondary School Principals, January, 1986.
12. *Healthy People: The Surgeon General's Report on Health Promotion and Disease Prevention.* Washington, D.C.: Department of Health, Education and Welfare, 1979.
13. Joint Committee on Health Problems in Education of the National Education Association and the American Medical Association. *School Health Services.* Washington, D.C.: National Education Association, 1964.
14. Means, Richard K. *Historical Perspectives On School Health.* Thorofare, New Jersey: Charles B. Slack, Inc., 1975.
15. National Comprehensive School Health Education Guidelines Committee. *Comprehensive School Health Education.* New York: National Center for Health Education, June, 1984.
16. National Education Association Commission on the Reorganization of Secondary Education. *Cardinal Principles of Secondary Education.* United States Department of the Interior, Bureau of Education, Bulletin No. 35. Washington, D.C.: Government Printing Office, 1918.
17. National Committee on School Health Policies. *Suggested School Health Policies.* Washington, D.C.: National Education Association, 1966.
18. Pine, Patricia. "Promoting Health Education in Schools—Problems and Solutions." *Critical Issues Report.* Arlington, Virginia: American Association of School Administrators, 1985.
19. Pollock, Marion. *Planning and Implementing Health Education in Schools.* Palo Alto, California: Mayfield Publishing Co., 1987.
20. Pentz, Mary Ann. "Community Organization and School Liaisons: How to Get Programs Started." *Journal of School Health. 56:*382–388, November, 1986.
21. *Prospects for a Healthier America (Proceedings): Achieving the Nation's Health Promotion Objectives.* Washington, D.C.: U.S. Department of Health and Human Services, November, 1984.
22. *Recommendations for School Health Education: A Handbook for State Policy Makers.* Denver, Colorado: Education Program Division, Education Commission of the States, 1981.
23. Russell, Robert D. for The Joint Committee on Health Problems in Education of The National Education Association and The American Medical Association. *Health Education.* Washington, D.C.: National Education Association, 1975.
24. *Schools for the Sixties*—A Report of the Project on Instruction, National Education Association. New York: McGraw-Hill Book Co., 1963.

25. *Schools for the 70's and Beyond: A Call to Action.* Washington, D.C.: National Education Association, 1971.
26. School Health Section. *Education For Health In The School Community Setting.* Washington, D.C.: American Public Health Association, 1975.
27. Special Feature: On Philosophical Directions For Health Education, *Health Education,* January / February, 1978.
28. "Special Issue on Community Programs for Drug Abuse Education." *Journal of School Health.* November, 1986.
29. Willgoose, Carl E. "Health Education as a Basic." *Health Education Today.* Reston, Virginia: Association for the Advancement of Health Education, October, 1985.
30. Wilson, Charles C. and Elizabeth A. Wilson, eds. *Healthful School Environment.* Washington, D.C.: NEA, 1969.

2

Determining The Content
of Health Instruction

The content of health instruction, to be relevant, should be based on data concerning health problems, needs and interests. Two sources from which significant information about health needs and interests and health problems can be generated are the *learner* and *society.* Information about the learner refers to data about individuals or groups of individuals of a particular age span such as ages 6 to 12, 15 to 17, 25 to 30. Specifically, this would include data about the level of health knowledge, kinds of health interests, health practices, and growth and development characteristics within a particular age group. Information about society refers to data concerning the general population without special reference to a specific age span. Thus data on the number of children age 15 through 17 who have contracted gonorrhea would be categorized as information about the learner. Data on the total number of cases of gonorrhea in a particular county, state, or in the nation would be categorized as information about society. The aforementioned data provide a "picture" of the health status of the learner and society at any one time. By attending to such data, health instruction can focus on that which is of most worth. That is, that which is relevant and that which will enhance the health status of the learner and society.

In this chapter illustrative data about both the learner and society is given. Examples of how this information can be used in identifying the content of health instruction also are shown.

THE LEARNER AS A DATA SOURCE

Numerous studies have been, and will continue to be, conducted about the learner. These are classified here as studies on health interests, growth and development, and health knowledge.

Health Interest Studies

A number of health interest studies have been conducted in the past. Information from such studies provide valuable clues as to what should be included in health instruction. The content of health instruction takes on a greater relevance for learners when their interests are considered.

Two early significant health interest studies were conducted by Lantagne (10) and the Denver public schools (3). Lantagne analyzed the health interests of 10,000 secondary school students from twenty-six high schools in ten different states. The Denver study was similar and involved grades kindergarten through twelve.

Another significant study concerning health interests of students was conducted in the state of Connecticut in 1969. This study involved over 5000 Connecticut students from kindergarten through grade twelve. The findings from this study are reported in the publication *Teach Us What We Want to Know* (1). Interests were reflected in questions asked by students about health in general; the body; food and nutrition; personal health and grooming; exercise and physical education; first aid and safety; babies; mental health; diseases; accidents; and drugs, smoking, and alcohol.

More recently an equally significant study of health interests was completed in 1984 by Trucano (18). This study, similar to the one conducted in Connecticut, was a survey of the health interests and concerns of over 5,000 Washington State students from kindergarten through grade twelve. These results were made available in the report *Students Speak* to provide a basis for planning classroom instruction. Health interests expressed by students in this study resulted in surfacing the following health related topics: handicapping conditions / birth defects, genetics, child and sexual abuse, fears and worries, self concept, understanding behavior, drugs, nutrition, aging, first aid / accident prevention, sexuality / families / babies / pregnancy.

While such interest studies serve a useful purpose, the world is ever changing and with it so do the health interests and concerns of young and old alike. One need only look to the recent awareness of such health problems as AIDS, toxic shock syndrome, crack or rock cocaine and smokeless tobacco. Thus, it is important for teachers to gather information about current health interests of students in their own classes if instruction is to be relevant and meaningful for the student.

Student interests can be obtained during the first week of class through informal discussions with students or by having students write about "What Health Means to Me." Another simple device that many teachers find useful is to have students list those things they most want to learn about health.

Health interests directly stated or implied can be used as one basis for identifying content to be included in health instruction. The example

Selected Health Interests and Their Use in Determining Health Content

Age Levels	Health Interests/Questions	Inferred Health Content
5–12	How does my body get made?	Growth/Development
	What makes people cry and laugh?	Emotions
	What makes you stop growing?	Duration of growth
	I am 9 years old and small. Do you think I will be 6 feet tall?	Patterns of growth
	Why are some people fat and some skinny?	Body types
	Why do only women have babies, not men?	Reproduction
	Why don't I have any friends?	Social growth
	How does reproduction work and what is it?	Reproduction
	Why are some kids smarter than others?	Intellectual growth
	Why do girls grow up faster than boys?	Rate of growth
	Why do girls have periods and boys don't?	Menstruation
13–20	What should you do if you are considering suicide?	Mental health
	How does it affect the baby if it does not have a father?	Family health
	How does chewing tobacco affect a person?	Drugs
	What is a good diet to go on if you are overweight?	Nutrition
	Why do some people get cancer and others don't?	Disease
	When is the right time to have sex?	Growth/development
	How can you handle stress?	Mental health
	How does physical fitness help or not help your body?	Exercise
	How can you tell if you have an STD?	Disease
	How can you tell if a doctor is a quack or not?	Health care
	How do you do CPR?	First aid

shown above illustrates inferred health content topics or areas from selected health interests.

Growth and Development Characteristics

Information about growth and development characteristics of children and youth provide additional insights into the health needs of learners and serve as another basis for identifying the content of health instruction (see references 2, 8, 9, 11). As individuals grow and develop from conception to death they experience certain predictable changes. These changes are referred to as growth and development characteristics and affect most individuals. Some of these characteristics are physical, some intellectual, others are emotional, some are social, some are gender related, and some are particular to those in the United States. Special attention to these characteristics is another means by which the content of health instruction can be "fine tuned" to be more learner relevant. The example on page 21 illustrates the utilization of selected growth and development characteristics as a basis for determining learner appropriate health content.

It should be noted that any significant existing or future studies that are concerned with the growth and development of individuals and their health interests should be utilized in the identification of health content.

Health Knowledge Studies

What children and youth already know or do not know about health can serve as another basis for selecting the content of health instruction. Several studies that assess health knowledge of children and youth have been conducted over the years. A significant national study was conducted in 1964 as a part of the School Health Education Study (12). This study indicated that many students had limited knowledge about or misconceptions about a number of health topics. Some selected examples of topics included: the use of dangerous drugs, weight control, how diseases are transmitted, reproduction and birth control, valid sources of health information, and the prevention and control of communicable and chronic diseases.

In 1988 the results of the National Adolescent Student Health Survey will be released. This survey will reveal the health-related knowledge, practices, and attitudes of the nation's youth in the following health areas:

- Consumer health
- Drug and alcohol use
- Injury prevention
- Nutrition
- Sexually transmitted disease and AIDS
- Suicide
- Violence

Several national professional organizations along with several federal agencies interested in health education have worked cooperatively in planning the survey. With the advice of representatives from these groups IOX Assessment Associates, an educational test development and research firm, developed and administered the survey (7).

Information from national surveys is useful in identifying the relevant content of health instruction. Of equal importance is information about health knowledge or lack of health knowledge among students in a given school district or school or in the teacher's own class. District or teacher-made tests can also be employed to assess the health knowledge of students.

Selected Growth and Development Characteristics and Their Use in Determining Health Content

Age Level	Growth and Development Characteristics	Inferred Health Content
5–9	• There is a need for 10 to 12 hours sleep	Sleep
	• Children tire easily	Fatigue
	• Children do not recognize their need for frequent periods of rest	Rest
	• This is a period of relatively slow growth, and muscular development is uneven and incomplete	Rate of growth
	• Nutritional problems may exist	Nutrition
	• There is a desire for independence yet there is a need for adult approval	Emotional independence
9–12	• Children have usually learned the difference between boys and girls and men and women	Sex differences
	• Children at this age can be expected to show increasing independence in caring for small wounds and taking medicine	Care of injuries
	• Children have an organic need for strenuous physical activity	Exercise
	• Children's social development is bound up with clubs and "special groups" of which they are enthusiastic members	Social growth
12–15	• Rest needs are approaching the rest needs of adults	Rest
	• Skin disorders, especially acne, are a major concern	Skin care
	• Girls are developing biological sexual maturity, and both boys and girls are very much aware of their bodies	Sexual development
	• Sometimes there is self-consciousness about undertaking new activities in which the individual is unskilled	Emotional growth
	• Children are broadening their understanding of group health problems such as contagious diseases and of the importance of preventive measures	Disease prevention
15–20	• Biological sexual maturity has already started in girls and is beginning to occur in boys	Physical growth
	• Members of this age group often resent parental suggestions concerning their health problems, yet they may eagerly buy and follow some manual prescribing a health program	Health care
	• Smoking and drinking may tend to be emotionally based symbols of revolt and sophistication	Reasons for using alcohol and tobacco
	• Young people of this age group become increasingly aware of the social, political and economic life of the community as a whole	Community health problems

Once the results of health knowledge tests have been analyzed, inferred health content can then be identified. The following is an example of such inferred health content which is based on selected misconceptions that might surface as a result of such analysis:

Misconception	Inferred Health Content
1. Nonprescription medicines are safe to purchase if recommended by a pharmacist	Criteria for purchasing medicines (consumer health)
2. The purpose of fluoridating water supplies is to purify water.	Use of fluorides (dental health)
3. Gonorrhea can be inherited.	Sexually transmitted diseases (communicable disease)
4. Carbohydrates should be eliminated from one's diet if weight reduction is desired	Selection of foods to control weight (nutrition)

Health Status of the Learner

The health status of students in a given school district, school, or particular classroom also should be considered when determining the content of health instruction. Students with specific health problems including vision and hearing disorders, improper diets, overweight and underweight, child abuse, emotional disturbances, drug abuse, physical handicaps, communicable disease, dental problems, and skin disorders often can be identified in the classroom. Health instruction that includes content relevant to the specific health needs of students in the class is more viable and more meaningful to students than is content that merely reflects generalized health problems and interests. Consultation with the school nurse, school psychologist, or counselor as well as with students and parents often uncovers significant health problems that can be helpful to the teacher. The cumulative health record that is kept for all students in most schools also provides valuable information about the students' health status.

SOCIETY AS A DATA SOURCE

The content of health instruction, as previously mentioned, also should be based upon those health problems confronting the nation or a particular community. One means of determining these problems is to examine and interpret morbidity and mortality statistics of the population. Morbidity refers to the relative incidence of disease or the number of cases of a disease in a given population. Mortality refers to the number of deaths in a given time and place or the proportion of deaths to population. Examples of morbidity and mortality statistics

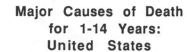

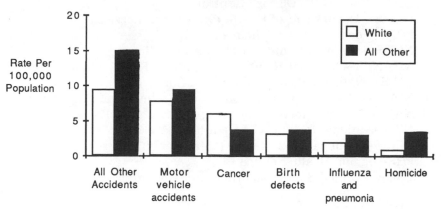

Source: Based on data from the National Center for Health
Statistics, Division of Vital Statistics

Figure 4.

are illustrated in Figures 4 and 5. Figure 4 (mortality) shows major
causes of death for ages 1 to 14 years. Figure 5 (morbidity) compares
male smokers and nonsmokers with regard to selected disease rates.

Many sources are available for obtaining data about morbidity and
mortality. Some of these sources are listed on page 24:

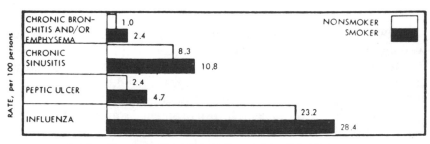

Data from *Cigarette Smoking and Health Characteristics, United States*

Figure 5.

1. National Level

ADAMHA—Alcohol, Drug Abuse, and Mental Health Administration
CDC—Centers for Disease Control
DHHS—Department of Health and Human Services
FDA—Food and Drug Administration
NCHS—National Center for Health Statistics
NHANES—National Health and Nutrition Examination Survey
NHIS—National Health Information Survey
NIAAA—National Institute on Alcohol Abuse and Alcoholism
NIDA—National Institute on Drug Abuse
NIH—National Institutes of Health
NIMH—National Institute of Mental Health
PHS—Public Health Service
USDA—United States Department of Agriculture

2. State and Local Level

Published health data from local and state health departments and other governmental agencies.

Published health data from local and state voluntary health agencies.

An analysis of health problems in the nation and community provides another basis for inferring or substantiating relevant content for health instruction. The following example illustrates how health content might be derived from data concerning societal health problems.

The document, *Promoting Health/Preventing Disease: Objectives for the Nation,* provides another example in which data concerning societal health problems have been used to infer relevant health content (13). This landmark public health effort not only pinpoints priority health content, but also includes specific changes related to this content which need to be realized. Issued in 1980, this document includes 226 health objectives aimed at reducing preventable death and disease in all age groups by the target year 1990. The examples on page 25 illustrate how national public health data can be used to pinpoint relevant health content for instruction.

By 1985 a review showed that nearly half of the 226 objectives were well on the way to being achieved (16). Already plans are being made for the specification of health objectives for the year 2000. Such national efforts at highlighting relevant health content need to be carefully considered when planning for health instruction.

Another reflection of societal health problems is found in the differing laws among states. Some states require or prohibit the teaching of certain aspects of health. Legal requirements vary from state to state and dictate the content that must be included in the health instruction program. These legal requirements are therefore a necessary criterion

Selected Data About Societal Health Problems and Inferred Health Content

Health Data	Inferred Health Content
Heart diseases are the number one cause of death in the United States.	Prevention of diseases and disorders
Accidents are the leading cause of death for age groups 1–15.	Safety and first aid
Communicable diseases in the United States disable more people than heart disease, cancer, and accidents combined.	Prevention of diseases and disorders
Sixty-one percent of high school seniors have used illicit drugs.	Drug use and misuse
In 1984, there were almost 10,000 recorded births to girls under age 15.	Family health
Lower class and lower-middle class people do not utilize available health services as effectively as do upper-middle class and upper class people.	Consumer health
People of lower class and lower-middle class do not have as high a regard for individual and community health as do people of upper-middle class and upper class.	Community health

Selected 1990 Health Objectives for the Nation

Health Data	Inferred Health Content (Objectives)
In 1979, the reported case rate for gonorrhea was 457 per 100,000 population.	Prevention of diseases and disorders—by 1990, reported gonorrhea incidence should be reduced to a rate of 280 cases per 100,000 population.
In 1978, the infant mortality rate was 13.8 per 1,000 live births.	Family health—by 1990, the national infant mortality rate (deaths for all babies up to one year of age) should be reduced to no more than 9 deaths per 1,000 live births.
In 1978, the motor vehicle fatality rate for children under 15 was 9.2 per 100,000 children	Accident prevention—fatality rate for children under 15 should be reduced to no greater than 5.5 per 100,000 children.
In 1979, the proportion of 12 to 18 year olds who smoked was 11.7%	Drug abuse prevention—by 1990, the proportion of children and youth aged 12 to 18 years old who smoke should be reduced to below 6%.

for determining content which must be included in the health instruction program.

OTHER SOURCES FOR SELECTING HEALTH CONTENT

Other sources for selecting the content of health instruction include: state education code requirements; content specialists; textbooks and other courses of study; and points of view in the community, school district, and school.

State Education Code Requirements

In over 40 states there are education code requirements for health as part of the public school curriculum. While in many states the word "health" is not defined, some states have additional code sections which define health and recommend specific health topics for the curriculum. There are certain mandated topics in health in every state. Instruction related to alcohol, tobacco, and drugs and their effects on health is the most common requirement (5:8–11). State legal requirements are therefore a necessary criterion for determining content which must be included in the health instruction program.

Content Specialists

Reputable content specialists can provide up-to-date scientific information that is useful in determining the content of health instruction. The specialist may be a physician, sociologist, anthropologist, biochemist, psychologist, or any other expert in some field related to the study of humans and their environment.

With the increasing knowledge of humans and the increasing complexity of the society in which they live, subject-matter specialists should be consulted and used frequently in order to maintain a viable health curriculum. These specialists can assist in bridging the gap between common knowledge and newly discovered scientific facts, principles, concepts, generalizations, or theories in their field of specialty as related to the health behavior of human beings.

In some cases content specialists such as pediatricians, cardiologists, exercise physiologists, dentists, nutritionists, or specialists in communicable disease control may come to the educational setting to inform teaching personnel of an existing health problem. Such information should be validated as to its accuracy and relevancy to the established points of view concerning health, education, and the school health program. Such a strategy will help minimize overreaction to special-interest groups which often pressure schools to develop "crash" or superficial programs of health instruction.

Textbooks and Other Courses of Study

An examination of textbooks and previously developed health courses of study also provides a basis for selecting health content. Health textbooks, for instance, reflect the thinking of individuals or a group of individuals generally considered to be experts in health education. Their writings reveal a qualified perspective of health content recommended for learners of a particular maturity level. Textbooks, however, should not be taken as sole determinants of the health curriculum. In the first place, they are often outdated by the time they are put to use by schools. This is particularly true in the area of health because of the vast amount of research being conducted in the fields of public health, medicine, and the behavioral and biological sciences. This research creates a continuous change in the body of health knowledge.

Secondly, the information within textbooks is of a general nature and does not take into account the unique health problems of the community or the individual health needs in a particular school or community.

Courses of study developed by other school districts or community agencies also may be appraised as to their worth in helping to identify relevant health content. They provide another means of utilizing the opinions and wisdom of others who have been confronted with the task of selecting viable health content. Courses of study, however, also tend to become outdated, and they are usually developed to meet the health needs of a specific group of individuals in a specific community. For reasons such as these a course of study from a school district or community agency might be adapted, perhaps, but not adopted by another school district or community agency. Even if courses of study are adapted, the health content presented should be evaluated as to its validity.

Points of View in the Community, School District, and School

Points of view concerning health and health education held within the community, the school board, and by the instructional staff of a school or school district or community agency cannot be ignored when selecting the content of health instruction. These points of view largely determine the scope of content to be covered in the instructional program. For instance, if the contention of school district personnel is that the schools have little responsibility for influencing the health knowledge and values of the learner, the probability of developing comprehensive health instruction adequate in scope is slim. Furthermore, if it is believed that health refers primarily, or solely, to physical fitness and the absence of disease, only content which relates to the physical health of the learner will be emphasized. In this instance very little attention will be given to that content which stresses mental and social well-being. Similarly, if the district point of view places emphasis only upon the health of the individual rather than upon a balance of individual, family, and community health, the content of the health curriculum will be narrowed to individual well-being.

Finally, the inclusion of controversial content in the health curriculum must depend on points of view held in the educational system and the community. If those in an instructional setting believe that particular topics such as sex education, suicide prevention, sexually transmitted diseases, death and dying, or any other controversial topic have no place in the health curriculum, these subjects will not be taught. This does not mean, however, that reasonable efforts cannot be directed toward modifying or changing beliefs concerning controversial health problems. It does mean that controversial content or issues should not be included in the health curriculum until a favorable climate for their inclusion has been created.

State education code requirements, content specialists, textbooks and courses of study, and points of view held in the community and the school or school district, in and of themselves, are not sole determinants of the health content. However, when these sources are considered collectively and in conjunction with health data about the learner and society, they provide a basis for making rational decisions about that health content which should be included in a viable health instruction program.

REFERENCES

1. Byler, Ruth, Gertrude Lewis, and Ruth Totman. *Teach Us What We Want To Know.* New York: Mental Health Materials Center, 1969.
2. *Child Development Research and Social Policy.* edited by Harold W. Stevenson and Alberta E. Siegel, Chicago: University of Chicago Press, 1984.
3. Denver Board of Education. *Health Interests of Children.* Denver: Denver Public Schools, 1954.
4. Education Commission of the States. *Recommendations for School Health Education: A handbook for State Policymakers.* Denver, Colorado, 1981.
5. Education Commission of the States. *State Policy Support for Schools Health Education: A Review and Analysis.* Denver, Colorado, 1982.
6. *Healthy People: The Surgeon General's Report On Health Promotion and Disease Prevention.* Public Health Service, Office of the Assistant Secretary for Health and Surgeon General, DHEW (PHS) Publication No. 79-55071.
7. "National Adolescent Student Health Survey." *Health Education.* October/November, *18*:83, 1987.
8. Kohlberg, Lawrence. *Child Psychology and Childhood Education: A Cognitive-Development View.* New York: Longman, 1987.
9. Kundu, Dibakar. "Creative Development In School Children." *The Education Quarterly.* *37*:6–7, 1985.
10. Lantagne, Joseph. "Health Interests of 10,000 Secondary School Students." *Research Quarterly.* *23*:330–346, October, 1952.

11. Lawrey, George H. *Growth and Development of Children.* 8th ed., Chicago: Year Book Medical Publishers, 1986.
12. Pine, Patricia. *Promoting Health Education In Schools.* Arlington, Virginia: American Association of School Administrators, 1985.
13. *Promoting Health/Preventing Disease: Objectives for the Nation.* U.S. Department of Health and Human Services, Public Health Service, 1980.
14. *Promoting Health/Preventing Disease: Public Health Service Implementation Plans for Attaining the Objectives for the Nation.* Public Health Reports, September–October 1983 Supplement. U.S. Department of Health and Human Services, Public Health Service, 1983.
15. Sliepcevich, Elena M. *School Health Education Study: A Summary Report.* Washington, D.C.: School Health Education Study, 1964.
16. *The 1990 Health Objectives for the Nation: A Midcourse Review.* U.S. Department of Health and Human Services, Public Health Service, Office of Disease Prevention and Health Promotion, 1986.
17. Trad, Paul W. *Infant and Childhood Depression: Developmental Factors.* New York: Wiley, 1987.

3

Structuring Knowledge for Health Instruction

The ever increasing amount of knowledge available has been coming forth in staggering quantities. For instance, it has been proposed that since the birth of Christ knowledge has doubled more than seven times. It is estimated that the first doubling of knowledge occurred in 1750, the second in 1900, the third in 1950, the fourth in 1960, the fifth and sixth in 1969 and 1977, respectively and the seventh a few short years later, in 1986. Since 1960, it has been estimated that knowledge will continue to double every 7 to 10 years. While knowledge is accumulating in such geometric proportions, the individual's capacity to assimilate this knowledge has not gained proportionately. There is a need, therefore, to better structure the vast amount of information available into some manageable form. This is of particular importance in health education because of the overwhelming amount of information continually being generated about the health of society and the individual.

Structuring health knowledge for the purpose of health instruction serves both the teacher and the learner. For the teacher attention to such a structure helps answer two fundamental teaching questions: What should be taught in the program of health instruction? and What can be done to help learners cope with the explosion of health knowledge? For the learner, who as a product of the instructional program assimilates a structure of health knowledge, this very structure provides a basis for categorizing knowledge "new" to the learner. This process of compartmentalizing related health knowledge can facilitate the assimilation of emerging new knowledge and in turn life-long learning.

Some kind of strategy is needed to structure health knowledge for the purpose of classroom instruction. The usefulness of a strategy is that it provides a systematic approach that can be repeated or followed by those who are concerned with better organizing and structuring health knowledge. The following is a suggested strategy that may be useful in moving from bits and fragments of health information to a systematic structure and organization of health knowledge for the purpose of planning and conducting meaningful health instruction:

- Step 1. Collecting health data or information.
- Step 2. Grouping similar health data or information under broad health areas, themes, or questions.
- Step 3. Formulating generalizations / topics to be stressed within each health information grouping.
- Step 4. Developing instructional goals and objectives for each generalization or topic to be stressed.
- Step 5. Periodically repeating steps 1 through 4 to identify, group, and accommodate new health knowledge.

COLLECTING DATA

The first step in structuring health knowledge for classroom instruction is data collection as described in Chapter 2. Specific reference was made to identifying data concerning the health needs of the learner and of society, drawn from the behavioral, biological, physical, and health sciences. Also mentioned was consideration of up-to-date valid health information from content specialists and the textbooks of individuals regarded as health experts. Examples of such data and information include:

- The basic elements of physical fitness are strength, flexibility, and endurance. Each one influences the other two.
- In boys, the prepubertal period begins at 12 or 13 years of age (sometimes much younger), and puberty (marked by mature spermatozoa) anywhere between 14 and 16 years. Females mature anywhere from 1 to 3 years earlier than males.
- Over 90% of the AIDS patients have been between the ages of 20 and 49 years; 48% have been 30 to 39 years old. Cases occurred among whites, blacks, and Hispanics in the United States. Only 67 (6%) cases of AIDS have been reported among females.
- Young children tend to be accident-prone. They need constant supervision for their own safety. Two-year-olds will climb slides and jump off walls, trusting your arms will catch them (even if you are several yards away). Four-year-olds will run pell-mell without watching the ground before them.
- In a study of high school students 39.4% of the students were interested in learning about habit forming substances.
- The suicide rate among persons 15 to 24 years of age has tripled since the 1950s.
- Late maturing boys are considered to be restless, bossy, and less grown up than early maturing boys.
- There is an estimated 20% of Americans who are overweight enough to be at risk for certain diet-related diseases and for every 100 children, 16 are obese.
- Non-drinking students conveyed in a Connecticut high school poll that they felt a sense of aloneness and differences among their peers.

- Gonorrhea is second only to the common cold as the most frequent infectious disease in America. More than a million cases reported annually.
- Each year, over 170,000 school age children sustain eye injuries—the majority in play or sports. And over 90% of these injuries are preventable.
- Approximately 89,000 people die of lung cancer in the U.S. per year and about 80% of lung cancer cases are related to smoking.
- The six most common causes of water pollution are: sewage pumped into the water supply, inadequate sewage treatment, industrial wastes, detergents, radioactive wastes, and chemical pesticides.
- Hypertension, which afflicts 23 million American men, women and children and kills 60,000 of them every year, becomes a distinct danger when the salt intake is 2.7% of the diet.
- "Some vigorous adolescent males at peak height velocity need a daily calorie intake comparable to that of a large adult doing heavy manual work, about 6,000 calories a day."
- Inhaling second-hand smoke makes the heart beat faster, blood pressure go up and the level of carbon monoxide in the blood increase.
- Young children frequently asked "What makes people cry, and laugh?"
- Alcohol is a depressant.
- Sexually transmitted diseases are caused by specific microorganisms.
- Carbon monoxide found in cigarette smoke has an affinity for red blood cells.
- Brushing the teeth after eating is an effective deterrent to gum disease and dental disease.

The foregoing example of data is but a microsample of the vast quantities of health data available. Once such data are collected they must be organized into a form that will be meaningful and manageable for both the learner and teacher in the teaching-learning situation.

GROUPING DATA

One approach for organizing health data is to group it into similar categories. A convenient way of doing this is to develop a classification system formulated around health topics, questions, or generalizations. The specific categories in such a system are themselves the product of data which suggest or give rise to the category. For example, there is no evidence of the category of environmental health in health education in the 1930s. No doubt this was so because there was insufficient data suggesting that environmental health was a need or concern of learners and of society. Regardless of the classification system utilized, the labels for the categories should be sufficiently representative of the health data grouped under the categories. The following are examples of categories using the system of health areas, themes, or questions.

Areas

- Consumer health
- Drug use and misuse

- Nutrition
- Diseases and disorders
- Environmental health
- Personal health

Themes

- Happiness, Health and Me
- Your Body
- Health Decisions
- Food for You
- Caring for Others
- Health Risks

Questions

- How can we prevent diseases and disorders?
- Why is proper nutrition important?
- What are some consequences of drug use?
- How do community health resources help protect people?
- How are health information, products, and services selected?

Refer now to the data listed on pages 31-32. Locate the specific data relative to alcohol being a depressant, carbon monoxide in cigarette smoke, interest in habit forming substances, nondrinking students, lung cancer deaths and smoking, and inhaling second hand smoke. Now consider how such health data might be related to the aforementioned examples of categories using broad health areas, themes, or questions. It would seem logical to place them under the area *Drug use and misuse,* or the theme *Health Risks,* or the question *What are some consequences of drug use?* In a similar fashion other health data can be grouped under related categories or organizers.

FORMULATING HEALTH GENERALIZATIONS

The next step in organizing health data or information is to specify the major ideas, those things to be stressed within a given health information grouping or category. This is the step that needs to be taken in order to provide greater specificity to the structure of health knowledge. If the broad areas, themes, or questions are the skeleton of the body of health knowledge then the vast amount of specific health data and information makes up the flesh supported by the skeleton.

One way to summarize the specific data and information within a broad health category is through the use of generalizations. Such generalizations reflect the meaning and scope of a given health category and serve as subcategories to provide focal points for health instruction. For instance, the category *consumer health* may have limited meaning for many and, therefore, provide a limited focus for classroom instruction. Formulating generalizations from specific data and information related to the area of consumer health can clarify the meaning of this health category and provide direction for classroom instruction. Consider for yourself what is meant by consumer health. Now reflect upon the following generalizations relative to consumer health:

- Individuals are responsible for their own health and for knowing when to seek help from others.
- Evaluative criteria are necessary for the selection and utilization of health information, products, and services.
- Choices of health information, services, and products are affected by one's feelings, values, and cultural experiences.
- The costs and benefits of health care affect the utilization of health services (10:44–46).

These four generalizations are an effort to reflect the sum total of data and information relative to consumer health and provide a better perception of what it means. In addition, they provide direction for the learnings to be stressed in classroom instruction with regard to this health category. Formulating generalizations for each of the health categories comprising a comprehensive health instruction program is an important process in developing the health curriculum and planning for health instruction. In essence it is a process which enables the teacher as curriculum developer to move from broad content (health categories) to less broad content (generalizations) in a systematic manner. In so doing the health data collected about the needs of the learner and of society as well as up-to-date health information can be used in formulating relevant health generalizations.

When formulating generalizations it is useful to follow certain processes. Data must be interpreted and explained, and relationships among data identified. Too, related data must be categorized. Once data are categorized it is necessary to synthesize the data and form summary statements about the data. These summary statements are, in fact, the generalizations.

Practice in each of the aforementioned processes—interpreting data, identifying relationships among data, categorizing data, synthesizing data, formulating summary statements from the data—is required if skill in formulating generalizations is to be developed.

In formulating health generalizations (summarizations of health data and information) certain criteria should be followed. Not all individuals working with such an approach would reach complete agreement on a list of such criteria. The questions below, however, have been successfully used as criteria for both formulating generalizations as well as evaluating existing ones as part of the process of developing a health instruction program.

1. Is the generalization a precise and understandable statement with a subject and a predicate.
2. Is the generalization consistent with current points of view concerning health and health education?
3. Is the generalization broad enough so that related data and information can be organized under it?
4. Is the generalization valid; can it be substantiated?
5. Is the generalization relevant to the age group and culture for which it is intended?
6. Is the generalization nonprescriptive or nondirective?

A Precise Statement. A precise statement is generally clearer and easier to understand than a single topic or word. Generally, there is little confusion about the intent of precise statements, whereas single topics or words tend to have several meanings. For example, the words *communicable disease* suggest a clear topic for consideration, but its meaning is broad and its intent for instruction seemingly boundless. One could consider etiology, prevention, control, socio-economics, public policy, recognition of diseases, treatment, patient management, and international efforts. On the other hand, the statement "Individuals can take personal actions to prevent and control communicable disease" is more definitive in its meaning and the intent for instruction is clearer. Here the explicit focus is on those personal actions for preventing and controlling communicable disease. Other examples of precise statements relative to communicable disease that could be used as generalizations for health instruction include: "Diseases can have immediate and long-range effects upon individuals," and "Many communicable diseases can be prevented."

In Keeping with Current Points of View. Health generalizations should stress principles of healthful living and should be in keeping with current points of view concerning health and health education. An example of a statement that would be questionable for emphasis in health education would be "Bacteria can be classified as gram positive or gram negative." While this is a precise statement, stress here is placed upon a bacteriological principle. More appropriate to health education would be a statement such as "Communicable diseases are caused by microorganisms and affect individuals physically, mentally, and socially." Understanding this generalization is primary to understanding the infectious disease cycle and actions useful in controlling communicable diseases. In addition, this generalization recognizes that communicable diseases impact the whole person—physically, mentally, and socially. It should cause health instruction to focus not only on the physical effects of specified communicable diseases, but also on the mental and social implications. For example, consider the common cold. The physical impact of the cold virus might include a runny nose, stuffiness, watery eyes, and maybe a headache. The impact of the cold mentally-emotionally might include the inability to concentrate, depression and maybe even anger. Socially, the cold might result in the desire to be away from people. Also, the cold virus is more readily spread in a social setting. Generalizations that recognize the whole person and give direction to actions which promote health provide the foundation for reality based health instruction.

Serves as an Organizer for Related Information. A generalization should be broad enough for a body of related facts to be organized under it. It should be pointed out that ideas (generalizations) may range from simple things to high-level abstractions rather far removed from the object level. If simple statements of fact are set forth as generalizations there is little value in using the generalization approach as a guide to instructional decisions. The number of health facts is overwhelming.

The statement "Carbon monoxide is a harmful substance found in smog" is a statement of fact rather than a big idea, or generalization. Little related information could be organized under it, except the *amount* of carbon monoxide found in smog. However, the statement "There are everchanging health hazards in man's environment" is broader and more appropriate for organizing related information; it could serve as an organizer for information concerning kinds of environmental health hazards—chemical pollutants, radioactive pollutants, man-made accidents, natural disorders; current environmental hazards of most concern to man and society, such as air, water, solid waste, and noise pollution; and factors causing health hazards to emerge or diminish, such as governmental controls, technology, production of goods and services, and population. Generalizations with a broader meaning, those which summarize a good deal of data, can help the teacher as well as the learner categorize, store, and retrieve information. Caution must be used, however, not to make the generalization too broad. For instance, the statement "Environment is influenced by man and in turn influences man" is perhaps too broad. All information relative to man and the environment can be organized under such a generalization. Formulating generalizations that are neither too broad nor too narrow in scope is a difficult task, and no precise yardsticks are available. For this reason it is useful to involve other professionals in formulating generalized statements and making judgments about their scope.

A Valid Statement. Misconceptions or erroneous ideas and unfounded theories or assumptions should not be used as a basis for formulating generalizations. A generalization should not encourage or support ideas which cannot be substantiated by scientific fact. For instance the statement "Knowledge of growth and development leads to practices that insure optimal well-being" is an unfounded statement. While such a "generalization" might sound good, there are no scientific data to support it. Knowledge may be useful in helping a person make health decisions, but it does not insure that he or she *will* make those decisions. Some valid generalizations relative to growth and development that can be substantiated by scientific evidence include:

1. "Growth and development follow a predictable pattern."
2. "Differences between boys and girls become greater as they are growing and developing."
3. "Human masculinity and femininity are determined by biological, emotional and social factors."

Relevant to Age Group and Culture. The generalization should be relevant to the age group toward which instruction is directed. In the primary grades generalizations should be simple, while at the upper grades they can be more complex. The statement "Communicable diseases affect the health and economy of the individual and society" might be appropriate for the upper grades but perhaps too complex for the primary grades. The statement would need to be altered so as to be within the frame of reference of the learner at the primary grades. For example, it might read "Diseases influence one's ability to work and play."

Another approach, however, is to use the same generalization at all age levels regardless of its complexity. In this instance relevancy to various age levels can be achieved through objectives developed for learners at particular age levels. The following serves as an example of this approach:

Generalization—Communicable diseases affect the health and economy of the individual and society.
Objective (ages 5 to 12)
Students can tell how diseases influence their ability to work and play.
Objective (ages 12 to 15)
Students can cite examples of how specific diseases have affected man and society.

Generalizations also should be relevant to the culture and environment of the individuals toward which they are directed. Imposing a generalization relative to birth control on a subculture that does not accept birth control would be questionable. Similarly, a generalization stressing middle class dietary and food selection practices, such as "The abundance of food in our society along with the mental-emotional condition of the individual influences food intake and may contribute to obesity," would probably be irrelevant in an economically deprived area. It does not take into account the economic and social conditions of people living in such an area, where the issue is not one of overabundance of food but rather an insufficient quantity of food or poor food selection from the sources available. Consequently, for the economically deprived, a more relevant generalization might be: "Obesity as well as nutrient deficiencies can result from improper food selection."

Nonprescriptive Statements. In our society stress is placed upon providing individuals with opportunities for making their own decisions. It would seem inconsistent to lay down prescriptive generalizations to be followed as rules in such a society. An example of such a generalization would be: "Everyone should utilize health department services in order to promote health." This "generalization" does not recognize the right of the individual to select the services he or she desires. It directs the individual to a particular source of health services that may or may not be appropriate for the individual's needs.

A more consistent approach would be the development of generalizations that provide individuals and families with a basis for making their own decisions consistent with their values and those of society. The following generalization is such an example: "Various health resources are available which are useful in promoting health." This generalization calls for providing learners with information relative to many available health resources. Based upon that information, individuals could make their own decisions as to which resource they or their families should use.

Values and Generalizations

Implicit in the aforementioned criteria for formulating or evaluating existing generalizations are individual values. What is viewed as good or bad, relevant or irrelevant, wise or unwise, useful or not useful, important or not important is based upon the values held by the individual formulating the generalizations.

Because we live in a multivalue society, it would seem appropriate to seek the opinions of others in the process of arriving at generalizations. To the extent that it is possible, a variety of opinions from professionals, the learner, and the community should be sought. When this is done, the generalizations will reflect more than merely one's own values and will be more likely accepted by those for whom they are intended.

A number of curriculum studies in many subject areas have made use of generalizations to represent that knowledge which ought to be emphasized in a subject area (9:13–46). Such an approach also has been utilized in health education. A review of these studies would be helpful to the planner who chooses to use generalizations in developing a health instruction program. In some cases the teacher/planner might wish to adopt generalizations identified in these studies in their entirety. In other instances such statements can be modified before they are used in the classroom to better meet the needs of the community and students. It is natural and normal to make value judgments when look-

ing at any health curriculum whether it is structured around generalizations or something else. Common responses include, "I sure like this
one!" or "This would be great material except for ..." or "If I were
to use this curriculum it would be like returning to the dark ages of
health education." Such judgments can be more rational when they
are based on an awareness of one's values and points of view concerning health and health education. And rational judgments may be
sobering when one is urged to jump on one or another health curriculum
bandwagon. Ultimately, successful implementation and use of any
health curriculum will rest, in part, on how closely the curriculum's
structure matches the users' values about health education. For example, one who values a health curriculum which includes generalizations (content) which recognizes the physical, mental-emotional, and
social dimensions of people is more apt to use such a curriculum.

School Health Education Study

The School Health Education Study employed a hierarchy of health
concepts and generalizations as a way to provide greater specificity
to the structure of health education from kindergarten through grade
twelve (13). This landmark effort represented a departure from structuring health knowledge through the use of traditional broad health
areas and related subtopics (drug use and abuse: legal and illegal drugs,
effects of drugs, consequences of misuse and abuse, why use and abuse,
personal-social skills for drug abuse prevention). While several decades have passed since this study, the generalizations formulated are
to this day exemplars of the use of generalizations to structure the
knowledge of health education. What follows is a description of this
structure.

Key Concepts. Three key concepts were identified. These are at the
highest level of generality and serve as the unifying elements of health
instruction. They also characterize processes underlying health. They
were labeled as: (1) *growing and developing,* (2) *decision making,* and
(3) *interacting.*

Concepts (Generalizations). Related to these key concepts, ten statements were identified. These statements (generalizations) or ideas are
next in order of generality on a descending scale, and represent the
scope of health instruction. They include the following:

1. ... Growth and development influences and is influenced by the structure and functioning of the individual.
2. ... Growing and developing follows a predictable sequence, yet is
   unique for each individual.
3. ... Protection and promotion of health is an individual, community,
   and international responsibility.

4. ... The potential for hazards and accidents exists, whatever the environment.
5. ... There are reciprocal relationships involving man, disease, and environment.
6. ... The family serves to perpetuate man and to fulfill certain health needs.
7. ... Personal health practices are affected by a complexity of forces, often conflicting.
8. ... Utilization of health information, products, and services is guided by values and perceptions.
9. ... Use of substances that modify mood and behavior arises from a variety of motivations.
10. ... Food selection and eating patterns are determined by physical, social, mental, economic, and cultural factors (13:20).

Subconcepts (Subgeneralizations). The final or lowest level of ideas (generalizations) was identified and labeled as subconcepts. Anywhere from two to four subconcepts were identified for each of the ten concepts for a total of thirty-one. Each of these subconcepts was represented in three dimensions: *physical, mental,* and *social.* It is important to note that these three dimensions are not isolated from one another or treated separately. Rather, these dimensions or aspects are interdependent and interacting. They recognize and represent a holistic health view of man. An example of this hierarchical structure of health knowledge is provided on page 42 (14:4).

California State Framework for Health Instruction

The *Health Instruction Framework for California Public Schools* (10) was developed to assist school district personnel in planning health instruction from kindergarten through grade twelve. The *Framework* was developed around ten health content areas. Each content area was further broken down into concepts (generalizations). This Framework is one representation of the structure of knowledge for health education. It is the structure recommended to the school districts in California.

Content Areas. Ten health content areas that represent the scope of health instruction were developed. These include (10:19):

    I. Personal Health
    II. Family Health
    III. Nutrition
    IV. Mental-Emotional Health
    V. Use and Misuse of Substances
    VI. Diseases and Disorders
    VII. Consumer Health
   VIII. Accident Prevention and Emergency Health Services
    IX. Community Health
    X. Environmental Health

Concepts (Generalizations). For each health content area several concepts (generalizations) were developed. These concepts (generalizations) are the major ideas that should be emphasized in each area. They serve as focal points for classroom instruction and provide for continuity and sequence in the instructional program. An example of generalizations for the health area of nutrition follows:

Health Area: Nutrition
- Food Choices—Daily food intake is related to the attainment of optimal health.
- Factors Influencing Choices—Life styles, peers, and individual family resources reflect similarities and differences in food choices.
- Food-related Careers—The food industry offers many employment and career opportunities.
- Consumer Competencies—Effective utilization of existing resources may enhance potential for satisfying individual and family nutritional needs and wants.
- Food Protection—The quality and safety of foods are influenced by the handling, processing, and preparing of foods.

USING AN ALTERNATIVE TO GENERALIZATIONS

A more traditional approach to developing and representing a structure of knowledge for the discipline of health education has been through the use of topics. Such an approach has involved the identification of several topics related to a particular health area, theme, or question. For example:

Health Area: Disease and Disorders
Related topics:
- Health and Illness
- Infectious Diseases
- Common Communicable Diseases
- Sexually Transmitted Diseases
- Common Chronic Disorders
- Prevention and Protection from Diseases and Disorders

In general, topics for a given health area are usually the product of health data and information which lend credence to the significance of the topics. By considering a range of health data and information indicative of the health needs of learners and society and related to a particular health category, inferences can be drawn about topics. Such topics will provide relevancy to both the structure of health knowledge and to the bases for the program of health instruction.

Care should be taken that topics are neither too broad nor too specific. For example, the topic communicable disease is quite broad and the focus for instruction is almost limitless. Yet, a topic like Acquired Immune Deficiency Disease (AIDS) is too specific. The focus here would be on one particular disease, albeit a significant one. When

GROWING AND DEVELOPING   INTERACTING   DECISION MAKING

Concept (Generalization): Use of Substances that Modify Mood and Behavior Arises from a Variety of Motivations

Subconcepts (Subgeneralizations)	Dimensions		
	Physical	Mental	Social
1 Substances that modify mood and behavior range from mild to strong, have multiple uses, and produce many and varied effects in individuals who use them.	Some mood and behavior modifiers as having noticeable effect on the body; others producing marked changes in body functioning and their regular, prolonged use resulting in serious structural or functional deterioration.	Some mood and behavior modifiers as agents to reduce feelings of fatigue, to elevate moods, and to aid relaxation; others serving to reduce inhibitions and producing unpredictable and often dangerous behavior (e.g., tranquilizers, alcohol, amphetamines, LSD, marijuana, and heroin).	Adult social custom as including use of some substances that modify mood and behavior; use of others as illegal and against general social mores (e.g., social drinking generally accepted as part of culture; strict laws against marijuana and heroin).
2 Use of substances that modify mood and behavior may result in health and safety problems.	Mood and behavior modifiers and their primary effect on the nervous and circulatory systems; physical dependence or accidental injury possibly resulting from use.	Possible modification of moods, perceptions of reality, and diminished emotional control from use of these substances.	Use of mood and behavior modifiers, often encouraged in social situations, as resulting in possible antisocial or dangerous behavior (e.g., alcoholism, narcotic addiction, accidents).
3 Many factors and forces influence the use of substances that modify mood and behavior.	Role of physical factors as influencing the use of mood and behavior modifying substances (e.g., fatigue, pleasure, boredom, craving, pain).	Desire for relaxation, loss of inhibitions, general change of mood, or discovery of "self" and its limits as reasons for use of such substances.	Social customers, family patterns, and desire to elicit group acceptance and approval as affecting the use of mood and behavior modifying substances.

identifying topics, the challenge is one that is somewhere in between too general and too specific. When considering data and information about AIDS, it might be well to recognize that it is a sexually transmitted disease. Therefore, it would seem that there is some logic in looking at any data and information about other sexually transmitted diseases. Such an observation would reveal other sexually transmitted diseases and in turn suggest that one relevant "middle of the road" topic under the Diseases and Disorders health area should be the topic of sexually transmitted diseases. Such a "middle of the road" topic provides direction for a manageable instructional focus. Consider that instruction which would focus on sexually transmitted diseases would focus on AIDS as well as other significant diseases such as chlamydia, herpes, gonorrhea, and syphilis. Furthermore, the topic of sexually transmitted diseases could be related to the broader topic of communicable diseases and learners would come to see that sexually transmitted diseases are a subset of communicable diseases.

Growing Healthy

The Growing Healthy program is a comprehensive education-for-health program aimed at elementary school age children (3). This curriculum was developed by the National Center for Health Education's School Health Education Project. The curriculum is structured around ten health areas. These areas are Growth and Development, Mental/Emotional Health, Personal Health, Family Life and Health, Nutrition, Disease Prevention and Control, Safety and First Aid, Consumer Health, Drug Use and Abuse, and Community Health Management. For each health area several related topics and lifestyle goals are specified. Also, student objectives are provided for grades kindergarten through seven. An example of topics for the health area called Family Life and Health includes:

> Health Area: Family Life and Health
>   Related Topics:
>   • Roles and interactions of individuals with the family life cycle
>   • Responsibilities and privileges experienced by each family member
>   • Physical, mental and social changes anticipated from birth to death
>   • Family's responsibility for the health, maturation, and socialization of children.

Wisconsin Guide to Curriculum Planning in Health Education

The Wisconsin curriculum guide was designed to assist those in local districts responsible for the development, implementation, and evaluation of comprehensive K-12 programs of health instruction (1:8). One feature of this guide is the inclusion of a recommended structure of knowledge for health education. This structure is intended as a roadmap for planning meaningful and relevant health instruction. The Wisconsin curriculum guide is structured around ten health content ares. These consist of Accident Prevention and Safety, Community Health, Consumer Health, Environmental Health, Family Life Education, Mental and Emotional Health, Nutrition, Personal Health, Prevention and Control of Disease, and Substance Use and Abuse. For each of these health areas, topics are provided as an overview of recommended content. These topics are identified at specified grade levels. An example of topics for the health areas of Accident Prevention and Safety and Community Health includes:

Major Content Area	Accident Prevention and Safety	Community Health
Grade Level		
K	–poison signs –protective behaviors –rules –life hazards	
1	–school safety –fire drills –bus and auto safety	
2	–water safety –electrical safety –basic first aid –fire escape plans –accident prevention	
3	–pedestrian safety –reflective clothing –home fires –safety patrols –safety laws	–characteristics of a healthy community –problem solving –assistance with health promotion
4	–hiking safety –first aid for bleeding –bike safety –minor injuries	–public health workers –disease prevention
5	–boating safety –water safety –choking symptoms	–health benefits –personal and family activities that promote health –community health issues –community health specialists
6	–shock –heart attack –safety attitude	–community health planning –community action –volunteer health agencies
7–9	–first aid for drug overdose –artificial respiration –first aid for choking victim	–community help for the aged –health organizations –community health careers
10–12	–careers in safety –CPR –bandaging –splinting –safety in sports and leisure	–individual versus community rights –medical care trends –personal action plan

HEALTH GENERALIZATIONS OR HEALTH TOPICS

Clearly, inferences drawn from health data and information can be represented as generalizations or topics. Either can be used to give meaning to and structure for any given health area, theme, or question. Both approaches require careful thought and consideration to adequately account for the great quantities of health data and information and to provide a structure for the health instruction program.

Of the two approaches, the formulation of generalizations is the more difficult. This is so because generalizations need to be precise and understandable statements, consistent with current points of view concerning health and health education, and nonprescriptive. All this requires added rigor when formulating generalizations. Yet, when properly formulated, generalizations can provide a clearer focus for health instruction. They can provide an explicit reference to actions which can promote health. Also, generalizations can include explicit references to the whole person and not just one dimension such as the physical. These explicit references which are or should be built into generalizations are not explicit in topics. Rather they are implicit in topics and as such can be easily "lost" or left unattended. The result can be a program of health instruction that lacks a thrust toward health behaviors which promote health and which ignores a holistic view of people.

Whether the preference is toward generalizations or topics, some such specification is a useful step in structuring health knowledge for classroom instruction. From either generalizations or topics the next step is one of developing goals and instructional objectives.

DEVELOPING GOALS AND INSTRUCTIONAL OBJECTIVES

A further step in structuring health knowledge for classroom instruction involves the development of goals and instructional objectives. In particular, the specification of goals and objectives provides the student and teacher with a discrete learning to focus on relative to a given health generalization or topic. As the development of goals and objectives is an involved process, the entire next chapter is devoted to this step.

REPEATING THE PROCESS

Our environment—socioeconomic, cultural, scientific, technological, as well as physical—is in a constant state of flux. With new health discoveries, with changing health conditions, with shifts in health priorities there is a need to reassess the structure of knowledge for health instruction. In essence the strategy suggested for structuring health knowledge needs to be repeated periodically.

Thus as new data concerning the health needs of the learner and society and up-to-date valid health information emerges it needs to be collected and grouped into similar categories. New health generalizations or topics, goals, and instructional objectives may have to be formulated. Existing generalizations or topics, goals, and objectives might have to be modified or discarded. When the process of structuring health knowledge is thus repeated periodically, health instruction will continue to be valid and relevant.

REFERENCES

1. *A Guide To Curriculum Planning In Health Education.* Madison, Wisconsin: Wisconsin Department of Public Instruction, 1985.
2. Allensworth, Diane D. and Cynthia A. Wolford. "Schools as Agents for Achieving The 1990 Health Objectives for the Nation." *Health Education Quarterly.* 15:3–15, Spring, 1988.
3. American Lung Association. *Growing Healthy Health Education Curriculum Progression Chart.* New York: American Lung Association, 1985.
4. Beane, James A., Conrad F. Toepfer, Jr., and Samuel J. Alessi, Jr. *Curriculum Planning and Development.* Newton, Massachusetts: Allyn and Bacon Inc., 1986.
5. Dobson, Russell L. and Judith E. Dobson. "Curriculum Theorizing." *The Educational Forum.* 51:275–284, Spring, 1987.
6. Duckworth, Eleanor. *The Having of Wonderful Ideas and Other Essays on Teaching and Learning.* New York: Teachers College Press, 1987.
7. Eisner, Elliot. *The Educational Imagination.* New York: Macmillan, 1985.
8. Glaser, Robert. "Education and Thinking: The Role of Knowledge," *American Psychologist.* 39: 93–104, February, 1984.
9. Goodlad, John I. *School Curriculum Reform.* New York: The Fund for the Advancement of Education, 1964.
10. *Health Instruction Framework for Public Schools.* Sacramento: California State Department of Education, 1978, 1985.
11. Perkins, D.N. *Knowledge As Design.* Hillsdale, N.J.: Lawrence Erlbaum Associates, 1986.
12. Portelli, John P. "Perspectives and Imperatives on Defining Curriculum." *Journal of Curriculum and Supervision.* 2: 354–367, Summer, 1987.
13. School Health Education Study. *Health Education. A Conceptual Approach; Experimental Curriculum Materials Project.* St. Paul: 3M Education Press, 1967.
14. School Health Education Study. *Teaching Learning Guides, Use of Substances that Modify Mood and Behavior Arises From a Variety of Motivations.* St. Paul: 3M Education Press, 1968.
15. Willgoose, Carl E. "Health Education As a Basic." *Health Education Today.* Reston, VA: Association for the Advancement of Health Education, October, 1985.

CHAPTER

4

Formulating Goals and Objectives for Health Instruction

Formulating goals and objectives serves to further specify that which is to be stressed in health instruction.

GOALS

The Value of Goals

Goals are statements of broad direction or intent. They provide direction in making instructional decisions. That is, goals are long-range targets toward which instruction is directed. They help clarify that which is to be emphasized (generalizations or topics). For some, generalizations or topics themselves may serve as goals to be attained by students. In such cases, while the behavior sought in the learner is not specified, it is implied that the learner is able to do something with the generalization or topic: understand it, become aware of it, or know it. For instance, the generalization "A variety of health resources are available which are useful in promoting health" can be converted to a goal by adding the phrase *The student understands that* a variety of health resources are available which are useful in promoting health. For others, several goals might be developed that are related to a generalization or topic and which further help to clarify it. For instance, with the topic, "health promotion resources," several goals might be identified, such as:

- The student will become increasingly aware of a variety of community health resources.
- The student will learn to utilize a variety of available appropriate resources in coping with individual and family health problems.

- The student will develop positive attitudes about the usefulness of those community health resources that help individuals and families cope with specific health problems.

Limitations of Goals

Goals are more general than objectives. They do not include a specification of achievement that can be readily assessed. For this reason it is difficult to determine when or if goals are attained by students. For example, a goal for health instruction might be that "the student will develop positive attitudes toward the utilization of health services, products, and information." The attainment of this goal would be difficult to assess, for several reasons. It is difficult to determine what is meant by positive attitudes. Does this mean the student likes to do something, feels that it is important to do something, or feels good about doing it? Too, what is meant by effective utilization of health services, health products, and health information? This portion of the goal is open to many and varied interpretations, making assessment virtually impossible.

Because of their breadth and generality goals tend to be timeless. That is, final attainment of the goal might never be fully realized. As the learner grows and develops, in one way or another, throughout his or her lifetime, there is a potential for further goal attainment. Consequently, final goal attainment is elusive and thus timeless.

OBJECTIVES

Through the stating of instructional objectives, increased specificity with regard to what should be taught in health instruction can be achieved. Such objectives are short-term, precise statements of end-results that build cumulatively to a goal and in turn a topic or generalization. As an analogy we can use the climber whose goal is to reach the highest peak. While the individual might spend a lifetime trying to achieve this goal, the immediate objective might be "that peak over there" or "this ridge here." After rest and nourishment higher peaks (objectives) might be set as steps toward achieving the ultimate goal.

Stating Objectives

To be effective, an objective should be stated so that the specific content to be studied by the student and the specific behavior that is sought with respect to this content is included. Each objective should have a *content dimension* and a *behavioral dimension.* If either of these dimensions is missing, the objective is incomplete. For example, the following "instructional objectives" omit the content dimension:

"To develop values"
"To develop the ability to appreciate"
"To develop the ability to evaluate"

These "objectives" fail to indicate specific areas of content in which behaviors are being sought. What are the values to be developed? What should the student appreciate? What should be evaluated?

Equally confusing and vague are statements presented as instructional objectives but which omit the behavioral dimension. Such "instructional objectives" might include:

"The causes of periodontal disease"
"Some drugs are stimulants"
"Immunity is a means of preventing communicable disease."

Objectives stated in this fashion fail to stipulate what the student is to do with this content. Are students expected to recall these statements or facts related to them? Are they to develop the ability to apply knowledge of these topics to their everyday living, or merely to develop an interest in these topics? Are they expected to judge the validity of these statements? When objectives are incomplete, that is, when either the content or the behavioral dimension is omitted, they fail to provide the necessary specifications useful for planning and implementing effective instruction.

Being Precise

In stating objectives as much precision as possible should be included in specifying both the content and behavioral dimensions. While an objective such as "The student *understands nutrition*" has a content dimension (nutrition) and a behavioral dimension (understands), it lacks precision. There is a lack of specific direction for both the teacher and the student. The content dimension is extremely broad. Volumes of written material have been devoted to the subject of nutrition. It would be impossible to ascertain the aspects of nutrition the student is to "learn" from this objective; further interpretation would be needed. To lend precision to the content, clarity must be applied in specifying the content dimension. This means that terms or phrases that make up this dimension should be specific and open to few interpretations. The following provide a contrast between less precise and more precise content terms and phrases:

Less Precise Content (Broad in meaning)	More Precise Content (More specific in meaning)
Nutrition	Cultural influences on eating habits
Growth and development	Specific secondary sex characteristics of boys and girls
Promoting health	Community and national responsibilties for promoting health
Hazards and accidents	Emotional factors that influence accidents
Cigarette smoking	Immediate physiologic effects of cigarette smoking

Similarly, the meaning of the verb *understands* in the aforementioned objective is vague and open to many interpretations. To what extent do students understand something? Does understand mean that students can remember or recall certain facts or that they can relate these facts to other ideas? Does understand mean that students identify important ideas? When students understand, do they value nutrition?

Behavioral terms that are open to several interpretations may lead to imprecise or "wandering" emphases by teachers. In turn, this may result in confusion on the part of students as to what specifically they are supposed to learn. Precise terms that describe or define behavior need to be identified and used in the stating of instructional objectives. The following list provides a contrast between verbs or phrases that are vague and open to varied interpretations and those that are more precise in describing behavior.

Less Precise Terms (Many interpretations)	More Precise Terms (Fewer interpretations)
Know	Discuss
Realize	Identify
Fully realize	List
Enjoy	Diagram
Believe	Compare
Understand	Contrast
Feel responsible for	Translate
Appreciate	Recall
Value	State
Comprehend	Select
Be aware	Illustrate
Tolerate	Interpret
Respect	Differentiate
Be familiar with	Summarize
Desire	Classify
Feel	Predict
	Apply
	Conclude
	Plan
	Theorize

It should be noted, however, that terms open to many interpretations (appreciate, understand, or value) may be used in stating instructional objectives when certain qualifications are met.

For instance, the intended meaning could be amplified:

> *The student understands the basic four food groups and indicates this understanding by naming at least one food in each group.*

Or a vague term might be used in an "overall' objective with a number of more specific objectives being developed that relate to the "overall" objective:

> *The Student Develops An Appreciation of Community Health Agencies.*
>
> - *describes three functions of the American Heart Association and the American Cancer Society*
> - *states at least four ways community agencies benefit society.*
> - *lists three ways individuals can cooperate with community health agencies.*
> - *Expresses opinions about the relative usefulness of community health agencies in dealing with health problems.*

Precision in formulating and stating objectives can contribute to more effective teaching. The teacher will be able to plan and implement instruction which will help students attain the specified objective and will be able to be more precise in evaluating student success. Too, Dalis showed that when students are made aware of the precise objectives in the teaching-learning situation they will better know what is expected of them and consequently will demonstrate enhanced achievement (2).

MEANINGFUL OBJECTIVES

Objectives can be stated precisely and still not be purposeful or meaningful to the student. For instance, the objective "The student can *identify twenty-five vitamins*" has both a content and a behavioral dimension and is precisely stated. Yet what is the necessity of having students know the names of twenty-five vitamins? The same would be true if for "twenty-five vitamins" we substituted "blood vessels in the thoracic cavity" or "nerves in the central nervous system." These phrases illustrate emphasis on anatomical structures. Such a structural emphasis is of minimum value when appraised in terms of points of view relative to health and health instruction. In health instruction, stress on anatomical structures is tenable only if there is an obvious health implication or opportunity for application of the content to health values, principles, or practices.

OBJECTIVES AND BEHAVIORS SOUGHT IN STUDENTS

Clearly, the major outcome of health education has been and continues to be learners who incorporate into their lifestyles actions or practices deemed to promote health. For example, such lifestyle practices as using time management to avoid or reduce stress, participating in 20 minutes of vigorous physical activity 3 to 4 times a week, flossing daily, performing the skill of saying no to drug use, obtaining recommended vaccinations and immunizations, and using the 911 emergency number to seek emergency care. Programs of health instruction have been designed to instill and/or strengthen health practices and to extinguish and/or limit health compromising practices.

Instructional approaches to the development of healthy lifestyle practices has varied over the years. At one time or another the focus has been primarily on arousing fear of actions deemed unhealthy, or on disseminating health information, or on the development of health cognition, or, more recently, on the enhancement of self concept. Each of these approaches was taken to rectify certain inadequacies in learners which hindered their assimilation of healthy practices. For example, the fear approach would be utilized in the belief that an individual who was not fearful of such a substance as alcohol was at risk of becoming a drunkard; therefore, fear of alcohol had to be instilled. Likewise, those who lacked health information, health cognition, or a healthy self concept were individuals at risk and therefore instructional approaches to remedy these deprivations were administered. Independently all of these approaches have proven to be rather ineffective.

Presently, increasing emphasis is being given to multiple or eclectic approaches in health instruction. Papenfuss et al. advocate that attention be given to a range of theories that help explain behavior formation (10). These include theories that focus on social learning, problem behavior, behavioral intention, communication, wellness, total person, self concept, coping, decision making, cognitive dissonance, and fear arousal. As a group, these theories are supportive of working on an array of learner outcomes as a way to facilitate the development of healthy lifestyle practices.

In summarizing research on emerging approaches to school based substance abuse prevention models, Botvin cited the efficacy of using both social influences as well as personal and social skills approaches (2). The social influences approach emphasizes awareness of social influences on behavior and correcting misperceptions of social norms; "not everybody is doing it." The personal and social skills approach calls for training in such areas as problem solving, decision making, cognitive skills for resisting harmful risk taking behavior, skills for increasing self control and self esteem, strategies for relieving stress and anxiety, interpersonal skills, assertive skills, and refusal skills.

While the effectiveness of these approaches was demonstrated initially with cigarette smoking, they have been used with both alcohol and marijuana use and teenage pregnancy prevention.

Since many, if not all, health behaviors are a product of psychosocial factors, it is reasonable to consider the aforementioned approaches when seeking to instill and/or strengthen health practices and extinguish and/or limit health compromising practices. Therefore, attention to these approaches needs to be given to health practices related to such issues as family planning, food intake, seat belts, salt intake, sexually transmitted diseases, immunization, pregnancy and infant care, control of stress, fluoridation and dental health, physical fitness and exercise, as well as smoking and misuse of alcohol and drugs.

Certain inferences can be drawn from theories as well as social influences and personal and social skills approaches which have proven to be useful in influencing health behavior. One important inference for those in health instruction is the necessity to focus on a range of behaviors for learners; not just fear or information or cognition or self concept behavior. This range of behaviors for learners should center around the general areas of *information acquisition, skill development, concept development, opinion expression* and *development, and values awareness* (8). In effect, these general areas represent categories of specific behaviors which need to be sought in learners in order to facilitate the development of health educated individuals.

The following is a description of the aforementioned general categories with examples of objectives related to these categories.

Information Acquisition

This category of objectives includes all those behaviors which require the learner to remember. While objectives in this category might be formulated by using a variety of verbs such as identify, describe, list, diagram or summarize, the fundamental outcome is that the learner can *recall* and/or *apply* the information. Examples of objectives related to information acquisition are:

- The student can list three immediate effects of smoking.
- The student can describe the growth changes that occur during adolescence.
- The student can name the seven United States Department of Agriculture dietary guidelines.
- The student can explain ways family members may help each other.

Evidence that the learner has attained objectives in this category is demonstrated when the learner is able to retrieve information verbally or in some written manner. Also, evidence may be demonstrated when the learner is able to cite the information acquired as a basis for a decision. For example, the learner chooses food A over food B because A has less sodium and is in keeping with the dietary guideline "avoid too much sodium."

Skill Development

Objectives in this category include all those behaviors which require the learner to *perform* a skill. The skill may be one which is intellectual or psychomotor in nature. Regardless of the type of skill, all skills are characterized by inherent steps. That is, a skill consists of two or more steps which may or may not need to be implemented in a particular order. Examples of objectives related to skill development are:

- The student can translate health data presented in graph form into a verbal form.
- The student can analyze advertisements of health products or services for unstated assumptions.
- The student can administer cardiopulmonary resuscitation (CPR).
- The student can demonstrate the steps of "saying no and keeping your friends".

With skill development objectives it is imperative that, for the purposes of instruction, the steps of a skill be identified. For example, the steps of the skill of "saying no and keeping your friends" have been identified as:

1. Ask questions.
2. Name the trouble.
3. Identify the consequences.
4. Suggest an alternative.
5. Move it, sell it, leave the door open (14).

While some learners intuitively acquire such skills, many do not. Some learners, frequently referred to as gifted, are able to replicate a skill after if it is demonstrated once or twice. Many, however, are unable to do so even after repeated demonstrations of the skill. In order to provide "equal opportunity" for all learners, the steps of a skill need to be taught explicity. If the steps are not available or known, then they must be "psyched out." This means doing a task analysis to determine, for example, what one does intellectually when translating health data presented in a graph form into a verbal form.

Evidence that the learner has attained a skill objective is demonstrated when the learner is able to demonstrate or do the skill. While skills involve remembering the steps or process, success in attaining the skill is not based on whether the learner can recount the steps but rather whether the learner can *perform* the steps. This then becomes a critical distinction between information acquisition and skill development.

Concept Development

In this category objectives include all those behaviors which require the learner to *use* a concept. To distinguish concepts from facts or bits of information it is useful to consider critical characteristics of concepts. These attributes are as follows:

- All concepts have a definition that includes a description of some relationship or a set of specific characteristics. For example, a definition including a relationship would be *immunity, that resistance usually associated with the presence of antibodies or cells having a specific action on the microorganism concerned with a particular infectious disease or on its toxin* (1). An example of a definition including a set of specific characteristics would be a *healthy daily diet* consisting of foods from (1) the vegetable-fruit group, 4 servings daily; (2) the bread-cereal group, 4 servings daily; (3) the milk-cheese group, on a daily basis, 3 servings for child, 4 servings for teenager, 2 servings for adult, 4 servings for pregnant woman; and (4) the meat-poultry and fish-bean group, on a daily basis, 2 servings, 3 servings for pregnant woman.
- All concepts have a label that substitutes for the concept definition. For example, *immunity* and *healthy daily diet.*
- All concepts can be used to do at least two of the following: build or design a product, categorize, explain, or predict. For example, it is possible to use the concept *healthy daily diet* to put together or *build* a diet for a teenager. This same concept can be used to examine the diets of a number of teenagers and *categorize* those diets that are healthy from those that are not. With the concept *immunity* it is possible to use it to *explain* why some individual has resistance to a particular infectious disease and another does not. This same concept also can be used to develop or *design* immunity to a particular infectious disease such as a real one like AIDS or a hypothetical one like the dreaded "Zorch Syndrome".

Examples of objectives related to concept development are:

- The student can develop a personal meal plan for 1 week consistent with the healthy daily diet concept.
- The student eats food consistent with the healthy daily diet concept.
- The student can use the concept of immunity to explain why some individuals have immunity to a particular infectious disease and others do not.
- The student can use the concept of dominant/recessive genes to predict color of eyes and hair and shape of nose.

Concepts are the inventions of humans. They function as intellectual tools which enable one to build or design a product (plan, model, regimen), explain, categorize, or predict. Evidence that the learner has attained objectives in the concept development category is demonstrated when the learner is able to not only recall the concept definition but more importantly *use* the concept.

Opinion Expression and Development

The emphasis of objectives in this category is on all those behaviors which call for the learner to express his or her own individual opinion(s) on some topic or issue. While the learner might report information or predictions related to a discussion topic the key outcome is one of expressing an opinion. Examples of objectives related to opinion expression and development are:

- The student can offer action(s) to take in specific sexually transmitted disease situations (e.g. how might an individual tell his/her parents if he/she thought they had a sexually transmitted disease).
- The student can state personal pros and cons of having a steady boyfriend/girlfriend.
- The student can present his/her point of view regarding the issue of abortion.
- The student can present thoughts and feelings about specific situation where individuals bully others.

Evidence that the learner has attained objectives in this category is demonstrated when the learner is able to *state/restate* an opinion and *consider* his or her own opinion or the opinion of others. To be valid, this evidence must come forth freely and responsibly from the learner. The act of stating/restating and of giving consideration should be at the volition of the learner and not in response to probing by the teacher or some discussion leader.

Values Awareness

With this category of objectives the focus is on all those behaviors which require the learner to demonstrate an awareness of his or her own values and the values of others. Awareness of values does not occur in a vacuum but rather in the context of some real or hypothetical issue. For example, issues such as the advertising of drugs on television, supplying sterile needles for intravenous drug users, using tax dollars for abortions, admitting to school students who have AIDS and the using of pesticides by farmers. Examples of objectives related to values awareness are:

- The student can name personal values related to a decision favoring or not favoring the establishment of high school health clinics.
- The student can name personal values about a decision to work hard to keep slim and physically fit.
- The student can cite personal values and/or the values of others related to actions to reduce gang violence.
- The student can identify personal values and/or the values of others related to judgments about visual pollution caused by billboards.

Evidence that the learner has attained an objective in this category is demonstrated when the learner is able to *identify* the value(s) he or she has related to a judgment or decision about a particular issue. Also, evidence of objective attainment includes instances where the learner is able to *decide* by using values. The act of identifying values and deciding consistent with personal values may occur voluntarily or it may occur in response to an invitation to do so by the teacher.

No longer should programs of health instruction focus only on one learner behavior such as the assimilation of pertinent health information or the expression of feelings linked to health issues. To facilitate rational and responsible healthy lifestyles, the learner needs to be empowered with a repertoire of learnings. A viable program of health instruction needs to include a thoughtful balance of specific learner objectives which focus on information acquisition, skill development, concept development, opinion expression and development, and values awareness.

PURPOSE OF OBJECTIVES

Objectives are vital in dynamic teaching. Properly stated they are not only useful but essential for both students and teachers. Objectives can provide valuable clues as to what should be taught, how it should be taught, and whether or not it is retained by the learner.

Thus, when properly stated, an objective is a guide to: (1) specific content to be studied by the student; (2) specific behavior changes sought in the student with respect to this content; (3) selection of the teaching strategy that best enables the learner to achieve the desired behavioral outcome; (4) what to evaluate in terms of the health content studied and the behavior sought in the learner; and (5) the evaluation of teacher effectiveness.

A Guide to the Selection of Specific Content

With a well-stated objective, the teacher has a guide for the selection of content to be emphasized. Guesswork is eliminated. Properly stated objectives enable the teacher to carry out instruction in an efficient manner. In so doing, the random coverage of irrelevant subject matter is minimized.

A Guide to Specific Behaviors Sought in the Learner

With a well-stated objective the teacher has a guide for the specific behavior to be developed. The efforts of the teacher can be directed to planning instruction which will assist learners to attain the specific behavior. By focusing the instruction on a specific behavior efficiency of teaching and learning can be achieved.

A Guide to the Selection of Teaching Strategies

A precisely stated objective can serve as a guide in the selection of a relevant teaching strategy. When using objectives for this selection, consideration should be given to the kinds of behaviors sought in the learner.

The behavior specified in an objective is the main determinant as to which teaching strategy is most appropriate for a given lesson. For example, when seeking to influence the learner's ability to recall, there is a need to utilize a teaching strategy somewhat different from one that would be used to influence the learner's ability to perform some skill. Since the behaviors *recall* and *perform* are different, the learner needs to do something different to attain them. To recall certain bits of information, the learner needs to be provided with opportunities to practice *recalling,* whereas to perform a particular skill the learner needs to be provided with opportunities to practice *performing* the skill. Therefore, the teacher needs to select and utilize a teaching strategy that causes the teacher to incorporate key events in the process of teaching that will facilitate the learner's attainment of the specific behavior. The critical events which need to occur for different teaching strategies is discussed further in Chapter 5.

A Guide to the Evaluation of Students

Objectives also serve as guides to evaluation by specifying the area of content to be dealt with by the student and the way in which the student is to deal with this content (behaviors sought). This reduces guesswork in evaluation and increases the precision of the evaluative process. In the absence of objectives, or with poorly stated objectives, there is a tendency to overlook the necessity of evaluating students for a variety of appropriate outcomes, and the evaluative process tends to be limited to an appraisal of facts or a test for recall.

With objectives that include both the content to be studied and the behaviors sought in the learner, the teacher is provided with a specific guide for evaluating the degree to which the objectives have been attained. Because of the importance of evaluation, Chapter 7 includes a focus on the evaluation of health instruction. In this section the discussion has been limited to the important role of objectives in the evaluative process.

A Guide to the Evaluation of Teacher Effectiveness

In addition to serving as a guide to the evaluation of student growth, well-stated objectives can help teachers assess their teaching effectiveness. The degree to which students achieve or do not achieve anticipated outcomes can serve as a basis for drawing inferences about the teacher's effectiveness in the teaching-learning situation. In those instances when teachers judge that they have not been effective in facilitating student achievement, alternate ways of working with students to attain desired outcomes should be considered.

LEVELS OF GOALS AND OBJECTIVES

Goals and objectives exist at the state, district, and classroom levels of school organization. The specificity with which goals and objectives are stated is determined by the level of school organization. That is, the closer they are to the classroom level, the greater should be their specificity. Both goals and objectives are essential since they are related to one another in the total health curriculum. Three levels at which objectives can be identified are: (1) state-wide curriculum planning; (2) local curriculum planning, the district setting; (3) teacher and student curriculum planning, the teaching-learning situation.

At the state level goals and objectives should be general, to provide the broad aims of health education within a state. Based upon these, school district personnel can develop goals and objectives applicable to the district, which in turn, offer further direction for more specific objectives planned by the teacher and applicable to students in a given teaching-learning situation.

RELATING OBJECTIVES AND GENERALIZATIONS/TOPICS

The identification of health generalizations or topics and objectives provides a structure for health instruction. For this structure to be viable, there must be a built-in relationship between such generalizations or topics and objectives. That is, any objective for health instruction should be relevant to an identified health generalization or topic.

In the teaching-learning situation several objectives may be related to one generalization. For instance, there may be a number of specified instructional objectives related to the generalization, "There is a direct relationship between dental health and nutrition," such as:

- The student can discuss the relationship of carbohydrates to tooth decay.
- The student can identify foods that are needed for sound tooth structure.

- The student eats food such as carrots and apples between meals to help keep the teeth clean.

The attainment of these objectives provides the student with a base for making health decisions relative to nutrition and dental health. The degree to which the student has attained the stated objectives, in fact, serves as one indication of the degree to which the generalization has been acquired. As a range of health generalizations or topics are acquired, students develop bases for making health decisions now and in the future.

The rationale for health instruction presented thus far has emphasized the importance of points of view concerning health and health education as a base upon which health instruction might be developed. A consideration also was given to health needs of individuals and society as necessary guides to determine the content of health instruction. A discussion of structuring health knowledge in terms of generalizations or topics and specified objectives followed. The next consideration will be the selection and utilization of relevant teaching strategies to assist students in the attainment of specified objectives.

REFERENCES

1. Beneson, Abram S. Editor. *Control of Communicable Diseases in Man.* Washington, D.C.: American Public Health Association, 1981, p. 412.
2. Botvin, Gilbert. "Substance Abuse Prevention Research: Recent Developments and Future Directions." *Journal of School Health. 58:*369–374, November, 1986.
3. Dalis, Gus T. "Effect of Precise Objectives Upon Student Achievement in Health Education." *The Journal of Experimental Education. 39:*-20-23, Winter, 1970.
4. Eisner, Elliott. "Educational Objectives: Help or Hindrance?" *American Journal of Education. 91:*549–60, Aug. 1983.
5. Ho, Curtis P., et al. "The Effects of Orienting Objectives and Review on Learning from Interactive Video." *Journal of Computer-Based Instruction. 13:*126–29. Autumn, 1986.
6. Heller, Mel. "Evaluation: Using Behavioral Objectives as the Framework." *NASSP Bulletin. 68:*47–49, February, 1984.
7. Lewis, James M. "Behavioral Objectives from Research to Reality." *Journal of Educational Technology System. 10:*285–91, 1981–82.
8. Loggins, Dennis, Ray Cowan, Gus Dalis, and Ben Strasser. "Elephants Are Easier to Recognize Than Good Lessons." *Thrust. 16:*40–43, October, 1986.
9. Mager, Robert F. *Goal Analysis.* Belmont, California: Pitman Management and Training, 1984.
10. Papenfuss, Richard L., Michael Hammes and Christina Perry. "School Health Education: A Vital Component in the Educational Process." (Unpublished paper) University of New Mexico.
11. Perry, Cheryl L. "A Conceptual Approach to School-Based Health Promotion." *Health Education. 15:*33–38, 1984.
12. Popham, W. James. *Modern Educational Measurement.* Englewood Cliffs, New Jersey: Prentice-Hall, 1981.
13. Popham, W. James. "Two-Plus Decades of Educational Objectives." *International Journal of Education Research. 11:*31–41, 1987.
14. Roberts, Fitzmahan and Associates and Educational Services District #121. *Here's Looking At You, 2000: A Teacher's Guide for Drug Education, Grade 4.* Seattle, Washington: Comprehensive Health Education Foundation, 1986, pp. 47–58.

5

Utilizing Appropriate Teaching Strategies for Health Instruction

The formulation and utilization of teaching strategies should be based, primarily, upon instructional objectives or ends students are to attain. Teaching strategies are means to ends. They are not ends in themselves and are of questionable value unless related to specified objectives. When related to instructional objectives, teaching strategies have a purpose. That purpose is to afford students the opportunity to attain desired outcomes.

TEACHING STRATEGIES

Numerous terms have been used by educators to describe those things used with or on students in order to accomplish the objectives of the instructional program. *Methods of instruction, learning experiences, learning activities, learning opportunities,* and more recently teaching strategies are some of the terms used. Of these, teaching strategies seems to describe most accurately the means by which instructional objectives are best attained. *Methods of instruction* might be too narrow a term and tends to imply only "teacher activities" in the classroom situation. The teaching-learning situation involves much more than classroom activities provided by the teacher. It also involves students interacting with that which is provided by the teacher. *Learning experience* implies that "learning" takes place. Learning may or may not take place. Because the teacher provides a situation or activity designed to bring about learning on the part of the student, it does not necessarily follow that the student will "experience" learning. *Learning activity* also implies that activity leads to learning, which may or may not be the case. The term further implies that the learner must engage in some kind of overt activity before learning can take place. However, one may contemplate an idea and "learn" covertly without any observable activity taking place. *Learning opportunities* carries with it a focus on the learner and what the learner does to attain a lesson objective. The implied emphasis on the learner is appealing since it is consistent with the widely held legitimate belief that the learner has to be involved with that which is to be learned if learning is to take place. This term, however, tends to ignore the role of the teacher in the teaching learning process.

Effective teaching is more complex than implementing a particular instructional method or arranging for a specific experience or opportunity for learners. Rather, such teaching requires the teacher to "orchestrate" a network of actions specific to the lesson objective and which will facilitate learner attainment of this objective. The term *teaching strategy* has been selected for the network of teacher actions.

Teaching Strategy Defined

Dalis and Strasser define a teaching strategy as a set of instructional decisions which when made and implemented yield a particular learner outcome (objective). Given an instructional objective this set of decisions centers around:

- What are the learning steps and how are they to be sequenced?
- What are the students to do as they come to grips with this particular learning task?
- What will the teacher do to initiate the lesson and to facilitate the student's growth toward the lesson objective (3)?

A teaching strategy is a network or set of *critical steps* used to promote learner attainment of an objective. These steps include explicit roles for both teacher and learner. Depending upon the instructional objective, the steps may or may not need to unfold in a particular order.

Of importance to a teaching strategy are those specific steps or events deemed critical to promoting learner attainment of the learning task (objective). To implement the steps, different methods of instruction can be utilized and a variety of experiences or activities or opportunities can be arranged for the learner.

Different Objectives Different Teaching Strategies

Not all instructional objectives are or should be the same. As discussed in Chapter 4, a viable program of health instruction needs to focus on developing a repertoire of learner behaviors or competencies in the area of health. With behaviors that are different, what the learner needs to do to assimilate them is different. For example, the learner has one set of needs in order to learn how to *use* a particular health concept and a different set in order to learn how to *identify* the values he or she has related to a particular health decision. Clearly, one generic teaching approach or strategy, regardless of the behavior specified in the objective, will not suffice. Rather, a teaching strategy which meets the learner's needs to acquire the behavior in the objective has to be utilized. Effective health instruction requires that the teacher match the appropriate teaching strategy to the objective for a given lesson.

Most health instruction objectives can or should be related to the following categories of objectives: information acquisition, skill development, concept development, opinion expression and development, and values awareness. The names of these categories can also serve as the name of the teaching strategy which is appropriate to facilitate learner attainment of objectives related to that category. This relationship of objective categories and related teaching strategies is illustrated in the following.

Health Objectives Categories		Appropriate Teaching Strategy
• Information Acquisition	→	Information Acquisition Teaching Strategy
• Skill Development	→	Skill Development Teaching Strategy
• Concept Development	→	Concept Development Teaching Strategy
• Opinion Expression and Development	→	Opinion Expression and Development Teaching Strategy
• Values Awareness	→	Values Awareness Teaching Strategy (12:41-42)

CRITICAL CHARACTERISTICS OF DIFFERENT TEACHING STRATEGIES

In the context of teaching strategies, critical characteristics are those steps or events which when implemented by the teacher facilitate learning. Successful implementation of these steps is one way to provide "equal opportunity" for all learners to attain the lesson objective. For different teaching strategies the set of characteristics is different. Again, the differences in sets of characteristics are dictated, in part, by the different needs learners have related to the assimilation of different behaviors or competencies. Other differences in sets of characteristics are an outgrowth of research on learning. For example, some research shows that learning is enhanced when learners are provided with an opportunity to practice or rehearse overtly that which they are trying to learn and some shows that learning is facilitated when learners know in advance of instruction what they are expected to learn (10).

The following includes the name, purpose, and the set of critical characteristics for each of 5 teaching strategies appropriate for health education.

Information Acquisition Teaching Strategy

The purpose of this teaching strategy is to promote students' acquisition of information. As an outgrowth of using this strategy, students should be able to demonstrate their ability to recall specified health information and, as appropriate, cite the information as one basis for a health decision. To implement this strategy the teacher:

- Informs the students of what is to be learned and describes how they will be evaluated.
- Makes the specific information available to the students and monitors to determine if information received is correct.
- Provides practice for all students in recalling the specific information by doing such things as identifying, distinguishing, listing, describing, and so on; monitors their practice, and provides feedback.
- Evaluates students' ability to recall the information (5).

Skill Development Teaching Strategy

The purpose of this teaching strategy is to promote students' development of a skill. As an outgrowth of using this strategy students should be able to demonstrate the performance of intellectual skills such as analyzing, inferring, interpreting, summarizing; or the performance of psychomotor skills such as brushing teeth, applying a pressure bandage, administering cardio-pulmonary resuscitation, and so on. To implement this strategy the teacher:

- Informs students of the skill to be learned and describes how they will be evaluated.
- Provides a demonstration and/or description of the skill and, if appropriate, points out the elements or steps involved in doing the skill and monitors for understanding.
- Provides:
  –guided practice for all students in performing each step one at a time, monitors and provides feedback after each step.
  –Independent practice for all students in performing all of the steps one or more times, monitors practice and provides feedback.
- Evaluates students' performance of the skill (7).

Concept Development Teaching Strategy

The purpose of this teaching strategy is to promote students' knowledge of a concept definition and their ability to use that concept. As an outgrowth of using this strategy students should be able to recall the definition of a health concept as well as use the concept to build or design a product (plan, model, regimen), explain consistent with the concept definition, categorize, or predict. To implement this strategy the teacher:

- Makes the concept definition available to the students or provides opportunities for them to "discover" the definition.
- Provides practice for all students in recalling the concept definition; monitors their practice, and provides feedback.
- Provides practice for all students in using the concept to build or design a product, explain, categorize, or predict; monitors their practice and provides feedback.
- Evaluates students' ability to use the concept in relation to a phenomenon different from that which was used in practice (4).

In the information acquisition, skill development, and concept development teaching strategies, the thrust is toward making it possible for students to learn particular information, a particular way to do a skill, or a particular concept, respectively. As a group these three teaching strategies are appropriate for promoting learning that is *convergent*. For example, through the appropriate teaching strategy, students are being guided to *converge* on the names of the seven USDA dietary guidelines, or the steps for administering cardio-pulmonary resuscitation, or the concept of immunity. With learnings that are convergent, the student has a need to know if they are "on course" in acquiring the information, skill, or concept. For this reason all three of the teaching strategies appropriate for these categories of learnings include providing feedback for the learner.

Opinion Expression and Development Teaching Strategy

The purpose of this teaching strategy is to promote students' more rational formulation and effective expression of opinions. As an outgrowth of using this strategy students should be able to rationally formulate and express their own opinions on given value-loaded health topics or issues, get responses or reactions from their peers, hear the opinions of others, and become effective in interacting with others. To implement this strategy the teacher:

- Presents one question for discussion rather than a sequence of questions.
- Uses a discussion question which makes it possible for students to express courses of action and value judgements, report or obtain information, and make predictions.
- Establishes and maintains a nonjudgemental environment which encourages voluntary participation and open, responsible communication among students.
- Does not directly or indirectly influence students' responses, summarize the discussion, or communicate his or her opinion about the discussion question (6).

Values Awareness Teaching Strategy

The purpose of this teaching strategy is to promote students' awareness of their own values and the values of others. As an outgrowth of using this strategy students should in relation to a value loaded health topic or issue be able to report those values which undergird preferred actions, decisions or judgments. To implement this strategy the teacher:

- Uses an activity or one question for discussion which makes it possible for students to make judgments or propose courses of action and report their reasons for those judgments or proposed actions.
- Provides for the identification of students' reasons for their courses of action or judgments as values.
- Establishes and maintains a nonjudgmental environment which encourages open, responsible communication among students.
- Does not directly or indirectly influence students' responses, summarize the discussion, or communicate his or her opinion (8).

With the opinion expression and development and values awareness teaching strategies, the thrust is toward making it possible for learners to learn about themselves; the opinions they have about health issues and the values they have about various health actions, decisions, and judgments. As a group these two teaching strategies are appropriate to facilitate learning which is *divergent*. For example, through the appropriate teaching strategy, students are provided with an opportunity to practice or rehearse proposing their own actions or decisions and sharing their own opinions related to a variety of health issues. With learnings that are divergent, the student needs a psychologically safe learning environment where he or she can, in a responsible way, present and consider different points of view. Such an environment needs to be free from "on course or off course" feedback from the teacher. For this reason the two teaching strategies appropriate for these categories of learnings include the absence of direct or indirect teacher feedback for the learner.

Regardless of the aforementioned five Teaching Strategies, the set of critical characteristics should not be viewed as "magic bullets.' That is, students will automatically learn everything they are supposed to learn when the teacher plans for and implements each characteristic of the teaching strategies. Rather, these characteristics are steps which will increase the chances for students to learn. They can provide more students with an equal opportunity to attain the lesson objective.

TEACHING TECHNIQUES

Teaching techniques are the specific tools of the teacher. They are means to ends. Generally, however, one specific technique is not suitable for implementing all of the steps of a particular teaching strategy. While the technique of using a teacher demonstration or a film might be suitable for illustrating the steps of a skill, a different technique would be necessary to engage learners in practicing this skill for themselves. Depending on the skill, practice of the skill by learners might take place on a worksheet, model, or with other learners.

Illustrative Teaching Techniques

A range of teaching techniques which can be categorized as educational media or individual and group processes can be utilized effectively by the resourceful teacher. Some of these include:

> *Educational media*
> > Books, pamphlets, and periodicals
> > Bulletin board
> > Chalk board
> > Demonstrations
> > Films
> > Film strips
> > Flannel board
> > Opaque projector
> > Overhead projector
> > Picture study
> > Records and audio tape recordings
> > Slides
> > Television or videotape recordings
> > Worksheets
> *Group and individual processes*
> > Brainstorming
> > Buzz sessions or small group discussions
> > Cooperative learning
> > Field trips
> > Large group or class discussion
> > Lecture
> > Panel discussion
> > Problem solving
> > Question and answer technique
> > Self appraisals
> > Sociodramas or role playing
> > Symposia or reports

Again, it should be emphasized that these teaching techniques are not in and of themselves teaching strategies. They are, however, integral to the implementation of teaching strategies.

Relationship of Techniques to Teaching Strategies

The implementation of the various teaching strategies steps is highly dependent upon the use of teaching techniques. These techniques are the means available to teachers to put these steps into action with learners. When, for example, the teaching strategy involves "informing students of what is to be learned" this can be done by using a lecture or chalkboard or both to communicate this information to learners.

When the teaching strategy involves "monitoring practice," this can be done by observing learners as they practice recalling on a prepared worksheet or by observing learners as they practice recalling on small individual chalkboards which they hold up for the teacher to observe. Or, the teacher may monitor learners' ability to recall by using a question and answer technique. A wide variety of teaching techniques are available to implement teaching strategies. Some of these techniques are more suitable for implementing certain steps than they are for others. The teacher needs to have skill in using a repertoire of teaching techniques and needs to be aware of the values and limitations of these techniques.

VALUES AND LIMITATIONS OF SELECTED TEACHING TECHNIQUES

No single teaching technique should be labeled as the "best" tool. Each of the various kinds of techniques has a place in health instruction. Each has certain values and certain limitations. By considering the following values and limitations the effective use of a variety of teaching techniques can be enhanced.

Educational Media

Books, Pamphlets and Periodicals (printed materials used for the acquisition of information).

Values
   Contain a core of information that is to be learned.
   Are economical in terms of relative amount of time expended in acquiring information.
   Are readily available.
   Expose students to a variety of printed information for a given area of study.
   Enable students to acquire information at their own pace.

Limitations
   May be inappropriate for a specific maturity level because of differing reading abilities among students.
   May not be appropriate for the maturity level of students because of the size of print.
   May be inaccurate because of outdated information.
   Are easily overused and relied upon as the sole tool to facilitate learning.
   May be inappropriate in terms of sequence of instructional objectives.
   May not be conducive to learning when the quality of paper and contrast of print are poor.

Bulletin Board (a device used to display graphic materials which are closely related to the interests and instructional objective attainment responsibilities of students).

Values

    May be used to motivate and arouse interest.

    May be used to graphically portray certain aspects of health.

    May be used to establish a visual environment conducive to learning.

    May be used to provide a focal point for more intensive research and study.

    May be used to stimulate student initiative in communicating ideas.

Limitations

    May become distracting if materials are not changed periodically.

    May become teacher centered if students are not provided an opportunity to work on the bulletin board.

    May become confusing if materials are too cluttered.

    May become a collection of unrelated materials and notices.

    May become time consuming and reduce available time for teaching.

Chalk Board (a familiar technique used in teaching which allows for the writing of words and drawing of diagrams and illustrations).

Values

    Is readily available.

    May be used as a means for attracting and holding the attention of students.

    Allows for the building of ideas in a graphic form.

    May be used to facilitate the giving of instructions and the following of special procedures.

    May be easily cleaned and made available for reuse.

Limitations

    May be ineffective when size of graphics or writing is inappropriate for class size or maturity level of students.

    May result in confusion when words or graphics are overcrowded or cluttered.

    May be ineffective when writing is not legible or when lighting is poor.

    May distract the teacher from focusing attention on students.

    May be distracting to students when words or graphics on the board do not relate to that which is being learned.

Demonstration (a technique used to demonstrate a sequence of steps inherent in a skill, show a procedure, or provide a basis for discussion).

Values

    May be used to illustrate visually a procedure or process.

    May be used to stimulate a variety of senses.

    Offers students an opportunity to participate.

    May be an effective means of monitoring the attainment of certain skills when demonstrations are conducted by students.

Limitations

    Requires adequate time for preparation and for obtaining materials.

    Requires adequate facilities.

    Is not profitable unless students see the relationship between the demonstration and specific instructional objective.

    May fail.

Film (an audiovisual technique that can be projected with or without sound. Its use in the classroom is intended to serve as a teaching tool rather than a source of entertainment).

   Values
      Provides realism and motion.
      Visually portrays that which is not readily available for individual or
         mass observation.
      Enables students through time-lapse photography to see in a few mo-
         ments a process that takes some time to occur.
      Presents processes which cannot be visualized by the human eye.
      May be used to stimulate discussion.

   Limitations
      May not be available for certain instructional objectives.
      Is susceptible to damage.
      Necessitates adequate equipment and facilities for viewing.
      Requires scheduling so that film coincides with current instructional
         objectives.
      Necessitates time-consuming preparation prior to use in class.
      May be difficult to preview due to scheduling problems and equipment
         availability.

Film Strip (a related sequence of transparent, still pictures or images on a strip of 35-mm film usually containing from 20 to 50 frames that can be projected on a screen, sometimes accompanied by a sound recording).

   Values
      Can be used at whatever pace is appropriate or desired.
      May be used to stimulate discussion.
      Takes up little space and is easily stored.
      May be used to project a single image on the screen for any desired
         length of time.
      Is effective in showing a sequence of events or series of steps.

   Limitations
      Does not effectively portray motion.
      Sequence cannot be easily altered.
      Necessitates adequate equipment and facilities for viewing.
      May be difficult to preview due to scheduling problems and equipment
         availability.
      Necessitates time-consuming preparations prior to use in class.

Flannel Board (a board covered with felt, flannel, or suede, and on which objects, graphs, pictures, words, and symbols cut out of light weight material and backed with felt, flannel, sandpaper, or velcro can be placed).

   Values
      Is an effective technique for putting many concepts, principles, gen-
         eralizations, and facts in a visual form.
      Provides the opportunity to rearrange visuals easily and quickly.

Is mobile and adaptable to many classroom situations.

Facilitates the use of relevant visual materials with any age group.

May be used to monitor student understanding.

Limitations

Requires time-consuming preparation of materials.

May result in the use of visual materials that are inappropriate for the maturity level of students or that are not relevant to the stated instructional objective.

May become distracting to students if visual materials do not adhere to the board.

Opaque Projector (projecting equipment designed to project printed materials and photographs).

Values

Can be conveniently used to project materials without a great deal of preparation.

Allows for the projection of visuals from a variety of sources.

Enables all students to see projected materials from a single source.

Limitations

Necessitates the darkening of classroom for viewing.

Is usually heavy and bulky.

Can lead to classroom control problems while trying to carry out discussion in a darkened classroom.

Overhead Projector (projecting equipment designed to project drawings, diagrams, graphs or charts utilizing transparent acetate material).

Values

Saves on class time when prepared transparency visuals are used.

Visuals can be viewed without darkening classroom.

Facilitates classroom control in that the teacher faces the class while presenting visuals.

Allows the teacher to build ideas by using a predetermined sequence of visuals.

Transparency visuals can be used to stimulate discussion and arouse interest.

Allows students to visualize that which is being studied.

Prepared transparency visuals can be arranged in any sequence desired.

Limitations

Requires time-consuming preparation of transparency visuals.

Can be overused because of ease of use.

Can be annoying to the viewer when transparency visuals contain small print or cluttered images.

Can be distracting when a clean lens is not used to project transparency visuals.

Can distort visuals if projector and screen are not properly aligned.

Picture Study (still prints used in the class to illustrate a topic under discussion).

Values
> Allows for the use of pictures that are readily available from a variety of sources.
> Can be utilized for a variety of content areas, generalizations or topics, and instructional objectives.
> Stimulates discussion and arouses interest.
> Enables the student to visualize that which is being studied.

Limitations
> May be ineffective if pictures do not relate to specified instructional objectives.
> May result in confusion among students if pictures are too complex.
> May be ineffective when pictures are too small to be seen clearly.
> May create misconceptions because of different perceptions among students.

Records and Audio Tape Recordings (recorded materials that can be amplified so that an individual or an entire class can hear previously prepared verbal material).

Values
> Serve as a means of preserving and presenting recent or dated verbal accounts of health content.
> Can be a useful audio supplement to available classroom visual or written resources.
> Can be used to provide audio accounts of health content without interference from other stimuli when earphones or individual listening stations are utilized.
> Can be easily reproduced and stored.

Limitations
> Require appropriate equipment and facilities.
> May not be readily available.
> May be ineffective for those who have difficulty learning through audio experiences.
> May be ineffective when the pacing and vocabulary are inappropriate for a particular maturity level.
> May be ineffective when recorded materials are of a poor quality.

Slides (lantern slides or 35-mm transparencies mounted in cardboard or plastic so that they may be projected on a screen).

Values
> Are relatively inexpensive and easily prepared.
> Can be arranged in any desired sequence.
> Can be projected on the screen for any length of time.
> Can serve to stimulate discussion during and after viewing.
> Are applicable to a variety of health content areas, generalizations or topics, and instructional objectives.

Limitations
> Can be placed incorrectly into the projector or out of the desired sequence.
> Do not portray motion effectively.

Necessitate appropriate equipment and facilities for viewing slides.
Require necessary material and time to prepare.

Television (live or videotape broadcast or videocassette or video-
disc, or live or recorded television presentations that can be viewed
by individuals or the entire class).

Values
May be used to view timely or current health content.
May be used without darkening the room.
Affords quiet viewing since there is no equipment noise.
(see also values of films, p. 70).

Limitations
May be difficult for entire class to see.
Broadcast schedule and school bell schedule may conflict.
May not get good reception in some areas.
May be too costly, difficult or impractical to preview materials.
Programming may not be available for the range of health content
    areas, generalizations or topics, and instructional objectives.
Requires use of costly equipment and materials.

Worksheets (printed or visual materials with space for students to
affix responses).

Values
Are easily reproduced so that each student may have a copy.
May be used to monitor student progress in attaining the lesson ob-
    jective.
May be used to achieve active student involvement.
May be used to motivate student accountability for learning.
Allows for students to practice what they are supposed to learn.

Limitations
Are easily overused as the sole technique for practice or to keep
    students busy.
May be unrelated to instructional objective.
Require time to create.
May be distracting to students when format and/or reproduction is
    poor.

Individual and Group Processes

Brainstorming (a technique used to stimulate the generation of ideas
and to facilitate expression). Spontaneous responses regarding a problem or topic are elicited from students. Students are free to make
suggestions they feel are pertinent to the topic or problem. There is no
criticism. All suggestions are recorded, and when there are no further
suggestions the class or a panel discusses the merits of various suggestions and, depending upon the instructional objectives, seeks agreement on the most appropriate ideas or solutions.

Values
    Provides for free expression of thought without the threat of criticism.
    Enables students to participate in a problem-solving technique.
    Enables student to exchange his or her ideas.
    Stimulates initiative of participants.
    Generates creative thinking.

Limitations
    May get out of hand.
    May lead to misconceptions without discussion and clarification of ideas presented.
    May not be productive if group is too large.
    Will be of limited profit unless students have some background of information.
    May become difficult to conduct because of the need for rapid recording of ideas presented.

Buzz Session or Small-group Discussion (a form of committee organization that takes its name from the "buzz" of participants interacting with one another in small groups). These groups are organized in order to discuss a topic, problem or various problems.

Values
    Provides for considerable spontaneous student interaction.
    May be used to stimulate oral discussion and participation.
    May be used to foster creative thinking.
    Gives students a feeling of worth by enabling them to identify and attack personal and community health problems.

Limitations
    Is of limited profit unless students have some background of information.
    May result in a few students dominating the discussion.
    May result in students pursuing unrelated topics if discussion is not coordinated or monitored.
    May result in classroom management problems because of discussion taking place in several small groups.
    May result in some students verbally abusing other students.

Cooperative Learning (structuring students' interactions so that each depends on and is accountable to the others in a group). One way to stimulate cooperation is to require a single product from a group of students and to guarantee that group members share a goal. Another way is to divide a learning into segments and have group members responsible for attaining a particular segment and teaching it to others in the group (11).

Values
    Provides psychological support for those students who lack confidence when initiating a new learning.
    Fosters teamwork and unavoidable concern about group members learning welfare.

Is consistent with the adage "the best way to learn something is to teach it."

Tends to lead to high achievement when compared to individualistic techniques for learning.

Enables the sharing of individuals talents and skills to benefit other students.

Limitations

Requires that students are adept at both learning something and communicating (teaching) it to others.

Necessitates specialized attention be given to students having difficulty in fulfilling their role as a group member.

Overuse may result in students becoming dependent upon learning only through this mode.

May result in conflict when individuals are judged or graded on the basis of the group effort.

Field Trip (any visitation outside of the classroom that enables the student to gain a first-hand experience of a process or structure).

Values

Provides opportunity for first-hand experience.

May be motivational and stimulate interest.

May provide the basis for further research and study.

May be used to facilitate understanding of community problems.

May be an effective introductory, concluding or summarizing activity.

Limitations

Is time consuming.

May be costly.

May require complex administrative arrangements.

May be too complex for the maturity level of students.

May become an entertainment excursion.

Is difficult to relate to instructional objectives because of varied student perceptions.

Large-group or Class Discussion (an open or closed ended discussion* of a specific topic with members of the class interacting with one another and with the teacher). There is a give-and-take session between students and the teacher.

Values

Allows for the involvement of all students.

Is conducive to group interaction and participation.

Enables students to discuss problems or topics of common interest.

Provides students with an opportunity to develop interpersonal and communication skills useful in working with people.

---

*As used here open ended refers to discussion which is not directed toward closure and is intended to promote or allow divergent thinking. Closed ended discussion, conversely, refers to discussion aimed at bringing about closure and is intended to help students converge on a particular idea; for example, the name of the nutrient that builds and repairs body tissue or the 6 warning signs of cancer.

Allows students to become aware of information and opinions other than their own or the teacher's.

Limitations
May result in the involvement of only a few students.
May be difficult for shy students.
Allows some students to become the focus of attention through unfavorable or disruptive behavior.
May be overused.
May not be profitable unless students have some background of information.
May be easily misused in that the type of discussion implemented may not match the student outcome indicated in the instructional objective.

Lecture (a discourse delivered on any subject). This technique is used so universally that many mistakenly use the term synonymously with teaching. Because of overuse and misuse, it is sometimes questioned as an effective method of teaching.

Values
Provides an opportunity to convey information that is not available through other media.
Is effective in presenting many facts in a relatively short period of time.
Is useful in integrating diverse materials and pulling various ideas and concepts into an orderly system of thought.
Allows the teacher to economically present a rich fund of information that might have been obtained through personal experiences.
Is conducive to presenting information to a large audience.

Limitations
Limits student participation.
May stifle creative thinking.
Does not allow for interaction between teacher and students and limits feedback.
Difficult to monitor student understanding of information being presented.
May become a lengthy and dull discourse that detracts from learning.
May detract from learning if the lecturer does not possess effective speaking skills.

Panel Discussion (the discussion of a problem or topic by two or more students). Members of the panel may ask questions of one another and may agree or disagree with each other. After the panel members have presented their points of view, a chairman usually opens up the discussion so that class members may ask questions and react to the ideas presented by panel members.

Values
Enables students to exchange ideas and to become aware of other views.
Allows students to interact with one another.

Provides an opportunity for evaluation; to gain insight into what students know and do not know.

May be an effective means of solving group problems.

May motivate students by creating an air of suspense.

Limitations

Is limited to topics of personal concern to students.

Requires that students possess adequate knowledge as well as communication skills to carry on a discussion.

May result in one or two panel or class members dominating the discussion.

May result in excessive discussion of irrelevant topics.

Results in a verbal exchange that may not be beneficial to slower students.

May leave students with misinformation.

Problem Solving (a technique considered by many to be comprehensive and conducive to the development of a wide range of health attitudes, values, practices, and cognitive skills). Problem solving refers to "discovery learning" and may employ other teaching techniques such as reading material, discussion, film, research and reporting. The essential steps that should be utilized in the problem-solving technique include: (1) identification of the problem, (2) analysis and clarification of the problem, (3) collection of data, (4) organization and use of data in the formulation of possible solutions to the problem, (5) anticipating consequences of each solution, (6) appraising the value of each solution, and (7) selecting and testing the best solution to the problem. While presented in a particular order, individuals can be creative in how they sequence or 'orchestrate" the use of these steps. Such creativity should be encouraged and individuals should not be forced into one particular sequence.

Values

Fosters creative thinking.

Provides opportunity for students to practice problem-solving skills.

Enables students to discover for themselves.

Enables students to savor the success of their prudent efforts as well as cope with the frustration that comes with incomplete or misdirected effort.

Allows students to organize knowledge in a personally meaningful way.

Provides for the use of a variety of sources of information.

Provides students with an opportunity to practice and develop a wide range of cognitive skills.

Limitations

Is time consuming.

Requires the availability of many resources.

May not be appropriate for all students because of varying abilities.

May lead to inaccurate conclusions.

May result in inappropriate solutions when students do not carry out each step of the problem-solving technique or carry out the steps in an ineffective manner.

Requires the teacher, within certain parameters, to be comfortable with student solutions which may not be to the teacher's liking. (Teacher may need to intervene if a solution is deemed imminently dangerous to a student).

Question and Answer Technique (an oral quiz or review technique). The teacher asks questions of students to elicit class discussion. It may be used as a monitoring practice or evaluating technique.

Values

Stimulates and motivates students by involving and challenging them.

May be used to subjectively monitor health attitudes, values, practices, and cognitive skills.

Useful for the review of content.

May encourage further study when questions are answered inappropriately or left unanswered.

Limitations

May develop into an argumentative session.

May result in calling upon only favored or reliable students.

May result in the embarrassment of students who cannot answer questions.

May encourage guesswork instead of thoughtful recall and critical thinking.

Fosters boredom or frustration or both when emphasis is placed only upon recall.

May lead to a discussion of irrelevant data.

Self-appraisal (a technique that requires individuals to appraise their own strengths and limitations). Students rate themselves in regard to some aspect of health, such as food eating habits, physical exercise, growth and development characteristics, rest and sleep, dental health practices, or immunization practices. This technique is often overlooked as being meaningful.

Values

Provides students with insight into their own health needs.

May motivate students toward self improvement.

Enables students to participate at their own rate.

Provides the basis for further study of individual health problems.

Limitations

May be ineffective when used to assess student achievement in class.

May lead to unnecessary concern over one's health when excessively utilized.

May be invalid if students are not motivated to appraise their strengths and limitations.

May be superficial when students merely seek to please the teacher, classmates, or provide the "right" appraisal.

Role Playing (a dramatization used as a means of exploring certain health problems, usually related to the area of human relations). Dramatizations can be extemporaneous or planned as students act out a "real-life" situation that provides the basis for discussion and analysis.

Values
Assists students in developing self-understanding by relating to the world in which they live.
Allows students to gain an understanding of others by "role" playing.
Enables students to engage in "life-like" activities as a way of learning.
Can route the "make-believe" or the "pretend" urges of students into suitable channels for learning.
Capitalizes on the imagination of students.
Holds the interest of the class.
Provides for interaction among students.

Limitations
May result in entertainment only rather than in the attainment of specified instructional objectives.
May not be an economical or efficient means of achieving desired instructional objectives.
May not allow all students to receive benefit or direct participation unless the "cast" is frequently changed.
May embarrass certain students.
May result in placing emphasis on drama "techniques" rather than on the attainment of desired instructional objectives.

Symposium or Reporting (symposium: a collection of comments or opinions from various students presented in a series before the class; reporting: an individual's comments on a particular subject or problem).

Values
Actively involves students in research and reporting.
Allows for some in-depth study on a particular health problem or issue.
Provides an opportunity to organize and present comments on a particular subject.
Offers an opportunity for gifted or verbally inclined students to express themselves orally as well as those not so inclined to foster oral language development.

Limitations
May be boring or distracting for the class if a student does not know the subject or cannot speak well.
May be uneconomical in terms of time spent in the achievement of specific instructional objectives.
May result in misconceptions and inaccurate information if students are not thoroughly prepared.
May be embarrassing to some students if they are forced to give a report.

Certainly not all values and limitations of the foregoing teaching techniques have been described. Depending on a variety of conditions and circumstances, other values and limitations may emerge. The teacher and his or her abilities will determine to a great extent whether the values of a particular technique outweigh the limitations. In other words, the teacher makes a difference. The resourceful teacher, when selecting and implementing teaching techniques for any teaching strategy, will carefully weigh the values and limitations so that the probability of learners' attaining specified objectives will be increased.

USING A VARIETY OF TEACHING TECHNIQUES

Different and varying teaching techniques should be used for more than just the sake of variety. A variety of techniques may be of value since variety tends to break the monotony for the teacher as well as for the student. There are, however, more important reasons for using different teaching techniques: (1) to meet a variety of objectives, (2) to meet a variety of student needs and interests, and (3) to stimulate a variety of senses.

To Meet a Variety of Objectives

In health education it is necessary to focus on a variety of objectives; including an emphasis on health information, skills, concepts, opinion expression, and values awareness. Such a range of learnings is requisite to installing and/or strengthening healthy practices and extinguishing and/or limiting health compromising practices. While the appropriate teaching strategy is critical to facilitating learner attainment of a particular objective, the implementation of the teaching strategy is reliant upon different teaching techniques. Some techniques may be more relevant for some teaching strategies and, therefore, the objectives for which these strategies are most appropriate. For example, for recall objectives and the information acquisition teaching strategy the lecture, chalkboard, book, and film strip teaching techniques might be most suitable. Whereas, for an opinion expression objective and the opinion expression and development teaching strategy the role playing, brainstorm, and large group discussion teaching techniques may be more suitable. With a variety of objectives there is a need for a variety of related teaching strategies and in turn a variety of suitable teaching techniques.

To Meet a Variety of Student Needs and Abilities

A variety of teaching techniques is necessary in order to meet the diverse needs and abilities of students. On this basis alone the using of one technique approach (using only a textbook, or only lectures, or only films) cannot be supported.

All students do not learn at the same rate, nor do they learn in the same way or by the same techniques. Some learn more slowly than others. Some learn better by seeing than others, while a few learn better by hearing. Flannel-board displays may be more meaningful to one student than to another. A group discussion on some topics might be quite relevant for one student and have little meaning to another. A research project may provide insight to one and seem pointless to another.

As teachers select and utilize teaching techniques within different teaching strategies, it is well for them to be familiar with the needs and abilities of their students. Therefore, the teacher should spend some time diagnosing individual learning needs, styles, and patterns among his or her students. This can be done by observing student participation as different technique are used. Reviewing student achievement records also may be helpful.

To Stimulate a Variety of Senses

Another substantiation for the use of different teaching techniques is that when different kinds of techniques are used a variety of senses are stimulated. In this way learning by one sense can be reinforced with learning by another sense. Verbal symbols that describe community health levels of organization, the infectious disease process, or ways of adjusting to different social situations can be reinforced by visual symbols placed on the chalk board or flannel board. These visual symbols may be further reinforced by feeling or manipulating objects that represent that which is to be learned.

CONSIDERATIONS FOR SELECTING TEACHING TECHNIQUES

In the selection of different teaching techniques a number of criteria should be considered, including:

Points of view in the school and community
Mastery of teaching skills
Psychology of learning
Maturity level of the learner
Content to be covered
Environmental conditions and equipment available
Time allotment
Class size
Time of day

Points of View in the School and Community

Points of view in the school and community play an important role in determining the specific teaching techniques to be used along with determining what to teach. The showing of a film, the assigning of reading, or the use of a particular sociodrama that is controversial or contrary to the wishes of the community may result in many problems. If a particular film, reading, or sociodrama activity is considered to be an important teaching technique, it is wise to "educate" the community as well as those in the schools (administrators, fellow teachers, counselors, etc.) regarding the instructional value of such techniques. Once this is accomplished, any technique can be used to accomplish what it was intended to without becoming the basis for an attack on a particular program.

Mastery of Teaching Skills

Perhaps the most crucial condition affecting the successful use of a particular teaching technique is the teacher's mastery of teaching skills. What the teacher does as well as does not do is critical to the successful implementation of any teaching technique. All teachers do not have the same skill or ability in utilizing different techniques. Some teachers can plan and carry out a sociodrama or can effectively utilize a flannel board, whereas others experience difficulty when trying to employ these same techniques.

The wise teacher will capitalize upon those skills in which he or she excels and play down skills in which he or she is less proficient. This does not mean that a teacher should incorporate lecture or small group discussions in various teaching strategies because the teacher possesses those skills useful in implementing these types of techniques. It does mean that the teacher should recognize his or her strengths and weaknesses. It should be noted that the mastery of a range of communication, interpersonal, and organizational skills is essential to good teaching. The more expertise the teacher can develop in these skill areas, the more effective will be the health instruction program. The teacher will have more tools with which to facilitate learning.

Psychology of Learning

Vital to the selection of suitable teaching techniques are various laws or principles of learning. These laws or principles serve as guidelines for the teacher in the selection of teaching techniques. Although the use of principles or laws does not necessarily assure that learning will take place, there is evidence to indicate that when they are used learning is enhanced. When teaching techniques are selected or designed for use within teaching strategies to assist students attain specific instructional objectives, it is well for the teacher to consider the following generally accepted principles of learning:

Principles Related to Motivating the Learner
- Learning is more effective when the learner is motivated by goals intrinsic to the activity.
- An individual learns best when he or she feels the need for learning.
- Learners can be helped in the acquisition of a concept, principle, or generalization through *varied* experiences relating to it and by applying the concept, principle, or generalization to a new or novel situation.
- Individuals tend to repeat behaviors that are rewarded (reinforced).
- Reward is most effective when it immediately follows and is related to the desired behavior.
- Fear and punishment have uncertain effects upon learning. They may facilitate or hinder learning.

Principles Related to the Needs and Abilities of the Learner
- When problems are a common concern, group thinking is an effective approach to learning.
- Behaviors sought should be within the range of possibility for the learner involved.
- The higher the educational level of any given group, the greater the reliance on printed symbols. The lower the educational level the greater the reliance on oral or picture media.
- There are marked inter- and intra-individual differences in any given group of learners.
- Individuals usually slant persuasive communications to fit their own predispositions.
- Creative individuals show a preference for the complex and the novel.

Principles Relating to the General Nature of Learning
- Learning is an active process that involves the dynamic interaction of the learner with that which is to be learned.
- In order for learning to occur repetition is usually required.
- Other things being equal, first experiences or first acts in a series tend to be favored.
- Other things being equal, recent experiences are more vivid than earlier ones.
- According to Gestalt psychology:
    Intellectual processes operate as a whole.
    The whole organism responds in a unified way.
    The organism reacts to the total situation.
    We understand the parts by understanding the whole.
    Learning proceeds from the general to the specific, then to the general (whole-part-whole).
- Transfer learning is not automatic. We must teach for transfer.
- Behaviors sought must be practiced or used.
- Learning generally progresses from the known to the unknown, from the concrete to the abstract, and from the simple to the complex.
- Periods of practice interrupted by periods of rest result in more efficient learning than do longer periods of practice with little or no interruptions.
- Time spent recalling what has been read facilitates learning more than does the mere act of rereading.

Maturity Level of the Learner

Teaching techniques should be selected so that they are neither too complex nor too simple for the learner. The maturity level and ability of students and their prior experiences must be taken into account if learning is to be effective and economical. Teaching techniques beyond the comprehension or capabilities of students may only confuse them and thereby interfere with the implementation of the teaching strategy and the learners' attainment of specified instructional objectives.

As students progress in their maturity, teaching techniques can become increasingly complex and abstract. For instance, at the elementary level analogies and visual illustrations may be necessary when discussing the role of germs or microorganisms as disease-causing agents. At the high-school level, verbal explanations may suffice when describing the relationship of microorganisms to disease.

Past experiences may affect the maturity level of students and also should be considered when selecting teaching techniques. Some students of low socioeconomic background may not have been exposed to as much written communication as students of a high socioeconomic background. In providing techniques for low socioeconomic background students, initial emphasis might best be placed upon nonwritten communication (visual, verbal) as preparatory for the use of written materials.

Content to be Covered

Consideration of the content to be covered provides clues as to the types of teaching techniques most appropriate for its study. For instance, in seeking the attainment of instructional objectives in the area of mental health, small-group discussions, role playing, or sociodramas might be appropriate. Demonstrations, individual reports, and field trips might be more effective to assist learners in the attainment of objectives related to the area of communicable disease.

Environmental Conditions

Environmental conditions such as lighting, heating, ventilation, acoustics, and general emotional tone of the class may enhance or deter learning. Teaching techniques need to be selected or modified depending upon environmental conditions. For example, if a film has been scheduled on a hot and humid day, it may be well to reschedule the film, make adjustments for showing it, or not show it at all. In such a situation a different technique, if appropriate to the objective and related teaching strategy, should be considered as a substitute.

Materials and Equipment Available

A practical consideration in selecting various teaching techniques is the availability of materials and equipment. The teacher must consider the availability of such things as bulletin-board materials, charts, films and film strips, supplemental reading materials, models, and other audiovisual equipment. It is generally recognized that there is an abundance of supplemental reading materials and posters. The problem is to select materials appropriate for a particular maturity level and to adapt materials to the techniques being used to implement a particular teaching strategy.

Time Allotment

Development and selection of teaching techniques should be carried out with a realistic consideration of the time alloted for health instruction. If a limited time allotment is provided for the health instruction program during a semester whether at the elementary or secondary level, varied and time-consuming teaching techniques would be impractical. In such short periods, it is difficult to do more than provide a superficial discussion of health. However, if a full semester is devoted to health instruction at the junior and senior high school, or a set block of time is allocated every day at the elementary level, varied and time intense teaching techniques can be utilized to implement teaching strategies.

Class Size

Some teaching techniques are more appropriate for use with relatively small groups: demonstrations, buzz groups, role playing, and brainstorming, for example. Other techniques such as lectures, films, question and answer techniques, and panel discussions can be used effectively with larger sized groups. The size of the class should be considered when determining the techniques to be used with different teaching strategies.

Time of Day

It is well for the teacher to consider the factor of fatigue as the day progresses and to select and utilize teaching techniques accordingly. A lecture or long reading assignment used to implement a particular teaching strategy step immediately after lunch may lull students to sleep rather than facilitate their attainment of the lesson objective.

Teaching techniques should be selected and developed on the basis of rational decisions rather than upon the whim or fancy of the instructor. The aforementioned criteria serve as a basis for making such decisions.

PLANS FOR IMPLEMENTING TEACHING STRATEGIES

For health instruction to have integrity, systematic planning is necessary. Here, integrity refers to logical relationships among health areas/themes/questions and generalizations/topics (Ch. 3), instructional objectives (Ch. 4), and teaching strategies (Ch. 5). Also, integrity refers to the presence of critical characteristics or steps within a given teaching strategy. With so many variables to account for, the integrity of health instruction can be compromised. Such a threat, however, can be minimized by having a plan.

A worthwhile plan needs to account for the aforementioned relationships. Also, the plan needs to include specific directions for how selected techniques will be used to implement the teaching strategy. The critical characteristics or steps of the appropriate teaching strategy can serve as a "road map" for developing directions for the teaching strategy portion of the plan. The following are examples of instructional plans for each of five categories of objectives and related teaching strategies; information acquisition, skill development, concept development, opinion expression and development, and values awareness.

*Example of Information Acquisition Teaching Strategy Plan**

AREA: Drug Use and Misuse
GENERALIZATION: Helpful as well as harmful substances can be taken
into the body in different ways.
GRADE LEVEL: 1
OBJECTIVE: The student can show three different ways substances can
enter the body.

Teacher Background Information
Substances can be taken into the body in three ways:
1. *Ingestion.* Substances taken by mouth pass through the stomach and into the small intestines. After being changed into a form the body can use, they may be absorbed into the bloodstream where they can travel to other parts of the body including the brain.
2. *Inhalation.* Substances breathed in pass through passages to the lungs where they can, after absorption into the bloodstream, travel to other parts of the body including the brain.
3. *Through the Skin.* Some substances placed on the skin may pass through it and enter the bloodstream. Substances can pass through the skin through an injection and then enter the blood-

---

*Adapted from a lesson developed by Joan Tandrow, student, Department of Health Science, California State University, Northridge.

stream. Through the bloodstream substances can reach other parts of the body including the brain.
4. Vocabulary Words: inhale, ointment, swallow, intestines, liquid, syringe, injection.

CHARACTERISTIC #1
INFORMS students of what is to be learned:
(1) Use a transparency of figure 6A to show a body outline. With a red transparency pen include the heart and lines from the heart to the extremities to represent the bloodstream.
(2) Ask students to tell what the lines show (bloodstream).
(3) Emphasize that students will learn that there are only three ways things can enter the body and reach the bloodstream.

DESCRIBES how students will be evaluated:
(1) Point out that at the end of the lesson students should be able to tell or show how different things enter the body and bloodstream.
(2) Overlay a transparency of figure 6B onto the transparency of figure 6A. Emphasize that at the end of the lesson students should be able to draw a line from each substance to the place on the body where it would enter. Illustrate by drawing a line from the apple to the mouth.

CHARACTERISTIC #2
MAKES information available:
(1) Display a simple poster of a child on the bulletin board next to the chalkboard or chart paper. (American Cancer Society poster, *My Wonderful Body Machine* can be used. See figure 6C for replica).
(2) Display several objects such as vitamin capsules, cough syrup, fruit and ask students how they enter the body.
(3) Point to the mouth on the poster and place the word mouth next to it. Ask students for other things that are swallowed. Place the word swallow under the word mouth and list items students say are swallowed.
(4) Describe how after substances are swallowed they pass into the stomach and then into the small intestines. Trace this flow on the poster. Point out that as foods are chewed, swallowed, and churned in the stomach they are in a watery form. Indicate that from the stomach the watery churned up food passes into the intestines where some of it passes into the bloodstream and from there to various parts of the body.
(5) Squirt some deodorizer in the air and ask students how this substance can enter the body. Invite several students to come to the poster and point to the area. Place the word nose next to the poster. Ask the class for other things that are inhaled or breathed in. Add the word inhale under nose and list the appropriate things suggested by students e.g. smoke, smog, dust.
(6) Point out that it is possible to inhale through the mouth. Direct everyone to pinch their nose and take a deep breath.
(7) Describe how after substances are inhaled they reach the lungs. Trace this route on the poster. Indicate that in the lungs some of the substances (chemicals) inhaled pass into the

bloodstream and from there go to various parts of the body including the brain.

(8) Show a muscle ache ointment tube and rub the ointment on the top of your hand. Describe its warmth. Ask students how they think the substance entered your body. Elicit the response "through the skin" and place these words next to the poster.

(9) Indicate that only a few special substances can go through the skin, such as certain chemicals in the ointment. Place the word ointment next to "through the skin."

(10) Invite students to tell how substances can be placed or forced through the skin. Elicit the response "shot" or "injection." Use a transparency of figure 6D to show a syringe and point out that doctors and some nurses use it to help them put medicine into the body through the skin. Add the words "injection" and "syringe" under "through the skin."

(11) Emphasize that many substances that pass through the skin affect the nerves in the immediate area by numbing them. Indicate that some substances can get into the bloodstream and go to all parts of the body including the brain.

MONITORS information received:

(1) Tell the students you are going to show them some substances and that at your direction they are to point to the part of their bodies where the substance would enter.

(2) Show several substances such as a lotion or cream containing aspirin, a pill, and ant spray. As students respond praise correct responses and with inappropriate responses reteach as necessary.

CHARACTERISTIC #3

PROVIDES recall practice for all students, MONITORS recall practice, and PROVIDES recall feedback:

(1) Distribute a copy of worksheet, figure 6E to each student. Review the worksheet to identify the six simple pictures: nose, mouth, hand (representing skin), syringe, shoe, and eye.

(2) Inform the students that they are to color the pictures, cut them out, and paste the three different ways substances can enter the body on each of three paper plates. Point to the three ways that are listed next to the poster, *My Wonderful Body Machine.* Emphasize that two plates should have one picture each and the third plate should have two pictures on it. Caution the students that there are two pictures on the worksheet that should not go on any plates. Indicate that it is their job to figure this out.

(3) Observe students as they work and assist and reteach individual students as necessary.

(4) Instruct the students to place the three plates with the pictures in front of them. Inform that you will "act out" substances being taken or not taken into your body. Point out that as you do so they are to vote, at your direction, in the following two ways:

• Hold thumbs up if the substance was taken in or thumbs down if it was not.

- Hold up the appropriate plate to show how the substance was taken in.
(5) Use a variety of props to "act out" substance use/non use. e.g., drink water, deeply smell a real flower, handle an unopened tube of ointment, look at an aerosol can, shake a bottle of furniture polish and open so students can smell aroma (be careful they do not breath deeply), pretend to give an injection. Let all students know the correct voting after each "act" and reteach as necessary.
(6) Distribute a copy of worksheet, figure 6F to each student. Instruct them to color the pictures and to draw a line from the substance to the place on the body where it would enter. As students work, assist them and reteach as necessary.
(7) After all students have completed the worksheet show a transparency of figure 6F with the lines correctly placed and ask students to check their work.

CHARACTERISTIC #4
EVALUATES students' ability to recall the information:
(1) Use the final practice activity, worksheet of figure 6F to informally judge students' ability to show three different ways substances can enter the body.
(2) As an alternative, distribute a worksheet that is a combining of figures 6A and B. Instruct students to draw a line from each substance to where it can enter the body and afterwards to color hair and clothing on the figure. Observe the students' work for correctness as they are occupied with the coloring.

Example of Skill Development Teaching Strategy Plan*

AREA: Environmental Health
GENERALIZATION: The presence of air pollutants and other environmental hazards can influence health decisions.
GRADE LEVEL: Senior High
OBJECTIVE: The student can interpret charts containing air quality data.

Teacher Background Information
1. Many local newspapers publish daily air quality charts for various regions in a geographic area. The ability to read such charts can help individuals see trends in air quality and thereby modify physical activities accordingly.
2. Steps in interpreting/reading air quality charts:
   - Identify the subject of the data (ozone, nitrogen dioxide, carbon monoxide).
   - Identify the scope of the data (regions within a given geographic area).
   - Determine date/day and time referrent (Saturday, 7 a.m. to 6 p.m., as indicated by the horizontal axis on the chart).

---

*Adapted from a lesson developed by Steven Wolff, Student, Department of Health Science, California State University, Northridge.

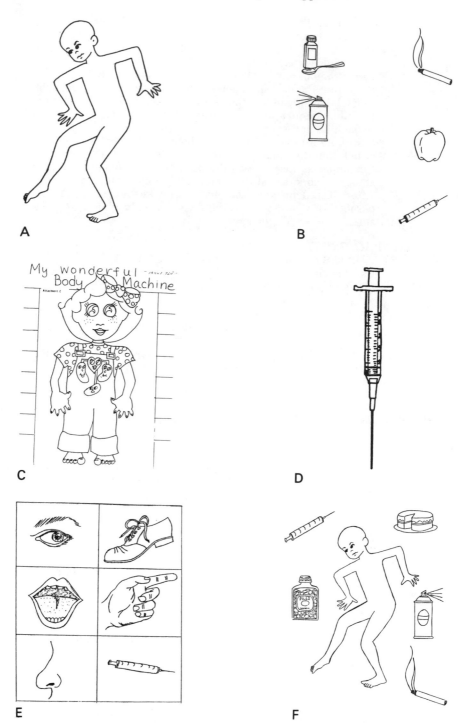

Figure 6.

- Identify air quality standard (O-S = clean air standard, S-1 = 1st stage episode, 1-2 = 2nd stage episode as indicated by the vertical axis on the chart).
- Make a vertical line from a desired time on the horizontal axis to the line symbol representing a specific pollutant (this can be estimated visually).
- Make a horizontal line from the point determined in the previous step to the vertical axis to determine air quality standard for the specific pollutant (this can be estimated visually).
- Formulate a summary statement that includes the subject, scope, day and time, and air quality.

CHARACTERISTIC #1

INFORMS students of the skill to be learned:
(1) Show a transparency of the chart contained on figure 7. Indicate to students that they are going to learn how to interpret/read air quality charts such as the one on the transparency.
(2) Point out that charts such as this one appear daily in newspapers and show a prediction of the air quality for the coming day. Invite students to share the significance of being able to read such air quality charts.

DESCRIBES how students will be evaluated:
(1) Show transparency of figure 7 and indicate that at the end of the lesson when students are given charts such as the one being shown they should be able to interpret/read them.
(2) Emphasize that students will demonstrate the ability to interpret air quality charts when they can make, in writing, a summary statement about the air quality for a particular air pollutant.
(3) Refer to the carbon monoxide data at 12 noon on the transparency of figure 7 and write on the chalkboard an example of a summary statement (e.g., In west Los Angeles carbon monoxide was at the clean air standard at 12 noon on Saturday.).

CHARACTERISTIC #2

DEMONSTRATES or describes the skill and POINTS out the elements or steps:
(1) Use transparency of figure 7 and direct students attention to the legend box. Invite students through questions to report the following:
- Day (Saturday).
- Time range (7 a.m. to 6. p.m.).
- Line symbol for ozone, nitrogen, and carbon monoxide.
- Meaning of O-S, S-1, and 1-2.
- Region (West Los Angeles).
(2) Specify that the steps for reading air quality charts will be discussed and shown. Direct students to write each of the seven steps.
(3) Use the transparency of figure 7 and refer to ozone, nitrogen dioxide, and carbon monoxide in the legend box. Indicate that on the chart this is called the subject of the data. Write on the chalkboard (1) IDENTIFY THE SUBJECT. Point out that this is one step in reading such a chart.

(4) Use the transparency again and refer to West L.A. Indicate that this is the scope of the data. Specify that scope means the specific geographic region to which the data applies. Add on the chalkboard (2) IDENTIFY SCOPE OF DATA. Point out that this is another step in reading such a chart.

(5) Refer to the transparency and to the bottom line with the numbers 7-6. Specify that this is the horizontal axis. Point out that the horizontal axis contains the time referrent which in this case is in hours, 7 a.m. to 6 p.m. Refer to the legend box and indicate that these data are for a Saturday and if this were in a newspaper the date would be found on the page. Add to the chalkboard (3) IDENTIFY THE TIME REFERRENT. Point out that this is another step in reading such a chart.

(6) Refer to the transparency and to S, 1, and 2 in the legend box. Point to the O-S-1-2 line and specify that this is the vertical axis. Indicate that the vertical axis contains the air quality standards. Note that there are three standards. Invite students to report each of the three standards; 0-S, S-1, and 1-2 and what they mean. Add to the chalkboard (4) IDENTIFY AIR QUALITY STANDARD. Point out that this is another step in reading such a chart.

(7) Use the same transparency and set up the following situation:
 • Suppose we want to know the air quality standard for ozone at 12 noon.
   Invite students to respond (answer: S-1, 1st stage episode). Ask students for the implications to individuals under such conditions. Make a vertical line on the transparency from N to the ozone line symbol. Add to the chalkboard (5) MAKE VERTICAL LINE FROM DESIRED TIME TO POLLUTANT SYMBOL OF INTEREST. Draw a horizontal line on the transparency from the point determined in step 5 to the vertical axis. Add to the chalkboard (6) MAKE HORIZONTAL LINE FROM POINT DETERMINED IN STEP 5 TO VERTICAL AXIS. Emphasize that such line drawings (steps 5 and 6) can be estimated or "eyeballed." Point out that steps 5 and 6 are additional steps in reading such charts.

(8) Refer to the steps on the chalkboard and indicate that while these steps are numbered in a sequence they need not necessarily be done in that order. Emphasize that the important task in this skill is to determine the data that each step yields.

(9) Use the transparency of figure 7 and present the following problem to students:
   From the chart what kind of a statement can be made about nitrogen dioxide at noon. Guide student responses to a statement such as:
   In West Los Angeles nitrogen dioxide was at the clean air standard at 12 noon on Saturday. Write such a statement on the chalkboard and invite students to analyze it to determine if the subject, scope, day and time, and air quality standard were included in the response to the problem presented. Add to the chalkboard (7) MAKE A SUMMARY STATEMENT (including subject, scope, day and time, and air quality).

MONITORS for understanding:
(1) Refer to the numbers of the 7 steps on the chalkboard and indicate that you are going to point to a particular place on the transparency of the chart you have been using. Emphasize that as you point to particular data on the chart you will ask all students to show you the number of the step that accounts for that data. Specify that they will show the number of the step by indicating the appropriate number of fingers.
(2) Point one at a time to the following: horizontal line, 7-6 (step 3); West L.A., (step 2); vertical line, 0-2 (step 4); ozone in the box, (step 1); draw a horizontal line from ozone at 1 p.m., (step 6); draw a vertical line from ozone to 1 p.m. (step 5).
(3) As students respond indicate correct answer and reteach as necessary.

CHARACTERISTIC #3
PROVIDES GUIDED PRACTICE for all students:
(1) Distribute to each student a copy of worksheet, figure 8.
(2) Use a transparency of the worksheet, figure 8 and direct students attention to chart #1. Indicate that everyone is going to practice reading this chart, one step at a time. Ask all students to do step one and to write down the information in the appropriate space under the chart. Caution students to do only step 1 and not to move ahead to the other steps. Tell students they may refer to the steps on the chalkboard.
(3) Monitor students work by observing them work. Invite students to give in unison, the answer to step 1 (ozone). Monitor students' responses.
(4) Write the correct answer in the appropriate space (subject) on the transparency of the worksheet.
(5) Proceed in the same manner for steps 2-6, monitoring students after each step and writing the correct information on the transparency.
(6) Ask students on a separate sheet of paper to place a numeral 1 for chart #1 and do step 7.
(7) Direct students to exchange papers with a partner and to "correct" each other's statements making sure that the subject, scope, day and time, and air quality standard are included.
(8) Monitor students' work as they analyze their partners' statement.
(9) Place a model statement on the chalkboard (e.g., In downtown the ozone was at the clean air standard at noon on Wednesday.).
(10) Reteach and provide additional guided practice as necessary.

PROVIDES INDEPENDENT PRACTICE for all students:
(1) Direct students to complete reading the remaining charts on the worksheet, figure 8. Indicate that step 7, the summary statement, is to be written on the same paper they used for chart #1 and to number from 2 to 6 to correspond to the remaining charts in the worksheet.
(2) Point out that for charts 5 and 6 the clues for the data for the steps are not provided. Emphasize that students should try to identify the data for each of the steps without the clues.

(3) Note, the practice sheet could be a homework assignment.

(4) Monitor students by observing them as they complete the practice sheet. Provide individual assistance as necessary.

(5) Inform students that after they have finished they can compare their work with answer sheets that have been placed in various classroom locations.

(6) As necessary, reteach and provide additional charts for independent practice.

CHARACTERISTIC #4

EVALUATES student's performance of the skill:

(1) Distribute several air quality charts and ask students to interpret them and write a summary statement for each.

(2) Check students summary statements to be sure they have included the subject, scope, day and time, and air quality standard.

Example of Concept Development Teaching Strategy*

AREA: Nutrition

GENERALIZATION: Nutrient content of food influences individual behavior and performance.

GRADE LEVEL: 5

OBJECTIVE: The student is able to use the concept of high energy food to categorize, design a product, and predict.

Teacher Background Information:

1. Food is necessary for the body's activities, both internal and external. Examples of internal activities are the beating of the heart, the breathing action of the body, and the digestion of food. Examples of external activities are running, swimming, and studying.

2. Some foods, because of the percentage of protein, carbohydrates, and fat contained in them provide more energy than others.

3. Foods that are particularly abundant in energy are called high energy foods.

4. A nonclinical definition of the concept, high energy foods, includes foods that contain the following per serving: (1) 100 calories or more, (2) low in protein (less than 30%), and (3) high in carbohydrate or fat or both (70% or more).

CHARACTERISTIC #1

MAKES concept definition available:**

---

*Developed by Nancy Cowan, teacher, Paramount Unified School District, Paramount, California and the Teaching Strategies Center, Los Angeles County Office of Education, Downey, California.

**Two different approaches can be taken to make the definition of a concept available to learners. A more traditional approach is to provide the definition by using such techniques as a lecture, pamphlet, or film. Another approach is to provide learners with a chance to "discover" the concept definition. In this approach learners are guided toward "discovery" as the teacher (1) provides exemplars of the concept, (2) invites observations as to how the exemplars are different (this process "clears the deck" for the next more critical process), (3) invites observations as to how the exemplars are alike (this process focuses on identifying the set of likenesses or critical attributes which is the concept definition, and (4) solicits a concept label for the definition or, if necessary, provides the concept label.

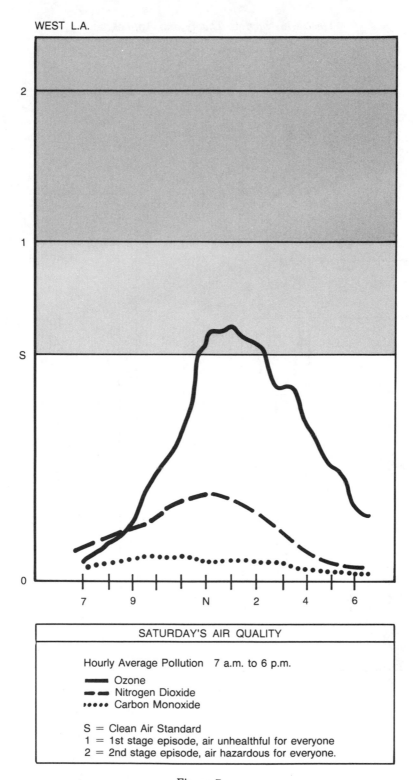

WEST L.A.

SATURDAY'S AIR QUALITY

Hourly Average Pollution   7 a.m. to 6 p.m.
━━━ Ozone
━ ━ Nitrogen Dioxide
••••• Carbon Monoxide

S = Clean Air Standard
1 = 1st stage episode, air unhealthful for everyone
2 = 2nd stage episode, air hazardous for everyone.

Figure 7.

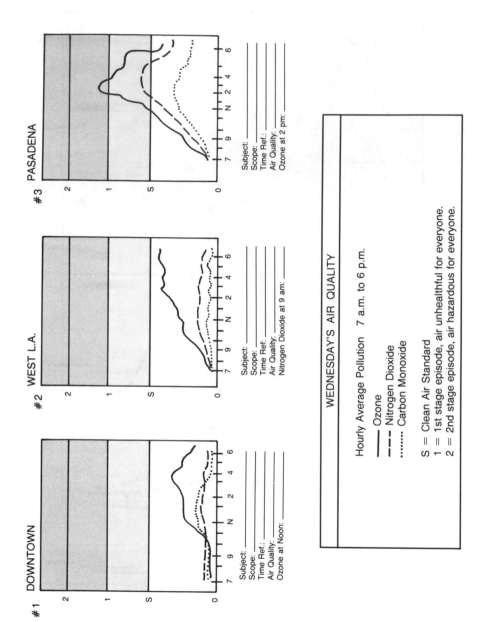

#1 DOWNTOWN

Subject: _____
Scope: _____
Time Ref.: _____
Air Quality: _____
Ozone at Noon: _____

#2 WEST L.A.

Subject: _____
Scope: _____
Time Ref.: _____
Air Quality: _____
Nitrogen Dioxide at 9 am: _____

#3 PASADENA

Subject: _____
Scope: _____
Time Ref.: _____
Air Quality: _____
Ozone at 2 pm: _____

WEDNESDAY'S AIR QUALITY

Hourly Average Pollution 7 a.m. to 6 p.m.

——— Ozone
– – – Nitrogen Dioxide
········· Carbon Monoxide

S = Clean Air Standard
1 = 1st stage episode, air unhealthful for everyone.
2 = 2nd stage episode, air hazardous for everyone.

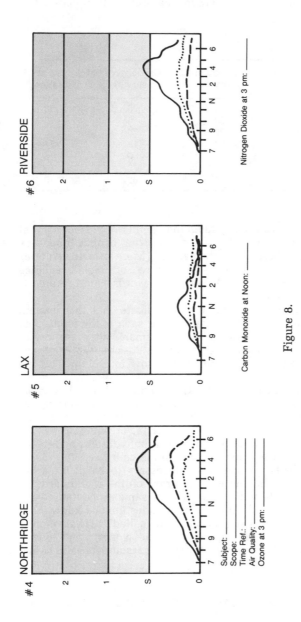

Figure 8.

(1) Use the following chart and show only the column with the list of foods. Ask questions to identify ways these foods are different (e.g., different food groups, natural foods, processed food, etc.).

Food	Total Calories / serving	% Protein / serving	% Carbohydrates / serving	% Fats / serving
Vanilla Ice Cream	138	8	38	53
Scrambled Eggs	111	28	5	67
Refried Beans	142	22	75	5
Peanut Butter	186	17	12	71
Pear	101	4	90	6
Hamburger Bun	119	11	73	15
Ear of Corn	114	9	82	10

(2) Next, reveal the total calories column then point out to students that the number of calories listed is for one serving of that food. Ask students "How are these foods the same?" (More than 100 calories per serving. If students use words like "more" or "high", rephrase into "more than 100 calories"). Write the words "more than 100 calories" on the chalkboard.

(3) Reveal percent of protein column and indicate that this column shows the percent of protein per serving for each of the foods. Ask students "now, how are these foods the same?" (they are low in protein. If they use words like, "not many" or "less than 28" rephrase into "low in protein"). Write the words "low in protein." on the chalkboard.

(4) Reveal the last 2 columns on the Chart and indicate that those columns are the percent of carbohydrates and fats per serving for each of the foods. Ask students, "now, how are these foods the same?" (they are high in carbohydrates or fat or both). It may be necessary to clue students by adding the carbohydrates and fats for vanilla ice cream and writing the sum on the chart, i.e. 38 + 53 = 91. Rephrase students' responses as necessary to "high in carbohydrates or fats or both." Write this phrase on the chalkboard.

(5) Point out that the foods on the chart are the same in the three ways written on the chalkboard. Ask students "does anyone know what foods that have these characteristics are called?" (High energy foods.) If students do not respond with the words "high energy foods" then indicate that foods with these characteristics are called "high energy foods."

CHARACTERISTIC #2
PROVIDES recall for all students, MONITORS recall practice, and PROVIDES recall feedback.

(1) Cover up the characteristics written on the chalkboard and ask individual students to name the characteristics of high energy foods. Provide feedback on student responses and, as necessary, rephrase responses into the terms written on the board.

(2) Cover the list of characteristics of high energy food on the chalkboard and have students write the three characteristics on a sheet of paper. Observe students as they work. Uncover the list and have students exchange papers and correct each others work. Reteach as necessary.

CHARACTERISTIC #3
PROVIDES practice for all students in using the concept (build or design a product, explain, categorize, predict), MONITORS for evidence of concept definition use, PROVIDES feedback:
(1) Distribute a copy of the following chart to each student.
(2) Use a transparency of the following chart to describe the high energy food concept using practice activity.

Food	Total Calories	% Protein /serving	% Carbohydrates /serving	% Fats /serving
Graham Crackers	54	7	72	20
Waffles	130	13	54	34
Apricots	39	7	92	2
Baked Potato	132	8	91	1
Meat Patty	186	53	0	47
Oatmeal	66	13	72	15
Cheddar Cheese	113	26	2	72

(3) Indicate that by using the definition (characteristics) of high energy foods students are to use the symbol HEF and place it next to those foods which have high energy (Waffles, baked potato, and cheddar cheese). Also, indicate that they are to place the symbol N next to those foods which are not high energy and to circle the data in the column(s) for that food which make it a non high energy food (graham crackers, apricots, meat patty, and oatmeal). Point out that after they have finished marking their chart they should be ready to tell why a particular food is or is not a high energy food.
(4) Allow work time.
(5) Use the transparency of the chart and inform students that as you point to each food they are to "vote" on whether it is or is not a high energy food. Indicate that they are to vote on your instructions by raising their hand with fist open if it is a HEF and with fist closed if it is N (not a HEF). After each "vote" call on students to tell why a particular food is or is not a high energy food.
(6) Monitor students' voting and explanations and reteach as necessary. Place the correct symbols next to the foods on the transparency and circle the appropriate column(s) for the non high energy foods during the voting to provide corrective feedback for all the students.
(7) For additional practice have students prepare in writing a 2-day menu plan for themselves. Indicate that the plan should represent a balanced diet and also contain at least one or two high energy foods for each meal and two snack periods. Provide students with

copies of a comprehensive list of foods which includes nutrient data (available through the National or State Dairy Council). Collect menus, monitor work, and provide feedback on each students' menu.

CHARACTERISTIC #4
EVALUATES students' ability to use the concept in relation to a different phenomenon:
(1) Tell students the following story:
There are two students in the same grade, Bob and Debbie. They have raced 10 times against each other during the year. Each race has been neck and neck with Bob winning 5 and Debbie winning 5. Now the school has a track meet. For lunch Bob only has graham crackers and Debbie only had a peanut butter sandwich.
(2) Ask students to use the concept, high energy foods, to predict whether Debbie or Bob would most *likely* win the race and to report the basis for their prediction.

Example of Opinion Expression and Development Teaching Strategy Plan

AREA: Mental-Emotional Health
GENERALIZATION: Freedom and responsibility are both part of growing and developing and tension between the two causes strong feelings.
GRADE LEVEL: 6
OBJECTIVE: The student is able to express opinions and hear the opinions of others regarding a situation involving freedom and responsibility.

CHARACTERISTIC #1-#2
PRESENTS ONE QUESTION for discussion rather than a sequence of questions and USES A DISCUSSION QUESTION which makes it possible for students to express courses of action and value judgments, report or obtain information, and make predictions:
(1) Have students view a video cassette of the 15-minute television program. Must I/May I from the Inside/Out television series, produced by the Agency for Instructional Television, Bloomington, Indiana.
(2) Introduce the program by using any part of the following Must I/May I Program synopsis (2:16):
In interwoven stories Debbie and Bobby must each deal with situations that try their growing sense of independence. Debbie is supposed to look after her younger cousins and get them safely to a day care center. Overwhelmed by the task of minding the children and being responsible for general housekeeping and cooking at home, she is distracted by other things she would rather be doing. Bobby, unlike her, has been given too little responsibility for his own actions. His mother constantly fusses over him and fails to let him do things for himself. Eventually he gets his chance when he is given a package to deliver. How the children resolve their separate problems is left for classroom discussion. The emotions they

feel as they work through their problems are clearly expressed.

(3) After viewing the program present the following questions as the focus for an open-ended discussion:

What should Debbie and Bobby do to resolve their problems?

(4) As students respond and discussion unfolds, implement Characteristic #3 and #4 of the teaching strategy.*

CHARACTERISTIC #3–#4

ESTABLISHES AND MAINTAINS a nonjudgemental environment which encourages voluntary participation and open, responsible communication among students. DOES NOT DIRECTLY OR INDIRECTLY INFLUENCE students' responses, SUMMARIZE the discussion, or communicate his or her opinion about the discussion question.

Examples of Values Awareness Teaching Strategy Plan

AREA: Environmental Health

GENERALIZATION: The individual, family, and society can collectively take action to promote and maintain a safe and healthful environment.

GRADE LEVEL: Junior High

OBJECTIVE: The student is able to cite his or her values and/or the values of others regarding the quality of life in a neighborhood/community.

CHARACTERISTIC #1

USES AN ACTIVITY OR ONE QUESTION** for discussion, which makes it possible for students to make judgements or propose courses of action and report their reasons for those judgements or proposed actions:

(1) Have one half the class find 2 to 3 pictures from magazines which show or illustrate aspects of a desirable neighborhood/community environment. Ask the remainder of the class to find 2 to 3 pictures which show aspects of an undesirable neighborhood/community environment.

(2) Conduct a short discussion on the meaning of the word environment. As necessary, point out that environment consists of physical, psychological, and social aspects.

(3) Students are invited to place their pictures under one of the two following headings previously placed on a bulletin board:
● Desirable Neighborhood/Community Environment
● Undesirable Neighborhood/Community Environment

(4) Have students observe the various objects and conditions depicted in the pictures mounted on the bulletin board.

---

*As students participate in the opinion expression and developmental lesson an alternative is for the teacher to use the Basic Teaching Behaviors (3:78–88).

**For this lesson example the following question could be used as the focus for a values awareness class discussion: "What should be done to improve the quality of life in neighborhoods/communities?" As students respond to the discussion question use the Basic and Values Awareness Goal Directed Teaching Behaviors (3:78–94).

(5) Place the following incomplete statement on the chalkboard:
A good neighborhood/community is one
which has _____.

(6) Ask students to volunteer and read and orally complete this sentence.

(7) List the students' responses on the chalkboards as they respond. Following are some illustrative responses:
- friendly, polite people
- clean air
- well maintained landscape areas
- nearby recreational facilities
- effective police and fire protection
- abundance of nearby medical-dental services
- quiet and serenity

CHARACTERISTIC #2

PROVIDES for the identification of students' reasons for their courses of action or judgments as values:

(1) After students have responded, point out that they have reported characteristics that are important to them—or values they hold about a neighborhood/community environment.

(2) Indicate to the students that with this list of desirable characteristics they can make a value statement about the environment of neighborhoods/communities. Model such a statement. For example, "One of my values about a neighborhood environment is *friendly, polite people.*"

(3) Invite students to make similar statements regarding what they consider to be their most important values about a neighborhood/community environment.

(4) As students participate in the activity and share their judgments and/or actions and related reasons implement characteristics #3 and #4 of the teaching strategy.

CHARACTERISTICS #3–#4

ESTABLISHES AND MAINTAINS a nonjudgmental environment which encourages voluntary participation and open, responsible communication among students.

DOES NOT DIRECTLY OR INDIRECTLY INFLUENCE students' responses, summarize the discussion, or communicate his or her opinion.

A PERSPECTIVE ON TEACHING STRATEGY LESSON PLANS

Any kind of a written plan, whether for conducting a lesson or programming a VCR, can be as detailed or as sketchy depending upon the developer of the plan. Perhaps critical in deciding the amount of detail to be included should be a consideration of who is to use the plan. If the lesson plan is intended for the developer, then written directions can be rather sketchy. The developer can be brief, use cryptic phrases and abbreviations, and place the directions on a small card. The only person that needs to understand and be guided by such a plan is the developer. If, however, the lesson plan is intended to be used by someone other than the developer, then far more is needed. Clear detailed directions are the only means available to communicate the lesson steps to someone else. More detail and direction, however, can cause the lesson to appear as though it will be a tedious exercise. Yet, not enough detail can result in confusion on the part of the user. The challenge in preparing lessons for others is to provide just enough detail in as concise a manner as possible.

Whether a lesson plan is developed for use by the developer or for someone else, it is essential that the lesson plan incorporate the critical characteristics of the teaching strategy to be used. This is necessary in order to assure equal opportunity for all students to attain the lesson objective.

REFERENCES

1. ASCD. *Developing Minds: A Resource Book for Teaching Thinking.* Alexandria, VA: Association for Supervision and Curriculum Development, 1985.
2. Agency for Instructional Television. *Inside/Out: A Guide For Teachers.* Bloomington, Indiana: Agency for Instructional Television, 1973.
3. Dalis, Gus T. and Ben B. Strasser. *Teaching Strategies for Values Awareness and Decision Making in Health Education.* Thorofare, New Jersey: Charles B. Slack, Inc., 1977.
4. Dalis, Gus T., Ben B. Strasser, Dennis Loggins, and Ray Cowan. *Concept Development Lesson Characteristics.* Downey, California: Los Angeles County Office of Education, 1986.
5. Dalis, Gus T., Ben B. Strasser, Dennis Loggins and Ray Cowan. *Information Acquisition Lesson Characteristics.* Downey, California: Los Angeles County Office of Education, 1986.
6. Dalis, Gus T., Ben B. Strasser, Dennis Loggins, and Ray Cowan. *Opinion Expression and Development Lesson Characteristics.* Downey, California: Los Angeles County Office of Education, 1981.
7. Dalis, Gus T., Ben B. Strasser, Dennis Loggins, and Ray Cowan. *Skill Development Lesson Characteristics.* Downey, California: Los Angeles County Office of Education, 1986.
8. Dalis, Gus T., Ben B. Strasser, Dennis Loggins, and Ray Cowan. *Values Awareness Lesson Characteristics.* Downey, California: Los Angeles County Office of Education, 1979.
9. Goodlad, John. *A Place Called School.* New York: McGraw Hill, 1984.
10. Joyce, Bruce and Marsha Weil. *Models of Teaching.* Englewood Cliffs, New Jersey: Prentice Hall, 1986.
11. Kohn, Alfie. "It's Harder to Get Left Out of A Pair." *Psychology Today.* October, 53–57, 1987.
12. Loggins, Dennis, Ray Cowan, Gus Dalis, and Ben Strasser. "Elephants Are Easier To Recognize Than Good Lessons." *Thrust.* 16:40–43, October, 1986.
13. Sine, Raymond L. "A Review of Methodology." *Health Education.* 9:24–27, November/December, 1978.
14. Sutherland, Mary and William Hemmer. "Effective Teaching: Variety In The Classroom." *Health Eduction.* 9:40–41, May/June, 1978.
15. Zumwalt, Karen K. Editor. *Improving Instruction 1986 ASCD Yearbook.* Alexandria, VA: Association for Supervision and Curriculum Development, 1986.

CHAPTER

6

Organizing Health Instruction

Regardless of the subject matter or instructional setting, organizing the curriculum is an essential process in planning for effective instruction. This process involves organizing the total curriculum, courses or offerings within the curriculum, units within each course or offering, and lessons within each unit.

Lesson. Organizing a lesson involves the ordering of generalizations / topics, objectives, content, teaching strategies, and evaluation procedures for that lesson. Relationships of a given lesson to previous lessons and to those that follow also need to be considered. As used here, a lesson consists of all those actions that both the teacher and students do to attain a given objective. One lesson might take as little as 10 minutes, while another might take several hours. In a class hour, it may be possible for students to attain more than one objective.

Unit. Unit organization deals with the ordering of a series of lessons around generalizations / topics, which in turn are related to either a health area, theme, or question. The relationship of one unit to another, or the way in which one unit relates to all the other units in a course is also a part of unit organization.

Course. In organizing a course the principal concerns are the ordering of units within a course and the relationship that the course has to other offerings in a school or community setting.

Curriculum. Organizing the total curriculum refers to structuring all offerings within the educational setting so that interrelationships among the offerings and sequential arrangements within and between offerings are provided for.

In this chapter a framework for identifying, ordering, and organizing all components of the health curriculum is provided. Topics covered include: (1) Vertical and Horizontal Organization, (2) Organizing Generalizations and Behaviors Sought, (3) Criteria for Organizing the Health Curriculum, (4) Principles of Curriculum Organization Applied to Health Instruction, (5) Organizing Health Instruction at the Classroom Level, and (6) Application to the Community Setting.

VERTICAL AND HORIZONTAL ORGANIZATION

The curriculum can be viewed as having both vertical and horizontal organization.

Vertical Organization

Vertical organization refers to the sequential arrangement of generalizations / topics, content, objectives or teaching strategies and techniques so that learnings build one upon the other. That is, initial learnings become the basis for subsequent learnings. In the school setting this means structuring the curriculum sequentially from grades K to 12 as well as sequentially structuring learnings within a lesson, unit, or course.

In a community setting, vertical organization does not generally refer to a sequential structuring among the various educational programs offered by a particular community health agency as such educational programs do not usually build one upon the other. It is more likely that vertical organization of an educational program offered by a community health agency would involve the sequential structuring of content, objectives, and teaching strategies for the specific educational program, group session or class. Figure 9 graphically illustrates vertical organization.

An important question that often arises in considering the vertical organization of the health curriculum in schools is, "How many health areas should be included at each grade?" With the number of health areas to be studied and with the growing concern about the crowded curriculum, it becomes obvious that not all areas can be included at each grade. School districts need to decide on the priority health areas to be included at the various grades. Such decisions need to be made rationally and not in some arbitrary manner.

Those concerned with the health and instruction of children and youth need to be involved in determining the priority health areas for the various grade / maturity levels. Some schools as well as school districts have found it useful to involve a wide range of people in this process, such as classroom teachers, parents, school nurses, physicians, dentists, counselors / psychologists, school administrators, and any other persons interested in the health of students. In deciding what health topics should be emphasized at each grade level, the following should be taken into consideration (1) the health needs and interests of the students, (2) the range of curriculum subject areas taught, (3) the relationship of the health areas to other subject areas (i.e. science,

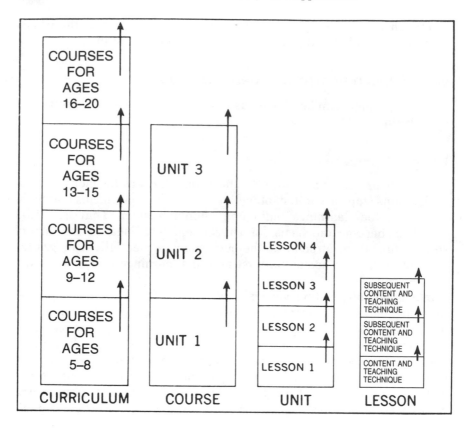

Figure 9. Vertical Organization for the Health Curriculum

social studies, etc.), (4) the availability of relevant instructional materials, and (5) any legal requirements. Figure 10 indicates the decisions made by one elementary-school district. In this example the Xs indicate the grade at which the particular health area will be emphasized.

Horizontal Organization

Horizontal organization refers to the building of interrelationships among courses, units, and lessons. In the school setting, this may mean building relationships between or among traditional courses. For instance, when preparing a unit in health education on communicable disease, relationships could be developed with a unit in science dealing with microorganisms. Similarly, learnings on preventing heart disease in health education could be related to learnings on cardiovascular fitness in a physical education class and to learnings on the structure and function of the circulatory system in a science class.

Subject Area	K	1	2	3	Grades 4	5	6	7	8
Community health			X	X	X	X	X	X	
Consumer health		X		X		X			X
Diseases and disorders	X	X			X	X	X	X	X
Drug use and misuse			X		X	X	X	X	X
Environmental health		X		X		X	X	X	X
Individual and family growth and development	X	X	X	X	X	X	X	X	X
Mental and social health	X	X	X	X	X	X		X	X
Nutrition	X		X		X		X		X
Personal health	X	X		X		X		X	
Safety and first aid	X	X	X	X	X	X	X		X

Figure 10. Health Education Scope and Sequence—School District A.

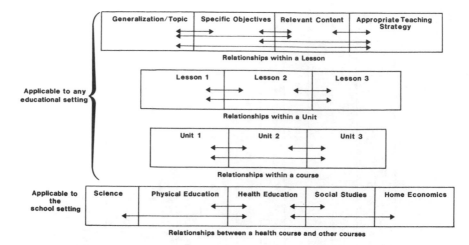

Figure 11. Horizontal Organization for the Health Curriculum

Horizontal organization also refers to the development of interrelationships within a lesson, unit, or course. For instance, within a lesson, horizontal organization means structuring a lesson so that relationships among the generalization/topic, specific related objective, relevant content and appropriate teaching strategy are shown (See examples of such lesson plans in chapter 5).

Horizontal organization within a unit refers to the structuring of several lessons so that the same generalization or topic is revisited. For instance, the generalization: "oral health problems can be reduced if current procedures regarding prevention and treatment are put into practice" may be revisited (reemphasized) in several lessons over a period of time as instruction focuses on different kinds of prevention and treatment of oral problems.

Within a course, horizontal organization would be used to show interrelationships that exist among several units. For instance, objectives dealing with a balanced diet in a nutrition unit could be revisited in a unit on physical fitness when teaching about the importance of a balanced diet to physical fitness. Similarly, the same objectives could be revisited in a unit on diseases and disorders when teaching about the role of nutrition in preventing certain diseases and disorders. Figure 11 gives a schematic of horizontal organization in the curriculum.

ORGANIZING GENERALIZATIONS/TOPICS AND BEHAVIORS SOUGHT

Because of the increase in both amount and complexity of knowledge in the health sciences, a more effective means of organizing the health curriculum in schools is necessary—in fact, required. A viable approach is to build the health curriculum around generalizations/topics to be stressed and behaviors sought in the learner; the idea is that students should be taught the unifying generalizations/topics of various health areas whereby specific facts can be related to these generalizations/topics. Teaching unifying generalizations, however, does not mean doing so merely at the verbal level. Rather it means creating situations whereby students can "discover" these generalizations for themselves. The key to creating such situations lies in the careful consideration of the behaviors sought in the learner (see also McNeil 13:149–152).

Basis for Emphasizing Generalizations/Topics

Broudy, et al. (2:93–94) indicated that Thorndike's learning theory places emphasis on establishing synaptic connections. This position is closely related to that of the associative school of psychology, that learning is an accumulation of conditioned responses. Both the associative school of psychology and Thorndike stress the gradual accumulation of learnings and do not recognize stages of development in the learner. Rather, differences in learning among and within individuals are seen as dependent upon the number of synaptic connections or associations that previously have been established (the previous experiences of the learner). According to this view, organization of the curriculum might best be based upon facts, concepts, principles and generalizations that have been acquired. Thus, topics or generalizations relative to health problems might be introduced early in the curriculum provided they are presented in a form appropriate to young children. In so doing, such topics or generalizations along with related facts, concepts, and skills will tend to serve as a basis for future learning.

Basis for Emphasizing Behaviors Sought in the Learner

A different theory of learning places emphasis upon the progressive emergence of inherent abilities. According to this theory, the child does not learn given behavior until a maturity level appropriate to that learning has been reached (2:92). This theory has been given added impetus as a result of the work by Piaget (14,15,16), Gesell and Ilg (4,5), and Havighurst (8).

In his works, Piaget identified the following stages of development for the school-age years:

Mental ages 4–7: Intuitive-thought stage
Mental ages 7–11: Concrete-operations stage
Mental ages 11–15: Formal-operations stage (14:245).

Piaget was quick to point out, however, that, while the learner goes through these stages of intellectual development, the time of their appearance may vary both with the individual and with society.

Intuitive-thought Stage. This stage refers to a crude trial-and-error operation. The thinking process has not yet been freed from perceptions. That is, the child must "see" in order to "learn" an idea. The child must manipulate or handle. He or she does not perceive ideas unless there is tangible evidence that the thought or idea exists. The child at this stage of development is not able to formulate effectively abstract thoughts or behaviors such as synthesizing and analyzing.

Concrete-operations Stage. At this stage the reasoning processes are logical but not altogether dissociated from concrete data. The child is able to study logically that which is encountered or experienced. He or she is not readily able to manipulate that which is not concrete or that which is not being experienced or encountered. This stage differs from the previous one in that the child goes beyond overt trial-and-error manipulation of objects or things. The child now can perform these trial-and-error manipulations in his or her head and can logically order that which is concrete (14:246). At this stage of development the child might be expected to perform a wide range of behaviors as these relate to familiar or concrete situations. Such behaviors include: applying knowledge (application); forming a whole out of parts (synthesis); making value judgments (evaluation); identifying the relationships that exist between parts and identifying the way parts are organized (analysis).

Formal-operations Stage. At this stage the child can operate on hypothetical propositions and can reason from the abstract or hypothetical. The child can go beyond the information given to a description of what else might occur. The learner can apply what he or she knows to unfamiliar or hypothetical situations. With regard to expected outcomes, the learner should be able to apply knowledge to new situations, form new generalizations or theories out of known parts on an abstract level of thinking, formulate criteria for making value judgments, and identify relationships.

By utilizing these developmental stages in the organization of the health curriculum, emphasis would not be given to prior learnings. Indeed, prior learnings would have little bearing upon what the child can learn in the future. Rather, organization of the curriculum, according to this point of view, would depend upon the developmental stages of the individual. The following description of a series of experiments by Inhelder (14:246) seems to support this view:

> ... children were invited to discover for themselves, with the help of simple apparatus, elementary laws of physics. Children during the "intuitive" stage varied conditions haphazardly and observed what happened in particular cases without deriving any general principles. During

the "concrete operations" stage, one factor at a time was varied and its effect noted. Not before the "formal operations" stage did the child plan truly scientific investigations, varying the factors in all possible operations in a systematic order. The instructional implications are unmistakable: Children with no previous instruction seem capable of learning scientific laws in this way with more zest and understanding than by traditional teaching methods. But timing is important—they are not able to do this before the formal operations stage has been reached.

Merging Two Points of View

Broudy, et al. (2:94) suggested that neither the associative-psychology nor the developmental-stages point of view is entirely correct (see also 14:239). Learning is dependent upon both maturation of the individual (developmental stages) and acquisition of neural connections or associations (accumulated facts, concepts, generalizations, or principles). The individual must have associative ideas in the environment as well as the maturation or inherent ability to handle this knowledge at a particular developmental level. This point of view seems to substantiate the use of both generalizations or topics and behaviors sought as a basis for organizing the health curriculum.

Generalizations/Topics As Organizers of Health Curriculum. Generalizations or topics are elements of the curriculum around which specific learnings are to be organized. They are the threads or themes running through the curriculum from kindergarten through grade 12 and are clues as to the health content that should be selected. They serve as guides for the teacher and curriculum worker in the rational selection of content.

Generalizations/topics as organizers of the health curriculum are revisited at various grade levels. They are the big ideas considered in increasing depth and complexity as the learner progresses throughout the curriculum. At the primary level the learner's generalization might be simple and introductory. At this level the learner may develop merely an awareness of the generalization based upon his or her background, frame of reference, and level of maturity. As the learner progresses through the health curriculum and as the generalization is revisited there is a more intricate and more functional understanding of the generalization and of the facts, concepts and skills relating to it. As an example, the following generalization relative to mental health might be one thread running through the curriculum: "Developing interpersonal relationships involves getting along with others." At the primary level this generalization may be emphasized as "getting along with playmates and family members." At the upper elementary level it may be emphasized as "getting along with people in the community." As the child matures this same generalization can become more involved by encompassing more complex interactions with peers, family, and community members.

An example of a topic is: "Prevention of Communicable Diseases." Using this topic as a curriculum organizer would involve study at the primary level centered around cleanliness and habits of hygiene (washing before eating and not drinking out of a common glass). At the upper elementary level, stress would be placed on prevention of communicable diseases through immunization and avoiding contact with infected persons. As the child grows older emphasis would be on a thorough understanding of the antigen-antibody reaction and community and international efforts to minimize diseases.

In the *School Health Education Study*, generalizations and subgeneralizations were used as curriculum organizers. The following example is from this study.

> *Health Area:* Growth and development—Growing and developing follows a predictable sequence, yet is unique for each individual.*

Subgeneralizations:

1. All individuals grow and develop in a similar predictable sequence.
2. Body parts, systems, and functions grow and develop in each individual in a unique way.
3. Unique differences in rate of growing and developing occur among individuals (17:4–5).

Generalizations also were used as organizers in the *Health Instruction Framework for California Public Schools* (3). For example, the following served to organize knowledge relative to drug abuse:

1. Many substances are beneficial to humanity.
2. All substances should be handled with care and caution.
3. The use and misuse of substances is an independent decision which is made on the basis of values and needs.
4. Individuals determine and choose appropriate alternatives to the use and misuse of substances.
5. The responsibility for initiating changes in practices relative to substance use and misuse belongs to individuals, families, and communities (3:40–42).

In the *Health Instruction Framework for California Public Schools* generalizations also were formulated for: consumer health; mental-emotional health; personal health; nutrition; diseases and disorders; environmental health; community health; accident prevention and emergency health services; and use and misuse of substances.

---

*Note that in the School Health Education Study the major health areas are formulated as generalizations.

Behaviors Sought in the Learner as Organizers of the Health Curriculum. Once generalizations or topics of the health curriculum have been selected, it is necessary to identify and organize the behaviors sought in the learner so that they relate to these generalizations and are appropriate to the maturity level of the learner. That is, it is necessary to identify and organize the specific kinds of behaviors expected of the learner at various grade levels from kindergarten through grade 12 with respect to each generalization or topic formulated. The three stages of intellectual development (intuitive-thought stage, concrete-operations stage, and formal-operations stage), as emphasized by Piaget, may serve as guidelines in determining the behavior appropriate to a given maturity level. The following treatment of the generalization "Developing interpersonal relationships involves getting along with others" illustrates this point.

Intuitive-thought Stage. At the intuitive-thought stage the learner's perception of interpersonal relations would probably be related to working and playing with classmates. A child learns to "get along with others" by trial and error. The child learns that he or she must follow certain "rules" in interpersonal relations. To do so, however, the child must be in a situation where interaction with others is taking place before he or she grasps the idea of what it takes to get along with them.

Concrete-operations Stage. In dealing with the idea of getting along with others at the concrete-operations stage, the learner should be able to analyze a situation in which he or she is interacting with others, and, on the basis of this analysis, adjust or modify behavior. The individual has now progressed from adjusting his or her behavior from overt trial-and-error experiences to adjusting his or her behavior on the basis of an analysis of a given situation. When put in a situation with other people, the learner recognizes the value of analysis of interpersonal relationships as a guide to behavior. The learner should also be able to make value judgments about others, be aware of such judgments, apply knowledge without trial and error, and integrate the factors involved in getting along with others into effective interpersonal relations in a given situation.

Formal-operations Stage. Finally, at the formal-operations stage, the learner, with respect to getting along with others, should be able to go beyond a given situation and apply knowledge about getting along with others to new or hypothetical situations. He or she should be able to predict adjustments and modifications of behavior for satisfactory interpersonal relations and demonstrate the ability to develop and apply criteria for making value judgments about self and others. In other words, the individual can function on the abstract level.

Other examples taken from the *School Health Education Study* and the *Health Instruction Framework for California Public Schools* are used to further illustrate how generalizations and related behaviors sought in the learner (objectives) function as curriculum organizers.

School Health Education Study (17:6–7)

Health Area: Growth and development—*Generalization:* Growing and developing follows a predictable sequence, yet is unique for each individual.

Subgeneralization: Unique differences in rate of growing and developing occur among individuals.

Objectives: Primary level
Cites examples showing how people of the same age differ and yet are similar while growing and developing.
Explains why differences in the rate of growing and developing among children of the same age are to be expected.
Describes how each person becomes unique.

Objectives: Upper elementary level
Identifies different ways children grow physically, mentally, and socially.
Differentiates among the various influences which continually affect growing and developing.

Objectives: Junior-high level
Identifies ways of enhancing physical, mental, and social growing and developing.
Concludes that wide differences in growing and developing in those of the same age are to be expected.
Predicts the kinds of behavior that may result when physical, emotional, and social needs are not adequately met.

Objectives: Senior-high level
Identifies the relationship of heredity to uniqueness of individual growing and developing.
Infers from a diversity of influences how individual patterns of growing and developing might be modified.
Analyzes trends of socialization which influence growing and developing.
Deduces that differences among individuals affect the quality of life.

Health Instruction Framework for California Public Schools (3:26–27)

Health Area: Family Health
Generalization (Concept C): Gender identity and roles are influenced by biological, emotional, and sociocultural factors.

Objective*: Preschool (ages 3 to 5)

---

*Only illustrative objectives were given in the *Framework*.

Makes friends with children of both sexes.

Objective: Early childhood (ages 6 to 8)
Cite examples of traditional and non traditional tasks performed by both men and women within the same and different cultures.

Objective: Preadolescent (ages 9 to 11)
Explore a wide range of family roles and future career opportunities, regardless of sex.

Objective: Adolescent (ages 12 to 15)
Analyze changing laws and customs dealing with sex discrimination.

Objective: Young adult (ages 16 to 18)
Assess gender identity and roles in interpersonal relationships and in preparation for marriage.

CRITERIA FOR ORGANIZING THE HEALTH CURRICULUM

In 1950, Tyler (19:55) identified three criteria for organizing the curriculum: *continuity, sequence* and *integration.* These criteria are still applicable today and are described here as they relate to health instruction.

Continuity

Continuity refers to repetition given to generalizations or topics as they are continuously revisited throughout the curriculum. Continuity should thus be built into lessons and courses. Continuity is provided when a particular generalization or topic is reemphasized in a lesson as different objectives related to these are dealt with. Too, the same generalization or topic might be reemphasized in a different unit or at a different grade or maturity level with different objectives. The following is an example of continuity found in the *California Framework for Health Education* as the generalization "Individuals determine and choose appropriate alternatives to the use and misuse of substances" is revisited at different maturity levels with different objectives:

Sequence of Objectives Emphasizing a Generalization

Generalization: Individuals determine and choose appropriate alternatives to the use and misuse of substances.

Maturity Level	Objectives
Preschool	List appropriate alternatives from the suggestions of others.
Early childhood	Choose pleasurable activities that can be used in unstructured time.
Preadolescent	Illustrate situations in which activities that promote well-being are likely to occur.
Young adult	Describe how life goals are achieved by identifying alternatives that provide acceptable risk and high return (3:38-39)

It is the revisiting of the generalization or topic at the various grade levels that provides for continuity. For additional information regarding the use of generalizations and objectives in organizing the curriculum see also McNeil (13:149–160).

Sequence

Sequence is related to continuity but goes beyond it. While continuity calls for the repetition of generalizations or topics, sequence emphasizes succeedingly higher levels of complexity. At each maturity level generalizations / topics and behaviors are considered in greater depth and breadth. The following is an illustration.

A Sequence of Content Related to a Generalization

Generalization: Biological and environmental, including social, factors influence growing and developing.

Maturity Levels	Content Sequence
Primary	"How different things grow and develop." "Differences between boys and girls."
Upper elementary	"How the body grows and develops." "Individual differences in body build and growth patterns."
Junior high	"How heredity and environment play a part in growth and development." "The nature of the cycle of human growth." "Social development as related to physical growth and development."
Senior high	"Relation of family life cycle to self and society." "Social implications of sexual behavior."

Sequence also might be demonstrated by looking at the behaviors sought at the various maturity levels for a given generalization. In developing sequence with respect to the behaviors sought in the learner, a range of behaviors for learners focusing on the general areas of information acquisition, skill development, concept development, opinion expression and development, and value awareness should be considered. By using cognitive skills, as an example, the arrangement of a sequence of behaviors can be illustrated. In review, these skills involve knowledge, comprehension, analysis, synthesis, and evaluation. Although this range of behaviors can be developed at all grade levels with varying degrees of complexity, it is suggested that consideration be given to the developmental maturity level and the abilities of students when behaviors are specified. The following illustrates the arrangement of a sequence of such behaviors sought in the learner.

A Sequence of Behaviors Sought Related to a Generalization

Generalization: Biological and environmental, including social, factors influence growing and developing.

Behavior Categories	Sequence of Behaviors Sought
Information acquisition	The student is able to recall specific ways in which all plants and animals grow and develop.
Skill development	Analyze data about selected life-style behaviors to determine the influence that these behaviors have on growth and development
Concept development	Use the concept of dominant/recessive genes to predict genetic disorders.
Opinion expression	Express their feelings about their own growth and development in relation to their peers.
Values awareness	Identify personal values and/or the values of others about sex role stereotyping.

While the task of arranging a sequence of behaviors is demanding and difficult, it is essential. Without conscious effort in arranging such a sequence, emphasis might be placed only upon recalling specific facts. By arranging a sequence of behaviors it is possible to emphasize a wider range of cognitive and behavioral outcomes.

Integration

Integration refers to the relationship of one subject-matter area to another or of one health area to another.

In the school setting, integration also relates learnings in science, social studies, physical education, and home economics to learnings in health education. It relates learnings in growth and development to learnings in nutrition, or learnings in nutrition to learnings in disease prevention. It provides the learner with a unified view of health rather than a segmented one.

Integration between Health Education and Other Subject-matter Areas. There are frequent opportunities in other subject areas to help learners develop a unified view of health. For instance, in science, when microorganisms are being studied, relationships to prevention of disease can be developed. In social studies, when communities are being studied, community organization for health can be examined. The principles of physical fitness that might be covered in health education can be related to physical education programs and applied in the physical education class. In mathematics, when interpreting and translating bar graphs, pie charts, and tables, materials depicting the incidence of social health problems might be used.

Integration among Health Areas. Within the subject of health education there are many opportunities to relate health areas to one another so that an integrated view is attained by the learner. Examples of such relationships include the following:

- As *growth and development* are discussed in terms of physical maturation, relationships to *mental and social health* are explored.
- As care of the *skin and teeth* is examined, the importance of *diet and nutrition* to health, skin and teeth is stressed.
- As *stimulant and depressant* substances such as alcohol and tobacco are studied, the relationship of these substances to *safety* is examined.
- As claims about the *nutritional* value of certain foods are examined, criteria for judging these claims in the interests of *consumer health* can be developed.
- As *prevention of diseases and disorders* is studied, *community health* efforts for disease control and prevention are identified.
- As *environmental health* conditions are examined, their effects on *growth and development* can be considered.
- As factors influencing the *environment* are considered, the role of *community health* efforts to insure the *safety* of the environment is explored (12:229).

PRINCIPLES OF CURRICULUM ORGANIZATION

Principles of organization should be utilized systematically in organizing the curriculum for continuity, sequence and integration. In health education, these principles should reflect a concern for the learner as well as a concern for the subject matter to be taught. In the following, principles consistent with these concerns are identified:

Principles Concerning the Learner

Principles of organization concerning the learner can be viewed individually or, because of their relatedness, collectively. Here they will be considered as interrelated principles closely involved with the individual's ability to learn.

Needs and Interests, Maturity Level, Readiness. Knowing when to introduce certain learnings into the curriculum is a problem which has plagued all curriculum development. By introducing and arranging into the health curriculum related generalizations/topics, objectives, content, and teaching strategies which take into account the learner's readiness, maturity level, and health needs and interests, it is possible to provide a relevant program of instruction. A thorough knowledge of the learner is necessary if learner readiness, maturity level, and needs and interests are to be utilized effectively. Knowledge of the learner can be gained through observation and research about his or her behavior. In the school setting, one way of accomplishing this is through a planned program of child study. With an understanding of children and their behavior a basis is provided for making decisions as to the time at which certain content should be introduced. For instance, the effect of smoking on health, in most curricula, has been introduced at the junior-high and senior-high levels, but studies show that the incidence of smoking at the upper elementary level is increasing. This would indicate that information on smoking should be introduced at the upper elementary grades because of the timing of the health hazard to the learner. To make instruction effective, however, it also would be necessary to provide learnings appropriate to the learner's readiness and maturity level (i.e., taking into consideration Piaget's maturity levels).

Geographic Extension. This principle refers to an extension geographically from the learner's immediate personal life. When introducing certain health learnings into the curriculum at the elementary level, a starting point might be the experiences close to the personal life of the learner. As the child matures and becomes increasingly aware of his or her environment, learnings initially might be related to the home, then to the school, and subsequently the community, the state, the nation and the world. This principle might well be applied to a topic such as prevention and control of diseases and disorders. In this instance learnings would first relate to individual practices regarding disease prevention. These learnings might then progressively extend to disease prevention practices at the international level.

The principle of geographic extension is illustrated in the following example:

Use of the Principle of Geographical Extension for Organizing Health Content to be Emphasized

Areas of Geographic Extension	Related Content in the Health Area: Prevention of Diseases and Disorders
Individual	Personal practices for disease prevention (i.e., personal cleanliness, nutrition, immunization, periodic dental and medical examinations)
Home	Establishment and reinforcement of personal practices for disease prevention (i.e., responsibility of individual to family and family to individual with respect to disease prevention and care of the sick)
School	Healthful school environment (i.e., sanitation of toilet and washing facilities, food handling practices, food storage and waste disposal, and adjusting to tension in the environment)
Community	Community organization related to prevention of diseases and disorders (i.e., local health department, voluntary health agencies, professional health groups)

State	Prevention of diseases and disorders at the state level (i.e., state department and public health, laws related to disease control and prevention)
Nation	National concerns for disease prevention and control (i.e., United States Department of Health and Human Services, federal laws)
World	International concerns for the prevention and control of disease (i.e., World Health Organization, interdependence of nations for the control of diseases, international cooperation for the control of disorders through joint research)

Principles Concerning the Subject Matter

In organizing the health curriculum, consideration also should be given to principles related to the body of knowledge which comprises health education facts, concepts and skills. Such principles include:

1. Logic of the Subject Matter
2. Simple to Complex
3. Concrete to Abstract

Logic of the Subject Matter. Some courses in the school curriculum lend themselves to the logical ordering of content by the very nature of the subject matter itself. This is true, for example, in mathematics, physics, and chemistry. In health education, however, because of the diversity of subject matter comprising the health curriculum, it is difficult to find an inherent, logical structure for all health knowledge. That is, in most instances, health instruction subject matter itself does not provide for a logical structuring of the knowledge to be taught. For this reason, in health education at least, the development of the scope and sequence of the curriculum, course, unit or lesson is more often based on the learners' readiness, health needs and interests and intellectual abilities than on the "inherent logical structure" of the health knowledge.

Some would argue, however, that certain units within health education could have a sequence of content based on the "logical structuring" of subject matter. The structure of content in a unit on nutrition, for instance, might focus on the anatomical parts involved in the digestive process, the digestive process itself, essential nutrients and foods in which essential nutrients are found. Similarly, content in a unit on communicable disease might focus on the infectious disease cycle whereby the relationship among disease-causing microorganisms, environmental factors and host factors are "logically" presented. When it is possible to "logically" structure the content in a health unit, this structuring also should take into account those principles of organization concerning the learner; readiness, health needs and interests and intellectual abilities.

Simple to Complex. This principle refers to organizing subject matter from a relatively simple level to a more complex or involved level. The principle of simple to complex seems rational and therefore appealing. It seems only natural that learners should progress from simple to complex. However, the difficulty occurs when deciding what is simple or complex, and what ranges in between. This problem is compounded by attempting to determine what is simple or complex from the view of the learner. Teachers often will arrange learnings on the basis of their perceptions while ignoring the learner's perceptions. For instance, a series of lessons on cigarette smoking and health might be organized so that initial lessons focus on "simple" facts to be recalled, such as the ingredients of cigarette smoke and the harmful effects of smoking. As the unit progresses, lessons become more "complex" and take up topics on motivational factors that cause people to smoke and how these factors need to be dealt with in preventing people from taking up smoking. While this structure may be progressing from simple to complex from the teacher's point of view, it may not be so perceived by students. For some students, merely recalling the ingredients of cigarette smoke or the harmful effects of smoking might be perceived as complex. Before this principle can be effectively applied, knowledge of the nature of the learners within any teaching-learning setting is necessary. What might be perceived as being simple to a high-ability group might, in fact, be most complex to a low-ability group.

Concrete to Abstract. This principle refers to the fact that one must deal with ideas, objects, events, conditions, and properties on a concrete level before one can effectively manage abstractions or symbols related to these. When introducing a topic such as nutrition at the primary level, it is suggested that the learner be provided with opportunities to deal with tangible or real objects related to nutrition before considering related abstractions. At the concrete level, immediate or real representations of food (pictures or models or the food itself) would be useful.

At a later stage the learner can use the verbal symbols for foods when discussing them in relation to diets and dietary needs. The teaching techniques used within any teaching strategy should be dependent upon the various levels of abstractions. The implication here is that the principle of concrete to abstract provides a basis for selecting and organizing teaching techniques to implement various teaching strategies. Another implication is that this principle can be used to help organize health content. Content, including facts, concepts, and skills that cannot be represented in some tangible way should not be introduced at the lower grade levels; rather, it should be offered at a time when the learner is capable of dealing with it in abstract form. For example, some would hold that when presenting lessons on communicable diseases at the primary level, it would be appropriate to introduce the broad concept of immunity but it would be inappropriate to introduce the concept of the antigen-antibody relationship. That concept should be reserved for a time when a learner is capable of conceptualizing this abstraction.

The aforementioned principles of organization have been used in the past to a greater or lesser degree in organizing the health curriculum so that *sequence, continuity,* and *integration* might be achieved. The problem is that there is little evidence to substantiate the validity of their use. However, because of their appeal these principles will continue to be used. If they are to be used effectively in health education, there is a need to answer such questions as: What is simple and what is complex? At what maturity level does the learner view something as simple or complex? Is there a logical sequence to the subject matter presented in health education? If so, is this sequence appropriate to the maturity level of the learner? At what point is the learner able to perceive abstractions in the various areas of knowledge that comprise health education?

When these or similar questions are answered, it may be possible to organize the health curriculum more effectively so that *continuity, sequence,* and *integration* can be better achieved. In the interim, teachers are urged to apply these principles and assess their validity.

ORGANIZATION OF HEALTH INSTRUCTION AT THE INSTRUCTIONAL LEVEL

At the instructional or classroom level, decisions concerning organization also must be made. That is, the teacher has the task of arranging objectives, content and teaching strategies for lessons and units of instruction.

Planning for Continuity, Sequence, and Integration

In preparing a specific lesson, the teacher should consider what has preceded and what will follow. In addition, the teacher should plan so that the composition of the specific lesson has order and systematic progression toward increasing complexity or depth. In so doing, the teacher will be making provisions for *vertical organization,* and the criteria of *continuity* and *sequence* will thereby be put into action.

It is important too that the teacher relate the lessons in specific health areas to one another and to the lessons in other related health areas. When planning a lesson or series of lessons, the teacher should establish relationships among generalizations / topics, objectives, related content, and teaching strategies. In fulfilling these tasks, the teacher will provide for *horizontal organization* and will be implementing the criterion of *integration.*

Teachers also should be concerned with arranging the study of health areas so that they relate to one another. The task is one of arranging these areas so that each provides the basis for succeeding ones. Such an arrangement allows students to pursue learning on an increasingly complex and in-depth level. For example, initial health units might be concerned with the learner's individual health needs. Succeeding units might progressively relate to family, community, and societal health needs. The teacher, by arranging health units in this fashion, is making provision for vertical organization as well as providing for sequence and continuity.

The teacher also can provide for horizontal organization and integration by building relationships among health areas. That is, learnings in one health area would relate to learnings in others. For instance, as nutrition is studied it also could be related to dental health, physical fitness, communicable disease, and so on. The many possible relationships that can and should exist in health education are further illustrated in Figure 12 (12:227).

Using Principles of Organization

As the teacher provides for horizontal and vertical organization and for integration, sequence, and continuity, the various principles of organization discussed previously also should be utilized. The use of one or more of these principles often depends upon the nature of the content and the learner. In certain situations one principle may be more appropriate than another. For example, the principle of geographic extension might not be as applicable when studying personal health or growth and development as it would be when studying community health, prevention of diseases and disorders, or nutrition. In organizing behavior that the learner is to attain, the learner's maturity level might be more important than the principle relating to the logical ordering of the subject matter.

Principles of organization should be applied when appropriate and when possible. These principles are not equally applicable in all situations. When organizing units and lessons the teacher should apply the principles by design and with discretion and should evaluate their effectiveness.

Application to the Community Setting

The organizing elements, criteria and principles described in this chapter can all be effectively applied in the community, medical care and work site settings as well as in the school setting. The primary

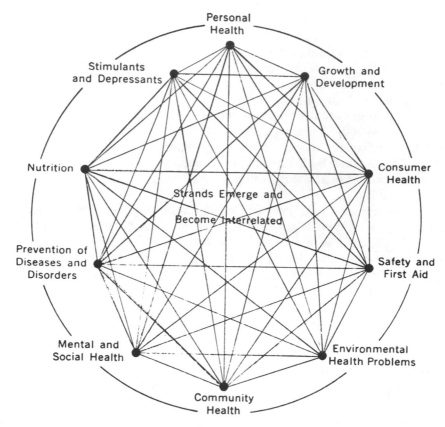

Figure 12.

difference would be that health education in a community setting (i.e. public health department, voluntary health organization, hospital) would focus on maturity levels (infants, children, adolescents, young adults, adults) or special target populations (young mothers, families of patients, patients, unwed pregnant girls) rather than on grade level subjects identified in the school curriculum. There are times, however, when health educators working for public health or voluntary health agencies prepare health instruction materials, lessons or units for use in the classroom. When this occurs, the organizing elements, principles and criteria as described relative to grade levels and subject areas should be applied.

Regardless of the instructional setting, organizing the health curriculum should be based on a planned strategy or rationale. A variety of people, including the target group teachers, administrators and supervisors should be involved in the curriculum planning and organizing process. Too, a multitude of factors must be considered. An example of such factors are classified in the following as *Source Factors, Design Factors* and *Operational Factors*—See also Beauchamp (1).

Factors to Consider in Developing
Health Education Curriculum

Source Factors
  Basis for content selection
  Individual and societal health needs
  Points of view concerning health and education
  Opinions of specialists
  Administrative and community support
  Financial support
Design Factors
  Rationale to be used
  Format and structure
  Organization
  Time allotment
  Relationship to other offerings
Operational Factors
  Implementation
  Personnel required
  In-service education needed
  Teaching facilities needed
  Materials required
  Selecting appropriate teaching strategies/techniques
  Evaluation
  Revisions and up-dating

The process of organizing the health curriculum is a time consuming and bewildering experience. Yet no one ever said developing effective health education would be easy.

REFERENCES

1. Beauchamp, George A. *Curriculum Theory.* Wilmette, Illinois: The Kagg Press, 1975.
2. Broudy, Harry S., B. Othanial Smith, and Joe R. Burnett. *Democracy and Excellence in American Secondary Education.* Chicago: Rand McNally & Co., 1964.
3. Curriculum Framework Criteria Committee on Health. *Health Instruction Framework for California Public Schools.* Sacramento: California State Department of Education, 1978.
4. Gesell, Arnold, and Frances L. Ilg. *The Child From Five to Ten.* New York: Harper & Brothers, 1946.
5. Gesell, Arnold, Frances L. Ilg, and L. B. Ames. *Youth—The Years from Ten to Sixteen.* New York: Harper & Brothers, 1956.
6. Goodlad, John I. *Facing the Future: Issues In Education and Schooling.* New York: McGraw-Hill, 1976.
7. Hass, Glen, Joseph Bondi, and Jon Wiles. *Curriculum Planning: A New Approach.* Boston: Allyn and Bacon, 1974.
8. Havighurst, Robert J. *Developmental Tasks and Education.* London: Longmans, Green & Company, 1957.
9. Havighurst, Robert J. "Nurturing the Cognitive Skills in Health." *The Journal of School Health,* 42:73–76, February, 1972.
10. Kemp, Jerrold E. *Instructional Design.* Belmont, California: Fearon Publishers, Inc. 1977.
11. Lawry, George H. *Growth and Development of Children.* 8th ed., Chicago: Year Book Medical Publishers, 1986.
12. Los Angeles County Superintendent of Schools Office. *A Guide to Curriculum Development and Course of Study for Elementary Schools of Los Angeles County.* Los Angeles; Published as Laco No. 79, 1965.

13. McNeil, John E. *Curriculum: A Comprehensive Introduction.* Boston: Little, Brown and Co., 1985.
14. National Society for the Study of Education. Sixty-third Yearbook. *Theories of Learning and Instruction.* Chicago: University of Chicago Press, 1964.
15. Piaget, Jean. *Logic and Psychology.* New York: Basic Books, 1957.
16. Piaget, Jean. *The Psychology of Intelligence.* London: Routledge and Kogan Press, 1950.
17. School Health Education Study. Teaching Learning Guide, *Growing and Developing Follows a Predictable Sequence Yet is Unique for Each Individual.* St. Paul: 3M Education Press, 1972.
18. Tanner, Daniel and Laurel N. Tanner. *Curriculum Development: Theory Into Practice.* New York: Macmillan Publishing Co., Inc. 1980.
19. Tyler, Ralph. *Basic Principles of Curriculum.* Chicago: University of Chicago Press, 1950.

7

Evaluating Health Instruction

Evaluation is one of the necessary components of a viable health education program. It helps determine the effectiveness of the program—assessing the degree to which desired outcomes have been achieved—and it helps identify strengths and weaknesses of the program—assessing the processes used to bring about desired changes.

To place evaluation in its proper perspective with regard to health instruction, the following questions will be examined in this chapter:

1. What are the purposes of evaluation?
2. What should be evaluated?
3. Who should be evaluated?
4. Who should evaluate?
5. When should evaluation be conducted?
6. How should evaluation be conducted?

WHAT ARE THE PURPOSES OF EVALUATION?

Evaluation is used to identify needs which help determine the scope and emphasis of health instruction, assesses strengths and weaknesses of the program and assesses the extent to which desired outcomes are attained.

To Assess Health Needs

Evaluation is conducted to assess individual, group, and societal needs for the purpose of determining the health content of the instructional program. Evaluation, thus, helps to provide for a meaningful health instruction program in that the program can be directed to meet individual, group, and societal needs. In this sense evaluation is integral to the development of the program.

To Determine Strengths and Weaknesses

Evaluation makes it possible to determine strengths and weaknesses of the instructional program in terms of the abilities of teaching personnel, the effectiveness of teaching strategies (including teaching techniques and human and material resources), and the organization of health instruction. Thus, through evaluation, the effectiveness of the instructional process is assessed; evaluation becomes the basis for improving instructional programs.

To Assess the Attainment of Desired Outcomes

Evaluation also is conducted to determine the extent to which students attain specified objectives. Well-stated objectives provide the basis for evaluation, in that they identify specifically the kinds of behavior changes sought in relation to specific health content. Those in health education should be concerned with evaluating a range of cognitive and behavioral outcomes.

Much has been said about the need for influencing health attitudes. If health educators are to do more than pay lip service to developing positive health attitudes (affective behavior), an attempt must be made to assess changes in the affective realm of behavior—attending or being receptive, responding or being impressed, and valuing or rating highly.

Ideally, the ultimate measure of success of the health instruction program is the degree to which sound health practices have been reinforced or developed by the learner. Do learners get an adequate amount of sleep? Do they participate in programs of physical fitness? Do they brush their teeth effectively? Do they select and eat a wholesome diet? Do they utilize effective preventive health measures such as immunization? Do they purchase health products on a rational basis? These questions imply present health practices. Consideration also should be given to practices that may not develop until some time in the future. Future health practices may result from an accumulation of cognitive and affective behavior over a period of time, or from changing motivations. For instance, young teenagers may not immediately put into practice the concept "Balanced Diet" to plan meals if, in fact, their meals are planned for them. However, these same teenagers, when they become parents and prepare meals for their families, may draw upon their previous learnings on preparing a well-balanced diet. In determining the value of health instruction or in evaluating the outcomes of health instruction, procedures should be developed so that both present and future health practices can be assessed.

A paradox in health education is that, while the development and evaluation of health practices are considered to be of utmost importance, the tools available for evaluating health practices are limited.

The development of instruments that can be used effectively to assess health practices is perhaps the single most important challenge to those concerned with evaluation.

Evaluation is necessary to determine what to teach, when to teach, and how to teach. Evaluation helps determine the health needs of children, youth and society. The effectiveness of teaching strategies and the degree to which the instructional objectives have been attained by the learner can be assessed through the evaluation process. The reasons for evaluation are often interrelated, and one reason is no more important than another. The development of an effective health instruction program can be more fully realized when the evaluative process is conducted so that the many purposes of evaluation are considered. Only after the purposes of evaluation are identified will it be possible to effectively determine what to evaluate, who to evaluate, who should evaluate, when to evaluate, and how to evaluate.

WHAT SHOULD BE EVALUATED?

Deciding on what to evaluate is largely dependent on the specific purpose of evaluation. Thus, after examining the purposes of evaluation, the focus of evaluation (what to evaluate) may be on values, needs and interests, content, objectives, teaching strategies/techniques, the process of curriculum development, the structure of the curriculum, the teaching environment, and the evaluative process itself.

Evaluating Values

There is a continual need to appraise values or points of view concerning *health, education,* and *school/community health programs.* In conducting such an appraisal it is important to consider the points of view held by personnel at the local, state and national levels. Such a process is necessary because of the importance of points of view on the development of an effective health instruction program. These appraisals may provide the basis for changing the points of view held, or for changing the instructional program.

Evaluating Needs and Interests and Societal Health Problems

If health instruction is to be based on needs and interests, it is necessary to determine the specific health needs and interests of learners and the health problems that exist within the community and within society. This would call for assessments to be made on:

- Maturation levels and health status of learners
- The learners' health knowledge

- Health attitudes held by learners
- Health practices of learners
- The learners' health concerns and health interests
- Local, state, and national morbidity and mortality statistics.

In Chapter 2 of this text, data sources and information regarding such health needs and interests were identified, and suggestions were given on how to utilize this information in selecting and substantiating the content of health instruction.

Evaluating Content

The content of health instruction also should be evaluated periodically if it is to be meaningful and realistic. Assessment should be made to determine if the content is:

- Up to date.
- Valid.
- In keeping with points of view held concerning health and health education.
- Based upon health needs and interests of the learner and of society.
- In keeping with the maturity level of the learner.
- Interrelated when possible.

Evaluating Objectives

Objectives need to be evaluated in that they are pivotal to the instructional program. As discussed in Chapter 4 of this text, objectives should serve as guides in the selection of specific health content (p. 57), as guides to specific behaviors sought in the learner (p. 57), as guides to the selection of appropriate teaching strategies and related teaching techniques (p. 58), and as guides to the evaluation of teacher effectiveness (p. 59). Questions that need to be asked when assessing instructional objectives include:

- Are objectives precisely stated?
- Are objectives accurate?
- Are objectives practical or feasible?
- Are objectives consistent with one another and with points of view held?
- Do objectives cover a range of cognitive and behavioral outcomes?
- Are objectives stated in terms of specific content and specific behaviors sought in the learner?

Evaluating Teaching Strategies/Teaching Techniques

Teaching strategies and techniques should be evaluated to determine the extent to which they help students attain objectives. In this regard, evaluation may center on a specific teaching strategy (i.e., opinion expression and development, information acquisition, skill development) or specific teaching techniques used in a lesson, such as demonstrations, small-group discussions, panel discussions, posters, bulletin boards, videos, films, computer software, text books, or any technique or process designed to help students attain specified objectives. The following questions will serve as guides when assessing teaching strategies or techniques:

- Is the teaching strategy appropriate for the objective?
- Are all of the critical steps of the teaching strategy included?
- Does the teaching strategy provide the learner with an opportunity to use or practice the behavior stipulated in the objective?
- Is the teaching technique appropriate for the maturity level of the learner?
- Is the teaching technique motivating or rewarding?
- When possible, does the teaching technique stimulate more than one sense?
- Does the teaching technique allow for the integration of related experiences?
- Does the teaching technique allow for individual differences and abilities of the learners?

Evaluating the Curriculum Development Process and the Structure of the Curriculum

A comprehensive evaluation of health instruction calls for the assessment of the curriculum development process and the structure of the curriculum itself. In making such an assessment, it would be necessary to ask:

- Who is responsible for developing the curriculum?
- Who participated in developing the curriculum?
- Were those who will utilize the curriculum involved in its development?
- What data sources and resource personnel were used in developing the curriculum?
- What was the philosophical basis for developing the curriculum?
- What was the theoretical basis for developing the curriculum?
- Have provisions been made for upgrading and revising the curriculum?
- Have provisions been made for teacher and student feedback?
- Have the principles of vertical and horizonal organization been utilized in the development of the curriculum?
- Has a plan for implementing the curriculum been established?
- Have provisions been made for in-service education for those who will teach the curriculum?

Evaluating the Teaching Environment

In assessing the health instruction program, the classroom setting should be evaluated to determine if the physical and emotional environment is conducive to learning. Some considerations concerning the physical environment would include:

- Class size
- Heating, lighting, ventilation, and acoustics
- Availability of materials and equipment
- Seating facilities and arrangements
- Proximity to noise created by such things as trains and automobile traffic

Some considerations concerning the emotional environment would include:

- Teacher-pupil relations (rapport)
- Student-student relations and teacher-teacher relations (morale)
- Frequency of interruptions
- Administration and instructional policies

Evaluating the Evaluative Process

Finally, it is necessary to evaluate the process of evaluation itself. Consideration should be given to the tools (or measuring devices) that are being used to determine whether or not objectives have been attained. In this regard, questions that might be asked include:

- Are evaluative instruments and techniques used valid and reliable?
- What measures of validity and reliability are used?
- Are the evaluative instruments and techniques based on specified objectives?
- What types of data analysis are used?
- Is evaluation an on-going process?

WHO SHOULD BE EVALUATED?

With the broad scope of evaluation presented thus far, that is, the varied purposes of evaluation and the number of things that are to be evaluated, it becomes apparent that there is a need to evaluate anyone directly or indirectly related to the instructional program. Certainly, effective evaluation involves students, teachers, supervisors, health personnel, administrators, parents, and the community as a whole. All of these individuals are accountable for the success of the instructional program. The specific individual to be evaluated at a given time will depend on the purpose of the evaluation and what is being evaluated. For instance, if the purpose of the evaluation is to determine needs and interests, then learners, family members and those in the larger community would need to be evaluated. If the strengths and weak-nesses of the program and the teaching process are to be assessed, the learners, teachers, administrators, and supervisors will be evaluated.

Evaluating Students

A primary concern in health instruction is the learner. Thus, evalu-ation must also focus on the learner. Of necessity, the process of eval-uation should be conducted to assess the health status of students. If health instruction is based upon the needs and interests of children and youth, individual as well as group needs and interests should be assessed prior to the development of the health instruction program. As health instruction progresses, the student is evaluated to determine the extent to which a range of cognitive and behavioral outcomes are attained.

Evaluating Teachers

The student is but one of the persons who should be evaluated if evaluation is to be meaningful and effective in planning and carrying out health instruction. Another is the teacher. Of utmost concern are the appropriateness and effectiveness of related teaching strategies used. Also of concern are teacher relationships with students and other school personnel. It is not suggested that someone should constantly check on teachers, but it is proposed that teachers periodically check on themselves. Teachers should assess their own teaching behavior, knowledge of subject matter, use of teaching strategies and related teaching techniques, and interpersonal relations as these relate to the objectives of the instructional program.

This appraisal need not be confined to self analysis, but often can be conducted effectively with the assistance of one in whom the teacher has confidence—a fellow teacher, mentor-teacher, administrator, de-partment head, supervisor, or coordinator. The important consideration is that teachers have trust and confidence in the person or persons assisting in their self evaluation.

Successful teachers will strive for continuous self improvement and usually will welcome evaluation. Those who are doing the least effec-tive teaching may be the most fearful of evaluation. Ironically, those who need it the most usually are the least likely to seek assistance through evaluation.

Evaluating Administrators and Supervisors

The performance of administrators and supervisors also needs to be assessed when evaluating the health instruction program. The ultimate success or failure of a program is the administrator's responsibility. The kind of personnel hired to carry out the instructional program, the importance placed upon health as a subject area for instruction, and administrative health instruction policies and procedures must all carefully be considered when evaluating administrators and supervisors.

Evaluating People in the Community

Effective health instruction also necessitates evaluating the health needs and interests of people in the community, for these are important considerations in deciding what to teach. Assessing health needs of individuals within the community over a long period of time may be an indirect means of determining the effectiveness of the existing health instruction program. The decline in accident fatalities in some areas and the decreasing incidence of communicable disease in other areas may be attributed, partially at least, to the health instruction program in effect in these areas. Too, communications with those in the community should be maintained to help ascertain points of view held about health education and the school health program.

Parents also may provide clues as to whether or not the objectives of health instruction are being achieved. Parent conferences and questionnaires can provide valuable information regarding the health values, attitudes and practices, and cognitive capabilities displayed by the student in his or her home.

The task of evaluating in the community should be a shared responsibility between those concerned with health in the community and those concerned with health in the schools. This approach is essential, for the task is too great for school personnel to manage by themselves.

WHO SHOULD EVALUATE?

Evaluation can be conducted by many different people, depending on the specific purpose of the evaluation. The "evaluator" may be an administrator or supervisor when assessments are made on teaching effectiveness. Teachers too may assess their own teaching effectiveness. Certainly, the teacher becomes the "evaluator" when assessments are made to determine the extent to which students have attained specified objectives. Students too can become "evaluators" when doing self appraisals and when assessing teaching effectiveness. Parents or other family members, through such groups as the PTA or Community Advisory Committee, become "evaluators" when assessing content to be taught or when assessing sensitive materials used in class.

Often, other professionals, such as medical doctors, public health officials, and dentists are asked to assess the efficacy of content being covered. In some cases, evaluation specialists are asked to conduct a formal evaluation of the instructional program or to assist in such evaluations.

WHEN SHOULD EVALUATION BE CONDUCTED?

Evaluation is sometimes incorrectly thought of as a terminal procedure. A program is developed, and then the effectiveness of the program is assessed. Evaluation should be broader than this. It should be concerned with process as well as with outcomes and should be conducted: (1) before instruction, (2) during instruction, and (3) after instruction. In other words, evaluation should be an ongoing process and should be an integral part of health instruction.

Before Instruction

Before the instructional program begins, health needs, interests and the health status of individuals and of society should be assessed to determine the nature and extent of the health instruction program. In this regard evaluation serves as a basis for shaping the program.

During Instruction

As instruction continues, progress that is being made toward stated objectives should be evaluated periodically. Teaching strategies, teaching techniques, and classroom environment, as well as pupil progress, should be assessed. Strengths and weaknesses of the program, as well as teaching effectiveness should be assessed. Ongoing evaluation provides feedback which enables the teacher to make sensitive adjustments in the instructional program so that health needs of the learner can better be met.

After Instruction

When instruction is completed, the extent to which stated objectives have been attained should be evaluated. The results of this evaluation will serve as a basis for redeveloping and improving the existing health instruction program.

HOW SHOULD EVALUATION BE CONDUCTED?

How to evaluate health instruction is concerned primarily with evaluative techniques or measuring devices. In determining what measuring devices to use, consideration should be given to the purpose of evaluation, what is to be evaluated and who is to be evaluated. Assessing the amount of knowledge gained by students as a result of instruction, for instance, will call for a different kind of evaluative instrument than will assessing changes in students' overt health behavior. Similarly, assessing the degree of student participation during discussion (process evaluation) will require a different evaluative technique or device than will assessing whether or not a text book contains up-to-date health content.

Evaluative devices may focus on students, family members, teachers, the environment, structure, and process. The primary focus of this chapter will be on evaluative techniques and instruments used in the teaching-learning situation. In this regard, two broad categories of evaluative techniques are discussed: (1) clinical or subjective techniques and (2) statistical or objective techniques. For a more detailed treatment of evaluation and measurement in health education the reader is referred to: L.W. Green and F.M. Lewis, *Measurement and Evaluation in Health Education and Health Promotion* (5). See also R.A. Windsor, T. Baranowski and N. Clark, *Evaluation of Health Promotion and Education Programs* (16); W.A. Mehrens and I.J. Lehmann, *Measurement and Evaluation in Education and Psychology* (11) and M. Solleder, *Evaluative Instruments in Health Education* (15). For a comprehensive assessment of school health education, see also *School Health Education Evaluation* (14).

Clinical or Subjective Evaluative Techniques

Clinical or subjective evaluative techniques include procedures that necessitate a subjective judgment or assessment of desired behavioral outcomes. Usually, but not always, this kind of evaluation is limited to the assessment of values, attitudes and practices. Although evaluation of this kind is dependent largely upon subjective data or value judgments, every effort should be made to make it as objective and as valid an assessment as possible. (See J. Lofland and L.H. Lofland, *A Guide to Qualitative Observation and Analysis* (8) and McLaughlin and Owen, "Qualitative Evaluation Issues in Funded School Health Projects" (10). For instance, the primary technique employed in this kind of evaluation is observation, but there are many ways of increasing the reliability and validity of observation as a tool for assessing attitudes and practices. Observations can be conducted in an informal setting rather than in a formal classroom situation so that assessment might be made in a "natural" environment. In the following, observations and techniques that make observations easier to conduct and record are discussed.

Observations. Observations can be made in formal and informal settings by teachers, teachers and parents, or students. Observations often provide valuable clues regarding attitudes and practices. For example, students might be observed in the classroom or on the playground to assess their: (1) ability to get along with peers, (2) respect for personal property, (3) habits of cleanliness, (4) participation in physical activities, and so on.

Check Lists. Check lists help quantify that which is being observed. If the intent is to observe the kind of foods students choose during lunch period, a check list of foods would be helpful. Check lists also might be of use in observations related to first aid, fire and safety procedures, pupil reactions to stress situations, or pupil reactions to peers or to teachers. Check lists may also be utilized by teachers or by pupils in self evaluation.

Anecdotal Records. Anecdotal records are short summary accounts of what a teacher has observed in a student. They are of value when the teacher is watching the progress of a student who might have a specific health problem. Daily or weekly accounts can be used to determine gains that have been made by the student in solving a specific problem. It should be emphasized that anecdotal records ought to include only that which is observed. Care must be taken not to include inferences or value judgments about the behavior taking place. Describing accurately what has been observed, however, is a difficult task when maintaining anecdotal records.

Questionnaires. Questionnaires covering a wide range of topics can be administered to students, teachers, family members, or members of the community when assessing the extent to which stated objectives have been attained. These instruments usually call for the opinions of those who are being evaluated. They may be used to obtain general data about an individual or about a community, or they may be attitude scales or practice inventories designed to obtain more specific information.

Interviews. Interviews with parents, students, teachers, nurses, or others can give the teacher insight as to whether or not certain attitudes, practices or cognitive skills have been changed. Here again, check lists, questionnaires, anecdotal records, or a combination of these can be effectively used during interviews. In some instances tape recordings also can be used.

Self Appraisals. Self appraisals by students or teachers also provide individuals with clues regarding their strengths and weaknesses and the extent to which they have attained specific objectives. The student's daily food intake, personal health habits, daily program of physical fitness, or immunization records might serve both as effective teaching techniques and as a means of determining the effectiveness of instruction. One objective in a health class might be to develop students' interest in appraising their own personal health habits. Evidence that students are evaluating their health habits could be a means of assessing the effectiveness of instruction in light of this one objective.

Sociodramas, Small-group Discussions, Informal Essays. Sociodramas and other teaching techniques such as small-group discussions or short essays can provide further evidence that students are attaining specified objectives, especially those dealing with attitude changes. The way a student reacts to a role-playing situation or sociodrama might give the teacher insight regarding the student's interpersonal relations.

The comments made by students during small-group discussions often indicate the kind of interest or enthusiasm that the teacher has been able to generate. Comments such as: "Do we have to?" or "How boring!" show a definite lack of interest, whereas comments such as: "When can we discuss this again?" or "We should do this more often!" indicate interest on the part of the student. Also, the facial expressions or gestures of students can indicate an attitude about the concept or topic under discussion.

Essays on topics such as "What Health Means to Me," "The Importance of Physical Exercise," or "Twenty-four Hours to Live" and student autobiographies also can help the teacher in evaluating the effectiveness of health instruction.

Collectively, or in combination, these subjective or "clinical" evaluative procedures can serve as effective tools to ascertain the extent to which a range of cognitive and behavioral outcomes have been attained.

Statistical or Objective Evaluative Techniques

Statistical or objective evaluative techniques refer to objective-type paper-and-pencil tests that can be quantified and analyzed. While these techniques are used to determine the knowledge, attitudes, and practices students possess, they are most effective when assessing the extent to which information, concepts, and skill objectives have been attained.

Two broad categories of instruments are used in relation to statistical or objective techniques: *teacher-made tests* and *standardized tests.* Teacher-made tests are those prepared by the classroom teacher for use in a particular setting. Standardized tests are those prepared by a professional or group of professionals in a field, for which reliability and validity coefficients have been established, and for which norms have been determined.

Teacher-made Tests. Most teachers experience difficulty in developing tests. It is extremely difficult to construct effective tests that accurately assess the attainment of a range of cognitive and behavioral outcomes. There are ways, however, of improving teacher-made tests.

In developing an effective test, consideration should be given to the specific objectives of the course, unit, or lesson. Each objective should be considered in preparing test items, or each test item should be related to a specific objective. When tests are constructed in this manner teachers can evaluate the effectiveness of instruction in terms of the degree to which learners have attained objectives.

The primary value of teacher-made tests is that they can be specifically related to stated objectives, thereby providing a somewhat valid means of assessing whether or not objectives have been attained by students. The tests generally cover the learnings that have been considered in class.

Construction of accurate test items that relate to specific instructional objectives is difficult and time-consuming. A primary limitation is that many teacher-made test items are constructed in haste, often resulting in vague or ambiguous items. Items are not generally tested for validity or reliability. Therefore, these tests may not measure accurately what they purport to measure, and may not measure it consistently. The limitations of teacher-made tests are further compounded by the fact that specific objectives with measurable behavior might not be provided, thereby making assessment of desired behavioral outcomes difficult, if not impossible.

Standardized Tests. Standardized tests also play an important role in the evaluative process, but for the most part they are used to compare the relative status of one group to another. Several standardized tests have been developed for the purpose of assessing the attainment of health attitudes, practices, and cognitive skills; a selection of such tests is available in the publication *Evaluation Instruments in Health Education* (10). While tests found in this publication can be used to advantage in the classroom setting, teachers or other school district personnel need to analyze these tests in terms of their value and limitations to their particular instructional setting. Because a test is standardized, it is not necessarily infallible. No attempt will be made to analyze individual standardized tests at this point. However, the following observations concerning the values and limitations of such tests may be helpful.

A primary value of standardized tests is that the content of test items is generally accurate. In this regard, most standardized tests have a high degree of content validity. That is, they assess what the test developers purport the tests are capable of assessing. Also, norms have been established that enable the teacher to compare a given class with the norm. If the test is standardized, reliability coefficients have been established and the test will yield consistent results. Another value of these tests is that students can use them in self appraisal. Finally, standardized tests can be used as teaching techniques because students can "learn" from reviewing and discussing test items.

A chief criticism of using standardized tests is that they do not always relate to specific objectives formulated for a particular group of learners. If a standardized test is not related to instructional objectives, it will not assess accurately the attainment of these objectives by students. In addition, instruction may be directed primarily toward the test rather than toward the stated objectives. However, teaching toward the test might be a desirable practice if the test items are sufficiently inclusive to reflect accurately stated objectives.

Another criticism of these tests is that they generally emphasize a low level of cognition, primarily recall of specific facts. The tests often omit items that assess the attainment of other cognitive skills such as comprehension, analysis, synthesis, and evaluation. Furthermore, the use of standardized tests is sometimes deemed questionable because rapid advances in the health sciences may render tests obsolete before they are published.

Finally, care must be taken when using some standardized attitude scales or standardized health practice inventories. Such tests may measure *knowledge* of desired attitudes or practices, rather than actual attitudes or practices.

In evaluating the effectiveness of health instruction, a range of subjective and objective techniques should be utilized to determine whether or not instruction has brought about behaviors sought in the learner.

RELATING TEST ITEMS TO OBJECTIVES

If test items are to assess the attainment of a range of cognitive and behavioral outcomes, objectives that identify such outcomes must be stated. The following are examples of specified objectives for a range of cognitive outcomes and related test items.

Objective (information/recall):
The student can identify foods in the basic food groups.

Test items:
True and False
(T)F   Beans and nuts are in the meat food group.
(T)F   Cheese is in the milk food group.
Multiple Choice
Eggs are in which of the following food groups:
(1.) Meat food group
2.   Milk and milk product food group
3.   Fruits and vegetables food group
4.   Bread and cereal food group

Objective (Skill/Translate):

The student can translate graphs depicting the incidence of community health problems into verbal form.

Test item:

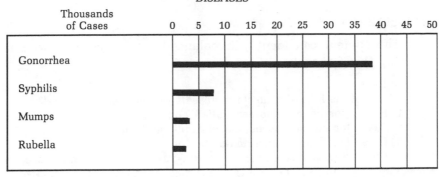

Ranking Communicable Diseases
Number of Reported Cases
DISEASES

According to the graph, how many cases of gonorrhea were reported?
1. Thirty-eight and one-half
2. Three thousand eight hundred and sixty.
3. Thirty-eight thousand six hundred.
4. Three hundred and eighty-six.

Objective (Skill/Synthesis):

The student can integrate data about a specific health problem into an effective plan for solving the problem.

Test Item:

Lung Cancer Death Rates per 100,000 Population
Men and Women, Ages 50–64

Age	Lung Cancer	
	Men	Women
50	18.5	4.0
58	29.5	5.0
64	38.0	7.0

Other Facts:
1. More men than women smoke.
2. Men start smoking at an earlier age than do women.
3. The longer one smokes the greater are his or her chances of getting lung cancer.

Response: (questions)

1. Using the data above explain the differences in the rate between males and females and among the different age groups.
2. In view of your explanation of the data, what proposals would you make for reducing the death rate due to lung cancer?

Note: the first question assesses the student's ability to interpret data. It is the second question which, in fact, enables one to assess whether or not the student is able to synthesize the information obtained.

Objective (Concept—Categorize):

The student can identify a balanced meal consistent with the Healthy Diet Concept.

Test Item:
Which of the following meals represents the most balanced diet?
1. Bread, porkchops, potatoes, coffee, and fruit.
2. Pasta, tomatoes, broccoli, carrots, milk, and cake.
3. Green salad, hamburger, milk, and fruit cocktail.
4. Fried chicken, biscuit, corn, soft drink, and apple and orange sections.

When constructing test items, a suggested practice is to identify the specific objective being assessed by each test item. This can be done by numbering each objective and writing the number next to the test item designed to assess the attainment of that objective. A simple chart could then be formulated charting objectives covered by test items (Fig. 13). Such a chart will give the instructor a quick visual indicating whether or not all objectives have been covered and the extent to which each objective is covered.

Two useful references for additional illustrations of test items related to cognitive skills are: *Modern Educational Measurement* by Popham

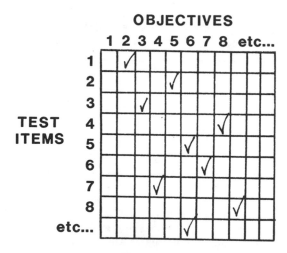

Figure 13.

(13) and *Handbook on Formative and Summative Evaluation of Student Learning* by Bloom, Hastings, and Madaus (2).

FIVE TYPES OF TEST ITEMS ANALYZED

The development of teacher-made test items, as previously indicated, is a formidable task which requires skill and practice on the part of the teacher. To assist teachers in constructing test items, the development of five kinds of test items will be reviewed: (1) true and false items, (2) multiple choice items, (3) matching items, (4) completion items, and (5) essay questions. For further references on test item construction see N.L. Gage and D.C. Berliner, *Educational Psychology* (6); W.A. Mehrens and I.J. Lehmann, *Measurement and Evaluation in Education and Psychology* (11) and Marion Pollock, Ch. 8 "Constructing and Using Evaluation Tools and Measures," *Planning and Implementing Health Education in Schools* (12).

True and False Test Items

True and false test items seem to be more ambiguous than other types. This is perhaps even more true in health instruction, because of the dynamic nature of the health sciences, the differences in and among individuals, and the varying circumstances that dictate courses of action. For example the statement: "When you have a headache, aspirin will relieve the pain," may or may not be true, depending upon the nature of the headache or its cause and a person's reaction to aspirin.

Another example illustrating the ambiguity of the true and false question in the area of health can be seen in the statement: "Chronic diseases can be transmitted from person to person." At first glance this may appear as a false statement. When analyzed further, however, other choices become evident: (1) the possibility of pathogenic organisms causing a disease categorized as a "chronic disease" (e.g., cancer-causing virus) and (2) the possible overlap in classifying chronic and communicable diseases. That is, some diseases may be communicable in origin and result in a chronic disorder (e.g., polio or rheumatic heart disease). Students who have in-depth insight, as contrasted with students who have a superficial familiarity with health problems, will be handicapped and will find it difficult, if not impossible, to say that statements such as those cited are completely true or false.

Another problem relating to true and false test items is in the construction of the item itself. The way in which the item is stated may make it ambiguous or obviously either true or false. The following items will serve to illustrate the point:

Item:
You should stop smoking because excessive smoking will give *you* cancer of the lung.

Although it has been demonstrated that smoking may cause lung cancer, it is quite possible that a person who smokes will not develop lung cancer. Therefore, the use of the personal pronoun *you* should be avoided in true and false test items.

Item:
Alcohol has a *bad effect* on the human body.

Value judgments (bad, good, essential, important) need further clarification. To classify alcohol as "bad," students must be able to ascertain the extent to which the effect is bad. They also must determine the degree to which alcohol has been used. In certain situations alcohol does have a "bad" effect (e.g., excessive and prolonged use may damage the brain and liver), and in other instances alcohol has a "good" effect (e.g., for medicinal purposes or to make you feel "good"). Furthermore, the use of descriptive terms or phrases which are value-laden may confuse the student. For example, in the above illustration the adjective "bad" may be somewhat perplexing to the student who witnesses the use of alcohol in religious services. However, the term "bad" will not bewilder the student whose religious beliefs advocate total abstinence.

Item:
No food, even when kept in a refrigerator, should *never* be stored in an open can.

Although this statement is obviously grammatically incorrect, it points out that care must be taken to avoid the trap of the double negative.

Item:
Claims made by advertisers of health products are *always* misleading.

Specific determiners such as *always* and *never* should be avoided because they do not allow for the exception. Students quickly learn to classify true and false test items containing these determiners as false.

Item:
During early adolescence there is a period of rapid growth and development. This is characterized by changing physical and psychological needs, which are generally recognized as normal signs of adolescence and which bring about certain problems that must be faced by the adolescent and his or her family.

Responding to extremely long test items such as this becomes a task of being able to decipher what the statement actually means rather than knowing if the statement is true or false. Dividing the above item into three true and false test items would make it more understandable, and the degree to which the student knows the material could still be assessed.

Item:
  Fluoridating the water supply reduces the incidence of tooth decay, *and it also purifies the water supply making it safe to drink.*

Unless the directions point out that if any part of the question is false it should be marked false, a test item such as the one above would be difficult to answer. It is true because evidence indicates that fluoridation does reduce the incidence of tooth decay. The statement is false in that there is no evidence that indicates fluoridation purifies the water. Test items with more than one meaning should be avoided.

The task of developing valid true and false test items is not an easy one. Caution must be exercised to eliminate, as much as possible, the ambiguity of statements. The following test items have been developed to avoid the previously discussed pitfalls of the true and false test item.

Ⓣ F 1. It has been demonstrated through scientific studies that there is a positive correlation between the smoking of cigarettes and the incidence of lung cancer.

T Ⓕ 2. Scientific evidence has demonstrated that people who smoke will develop lung cancer.

Ⓣ F 3. Drinking one highball with one ounce of whiskey can reduce peripheral vision and visual acuity.

Ⓣ F 4. Smoking one cigarette will cause the pulse rate to increase whether or not one smokes filtered or nonfiltered cigarettes.

T Ⓕ 5. Fluoridating the water supply will rid the water of microorganisms.

T Ⓕ 6. Storing foods in an open can in a refrigerator will result in contamination by microorganisms.

Multiple Choice Test Items

Multiple choice test items are considered to be more effective in measuring cognition than are true and false test items. However, a poorly stated multiple choice question can be confusing and may not actually assess students' cognitive skills. Some general considerations in developing such test items follow.

In general, it is a better practice to provide a longer stem and a shorter response than vice versa.

Example:
  (poor) Do not:
    1. smoke cigarettes if you want to stay healthy.
    2. bring water to a boil before you put vegetables in the water.
    3. consult a physician every time you have a cold.
    4. buy fish from fresh-fish markets because these markets are not properly supervised.

(better) Which of the following diseases has been shown to be related to smoking?
1. Buerger's disease
2. Parkinson's disease
3. Addison's disease
4. Hodgson's disease

There are fewer pitfalls for the person who has not constructed many tests if the stem is in the form of a question rather than a continuing statement. Grammatical errors are less likely to occur and the continuity between stem and alternatives is apt to be more consistent.

Example:

(poor) USP on a label of a medicine or drug:
1. certain standards have not been met.
2. certain standards have been met.
3. certain standards are not required.
4. certain standards are pending.

(better) What do the letters "USP" on the label of a drug or bottle of medicine mean?
1. Certain standards have not been met.
2. Certain standards have been met.
3. Certain standards are not required.
4. Certain standards are pending.

Responses should be similar or fall into the same category. This practice makes the answer less obvious and requires greater discrimination on the part of students.

Example:

(poor) Which of the following agencies is classified as a voluntary health organization?
1. American Heart Association
2. the church
3. the school
4. U.S. Public Health Service

(better) Which of the following agencies is classified as a voluntary health organization?
1. American Heart Association
2. World Health Organization
3. American Medical Association
4. U.S. Public Health Service

It is better to use four or five responses. More than five responses become cumbersome to handle. Less than four responses increases the possibility of guessing the correct answer.

When writing multiple choice test items, do not try to hide qualifiers such as best, not, does, does not. These terms should be underlined. The purpose of the test is not to try to fool or trick the student.

Example:

> Which <u>one</u> of the following *does not* respond to antibiotics?
> (1.) Virus
> 2. Fungus
> 3. Bacterium
> 4. Bacillus

Matching Items

Matching items can be used to measure the student's ability to recall information and to identify relationships. Such items can be confusing to the student if they are poorly prepared. By considering the following points when preparing matching items some of the ambiguities and difficulties can be avoided.

A set of matching test items should not include more than 10 or less than 5 choices. When there are more than 10 items it is difficult for students to keep track of or sort out relationships. Too many matching items tend to test the students' organizational abilities rather than measure their ability to identify relationships among the items.

When there are fewer than 5 items the possibility of guessing the correct answer is increased.

In matching test items the numbers of alternatives to choose from should exceed the number of items. This minimizes matching items through the process of elimination and more accurately measures students' knowledge.

Example:

Match the function in column B with the list of reproductive organs in
Column A.

		Column A		Column B
C	1.	Ovary	A.	Houses fertilized egg
B	2.	Fallopian tube	B.	Passageway for ova
A	3.	Uterus	C.	Prepares reproductive cells
D	4.	Labia	D.	Folds of skin that protect reproductive system
E	5	Vagina	E.	Passageway for baby at birth
			F.	Supplies developing baby with nutrients
			G.	Secretes follicle-stimulating hormone

Each set of matching test items should fall into the same or similar category or class of information. This practice forces students to be more discriminating in identifying the correct relationships.

Example:

(poor): Match items in Column A with appropriate response in Column B

	Column A		Column B
F	1. Carbohydrate	A.	Muscle that flexes the elbow
D	2. Amphetamines	B.	Nutrient that regulates metabolism
C	3. Aorta	C.	Carries blood from the heart
E	4. FSH	D.	Stimulates heart rate
A	5. Biceps	E.	Hormone that stimulates the growth of ova
		F.	Nutrient that provides energy
		G.	Hormone that regulates sugar metabolism

Example:

(better): Match the drug effects in Column B with the correct class of drugs in Column A

	Column A		Column B
B	1. Hallucinogens	A.	Deadens feelings
D	2. Amphetamines	B.	Disturbs perception
F	3. Barbiturates	C.	Hypnotizes
A	4. Opiates	D.	Stimulates
G	5. Tranquilizers	E.	Improves memory
		F.	Induces sleep
		G.	Calms nerves

Completion Items

Completion items are used primarily to test students' ability to recall facts. Such items should be used with caution because in most instances the student is required to form a mind set identical with that of the test developer. That is, students must view the incomplete statement in the same context as the one who has developed the test item or their chances of finding the correct response are remote. Students may give a "correct" response in accordance with their interpretation but not in accordance with what was intended by the test developer.

By observing the following practices in developing completion test items, some pitfalls can be avoided.

The incomplete statement should call for a precise term or phrase.

Example:

(poor)   Essential for building and repairing is _____ (protein).

(better) The name of the nutrient essential for building and repair of body tissue is _____ (protein).

The portion of the statement to be completed should not call for more than one or two terms. If too many blanks are to be completed, it is difficult, if not impossible, to interpret the meaning of the statement.

Example:

(poor) The _____ (nicotine) found in cigarettes causes _____ (increased heart rate).

(better) The nicotine found in cigarette smoke causes the heart rate to _____ (increase).

There is less chance of ambiguity if the completion portion of the statement comes at the end of the sentence rather than at the beginning or middle. This approach tends to provide students with a clearer meaning of the statement and thereby better enables them to provide the appropriate response.

Example:

(poor) _____ (Milk and dairy products) provide essential nutrients.

(better) The name of the food group that includes cheese is _____ (milk and dairy products).

Essay Questions

The most common failing of essay questions is that they are too general, and their lack of specificity makes it difficult to assess students' cognitive skills. Furthermore, it is hard for students to determine just how much or how little to write. The following examples illustrate this point.

Item (poor):
Discuss the effects of smoking.

How much of a discussion is called for in this test item? The item does not prescribe the boundaries within which the student should operate. What kinds of effects are called for? Should economic, or social, or physiologic effects be discussed?

Item (poor):
Why should people stop smoking?

Whenever an essay item is developed in question form, and there are several possible answers, students should be told whether they are expected to discuss all possibilities or just one of the possible responses.

Some general considerations regarding essay questions might help the reader to develop items that are clear and consequently make assessing cognitive skills an easier task:

Spell out specifics you want students to discuss.

Example:

Compare and contrast syphilis and gonorrhea in terms of:
1. etiologic agent
2. mode of transmission
3. host
4. symptoms
5. treatment

Use terms such as analyze, describe, defend, criticize, and compare, so as to measure more than simple recall of knowledge.

Example:
Describe the values and limitations of three different birth control methods. Your discussion should include at least two (2) values and two (2) limitations for each method.
or
Defend and *criticize* both government-sponsored and privately-sponsored insurance health plans. Your discussion should include a consideration of (1) economic factors, (2) political factors, and (3) social factors

Assign a point value to essay test items or to parts of these items. This will enable students to pace themselves, and it will make assessment of cognitive skills called for in the test item more consistent.

Example:
(14 points) Compare and contrast syphilis and gonorrhea in terms of:

(2 points)   1. etiological agent
(2 points)   2. mode of transmission
(2 points)   3. host
(4 points)   4. symptoms
(4 points)   5. treatment

or

(30 points) Defend and criticize both government-sponored and privately-sponsored insurance health plans. Your discussion should include a consideration of:
(10 points) 1. economic factors
(10 points) 2. political factors
(10 points) 3. social factors

Regardless of the techniques utilized, evaluation should be based upon specified objectives. Without objectives evaluation becomes aimless—an end rather than a means to an end. The greater the clarity and specificity of objectives the greater is the opportunity to select or develop more precise evaluative techniques or instruments.

MAKING EVALUATION MEANINGFUL

One way to help make evaluation more meaningful is to provide students with test results as quickly as possible. Students profit from immediate knowledge of test results in that correct responses are reinforced and mistakes are corrected.

In addition evaluative technique should enable students as well as teachers to assess the degree to which objectives have been attained. Furthermore, evaluation should foster in students a desire for self appraisal and the ability to recognize when and how to evaluate their own health behavior.

REFERENCES

1. Bloom, Benjamin S. (ed.). *Taxonomy of Educational Objectives. Handbook I: Cognitive Domain.* New York: David McKay Co., 1956.
2. Bloom, Benjamin S., J. Thomas Hastings, and George F. Madaus. *Handbook on Formative and Summative Evaluation of Student Learning.* New York: McGraw-Hill Book Co., 1971.
3. Dignan, Mark B. *Measurement and Evaluation of Health Education.* Springfield: Charles C Thomas, 1986.
4. Green, L.W. "Modifying and Developing Health Behavior." *Annual Review of Public Health.* 5:215–236, 1984.
5. Green, L.W. and F.M. Lewis. *Measurement and Evaluation in Health Education and Health Promotion.* Palo Alto, California: Mayfield Publishing Co., 1986.
6. Gage, N.L. and David C. Berliner, *Educational Psychology.* Chicago: Rand McNally College Publishing Co., 1979, pp. 684–700.
7. Johnson, David W., *Educational Psychology.* Englewood Cliffs, N.J.: Prentice-Hall, Inc., 1979, pp. 446–481.
8. Lofland, J. and L.H. Lofland. *Analyzing Social Settings: A Guide to Qualitative Observation and Analysis.* Belmont Hills, California: Wadsworth Publishing Co., 1984.
9. McLaughlin, Judith. "Reliability and Validity Issues in School Ethnography and Qualitative Research." *Journal of School Health.* 56:187–189, May, 1986.
10. McLaughlin, Judith and Sandra L. Owen. "Qualitative Evaluation Issues in Funded School Health Projects." *Journal of School Health.* 57:119–121, March 1987.
11. Mehrens, William A. and Irvin J. Lehmann. *Measurement and Evaluation in Education and Psychology.* New York: Holt, Rinehart and Winston, 1984
12. Pollock, Marion. "Constructing and Using Evaluation Tools and Measures." *Planning and Implementing Health Education in Schools.* Palo Alto, California: Mayfield Publishing Co., 1987.
13. Popham, W.J., *Modern Educational Measurement.* Englewood Cliffs, N.J.: Prentice-Hall, Inc., 1981.
14. School Health Education Evaluation. Special Issue, *Journal of School Health.* October, 1985.
15. Solleder, Marian K. *Evaluation Instruments in Health Education.* Waldorf, Maryland: AAHPERD Publications, 1979.
16. Windsor, R.A., et al. *Evaluation of Health Promotion and Education Programs.* Palo Alto, California: Mayfield Publishing Co., 1984.

8

Identifying Competencies of Those Teaching Health

Regardless of the setting, no plan of curriculum organization can take the place of good teaching, even though effective planning is necessary to provide an atmosphere for inspirational teaching and productive learning. The teacher is the most important element in a sound health instruction program. With unqualified or poorly prepared teachers, fads rather than facts may be stressed. Irrelevant content may be emphasized. Exciting or interesting teaching strategies might be utilized but may be totally unrelated to instructional objectives. When this is the case, students may enjoy themselves but this will not insure the attainment of specified objectives. Finally, unqualified teachers may select limited or poorly developed evaluation techniques to determine the needs of children and youth and to appraise the learner's achievement.

What are the competencies of those teaching health? What should be the training and preparation for those teaching health at the elementary level? Who is best qualified to teach health classes at the secondary level? If health is taught in relation to other subjects at the secondary level, what background and preparation should teachers of these subjects have to carry out effective health instruction? What should be the training and preparation of those teaching health outside the school setting?

PREPARATION OF ELEMENTARY SCHOOL TEACHERS

In many states, certain aspects of health must be included in the course of study at the elementary level. In some states, one or more courses of health education are included in the certification requirements for classroom teachers. In other states, teachers may be required to teach about "health" even though they are not required to have preparation in health education.

If health content is to be included in the curriculum of the elementary school, teachers in these schools should be required to have adequate preparation. Minimum requirements would include preparation in: (1) health problems of elementary school-age children, (2) teaching of health at the elementary level, and (3) the function, purpose, and organization of the school health program.

In some states the trend is to develop a diversified or multisubject major for those preparing to teach in elementary schools. If such a major is offered, health education should be one of the components. If teachers are required to teach health at the elementary level, they should be prepared to teach accurately and effectively. Teachers are not expected to teach mathematics or reading without adequate preparation in these subjects. They should not be expected to teach "health" without adequate preparation in health education.

PREPARATION OF SECONDARY SCHOOL TEACHERS

In some secondary schools health instruction is correlated or integrated with other subject-matter areas. Correlation generally means that health concepts are dealt with in other subject areas, such as physical education, science, home economics, and social studies. For instance, when microorganisms are being studied in a science class, their impact on health might be considered.

Integration generally means that several subjects are offered as a core in a given block of time. For example, social studies, english and health might be combined in such an offering. As major themes are examined, the social science, English, and health aspects of these themes are studied. When students study "the westward movement," health, social and economic problems associated with this movement, and the ways in which these problems were confronted, might be considered and written reports prepared. Literary works expressing the health, economic, political, and historical dimensions of the "westward movement" also could be utilized.

Health instruction by means of correlation or integration alone is generally not as effective as health instruction in a separate course. Everyone's business to teach health often becomes no one's business— "let the other teachers do it." In some cases, however, health instruction by correlation or integration can be most effective. The success or failure of health instruction by these two approaches, or by any approach for that matter, is primarily dependent upon the qualification and competency of the individual teaching the class. When correlated or integrated programs have effective health instruction, the instructor usually has had some preparation in health, either as a major or minor, or through graduate courses or in-service programs and recognizes the value of health instruction. Most teachers teaching health by correlation or integration, however, have majored or minored in other subject areas. A science teacher responsible for correlating some health instruction in the science class may not have adequate preparation in health and may have little interest in correlating health with the science content of the class. Furthermore, because of the demands for teaching science, little time may be available for health instruction in the science class.

If health instruction is to be conducted by correlation or integration with other subject areas, teachers of these subjects should have adequate preparation in health education, similar to the preparation proposed previously for elementary teachers. The main difference in preparation would be that secondary teachers concern themselves with a study of adolescents, their characteristics and health problems.

In many instances, health is taught as a separate course. Persons assigned to teach this course should be fully qualified health educators. They should not be assigned to teach the course because they are physical educators, science teachers, or home economics teachers. While the fields of physical education, science, and home economics bear a relationship to health, teachers in these fields do not necessarily possess the needed subject-matter competencies to teach the health course.

If teachers have a responsibility for health instruction but are prepared in physical education, biology, sociology, or psychology and not in health education, they are likely to emphasize one aspect of health— physical, biological, physiological, social, or emotional. Such overemphasis on any one of these important aspects minimizes the interrelatedness of physical, mental, and social perspectives of health. Only when all aspects of health are studied collectively, without undue emphasis on one at the risk of neglecting the others, will there be a balanced program of health instruction.

Unless teachers have a well-developed and well-rounded preparation in health education or health science, they will not be prepared to carry out an instructional program which emphasizes the dynamic interrelationships that exist among physical, mental, and social well-being. Therefore, those teaching separate courses in health should have a major or minor preparation in this field.

Preparation in Health Education

There are at least three primary areas of preparation recommended for those preparing to teach in health education: (1) common personal and community health needs; (2) related areas (sociology, psychology, bacteriology, public health, physiology and anatomy); and (3) structure and process of school health programs and modern concepts of health instruction (1,3,4,6). A 60-unit program of studies for developing well-qualified health educators who are proficient in these three areas is offered at California State University, Northridge (2). This program includes:

Lower Division Requirements	*Semester Units*
Introductory Health	2
Human Physiology	3
Introductory Chemistry	3
General Biology	4
College Algebra or Introductory Statistics	3
Introductory Psychology	3
Introductory Sociology	3
Biology Elective	2
Upper Division Requirements	
Biostatistics	4
Health Behavior	3
Solving School/Community Health Problems	3
School Health Education	3
Teaching Strategies in Health Education	3
Epidemiology	3
Community Health Education	3
Intercultural Communications	3

Electives
Credential candidates are to select 12 units from the following:

	Semester Units
Nutrition	3
Family Health	3
Environmental Health	3
Mental Health	3
Drug Use and Abuse	3
Emergency Procedures	2
Health Problems of the Disadvantaged	3
	Total = 60 units

A similar program of studies is offered at most institutions that have a major in health education.

PROFESSIONAL COMPETENCIES

Identifying the professional competencies of health educators has been a continuing effort for a number of years. One of the first attempts took place in 1948 at Jackson's Mill, West Virginia (5). The focus was on the undergraduate professional preparation needed to develop professional health education competencies. In 1950 a similar effort with focus on graduate preparation was conducted at Pere Marquette State Park, Illinois (9). Sliepcevich, in 1965, specified a number of professional competencies in her presentation entitled, "Implications of the School Health Education Study for Professional Preparation of Teachers" (12). Fodor, Johns, and Sutton, in 1972, identified specific professional competencies and professional preparation needed for health educators in a paper entitled "The Significance of Professional

Preparation in Health Education" (3). A more recent effort to identify professional competencies of health educators was initiated by the National Center for Health Education in a project entitled "The Role Delineation Project" (13). This project, first funded in 1978, resulted in the establishment of the National Task Force for the Preparation and Practice of Health Educators. In 1985, the Task Force identified seven responsibilities of health educators. These included:

1. Assessing individual and community needs for health.
2. Planning effective health education programs.
3. Implementing health education programs.
4. Evaluating the effectiveness of health education programs.
5. Coordinating provisions of health education services.
6. Acting as a resource person in health education.
7. Communicating health education needs, concerns and resources (6).

These responsibilities were identified by the Task Force as the framework for developing competencies of the generic health educator, whether in the school, community, medical, or work site setting. For each responsibility a set of competencies, subcompetencies and related objectives were developed.

In 1988, the Task Force announced the establishment of the National Commission for Health Education Credentialing. The aforementioned seven responsibilities of health educators will be used by the Commission to: (1) certify health education specialists, (2) promote professional development and (3) strengthen professional preparation. The ultimate goal is to eventually institute a national certification or credentialing process for the preparation of health educators. The competencies developed by the Task Force are being used by a number of universities in the revision and development of professional preparation programs in health education. An example of such utilization is found in "Application of the Role Delineation Project 'Framework' to a Professional Preparation Program" (1).

In the tables on pages 157, 158, and 159, the authors have used the framework of this text for classifying selected competencies from these studies relative to: (1) administering and coordinating the health instruction program, (2) teaching health and (3) utilizing school and community resources.

The Health Education Specialist

There is an increasing emphasis on preparing health educators who have competencies in both school and community health education. The notion is that regardless of the setting, health educators essentially need the same kinds of competencies. The community health educator is required more and more to possess teaching and curriculum devel-

Administering and Coordinating the Health Instruction Program

Areas	Competencies
Point of view	Is able to interpret the health instruction program, including modern points of view of health and health education, to other school community personnel and to lay groups.
Basis for content—learner	Can encourage school personnel to identify, record, and share information pertaining to the health of students.
	Can encourage teachers concerned with health instruction to utilize specific health needs of children and youth as a basis of the health instruction program.
Basis for content—society	Is able to plan and organize the health instruction program by recognizing the health needs of society.
Structuring health knowledge— content and generalizations/ topics	Is able to plan and contribute to in-service programs that enrich the health knowledge of teachers.
Goals and objectives	Is able to involve the community and professional staff in establishing and reviewing goals and objectives for health instruction.
Teaching strategies / techniques	Can marshal available human and material resources to enrich the health instruction program.
Organization	Is able to plan and coordinate the health instruction program by relating health instruction to the total school/community health program.
Evaluation	Is able to integrate the results of evaluation into an effective health instruction program.

opment skills. These skills are being put to use in a variety of settings, including hospitals, churches, community agencies, private industry and schools. Community health educators often work directly with school district personnel in planning and implementing health education curricula. Conversely, school health educators increasingly need the skills necessary to work with small community groups of parents and health professionals in school-community coordinated health instruction programs. The school health educator needs the same community organization and health promotion skills required of the community health educator. This trend is supported by the recommendations of the Task Force on the Preparation and Practice of Health Educators in their identification of competencies for the generic health educator regardless of work setting. Too, a number of states, including California, Illinois, Oregon, Wisconsin, and New York, to name a few, have initiated Comprehensive Health Education Programs that require cooperative efforts between community and school personnel in solving health problems. For these reasons, some institutions are beginning to

Teaching Health

Areas	Competencies
Point of view	Can relate the health instruction program to points of view held concerning health, education, and school/community health programs.
Basis for content—learner	Is sensitive to the inter- and intra-individual differences of students.
Basis for content—society	Can relate the health needs of society to the health instruction program.
Structuring health knowledge—content and generalizations/topics	Possesses skills in oral and written communication.
	Possesses a command of the fundamental concepts comprising the content or substance of health instruction, including a background in the behavioral and biological sciences.
Goals and objectives	Can formulate goals and objectives for health instruction.
Teaching strategies/techniques	Possesses and is able to utilize principles of learning in motivating the learner toward the development of optimum health.
	Can utilize appropriate teaching strategies and teaching techniques so that learners can effectively attain objectives.
Organization	Is able to integrate the physical, mental, and social perspectives of health in presenting health issues, problems, and topics.
	Can plan lessons effectively so that sequence, continuity and integration are provided in health instruction.
Evaluation	Can assess the health needs and interests of the learner through the use of such techniques as observation; conferences with children, parents, and teachers; consultation with medical personnel; analysis of health records; analysis of check lists and questionnaires.
	Can evaluate the health instruction program in terms of how effectively learners attain instructional objectives.

offer common undergraduate and graduate programs for both school and community health educators. At California State University, Northridge, for example, the school health and community health options have been merged into the "Health Education Option." Whether their interests are in schools or communities, students take a common undergraduate and graduate professional preparation program in the major. Those students wishing to teach in public schools also must take courses in teacher preparation specified by the state for the teaching credential. Graduates from this program are commonly referred to as

Utilizing School and Community Resources

Areas	Competencies
Point of view	Is able to select community resources that are not in conflict with the points of view held concerning health, education, and school/community health programs.
Basis for content—learner	Can select and utilize resource materials suitable to the maturity level of the learner.
Basis for content—society	Can use effectively school and community resources for health instruction.
Structuring health knowledge—content and generalizations/topics	Is able to choose materials that contain valid health content and concepts for the instructional program.
Goals and objectives	Is able to utilize school and community health resources in establishing and reviewing goals and objectives for health instruction.
Teaching strategies/techniques	Is able to identify those school and community resources that can be used within teaching to enrich the health instruction program.
Organization	Is able to organize and coordinate school and community resources utilized in the health instruction program.
Evaluation	Can assess the educational validity of human and material resources as they relate to health instruction.

health education specialists and possess a broad range of professional competencies that enable them to function effectively as health educators in a variety of settings, including schools, hospitals, official and voluntary health agencies and private industry.

PERSONAL COMPETENCIES

In addition to professional competencies for those who are going to teach health, important personal competencies should be considered. Whether health teachers like it or not, what they are and what they do will often have a greater effect on the behavior of students than what they tell them. As with professional competencies, personal competencies of health educators have been classified into areas related to the framework used for this text. The table on page 160 is an example of such a classification.

As with the identification of professional competencies, this list was not intended to be exhaustive. Rather, it is presented as an example of personal competencies of the teacher of health.

Personal Competencies

Areas	Competencies
Point of view	Has a zest for living and appreciates and values health. Desires to improve professional competencies.
Basis for content—learner	Relates to children, youth, and adults and appreciates and understands individual differences.
Basis for content—society	Values people and their needs.
Structuring health knowledge— content and generalizations/ topics	Seeks to keep abreast of emerging up-to-date health concepts and content.
Goals and objectives	Seeks continually to update goals and objectives for health instruction.
Teaching strategies / techniques	Has a positive and inquiring attitude when teaching, rather than a dogmatic or moralistic one.
Organization	Is organized and recognizes the value of planning, yet is flexible in adjusting to changing conditions and situations.
Evaluation	Is willing to take time to gather data to assess student needs and achievement.

KEEPING UP TO DATE

Because health education is a dynamic and changing field, those who teach it cannot rely solely on their past preparation and experiences. Adequate undergraduate and graduate preparation in health education alone does not insure continued competency. The health educator should keep abreast of latest developments in the fields of medicine, dentistry, and the biological and behavioral sciences. What is fiction today may be fact tomorrow. Not many years ago, the idea that a virus might be a possible cause of cancer was regarded as a daydream. Today, it is a prevalent theory. Health educators should find ways to keep informed about current health findings. This is essential if they are to help students translate what is known about health into desired health practices.

In-Service Education

In-service education is one means by which the teacher can keep up to date. This kind of education is concerned with activities engaged in by professional teaching personnel and planned by school or professional organizations and agencies or both. Its purposes are to improve teacher competencies in teaching and to improve the standards of the profession in general. Activities often take the form of a single meeting or a series of meetings referred to as workshops or institutes.

One-meeting Approach. The one-meeting approach to in-service education is limited because it is likely to be a poor learning situation. There is generally little opportunity for teachers to exchange ideas with resource persons or with one another or to explore subjects in depth. Furthermore, the one-meeting approach does not offer resource personnel the opportunity of obtaining feedback from the audience, and thus they may have difficulty in adjusting the program to meet the needs of the audience.

Series Approach. A series of meetings is perhaps more beneficial in terms of enriching the background of teaching personnel than is the one-meeting approach. A series provides an opportunity for teachers to become actively involved in the in-service program. This approach enables teachers to study a particular problem, issue, topic or teaching strategy in some depth. It also provides an atmosphere for the exchange of ideas with resource persons and with colleagues. This in turn affords resource personnel an opportunity to adjust the program to better meet the needs of individual teachers. Over the period of time provided in the series approach, teachers can utilize knowledge, teaching strategies / techniques, principles, or skills derived from the in-service program in a personally meaningful way.

In one of the studies conducted as part of the *School Health Education Evaluation,* it was shown that teachers who received at least 40 hours of specified in-service education over a period of time did a more effective job of health education—completed a greater percentage of the program with greater fidelity—than did teachers with partial training. However, those who only received partial training implemented programs more fully than did teachers with no in-service education at all (10:318). While this study supports the value of the series approach to in-service education, it also shows that some in-service education is better than none.

Regardless of the approach used, in-service activities should be based upon specific individual needs related to cognitive skills, attitudes, and techniques essential to successful teaching and to successful administration. These activities should cover a variety of health subjects and teaching strategies and should utilize a variety of meaningful teaching techniques. They also should be evaluated in terms of their value in meeting the specific needs of the professional staff. In-service activities should be flexible in meeting the ever-changing needs of teachers, and they should reflect something more permanent and penetrating than a collection of facts unrelated to the instructional program and to the needs of teachers.

Organizing Resource Materials

Those involved in health education, in order to keep abreast of current information, should be familiar with a variety of resources, including resource people and reference materials. With a knowledge of the various resources and with an accumulation of resource materials, the teacher should be able to organize or file this information in a way that it can be readily retrieved so that it can be used effectively in the health instruction program. Again, the framework for this text offers one way of organizing this information. The following serves as an example:

1. Points of view
   A. Concerning health
   B. Concerning education
   C. Concerning health education.
2. Basis for health content
   A. Individual needs and interests
   B. Societal needs.
3. Structuring health knowledge
   A. Health areas/themes/questions (e.g., information relative to consumer health; mental-emotional health; family health, drug use and misuse; diseases and disorders; exercise, rest, posture; environmental health hazards; community health resources; and vision, hearing, and oral health)
   B. Health generalizations/topics within each area/theme/question.
4. Goals and objectives for health instruction
   A. Goals relative to the entire program and for each area/theme/question.
   B. Objectives relative to generalizations/topics within each area/theme/question.
5. Teaching Strategies/Teaching Techniques
   A. Education media (general and related to objectives)
   B. Individual and group processes (general and related to objectives).
6. Organization of health instruction
   A. Scope and sequence of curriculum
   B. Course outlines
   C. Units of instruction
   D. Daily lessons.
7. Evaluation
   A. Subjective or clinical evaluative techniques/instruments
   B. Objective or statistical evaluative techniques/instruments
   C. Test items for specific objectives.
8. Professional and personal competencies
   A. Professional competencies.
   B. Personal competencies.

Whether one uses this approach or another, the point is that some system is needed for keeping up to date and for logically retrieving information.

SUMMARY

If a planned rationale is used for developing health instruction and for securing health materials, information, and teaching personnel, consistency will be evident in the health instruction program. The success of the health instruction program depends greatly upon the acquisition of teachers who are able and willing to work within an organization's program. For example, a school district or hospital might develop its program of health instruction by using the rationale for health instruction presented in this text. If this were the case, it would be inconsistent for the district or hospital to secure teachers who are either unable or unwilling to use objectives as guides for selecting appropriate teaching strategies. Similarly, it would be a poor practice for these organizations to secure teachers who base their evaluations only on recall of information rather than on a range of cognitive skills.

For effective health instruction, the school should possess a modern point of view of health and should place health knowledge and values high on their priority list of educational outcomes. To perpetuate an effective program of health instruction, it is necessary to secure teachers with the necessary professional competencies and personal qualifications to teach health education. In the final analysis viable health instruction depends upon those who teach it.

REFERENCES

1. Bruess, Clint E., et al. "Application of the Role Delineation Project 'Framework' to a Professional Preparation Program." *Journal of School Health. 57:*183-185, May, 1987.
2. California State University Northridge, Department of Health Science. *Catalogue,* 1987-88, "Major in Health Education," Sacramento: State Printing Office, 1987.
3. Fodor, John T., Edward B. Johns, and Wilfred Sutton. "The Significance of Professional Preparation in Health Education." *School Health Review,* 3:27-30, September-October, 1972.
4. Kuntstel, Frank. "Assessing Community Needs: Implications for Curriculum and Staff Development in Health Education," *Journal of School Health, 48:*220-224, April, 1978.
5. *National Conference on Undergraduate Professional Preparation in Physical Education, Health Education and Recreation.* Jackson's Mill, West Virginia, May 16-27, 1948. Chicago: The Athletic Institute, 1948.
6. National Task Force on the Preparation and Practice of Health Educators. *A Framework for the Development of Competency based Curricula for Entry Level Health Educators.* New York: National Task Force on the Preparation and Practice of Health Educators, Inc., 1985.
7. Osman, Jack. "Reflections on the Health Major Curriculum," *Health Education, 12,* May/June, 1977.
8. Pigg, Morgan. "National Study of Competency Based Health Education Programs," *Health Education, 32,* May/June, 1977.
9. *Report of the National Conference on Graduate Study in Health Education, Physical Education, and Recreation.* Pere Marquette State Park, Illinois, January, 1950. Chicago: The Athletic Institute, 1950.
10. "Results of the School Health Education Evaluation." Special Edition—*Journal of School Health. 55:* October, 1985.
11. Schaller, Warren E. "Professional Preparation and Curriculum Planning," *Journal of School Health, 48:*236-240, April, 1978.

12. Sliepcevich, Elena M. "Implications of the School Health Education Study for Professional Preparation of Teachers." AAHPER Convention, Dallas, Texas, March 21, 1965.
13. *The Role Delineation Project.* San Francisco: National Center for Health Education, 1978.

EPILOG

The theme provided in this text is one of rational decision making in the process of health instruction and curriculum development. While the process was presented in a particular order, it is not necessary to follow this order in planning for health instruction. The various steps in the process are dynamically interrelated and several can occur simultaneously as health instruction is being planned.

Care should be taken not to accept the rationale presented as an absolute formula or blueprint for developing health instruction. Rather, it should be considered as a basis for making curriculum and instruction decisions, and should serve as a springboard for productive and creative efforts to upgrade health instruction and give direction to those responsible for implementing it. Inquiry about instruction and curriculum development needs to be ongoing to account for new technology and emerging insights into teaching and learning.

Index